THE PAPERS OF
WOODROW WILSON
VOLUME 36
JANUARY 27–MAY 8, 1916

SPONSORED BY THE WOODROW WILSON
FOUNDATION
AND PRINCETON UNIVERSITY

THE PAPERS OF

WOODROW WILSON

ARTHUR S. LINK, *EDITOR*

DAVID W. HIRST, *SENIOR ASSOCIATE EDITOR*

JOHN E. LITTLE, *ASSOCIATE EDITOR*

ANN DEXTER GORDON, *ASSISTANT EDITOR*

PHYLLIS MARCHAND AND MARGARET D. LINK,
EDITORIAL ASSISTANTS

Volume 36
January 27–May 8, 1916

PRINCETON, NEW JERSEY
PRINCETON UNIVERSITY PRESS
1981

Note to scholars: Princeton University Press subscribes to the Resolution on Permissions of the Association of American University Presses, defining what we regard as "fair use" of copyrighted works. This Resolution, intended to encourage scholarly use of university press publications and to avoid unnecessary applications for permission, is obtainable from the Press or from the A.A.U.P. central office. Note, however, that the scholarly apparatus, transcripts of shorthand, and the texts of Wilson documents as they appear in this volume are copyrighted, and the usual rules about the use of copyrighted materials apply.

Publication of this book has been aided by a grant from the National Historical Publications and Records Commission.

Printed in the United States of America
by Princeton University Press
Princeton, New Jersey

INTRODUCTION

The beginning of this volume finds Wilson in New York to inaugurate a speaking campaign on behalf of preparedness that carries him deep into the Middle West, where opposition to the administration's program is said to be strongest. Wilson arouses great enthusiasm on his tour. However, he returns to Washington to find the House Military Affairs Committee still adamant against a main feature of the administration's program—a national Continental reserve force of some 400,000 men. Wilson accepts a compromise plan to substitute a greatly enlarged National Guard under strict federal control for the Continental Army. Wilson also wins a measure to undertake a large program of naval construction. Meanwhile, Secretary of War Lindley M. Garrison has resigned in protest against Wilson's acceptance of the National Guard compromise and been replaced by Newton D. Baker of Cleveland.

Relations with Mexico, which have been unusually friendly since Wilson's *de facto* recognition of the government of Venustiano Carranza in October 1915, become heated again. Pancho Villa, who still controls large sections of northern Mexico, raids and burns the border town of Columbus, New Mexico, on March 19, 1916, and kills nineteen inhabitants. Wilson sends General John J. Pershing and a Punitive Expedition into Mexico to pursue and apprehend Villa. The *Carrancista* authorities acquiesce at first; indeed, for a time they assist in the chase. However, the cunning Villa draws Pershing some 300 miles deep into Mexico, and Carranza, under heavy domestic pressure, demands that the Punitive Expedition be withdrawn entirely from Mexico. There is a bloody clash between American and Mexican troops at Parral on April 12, and a potentially deadly crisis in Mexican-American relations is developing as this volume ends.

The opening of this volume also finds Colonel Edward M. House, Wilson's confidant, in Europe on his second peace mission. He concludes an agreement with Sir Edward Grey, the British Foreign Secretary, for Anglo-American cooperation in a peace plan, to be put into effect when the British and French governments decide that the time is ripe. House returns to the United States in early March 1916 and informs Wilson that the opportunity for which Wilson has long been seeking—mediation of the war—is at hand.

German-American relations reach a new crisis when a submarine torpedoes an unarmed Channel packet, *Sussex*, on March 24, 1916. House and Secretary of State Robert Lansing urge Wilson to break diplomatic relations with Germany at once. Wilson, however, again, as in former crises with Germany, patiently negotiates with the German government. The Germans do not respond positively, and Wilson, on April 18, 1916, sends an ultimatum to Berlin. It warns that the United States will break diplomatic relations with Germany unless she abandons her unrestricted submarine campaign against all merchant shipping. As this volume ends, the Germans have just capitulated to Wilson's demand, and German-American peace seems assured for a time.

The documents in this volume fully illustrate all the foregoing events. Like preceding volumes in *The Papers of Woodrow Wilson*, this volume includes numerous other documents that chronicle Wilson's relations with Congress; it also includes all of Wilson's speeches for the period covered by this volume and many personal letters that reveal Wilson's many faceted personality.

"VERBATIM ET LITERATIM"

In earlier volumes of this series we have said something like the following: "All documents are reproduced *verbatim et literatim*, with typographical and spelling errors corrected in square brackets only when necessary for clarity and ease of reading." The following essay explains our textual methods and review procedures.

We have never printed and do not intend to print, critical, or corrected, versions of documents. We print them exactly as they are, with a few exceptions which we always note. We never use the word *sic* except to denote the repetition of words in a document; in fact, we think that a succession of *sics* simply defaces a page.

We repair words in square brackets when letters are missing. As we have said, we also repair words in square brackets for clarity and ease of reading. Our general rule is to do this when we ourselves cannot read the word without stopping to determine its meaning. Jumbled words and names misspelled beyond recognition of course have to be repaired. We correct the misspelling of a name in the footnote identifying the person.

However, when an old man writes to Wilson saying that he is glad to hear that Wilson is "comming" to Newark, or a semiliterate farmer from Texas writes phonetically, we see no reason to correct spellings in square brackets when the words are perfectly understandable. We do not correct Wilson's misspellings unless they are unreadable, except to supply in square brackets letters missing in words. For example, for some reason he insisted upon spelling "belligerent" as "belligerant." Nothing would be gained by correcting "belligerant" in square brackets.

We think that it is very important for several reasons to follow the rule of *verbatim et literatim*. Most important, a document has its own integrity and power, particularly when it is not written in perfect literary form. There is something very moving in seeing a Texas dirt farmer struggling to express his feelings in words, or a semiliterate former slave doing the same thing. Second, in Wilson's case it is crucially important to reproduce his errors in letters that he typed himself, since he always typed badly when he was in an agitated state. Third, since style is the essence of the person, we would never correct grammar or make tenses consistent, as one correspondent has urged us to do. Fourth, we think that it is obligatory to print typed documents *verbatim et literatim*. For example, we think that it is very important that we print exact transcripts of Charles L. Swem's copies of Wilson's letters. Swem made many mistakes (we correct them in footnotes from a reading of his shorthand books), and Wilson let them pass. We thus have to assume that Wilson did not read his letters before signing them, and this, we think, is a significant fact. Finally, printing letters and typed documents *verbatim et literatim* tells us a great deal about the educational level of the stenographic profession in the United States during Wilson's time.

We think that our series would be worthless if we produced unreliable texts, and we go to some effort to make certain that the texts are authentic.

Our typists are highly skilled and proofread their transcripts carefully as soon as they have been typed. The Editor sight proofreads documents once he has assembled a volume and is setting its annotation. The Editors who write the notes read through documents several times and are careful to check any anomalies. Then, once the manuscript volume has been completed and all notes checked, the Editor and Senior Associate Editor orally proofread the documents against the copy. They read every comma, dash, and character. They note every absence of punctuation. They study every nearly illegible word in written documents.

Once this process of "establishing the text" is completed, the manuscript volume goes to our editor at Princeton University Press, who checks the volume carefully and sends it to the printing plant. The volume is set by linotype by two typographers who have been working on the Wilson volumes for years. The galley proofs go to the proofroom, where they are read orally against copy. And we must say that the proofreaders at the Press are extraordinarily skilled. Some years ago, before we found a way to ease their burden, they used to query every misspelled word, absence of punctuation, or other such anomalies. Now we write "O.K." above such words or spaces on the copy.

We read the galley proofs three times. Our copyeditor gives them a sight reading against copy to look for remaining typographical errors and to make sure that no line has been dropped. The Editor and the Senior Associate Editor sight read them against documents and copy. We then get the page proofs, which have been corrected at the Press. We check all the changes three times. In addition, we get *revised* pages and check them twice.

This is not the end. Our indexer of course reads the pages word by word. Before we return the pages to the Press, she comes in with a list of queries, all of which are answered by reference to the documents.

Our rule in the Wilson Papers is that our tolerance of error is zero. No system and no person can be perfect. We are sure that there are errors in our volumes. However, we believe that we have done everything humanly possible to avoid error; the chance is remote that what looks at first glance like a typographical error is indeed an error.

The Editors take this occasion to thank Professors John Milton Cooper, Jr., William H. Harbaugh, and Richard W. Leopold for their careful reading of the manuscript of this volume and for their helpful suggestions. We are also indebted to the continuing assistance of Judith May, our editor at Princeton University Press.

THE EDITORS

Princeton, New Jersey
October 29, 1980

CONTENTS

CONTENTS   xiii

ILLUSTRATIONS

Following page 326

ABBREVIATIONS

AL	autograph letter
ALI	autograph letter initialed
ALS	autograph letter signed
ASB	Albert Sidney Burleson
CC	carbon copy
CCL	carbon copy of letter
CLS	Charles Lee Swem
CLSsh	Charles Lee Swem shorthand
EBG	Edith Bolling Galt
EBW	Edith Bolling Wilson
EBWhw	Edith Bolling Wilson handwriting, handwritten
EMH	Edward Mandell House
FR	*Papers Relating to the Foreign Relations of the United States*
FR-LP	*Papers Relating to the Foreign Relations of the United States, The Lansing Papers*
FR-WWS 1916	*Papers Relating to the Foreign Relations of the United States, 1916, Supplement, The World War*
Hw	handwriting, handwritten
HwC	handwritten copy
HwCL	handwritten copy of letter
HwLS	handwritten letter signed
HwS	handwritten signed
JPT	Joseph Patrick Tumulty
JRT	Jack Romagna typed
LMG	Lindley Miller Garrison
MS	manuscript
MSS	manuscripts
NDB	Newton Diehl Baker
RG	record group
RL	Robert Lansing
T	typed
T MS	typed manuscript
T MSS	typed manuscripts
TC	typed copy
TCL	typed copy of letter
TI	typed initialed
TL	typed letter
TLI	typed letter initialed
TLS	typed letter signed
TS	typed signed
WHP	Walter Hines Page
WW	Woodrow Wilson
WWhw	Woodrow Wilson handwriting, handwritten
WWsh	Woodrow Wilson shorthand
WWT	Woodrow Wilson typed
WWTL	Woodrow Wilson typed letter
WWTLI	Woodrow Wilson typed letter initialed
WWTLS	Woodrow Wilson typed letter signed

ABBREVIATIONS FOR COLLECTIONS
AND REPOSITORIES
Following the National Union Catalog of the
Library of Congress

AFL-CIO-Ar	AFL-CIO Archives
AGO	Adjutant General's Office
CtY	Yale University
DeU	University of Delaware
DJR	Department of Justice Records
DLC	Library of Congress
DNA	National Archives
FFM-Ar	French Foreign Ministry Archives
FO	British Foreign Office
GFO-Ar	German Foreign Office Archives
InU	Indiana University
MH	Harvard University
Nc-Ar	North Carolina State Department of Archives and History
NcD	Duke University
NjP	Princeton University
NN	New York Public Library
NNC	Columbia University
PRO	Public Record Office
RSB Coll., DLC	Ray Stannard Baker Collection of Wilsoniana, Library of Congress
ScCleU	Clemson University
SDR	State Department Records
TxHr	Rice University
ViU	University of Virginia
WDR	War Department Records
WP, DLC	Woodrow Wilson Papers, Library of Congress

SYMBOLS

[Jan. 27, 1916]	publication date of a published writing; also date of document when date is not part of text
[*March 25, 1916*]	composition date when publication date differs
[[Feb. 26, 1916]]	delivery date of speech if publication date differs
* * * *	text deleted by author of document

THE PAPERS OF
WOODROW WILSON

VOLUME 36
JANUARY 27–MAY 8, 1916

THE PAPERS OF
WOODROW WILSON

Remarks in New York to a Suffrage Delegation[1]

[Jan. 27, 1916]

Ladies: I ought to say, in the first place, that the apologies I think ought to come from me, because I had not understood that an appointment had been made. On the contrary, I supposed none had been made and therefore had filled my morning with work from which it did not seem possible to escape. I can easily understand the embarrassment of any one of your representatives in trying to make a speech in this presence. I feel that embarrassment very strongly myself, and I wish very much that I had the eloquence of some of your speakers so that I could set my views forth as adequately as they set theirs forth. It may be, ladies, that my mind works slowly. I have always felt that those things were most solidly built that were built piece by piece, and I have felt that the genius of our political development in this country lay in the processes of our states and in the very clear definition of the difference of sphere between the state and federal governments. It may be that I am a little old fashioned in that.

When I last had the pleasure of receiving some ladies urging the amendment that you are urging this morning,[2] I told them that my own mind was unchanged, but I hoped open, and that I would take pleasure in conferring with the leaders of my party and the leaders of Congress with regard to this matter. I have not fulfilled that promise, and I hope you will understand why I have not fulfilled it, because there seemed to be questions of legislation so pressing in their necessity that they ought to take precedence of everything else; that we could postpone fundamental changes to immediate action along lines in the national interest. That has been my reason, and I think it is a sufficient reason. The business of government is a business from day to day, ladies, and there are things that cannot wait. However great the principle involved in this instance, action must of necessity in great fundamental constitutional changes be deliberate, and I do not feel that I have put the less pressing in advance of the more pressing in the course that I have taken. I have not forgotten the

promise that I made, and I certainly shall not forget the fulfillment of it, but I want always to be absolutely frank. My own mind
is still convinced that we ought to work this thing out state by
state. I did what I could to work it out in my own state in New
Jersey, and I am willing to act there whenever it comes up. But
that is, so far, my conviction as to the best and solidest way to
build changes of this kind. And I, for my own part, see no reason
for discouragement on the part of the women of the country in
the progress that this movement has been making. It may move
like a glacier, but when it does move, its effects are permanent.
I had not expected to have this pleasure this morning and therefore am simply speaking offhand and without consideration of
my phrases, but I hope in entire frankness. I thank you sincerely
for this opportunity.

T MS (WP, DLC).

[1] Wilson spoke to two hundred members of the Congressional Union, led by
Edith LaBau (Mrs. E. Tiffany) Dyer, in the East Room of the Waldorf-Astoria
Hotel. Considerable confusion had arisen over the question of whether they had
made an appointment, and Wilson at first refused to meet with the group.
However, the women said that they would wait "as long as necessary," and
messengers conferred with Tumulty throughout the morning until Wilson
agreed to speak. After Wilson had spoken, the suffragists asked him to campaign
for a federal suffrage amendment during his forthcoming preparedness tour.
They also challenged his position on suffrage, particularly his conviction that
each state should decide the question for itself. Mary Ritter (Mrs. Charles A.)
Beard tried Wilson's patience by asking whether the Clayton Act had been
enacted state by state, and the meeting came to an end. See Edith L. Dyer to
WW, Jan. 27, 1916 (2), ALS (WP, DLC); JPT to Edith L. Dyer, Jan. 27, 1916,
TLS (WP, DLC); *The Suffragist*, Feb. 5, 1916; and the *New York Times*, Jan.
28, 1916.

[2] Wilson had received a delegation of the National American Woman Suffrage Association, led by Dr. Anna Howard Shaw, at the White House on December 14, 1915. For an account of this meeting, see the *New York Times*, Dec. 15,
1915.

Remarks to the Clerical Conference of the New York Federation of Churches[1]

[Jan. 27, 1916]

Mr. Chairman and gentlemen: You have paid me a great honor
today, and I want to say how deeply and from the heart I appreciate it. I feel that you have unduly honored me as a man,
and that most of the things you have been pleased to say can be
truly said of me only as a representative of the great people whom
we all love. Because, in my efforts for peace, I have been conscious of representing the spirit of America and no private convictions merely of my own. It is hard to hold the balance even,
where so many passions are involved, but I have known that, in
their hearts and by their purpose, the people of America were

seeking to hold the balance even. The neutrality of the United States has not been a merely formal matter. It has been a matter of conviction and of the heart. And, in reflecting upon peace and the means of maintaining it, one is obliged to search for the foundations of peace. I can find no other foundation for peace than is laid in justice without aggression. If you wish to be just and insist upon being justly treated, and have no motive of covetousness or aggression, I believe you stand upon the only firm foundations which will sustain peace.

The greatest thing in the world, the greatest force in the world, is character. And I believe that character can be expressed upon a national scale and by a nation; that every act of a nation, at any rate of a nation which opens its counsels to the voices of the people themselves, expresses its character in its attitude towards its own affairs and in its attitude towards the affairs of other nations. America has always stood resolutely and absolutely for the right of every people to determine its own destiny and its own affairs. I am so absolute a disciple of that doctrine that I am ready to do that thing and observe that principle in dealing with the troubled affairs of our distressed neighbor to the south. And, similarly, it is the passion of America to be permitted to live her own life according to her own principles. The only thing that she profoundly resents, or will ever profoundly resent, is having her life and freedom interfered with. These are the terms of self-respect upon which to deal with one another as individuals, and these are the terms of self-respect upon which nations deal with one another. Because character is determined, at any rate is manifested, by what an individual and a nation most quickly respond to. I have never found audiences in America responding to any doctrine or purpose of aggression, but I have found them responding instantly, as the instrument responds to the hand of the musician, to every sentiment of justice and every ideal of liberty and every purpose of freedom.

America has not grown cold with regard to the great things for which she created a government and a nation, and these are the only things that stir her passion. And surely it is a handsome and elevated passion, a disinterested passion, because at its heart dwells the interest of every man and every woman within her confines. There is a further foundation for peace additional to this conception of justice and of fairness to others. That is our internal attitude toward each other. America has been hospitable in an unprecedented degree toward all nations, all races, all creeds. She has seemed almost to desire to be made up of all the stocks and influenced by all the thoughts of the wide world.

She has seemed to realize that she could be fertile only if every great impulse were planted amongst her. So she has set for herself in this process, which is still unfinished, of uniting and amalgamating these things, the problem of making disparate things live together in peace and accommodation and harmony. The peace of America depends upon the attitude of the different elements of race and thought of which she is made up towards one another.

I have been deeply disturbed, gentlemen, I think every thoughtful American has been deeply disturbed, at the evidence afforded in recent days of the recrudescence of religious antagonisms in this country. That is a very dangerous thing which cuts at the very root of the American spirit. If men do not love one another, they cannot love peace. If men are intolerant of one another, they will be intolerant of the processes of peace, which are the processes of accommodation. "Live and let live" is a very homely phrase, and yet it is the basis of social existence. I have neighbors whose manners and opinions I would very much like to alter, but I entertain a suspicion that they would, in turn, very much like to alter mine. And I am afraid that, if I began the process in their direction, they might insist upon it in mine; and upon reflection, as I grow older, I agree to live and let live. Birrell says somewhere, "The child beats its nurse and cries for the moon; the old man sips his gruel humbly and thanks God that nobody beats him." I have not yet quite reached that point of humility, and I always accept, perhaps by some impulse of my native blood, the invitation to a fight. But I hope I always conduct the fight in knightly fashion. I hope I do not traduce my antagonists. I hope that I fight them with the purpose and intention of converting them. And I know that I wish that the best argument and the right purpose shall prevail. It is not a case of knock down and drag out; it is a case of putting up the best reason why your own side should survive. These franknesses of controversy, these knightly equalities of condition in the fight, are the necessary conditions precedent to peace. Peace does not mean inaction. There may be infinite activity; there may be almost violent activity in the midst of peace.

Peace dwells, after all, in the character and in the heart, and that is where peace is rooted in this blessed country of ours. It is rooted in the hearts of the people. The only place where tinder lies and the spark may kindle a flame is where still deeper things lie which they love—the principles and independence of their own life. Let no man drop fire there, because peace is inconsistent with the loss of self-respect. More than that, peace is inconsistent with the abandonment of principle.

But these things are not to be thought of. These things, I pray God, may never be challenged. I mention them merely that we may frankly remind each other of the conditions under which we live. We believe in peace, but we believe also in justice and right-eousness and liberty, and peace cannot subsist without these. In what you have too generously praised me for, therefore, gentle-men, I have conceived myself merely as the spokesman of your-selves and of all other Americans who, like yourselves, are thoughtful of the welfare and ideals of America. These are very responsible days. I do not see how any man dares utter anything but the truth in this tense atmosphere. I do not see how any man can in conscience display narrow or partisan passion. We are all of one spiritual kith and kin, and a great family is building up here, which I believe in my heart will set an example to the world of those things which elevate and purify and strengthen mankind.

Printed in *Addresses of President Wilson January 27-February 3, 1916* (Wash-ington, 1916). This is a collection of Swem's transcripts of Wilson's speeches on his tour for preparedness. The Editors have, as usual, read Swem's transcripts against his shorthand notes and have made numerous silent corrections. The Editors have also compared Swem's transcripts and shorthand notes against as many independent variant texts as could be found. They have made corrections of the Swem versions silently.

  1 In Aeolian Hall before an audience of seven hundred clergymen of all faiths and denominations. The Rev. Dr. Samuel Edward Young, chairman of the Clerical Conference of the New York Federation of Churches, presided over the meeting. The federation called the meeting to express its appreciation to Wilson for his efforts in behalf of peace. Wilson's speech was preceded by the reading of a message from John Murphy Cardinal Farley, which eulogized Wilson and promised the support of the Roman Catholic Church in restoring peace. The assembled ministers interrupted the Cardinal's spokesman three times by ap-plause.

An Address in New York on Preparedness[1]

[Jan. 27, 1916]

Mr. Toastmaster, ladies, and gentlemen: The exactions of my official duties have recently been so great that it has been very seldom, indeed, that I could give myself so great a pleasure as that which I am enjoying tonight. It is a great pleasure to come and be greeted in such generous fashion by men so thoughtful as yourselves and so deeply engaged in some of the most im-portant undertakings of the nation, and I consider it a privilege to be permitted to lay before you some of the things to which we ought to give our most careful and deliberate consideration. The question, it seems to me, which most demands clarifica-

  1 To the seventh annual dinner of the Railway Business Association, held at the Waldorf-Astoria Hotel. George Adams Post, manufacturer and president of the association since 1909, introduced Wilson.

tion just now, is the question to which your toastmaster has referred—the question of preparation for national defense. I say that it stands in need of clarification because, singularly enough, it has been deeply clouded by passion and prejudice. It is very singular that a question, the elements of which are so simple and so obvious, should have been so beclouded by the discussion of men of high motive, men of purpose as handsome as any of us may claim, and yet apparently incapable of divesting themselves of that sort of provincialism which consists in thinking the contents of their own mind to be the contents of the mind of the world. For, gentlemen, while America is a very great nation, while America contains all the elements of fine force and accomplishment, America does not constitute the major part of the world. We live in a world which we did not make, which we cannot alter, which we cannot think into a different condition from that which actually exists. It would be a hopeless piece of provincialism to suppose that, because we think differently from the rest of the world, we are at liberty to assume that the rest of the world will permit us to enjoy that thought without disturbance.

It is a surprising circumstance, also, that men should allow partisan feeling or personal ambition to creep into the discussion of this fundamental thing. How can Americans differ about the safety of America? And I, for my part, am ambitious that America should do a greater and more difficult thing than the great nations on the other side of the water have done. In all the belligerent countries, men without distinction of party have drawn together to accomplish a successful prosecution of the war. Is it not a more difficult and a more desirable thing that all Americans should put partisan prepossession aside and draw together for the successful prosecution of peace? I covet that distinction for America; and I believe that America is going to enjoy that distinction. Only the other day, the leader of the Republican minority in the House of Representatives[2] delivered a speech which showed that he was ready and, I take it for granted, that the men behind him were ready, to forget party lines in order that all men may act with a common mind and impulse for the service of the country, and I want, upon this first public occasion, to pay my tribute of respect and obligation to him.

I find it very hard, indeed, to approach this subject without very deep emotion, gentlemen, because when we speak of America and the things that are to be conserved in her, does it not call a wonderful picture into your mind? America is young still;

2 James R. Mann of Illinois.

she is not yet even in the heyday of her development and power. Think of the great treasures of youth and energy and ideal purpose still to be drawn from the deep sources from which this nation has always drawn its life! Think of the service which those forces can and must render to the rest of the world! Think of the position into which America has been drawn, almost in spite of herself, by the circumstances of the present day! She alone is free to help fine things wherever they show themselves in the world. And she is forced, also, whether she will or no, in the decades immediately ahead of us, to furnish the world with its chief economic guidance and assistance.

It is very fine to remember what ideals will be back of that assistance. Economic assistance in itself is not necessarily handsome. It is a legitimate thing to make money, but it is not an ideal thing to make money. Money brings with it power which may be well or ill employed, and it should be the pride of America always to employ her money to the highest purpose. And yet if we are drawn into the maelstrom that now surges across the water, swirls even in the western regions of the world, we shall not be permitted to keep a free hand to do the high things that we intend to do. And it is necessary that we should examine ourselves and so order that can make certain that the tasks imposed upon us will be performed, well performed, and performed without interruption.

America has been reluctant to match her wits with the rest of the world. When I face a body of men like this, it is almost incredible to remember that only yesterday they were afraid to put their wits into free competition with the world. The best brains in the world afraid to match brains with the rest of the world! We have preferred to be provincial. We have preferred to stand behind protecting devices. And now, whether we will or no, we are thrust out to do, on a scale never dreamed of by recent generations in America, the business of the world. We can no longer be a provincial nation.

Let no man dare to say, if he would speak the truth, that the question of preparation for national defense is a question of war or of peace. If there is one passion more deep-seated in the hearts of our fellow countrymen than another, it is the passion for peace. No nation in the world ever more instinctively turned away from the thought of war than this nation to which we belong. Partly because in the plenitude of its power, in the unrestricted area of its opportunities, it has found nothing to covet in the possessions and power of other nations. There is no spirit of aggrandizement in America. There is no desire on the part of any thoughtful and conscientious American man to take one foot of territory from any other nation in the world. And I, myself, share to the bottom of my heart that profound love for peace. I have sought to maintain peace against very great and sometimes very unfair odds. And I am ready, at any time, to use every power that is in me to prevent such a catastrophe as war coming upon this country. So that it is not permissible for any man to say that anxiety for the defense of the nation has in it the least tinge of desire for a power that can be used to bring on war.

But, gentlemen, there is something that the American people love better than they love peace. They love the principles upon which their political life is founded. They are ready at any time to fight for the vindication of their character and of their honor. They will at no time seek a contest, but they will at no time cravenly avoid it. Because, if there is one thing that the country ought to fight for, and that every nation ought to fight for, it is the integrity of its own convictions. We cannot surrender our convictions. I would rather surrender territory than surrender those ideals which are the staff of life of the soul itself.

And, because we hold certain ideals, we have thought it was right that we should hold them for others as well as for ourselves. America has more than once given evidence of the generosity and disinterestedness of its love of liberty. It has been willing to fight for the liberty of others, as well as for its own liberty. The world sneered when we set out for the liberation of Cuba, but the world does not sneer any longer. The world now knows, what it was then loath to believe, that a nation can sacrifice its own interests and its own blood for the sake of the liberty and happiness of another people. And whether by one process or another, we have made ourselves, in some sort, the champions of free government and national sovereignty in both continents of this hemisphere; so that there are certain obligations which every American knows that we have undertaken.

The first and primary obligation is the maintenance of the integrity of our own sovereignty, which goes as of course. There is also the maintenance of our liberty to develop our political institutions without hindrance. And, last of all, there is the determination and the obligation to stand as the strong brother of all those in this hemisphere who will maintain the same principles and follow the same ideals of liberty.

May I venture to insert here a parenthesis? Have any of you thought of this? We have slowly, very slowly, indeed, begun to win the confidence of the other states of the American hemisphere. If we should go into Mexico, do you know what would happen? All the sympathies of the rest of America would look across the water and not northward to the great republic which we profess to represent. And do you not see the consequences that would ensue in every international relationship? Have gentlemen who have rushed down to Washington to insist that we should go into Mexico reflected upon the politics of the world? Nobody seriously supposes, gentlemen, that the United States needs to fear an invasion of its own territory. What America has to fear, if she has anything to fear, are indirect, roundabout, flank movements upon her regnant position in the western hemisphere. Are we going to open these gates, or are we going to close them? For they are the gates to the hearts of our American friends to the south of us, and not gates to the ports. Win their spirits and you have won the only sort of leadership and the only sort of safety that America covets. We must, all of us, think, from this time out, gentlemen, in terms of the world and must learn what it is that America has set out to maintain as a standard bearer for all those who love liberty and justice and the righteousness of political action.

But, gentlemen, we must find means to do this thing which are suitable to the time and suitable to our own ideals. Suitable to the time? Does anybody understand the time? Perhaps when you learned, as I dare say you did learn beforehand, that I was expecting to address you on the subject of preparedness, you recalled the address which I made to Congress something more than a year ago,[3] in which I said that this question of military preparedness was not a pressing question. But more than a year has gone by since then, and I would be ashamed if I had not learned something in fourteen months. The minute I stop changing my mind as President, with the change of all the circumstances in the world, I will be a back number.

There is another thing about which I have changed my mind. A year ago, I was not in favor of a tariff board, and I will tell you why. Because then the only purpose of a tariff board was to keep alive an unprofitable controversy. If you set up any board of inquiry whose purpose it is to keep business disturbed and to make it always an open question what you are going to do about the public policy of the government, I am opposed to it. And the very men who were dinning it into our ears that what business wanted was to be let alone were, many of them, men who were insisting that we should stir up a controversy, which meant that we could not let business alone. There is a great deal more opinion vocal in this world than is consistent with logic. But the circum-

[3] His Annual Message to Congress of 1914, printed at Dec. 8, 1914, Vol. 31.

stances of the present time are these: There is going on in the world, under our eyes, an economic revolution. No man understands that revolution; no man has the elements of it clearly in his mind. No part of the business of legislation with regard to international trade can be undertaken until we do understand it; and members of Congress are too busy, their duties are too multifarious and distracting, to make it possible, within a sufficiently short space of time, for them to master the change that is coming.

I hear a great many things predicted about the end of the war; but I do not know anything about what is going to happen when the war is over, and neither do you. There are two diametrically opposed views as to immigration. Some men tell us that at least a million men are going to leave the country and others tell us that many millions are going to rush into it. Neither party knows what they are talking about, and I am one of those prudent individuals who would really like to know the facts before he forms an opinion; not out of wisdom, but out of prudence. I have lived long enough to know that if I do not, the facts will get away with me. I have come to have a wholesome respect for the facts. I have had to yield to them sometimes before I saw them coming, and that has led me to keep a weather eye open in order that I may see them coming. There is so much to understand that we have not the data to comprehend that I, for one, would not dare, so far as my advice is concerned, to leave the government without the adequate means of inquiry. But that is another parenthesis.

What I am trying to impress upon you now is that the circumstances of the world today are not what they were yesterday, or ever were in any of our yesterdays, and that it is not certain what they will be tomorrow. I cannot tell you what the international relations of this country will be tomorrow, and I use the word literally. And I would not dare keep silent and let the country suppose that tomorrow was certain to be as bright as today. America will never be the aggressor. America will always seek, to the last point at which her honor is involved, to avoid the things which disturb the peace of the world. But America does not control the circumstances of the world, and we must be sure that we are faithful servants of those things which we love and are ready to defend them against every contingency that may affect or impair them.

But, as I was saying a moment ago, we must seek the means which are consistent with the principles of our lives. It goes without saying, though apparently it is necessary to say it to some excited persons, that one thing that this country never will endure is a system that can be called militarism. But militarism consists in this, gentlemen: It consists in preparing a great machine whose only use is for war and giving it no use to which to apply itself. Men who are in charge of edged tools and bidden to prepare them for exact and scientific use grow very impatient if they are not permitted to use them, and I do not believe that the creation of such an instrument is an insurance of peace. I believe that it involves the danger of all the impulses that skillful persons have to use the things that they know how to use.

But we do not have to do that. America is always going to use her army in two ways. She is going to use it for the purposes of peace, and she is going to use it as a nucleus for expansion into those things which she does believe in, namely, the preparation of her citizens to take care of themselves. There are two sides to the question of preparation. There is not merely the military side, there is the industrial side. And the ideal which I have in mind is this, gentlemen: We ought to have in this country a great system of industrial and vocational education under federal guidance and with federal aid, in which a very large percentage of the youth of this country will be given training in the skillful use and application of the principles of science in manufacturing and business. And it will be perfectly feasible and highly desirable to add to that, and combine with it, such a training in the mechanism and use and care of arms, in the sanitation of camps, in the simpler forms of maneuver and organization, as will make these same men, at one and the same time, industrially efficient and immediately serviceable for national defense. The point about such a system will be that its emphasis will lie on the industrial and civil side of life, and that, like all the rest of America, the use of force will only be in the background and as the last resort. So that men will think first of their families and their daily work, of their service in the economic fields of the country, of their efficiency as artisans, and only last of all of their serviceability to the nation as soldiers and men at arms. That is the ideal of America.

But, gentlemen, you cannot create such a system overnight; you cannot create such a system rapidly. It has got to be built up, and I hope it will be built up, by slow and effective stages. And there is something to be done in the meantime. We must see to it that a sufficient body of citizens is given the kind of training which will make them efficient now for call into the field in case of necessity. It is discreditable to this country, gentlemen—for this is a country full of intelligent men—that we should have exhibited to the world the example we have sometimes exhibited to it of stupidity and brutal waste of force. Think of asking men who can be easily drawn to come into the field—crude, ignorant, inexperienced, and merely furnish the stuff for camp fever and the bullets of the enemy. The sanitary experience of our army in the Spanish-American War was merely an indictment of America's indifference to the manifest lessons of experience in the matter of ordinary, careful preparation. We have got the men to waste, but God forbid that we should waste them. Men who go as efficient instruments of national honor into the field afford a very handsome spectacle, indeed. But the men who go in, crude and ignorant boys, only indict those in authority for stupidity and neglect. So it seems to me that it is our manifest duty to have a proper citizen reserve.

I am not forgetting our National Guard. I had the privilege of being governor of one of our great states—a state which furnishes this city with a great deal of its intelligence. Some Jerseymen on either side here enjoy that very much. And as Governor of New Jersey, I was brought into association with what I am glad to believe is one of the most efficient portions of the National Guard of the United States. I learned to admire the men, to respect the officers, and to believe in the National Guard. And I believe that it is the duty of Congress to do very much more for the National Guard than it has ever done heretofore. I believe that that great arm of our national defense should be built up and encouraged to the utmost. But you know, gentlemen, that, under the Constitution of the United States, it is under the direction of more than twoscore states, and that it is not permitted to the national government directly to direct its development and organization; and that only upon occasion of actual invasion has the President of the United States the right to ask those men to leave their respective states. I, for my part, am afraid, though some gentlemen differ with me, that there is no way in which that force can be made a direct resource as a national reserve under national authority.

What we need is a body of men trained in association with units of the army, a body of men organized under the immediate direction of the national authority, a body of men subject to the immediate call to arms of the national authority, and yet men not put into the ranks of the regular army—men left to their tasks of civil life, men supplied with equipment and training, but not drawn from the peaceful pursuits which have made America great and must keep her great. I am not a partisan of any one plan. I have had too much experience to think that it is right to say that the plan that I propose is the only plan that will work, because I have a shrewd suspicion that there may be other plans which will work. But what I am for, and what every American ought to insist upon, is a body of at least half a million trained citizens who will serve under conditions of danger as an immediately available national reserve.

I am not saying anything about the navy. I don't want to go to sea. I want to stick to the one theme tonight because, for some reason, there is not the same controversy about the navy that there is about the army. The navy is obvious and easily understood; the army, apparently, is very difficult to comprehend and understand. We have a traditional prejudice against armies, which makes us stop thinking the minute we begin talking about them. We suppose that all armies are alike and that there cannot be an American system in this instance, but that it must be the European system, and that is what I, for one, am trying to divest my own mind of. The navy is so obvious an instrument of national defense that I believe that, with differences of opinion about the detail, it is not going to be difficult to carry out a proper and reasonable program for the increase of the navy.

But that is another story. And you know I have to give a good many speeches in the near future, and I must save something for subsequent days. My theme tonight is national defense on land where we seem most ignorant of it and negligent about it. And I do not want to leave upon your minds the impression that I have any anxiety as to the outcome, for I have not the slightest. There is only one way that parties and individuals win the confidence of this nation, and that is to do the things that ought to be done. Nobody is going to be deceived. Speeches are not going to win elections. The facts are going to speak for themselves, and speak louder than anybody who controverts them. No political party or group of men can ever disappoint America. This is a year of political accounting, and Americans in politics are rather expert accountants. They know what the books contain, and they are not going to be deceived by it. No man is going to hide behind any excuses; the goods must be delivered or the confidence will not be enjoyed. For my part, I hope that every man in public life will get what is coming to him.

But if this is true, gentlemen, it is because of things that lie much deeper than laughter, much deeper than cheers; that lie down at the very roots of our life. America refuses to be deceived about the things which most concern her national honor and national safety, that lie at the foundation of everything that you love. It is a solemn time when men must examine, not only their purposes, but their hearts, when men must purge themselves of individual ambition, when men must see to it that they are ready for the utmost self-sacrifice in the interests of the common welfare. Let no man dare to be a marplot. Let no man bring partisan passion into these great things. Let men honestly debate the facts and courageously act upon them. Then there will come that day when the world will say, "This America, that we thought was full of a multitude of contrary counsels, now speaks with the great volume of the heart's accord, and that great heart of America has behind it the supreme moral force of righteousness and hope and the liberty of mankind."

Printed in the New York *World*, Jan. 28, 1916, with minor corrections from the text printed in *Addresses of President Wilson*.

After-Dinner Remarks in New York to the Motion Picture Board of Trade[1]

[Jan. 27, 1916]

Mr. Toastmaster and ladies and gentlemen: I wondered when I was on my way here what would be expected of me. It occurred to me that perhaps I would only be expected to go through the motions of a speech, and then I reflected that, never having seen myself speak and generally having my thoughts concentrated upon what I had to say, I had not the least notion what my motions were when I made a speech. Because it has never occurred to me, in my simplicity, to make a speech before a mirror. If you will give me time, I will rehearse this difficult part and return and perform it for you.

I have sometimes been very much chagrined in seeing myself in a motion picture. I have wondered if I really was that kind of a "guy." The extraordinary rapidity with which I walked, for example, the instantaneous and apparently automatic nature of my motion, the way in which I produce uncommon grimaces, and altogether the extraordinary exhibition I make of myself sends me to bed very unhappy. And I often think to myself that, although all the world is a stage and men and women but actors upon it, after all, the external appearances of things are very superficial, indeed. I am very much more interested in what my fellow men are thinking about than in the motions through which they are going. While we unconsciously display a great deal of human nature in our visible actions, there are some very deep waters which no picture can sound.

When you think of a great nation, ladies and gentlemen, you are not thinking of a visible thing; you are thinking of a spiritual thing. I suppose a man in public office feels this with a peculiar poignancy, because what it is important for him to know is the real, genuine sentiments and emotions of the people that make up the nation. I found out what was going on in Mexico in a very singular way—by hearing a sufficiently large number of liars talk about it. I think the psychological explanation will interest you.

You know that the truth is consistent with itself; one piece matches another. Now, no man is an inventive enough liar not to bring in large sections of truth in what he says, and, after all the liars are done talking to you about the same subject, it will come to your consciousness that long and large pieces of what they said matched; that in that respect they all said the same thing; that the variations are lies, and the consistencies are the truth. They will not all tell you the same piece of the truth, so that if you hear enough of them, you may get the whole of the truth. And yet it is very tedious to hear men lie, particularly when you know they are lying. You feel like reminding them that, really, your time is important to you, and that you wish they would get down to business and tell you what is really so. But they do not. They want this adventure of their invention; they want to give an excursion to their minds before they get down to business. What I particularly object to is a very able man, with a lot of inventions, coming to me and lying to me, because then the interview is very tedious and long before we get down to business. I got to know that story so by heart that, the last time a deputation visited me about Mexico, I thought I would save time, and I told them exactly what they were going to say to me. They went away very much confused; they wondered how I had heard it, because they knew it was not so.

Yet underneath all of this are those great pulses which throb in great bodies of men and drive the great powers of state, and I wonder how men venture to try to deceive a great nation. There never was a profounder saying than that of Lincoln, that you can fool all the people some of the time and some of the people all of the time, but you cannot fool all of the people all of the time. And the best way in which to silence any friend of yours whom you know to be a fool is to induce him to hire a hall. Nothing chills pretense like exposure. Nothing will bear the tests of examination for a shorter length of time than pretense. At least, so I try to persuade myself, and yet there are some humbugs that have been at large for a long time. I suppose that there is always a rising generation whom they can fool, but the older heads ought not to permit themselves to be fooled.

I should think that in a year like the year 1916, when there is to be a common reckoning for everybody, men would hurry up and begin to tell the truth. They are not hurrying about it; they are taking their time. But the American people are going to insist upon it, before this year is over, that everybody comes up and is counted on the great questions of the day. They are not going to take any excuses, they are not going to take any pretenses; they are going to insist upon the goods being delivered on the spot, and anybody that declines to deliver them is going to go bankrupt, and ought to go bankrupt. Everybody ought to get what is coming to him.

But I came here to say that I hoped you would not believe that I am what I appear to be in the pictures you make of me. I really am a pretty decent fellow! And I have a lot of emotions that do not show on the surface, and the things that I do not say would fill a library. The great curse of public life is that you are not allowed to say all the things that you think. Some of my opinions about some men are extremely picturesque, and, if you could only take a motion picture of them, you would think it was Vesuvius in eruption. Yet all these volcanic forces, all these things that are going on inside of me, have to be concealed under a most grave and reverend exterior, and I have to make believe that I have nothing but respectable and solemn thoughts all the time. There is a lot going on inside of me that would be entertaining to any audience anywhere.

I am very much complimented that you should have allowed me to come in at this late hour in your feast and, without partaking of the pleasures of conversation, to make you all, whether you would or not, listen to me talk. My object in life is not talking. I wish there were less talking to do. I wish that not everybody had to be persuaded to do the right thing. I wish that the things that are obvious did not have to be explained. I wish that principles did not have to be re-expounded. We all, in our hearts, agree upon the fundamental principles of our lives and of our life as a nation. Now, we ought to tax ourselves with the duty of seeing that those principles are realized in action, and no fooling about it. The only difficult things in life, ladies and gentlemen, are the applications of the principles of right and wrong. I can set forth the abstract principles of right and wrong, and so can you. But when it comes down to an individual item of conduct, whether in public affairs or in private affairs, there comes the pinch—in the first place, to see the right way to do it; and, in the second place, to do it that way. If we could only agree that in all matters of public concern we would adjourn our private interests, look each other frankly in the face and say, "We are all ready at what-

ever sacrifice of our own interest to do in common the thing
that the common weal demands," what an irresistible force
America would be! I can point out to you a few men—of course,
I am not going to name them now—whom every man ought to be
afraid of, because nothing but the truth resides in them. I have
one in particular in mind whom I have never caught thinking
about himself. I would not dare make a pretense in the presence
of that man, even if I wanted to. His eyes contain the penetrating
light of truth before which all disguises fall away.

Now, suppose we were all like that! It would hasten the mil-
lenium immensely. And if Americans were always to do what,
when the real temper of America is aroused they do, the world
would always turn to America for guidance, and America would
be the most potent and influential force in all the world. So that
when I look at pictures, whether they move or whether they do
not move, I think of all the deep sources of happiness and of pain,
of joy and of misery, that lie beneath that surface, and I am interested chiefly in the heart that beats underneath it all. For I
know that there lies the pulse and the machinery of all the great
forces of the world.

Printed in *Address of President Wilson at the First Annual Banquet of the
Motion Picture Board of Trade* (Washington, 1916), with a few corrections from
the incomplete text in the New York *World*, Jan. 28, 1916.
    [1] At the Biltmore Hotel. James Stuart Blackton, vice-president of the Vita-
graph Co. and founder and president of the Motion Picture Board, offered the
toast to Wilson.

From William Kent

Personal.

My dear Mr. President: Washington, D. C. January 27, 1916.

I trust you will pardon me for taking up such an important
matter with you. I have been doing some thinking and consulting with people concerning the vacancy on the Supreme Bench
and I wish to suggest to your most careful consideration our
friend, Mr. Louis Brandeis. There is no one in the country better
known for clear-headed, forward-looking constructive statesmanship. He has been advertised by his good works and his clear
thought.

You know, as well as I do, that the Supreme Court of the United
States is the real living Constitution and therefore see clearly the
necessity of having on the bench men with a vision of improving
average human conditions, which is the end and the aim of
democracy.

I have never known Mr. Brandeis too busy to take up the cudgels for a good cause and there is no man in the country more free from suspicion of sordid motives, although the enemies of progress and the friends of special privilege have made it their end and object to discredit him.

Among those from whom I have heard expressions of opinion, I would mention Senator La Follette, Mr. Charles R. Crane and Mr. Amos Pinchot.

I should never recommend to your attention any man for an important office on a basis of politics, much less for an office of this tremendous importance, but it can do no harm to state that I know of no appointment that would more surely rally to your support the thoughtful independent vote of the country.

Permit me, in closing, to state that I regard it as my duty to my country to do everything possible toward your re-election and therefore shall not hesitate to make political suggestions from time to time.   Yours truly,   William Kent

TLS (WP, DLC).

From John Sharp Williams, with Enclosure

My dear Mr. President: [Washington] January 27, 1916.

I recently had occasion to write a letter to a gentleman who wrote to me complimenting me upon my reply to Smith, etc.,[1] and I especially wrote a reply to a criticism he made of a phrase, which you failed to condition: "We are too proud to fight." I thought you would be interested in the manner which I took, at any rate, to explain what you meant; so I send you a carbon copy of my reply to his letter.

I am, with every expression of regard,
                    Very truly yours,   John Sharp Williams

TLS (WP, DLC).
  [1] In a debate in the Senate on January 20, Hoke Smith had attacked the British blockade and advocated a sweeping embargo against Britain to bring her to terms. Williams had replied in defense of Wilson's policies. He pointed out, first, that Smith's proposal would result in nonintercourse with the Allies and cause considerably more harm to the cotton trade than British policies did. Moreover, it was absurd to think that the British would stand bullying "from a people who cannot bully because they have nothing behind them to bully with, who cannot bluff because they hold no hand." Williams then attacked the practice of arguing great international questions from the standpoint of special interests. No property, including cotton, could be equated with human life, and human life should always take precedence over property in the defense of neutral rights. *Cong. Record*, 64th Cong., 1st sess., pp. 1295-1309.

ENCLOSURE

John Sharp Williams to Walter O. Borcherdt[1]

My dear sir: [Washington] January 27, 1916.

I have your letter of January 26th. I appreciated very much indeed the thoughtfulness and consideration which led you to write it.

I expect your criticism of me is correct. I somehow haven't taken as much interest in the business of the Senate as I used to take in that of the House. The average Senator makes set speeches and there is very little real debate—that is of the extemporaneous, catch-as-catch-can sort.

I am very sorry, however, that you made one criticism of the President that is absolutely uncalled for. The President did say that a man or a nation might very well be "too proud to fight," but he said it when we were discussing the Mexican question. He meant that a man might be too proud to fight a child and that the United States might be too proud to fight Mexico. He made the mistake of not sufficiently elaborating the condition in which it was used. We all must be subject to the risk of making that mistake when in public life we speak with our thoughts absorbed by the immediate question and with our minds assuming that everybody will confine what we say to the immediate question.

If I went out on the street and found a little, foolish six or seven-year-old boy trying to kill me with a pistol I would get out of his way and manage to evade his aim, get behind him, if I could, and disarm him; then I would take the little chap up in my arms and tell him that we were good friends, or, at any rate, ought to be. That is what the President meant.

Of course, as you say, a gentleman is proud to fight in many causes. But still, there are times when a gentleman might well be too proud to fight a woman, or a child, or something weak.

I agree with you substantially with regard to your views as to preparedness. What we want is a navy which will make anybody in this world think twice before he insults us.

I am, with every expression of regard,
             Very truly yours,   [John Sharp Williams]

CCL (WP, DLC).
[1] Mining engineer of Austinville, Va.

From Amos Richards Eno Pinchot

My dear Mr. President: New York January 27, 1916.

I understand that you are considering the advisability of appointing Louis Brandeis to the bench of the Supreme Court. I want to say that I believe that such an appointment would be a large service to the country, and a credit to yourself and the democratic administration.

Two years ago, I would not have said this, although I believed then, as much as I do now, that Brandeis would make a sound and strong judge. But I think that at that time the country would not have been ready for his appointment; for, the wisdom of the things he said and did had not then been proved as it is now. Then, it might have been considered an appointment a little ahead of the times; now, the public has caught up with Brandeis, has accepted him and is deeply grateful for his work. We see Brandeis now as a man who has been fighting rather an uphill battle, the sane usefulness of which has been justified by events.

I have known Brandeis pretty intimately since 1899, and I feel that there is in him a gatheredness and a power, which comes from his always keeping well within his facts, his thinking—in short, his strength.

Brandeis is a just man and a real democrat. We need his kind, especially now when there is such a powerfully driving impulse away from the democratic idea.

The doctrine, that private industrial monopoly is a necessity in order to achieve industrial efficiency, has been gathering force lately. Some very distinguished persons, who ought to know better, have come pretty near persuading the public that the people, who are against private monopoly and for industrial democracy, are trying to reduce the steel industry to the black-smith shop, and the railroad to the stage-coach. (I trust I am not giving away Progressive Party secrets.) They are insisting that business must be conducted in America, either by huge and efficient monopoly groups, or by small and inefficient units of production. They deny the possibility of competitive production between large integrated units. They are getting away with this, too, and the shouters for exorbitant armament are using preparedness as an argument with which to intrench more firmly the doctrine of the sacredness of monopoly and extortion.

I know, Mr. President, that you see the immense importance of putting America on a sound industrial basis. I believe that, when you read the message to Congress, in which you said that industrial monopoly was intolerable and indefensible, you had the public behind you. I believe that, when you are elected a second time and when the war is over, the large service that you will do for the United States will be in making plain to its people the necessity of economic democracy, and the way to get it. I sincerely hope that you will make us all understand, that political democracy alone does not mean democracy; that economic power is the great power of the world, and, while this is in the hands of a few people, fit to rule or otherwise, there will be no real democracy. And, in this fight of education and constructive statesmanship, the presence of a man like Brandeis in the Supreme Court will be extremely valuable.

With sincere congratulations for your Mexican policy, and for your determination, which I think is generally understood and appreciated, not to encourage the United States to go to war without a legitimate cause of war, I am

Sincerely yours,   Amos Pinchot

TLS (WP, DLC).

Joseph Patrick Tumulty to Amos Richards Eno Pinchot

My dear Mr. Pinchot: The White House January 28, 1916

The President directs me to acknowledge the receipt of your letter of January 27th, and to say that he is glad to learn that you think so highly of Mr. Brandeis, whose nomination for the vacancy on the Supreme Bench he is today sending to the Senate.

Assuring you that the President deeply appreciates your generous expressions, I am   Sincerely yours,   J. P. Tumulty

TLS (A. Pinchot Papers, DLC).

From Samuel Gompers

Sir: Washington, D. C., Jan. 28, 1916.

A piece of most astonishing information came to me this morning, that is, that there has been put into operation a movement to urge Honorable William B. Wilson to become a candidate for the nomination of United States Senator from the State of Pennsylvania; that pressure has been brought to bear upon him from some of the leading Democrats of that state: that it was urged upon him that he should be willing to make the sacrifice of the Secretaryship of the Department of Labor in order to make the race in the interests of the Democratic Party. I received this information from a friend who was as much astonished at the proposition as I was.

I took the liberty to call Secretary Wilson over the telephone and asked him whether he could not meet me at his office some time this afternoon, where I had the opportunity of conference with him for about half an hour. I found the situation as I have stated it, with the addition that Secretary Wilson stated in reply to the gentlemen who approached him on the subject that he felt he ought not to make such a race: that there are many reasons which he assigned for his declination of the offer, but that of course if his Chief, that is, you, the President of the United States, affirmatively asked him to make the race, he would feel it his bounden duty to comply. I stated to Secretary Wilson that I shall take the liberty of writing to you upon this subject, and I am doing so to ask you, aye, to prevail upon you, not to ask Mr. Wilson to make the race for the nomination for the Senatorship.

The law creating the Department of Labor became operative upon the day you were inaugurated President of the United States, a little more than two years ago. It was my privilege, as the representative of the organized labor movement, the American Federation of Labor, to submit to your favorable consideration the name of Honorable William B. Wilson for your appointment as Secretary of the Department of Labor, as a member of your Cabinet. It was the first time in the history of our government that a workman, truly representative of the human side of the rights[,] the interests, and the welfare of the working people of America, was the head of a great department of the government of the United States: the first time that a workman, a representative of the workers, became a member of the Cabinet of the President.

It is quite unnecessary, I take it, for me to call to your attention the many prejudices, difficulties, and obstacles which Secretary Wilson and the Department have had to overcome. He is the right man in the right place. It would not be an easy matter to find his successor, with all the qualifications so necessary to the performance of the delicate and difficult duties which the Secretary is required to perform. In appointing Mr. Wilson Secretary of the Department of Labor, he is not only your choice, he is not only the representative of the democracy, of the Democratic Party of Pennsylvania, he is not only a member of the Democratic Party of the United States, but he is in addition a direct representative of labor, and I am quite confident that his retirement from the position of Secretary of that Department to enter into the hopeless race for an election will disappoint and dishearten the men in the labor movement of America, as well as the hundreds of thousands of men who have learned to respect and honor him, men who find in him a high-minded, intelligent, sympathetic, yet stout hearted advocate and spokesman for the masses of the people in our republic.

Of course the position of a Senator is of great importance and far reaching influence, particularly a man of the ability and faithfulness of Mr. Wilson. There would be no question but that he would make his mark in the United States Senate as he has made and will make wherever he may be placed. But in the present situation, and until a considerable period of time elapses, I am strongly of the opinion that there is no position in our country in which Honorable William B. Wilson can serve the people quite so well as in the office of Secretary of the Department of Labor. In addition, there is this fact, that unless a political revolution takes place in the minds of the people of Pennsylvania, the nomination of any democrat in Pennsylvania for the United States Senatorship is doomed to failure in advance. I am of the opinion that it is neither fair nor just to lead Mr. Wilson to political slaughter. Confident that you share this last expression of mine, I write you in the hope that having the above facts and opinions before you, you may retain in your Cabinet the loyal, able, and faithful service of Secretary Wilson and give him the fuller and larger opportunity to aid his Chief wherever he may lead.   Very respectfully yours,   Saml. Gompers.

TLS (WP, DLC).

Norman Hapgood to Joseph Patrick Tumulty

Dear Mr. Tumulty: Washington, D. C. Jan 28 [1916]

What I had in mind was this:

Mr. Brandeis's purely legal qualifications are not surpassed by those of any other lawyer in the United States. He has been concerned in many of the most important cases of recent years. Some of his arguments before the Supreme Court, as in the Oregon Case on hours of labor for women,[1] have become classic. (Also arguments on the minimum wage I think, but am not sure of this. It would have to be looked up.) His practice has been very extensive and very important.

But there is a point much more exceptional than this. The title "the people's lawyer" is spontaneous and country-wide. Why? Because he, a man of the highest professional ability and earning power, chose to give a larger part of his time not to working for money but for working free for the public. This began back in Boston, as when he made a brilliant contract with the gas companies in behalf of the consumers.[2] And it has constantly increased in amount, until of recent years the greatest part of his time goes into big public work for which he is unwilling to be paid. Often big fees are offered for such work and refused, as he makes it a point never to take a cent for his public services.

(I suppose controversial work, as in the Ballinger case, the railroad cases, and the Riggs bank case, would better not be specially mentioned.)[3]

Yrs sincerely　Norman Hapgood

ALS (WP, DLC).

[1] That is, Muller *v.* Oregon (1908), in which Brandeis successfully defended an Oregon statute limiting the hours of labor by women to ten a day. In an attempt to demonstrate that the law and the needs of the economy were not mutually exclusive, Brandeis prepared a new kind of brief. He devoted but two pages to legal precedents and over a hundred pages to economic and social data concerning the effects of adverse working conditions on women. See Alpheus T. Mason, *Brandeis: A Free Man's Life* (New York, 1946), pp. 248-54, and Melvin I. Urofsky, *A Mind of One Piece: Brandeis and American Reform* (New York, 1971), pp. 39-42.

[2] This contract served as a model for the Sliding Scale Gas Act adopted by the Massachusetts legislature in May 1906. It provided that, as dividends increased, the price of gas should decrease on a sliding scale. See Mason, *Brandeis*, pp. 128-39.

[3] About the celebrated Ballinger controversy, see Alpheus T. Mason, *Bureaucracy Convicts Itself: The Ballinger-Pinchot Controversy of 1910* (New York, 1941), and George E. Mowry, *Theodore Roosevelt and the Progressive Movement* (Madison, Wisc., 1946), pp. 73-82. About the "railroad cases," see Henry L. Staples and Alpheus T. Mason, *The Fall of a Railroad Empire: Brandeis and the New Haven Merger Battle* (Syracuse, N. Y., 1947). The lesser known Riggs bank case involved a suit brought in April 1915 by the Riggs National Bank of Washington against McAdoo and other treasury officials for conspiring to wreck the bank. Brandeis was chief counsel for the government. The suit was still in the courts at the time Hapgood wrote this letter. The suit ended when several of the directors, who had meanwhile been indicted for perjury, promised to comply strictly with the law in the future.

An Address in Pittsburgh on Preparedness[1]

[Jan. 29, 1916]

Mr. Chairman, ladies, and gentlemen: I am conscious of a sort of truancy in being absent from my duties in Washington. And yet it did seem to me to be clearly the obligation laid upon me by the office to which I have been chosen that, as your servant and representative, I should come and report to you upon the progress of public affairs.

It has always been a feeling of mine that the best place for public servants was in the presence of those they serve, and that it was the obvious duty of every public man to hold frank counsel with the people themselves. I must frankly admit, with apologies

[1] In the auditorium of Soldiers' Memorial Hall. James Francis Burke, former congressman from Pennsylvania, introduced Wilson to an audience of more than four thousand persons.

to the chairman of the meeting and his associates, that I get a great deal more inspiration outside of Washington than inside of it; not because others are not as devoted as I am to the performance of their duties, but because you, the people of the United States, live outside of Washington. And the subject upon which I have come to address you is one upon which frank counsel is particularly needed.

You know that there is a multitude of voices upon the question of national defense, and I, for my part, am not inclined to criticize any of the views that have been put forth upon this important subject, because if there is one thing that we love more than another in the United States, it is that every man should have the privilege, unmolested and uncriticized, to utter the real convictions of his mind. Some of the things that are being said proceed from sentiment, and I would be the last to detract from genuine sentiment. I feel myself moved by some of the sentiments with the conclusions of which I cannot agree, just as much as the gentlemen are moved themselves who utter them. I believe in peace. I love peace. I would not be a true American if I did not love peace. But I know that peace costs something, and that the only way in which you can maintain peace is by thoroughly enjoying the respect of everybody with whom you deal. And while, therefore, I can subscribe to every desire which those fine people have who are counseling us against assuming arms in this country, I must ask them to think a second time about the circumstances under which we are living.

There are other counselors, the source of whose counsel is passion, and with them I cannot agree. It is not wise, it is not possible, to guide national policy under the impulse of passion. I would be ashamed of the passion of fear, and I would try to put the passion of aggression entirely aside in advising my fellow citizens what they should do at any great crisis of their national life. America does not desire anything that any other nation can give it, except friendship and justice and right conduct. I have been given the counsel of some people who are governed by the spirit of sympathy. I know it is difficult while some of the European countries are engaged in warfare and the world is aghast at the bloodshed and heroic sacrifices which are being made upon the battlefields. And I am sorry, for my part, to see any passion, whether of fear or of dislike, stir the counsels of America. I have counseled my fellow citizens, not only to be neutral in action in the presence of the present great European struggle, but also to be neutral in spirit and in feeling, and I have tried, for my own part, to hold off from every passion. I know it is not easy. When

the world is running red with blood, it is hard to keep the judgment cool. When men are suffering and offering up heroic
sacrifices, it is hard not to let the passion of sympathy take precedence over cool judgment. But, while I can understand the
excitements of the mind which circumstances have generated, I
would tremble to see them guide the decisions of the country.

And there is other advice which we get, which proceeds from
professional enthusiasm. I am glad that the soldiers and sailors
of the United States have professional enthusiasm, but I would
not like them to run away with me, any more than I would like
the passions and sympathies of my fellow countrymen to run
away with me. While we admire their zeal, we must square their
judgment with other standards than the professional standard.
I admire every man's professional enthusiasm, but I would not
wish to be guided by every man's professional enthusiasm. It is
time, therefore, that we attempted, at any rate, to apply the
standards of our own situation and of our own life to this great
question of national defense.

What is it that we want to defend? You don't need to have me
answer that question for you. It is in your own thought. We want
to defend the life of this nation against any sort of interference.
We want to maintain the equal right of this nation as against
the action of all other nations, and we wish to maintain the peace
and unity of the western hemisphere. Those are great things to
defend, and in their defense, sometimes, our thought must take a
great sweep, even beyond our own borders. Do you never stop
to reflect just what it is that America stands for? If she stands
for one thing more than another, it is for the sovereignty of self-
governing peoples, and her example, her assistance, her encouragement, has thrilled two continents in this western world with
all the fine impulses which have built up human liberty on both
sides of the water. She stands, therefore, as an example of
independence, as an example of free institutions, and as an example of disinterested international action in the maintenance
of justice. These are very great things to defend, and, wherever
they are attacked, America has at least the duty of example,
has at least the duty of such action as it is possible for her with
self-respect to take, in order that these things may not be
neglected or thrust on one side.

So it seems to me that the thing that we are in love with in
America is efficiency. Not merely business efficiency; not merely
efficiency in manufacturing and in the professions; not merely
the raising of great crops and the getting of our treasure out of
the bowels of the earth and the manufacture of our raw materials

into the things that are most useful to civilization. That efficiency merely underlies and furnishes a foundation for something a great deal bigger than that. We want the spirit of America to be efficient. We want American character to be efficient. We want American character to display itself in what I may perhaps be allowed to call spiritual efficiency—clear, disinterested thinking and fearless action along the right lines of thought. America is nothing if it consists merely of each of us; it is something only if it consists of all of us. And it cannot consist of all of us unless our spirits are banded together in a common enterprise. That common enterprise is the enterprise of liberty and justice and right. Therefore, I, for my part, have a great enthusiasm for rendering America spiritually efficient, and that conception lies at the basis of what seems very far removed from it, namely, the plans that have been proposed for the military efficiency of this nation.

Those plans do not involve a great army, because that is not America's way of being efficient in respect of her physical force. We do not intend, we never intend, to have a standing army greater than is necessary for the ordinary uses of peace. But we want to have, back of that army, a people who can rally to its assistance in the most efficacious fashion at any time they are called on to do so, but who, in the meantime, are not professional soldiers, who do not take the professional soldier's point of view in respect of public affairs, whose thought is upon their daily tasks of peaceful industry, and who know that in the United States the civilian takes precedence of the soldier.

Your chairman has just told you that the Constitution of the United States makes the President commander in chief of the armies and navies of the United States, and not often has the President been a soldier. I have sometimes said playfully that it was very awkward when, dressed in a frock coat and a silk hat, I had to ride a horse and review troops.[2] And the only reason I have consented to do so is because those formal garments—the very somber and formal garments which constitute a man's full dress in the daytime—are the symbol upon such occasions of the supremacy of the civil power over the military. A plain gentleman in black—sometimes a very plain gentleman—presides over the military force of the nation, and the thing is symbolic. We think first of peace, we think first of the civilian life, we think first of industry. We want the men who are going to defend the nation to be immersed in these pursuits of peace. But we want them to know

[2] See the picture of Wilson reviewing the New Jersey National Guard in Vol. 23.

how, when occasion arises, to rally to the assistance of the professional soldier of the country and show the nations of the world the might of America. Such men will not seek war. Such men will dread it as we all dread it. Such men will know that the happiness of their families and the prosperity of their countrysides and the wealth of their cities and everything upon which their life depends is rooted and grounded in peace. But they will also know that, upon occasion, infinite sacrifice must be made of life and of wealth, and that there are things that are higher than the ordinary occupations of life, namely, all assertions of the ideals of right.

I am not going before audiences like this to go into the details of the program which has been proposed to the Congress of the United States, because, after all, the details do not make any difference. I believe in one plan; others may think that an equally good plan can be substituted, and I hope my mind is open to be convinced that it can. But what I am convinced of, and what we are all working for, is that there should be provided, not a great militant force in this country, but a great reserve of adequate and available force which can be called on upon occasion. I have proposed that we should be supplied with at least half a million men accustomed to handle arms and to live in camps; and that is a very small number as compared with the gigantic proportions of modern armies. Therefore, it seems to me that no man can speak of proposals like that as if they pointed in the direction of militarism.

When men talk of the threat of what is proposed, I wonder if they have really stopped to consider what is actually proposed. It is astonishing how many men of straw are set up and gallantly knocked down. It is astonishingly easy to prove that something is wrong which nobody has proposed, and this nation is not going to be deceived by the fears of gentlemen who are fearful only of the things which they have imagined. We are not going to be stalked and daunted by ghosts and fancies. We are proposing a very businesslike thing. I, for my part, believe that I am proposing a thoroughly businesslike thing. For I am proposing something more than what is temporary. It is my conception that, as the Government of the United States has done a great deal, though even yet probably not enough, to promote agricultural education in this country, it ought to do a great deal to promote industrial education in this country. And, along with thoroughgoing industrial and vocational training, it is perfectly feasible to instruct the youth of the land in the mechanism and use of arms, in the sanitation of camps, in the more rudimentary principles and practices of modern warfare, and so not to bring about occasions such as we have sometimes brought about, when, upon a sudden danger, youngsters were summoned by the proclamation of the President out of every community, who came crude and green and raw into the service of their country—infinitely willing but also wholly unfitted for the great physical task which was ahead of them. No nation should waste its youth like that. A nation like this should be ashamed to use an inefficient instrument when it can make its instrument efficient for everything that it needs to employ it for, and can do it along with the magnifying and ennobling and quickening of the tasks of peace.

But we have to create the schools and develop the schools to do these things, and we cannot at present wait for this slow process. We must go at once to the task of training a very considerable body of men to the use of arms and the life of camps, and we can do so upon one condition, and one condition only. The test, ladies and gentlemen, of what we are proposing is not going to be the action of Congress; it is going to be the response of the country. It is going to be the volunteering of the men to take the training and the willingness of their employers to see to it that no obstacle is put in the way of their volunteering. It will be up to the young men of this country and to the men who employ them. Then, and not till then, we shall know how far it is true that America wishes to prepare itself for national defense —not a matter of sentiment, but a matter of hard practice.

Are the men going to come out, and are those who employ them going to facilitate their coming out? I, for one, believe that they will. There are many selfish influences at work in this country, as in every other. But when it comes to the large view, America can produce the substance of patriotism as abundantly as any other country under God's sun. I have no anxiety along those lines, and I have no anxiety along the lines of what Congress is going to do. You elect men to Congress who have opinions, and it is not strange that they should have differing opinions. I am not jealous of debate. If what I propose cannot stand debate, then something ought to be substituted for it which can. And I am not afraid that it is going to be all debate. I am not afraid that nothing is going to come out of it. I am not afraid that we shall fail to get out of it the most substantial and satisfactory results. Certainly, when I talk a great deal myself, I am not going to be jealous of the other man's having a chance to talk also. We are talking, I take it, in order to get at the very final analysis of the case—the final proof and demonstration of what we ought to do.

My own feeling, ladies and gentlemen, is that it is a pity that this is a campaign year. I hope, with the chairman of the meeting, that the question of national preparation for defense will not by anybody be drawn into campaign uses or partisan aspects. There are many differences between Democrats and Republicans—honest differences of opinion and of conviction—but Democrats do not differ from Republicans upon the question of the nation's safety, and no man ought to draw this thing into controversy in order to make party or personal profit out of it. I am ready to acknowledge that men on the other side politically are just as deeply and just as intelligently interested in this question as I am, of course, and I shall be ashamed of any friends of mine who may take any different view of it.

I want you to realize just what is happening, not in America, but in the rest of the world. It is very hard to describe it briefly. It is very hard to describe it in quiet phrases. The world is on fire, and there is tinder everywhere. The sparks are liable to drop anywhere, and somewhere there may be material which we cannot prevent from bursting into flame. The influence of passion is everywhere abroad in the world. It is not strange that men see red in such circumstances. What a year ago was incredible has now happened, and the world is so in the throes of this titanic struggle that no part of it is unaffected.

You know what is happening. You know that, by a kind of improvidence which should be very uncharacteristic of America, we have neglected for several generations to provide the means to carry our own commerce on the seas. And, therefore, being dependent upon other nations for the most part to carry our commerce, we are dependent upon other nations now for the movement of our commerce when other nations are caught in the grip of war. So that every natural impulse of our peaceful life is embarrassed and impeded by the circumstances of the time. And wherever there is contact, there is apt to be friction. Wherever the ordinary rules of commerce at sea and of international relationship are thrust aside or ignored, there is danger of the more critical kind of controversy. Where nations are engaged, as many nations are now engaged, they are peculiarly likely to be stubbornly steadfast in the pursuit of the purpose which is the main purpose of the moment. And so, while we move among friends, we move among friends who are preoccupied, preoccupied with an exigent matter which is foreign to our own life, foreign to our own policy, but which nevertheless inevitably affects our own life and our own policy. While a year ago it seemed impossible that a struggle upon so great a scale should last a whole twelvemonth, it has now lasted a year and a half, and the end is not yet. And all the time things have grown more and more difficult to handle.

It fills me with a very strange feeling sometimes, my fellow citizens, when it seems to be implied that I am not the friend of peace. If these gentlemen could have sat with me, reading the dispatches and handling the questions which arise every hour of the twenty-four, they would have known how infinitely difficult it had been to maintain the peace, and they would have believed that I was the friend of peace. But I also know the difficulties, the real dangers, dangers not about things that I can handle, but about things that the other parties handle and I cannot control.

It amazes me to hear men speak as if America stood alone in the world and could follow her own life as she pleased. We are in the midst of a world that we did not make and cannot alter. Its atmospheric and physical conditions are the conditions of our own life also. And, therefore, as your responsible servant, I must tell you that the dangers are infinite and constant. I should feel that I was guilty of an unpardonable omission if I did not go out and tell my fellow countrymen that new circumstances have arisen which make it absolutely necessary that this country should prepare herself, not for war, not for anything that smacks in the least of aggression, but for adequate national defense.

So I have come out from the seclusion of Washington and have broken what I hope you consider a good rule, namely, that a man ought steadfastly to attend to business. Counsel has become the most necessary business of the hour. The most necessary thing to do now is to make America acquainted with her own situation in the world and acquainted with the fact that not all the processes of conduct are within her own control; that, on the contrary, they are daily and hourly affected by things which she cannot govern or direct. Appeals of this sort are apt to be only too adequate. I am not afraid that America will do nothing. I am only desirous that she should be very coolly considerate of what she does. One cool judgment is worth a thousand hasty counsels. The thing to be supplied is light, not heat. But if heat, then white heat, not spluttering heat, which has a tendency to spread the fire. There ought, if there is any heat at all, to be that warmth of the heart, which makes every man thrust aside his own personal feelings—his own personal interests—and take thought of the welfare and benefit of others.

We seem sometimes, ladies and gentlemen, to be very careless in our use of words, and yet there are some words about which we are very careful. We call every sort of man who has displayed unusual powers "great"; we call some bad men "great." But we reserve the word "honorable" for those who are great but spend their greatness upon others rather than upon themselves. You erect statues to men who have made great sacrifices or to men who have given great beneficences. You do not erect statues to men who have served only themselves. There is a patriciate even in democratic America. Our peers are the men who have spent their great energies outside the narrow circle of their own self-interest, and who have seen to it that great largess of intellectual effort was given for the benefit of the communities in which they lived. These are the men we honor; these are the men who are the characteristic Americans. America was born into the world to do mankind service, and no man is a true American in whom the desire to do mankind service does not take precedence over the desire to serve himself. If I believed that the might of America was a threat to any free man in the world, I would wish America to be weak. But I believe the might of America is the might of righteous purpose and of a sincere love for the freedom of mankind.

For my own part, I am very much stirred by every sight that I get of the flag of the United States. I did not use to have the sentiment as poignantly as I have it now. But, if you stood in my place, ladies and gentlemen, and felt that, in some peculiar and unusual degree, the honor of that flag was entrusted to your keeping, how would you feel? Wouldn't you feel that you were a sort of trustee for the ideals of America? Wouldn't you feel that you ought to go out and seek counsel of your fellow citizens as to what they thought America to be and what they thought you ought to do honorably and perfectly to represent America? Wouldn't you feel that, if anything were incumbent upon you, more than another, it was to understand what that flag stands for? That flag was originally stained in very precious blood—blood spilt, not for any dynasty, not for any small controversies over national advantage, but in order that a little body of three million men in America might make sure that no man was their master. And, as this nation has accumulated in population and in power, as the tread of it has shaken every foot of this great continent, as we have built up great wealth and majestic cities and made fertile farms to bloom from one side of it to the other, there have been built up men who were calling constantly upon their public representatives to be trustees of that original conception.

America can't afford to be weak, and she can't afford to use her strength for anything which does not honor the Stars and Stripes. What I want you to do is this: I do not want you merely to listen to speeches. I want you to make yourselves vocal. I want you to let everybody who comes within earshot of you know that you are a partisan for the adequate preparation of the United

States for national defense. I have come to ask you, not merely to go home and say, "The President seems to be a good fellow and to mean what he says." I want you to go home determined that, within the whole circle of your influence, the President—not as a partisan, but as the representative of the national honor—shall be backed up by the whole force that is in the nation.

I know that that appeal is not in vain, for I know what deep fountains of sentiment well up in America. I know that the surface of our life sometimes seems sordid. I know that the men who do most of the talking do not always hear the undertones of our life. But I know that the men who go in and out of the farm, the men who go in and out at the factory door, the men who go in and out of the offices, the men who go abroad upon ships, the men who travel up and down the country to quicken the courses of our commerce—underneath the surface of every one of these men there is the beating of a heart which is willing to make a profound sacrifice for the country that we all love. And those hearts are now going to be guided by very hardheaded minds, by minds that know how to think and plan and insist. And out of what seems an intricate debate, there is going to come a great plan for national defense of which we will all be proud and which will lead us to forget partisan differences in one great enthusiasm for the United States of America.

Printed in *Addresses of President Wilson*, with additions and corrections from the text printed in the *Pittsburg Post*, Jan. 30, 1916.

An Address in Pittsburgh to an Overflow Meeting[1]

[Jan. 29, 1916]

Mr. Chairman, ladies, and gentlemen: I feel that I was lured here under false pretenses. I was told that I was to address an audience of women, and the men, as usual, have been usurpers and have come in. So they need not listen (Laughter). When I reflected what I should say to a body of women about military preparation for national defense, it seemed to me that there was no excuse for making any difference between what I should say to them and what I should say to any other body of citizens of the United States, unless, indeed, there was this reason for a distinction: There is a sense in which the women of the country live closer to the life of it than the men. The preoccupations of

[1] In the banquet room of Soldiers' Memorial Hall before an audience composed mainly of women. As no tickets had been handed out for this occasion, a crowd of more than two thousand persons had thronged the room, and another five thousand were waiting to get in. Wilson was again introduced by James F. Burke.

business for the man who has to work for his daily bread, and for the bread of those whom he loves and who are dependent upon him, are such that, sometimes, the material side of life seems to him the only real side of life. I find that very few men stop to think of the life of the family, of the life of the community, of the life of the state and of the nation. Their absorption is necessarily so great in the daily task that the spiritual needs do not often or very closely touch them, and it has seemed to me that in the home, in the contact with the children, in the anxieties for the moral and the daily conduct of this life which they live, the women perhaps feel the pulse of the country more than the men do. And it is in order that we may preserve the thoughtful ideals of America that it is necessary we should make preparation for national defense.

The old plea for the defense of our hearth and our home does not seem to me a very handsome appeal. It is easy to love what is your own, and it is easy to fight for what is your own. No man who has a drop of manliness in him would do anything else. But the thing that is hard, and the thing that challenges him, is to fight for the things that do not immediately touch him—in order that others may live, whom we do not love and do not even know, in order that the great rivers of the national life may flow free and unobstructed, in order that the great ideals and purposes and longings of the people we never see might be realized. That is the life of a nation. No man ever saw the people of whom he forms a part. No man ever saw a government. I live in the midst of the Government of the United States, but I never saw the Government of the United States. Its personnel extends through all the nations and across the seas and into every corner of the world— in the presence of the representatives of the United States in foreign capitals and in foreign centers of commerce. I never saw the Government of the United States. It is an ideal thing, and I must share its spirit by the use of my imagination. I must make myself part of it by thinking the things which, separately and of myself, I would not think—the thoughts that are national, the things that move great bodies of men to devote themselves to great tasks and even to great adventures.

I suppose that, as the women of the country look upon the life that surges around them, there must very often come into their hearts something of the profound feeling that pulses through great national existences. I do not believe that the women of this country are interested in national defense merely in order that they may be physically protected. If that is all we cared for, there would not be any great spirit of America. The flag would not

stand for anything if it was merely a roof over my head or a bul-
wark against an attack upon me. The flag stands for something
for which we are all trustees—the great part that America is to
play in the world.

And what is the great part that America is to play in the world?
America stands, first of all, for the right of men to determine
whom they will obey and whom they will serve; for the right of
political freedom and a people's sovereignty. And anybody who
interferes with this conception by touching the affairs of America makes it necessary that America should assert her rights.
America has, not only to assert her right to her own life within her
own borders, but she has to assert her right to the equal and just
treatment of her citizens wherever they go. And she has something even more than that to insist upon, because she has made
up her mind long ago that she is going to stand, so far as this
western hemisphere is concerned, for the right of peoples to
choose their own polities without foreign influence or interference. So she has a gigantic task which she cannot shirk without
disgrace.

In ordinary circumstances, it has not been necessary for her
to think of force, because everybody knows that there is latent
in her as much force as resides anywhere in the world. This great
body of 100,000,000 people has an average of intelligence and
resourcefulness probably unprecedented in the history of the
world. Nobody doubts that, give us time enough, we can assert
any amount of force we please to assert. But when the world is
on fire, how much time do you want to take to be ready? When
you know that there are combustible materials everywhere in
the life of the world and in your own national life, and that the
sky is full of floating sparks from a great conflagration, are you
going to sit down and say it will be time enough, when the fire
begins, to do something about it? I do not believe that the fire
is going to begin, but I would be surer of it if we were ready for
the fire. And I do want to come as your responsible servant and
tell you this—that we do not control this fire. We are under the
influence of it, but we are not at the sources of it. We are where
it any time may affect us, and yet we cannot govern its speed
and progress. And if it once touches us, it may touch the very
sources of our life, it may touch the very things we stand for and
fight for, too late to enable us successfully to vindicate or defend.
I have not come here to tell you of any immediate threat of a
definite danger, because by very great patience, by making our
position perfectly clear, and then steadfastly maintaining the
same attitude throughout great controversies, we have so far

held difficulty at arm's length. But I want you to realize the task you have imposed upon your government.

There are two things which practically everybody who comes to the Executive Office in Washington tells me. They tell me, "The people are counting upon you to keep us out of this war." And, in the next breath, what do they tell me? "The people are equally counting upon you to maintain the honor of the United States." Have you reflected that a time might come when I could not do both? And have you made yourselves ready to stand behind your government for the maintenance of the honor of your country, as well as for the maintenance of the peace of the country? If I am to maintain the honor of the United States, and it should be necessary to exert the force of the United States to do it, have you made the force ready? You know that you have not, and the very fact that the force is not ready may make the task you have set me all the more delicate and all the more difficult. And so I have come away from Washington to remind you of your part in this great business. There is no part that belongs to me that I wish to shirk, but I wish you to remember the part that belongs to you. I want every man and woman of you to stand behind me in pressing a reasonable plan for national defense.

The only possible reasonable plan is an American plan. The American plan is not a great military establishment. The American plan is a great body of citizens who are ready to rally to the national defense and adequate to serve the national defense when it is necessary to do so. And, as the heart of our politics lies in the breast of the average man, so the strength of the nation rests in the capacity of the individual man. He ought to know how modern arms are made and how they ought to be handled; he ought to know the rudimentary principles of camp sanitation; he ought to know the elements of military discipline, so that when he goes to the defense of his nation he won't be a raw recruit, but a man who knows what is expected of him and needs only the guidance of competent officers to do it.

You know how every constitution in the United States—the Constitution of the nation and the constitutions of the states—lays it down as a principle that every man in America has the right to carry arms. He hasn't the right to conceal them, because you would converse with a man who had a gun over his shoulder perhaps in a different tone of voice from that in which you would converse with him if you didn't see a gun. Concealed arms are not the constitutional privilege of anybody, but obvious arms are the constitutional privilege of everybody in the United States. For the very conception of our polity is that the country is going to be taken care of by the men who live in the country, and that they are not going to depute the task. Every audience still, after the passing of more than a hundred years, is stirred by the stories of the embattled farmers at Lexington—the men who already had arms, who seized them and came forth in order to assert the independence and political freedom of themselves and their neighbors. That is the ideal picture of America—the rising of the nation. But do we want the nation to rise unschooled, inexperienced, ineffective, and furnish material for powder and shot before they realize how to defend themselves at all?

I am not going to expound to you a particular plan for training a great citizen reserve, because the detail of the plan is not the important part of it. The important part is that it is necessary that we should have a plan, have it early, and put it into execution at the earliest possible moment, by which we will have a great reserve of men sufficiently trained to know what service is and to be ready for it when called. These are the things we are going to have. I say that because I believe it to be a national necessity. And I say it because I am confident that the members of Congress know a national necessity when they see it. There is going to be a great deal of debate, there is going to be many differences of opinion—many honest and intelligent differences of opinion— as to how the thing ought to be done, but there is not going to be any difference of purpose as to what ought to be done.

Of course, there are some gentlemen who allow themselves to be deceived by very handsome sentiments. If a man is so in love with peace that he can't imagine any kind of danger, I almost envy him the trance that he is in. And so long as he is in the trance, he is not going to do anything but enjoy the vision. But such men are not many. America is a hard-headed nation, and Americans generally want to see the facts as they come before they act. And the facts of the world are such that it is my duty to counsel my fellow citizens that preparation for national defense cannot any longer be postponed.

I am not one of those who believe that a great standing army is the means of maintaining peace, because; if you build up a great profession, those who form parts of it want to exercise their profession, and I cannot blame them for it. I should, myself, hate to be ready to do an expert thing and never be permitted to do it. But, for my part, we have never wanted, we have never encouraged in America the spirit of militarism, and we shall never have the fact of militarism in the United States. What I am particularly interested in is that my fellow citizens should make a distinction between militarism in any form and the things that are now being proposed to the Congress of the United States. If men are engaged nine months out of the twelve in the pursuits of commerce and manufacturing and agriculture and are in camp to do a little training only two or three months in the year, do you suppose they are going to have the spirit of the three months and not the spirit of the nine months? Don't you see that they are immersed in the civil and economic life of the nation? They know what a war means, what it will cost, what it will cost them and those who are dependent upon them. There will be bred in them no spirit of military ardor. There will be bred in them the sober spirit of being ready to defend peace and fend off war, to make good the safety, the ideals of America, and the performance of all the great tasks which she has set herself. And there will be bred in them also something very useful—the spirit of discipline, the spirit of obedience, the consciousness of having some kind of personal connection with the great body politic which they profess as citizens to serve. And there will well up in them, unless I am very much mistaken, great fountains of sober sentiment which will affect their neighbors as well as themselves, and Americans will be a little less careless of the general interest of the nation, a little less thoughtful of their own peculiar and selfish interests. And something of the old spirit of '76, which was not the spirit of aggression, but the spirit of love of country and pure and undefiled patriotism, will grow stronger and stronger in this country that we love.

And so, my fellow citizens, what I am pleading for with the utmost confidence is the revival of that great spirit of patriotism for which a hall like this stands as a symbol. I was saying the other night that it was a very interesting circumstance that we never hang a lad's yardstick up over the mantelpiece, but we do hang his musket up when he is gone. Not because the musket stands for a finer thing than the yardstick in itself—it is a brutal thing to kill—but that the musket stood for the risk of life, for something greater than the lad's own self. It stood for infinite sacrifice to the point of death. And it is for that sentiment of willingness to die for something greater than ourselves that we hang the musket up over the mantelpiece, and in doing so make a sacred record of the high service of the family to which we belong.

It is for that reason that we erect buildings like this. It is for that reason that we make monuments to those who serve us and forget ourselves. And when we summon the young men of this country to volunteer for brief training every year in order that they may be a source of security for the nation and its ideals, I know that the response will bring something more than a few hundred youngsters into the field. It will bring the spirit of America back to self-consciousness, and we shall again know what it is to belong to a country that throbs with a spirit of life that will arrest the attenion of mankind.

Printed in the *Pittsburg Post*, Jan. 30, 1916, with a few corrections from the text printed in *Addresses of President Wilson*.

An Address in Cleveland on Preparedness[1]

[Jan. 29, 1916]

Mr. President and fellow citizens: I esteem it a real privilege to be in Cleveland again and to address you upon the serious questions of public policy which now confront us. I have not given myself this sort of pleasure very often since I have been President, for I hope that you have observed what my conception of the office of President is. I do not believe that, ordinarily speaking, it is a speech-making office. I have found the exactions of it such that it was absolutely necessary for me to remain constantly in touch with the daily changes of public business, and you so arranged it that I should be President at a time when there was a great deal of public business to remain in touch with. But the times are such, gentlemen, that it is necessary that we should take common counsel together regarding them.

I suppose that this country has never found itself before in so singular a position. The present situation of the world would, only a twelvemonth ago, even after the European war had started, have seemed incredible, and yet now the things that no man anticipated have happened. The titanic struggle continues. The difficulties of the world's affairs accumulate. It was, of course, evident that this was taking place long before the present session of Congress assembled, but only since the Congress assembled has it been possible to consider what we ought to do in the new circumstances of the times. Congress cannot know what to do unless the nation knows what to do; and it seemed to me, not only my privilege, but my duty to go out and inform my fellow countrymen just what I understood the present situation to be.

What are the elements of the case? In the first place, and most

[1] In The Grays' Armory. Bascom Little, president of the Chamber of Commerce of Cleveland, introduced Wilson. Also on the speaker's platform were Newton D. Baker, Senator Atlee Pomerene, and Mayor Harry L. Davis. After this address, Wilson spoke informally from the balcony of the Hollender Hotel to a crowd of several thousand persons who stood in the rain. Swem did not record this speech, and the Cleveland newspapers only mentioned it.

obviously, two thirds of the world are at war. It is not merely a European struggle. Nations in the Orient have become involved, as well as nations in the West. And, everywhere, there seems to be creeping, even upon the nations disengaged, the spirit and the threat of war. All the world outside of America is on fire.

Do you wonder that men's imaginations take color from the situation? Do you wonder that there is a great reaction against war? Do you wonder that the passion for peace grows stronger as the spectacle grows more tremendous and more overwhelming? Do you wonder, on the other hand, that men's sympathies become deeply engaged on the one side or the other? For no small things are happening. This is a struggle which will determine the history of the world, I dare say, for more than a century to come. The world will never be the same again after this war is over. The change may be for weal or it may be for woe, but it will be fundamental and tremendous.

And in the meantime we, the people of the United States, are the one great disengaged power, the one neutral power, finding it a little difficult to be neutral, because, like men everywhere else, we are human. We have the deep passions of mankind in us. We have sympathies that are as easily stirred as the sympathies of any other people. We have interests which we see being drawn slowly into the maelstrom of this tremedous upheaval. It is very difficult for us to hold off and look with cool judgment upon such tremendous matters.

And yet we have held off. It has not been easy for the government at Washington to avoid the entanglements which seemed to beset it on every side. It has needed a great deal of watchfulness and an unremitting patience to do so. But, all the while, no American could fail to be aware that America did not wish to become engaged, that she wished to hold apart, not because she did not perceive the issues of the struggle, but because she thought her duties to be the duties of peace and of separate action. And, all the while, the nations, themselves, that were engaged seemed to be looking to us for some sort of action, not hostile in character, but sympathetic in character. Hardly a single thing has occurred in Europe which has in any degree shocked the sensibilities of mankind that the Government of the United States has not been called upon by the one side or the other to protest and intervene with its moral influence, if not with its physical force. It is as if we were the great audience before whom this stupendous drama is being played out, and we are asked to comment upon the turns and crises of the plot. And not only are we the audience, and challenged to be the umpire, so far as the opinion of the world is concerned, but all the while our own life touches these matters at many points of vital contact.

The United States is trying to keep up the processes of peaceful commerce while all the world is at war and while all the world is in need of the essential things which the United States produces. And yet, by an oversight for which it is difficult to forgive ourselves, we did not provide ourselves, when there was proper peace and opportunity, with a mercantile marine by means of which we could carry the commerce of the world without the interference of the navies of other nations which might be engaged in controversy not our own. And so the carrying trade of the world is for the most part in the hands of the nations now embroiled in this great struggle. Americans have gone to all quarters of the world. Americans are serving the business of the world in every part of it. And every one of these men, when his affairs touch the regions that are on fire, is our ward, and we must see to his rights and that they are respected. Do you not see how all the sensitive places of our life touch these great disturbances?

Now, in the midst of all this, what is it that we are called on to do as a nation? I suppose that, from the first, America has had one peculiar and particular mission in the world. Other nations have grown rich, my fellow citizens; other nations have been as powerful as we in material resources in comparison with the other nations of the world. Other nations have built up empires and exercised dominion. We are not peculiar in any of these things. But we are peculiar in this—that, from the first, we have dedicated our force to the service of justice and righteousness and peace. We have said: "Our chief interest is not in the rights of property, but in the rights of men. Our chief interest is in the spirits of men that they might be free; that they might enjoy their lives unmolested so long as they observed the just rules of the game; that they might deal with their fellow men with their heads erect, the subjects and servants of no man—the servants only of the principles upon which their lives rested." And America has done more than care for her own people and think of her own fortunes in these great matters. She has said, ever since the time of President Monroe, that she was the champion of the freedom and the separate sovereignty of peoples throughout the western hemisphere. She is trustee for these ideals, and she is pledged, deeply and permanently pledged, to keep these momentous promises.

She not only, therefore, must play her part in keeping this conflagration from spreading to the people of the United States. She must also keep this conflagration from spreading on this side of the sea. These are matters in which our very life and our whole pride are embedded and rooted, and we can never draw back from them. And I, my fellow citizens, because of the extraordinary office with which you have entrusted me, must, whether I will or not, be your responsible spokesman in these great matters. It is my duty, therefore, when impressions are deeply borne in upon me with regard to the nation's welfare, to speak to you with the utmost frankness about them. And that is the errand upon which I have come away from Washington.

For my own part, I am sorry that these things fall within the year of a national political campaign. They ought to have nothing whatever to do with politics. The man who brings partisan feeling into these matters and seeks partisan advantage by means of them is unworthy of your confidence. I am sorry that, upon the eve of a campaign, we should be obliged to discuss these things for fear they might run over into the campaign and seem to constitute a part of it. Let us forget that this is a year of national elections. That is neither here nor there. The thing to do now is for all men of all parties to think along the same lines and do the same things and forget every difference that may have divided them.

And what ought they to do? In the first place, they ought to tell the truth. There have been some extraordinary exaggerations both of the military weakness and the military strength of this country. Some men tell you that we have no means of defense, and others tell you that we have sufficient means of defense. And neither statement is true. Take, for example, the matter of our coast defenses. It is obvious to every man that they are of the most vital importance to the country. Such coast defenses as we have are strong and admirable, but we have not got coast defenses in enough places. Their quality is admirable, but their quantity is insufficient. The military authorities of this country have not been negligent. They have sought adequate appropriations from Congress, and in most instances have obtained them, so far as we saw the work in hand that it was necessary to do. And the work that they have done in the use of these appropriations has been admirable and skillful work. Do not let anybody deceive you into supposing that the army of the United States, so far as it has had opportunity, is in any degree unworthy of your confidence.

And the navy of the United States? You have been told that it is the second in strength in the world. I am sorry to say that experts do not agree with those who tell you that. Reckoning by its actual strength, I believe it to be one of the most efficient navies in the world, but in strength it ranks fourth, not second. You must reckon with the fact that it is necessary that that should be our first arm of defense, and you ought to insist that everything should be done that it is possible for us to do to bring the navy up to an adequate standard of strength and efficiency.

Where we are lacking in preparation is on land and in the number of men who are ready to fight. Not the number of fighting men, but the number of men who are ready to fight. Some men are born troublesome, some men have trouble thrust upon them, and other men acquire trouble. I think I belong to the second class. But the characteristic desire of America is, not that she should have a great body of men whose chief business it is to fight, but a great body of men who know how to fight and are ready to fight when anything that is dear to the nation is threatened. You might have what we have—millions of men who had never handled arms of war, who are mere material for shot and powder if you put them in the field. And America would be ashamed of the inefficiency of calling such men to defend the nation. What we want is to associate in training with the army of the United States men who will volunteer for a sufficient length of time every year to get a rudimentary acquaintance with arms, a rudimentary skill in handling them, a rudimentary acquaintance with camp life, a rudimentary acquaintance with military drill and discipline. And we ought to see to it that we have men of that sort in sufficient number to constitute an initial army when we need an army for the defense of the country.

I have heard it stated that there are probably several million men in this country who have received a sufficient amount of military drill, either here or in the countries in which they were born and from which they have come to us. Perhaps there are. Nobody knows, because there is no means of counting them. But if there are so many, they are not obliged to come at our call; we do not know who they are. That is not military preparation. Military preparation consists in the existence of such a body of men known to the federal authorities, organized provisionally by the federal authorities, and subject by their own choice and will to the immediate call of the federal authorities.

We have no such body of men in the United States except the National Guard. Now, I have a very great respect for the National Guard. I have been associated with one section of that guard in one of the great states of the Union, and I know the character of the officers and the quality of the men, and I would trust them unhesitatingly both for skill and for efficiency. But the whole National Guard of the United States falls short of 130,000 men.

It is characterized by a very great variety of discipline and efficiency as between state and state, and it is, by the Constitution itself, put under authority of more than twoscore state executives. The President of the United States has not the right to call on these men except in the case of actual invasion, and, therefore, no matter how skillful they are, no matter how ready they are, they are not the instruments for immediate national use. I believe that the Congress of the United States ought to do, and that it will do, a great deal more for the National Guard than it ever has done, and everything ought to be done to make it a model military arm.

But that is not the arm that we are immediately interested in. We are interested in knowing that there are men all over the United States prepared, equipped, and ready to go out at the call of the national government upon the shortest possible notice. You will ask me, "Why do you say the shortest possible notice?" Because, gentlemen, let me tell you, very solemnly, you cannot afford to postpone this thing. I do not know what a single day may bring forth. I do not wish to leave you with the impression that I am thinking of some particular danger. I merely want to leave you with this solemn impression—that I know that we are daily treading amidst the most intricate dangers, and that the dangers that we are treading amongst are not of our making and are not under our control, and that no man in the United States knows what a single week or a single day or a single hour may bring forth. These are solemn things to say to you, but I would be unworthy of my office if I did not come out and tell you with absolute frankness just exactly what I understand the situation to be.

I do not wish to hurry the Congress of the United States. These things are too important to be put through without very thorough sifting and debate, and I am not in the least jealous of any of the searching processes of discussion. That is what free people are for—to understand what they are about and to do what they wish to do only if they understand what they are about. But it is impossible to discuss the details of plans in great bodies, unorganized bodies, of men like this audience, for example. All that I can do in this presence is to tell you what I know of the necessities of the case and to ask you to stand back of the executive authorities of the United States in urging upon those who make our laws as early and effective action as possible.

America is not afraid of anybody. I know that I express your feeling, and the feeling of all our fellow citizens, when I say that the only thing I am afraid of is not being ready to perform my duty. I am afraid of the danger of shame; I am afraid of the danger of inadequacy; I am afraid of the danger of not being able to express the great character of this country with tremendous might and effectiveness whenever we are called upon to act in the field of the world's affairs.

For it is character we are going to express, not power merely. The United States is not in love with the aggressive use of power. It despises the aggressive use of power. There is not a foot of territory belonging to any other nation which this nation covets or desires. There is not a privilege which we ourselves enjoy which we would dream of denying any other nation in the world. If there is one thing that the American people love and believe in more than another, it is peace and all the handsome things that belong to peace. I hope that you will bear me out in saying that I have proved that I am a partisan of peace. I would be ashamed to be belligerent and impatient when the fortunes of my whole country and the happiness of all my fellow countrymen were involved. But I know that peace is not always within the choice of the nation, and I want to remind you, and remind you very solemnly, of the double obligation you have laid upon me. I know you have laid it upon me because I am constantly reminded of it in conversation, by letter, in editorial, by means of every voice that comes to me out of the body of the nation. You have laid upon me this double obligation: "We are relying upon you, Mr. President, to keep us out of this war, but we are relying upon you, Mr. President, to keep the honor of the nation unstained."

Do you not see that a time may come when it is impossible to do both of these things? Do you not see that, if I am to guard the honor of the nation, I am not protecting it against itself, for we are not going to do anything to stain the honor of our own country. I am protecting it against things that I cannot control—the actions of others. And where the actions of others may bring us, I cannot foretell. You may count upon my heart and resolution to keep you out of the war, but you must be ready, if it is necessary, that I should maintain your honor. That is the only thing a real man loves above himself. Some men who are not real men love other things above themselves. But the real man believes that his honor is dearer than his life; and a nation is merely all of us put together. And the nation's honor is dearer than the nation's comfort and the nation's peace and the nation's life itself. So that we must know what we have thrown into the balance; we must know the infinite issues which are impending every day of the year. And when we go to bed at night, and when we rise in the morning, and at every interval of the rush of business, we must remind ourselves that we are part of a great body politic in which are vested some of the highest hopes of the human race.

Why is it that all nations turn to us with the instinctive feeling that, if anything touches humanity, it touches us? Because it knows that, ever since we were born as a nation, we have undertaken to be the champions of humanity and of the rights of men. Without that ideal there would be nothing that would distinguish America from her predecessors in the history of nations. Why is it that men who loved liberty have crowded to these shores? Why is it that we greet them as they enter the great harbor at New York with that majestic Statue of Liberty holding up a torch whose visionary beams are supposed to spread abroad over the waters of the world, and to say to all men: "Come to America where mankind is free and where we love all the works of righteousness and of peace."

Printed in *Addresses of President Wilson*, with a few corrections from the complete text printed in the *Cleveland Plain Dealer*, Jan. 30, 1916.

From Gifford Pinchot

My dear Mr. President: Washington, D. C. January 29, 1916.

I am writing on behalf of the National Conservation Association to call your attention to the threat against the public welfare presented by the water power situation in Congress. This threat is so pressing, and the certain consequence of failure to meet it so disastrous, that it deserves your consideration and that of the whole people of the United States. In defense of the general interest, therefore, I shall take the liberty of making this letter public.

There is a bill on the calendar of the Senate whose passage would be a public misfortune. It is the Shields Bill for the disposal of water power on navigable streams. The great water power interests are behind it, and an effort to pass it is to be made next week.[1]

This is the second time the Shields Bill has been reported in the Senate. Last year the friends of Conservation were able to prevent its passage. This year, thanks to a skillful and elaborate campaign conducted by the water power interests, there is grave danger that it will pass.

The Shields Bill gives the use of enormously valuable public property to the water power interests without compensation. Ostensibly it provides for a method of restoring its own property to the public at the end of fifty years. As a matter of fact, it has been so drawn as to make it practically impossible for the people to take their own water powers back into their hands. This it does by opening the way for indefinite litigation, and by the use of language under which the United States might be required to take over and pay for the whole electric lighting systems of cities or the whole equipment of manufacturing plants in order to get possession again of water powers owned by the people.

The bill interposes every possible legal delay between the violator of a government permit and the chance of effective enforcement. It fails to require the necessary publicity and uniformity of accounts, and so makes the effective supervision of water power corporations impossible.

The Shields Bill gives to the water power interests the right to condemn or take any land they choose, public or private,—rights which they should never have, but which should be exercised when required for water power development either by the States or the National Government. It forces the people, when they take back the public property whose use they have granted, to pay the unearned increment on land condemned or otherwise acquired by the grantee. In not a few of its provisions the actual form of words prepared by the representatives of the water power interests have been incorporated.

These are by no means all of its defects, but they will suffice to make it plain that the Shields Bill has been astutely drawn for the benefit of the water power interests, and ought not to pass.

This is a public matter wholly removed from partisanship. You yourself have taken strong ground against the grabbing of our natural resources, of which none is more valuable in peace or war than water power. President Roosevelt vetoed the James River Bill in 1909, and President Taft vetoed the Coosa River Bill in 1911 because they gave away the public property for nothing. That is precisely what the Shields Bill would do today.

Natural resources lie at the foundation of all preparedness, whether for peace or for war. No plan for national defense can be effective unless it provides for adequate public control of the raw materials out of which the defensive strength of a nation is made. Of these raw materials water power is the most essential, because without electricity generated from water power we can not manufacture nitrates, and nitrates are the basis of gun powder. There are no great natural deposits of nitrates in the United States as there are in Chili. If we are to depend upon ourselves for our supplies, as we should, we must be prepared to produce our nitrates electrically from the air.

It would be folly to allow the public water powers, which can supply the indispensable basis of national defense, to pass out of effective public control. In the light of recent events, it would be especially shortsighted not to provide for the manufacture of nitrates and other munitions by means of the public water powers, if necessary in the event of war. The terms and conditions under which this could be done should be so fixed in advance as to forbid private greed to profit unduly from the public necessity. Under the law in France a man was recently charged with that specific offense, found guilty, and sent to prison.

There is another bill before the Senate to which I desire to call your attention. This is the Ferris Bill for the control of water power on the public lands and National Forests. The Ferris Bill, in the form in which it passed the House, is in accord with the principles of conservation. As it has been reported to the Senate it contains indefensible changes. It actually encourages monopoly by compelling the Secretary of the Interior to grant forthwith to any corporation all the power sites it may choose to ask for. Under it power corporations could seize upon any part they choose of the Grand Canyon of the Colorado, a natural wonder far greater than Niagara, and no one could stop them. These are but two of its faults.

The Senate form of the Ferris Bill should be killed, and the House form should pass, after it has been amended into conformity with the public interest, and so that it will no longer take the care of water powers on the National Forests away from the experienced and competent Forest Service, where it now lies. The Ferris Bill has already twice passed the House. It already has your endorsement, but without the active support of the Administration it will fail.

For every reason of national prosperity and national defense the development of our water powers is desirable. But the claim of the water power interests that free gifts of public property to themselves are needed to promote development is false. It is disproved, officially and finally, by Secretary Houston's recent report on water power, the most searching and exhaustive ever made.[2] The Houston report shows that where the public interest has been most carefully protected, on the National Forests, there development has been most rapid and the largest ratio of increase in capital invested has taken place. More than half of the water power developed in the West is on the public lands and the National Forests. In the eleven Western States water power development from 1902 to 1912 was nearly five times as rapid as in the rest of the country, and since 1912 the annual increase is greater than ever. In California, which has the largest area of National Forests, and in Oregon and Washington, development has gone on until it is now actually in excess of market requirements. It is clearly evident that fair Government regulation does not hamper development and use. No farmer, for example, will be deprived of nitrate fertilizer at a fair price because of reasonable Government control of public water powers.

I have ventured by this letter to call your special attention to the fact that the public interest in the public water powers is in danger. To set that danger aside, your opposition to the Shields Bill and your support of the Ferris Bill, properly amended in the Senate, are vitally needed. I need hardly add they will be vigorously seconded by the National Conservation Association, which, under every Administration since it was founded, has supported the officers of our Government in every effort they have made to promote the public welfare through the conservation of natural resources.   Very respectfully,   Gifford Pinchot

TLS (WP, DLC).
    [1] For an extended commentary on the Shields and Ferris bills, mentioned later in this letter, see F. K. Lane to WW, March 2, 1916.
    [2] *Electric Power Development in the United States*, Senate Doc. No. 316, 64th Cong., 1st sess. (Washington, 1916).

From Robert Latham Owen

My dear Mr. President: New York City, January 29th, 1916.

I am delighted with your nomination of Louis Brandeis. You could not have made a better selection, and I am more pleased at the point of view which you have shown in this selection than I can well express.

With greatest respect,
            Your obedient servant,   Robt. L. Owen

TLS (WP, DLC).

From Thomas Bell Love

Dallas Tex Jany 29 1916

The Brandeis appointment is one of the big things for the people in this administration made up of big things it could not be better   Thos. B. Love.

T telegram (WP, DLC).

Charles Lee Swem to Rudolph Forster

Cleveland, Ohio, January 30-31, 1916.

If letter from Col. House has or does come President asks that it be forwarded at once.   Chas. L. Swem.

T telegram (WP, DLC).

From Edward Mandell House

[Bern, Switzerland, Jan. 30, 1916]

The situation is like this. A great controversy is now going on in Germany regarding under-sea warfare. The navy, backed more or less by the army believe that England can be effectively block-aded provided Germany can use their new and powerful sub-marines indiscriminately and not be hampered by any laws whatsoever. They also believe failure has resulted from our [inter-ference][1] and Germany's endeavour to conform to our demands. They think war with us would not be so disastrous as England's blockade. The civil government believe that if the blockade con-tinues they may be forced to yield to the navy; consequently they are unwilling to admit the illegality of their under-sea warfare. They will yield anything but this. If you insist on that point, I believe war will follow. Gerard understands the question and I would suggest letting him try to arrange something [satisfactory] direct. I hope final action may not be taken until I have had an opportunity of talking with you. Do you [This, I] think it is of great importance since there [these] are phases of the situation that cannot be conveyed by cable or letter? Have you received my letters consecutively [four] to seven? I reach Paris Tuesday [morn-ing].   Edward House.

WWT decode of T telegram (WP, DLC).
[1] Words in brackets in House's telegrams are from the T copies in the E. M. House Papers, CtY.

Remarks from a Rear Platform in Waukegan, Illinois

[Jan. 31, 1916]

Ladies and gentlemen: I need not tell you how gratified I am that so large a number of you should have come out to bid me welcome. It looks like a holiday crowd and yet, as you know, I am not on a holiday errand. I have come away from Washington because I thought it absolutely necessary that I should interest my fellow citizens in the immediate question of the hour, which is the question of the preparation of the United States for national defense.

It is impossible in circumstances like these to discuss this very important question, but I take this very crowd as an evidence of your spontaneous interest in it, and I am reassured with regard to the attitude of my fellow countrymen concerning this great matter. You have not come out, I believe, to greet me as an individual, but to show your interest in and loyalty to the Government of the United States. I welcome this manifestation of your interest as an evidence of that, and I shall go forth on my errand with the more encouragement because of the greeting you have given me here this morning.

It is very delightful to have this immediate contact with you. I wish with all my heart that I could shake hands with all of you. I can only give you my very best wishes and say that you may take it for granted that we will do the best we can to take care of your interests. May I not thank you for your presence here this morning?

T MS (WP, DLC).

Remarks from a Rear Platform in Kenosha, Wisconsin

[Jan. 31, 1916]

Fellow citizens: I know that you are aware of the important errand upon which I have come away from Washington. You will hardly expect me in these circumstances to enter into a discussion of its serious features. I can only say to you that it is a very gratifying evidence to me of the interest of my fellow countrymen, in this great matter of preparation for national defense, that you should have come out to greet me in such numbers and with such a spirit of cordiality. It is equally gratifying to me to have an opportunity to come in contact with great bodies of men and women like this, and I believe that it is my duty, as well as my privilege, to report to you upon the condition of the nation.

I can only say in these circumstances, ladies and gentlemen, that the Government of the United States, which you have temporarily entrusted to us, is taking very serious thought, not only for the welfare of the nation, but also for its safety, and that it is our sincere and deliberate conviction that adequate preparation has not yet been made for the safety of the nation; that it is immediately necessary that it should be made. And I think I can report to you, with a good deal of confidence, that it certainly will be made. There will be a good deal of discussion as to how it will be done, but none as to whether or not it is to be done. (Train pulls out)

T MS (WP, DLC).

Remarks from a Rear Platform in Racine, Wisconsin

[Jan. 31, 1916]

Ladies and gentlemen: It is a great pleasure to find myself back in Wisconsin again. I wish I were here on more of a holiday errand, so that I could enjoy it with less preoccupation as to the errand upon which I have come. But, as you know, I have come upon a very serious errand, indeed. I do not believe that you really need to be enlisted in the cause of national preparation for defense. But I am very anxious, indeed, that you should know that, from the point of view of the government itself, that preparation cannot any longer wisely be postponed. And I have come to ask for your influence and support in insisting that it be very early attended to, and very thoroughly attended to.

There are some things that are being said which I hope you will not believe. It is being said, among other things, that this agitation for preparations for national defense comes chiefly from those who are interested in supplying the government with the munitions of war and from those who are interested in supplying our battleships with their armament. Gentlemen, do not allow yourselves to be misled by statements of that sort! Anything that the government does, somebody is going to make some money out of; but the impulse for this thing does not come from those quarters. The impulse comes from men disinterested, men who know the actual circumstances of the country and who know that these things are immediately necessary. And I, for my part, have all along advocated, and always shall advocate, that the government, so far as possible, manufacture these things for itself, in order that, at any rate, it may control the prices at which these articles will be sold to the government. If it is necessary to protect ourselves against those who would make money out of the necessities of the nation, there are adequate means of defending ourselves, and we will use those means. But I do not believe that the impulse comes from those quarters; I do not believe that in those quarters there is patriotism lacking any more than there is patriotism lacking in other quarters.

Neither do I want you to believe that the necessity for defense is sudden and recent. We have always been too easygoing in these matters, and it has long been necessary that we should make careful preparation. Now we are acutely brought to the consciousness of the necessity.

(Train pulls out) I am not going to be allowed to finish that argument.

T MS (WP, DLC).

An Address in Milwaukee on Preparedness[1]

[Jan. 31, 1916]

Mr. Chairman and fellow citizens: I need not inquire whether the citizens of Milwaukee and Wisconsin are interested in the subject of my errand. The presence of this great body in this vast hall sufficiently attests your interest. But I want at the outset to remove a misapprehension that I fear may exist in your minds. There is no sudden crisis; nothing new has happened. I am not out upon this errand because of any unexpected situation. I have come to confer with you upon a matter upon which it would, in any circumstances, be necessary for us to confer when all the rest of the world is on fire and our own house is not fireproof. Everywhere the atmosphere of the world is thrilling with the passion of a disturbance such as the world has never seen before. And it is wise, in the words just uttered by your chairman, that we should see that our own house is set in order and that everything is done to make certain that we shall not suffer by the general disturbance.

There were some dangers to which this nation seemed at the outset of the war to be exposed, which, I think I can say with confidence, are now passed and overcome. America has drawn her blood and her strength out of almost all the nations of the world. It is true of a great many of us that there lies deep in our hearts the recollection of an origin which is not American. We are aware that our roots, our traditions, run back into other national soils. There are songs that stir us; there are some faraway historical recollections which engage our affections and stir our memories. We cannot forget our forebears; we cannot altogether ignore the fact of our essential blood relationships. And, at the outset of this war, it did look as if there were a division of domestic sentiment which might lead us to some errors of judgment and some errors of action. But I, for one, believe that that danger is passed. I never doubted that the danger was exaggerated, because I had learned long ago—and many of you will corroborate

[1] In the Auditorium, before an audience of eight thousand persons. General Frederick C. Winkler, a German-American Civil War veteran, introduced Wilson.

me by your experience—that it is not the men who are doing the talking always who represent the real sentiments of the nation. I, for my part, always feel a serene confidence in waiting for the declaration of the principles and sentiments of the men who are not vociferous, do not go about seeking to make trouble, do their own thinking, attend to their own business, and love their own country.

I have at no time supposed that the men whose voices seemed to contain the threat of division amongst us were really uttering the sentiments even of those whom they pretended to represent. I, for my part, have no jealousy of family sentiment. I have no jealousy of that deep affection which runs back through long lineage. It would be a pity if we forget the fine things that our ancestors have done. But I also know the magic of America. I also know the great principles which thrill men in the singular body politic to which we belong in the United States. I know the impulses which have drawn men to our shores. They have not come idly. They have not come without conscious purpose to be free. They have not come without voluntary desire to unite themselves with the great nation on this side of the sea. And I know that, whenever the test comes, every man's heart will be first for America. It was principle and affection and ambition and hope that drew men to these shores, and they are not going to forget the errand upon which they came and allow America—the home of their refuge and hope—to suffer by any forgetfulness on their part. And so the troublemakers have shot their bolt, and it has been ineffectual. Some of them have been vociferous; all of them have been exceedingly irresponsible. Talk was cheap, and that was all it cost them. They did not have to do anything. But you will know, without my telling you, that the man who, for the time being, you have charged with the duties of President of the United States must talk with a deep sense of responsibility. And he must remember, above all things else, the fine traditions of his office, which some men seem to have forgotten. There is no precedent in American history for any action of aggression on the part of the United States or for any action which might mean that America is seeking to connect herself with the controversies on the other side of the water. Men who seek to provoke us to such action have forgotten the traditions of the United States. But it behooves those with whom you have entrusted office to remember the traditions of the United States and to see to it that the actions of the government are made to square with those traditions.

But there are other dangers, my fellow citizens, which are not past and which have not been overcome, and they are dangers which we cannot control. We can control irresponsible talkers amidst ourselves. All we have got to do is to encourage them to hire a hall, and their folly will be abundantly advertised by themselves. But we cannot in this simple fashion control the dangers that surround us now, and have surrounded us since this titanic struggle on the other side of the water began. I say on the other side of the water. You will ask me, "On the other side of which water?", for this great struggle has extended to all quarters of the globe. There is no continent outside, I was about to say, of this western hemisphere which is not touched by it. But I recollected, as I began the sentence, that a part of our own continent was touched with it, because it involves our neighbors to the north in Canada. There is no part of the world, except South America, to which the direct influences of this struggle have not extended, so that now we are completely surrounded by this tremendous disturbance. And you must realize what that involves.

Our thoughts are concentrated upon our own affairs and our own relations to the rest of the world. But the thoughts of the men who are engaged in this struggle are concentrated upon the struggle itself, and there is daily and hourly danger that they will feel themselves constrained to do things which are absolutely inconsistent with the rights of the United States. They are not thinking of us. I am not criticising them for not thinking of us. I dare say if I were in their place neither would I think of us. They believe that they are struggling for the lives and honor of their nations, and that, if the United States puts its interests in the path of this great struggle, she ought to know beforehand that there is danger of very serious misunderstanding and difficulty. So that the very uncalculating, unpremeditated, one might almost say accidental, course of affairs may touch us to the quick at any moment. And I want you to realize that, standing in the midst of these difficulties, I feel that I am charged with a double duty of the utmost difficulty. In the first place, I know that you are depending upon me to keep this nation out of the war. So far I have done so. And I pledge you my word that, God helping me, I will if it is possible. But you have laid another duty upon me. You have bidden me see to it that nothing stains or impairs the honor of the United States. And that is a matter not within my control. That depends upon what others do, not upon what the Government of the United States does. Therefore, there may at any moment come a time when I cannot preserve both the honor and the peace of the United States. Do not exact of me an impossible and contradictory thing, but stand ready and insistent that everybody who represents you should stand ready to provide the necessary means for maintaining the honor of the United States.

I sometimes think that it is true that no people ever went to war with another people. Governments have gone to war with one another. Peoples, so far as I remember, have not, and this is a government of the people, and this people is not going to choose war. But we are not dealing with people; we are dealing with governments. We are dealing with governments now engaged in a great struggle, and therefore we do not know what a day or an hour will bring forth. All that we know is the character of our own duty. We do not want the question of peace and war, or the conduct of war, entrusted too entirely to our government. We want war, if it must come, to be something that springs out of the sentiments and principles and actions of the people themselves. And it is on that account that I am counseling the Congress of the United States not to take the advice of those who recommend that we should have, and have very soon, a great standing army, but, on the contrary, to see to it that the citizens of this country are so trained, and that the military equipment is so sufficiently provided for them, that, when they choose, they can take up arms and defend themselves.

The Constitution of the United States makes the President the commander in chief of the army and navy of the nation, but I do not want a big army subject to my personal command. If danger comes, I want to turn to you and the rest of my fellow countrymen and say, "Men, are you ready?" And I know what the response will be. I know that there will spring up out of the body of the nation a great host of free men. And I want those men not to be mere targets for shot and shell. I want them to know something of the arms they have in their hands. I want them to know something about how to guard against the diseases that creep into camps where men are unaccustomed to live. I want them to know something of what the orders mean that they will be under when they enlist under arms for the Government of the United States. I want them to be men who can comprehend and easily and intelligently step into the duty of national defense. That is the reason that I am urging upon the Congress of the United States, at any rate, the beginnings of a system by which we may give a very considerable body of our fellow citizens the necessary training.

I have not forgotten the great National Guard of this country, but in this country of one hundred million people there are only 129,000 men in the National Guard. And the National Guard, fine as it is, is not subject to the orders of the President of the United States. It is subject to the orders of the governors of the several states. And the Constitution itself says that the President has no right to withdraw them from their states even, except in the case of actual invasion of the soil of the United States. I want the Congress of the United States to do a great deal for the National Guard, but I do not see how the Congress of the United States can put the National Guard at the disposal of the national authorities. Therefore, it seems to me absolutely necessary that, in addition to the National Guard, there should be a considerable body of men with some training in the military art who will have pledged themselves to come at the call of the nation.

I have been told by those who have a greater knack at guessing statistics than I have that there are probably several million men in the United States who, either in this country or in other countries from which they have come to the United States, have received training in arms. It may be; I do not know, and I suspect that they do not either. But even if it be true, these men are not subject to the call of the federal government. They would have to be found; they would have to be induced to enlist; they would have to be organized; their numbers are indefinite; and they would have to be equipped. Such are not the materials which we need. We want to know who these men are and where they are and to have everything ready for them if they should come to our assistance. For we have now got down, not to the sentiment of national defense, but to the business of national defense. It is a business proposition, and it must be treated as such. And there are abundant precedents for the proposals which have been made to the Congress. Even that arch democrat, Thomas Jefferson, believed that there ought to be compulsory military training for the adult men of the nation, because he believed, as every true believer in democracy believes, that it is upon the voluntary action of the men of a great nation like this that it must depend for its military force.

There is another misapprehension that I want to remove from your minds: Do not think that I have come to talk to you about these things because I doubt whether they are going to be done or not. I do not doubt it for a moment. But I believe that, when great things of this sort are going to be done, the people of this country are entitled to know just what is being proposed. As a friend of mine says, I am not arguing with you, I am telling you. I am not trying to convert you to anything, because I know that in your hearts you are converted already. But I want you to know the motives of what is proposed and the character of what is proposed, in order that we should have only one attitude and counsel with regard to this great matter.

It is being very sedulously spread abroad in this country that the impulse back of all this is the desire of men who make the materials of war to get money out of the Treasury of the United States. I wish the people that say that could see meetings like this. Did you come here for that purpose? Did you come here because you are interested to see some of your fellow citizens make money out of the present situation? Of course you did not. I am ready to admit that probably the equipment of those men whom we are training will have to be bought from somebody. And I know that, if the equipment is bought, it will have to be paid for, and I dare say somebody will make some money out of it. It is also true, ladies and gentlemen, that there are men now, a great many men, in the belligerent countries who are growing rich out of the sale of the materials needed by the armies of those countries. If the government itself does not manufacture everything that an army needs, somebody has got to make money out of it. And I, for my part, have been urging the Congress of the United States to make the necessary preparations by which the government can manufacture armor plate and munitions, so that, being in the business itself, and having the ability to manufacture all it needs, if it is put upon a business basis, it can, at any rate, keep the price that it pays within moderate and reasonable limits. The Government of the United States is not going to be imposed upon by anybody. And you may rest assured, therefore, that, while I believe you prefer that private capital and private initiative should bestir themselves in these matters, it is also possible—and I assure you that it is most likely—that the Government of the United States will have adequate means of controlling this matter very thoroughly, indeed. There need be no fear on that side. Let nobody make you suppose that this is a money-making agitation. I would, for one, be ashamed to be such a dupe as to be engaged in it if it had any suspicion of that about it. But I am not as innocent as I look. And I believe that I can say for my colleagues in Washington that they are just as watchful in such matters as you would desire them to be.

And there is another misapprehension that I do not wish you to entertain. Do not suppose that there is any new or sudden or recent inadequacy on the part of this government in respect of preparation for national defense. I have heard some gentlemen say that we have no coast defenses worth talking about. Coast defenses are not nowadays advertised, you understand, and they are not visible to the naked eye, so that if you passed them and nothing exploded, you would not know they were there. The coast defenses of the United States, while not numerous enough, are equipped in the most modern and efficient fashion. You are told that there has been some sort of neglect about the navy. There has not been any sort of neglect about the navy. We have been slowly building up a navy which in quality is second to no navy in the world. The only thing it lacks is quantity. In size, it is the fourth navy in the world, though I have heard it said by some gentlemen in this very region that it was the second. In fighting force, though not in quality, it is reckoned by experts to be the fourth in rank in the world. And, yet, when I go on board those ships and see their equipment and talk with their officers, I suspect that they could give an account of themselves which would raise them above the fourth class. It reminds me of that very quaint saying of the old darky preacher, "The Lord said unto Moses, come fourth, and he came fifth and lost the race." But I think this navy would not come fourth in the race, but higher.

What we are proposing now is not the sudden creation of a navy, for we have a splendid navy, but the definite working out of a program by which, within five years, we shall bring the navy to a fighting strength which otherwise might have taken eight or ten years, along exactly the same lines of development that have been followed, and followed diligently and intelligently, for at least a decade past. There is no sudden panic, there is no sudden change of plan. All that has happened is that we now see that we ought more rapidly and more thoroughly than ever before to do the things which have always been characteristic of America. For she has always been proud of her navy and has always been addicted to the principle that her citizenship must do the fighting on land. We are working out American principles a little faster, because American pulses are beating a little faster, because the world is in a whirl, because there are incalculable elements of trouble abroad which we cannot control or alter. I would be derelict to the duty which you have laid upon me if I did not tell you that it was absolutely necessary to carry out our purpose in this matter now and at once.

And yet, all the time, my fellow citizens, I believe that, in these things, we are merely interpreting the spirit of America. Who shall say what the spirit of America is? I have many times heard orators apostrophise this beautiful flag which is the emblem of the nation. I have many times heard orators and philosophers speak of the spirit which was resident in America. I have always, for my own part, felt that it was an act of audacity to attempt to characterize anything of that kind. And when I have been outside of the country, in foreign lands, and have been asked if this, that, or the other was true of America, I have habitually said, "Nothing stated in general terms is true of America, because it is the most variegated and varied and multiform land under the sun." Yet I know, my fellow citizens, that, if you turn away from the physical aspects of the country, if you turn away from the variety of the strains of blood that make up our great population, if you turn away from the great variations of occupation and of interest among our fellow citizens, there is a spiritual unity in America. I know that there are some things which stir every heart in America, no matter what the racial derivation or the local environment. And one of the things that stirs every American is the love of individual liberty. We do not stand for occupations. We do not stand for material interests. We do not stand for any narrow conception even of political institutions. But we do stand for this—that we are banded together in America to see to it that no man shall serve any master who is not of his own choosing. And we have been very liberal and generous about this idea. We have seen great peoples, for the most part not of the same blood with ourselves, to the south of us build up polities in which this same idea pulsed and was regnant—this idea of free institutions and individual liberty. And when we have seen hands reached across the water from older political polities to interfere with the development of free institutions in the western hemisphere, we have said: "No, we are the champions of the freedom of popular sovereignty wherever it displays or exercises itself throughout both Americas."

We are the champions of a particular sort of freedom, the sort of freedom which is the only foundation and guarantee of peace. Peace lies in the hearts of great industrial and agricultural populations, and we have arranged a government on this side of the water by which their preferences and their predilections and their interests are the mainsprings of government itself. And so, when we prepare for national defense, we prepare for national political integrity. We prepare to take care of the great ideals which gave birth to this government. We are going back in spirit and in energy to those great first generations in America, when men banded themselves together, though they were but a handful upon a single coast of the Atlantic, to set up in the world the standards which have ever since floated everywhere that Americans asserted the power of their government. As I came along the line of the railway today, I was touched to observe that everywhere, upon every railway station, upon every house, where a flag could be procured, some temporary standard had been raised from which there floated the Stars and Stripes. They seemed to have divined the errand upon which I had come—to remind you that we must subordinate every individual interest, and every local interest, to assert once more, if it should be necessary to assert them, the great principles for which that flag stands.

Do not deceive yourselves, ladies and gentlemen, as to where the colors of that flag came from. Those lines of red are lines of blood, nobly and unselfishly shed by men who loved the liberty of their fellow men more than they loved their own lives and fortunes. God forbid that we should have to use the blood of America to freshen the color of that flag. But if it should ever be necessary again to assert the majesty and integrity of those ancient and honorable principles, that flag will be colored once more, and in being colored will be glorified and purified.

Printed in *Addresses of President Wilson*, with corrections from the complete text in the *Chicago Daily Tribune*, Feb. 1, 1916.

An Address in Chicago on Preparedness[1]

[Jan. 31, 1916]

Mr. Chairman and fellow citizens: You put me under a great obligation to you by the generosity of your reception, and I am quite aware that it is largely because you know how desirous I am to speak to you with the utmost frankness upon some of the most essential issues of our national life. The Constitution of the United States explicitly lays upon the President the duty of reporting, at the beginning of each annual session of Congress, to the representatives of the people concerning the state of the Union. And it seems to me that it is a very natural inference from that command that the President should, from time to time, when unusual circumstances arise, make his report, so far as it is possible for him to do so, directly to the people themselves. It is with that conception in view that I have taken the liberty of coming to you tonight. I have not permitted myself the privilege of leaving my duties at Washington very often, because they have been very exacting and very anxious duties, and there is a very clear sense in which it is my duty to be constantly there and constantly watchful of the changing circumstances of the day. But I thought you would feel me justified, in the unusual circumstances of the time, if I left my duties there for a little while and came to explain a few matters to you.

A year ago, though the war in Europe had then been six months in progress, I take it it would have seemed incredible to all of us that the storm should continue to gather in intensity instead of

[1] In the Auditorium. Wilson was introduced by Frank Congleton Caldwell, president of the Industrial Club, which sponsored the event. Governor Edward Fitzsimmons Dunne, Democrat, was also on the stage.

spending its force. I suppose that twelve months ago no one could have predicted the extraordinary way in which the intensity of the struggle has increased from month to month. And the difficulties involved by reason of that war have also increased beyond all calculation. A year ago, it did seem as if America might rest secure without very great anxiety and take it for granted that she would not be drawn into this terrible maelstrom. But those first six months were merely the beginning of the struggle. Another year has been added, and now no man can confidently say whether the United States will be drawn into the struggle or not. Therefore, it is absolutely necessary that we should take counsel together as to what it is necessary that we should do. The circumstances of the day are so extraordinary that perhaps it is not prudent for a man upon whom the responsibility of affairs are laid to know too particularly the details of what is happening. The trouble with a great many of our fellow citizens is that they have let their imaginations become so engaged in this terrible affair that they cannot look upon it as those should who wish to keep a cool head and a detached judgment. So many men on this side of the water are seeing red that we seem to see in their thoughts the reflection of the blood that is being spent so copiously on the other side of the sea. It is not wise for us to let our thoughts become so deeply involved that we cannot think separately and must think with a sort of personal immersion in this great struggle.

I must admit to you, very frankly, that I have been careful to refrain from reading the details in the newspaper reports. I wish to see the thing and realize it only in its large aspects and to keep my thoughts concentrated on America—her duty, her circumstances, her tasks. And her tasks have been very difficult. They have not been merely negative. Have you not realized how all the world seems to have been constantly conscious from the beginning of this struggle that America was, so to say, the only audience before whom this terrible plot was being worked out; how everybody engaged in the struggle has seemed to turn to America for moral judgments concerning it; how each side in the titanic struggle has appealed to us to adjudge their enemies in the wrong; how there has been no tragical turn in the course of events that America has not been called on for some sort of protest or expression of judgment? And, so, those of us who are charged with the responsibility of affairs have realized very intensely that there was a certain sense in which America was looked to to keep even the balance of the whole world's thought.

And America was called upon to do something very much more

than that, even, profoundly difficult, if not impossible, though that be. She was called upon to assert in times of war the standards of times of peace. There is an old saying that the laws are silent in the presence of war. Alas, yes! Not only the civil laws of individual nations, but also apparently the law that governs the relation of nations with one another must at times fall silent and look on in dumb impotency. And yet it has been assumed throughout this struggle that the great principles of international law and of international comity had not been suspended. And the United States, as the greatest and most powerful of the disengaged nations, has been looked to to hold high the standards which should govern the relationship of nations to each other.

I know that on the other side of the water there has been a great deal of cruel misjudgment with regard to the reasons why America has remained neutral. Those who look at us at a distance, my fellow citizens, do not feel the strong pulses of ideal principle that are in us. They do not feel the conviction of America—that her mission is a mission of peace, and that righteousness can be maintained as a standard in the midst of arms. They do not realize that, back of all our energy by which we have built up great material wealth and created great material power, we are a body of idealists, much more ready to lay down our lives for a thought than for a dollar. They suppose, some of them, that we are holding off because we can make money while others are dying—the most cruel misunderstanding that any nation has ever had to face, so wrong that it seems almost useless to try to correct it, because it shows that the very fundamentals of our life are not comprehended and understood.

I need not tell you, my fellow citizens, that we have not held off from this struggle from motives of self-interest, unless it be considered self-interest to maintain our position as the trustees of the moral judgment of the world. We have believed, and I believe, that we can serve even the nations at war better by remaining at peace and holding off from this contest than we could possibly serve them in any other way. Your interest, your sympathy, your affections may be engaged on the one side or the other. But no matter which side they are engaged on, your duty to your affections in that matter is to stand off and not let this nation be drawn into the war. Somebody must keep the great stable foundations of the life of nations untouched and undisturbed. Somebody must ..eep the great economic processes of the world of business alive. Somebody must see to it that we stand ready to repair the enormous damage and the incalculable losses which will ensue from this war, and which it is hardly credible could be repaired if every great nation in the world were drawn into the contest. Do you realize how nearly it has come about that every great nation in the world has been drawn in? The flame has touched even our own continent by drawing in our Canadian neighbors to the north of us, and, except for the South American continent, there is not one continent upon the whole surface of the world to which this flame has not spread. And when I see some of my fellow citizens spread tinder where the sparks are falling, I wonder what their ideal of Americanism is.

I dare say you realize, therefore, the solemnity of the feeling with which I come to audiences of my fellow citizens at this time. I cannot indulge the reckless pleasure of expressing my own private opinions and prejudices. I speak as the trustee of the nation, called upon to speak its sober judgments and not its individual opinions. And, therefore, it is with the feeling of this responsibility upon me that I have come to you tonight and have approached the other audiences that I have had the privilege of addressing upon this journey. Do you realize the peculiar difficulty of the situation in which your Executive is placed? You have laid upon me, not by implication, but explicitly—it has come to me by means of every voice that has been vocal in the United States—you have laid upon me the double obligation of maintaining the honor of the United States and of maintaining the peace of the United States. Is it not conceivable that the two might become incompatible? Is it not conceivable that, however great our passion for peace, we would have to subordinate it to our passion for what is right? Is it not possible that, in maintaining the integrity of the character of the United States, it may become necessary to see that no man does that integrity too great violence?

It is a very terrible thing, ladies and gentlemen, to have the honor of the United States entrusted to your keeping. It is a great honor, that honor of the United States! In it runs the blood of generations of men who have built up ideals and institutions on this side of the water intended to regenerate mankind. And any man who does violence to right, any nation that does violence to the principles of just international understanding, is doing violence to the ideals of the United States. We observe the technical limits. We assert these rights only when our own citizens are directly affected. But you know that our feeling is just the same whether the rights of those individual citizens are affected or not, and that we feel all the concern of those who have built up things so great that they dare not let them be torn down or touched with profane hands.

Look at the task that is assigned to the United States—to assert the principles of law in a world in which the principles of law have broken down—not the technical principles of law, but the essential principles of right dealing and humanity as between nation and nation. Law is a very complicated term. It includes a great many things that do not engage our affections. But at the basis of the things that we are now dealing with lie the deepest affections of the human heart—the love of life, the love of right-eousness, the love of fair dealing, the love of those things that are just and of good report. The things that are rooted in our very spirit are the stuff of the law that I am talking about now.

We may have to assert these principles of right and of human-ity at any time. What means are available? What force is at the disposal of the United States to assert these things? The force of opinion? Opinion, I am sorry to say, my fellow citizens, did not bring this war on, and I am afraid that opinion cannot stay its progress. This war was brought on by rulers, not by peoples; and I thank God that there is no man in America who has the author-ity to bring war on without the consent of the people. No man for many a year yet can trace the real sources of this war. But this thing we know—that opinion did not bring it on, and that the force of opinion, at any rate the force of American opinion, is not going to stop it.

I admire the hopeful confidence of those of our fellow citizens who believe that American opinion can stop it. But, being some-what older than some of them, and having run through a rather wide gamut of experience, I am prevented from sharing their hopeful optimism. I would not belittle the influences of opinion, least of all the influences of American opinion—it is very influen-tial—but it will not stop this overwhelming flood. And, if not the force of opinion, what force has America available to stop the flood from overflowing her own fair area?

We have one considerable arm of force, a very considerable arm of force, namely, the splendid navy of the United States. I am told by the experts, to whose judgment I must defer in these matters, that the navy of the United States, in respect of its enumerated force, ranks only fourth among the navies of the world. I entertain and I indulge myself with the opinion that, in quality, it ranks very much higher than fourth place. The United States has never been negligent of its navy, despite what some gentlemen may say; least of all has it been negligent in recent years. Three years ago there were 182 vessels in commission in that navy; there are now 238. Three dreadnoughts and fifteen subordinate craft will be added within a month or two. There have been added 6,000 capable sailors to the ranks of the enlisted men of that navy. The Congress of the United States, in the last three years, has poured out more money than was poured out on the average in any previous years in the history of the United States for the maintenance and upbuilding of the United States Navy. It has spent $44,000,000 a year, as contrasted with a previous average of not more than $33,500,000. All the subsidiary arms of the service have been built up. Three years ago, there were four officers assigned to duty connected with aviation, and they did not have a single available—at any rate usable—craft at their service. Now there are thirty-seven airships, 121 commissioned officers, and a large number of noncommissioned officers and a sufficient force of enlisted men in the school of practice at Pensacola. And that is only the beginning, because the Sixty-third Congress, the last Congress, was the first to make a specific appropriation for aviation in connection with the navy.

We have given to the present fleet of the United States an organization such as it never had before, I am told by Admiral Fletcher, and we have made preparations for immediate war, so far as the navy is concerned. The trouble is not with the quality or the organization of the existing navy. It is merely that we have followed plans piecemeal, a little bit at a time, now in this direction, now in that direction; that we have never had a plan thought out to cover a number of years in advance; that we have never set ourselves a definite goal of equipment and set our resolutions to attain that goal within a reasonable length of time. The plans that are being proposed to the present Congress, and which the present Congress will adopt, are plans to remedy this piecemeal treatment of the navy and bring it to its highest point of efficiency by steady plans carried out from month to month and year to year. It is going to cost a good deal of money, and I find that the difficulty with some members of Congress is, not what ought to be done about the navy, but what they are going to tax in order to get the money. I do not happen to be a member of Congress, but I would be willing to go before any constituency in the United States in the confidence that they were willing to pay for the defense of the nation. We are neither poor nor niggardly. We know how things cost, and we intend to pay for them; and we do not intend to pay for them more than they are worth.

That is a matter which is troubling a good many people. I have proposed to the Congress that, for one thing, we at once build our own armor plant, not for the purpose of making all the armor that our ships need, unless that should become necessary, but for the purpose of keeping the price within sight. I have proposed to the Congress that we prepare to manufacture also the munitions which the government may need for the same purpose—not to drive other people out of business, but merely to serve other people with notice that, if necessary, we will manufacture all the munitions we need. We have had some experience in this matter. The navy now makes a very large proportion of its own powder. Before it began, it paid fifty-three cents a pound for it, and now it pays thirty-six cents. That shows the very interesting effect of governmental competition upon the price. So all along the line we mean business, and we are going to see that business characterizes the processes of national defense. We would not be Americans if we did not.

But what army have we available? I can tell you, because it has been necessary for us to take care of the patrolling of a very long southern border between us and Mexico. We have not men enough in the United States Army for the routine work of peace, and the increase in the regular army that is being proposed to the present Congress is intended only to bring the regular army up to an adequate peace establishment. I say that that is all that is being proposed with regard to the regular army. The United States has never, my fellow citizens, depended upon the regular army to conduct its wars. It has depended upon the volunteers of the United States, and it has never been disappointed, either in their numbers or in their quality. But modern warfare is very different from what warfare used to be. Warfare has changed so within the span of a single life that it is nothing less than brutal to send raw recruits into the trenches and into the field. I am told by gentlemen who are very much more expert in knowing things that nobody else knows than I am that there are probably several million men in this country who have been trained to arms, either in this country or in the country of their nativity. It may be, but who has a list of them? Where are they? What law lays upon them the duty of coming into the ranks of the armed forces of the United States if it should be necessary to call for volunteers? How are they organized? Who can reach them? Who can command them? There might be several million men with that training, but if they would not come upon the call, they would be of no immediate use to the United States.

What we wish is a definite citizen reserve of men trained to arms to a sufficient extent to make them quickly transformed into a fighting force—organized under the immediate direction of the United States, subject to a definite pledge to serve the United States, and pledged to obey immediately the call of the President when Congress authorizes him to call them to arms. We do not want men to devote the greater part of their time to training in arms. We want men whose occupation and passion and habit is peace, because they are the only men who can carry into the field the spirit of America, as contrasted with the spirit of the professional soldier. I would not have you for a moment understand me as detracting from the character and reputation of the professional soldier as we know him in the United States. I have dealt with him; he is as good an American as I am. He has a degree of intelligence and of devotion to his duty which command my entire admiration. But the spirit of every profession is different from the spirit of the community. I would not trust any particular business to any particular profession exclusively if it were the public business, because every profession that I know anything about has its special point of view. But when a man has to defend his country outside the circle of the things that he ordinarily does, he has, I believe, the spirit of his country in a degree that he would not have it if he were merely performing a professional duty.

Have you looked at the most valued souvenir of families in America? Have you never seen a rusty sword treasured from the days of the Revolution or from the days of the Civil War? Have you never seen an old-fashioned musket hung up in some conspicuous place of honor? Did you ever see a spade hung up, or a pick hung up, or a yardstick hung up, or a ledger hung up? Did you ever see in such place of honor any symbol of the ordinary occupations of peace? Why? Because America loves war and honors it more than she loves peace? Certainly not! But because America honors utter self-sacrifice more than she honors anything else. It is no self-sacrifice to earn your daily bread. It is a necessity—a necessity which, if you accomplish it with success, you are deserving of all praise. But it is not self-sacrifice. It is no self-sacrifice to work for yourself and the people you love. The self-sacrifice comes when you are ready to forget yourself, forget your loved ones, forget everything, even your love of life itself, to serve an invisible master—the great spirit of America herself. We dread war, we condemn war in America. We love peace. But we know that the lads who carried those swords and those muskets loved something more even than they loved peace—that they loved honor and the integrity of the nation.

And so, ladies and gentlemen, we have to prepare ourselves not to be unfair to the men who are going to make this self-sacrifice should the terrible necessity arise for them to make it. We ought to make sure that we are not responsible for leaving them unprepared in knowledge and in training. And we ought to make it the pride of America that great bodies of men greater than the government calls for are ready to prepare themselves for the day of exigency and the day of sacrifice. Every lad that did this would feel better for it. Every lad that obeyed his officers in the process of training would feel that he was obeying something greater than the officer—that he was obeying the instinct of patriotic service and clothing himself with a new nobility by reason of the process.

I have been asked by questioning friends in Washington whether I thought a sufficient number of men would volunteer for the training or not. Why, if they would not, it is not the America that you and I have known; something has happened. They have said, "Do you suppose that the men who employ young men would give them leave to take this training?" I say, "Certainly I suppose it. I know it." Because I know that the patriotism of America is not a name and an empty boast, but a splendid reality. If they did not do it, I should be ashamed of America, and I never expect to see the day when America gives me the slightest reason to be ashamed of her. I am sorry for the skeptics who believe that the response would not be tremendous, not grudging but overflowing in its abundant strength. And it is to prove that that we want to try the plans that are before the present Congress.

You will remind me of the great National Guard of the country, but how great is it, ladies and gentlemen? There are one hundred million people in this country, and there are only 129,000 men in the National Guard. And those 129,000 men are under the direction, by the constitutional arrangement of our system, of the governors of more than twoscore states. The President of the United States is not at liberty to call them out of their states except upon the occasion of actual invasion of the territory of the United States. We are not now thinking of invasion of the territory of the United States. That is not what is making us anxious. We are not asking ourselves, "Shall we be prepared to defend our own shores and our own homes?" Is that all that we stand for—to keep the door securely shut against enemies? Certainly not. What about the great trusteeship we have set up for liberty of government and national independence in the whole western hemisphere? What about the pledges back of that great principle that has been ours and guided our foreign affairs ever since the day of President Monroe? We stand pledged to see that both the continents of America are left free to be used by their peoples as those peoples choose to use them, under a principle of national popular sovereignty as absolute and unchallenged as our own. And, at this very moment, as I am speaking to you, the Americas are drawing together upon that handsome principle of reciprocal respect and reciprocal defense.

When I speak of preparation for national defense, I am speaking of something intangible and visionary. I am looking at a vision of the mind. America has never seen its destiny with the physical eye. The destiny of America lies written in the lines of poets, in the characters of self-sacrificing soldiers, in the conceptions and ambitions of her greatest statesmen; lies written in the teachings of her schoolrooms, in all those ideals of service of humanity and of liberty for the individual which are to be found written in the very schoolbooks of the boys and girls whom we send to be taught to be Americans. The destiny of America is an ideal destiny. America has no reason for being unless her destiny and her duty be ideal. It is her incumbent privilege to declare and stand for the rights of men. Nothing less is worth fighting for, nothing less is worth sacrificing for. The men and women of the American colonies were physically comfortable. Even the much complained of arrangements of trade in those days were not unfair in the sense that they did not bring prosperity. America was offended and restless under the mere suggestion that she was not allowed to get her prosperity in her own way and under the command of her own spirit and purpose, and the American Revolution was fought for an ideal. We would have been as prosperous under the British crown, but we should not have been as happy, and we should not have respected ourselves as much.

Therefore, what America is bound to fight for when the time comes is nothing more nor less than her self-respect. There is no immediate prospect that her material interests may be seriously affected. But there is constant danger, every day of the week, that her spiritual interests may suffer serious affront. And it is in order that they may be safeguarded, in order that America may show that the old conceptions of liberty are ready to translate themselves in her hands into conceptions and manifestations of power at any time, that it is necessary so to transform them, that we must make ourselves ready. You have not sent your representatives to Washington, ladies and gentlemen, to represent your business merely, to represent your ideals of material life. You have sent them there to represent you in your character as a nation. And it is only from that point of view that they can counsel you; it is only upon that footing that they can appeal to you. I feel this so profoundly that I want to add this: I did not come away from Washington because I had the least misgiving as to what the United States was going to do. You must not get impatient because there are long processes of debate at Washington. Wait for the end of the debate. The things that are necessary to be done are going to be done, and thoroughly done. I, for my part, would be sorry for the man who did not take part in doing them if he had to stand up and give the reasons why, and I hope that every man who does not consent to do them will be made to stand up and give the reasons why. But it is empty to say that, because there is no danger. The things are going to be done. I came merely in order that you might understand the spirit in which they are proposed and also receive from my lips the assurance of the absolute necessity that they should be done thoroughly, and done very soon. For if they are not done, and thoroughly done, and done very soon, it may turn out that you have laid upon me an impossible task, and that I should have to suffer the mortification and you the disappointment of having the combination of peace with honor prove to be impossible.

It is not a happy circumstance to have these tense moments of national necessity arise, and yet I, for my part, am not sorry that this necessity has arisen. It has awakened me, myself, I frankly confess to you, to many things and many conditions, which a year ago I did not realize. Then I did not believe that many things were possible which have since become actual facts. I am glad that I know better than I knew then exactly the sort of world we are living in. I would be ashamed of my intelligence if I did not understand the significance of indubitable facts. And it may be that large bodies of our fellow citizens were resting in a false security, based upon an imaginary correspondence of all the world with the conceptions under which they were themselves conducting their own lives. It is probably a fortunate circumstance, therefore, that America has been cried awake by these voices in the disturbed and reddened night, when fire sweeps sullenly from continent to continent. And it may be that in this red flame of light there will rise again that ideal figure of America holding up her hand of hope and of guidance to the people of the world and saying: "I stand ready to counsel and to help. I stand ready to assert, whenever the flame is quenched, those infinite principles of rectitude and peace which alone can bring happiness and liberty to mankind."

Printed in *Addresses of President Wilson*, with many changes from the complete text in the *Chicago Daily Tribune*, Feb. 1, 1916.

From Robert Lansing, with Enclosure

My dear Mr. President: [Washington] January 31, 1916.

I enclose flimsies of two telegrams—numbers 4006 and 4008, received from Berlin, relative to the LUSITANIA case.[1]

I call your particular attention to number 4008 because the suggestion made by Gerard, in which he says that "Colonel House concurs" is, to my mind, exactly in line with the memoranda which we have received from Count Bernstorff. I am very much afraid that Gerard, and possibly House, do not appreciate the real point at issue—namely, that the German Government should admit the wrong-doing of the submarine commander who torpedoed the vessel. I am also afraid that they have held out hopes to Zimmerman that a declaration such as is suggested would be acceptable to you. It shows the danger of attempting to negotiate at two ends of the line.

Do you wish to suggest a reply to Gerard or shall I prepare one, explaining the point at issue, so that he may disabuse Zimmerman of the idea that the suggested declaration would be acceptable.

I congratulate you upon the splendid reception you are receiving from the people whom you have addressed in behalf of preparedness.   Faithfully yours,   Robert Lansing

P.S. Please telegraph me an answer. I enclose also copy of a telegram which I have just sent Gerard.

TLS (Lansing Letterpress Book, SDR, RG 59, DNA).
¹ They are missing in WP, DLC, but are printed in *FR-WWS 1916*, pp. 153-54. In the first telegram (number 4006, changed to 3406), Gerard reported that Zimmermann had said that the *Lusitania* note proposed by Bernstorff would be unacceptable to the German people and government. In the second telegram (number 4008, changed to 3408), Gerard offered his own solution of the *Lusitania* case which, he said, was acceptable both to Colonel House and the German government. Gerard's suggested formula follows:
"Why not close the submarine incidents as follows: Give out a statement stating that Germany in the settlement of the *Arabic* case and in the *Frye* note had stated (quote from these notes); and that now, following this, and with reference to the *Lusitania* case the German Government had stated that it had commenced its submarine warfare in retaliation for the illegal acts of England; that the sinking of the *Lusitania*, in the carrying out of this retaliation, had affected neutral American rights which was contrary to the intention of the German Government; that the German Government has expressed profound regret that citizens of the United States suffered by the sinking of the *Lusitania* and has offered to make reparation by the payment of a suitable indemnity and has given the instructions referred to in the above notes with reference to the placing of the passengers and crews in safety before the sinking of any ship."
TC telegram (SDR, RG 59, 763.72/2364, DNA).

E N C L O S U R E

                                    Washington, January 31, 1916. 10 am
Your 4008. Offer no encouragement that the suggested statement would be at all acceptable. It has already been several times submitted to this Government. Will advise you later.
                                                          Lansing.

TC telegram (SDR, RG 59, 763.72/2364, DNA).

Remarks from a Rear Platform in Davenport, Iowa

[Feb. 1, 1916]

Fellow citizens: I want to express my very deep obligation that you should come out in such numbers to greet me, and I want you to know that I feel the very great seriousness of the errand upon which I have come. I know that there is a great deal of misunderstanding about the results of the policies which I am proposing in the matter of national defense, chiefly along one line. It seems to be supposed that a small body of men, who have a chance to make money out of the manufacture of munitions, have something to do with the policy of the Government of the United States. I have yet to discover any such influence, gentlemen, and I am proposing to the Congress of the United States, as I believe you know, that the government itself should take sufficient steps to control the manufacture of armament for our ships and munitions for our men who go into the field—absolutely to control the price of these things and prevent any undue profit to anybody. It is out of the question that a great national policy should either be guided, or constrained, or controlled, by any one interest or any one class of persons. There need not be the least apprehension, I take it, that any such thing will happen.

I have come out to tell you from my own knowledge that circumstances over which we have no control may at some time, whether we will or not, draw us into difficulties which will make it absolutely necessary that we should be adequately prepared for national defense. I need not tell you, my fellow citizens, that I love peace profoundly, and that I will do everything within my power to preserve it. I know that the love of peace is the predominant passion of the American people, but in the world, as it is now disturbed, we do not control the movement of affairs. There may arise, at any time, a condition of things when I will have more adequately to protect the honor and majesty and character of the United States. And when that time comes, I know that you will be ready to stand by the government. But I must be ready, and everybody connected with the government, to supply you with the adequate means of standing by it if it should, unhappily, become necessary for you to do it. So this is not a matter of an American choice of policy. It is a matter of the condition of the world at a time of unprecedented crisis, when America may be drawn into the maelstrom whether she would or not, and I know the men I can count on in these circumstances. (Train pulls out)

T MS (WP, DLC).

Remarks from a Rear Platform in Iowa City

[Feb. 1, 1916]

My fellow citizens: It is really difficult in these circumstances to speak upon the serious subject upon which I have come out from Washington. They told me before I left Washington that there was some kind of lethargy and indifference in this part of the country to the preparation for national defense, but I have seen evidence to me that there is nothing of the kind. I can see, by your numbers and by your whole manner, that you are as deeply interested in this great subject as I am.

I have come out here with the utmost confidence to appeal to you to realize that the nation stands in a very critical danger of being involved, in spite of its desire to keep out, in this great European struggle. And I have come in the confidence that you will sustain the government, which you have created, in preparing itself for the adequate defense of all the things that we hold dear in this country. And there need be no uneasiness on your part that there is a sordid motive at the bottom of this great agitation for national defense. No doubt when we prepare, we shall have to buy the materials for war from somebody, and somebody will have to be paid for them, and no doubt somebody will make money out of them. But you, perhaps, know already that I have repeatedly urged the Congress of the United States to prepare the government to manufacture its own armor plate and its own munitions, so that there might be an adequate control of this important matter of the cost of national defense. (Train pulls out)

T MS (WP, DLC).

Remarks from a Rear Platform in Grinnell, Iowa

[Feb. 1, 1916]

It is very fine of you, my fellow citizens, to come out in such numbers and with such a cordial spirit to welcome me to Grinnell. I have had a good many friends in Grinnell in times past, and I am glad to see their numbers growing.

Of course, I need not tell you that, although I have come out to advise the country that it is necessary to make more serious preparations for national defense, my real interest is in peace. I suppose you know some of the difficulties against which and in the face of which I have maintained peace, but perhaps there are some difficulties which you do not realize. (Train pulls out)

T MS (WP, DLC).

An Address in Des Moines on Preparedness[1]

[Feb. 1, 1916]

Mr. Chairman, Your Excellency, and fellow citizens: I am greatly cheered, as well as greatly honored, by the sight of this great audience. I have been very much impressed by being told that you have been waiting here patiently for more than two hours for the exercises of the evening, and I think I know, I hope I know, what that means. It is not only that, in your gracious courtesy, you have waited to greet the President of the United States, but that, knowing the errand upon which he has come, you are profoundly interested, as he is, in the candid discussion of some of the chief things which concern the welfare and the safety of the nation.

Someone who does not know our fellow citizens quite as well as he ought to know them told me that there was a certain degree of indifference and lethargy in the Middle West with regard to the defense of the nation. I said, "I do not believe it, but I am going out to see." And I have seen. I have seen what I expected to see—great bodies of serious men, great bodies of earnest women, coming together to show their profound interest in the objects of this visit of mine. I know, therefore, that it is my privilege to address those who will realize the spirit of responsibility in which I speak to them.

My fellow citizens, it would be easy, if I permitted myself to do so, to draw a picture of the present situation of the world which would deeply stir your feelings and perhaps deeply excite your apprehension. But you would not think that it was right for your Chief Magistrate to speak any word of excitement whatever. I want you to believe that, in what I say to you, I am endeavoring, as far as extemporaneous speech will permit, to weigh every word that I say. I said a moment ago that you know the errand upon which I have come to you. But do you know the reasons why I have undertaken that errand? There are some very conclusive and imperative reasons. Some of our fellow citizens are seeking to darken counsel upon this great matter, not, I hope and believe, out of mistaken motives, but certainly, I believe, out of mistaken conceptions of the duty and interest of America.

On the one hand, there is a considerable body of men who are trying to stir the very sort of excitement in this country upon which every true, well-balanced American ought to frown. There

[1] In the Coliseum, before an audience of eight thousand persons; among the guests was the Republican governor, George Washington Clarke. Harry Herndon Polk, president of the Greater Des Moines Society, who introduced Wilson, emphasized the nonpartisan character of the meeting.

are actually men in America who are preaching war, who are preaching the duty of the United States to do what it never would before seek—entanglement in the controversies which have arisen on the other side of the water and abandon its habitual and traditional policy and deliberately engage in the conflict which is now engulfing the rest of the world. I do not know what the standards of citizenship of these gentlemen may be. I only know that I, for one, cannot subscribe to those standards. I believe that I more truly speak the spirit of America when I say that that spirit is a spirit of peace. Why, no voice has ever come to any public man more audibly, more unmistakably, than the voice of this great people has come to me, bearing this impressive lesson: "We are counting upon you to keep this country out of war." And I call you to witness, my fellow country men, that I have spent every thought and energy that has been vouchsafed me in order to keep this country out of war. It cannot be disclosed now, perhaps it can never be disclosed, how anxious and difficult that task has been. But my heart has been in it. I have not grudged a single burden that has been thrown upon me with that end in view, for I knew that, not only my own heart, but the heart of all America was in the cause of peace.

Yet, my fellow citizens, there are some men amongst us preaching peace who go much further than I can go. Not further than I can go in the sentiment of peace; not further than truth warrants them in going in interpreting the desire and sentiment of America, but further than I can follow them, further, I believe, than you can follow them, in preaching the doctrine of peace at any price and in any circumstances. There is a price which is too great to pay for peace, and that price can be put in one word. One cannot pay the price of self-respect. One cannot pay the price of duties abdicated, of glorious opportunities neglected, of character, national character, vindicated and exemplified in action. America has a character as distinct as the character of any individual amongst us. We read that character in every page of her singular and glorious history. We believe that that character is written in invisible signs which, nevertheless, our spirits can decipher upon the very folds of the flag which is the emblem of our national life.

The gentlemen who are out-and-out pacifists are making one fundamental mistake. That is not a mistake about the sentiments of America, but a mistake about the circumstances of the world. America does not constitute the world. In many of her sentiments and predilections, she does not represent or influence the world. The dangers to our peace do not come any longer from within our own boundaries. I could not have said that a few months ago. Passion was astir in this country. There was a clash of sympathies and a heat of passion, which made our air tense and made men hold their breath for fear some of our fellow countrymen would forget that their first loyalty was to America and their second loyalty only to the ancient affections which bound them, and honorably bound them, to some older country and polity. But these dangers have passed. America has regained her self-possession. Men are now ready to feel and to act in common in the great cause of the national life, and no influence within America is going to disturb the peace of America.

But America cannot be an ostrich with its head in the sand. America cannot shut itself out from the rest of the world, because all the dangers at this present moment—and they are many —come from her contacts with the rest of the world. Those contacts are going to be largely determined by other nations, and not determined by ourselves. I have not come to tell you that there is any danger to our national life from anything that your government may do or your Congress propose. I have come to tell you that there is danger to our national life from what other nations may do. And let me say, ladies and gentlemen, that I would not speak of other nations in a spirit of criticism. Not only would it not become me to do so, as your spokesman and representative, but I would not be interpreting my real feeling if I did so. Every nation now engaged in the titanic struggle on the other side of the water believes, with an intensity of conviction that cannot be exaggerated, that it is fighting for its rights, and in most instances that it is fighting for its life; and we must not be too critical of the men who lead those nations. If America's liberty were involved, if we thought that America's life was involved, would we criticize our leaders and public men because they went every length of even desperate endeavor to see that the nation did not suffer and that the nation did triumph? I have it not in my heart to criticize these men. But I want you to know the dangers that they are running, and that the dangers they are running are dangers which involve us also.

Look what it is that America is called upon to do. I can tell you what America is called on to do, because there is hardly a day goes by that some bit of news does not bear to my office some kind of appeal. There is hardly a week goes by that some delegation does not come to the Executive Office in Washington bearing some kind of protest, some kind of request, some kind of urgent message, looking towards interference in the interest of peace. Why, I have talked with earnest men and women, not of our own citizenship, but come out of the body of these other great nations, who pleaded with me to put the moral force of the Government of the United States into one or other of the European scales, so as to see that this struggle was the sooner brought to a peaceful conclusion. America is looked upon to sit in a sort of moral judgment upon the processes of war. And the processes of what a war! The world, my fellow citizens, never witnessed a struggle like this before. Do you know that there is not a single continent, except the continent of South America, that has not been touched by the flame of this terrible conflagration? Do you know that there is not a single country in the world, not even excepting our own, into which the influences of this tremendous struggle have not been thrust by way of political influence and effect? The whole world is tremulous with the great influences of passion and of desperate struggle, and the only great disengaged nation is this nation, which we love and whose interests we would conserve.

What is America expected to do? She is expected to do nothing less than keep law alive while the rest of the world burns. You know that there is no international tribunal, my fellow citizens. I pray God that, if this contest have no other result, it will at least have the result of creating an international tribunal and producing some sort of joint guarantee of peace on the part of the great nations of the world. But it has not yet done that, and the only thing, therefore, that keeps America out of danger is that, to some degree, the understandings, the ancient and honorable understandings, of nations with regard to their relations to one another and to the citizens of one another are to some extent still observed and followed. And whenever there is a departure from them, the United States is called upon to intervene—to speak its voice of protest, to speak its voice of insistence.

Do you want it to be only a voice of insistence? Do you want the situation to be such that all that the President can do is to write messages, to utter words of protest? If these breaches of international law, which are in daily danger of occurring, should touch the very vital interests and honor of the United States, do you wish to do nothing about it? Do you wish to have all the world say that the flag of the United States, which we love, can be stained with impunity? Why, to ask the question is to answer it. I know that there is not a man or woman in the hearing of my voice who would wish peace at the expense of the honor of the United States.

I said just now that an unmistakable voice had come to my ears from out the great body of this nation, saying, "We depend upon you to keep us out of war." But that same voice added always this sentence also, "But we depend upon you to maintain unsullied and unquestioned the honor and integrity of the United States." And many a night, when it has seemed impossible for me to sleep, because of the thought of the apparently inextricable difficulties into which our international relations were drifting, I have said to myself, "I wonder if the people of the United States fully realize what that mandate means to me?" And then sleep has come because I have known, as I have known in my own mind and in my own heart, that there was not a community in America that would not stand behind me in maintaining the honor of the United States.

My fellow citizens, you may be called upon any day to stand behind me to maintain the honor of the United States. And how are you going to do it? There are two ways of doing it. One is the careless, easygoing, wasteful way in which we have done these things hitherto. You say: "There are plenty of fighting men in the United States; there are unexhausted and inexhaustible material resources in the United States; nobody could do more than put us at a disadvantage for a little while." Yes, there are plenty of fighting men in the United States. But do they know how modern war is conducted? Do they know how to guard themselves against disease in the camp? Do they know what the discipline of organization is? Shall we send the whole body of those men who first volunteer to be butchered because they did not know how to make themselves immediately ready for the battlefield and the trench, because they did not know anything about the terrible vicissitudes and disciplines of modern battle?

Why, war has been transformed almost within the memory of men. The mere mustering of volunteers is not war. Mere bodies of men are not an army, and we have neither the men nor the equipment for the men if they should be called out. It would take time to make an army of them—perhaps a fatal length of time— and it would take a long time to provide them with the absolute necessities of warfare. America is not going to sacrifice her youth after that fashion. America is going to prepare for war by preparing citizens who know what war means and how war can be conducted. It is going to increase its standing army up to the point of efficiency for the present uses for which it is needed, and it is going to put back of that army a great body of peaceful men, following their daily pursuits, knowing that their own happiness, and the happiness of everybody they love, depends upon peace, who, nevertheless, at the call of their country, will know how immediately to make themselves into an army and to come out and face an enemy in a fashion which will show that America can neither be daunted nor taken by surprise.

I spoke just now of equipment. I know that there is a very

general impression that influences are at work in this country whose impulse does not come from a thoughtful conviction of danger, but which is said to come from a very thoughtful prospect of profit. I have heard the preposterous statement made that the agitation for preparation for national defense has come chiefly from the men who make armor plate for the ships and munitions for the army. Why, ladies and gentlemen, do you suppose that all the thoughtful men who are engaged upon this side of this great question are susceptible of being led by influences of that sort? Do you suppose that they are so blind to the manifest opportunities for that sort of profit that they do not know the influences that are abroad and active in these matters? I have not found the impulse for national defense coming from those sources. I have found it coming from the men with whom I rubbed shoulders on the street and in the factory. I have found it coming from the men who have nothing to do with the making of profits, but who have everything to do with the making of the daily life of this country. And it is from them that I take my inspiration. But I know the points of danger, and, from the first, ladies and gentlemen, I have been urging upon Congress—I urged upon Congress before this war began—that the Government of the United States supply itself with the necessary plants to make the armor for the ships and to make the munitions for the guns and the men. And I believe, and confidently predict, that the adoption of measures of that sort will be part of the preparation for national defense; not in order, for it is not necessary, that the government should make all the armor plate needed for the fleet or all the munitions needed for the men and the guns, but in order that it should make enough to regulate and control the price.

We are not theorists in this matter. We have tried it in one field. The government is now manufacturing a very considerable proportion of the powder needed for the navy. The consequence is that it has reduced its price from fifty-three cents to thirty-six cents. The point is that it can now get its powder from the private manufacturers of powder at thirty-six cents, because they know that it can be manufactured for that with a reasonable profit, and that, if the government cannot buy it from them, it will make it for itself.

Of course, somebody is going to make money out of the things privately manufactured, manufactured by private capital. There are men now in the great belligerent countries making, I dare say, vast sums of money out of the war, but making it perfectly legitimately, and I for one do not stand here to challenge or doubt their patriotism in the matter. America is not going to be held back from any great national enterprise by any great financial interest of any sort, because America, of all places in the world, is alive to things of that sort and knows how to avoid the difficulties which are involved. If there is any thought on the part of those who make armor plate and munitions that they will get extraordinary profit out of preparation for national defense, all I have to say is that they will be sadly disappointed. But these are things which, to my mind, go without saying, for, ladies and gentlemen, if it is necessary to defend this nation, we are going to defend it, no matter who makes money and no matter what it costs.

I have heard some gentleman say, "My constituents do not object to the program, but they do object to the bills that will have to be paid afterward." I would be very sorry to give that account of any constituency in the United States. I would be very sorry to believe, and I do not believe, that any constituency in the United States will be governed by considerations of that sort. Of course, it is going to cost money to prepare for defense, but equally, of course, the American people are going to pay for it, and pay for it without any grumbling whatever. We are not selfishly rich. We are a very rich people, but we cannot be rich as people unless we maintain our character and integrity as a people. Life is not worth anything for us as a nation if the very issues of life for the nation itself are put in jeopardy by the action which we neglect to take. So I have come out on this errand merely to get into touch with you, my fellow citizens, merely to let you know, in temperate words from my own lips, that the men who are saying that preparation for national defense is necessary, and immediately necessary, are speaking the sober truth. And I believe that you will credit the statement that no man is in a better position to know that than I am.

One aspect of this matter makes me very glad, indeed. Party politics, my friends, sometimes plays too large a part in the United States. Parties are worthwhile only when their differences are based upon absolute conviction. They are not worthwhile when they are based upon differences of personal ambition. Parties are dignified and worthy of the consideration of a nation only when their arguments are for the national benefit, each arguing according to their genuine opinion, their real observation of facts, their real ardor for the national welfare. And it is very delightful sometimes, as upon this occasion, to find an issue regarding which no line can be drawn between one party and another. I have not the embarrassment in standing before you tonight of making the impression that I am urging the advantage of a party or the advantage of an individual. There are just as many men interested in national defense on the one side as on the other. They are all actuated by the same motives. They may differ as to details, but they do not differ as to their objects. And I thank God that there is no party politics when it comes to the life and welfare of the United States. Do you suppose that, if the country were in danger, any man would hesitate to volunteer on the ground that he belonged to this party or to the other? Do you suppose that, if a Republican administration were in power at Washington, any Democrat would hesitate to enlist, or that, a Democratic administration being there, any Republican would hesitate to enlist? Why, the whole history of the country gives an emphatic negative to that question. We are not Democrats or Republicans tonight. We are Americans.

It was a very thrilling thing to me, as I came into this hall, to see the multitude of American flags that waved about the heads of this audience. And upon every stage of my journey since I left Washington, on Friday last, I have seen flags—big flags, little flags, flags of every sort, old flags torn with use, new flags brought out for the first time—displayed any way—upon improvised poles, upon the rooftops of houses, upon chimneys, upon any point of vantage where somebody might throw to the breeze this thrilling signal of our national life. And it has seemed to me that, as each stage of the journey was accomplished, there was imprinted still deeper upon my heart this solemn reflection—that the honor of that flag was in my keeping, not only, but in the keeping of the people who displayed it. For, ladies and gentlemen, the impulses of government in this country do not come from the rulers, they come from the people. I was saying the other night that I knew of no case where one people made war upon another people. I know only of cases where one government made war upon another government. No government can make war in the United States. The people make war through their representatives. The Constitution of the United States does not give the President even a participating part in the making of war. War can be declared only by the Congress, by an action which the President does not take part in and cannot veto. I am literally, by constitutional arrangement, the mere servant of the people's representatives.

I know that a great pulse of feeling underlies the thought of every one of you, as it underlies my thought. We teach our children, ladies and gentlemen, the history of the United States, and I suppose we do incidentally point out to them the great material growth and tremendous physical power of this country. But that is not what we emphasize in our history. We tell them the stories (how proudly we tell them the stories!) of the men who have died for their country without any thought of themselves; of the great ideal principles for the vindication of which America was set up, and which the flag that we honor was designed to represent. And, as I look at that flag, I seem to see many characters upon it which are not visible to the naked eye. There seem to move there ghostly visions of devoted men who, looking to that flag, thought only of liberty, of the rights of mankind, of the mission of America to show the way to the world for the realization of the rights of mankind. And every grave of every brave man of the country would seem to have upon it the colors of the flag, if he was a true American; would seem to have on it that stain of red which means the true pulse of blood, and that beauty of pure white which means the peace of the soul. And, then, there seems to rise over the graves of these men and to hallow their memories that blue space of the sky in which stars swim, those stars which exemplify for us that glorious galaxy of the states of the Union— bodies of free men banded together to vindicate the rights of mankind.

Printed in the Des Moines *Register and Leader*, Feb. 2, 1916; with corrections from the text printed in *Addresses of President Wilson*.

From Edward Mandell House

[Paris, Feb. 1, 1916]

I doubt whether a crisis with Germany can long be avoided. The petty annoyances (?) [pinch] of the blockade will make the demand imperative that an attempt be made to break it by the transcendent sea warfare. We will then be compelled to sever relations and our position will be far better than if we do so over a nine months' old issue and largely upon the wording of a suitable apology. I think reference to the freedom of the seas in Bernstorff's proposed apology is unfortunate. It will irritate the Allies and give Germany hope where there is none. The rules of the sea cannot be changed during the war and it will be hurtful to all concerned to encourage such a delusion.

Edward House.

WWT decode of T telegram (WP, DLC).

Robert Lansing to Brand Whitlock

Washington, February 1, 1916.

Strictly Confidential, for Minister.

Marye having resigned the President desires to appoint you as Ambassador to Russia, and wishes to know that you would accept before requesting your recognition by the Russian Government.   Lansing.

T telegram (SDR, RG 59, 123 W59/117a, DNA).

Norman Hapgood to Joseph Patrick Tumulty, with Enclosure

Dear Mr. Tumulty: Washington, D. C. Feb. 1 [1916]

Many thanks for your note sent en route.

Fortunately the vague charges against Mr. Brandeis are to be heard definitely before the special sub-committee, of which Senator Chilton[1] is Chairman. It seems to me important that the Committee should have the documents I telephoned you about, answering explicitly and authoritatively the same charges. The hearings begin tomorrow afternoon.

I thought the President might be amused by the inclosed fragment of a letter from Amos Pinchot.

Yrs sincerely   Norman Hapgood

ALS (WP, DLC).

[1] William Edwin Chilton, Democrat of West Virginia, chairman of the sub-committee of the Committee on the Judiciary on the Brandeis nomination.

E N C L O S U R E

(to Norman Hapgood)

Louis Brandeis. It is the best news for the United States I've heard for many years.

Incidentally it, in my opinion, goes far toward illiminating the Colonel[1] from the list of presidential probabilities; for, although I dont think the appointment was political, Brandeis will pull a strong oar for Wilson in Wis, Minn, S & N Dakota and other Roosevelt strongholds. It took courage & sense to make this appointment & I take off my chapeau to the President.

I have been violently assailed down town & in this club on account of my admiration for Louis & my belief that the appointment proves the existance of a personal God.

Love to Ruth[2]   A. P. (Pinchot)

Hw MS (WP, DLC).
   1 Theodore Roosevelt.
   2 Hapgood's daughter.

An Address on Preparedness in Topeka[1]

[Feb. 2, 1916]

Mr. Chairman, Your Excellency, fellow citizens: It is a genuine satisfaction on my part to find myself in Kansas again. I feel that every word that your Governor has said about Kansas is true. It likes to know what the facts are, and it likes to give them an open and frank consideration. Moreover, I believe that you realize that I would not have come away from Washington except upon a very unusual occasion. Obviously, it is my duty, so far as possible, to be always in Washington during these critical times of change, when nobody knows what an hour will bring forth or what delicate question will assume some new aspect. You will realize, therefore, that it was only because I felt it my imperative and supreme duty to come out and discuss matters with you that I have left Washington at all, and that only for a few days.

I have come, not to plead a cause—the cause I would speak for does not need to be pled for—but because I would assist, if I could, to clarify judgment and to sweep away those things irrelevant and untrue which are likely to cloud the issue of national defense if they be not very candidly spoken about. You will ask me, "Is there some new crisis that has arisen?" I answer: "No, there is no special, new, critical situation which I have to discuss with you. But I want you to understand that the situation every day, every hour, is critical while this great contest continues in Europe." I need not tell you what my own attitude towards that contest is. I have tried to live up to the counsel which I have given my fellow citizens, not only to be neutral in action, but also to be neutral in the genuine attitude of my thought and mind. It is easy to refrain from unneutral acts, but it is not easy, when the world is swept by storm, to refrain from unneutral thought. Moreover, America is a composite nation. You do not realize it quite so much in Kansas as it is realized in some other parts of the Union. So overwhelming a proportion of your population is native born that you naturally feel your first consciousness to be of America and things American. But imagine those communities— and they are many—which contain very large bodies of men

1 In the Auditorium, before an audience of more than five thousand persons. More than half of them were members of the Kansas Farmers' Elevator and Cooperative Union, which, on the same day, had expressed its opposition to preparedness. Republican Governor Arthur Capper, in introducing Wilson, scarcely concealed his opposition to the administration's program.

whose birthplace, whose memories, whose family connections are on the other side of the sea, in places now swept by the flame of war—men for whom every mail brings news of some disaster that, it may be, has touched those whom they love or has swept the face of some countryside which they remember in association with the days of their youth.

Their intimate sympathies are with some of the places now most affected by this titanic struggle. You cannot wonder—I do not wonder—that their affections are stirred, old memories awakened, and old passions rekindled. The majority of them are steadfast Americans, nevertheless. Look what happened to them, my fellow citizens. You and I were born in America; they chose to be Americans. They deliberately came to America, beckoned hither by some of the fairest promises and prospects ever offered to mankind. They were told that this was a land of liberty and of opportunity, as it is. They were told that this was a land in which they could throw off some of the restraints and trammels under which they had chafed in the older countries. They were told that this was the place for the feet of young men who had ambition and who wished untrammeled hope to be their only leader. And, of their own free and deliberate choice, they crossed the waters and joined their destinies with ours. And the vast majority of them have the passion of American liberty in their hearts just as much as you and I have. I do not want any American to misunderstand the real situation, and I believe that to be the real situation. Some men of foreign birth have tried to stir up trouble in America, but, gentlemen, some men of American birth have tried to stir up trouble in America, too. If you were to listen to the counsels that are dinned into my ears in the Executive Office in Washington, you would find that some of the most intemperate of them came from the lips of men whose people have for generations together been identified with America, but who, for the moment, have been so carried away by their sympathies that they have ceased to think in the terms of American tradition and American policy.

So that the situation for us is this: There is no country in the world, I suppose, whose heart is more open to generous emotions than this dear country which we love. You have seen what the result was in the extraordinary amount of assistance which we have tried to render to those who are suffering most grievously from the consequences of the war on the other side of the sea. I express no judgment concerning any matter with regard to the conduct of the war, but the heart of America has bled because of the condition of the people in Belgium. And you know how we

have poured out of our sympathy and of our wealth to assist in
the relief of suffering in that sorrow-swept land. America looks
to all quarters of the world and sympathizes with mankind in its
sufferings wherever those sufferings may be displayed or undergone.

What you have to realize is that everywhere throughout America there is combustible material—combustible in our breasts. It
is easy to take fire where everything is hot. It is easy to start a
flame when the air is full of the floating sparks of a great conflagration. We have got to be on our guard, and it has been our
hourly and daily anxiety in Washington to see that the exposed
tinder was covered up and the sparks prevented from falling
where there were magazines.

I was told, before I came here, and I read in one of your papers
this morning, that Kansas was not in sympathy with any policy
of preparation for national defense.[2] I do not believe a word of
it. I long ago learned to distinguish between editorial opinion and
popular opinion. Moreover, having been addicted to books, I
happened to have read the history of Kansas. And, if there is any
place in the world fuller of fight than Kansas, I would like to hear
of it—any other place fuller of fight on the right lines. Kansas is
not looking for trouble, but Kansas has made trouble for everybody that interfered with her liberties or her rights. And, if I
were to pick out one place which was likely to wince first and get
hot first about the invasion of the essential principles of American
liberty, I certainly would look to Kansas among the first places
in the country. If Kansas is opposed, or has been opposed, to the
policy of preparation for national defense, it has been only because somebody has misrepresented that policy, and Kansas does
not know what it is.

What is the issue? Why, of course, there are some men going
about proposing a great military establishment for America, but
you have not heard anybody connected with the administration
who did. You have not heard anybody in any responsible situation,
who could carry out that plan, propose it. The singular thing
about this situation is that the loudest voices have been the irresponsible voices. It is easy to talk and to say what ought to be

2 Wilson here referred to an editorial in the Topeka *Daily Capital* (owned by
Governor Capper), Feb. 2, 1916. The editorial said that, although President Wilson would receive a cordial welcome in Kansas, the people of the state would
not approve all of his policies or agree with all of his opinions, especially on
preparedness. "We do not expect," it concluded, "to see Kansas sentiment
materially affected on military preparedness by the President's visit to this
State. The arguments on both sides have been listened to by Kansas people
attentively and with open minds, and the Kansas verdict is not likely to be
changed by repetitions of what has already been said."

done when you know that you do not have to do it. Nobody in authority, nobody in a position to lead the policy of the country, has proposed great military armaments, and nobody who really understands the history or shares the spirit of America could or would propose a great military establishment for America. But I have heard of men in Kansas who owned their own firearms and knew how to use them. And if there is any place in the Union more than another where you ought to understand what it is to be ready to take care of yourselves, this is the place. All that anybody in authority has proposed is that America should be put in such a position that her free citizens should know how to take care of themselves and their country when the occasion arose.

We have been proposing only a very moderate increase in the standing army of the country because it is already too small for the routine uses of peace. I have not had soldiers enough to patrol the border between here and Mexico. I have not had soldiers enough for the ordinary services of the army. And there are many things that it has been impossible for me to do, which it was my duty to do, because there were not men to do them with. You are not, I am sure, going to be jealous of an increase of the army merely sufficient to enable the Executive to carry out his constitutional responsibilities. Over and above that, we have proposed this —that a sufficient number of men, out of the ranks of the civil pursuits of the country, should be trained in the use and keeping of arms, in the sanitation of camps, in the maneuvers of the field, and in military organization; to be ready, and pledged to be ready, if the call should come upon act of Congress, to unite their force with the little force of the army itself and make a great multitude of armed men who were ready to vindicate the rights of America.

Is there anything inconsistent with the traditions of Kansas or with the true traditions of America in a proposal like that? The very essence of American tradition is contained in this proposal. Every constitution of every state in the Union forbids the state legislature to abridge the right of its citizens to carry arms. At the very outset, the makers of our very institutions realized that the force of the nation must dwell in the homes of the nation. I do not mean the moral force merely; I mean the physical force also. They realized that every man must be allowed, not only to have a vote, but, if he wanted to, to have a gun, too, so that, when the voices of peace did not suffice, the voices of force would prevail; knowing that great bodies of men do not use force to usurp their own liberties, but to declare and vindicate their liberties, and that there will be no collusion among free men to upset free institutions; that, whereas cliques and coteries and professional groups may conceive it to be in their interest to interfere with the peaceful life of the country, the general body of citizens would never so conceive it.

What we are asking is this, that the nation supply arms for those of the nation who are ready, if occasion should arise, to come to the national defense, and that it should do this without withdrawing them from their pursuits of industry and of peace, in order that America should know that, in the fountains from which she always draws her strength, there welled up the inexhaustible resources of American manhood. This is not a military policy; this is a policy of adequate preparation for national defense. And any man who represents it in any other light must either be ignorant or is consciously misrepresenting the facts.

You will say, "We have a National Guard." Yes, we have a National Guard, and the units of it, so far as I have observed them, command my admiration and respect. But there are only 129,000 enlisted men in the National Guard, taking the nation as a whole, and they are divided up into as many units as there are states. The Constitution of the United States puts them under the direct command and control of the governors of the states, not of the President of the United States, and the national authority has no right to call upon them for any service outside their states unless the territory of the nation is actually invaded.[3] I want to see Congress do everything that it can to enhance the dignity and the force and to assist in the development of the National Guard. But the National Guard is a body of state troops, and not a body of national reserves, because the Constitution makes them so, no matter whether we now think those are the best arrangements or not.

The other matter I want to speak to you about is not the plan itself, for that is a question of detail. I have given you the idea of it, and time does not suffice to discuss the detail in meetings of this sort. The detail is printed, for that matter, for anybody to see who wants it. The other matter is this: Suppose you had a great body of, let us say, half a million men sufficiently trained to arms to make the nucleus of a great army if it were necessary to create a great army? What would be your idea that you would do with it? That is the matter that we need to clear up most of all. There are all sorts of people in the United States, and there are people who think that we ought to use the force of the United States to get

[3] "The crowd outside at the door rushed the guards and created a commotion in the hall. The President paused and waited till it died down. 'That's somebody overeager for national defense,' he said, and the crowd laughed." *Kansas City Star*, Feb. 2, 1916.

anything we can get with it. But you don't think that. I don't think that. And not one American in a hundred thousand thinks that. We would never use this force to carry out any policy that even smacked of aggression of any kind, because this nation loves peace more than it loves anything else except honor.

I like that exclamation of Henry V in that stirring play of Shakespeare's, "If it be an offense to covet honor, then am I the most offending soul alive." And I believe that could be said of America. If it be an offense against the peace of the nations to covet honor, then is America the most offending nation in the world. But she knows the basis of honor—that the basis of honor is right, is peaceful intention, is just action, is the treatment of others as we would wish to be treated ourselves, is the insistence upon the rule of a free field and no favor. The spirit of America would hold any Executive back, would hold any Congress back, from any action that had the least taint of aggression upon it. We are not going to invade any nation's territory. We are not going to covet any nation's possessions. We are not going to invade any nation's rights. But suppose, my fellow countrymen, some nation should invade our rights? What then? What would Kansas think? What would Kansas do then? What would America, speaking by the voice of Kansas or any other state in the Union, think and do then? I have come here to tell you about the difficulties of our foreign policy. The delicate questions of our foreign relationships do not diminish either in number or in delicacy and difficulty, but, on the contrary, daily increase in number and in intricacy and in danger. And I would be derelict to my duty to you if I did not deal with you in these matters with the utmost candor and tell you what it may be necessary to use the force of the United States to do.

For one thing, it may be necessary to use the force of the United States to vindicate the right of American citizens everywhere to enjoy the protection of international law. There is nothing you would be quicker to blame me for than neglecting to safeguard the rights of Americans, no matter where they might be in the world. There are perfectly clearly marked rights guaranteed by international law, which every American is entitled to enjoy, and America is not going to abide the habitual or continued neglect of those rights. Perhaps not being as near the ports as some other Americans, you do not travel as much and you do not realize the infinite number of legitimate errands upon which Americans travel—errands of commerce, errands of relief, errands of business for the government, errands of every sort which make America useful to the world. Americans do not travel to disturb the world. They travel to quicken the processes of the interchange of life and of goods in the world, and their travel ought not to be impeded by a reckless disregard of international obligation.

There is another thing that we ought to safeguard, and that is our right to sell what we produce in the open neutral markets of the world. Where there is a blockade, we recognize the right to blockade. Where there are the ordinary restraints created by a state of war, we ought to recognize those restraints. But the world needs the wheat off the Kansas fields and off the other great flowering acres of the United States, and we have a right to supply the rest of the world with the products of those fields. We have a right to send food to peaceful populations wherever the conditions of war make it possible to do so under the ordinary rules of international law. We have a right to supply them with our cotton to clothe them. We have a right to supply them with our manufactured products.

We have made some mistakes, my fellow citizens. For several generations past, we have so neglected our merchant marine that one of the difficulties we are struggling against has nothing to do with international questions. We have not got the American ships to send the goods in, and we have got to get them. I am going to ask you to follow the fortunes of the so-called shipping bill in the present Congress and make suggestions to your congressmen as to the absolute necessity of getting your wheat and your other products out of the ports and upon the high seas where they can go, and shall go, under the protection of the laws of the United States.

But that is a mere parenthesis. Aside from that, so far as there are vehicles to carry our trade, we have the right to extend our trade for the assistance of the world. For we have not been selfish in this neutral attitude of ours. I resent the suggestion that we have been selfish, desiring merely to make money. What would happen if there were no great nation disengaged from this terrible struggle? What would happen if every nation were consuming its substance in war? What would happen if no nation stood ready to assist the world with its finances and to supply it with its food? We are more indispensable now to the nations at war by the maintenance of our peace than we could possibly be to either side if we engaged in the war. And, therefore, there is a moral obligation laid upon us to keep out of this war if possible. But, by the same token, there is a moral obligation laid upon us to keep free the courses of our commerce and of our finance, and I believe that America stands ready to vindicate those rights.

But there are rights higher than either of those, higher than the rights of individual Americans outside of America, higher and greater than the rights of trade and of commerce. I mean the rights of mankind. We have made ourselves the guarantors of the rights of national sovereignty and of popular sovereignty on this side of the water in both the continents of the western hemisphere. You would be ashamed, as I would be ashamed, to withdraw one inch from that handsome guarantee, for it is a handsome guarantee. We have nothing to make by it, unless it be that we are to make friendships by it, and friendships are the best usury of any sort of business. So far as dollars and cents and material advantage are concerned, we have nothing to make by the Monroe Doctrine. We have nothing to make by allying ourselves with the other nations of the western hemisphere in order to see to it that no man from outside, no government from outside, no nation from outside attempts to assert any kind of sovereignty or undue political influence over the peoples of this continent.

America knows that the only thing that sustains the Monroe Doctrine and all the influences that flow from it is her own moral and physical force. The Monroe Doctrine is not part of international law. The Monroe Doctrine has never been formally accepted by any international agreement. The Monroe Doctrine merely rests upon the statement of the United States that, if certain things happen, she will do certain things. So, nothing sustains the honor of the United States in respect of these long cherished and long admired promises except her own moral and physical force.

Do you know what has interfered more than anything else with the peaceful relations of the United States with the rest of the world? The incredulity of the rest of the world when we have made statement of our sincere unselfishness in these matters! The greatest surprise the world ever had, politically speaking, was when the United States withdrew from Cuba. We said, "We are fighting this war for the sake of the Cubans, and, when it is over, we are going to turn Cuba over to her own people." And statesmen in every capital in Europe smiled behind their hand. They said: "What! That great rich island lying directly south of the foot of your own Florida! Plant your flag there and then haul it down?" Some Americans even said, "We will never raise the flag of the United States anywhere and then haul it down." And, then, when the American people saw that the time had come when her promises were to be fulfilled, down came that fluttering emblem of our sovereignty, and we were more honored in its lowering than we had been in its hoisting. The American people feel the same way about the Philippines, though the rest of the world does not yet believe it. We are trustees for the Filipino people, and just so soon as we feel that they can take care of their own affairs without our direct interference and protection, the flag of the United States will again be honored by the fulfillment of a promise. That flag stands for honor, not for advantage. That flag stands for the rights of mankind, no matter where they be, no matter what their antecedents, no matter what the race involved. It stands for the absolute right to political liberty and free self-government, and wherever it stands for the contrary, American traditions have begun to be forgotten.

But, my friends, the world does not understand that yet. It has got to have a few more demonstrations like the demonstration in Cuba. It has got to have a few more vindications of the American name. When those vindications have come, I believe that nothing but peace will ever reign between the United States and the nations of the rest of the world. For every man who minds his own business is sure of peace. Every man who respects his own character and observes the rights of others is sure of peace. And every nation that makes right its guide and honor its principle is sure of peace. But until these things are believed of us, we must be ready, with the hand of force, to hold others off from the invasion of any right which we hold sacred.

I have come to you with the utmost confidence that the moment you understood the issue, all differences of party, all differences of individual judgment, all differences of point of view would fall away, and, like true Americans, we should all stand shoulder to shoulder in a common cause—America first and her vindication the sacred law of our life. For, ladies and gentlemen, it is only upon the most solemn occasions that I would appeal to you as I have been appealing today. The final test of the validity, the strength, the irresistible force of the American ideal, has come. The rest of the world must be made to realize from this time out just what America stands for. And when that happy time comes, when peace shall reign again, and America shall take part in the undisturbed and unclouded counsels of the world, it will be realized that the promises of the fathers, the ambitions of the men who fought for the bloody soil of Kansas, the ideals of the men who thought nothing of their lives in comparison with their ideals, will have been vindicated, and the world will say: "America promised to hold this light of liberty and right up for the guidance of our feet, and behold she has redeemed her promise. Her men, her leaders, her rank and file are pure of heart. They have purged their hearts of selfish ambition, and they have said to all mankind, 'Men and brethren, let us live together in righteousness and in the peace which springeth only from the soil of righteousness itself.'"

Printed in *Addresses of President Wilson*, with a few corrections from the incomplete text in the *Kansas City Star*, Feb. 2, 1916.

An Address to an Overflow Meeting in Topeka[1]

[Feb. 2, 1916]

Mr. Chairman, Your Excellency, and fellow citizens: I am very much tempted in this environment and in this presence to go back in mind to my old days as schoolmaster, because many of the sounds I have heard here this morning are very familiar. They remind me of the story of a friend of mine who dropped in at the Players' Club in New York. He was sitting quietly at his lunch, when a man whom he did not know at all came by and gave him a resounding whack on the shoulder and said, "Hello, Ollie, old boy, how are you?" He looked up rather coldly and said, "I don't know who you are; I don't know your name; but your manners are very familiar." I don't know your names, but your manners are very familiar. And I assure you that your welcome to me makes me feel very much at home.

I wonder how many persons have been infected with the wrong idea of war in talking nowadays, when they are talking about national defense. I find that a great many persons feel that we are trying to stir up in the United States a military spirit. In some instances, it would be difficult to stir up a military spirit in the United States and undesirable. I have been bred, and a good many Kansans have been bred, in a pretty stern school of religion, and there are some religions that have been worth fighting for. There are some political religions that are worth fighting for, and I would not care to hold any conviction that I was not ready to fight for if that conviction were too rudely challenged. I believe that the only thing necessary to stir up a military spirit in America is to drop a spark on the hearth where have been kindled all the fine emotions that have built up American life and where have been kept all the fine traditions that have consolidated American families and made American sentiment what it is.

There is a difference between one sort of military sentiment and another. If by military sentiment you mean a preference for standing armies, if you mean putting the nation upon a military basis, nobody in his senses is proposing anything of that

[1] In the auditorium of the local high school, before an audience of 1,000 men, women, and school children. Wilson was again introduced by Governor Capper, who emphasized the nonpartisan character of Wilson's visit.

sort. What we are proposing is what every woman's heart, as well as every man's heart, should dearly desire, and that is that the men of the nation should not only be willing to vindicate the honor of the nation, but should know how to do it when it is necessary to do it. Because one of the cruelest mistakes that a nation can make is to send crude boys into the trenches and into the battlefields who will be mere targets for powder and shell, eaten up by the great Gorgon of war before they know what the business is. Modern warfare is not what it used to be even so short a time ago, reckoning by the time of history, as the time of the American Revolution. Then farmers, taking their muskets from behind the door and going to some place of cover, infested the roads and drove the Redcoats back to Boston and, manning the trenches and earthworks on Bunker Hill, made the shots ring around the world that declared the voice of liberty. War is not conducted in that individual, easygoing, gathering-of-the-neighborhood fashion that it was conducted in those days. There are dreadful scientific processes of war, and if America is going to take care of herself in the time of her need, she must have bodies of men who understand those scientific processes of war—men who can command, men who can intelligently obey, men who know the materials of war and who know how to handle the materials of war. And the only American way of doing that is not to build up a great standing army, but to build up a body of men who understand these things, and yet diligently and for the most part—nine months out of the twelve—go about their peaceful occupations of commerce and industry and farming.

Have you met any of the men—they are not many in number, but very interesting in spirit—who volunteered to go to some of those camps that were established last summer in connection with some of the military posts of the United States?[2] Cultivated gentlemen, men engaged in the professions, men leading the great manufacturing processes of the country, intelligent farmers, men out of every intelligent occupation went to those camps, and they came back from them with several very interesting impressions. They realized that, in those few weeks, they had learned only the first rudiments of a tremendous business, but that they had learned the influence and the serviceability of discipline, and they had got something of the spirit of obedience. And, above all, they had had some little vision of what it was necessary to do in order to defend America if she should need to be defended. Ought we not to systematize that thing? Ought we not to see that camps

[2] About this, the so-called Plattsburg movement, see EMH to WW, Aug. 8, 1915, n. 1, Vol. 34.

of instruction are established in sufficient number, and that men volunteer in sufficient number, to take the instruction, so that, if the time should ever come in the tragedy of events when Americans should be called upon to volunteer to take arms in defense of their country, there would be men who would form the nucleus —a competent body of men at arms—who would see to it that the initial steps of war were not steps of disaster. Give us time enough; let us have but a little space to work in, and we can rally a responsible force in this country. But the first steps might be steps of shame and disaster. And we ought to be prepared to see that the first steps are rightly begun and the foundations solidly and rightly built.

You will say, "Have you come to tell us that there is going to be war?" God forbid, my fellow citizens. I do not know whether there is going to be war or not. I have tried through anxious months to make it impossible that war should touch this beloved country. My heart is absolutely and inalienably engaged in the cause of peace, as your hearts are. But I know, as perhaps nobody else in the country can know, what delicate and difficult and threatening matters we are dealing with every day in Washington. It seems to me that not a single day passes by that some new difficulty, that challenges every resource of our judgment, does not present itself for settlement, or, at any rate, for that temporary treatment which will postpone settlement. I would be derelict to my duty if I did not come and tell you that you cannot predict what a day will bring forth. The trials that make our fortunes as a nation in respect to our relations with other countries depend upon those other countries, and not upon ourselves.

Gentlemen go about and proclaim peace in this country, as if it were necessary to proclaim peace so far as the sentiments and wishes and purposes of America are concerned. But do they suppose that America is the only country in the world? Do they suppose that we live in a fireproof dwelling while all the rest of the world is on fire? Can they control the processes of politics in foreign capitals? Can they guide the heart and purpose of foreign ministers and heads of armies, and commanders of ships at sea? Why, the number of points at which America touches the other nations of the world is incalculable. It is as if every sensitive point of the whole circumference of our affairs touched somewhere the regions aflame in Europe. And you know how the fire has spread. It has spread to Asia. It has spread to Africa. It involves some portions of our own continent—in the Canadian Dominion. It has touched every part of the world except the continent of South America. And in the midst of this fire, friends say: "Never mind, the roof is made of shingles, but nothing ever catches on fire in America." Do you not know that some of our hearts have already caught on fire? Do you hear no intemperate speeches in America? Do you know of no passionate influences in America? Do you know of nobody who is trying to draw America into this struggle? If you sat at Washington, you would know how many are trying, by every sort of means, to draw America into this struggle. They are almost offering tinder to the flames.

So I have come to say to you that it is not in my power to be certain that we shall not have to exert ourselves for the vindication and defense of our national principles and our national honor, for we cannot allow America to be put upon beyond a certain point. We cannot lose our self-respect for the sake merely of keeping out of trouble. There is such a thing as losing your character in keeping the peace. There is a point beyond which the individual honor cannot let others go; there is a point beyond which the nation cannot let others go. And I am just as confident as I am of anything that there is no part of the country from which the resistance will be more instantaneous than from those old fighting men of Kansas. Why, Kansas was at one time made up of men who were just spoiling for a fight. They heard away back in New England that there was a fight going on in Kansas, and they flocked out here to take part. They were all men like the Irishman who went into a large barroom where two men were fighting in one corner of the rear, and he asked the bartender, "Is this a private fight, or can anybody get in?" It was obvious that, when the fight was going on to determine whether Kansas should be free ground or not, that men all over the country said, "This is not a private fight; let us get in." And they flocked to Kansas with arms in order to vindicate what? An idea, nothing more—an idea of freedom. They were comfortable where they were; they could make a living; nobody was interfering with them. The mere abstract idea of individual liberty and the existence of slavery somewhere else made them come down to Kansas and fight with the unstinted shedding of their blood. If Kansas will not fight, who will? Fight, that is to say, for the same sort of thing: Fight for principle, fight for an idea, fight for character, fight for a right. There is no other place in the Union more likely to fight than Kansas.

I read in one of your morning papers that you were not in sympathy with the policy of preparedness, and I reflected to myself, "Then they must be prepared already." If you are and will come out and enroll, it is all right; I will not talk to you any more. Let us know your name in order that we can call on you in time of trouble, and I will go home with a very quiet mind. I know what fine stuff will come out of your midst. I do not believe what I read in the newspapers—this with apology to the very engaging gentlemen who go around with me. I mean I do not believe the opinions that I see in the newspapers, because I know how few persons direct them, and I know how many persons must be united in spirit to make a great popular opinion.

One of the difficulties of public life, ladies and gentlemen, is that the great body of the people are inaudible. You just have to make up in your mind, by being an American yourself, what is sure to be an American opinion. And I believe I have been so ingrained by the study of the history of this country with the ideas that are American that I can make a better case than some other people as to what American opinion is. Anybody who runs can read what would be likely to be the opinion of Kansas upon any subject of human rights. And the only thing we are ever going to fight for again, my fellow citizens, is human rights in one shape or another. And they are worth fighting for.

Our life is but a little span. One generation follows another very quickly. If a man with red blood in him had his choice, knowing that he must die, he would rather die to vindicate some right unselfish to himself, than die in his bed. We are all touched with the love of the glory which is real glory, and the only glory comes from utter self-forgetfulness and self-sacrifice. We never erect a statue to a man who has merely succeeded. We erect statues to men who have forgotten themselves and been glorified by the memory of others. This is the standard that America holds up to mankind in all sincerity and in all earnestness. Let no man trifle with those rights of humanity which are in America's keeping. And let no American hold back from making this nation ready, upon the instant, to vindicate those rights of humanity which are entrusted to our keeping.

T MS (WP, DLC).

An Address on Preparedness in Kansas City[1]

[Feb. 2, 1916]

Mr. Chairman and fellow citizens: You have certainly given me a most royal welcome to Kansas City, and I esteem it a very great privilege to deliver the message which I have come to deliver to this great throng of intelligent people. My natural duty to you, ladies and gentlemen, is in Washington, not here. I have a certain

[1] In the Kansas City Convention Hall. Governor Capper again presented Wilson to an audience estimated at fifteen thousand persons.

scruple of conscience in being away from Washington for many days at a time, because it is one of the interesting circumstances of the moment that there is hardly a day which does not in some degree alter the aspect of affairs. It is important for your sake, and, I venture to add, for the sake of the peace of the world, that those who represent you in responsible stations should keep in constant touch with these changes. You will, therefore, credit me when I say that it is only an extraordinary occasion which draws me away from duties needing such constant attention.

I would not have come away from Washington had I not believed that there was a stronger compulsion of conscience to acquaint you with the state of affairs than there was to remain during this week at the place of guidance. You will know, without my describing it to you, what the task assigned me has been. It has been the task of keeping the scales so poised from day to day that no man should throw into one scale or the other any make-weight which would imperil the peace of the United States, for I have felt that you were depending upon your government to keep you out of this turmoil which is disturbing the rest of the world. You are counting upon me to do more than keep you out of trouble, however. You are counting upon me to see to it that the rights of citizens of the United States, wherever they might be, are respected by everybody. You have counted upon me to see that your energies should be released along the channels of trade in order that you might serve the world as the only nation disengaged and ready to serve it. You have expected me to see that the rest of the world permitted America thus to express and exercise her humane and legitimate energy.

I have come out to ask you what there was behind me in this task. You know the lawyers speak of the law having a sanction back of it. The judge, as he sits on his bench, has something back of him. He has the whole physical force of the nation back of him. The laws reside and sit upon him, no matter how commonplace his individual aspect, with a sort of majesty, because there is the sovereignty of the people and of the people's government back of him. When he utters a judgment, the man against whom it is uttered knows that he dare not resist it. But when I, as your spokesman and representative, utter a judgment with regard to the rights of the United States in its relations to other nations, what is the sanction? What is the compulsion? What lies back of that? You will say, "The force and majesty of the United States." Yes, the force and majesty of the United States. But is it ready to express itself? If you resist the judge, there are the bailiffs of the court. If you resist the bailiffs of the court, there are those who assist the sheriff of the county. If you resist the sheriff, there is the National Guard. If you resist the National Guard, there is the army of the United States. But if you ignore in some foreign capital what the President of the United States urges as the rights of the people and Government of the United States, what is there back of that?

It is necessary, my fellow citizens, that I should come and ask you this question, because I do not know how long the mere word and insistence of your government will prevail to maintain your honor and the dignity and power of the nation. There may come a time—I pray God it may never come, but it may, in spite of everything we do, come upon us, and come of a sudden—when I shall have to ask: "I have had my say; who stands back of me? Where is the force by which the majesty and right of the United States are to be maintained and asserted?" I take it that there may, in your own conviction, come a time when that might and force must be vindicated and asserted. You are not willing that what your government says should be ignored.

I have seen editorials written in more than one part of the United States sneering at the number of notes that were being written from the State Department to foreign governments, and asking, "Why does not the government act?" And, in those same papers, I have seen editorials against the preparation to do anything whatever effective if those notes are not regarded. Is that the temper of the United States? It may be the temper of some editorial offices, but it is not the temper of the people of the United States.

I came out upon this errand from Washington, and see what happened. Before I started, everybody knew what errand I was bound on. I expected to meet quiet audiences and explain to them the issues of the day, and what did I meet? At every stop of the train, multitudes of my fellow citizens crowded out, not to see the President of the United States merely—he is not much to look at—but to declare their ardent belief in the majesty of the government which he stands for and for the time being represents, and to declare in one fashion or another, if it were only by cheers, that they stood ready to do their duty in the hour of need. I have been thrilled by the experiences of these few days, and I shall go back to Washington and smile at anybody who tells me that the United States is not wide-awake. But, gentlemen, crowds at the stations, multitudes in great audience halls, cheers for the government, the display—the ardent display, as from the heart—of the emblem of our nation, the Stars and Stripes, only express the spirit of the nation. They do not express the organized force of the nation. And, while I know, and knew before I left Washington, what the spirit of the people was, I have come out to ask them what their organization is and what they intend to make it.

Modern wars are not won by mere numbers. They are not won by mere enthusiasm. They are not won by mere national spirit. They are won by the scientific conduct of war, the scientific application of irresistible force. And what is there behind the President of the United States? Well, in the first place, there is a navy, which, for my part, I am very proud of; a navy, which for its numbers, ship by ship, man by man, officer by officer, I believe to be the equal of any navy in the world. But look at the great sweep of our coasts. Mind you, this war has engaged all the rest of the world outside of South America and the portion of North America occupied by the United States, and if this flame begins to creep in upon us, it may, my fellow citizens, creep in towards both coasts, and here are thousands upon thousands of miles of coast. Do you know that the great sweep from the canal up the coast to Alaska is something like half the circumference of the world? Do you remember the great reaches of sea from the canal up to the St. Lawrence River? Do you know the bays, the inviting harbors, the great cities which cluster upon those coasts? And do you think that a navy that ranks only fourth in the world in force is enough to defend the coasts and make secure the territory of a great continent like this?

We have been interested in our navy for a great many years, and we have been slowly building it up to excellent force, but we have done it piecemeal and a little at a time. There has been a party in Congress that was for a little navy, as well as a party in Congress that was for a big navy, and it seemed to be a sort of theoretical situation as to whether we wanted a navy to be proud of or not. No nation ought to wish either an army or navy to be proud of, to make a display with, to make a toy of. It is the arm of force which must lie back of every sovereignty in the world, and the navy of the United States must now be as rapidly as possible brought to a state of efficiency and of numerical strength which will make it, practically, impregnable to the navies of the world. The fighting force of the navy now is splendid, and I should expect very great achievements from the fine officers and trained men that constitute that great navy. But it is not big enough; it is not numerous enough; it is incomplete. It must be completed, and what the present administration is proposing is that we limit the number of years to five within which we shall complete a definite program which will make that navy adequate for the defense of both coasts.

But, on land, what stands behind the President, if he should have to act in your behalf to enforce the demands of the United States for respect and right? An army so small that I have not had men enough to patrol the Mexican border. The Mexican border is a very long border, I admit. It runs the whole southern length of Texas and the whole southern length of New Mexico and Arizona besides, and that is a great strip of noble territory. But what is that single border to the whole extent and coast of the United States? I have not had men enough to prevent bandits from raiding across the border of Mexico into the United States. It has been a very mortifying circumstance, indeed. I have been tempted to advise Congress to help Texas build up its little force of Texas Rangers. And now, if you please, because I am asking the Congress to give the government an army adequate to the uses of peace, to the uses of the moment, some gentlemen go about and prate of military establishments. They see phantoms, they dream dreams. Militarism in the United States springing out of any of the proposals of this administration is—why, a man must have a very strong imagination, indeed, to conceive any such nonsense as that! I am not asking, the administration is not asking, to be backed by any bigger standing army than is necessary for the uses of the moment, but it is asking this.

Do you remember the experiences of the Spanish-American war? That was not much of a war, was it? It did not last very long. You remember the satirical verses that some newspaper man wrote about it:

> War is rude and impolite.
> It quite upsets a nation.
> It's made of several weeks of fight,
> And years of conversation.[2]

A war which was parodied in verse! What happened? You sent thousands of men to their death because they were ignorant. They did not get any further than the camps in Florida. They did not get on the water even, much less get to Cuba, and they died in the camps like flies, of all sorts of camp diseases, of all sorts of diseases that come from the ignorance of medical science and camp sanitation. Splendid boys, boys fit, with a little training, to make an invincible army, but sent to their death by miserable disease, the soil of which was ignorance, helpless ignorance. Why, the percentage of our loss in that war by disease in the camp was greater than the percentage of the loss of the Japanese by disease and battle together in their war with Russia.

[2] See n. 6 to the address to the Newark Board of Trade, printed at Jan. 25, 1911, Vol. 22.

It is a very mortifying thing. There is not any place in the world where medical science is more nobly studied or more adequately applied than in the United States. But we poured crude, ignorant, untrained boys into the ranks of those armies, and they died before they got sight of an enemy. Do you want to repeat that? And while that is going on, what may happen? What sort of disaster may come to you while you are trying to make an army out of absolutely raw material? Why, it seems almost ridiculous to state how little the present administration is asking for. It is asking that you give it something that is not sheer raw material out of which to begin to make an army, when it is absolutely necessary to make an army. It is asking that five hundred thousand men be asked to volunteer to take a little training every year for three years, not more than two or three months out of the year, in order that, when volunteers are called for in the case of war, we may have men, at least five hundred thousand of them, who know something about the use of arms, something about the sanitation of camps, something about the organization and discipline of war in the field and in the trenches. That is all that we are asking for at the present time, and if there is any criticism to be made upon it, it is that it is too little, not too much.

There are men in Congress asking, "Can you get the five hundred thousand men? Will they volunteer?" Why, I believe you could get them out of any one state in the Union. You could almost get five thousand of them out of this audience. But, ladies and gentlemen, do not forget that that is not all there is to this problem. Suppose that I knew that, back of the insistence of the United States upon its rights, was a great navy that ranked first in the world and a body of men trained to arms adequate, at any rate, to fend off any initial disaster to the United States while we were making an army ready? That would be only the beginning. There are other things that we have been very much concerned about in Washington and that we are taking steps to attend to. The railroads of this country have never been drawn into the counsels of the government, never until recently, in such fashion as to make plans for coordinating all of them to transport troops and transport provisions and transport munitions in such a way as to be the effective arteries of the red blood and energy of the nation. Never, until recently, though we are beginning to do it, for we called the businessmen and the engineers of the country into counsel to say: "What are the resources of manufacture in this country, and how can we coordinate them and put them into cooperation, so that there will be no waste of time, no duplication of effort, and no failure to get every part of the machinery into operation should we need to use them in case of war?" We are taking counsel with regard to that now. But, mark you, the munitions of war are made in this country almost exclusively near the borders of the country, and for the most part upon the Atlantic seaboard. And any initial disaster to the force of the United States might put the greater part of them, if not all of them, in the possession of an enemy. So that you see that the circle of my argument leads right back to the necessity for a force of men who can prevent an initial disaster, so that there will be no first failure, a first invasion, a first disaster.

Did you ever hear more momentous things spoken of than these? Did it ever before occur to you that you must put more than the authority of words into the mouths of the men who speak for you? I have been wringing my heart and straining every energy of mind and heart that I have to preserve the honor and integrity and peace of the United States. But think of what must lie at the back of my thought. I know what you want me to do. I would be ashamed if I did not use the utmost powers that are in me to do it. But suppose that some morning I should have to turn to you and say, "Fellow citizens, I have done as much as I can; now I must ask you to back me up with the force of the nation." And suppose that I should know, before I said it, that I had not told you what that meant, as I am telling you tonight? Suppose that I had not warned you of what was involved? Suppose that I had not challenged you in a moment of peace to make ready? Do not suppose, however, that I am afraid that it is not going to be done. I would not do the injustice that that implication would involve to the gallant men upon the Hill yonder in Washington, who make the laws of the nation. They are going to do a good deal of debating, but they are going to deliver the goods. Do not misunderstand me. I do not mean that I can oblige them to deliver the goods. They are going to deliver the goods because you want them delivered.

I am a believer, not only in some of the men who talk, though not all of them, but also in that vast body of my fellow citizens who do not do any talking. I would a great deal rather listen to the still, small voice that comes out of the great body of the nation to all the vocal orators in the land. But there are times when I must come out and say, "Do not let the voice be too small and too still"; when I must come out and say, "Fellow citizens, get up on your hind legs and talk and tell the people who represent you, wherever they are—in your state capital or in your national capital—what it is that the nation desires and demands." The thing that everybody is listening for in a democracy is the tramp, tramp, tramp of the facts.

Did you ever realize what the force of a democracy is? May I give you a small, whimsical example? A cynical English writer once said that the problem in every nation was how, out of a multitude of knaves, to make an honest people. Now, I, for my part, deny utterly that any nation is a multitude of knaves. But if it were a multitude of knaves as numerous as the people of the United States, you could make an honest nation out of them in this way: They are not all selfishly interested in the same things at the same time. They are going to take care of each other and neutralize each other and inspire one another. Suppose that an audience as great as this surrounded, let us say, a football field, too far away from the field to hear anything that was said out in the middle of the field itself. And suppose two men, dressed in ordinary street dress and not expected to pummel each other as the players perhaps are, should come out before the players and, standing in the sight of that great multitude, should suddenly fall to blows. You know what would happen. A great outcry would be raised, "Put them out! Put them out!" And there would be universal indignation that they should have lost their self-possession and forgotten their decency. Now, what happened? Perhaps one of those men said to the other something that nobody would allow another man to say to him without hitting him. Perhaps there was not a man in the whole body of the audience who would not have struck the first blow upon the same provocation. But it was not his provocation. He did not hear what was said; if he did, it was not addressed to him, and he is cool while they are hot.

Now, that is the way to answer the Englishman's cynical question. This country is so vast, its interests are so various, there are so many competing interests in it, that, while any body of citizens is hot, the vast majority are cool. And the vast majority are going to sit in judgment on the minority and tell them they have got to keep their heads and decide the quarrel in decent fashion. That is the way a democracy works. We are all of us fit to be judges about what is none of our business, and that is the way that great bodies of men come to the most cool-headed judgments. Their passions are not involved, their special interests are not involved; they are looking at the thing with a certain remove, with a certain aloofness of judgment.

I am anxious, therefore, my fellow citizens, that you should look at the hot stuff of war before you touch it; that you should be cool; that you should apply your hard business sense to the proposition. Shall we be caught unawares and do a scientific job like tyros and ignoramuses? Or shall we be ready? Shall we know how to do it, and, when it is necessary to do it, shall we do it to the queen's taste? I know what the answer of America is, but I want it to be unmistakably uttered, and I want it to be uttered now. Because, speaking with all solemnity, I assure you that there is not a day to be lost. Not, understand me, because of any new or specially critical matter, but because I cannot tell twenty-four hours at a time whether there is going to be trouble or not. And whether there is or not does not depend upon what I do or what I say, or upon what any man in the United States does or says. It depends upon what foreign governments do; what the commanders of ships at sea do; what those in charge of submarines do; what those who are conducting blockades do. Upon the judgment of a score of men, big and little, hang the vital issues of peace or war for the United States.

This month should not go by without something decisive being done by the people of the United States by way of preparation of the arms of self-vindication and defense. My heart burns within me, my fellow citizens, when I think of the importance of this matter and of all that is involved. I am sorry that there should be anybody in the United States who goes about crying out for war. There are such men, but they are irresponsible men who do a great deal of talking, and they are appealing to some of the most fundamental and dangerous passions of the human heart. And yet they are appealing, it must also be said, to some of the handsomest passions of the human heart. If I see somebody suffering, suffering cruelly, suffering unjustly, and believe that, by the exercise of force on my part, I can stop the suffering, it is not a low but an exalted passion which leads me to wish to go in and help. And there are men in this country, men by the thousand, who believe that we ought to intervene to stop the intolerable suffering which is involved in some of the processes of this terrible war. Yet I, for my part, am so convinced that we can help better by keeping out of the war, by giving our financial resources to the use of the injured world, by giving our cotton and our woolen stuffs to clothe the world; I am so convinced that the processes of peace are even now the helpful and healing and redeeming forces that I do not see how any man can think that, by adding to the number of guns, you can decrease the suffering or the tragedy of the world.

There is tragedy abroad in the world, my fellow citizens. We, in these peaceful areas of this blessed country, go about our daily tasks unmolested and unafraid. It seems very strange that this tragedy should be enacted while we lie so still and peaceful in our own abodes. But the world has never before in the history of mankind seen war upon such a scale, seen war with so many terrible features, seen the sweep of destruction comparable to that which is now devastating the fields of Europe. We think our own Civil War one of the bloodiest wars in history, but all the suffering of all the four years of that war are as dust in the balance as compared to the losses and sufferings and sacrifices which are being witnessed in Europe and upon the seas today. We are witnessing a cataclysm, and God only knows what the issue will be.

See, therefore, the noble part that is assigned to America—to stand steady, to stand cool, to keep alive all the wholesome processes of peace. And we, who are trustees to repair the world when the damage is done, must take counsel with one another how we shall see to it that we shall not be prevented from the efficacious performance of that task. I would not condescend to appeal to your passions. I would be ashamed of myself if I tried to do anything but quiet your judgments. I do not wish you to be any more excited than I am. I am too solemn to be excited. I would not draw a passionate breath for fear I might disturb the nice equipoise of the peace of this part of the world. But, ladies and gentlemen, one cannot help seeing visions, one cannot help realizing what it means to stand for the honor of a great nation like this. You little realize the feeling that it gives me when I see those little flags lifted in the air and know that every one of them is a symbol of the solemn duty laid upon those selected to represent you in the counsels of the world. And I have come in all solemnity to ask you to sustain the judgment of those who represent you in applying the means, the necessary means, the only means which will make it certain that those great interests may be conserved and cared for.

I am going away from here reassured beyond even the hope that I entertained when I came here. And, yet, I want to beg of you that you do not let the impressions of this hour die with the hour. Let every man and woman in this place go out of here with the feeling that he must concentrate his influence from this moment until the thing is accomplished upon making certain the security and adequacy of national defense. Because, if America succumbs, all the world loses its equipoise. Madness has entered into everything. And that serene flag, which we have thrown to the breeze upon so many occasions as the beckoning finger of hope to those who believe in the rights of mankind, will itself be stained with the blood of battle, and, staggering here and there among its foes, will lead men to wonder where the star of America has gone and why America has allowed herself to be embroiled when she might have carried that standard serenely forward to the redemption of the affairs of mankind. I beg of you to stand by your government with your minds as well as your hearts, and let us redeem America by applying our judgments to the wholesome process of national defense.

I am going to ask if the men in the band yonder will not allow me to conclude my address by allowing me to join with you in singing "America."

Printed in the *St. Louis Post-Dispatch*, Feb. 3, 1916, with a few corrections from the text printed in *Addresses of President Wilson.*

To Robert Lansing

Kansas City, Missouri. February 2, 1916.

Your letter of January 31st received. Please frame and send message you suggest explaining the point at issue.

Woodrow Wilson

T telegram (SDR, RG 59, 763.72/2389½, DNA).

An Address to the Business Men's League of St. Louis[1]

[Feb. 3, 1916]

Mr. Chairman, ladies, and gentlemen: I cannot stand here without remembering the last time that I had the pleasure of standing in this spot.[2] Your Civic League had paid me the compliment of supposing that I knew something about the government of cities, and I undertook at their invitation to be very instructive and to lead you in the way in which you should go with regard to a new charter for the city of St. Louis. I hope that you have forgotten that speech. I say I hope that you have forgotten it because I had forgotten it myself until somebody unexpectedly produced a copy of it and cited opinions in it from some of which I had departed. It is just as well to shed your speeches as you go.

As I think of the trip that I am now making, my own chief regret about it is the number of speeches with which I am expected to be loaded so that I can go off at any time. And yet I am

[1] At a breakfast meeting at the Hotel Jefferson of five hundred and sixty members of the Business Men's League of St. Louis, the president of which, Clarence Henry Howard, introduced Wilson.

[2] When he had addressed the Civic League of St. Louis on March 9, 1909. His speech is printed at that date in Vol. 19.

expected to speak exclusively of the preparation of the nation for national defense. And, of course, I do that with a great deal of ardor and zest, because that is the most pressing and immediate question ahead of us. One must first emphasize the things which admit of no delay. And, yet, there are many things that I would like to talk about to a company like this. Not only is it necessary that we should prepare, gentlemen, to mobilize the forces of the nation if necessary for the defense of the country—if it should, unhappily, become necessary to use them for that purpose. But it is also necessary to mobilize the economic forces of this country better than they have ever been mobilized before for the service of the world after this great war is over.

I am not looking forward to war. I am looking forward with the greatest ardor and interest to peace and to the services which this country may render the rest of the world in the times of peace and healing and restoration which will undoubtedly follow this great struggle. On the surface, gentlemen, there are many signs of bitterness and passion, but only on the surface. Men who are in contest with one another can sometimes hate one another, but no great people ever hated another great people. I believe that, underlying all the contests of the world, there is a true instinct of friendship among the peoples of the world, provided that the contests are righteous contests based upon merit and efficiency, and not based upon the seeking of unfair advantage. America will be infinitely efficient in the world of business if she is punctiliously righteous in the field of business, and it is with the greatest interest and hope that I have seen the many movements abroad in this country, movements which may be illustrated by one, though that not the chief one.

You know how the advertising men of this country have banded themselves together to see that advertisements speak the truth. Now, that is an index of what is happening in America. We have, upon some occasions, drawn it a little strong with regard to our individual business. Now we are beginning to realize that the real efficacy is in the facts as they are, because they are going to be uncovered sooner or later anyhow in the process of business. You cannot sell a thing that is not what you represent it to be without your customers ultimately finding out that it is not what you represent it to be. So that, even upon an instinct of preservation, if you put it upon no higher plane, you had better anticipate the facts when you see them coming and not get caught by them. The truth is stronger and mightier than any other influence in the world in the long run.

America is now going to be called out into an international

position such as she has never occupied before. For some reason that I have never understood, America has been shy about going out into the great field of international competition. She has sought, by one process or another—incomprehensible to me as a policy—to shut her doors against matching the wits of America with the wits of the world. I am willing to match the business capacity and the moral strength of American businessmen with, and to back them, against all the world.

We have left it, until very recently, to foreign corporations to conduct the greater part of the banking business in foreign bills of exchange. We have seemed to hold off from handling the very machinery by which we are to serve the rest of the world by our commerce and our industry. And now, with the rest of the world impaired in its economic efficiency, it is necessary that we should put ourselves at the service of trade and finance in all parts of the world. That is one of the reasons, gentlemen, why we are trying—trying so diligently, trying so patiently—to avoid being drawn into this great struggle now going on on the other side of thè sea. We must keep our resources and our thoughts and our strength untouched by that flame in order that they may be in a condition to serve the restoration of the world—the healing processes, the processes which will put the world upon a footing of peace, which, in the providence of God, we all pray may last for many a generation after. The world will not endure, I believe, another struggle like that which is going on now. It cannot endure it. The heart of man cannot stand it. And I believe that, after this war is over, we shall have been set further forward toward permanent peace than perhaps any other process would have set us. Man is slow to learn; he has to have it burned in; but when it is burned in, the lesson is finally comprehended.

I believe that the message which all men, such as sit in this room today, ought to carry at their hearts is the message of preparation for peace. Unhappily, you have to tread another way to approach that preparation. Unhappily, the conditions of peace are not established by us, but established by the rest of the world. We do not have to defend ourselves against ourselves; we may have to defend ourselves against the invasion of those processes of passion which are now shaking the whole round globe with their disturbance. We must be ready to see that America shall remain untouched, because America is too valuable to the world now to allow herself to be touched by this disturbance.

When we have settled this great question, as we shall presently settle it, of reasonable and rational and American preparation for national defense, then we shall talk about these other matters.

Then we shall set our house in order. Then we shall see the facts and act upon the facts. That is the reason that some of us have had to change our minds about certain things, gentlemen. I have changed my mind, for example, about the advisability of having a tariff board, and I have done it for this reason: Before this war began and the universal sweep of economic change set in, I believed, and I think I was justified in believing, that a tariff board was meant merely to keep alive the question of protection. Now, the sweep of this change has been so universal that an unprejudiced, nonpartisan board is absolutely necessary in order to find how far and in what way the facts have been changed. Because we cannot pretend that any man now living can predict or foresee or guide the policy of the United States with regard to her legislation in economic matters. We need the facts, and we need them from the most unprejudiced and undisturbed quarters that we can get them from.

Personally, I look forward to the establishment of a tariff board with some misgivings, because I will have to choose the men that make it up. And I tell you that men without prepossessions are hard to find, and, when you find them, they are generally empty of everything else. Gentlemen who have not done a lot of thinking and formed some very definite convictions are now very service-able in public affairs. And, knowing that I have my due quota of prejudices and prepossessions myself, and that I hold even my untested convictions in fighting spirit, I am not sure that I would be a suitable member of a tariff board. Yet I shall have to choose suitable members for a tariff board, for I feel great confidence that we shall have one, and I want the best counsel I can get. I want the best guidance I can get in the choosing of the men who shall make it up. If I make mistakes, they will not be mistakes of intention, but mistakes of lack of information. It is very in-teresting how important men feel after they get put on a fed-eral board. They are thereafter hardly approachable. They are jealous of nothing so much as being spoken to too familiarly by the President, who seems to be regarded as some sort of sus-picious political influence. You do not know how interesting it is, gentlemen, to be regarded as the positive pole of a political bat-tery, throwing out all sorts of electrifying influences which are supposed to be meant to increase the vitality of democratic poli-tics. I do not think that democratic politics needs any increase of vitality.

You will see that I am merely uttering to you the casual thoughts of an unprepared address, but it always stimulates me to say some of the things that are in my mind in face of a company like this. I have been in St. Louis so often, and have always enjoyed my visits here so much, that I have had the pleasure of making a great many friends here. When I arrived in Kansas City the other day, the reception committee said, "Mr. President, this is your fifth visit here." "Yes," I said, "my fifth visit since you began counting." And I made a good many visits to St. Louis before you began counting, sometimes merely as a Princeton man interested in the Princeton crowd, and sometimes upon purely private errands, but always with the renewed pleasure of meeting the substantial and thoughtful men who here vitalize the life of the business world in America.

There is one thing, gentlemen, I want you to relieve yourselves of—and that is the suspicion that there is a Middle West as distinguished from the rest of America. As I say, I have sampled your quality a great many times, and I have never found your quality to be anything but thoroughly American, suitable for any part of the continent. The distance between you and the Pacific coast or the Atlantic coast is not a distance that separates you or makes you different in sympathy and in impulse. On the contrary, standing somewhat nearer the middle of the continent than some other people, your horizon is the more symmetrical.

I have come out to appeal to America, not because I doubted what America felt, but because I thought America wanted the satisfaction of uttering what she felt, and of letting the whole world know that she was a unit in respect of every question of national dignity and national safety.

Printed in *Addresses of President Wilson*, with a few corrections from the complete text printed in the *St. Louis Republic*, Feb. 4, 1916.

An Address in St. Louis on Preparedness[1]

[Feb. 3, 1916]

Mr. Chairman and fellow citizens: I came out into the Middle West to find something, and I found it. I was told in Washington that the Middle West had a different feeling from the portions of the country that lie upon either coast, and that it was indifferent to the question of preparation for national defense. I knew enough of the Middle West of this great continent to know that the men who said that did not know what they were talking about. I knew the spirit of America dwelt as much in this great section of the country as in any other section of it. And I knew that the men of these parts loved the honor and safety of Amer-

[1] In the Coliseum at 10:45 A.M., before a capacity crowd of twelve thousand. Clarence H. Howard again introduced Wilson.

ica as much as Americans everywhere love it and are ready to stand by it. (Applause.) I didn't come out to find out how you felt or what you thought, but to tell you what was going on. I came out here in order that there might be an absolute clarification of the issues immediately confronting us, because I, for one, have an absolute faith in the readiness of America to act upon the facts just as soon as America knows what the facts are.

Now, the facts are very easily and briefly stated. What is the situation? The situation is that America is at peace with all the world, and desires to remain at peace with all the world. (Applause.) And it is not a shallow peace. It is a genuine peace, based upon some of the most fundamental principles of international intercourse. America is at peace with all the world because she entertains a real friendship for all the nations of the world. It is not, as some have mistakenly supposed, a peace based upon self-interest. It is a peace based upon some of the most generous sentiments that characterize the heart.

You know, my fellow citizens, that this nation is a composite nation. It has a genuine friendship for all the nations of the world because it is drawn from all the nations of the world. The blood of all the great national stocks runs, and runs red and strong, in the veins of America, and America understands what the genuine ties of friendship and affection are. It would tear the heartstrings of America to be at war with any of the great nations of the world. (Applause.) Our peace is not based upon the mere conveniences of our national life. For great issues, which it is our honorable obligation to defend, we would not be at peace, but would plunge into any trouble necessary in order to defend our honor and integrity, the honor and integrity of our nation. But we believe, my fellow citizens, that we can show our friendship for the world and our devotion to the principles of humanity better and more effectively by keeping out of this trouble than by getting into it.

I did not misread the heart of this great country. The heart of this great country is sound and is made up of fundamental principles of human sympathy which move all men when they are permitted free scope and are not interfered with by the politics of groups of men and the suggestions of those who do not represent the people themselves. I have no indictment against any form of government, but I do believe in my heart that the world has never witnessed a case, and never will witness a case, where one people desired to make war upon another people. And I believe that the security of America rests in the fact that no man is master of America, that we know that no man can lead whither the people do not desire to be led. I believe it to be my duty, whatever my individual opinions might be, whatever my individual sympathies, whatever my individual points of view, to subordinate everything to the conscientious attempt to interpret and express, in the international affairs of the world, the genuine spirit of my fellow citizens.

So far as America is concerned, no man need go about amongst us preaching peace. We are disciples of peace already, and no man need preach that gospel amongst us. I, in my individual capacity, am also a disciple of domestic peace and security. (Applause.) But, suppose that my neighbor's house is on fire and my roof is of combustible shingles; that the fire eats into the wood, the flame leaps from timber to timber? Is it my fault, because I love peace and security, that my doors are battered in recklessly? The danger is not from within, gentlemen, it is from without. (Applause.) And I am bound to tell you that that danger is constant and immediate, not because anything new has happened, not because there has been any change in our international relationship within recent weeks or months, but because the danger comes with every turn of events. Why, gentlemen, the commanders of submarines have their instructions, and those instructions are consistent for the most part with the law of nations. But one reckless commander of a submarine, choosing to put his private interpretation upon what his government wishes him to do, might set the world on fire. There are not only governments to deal with, but the servants of governments; there are not only the contacts of politics, but also those infinitely varied contacts which come from the mere movement of mankind, the quiet processes of the everyday world. There are cargoes of cotton on the seas; there are cargoes of wheat on the seas; there are cargoes of manufactured articles on the seas. And every one of those cargoes may be the point of ignition, because every cargo comes into the field of fire, comes where there are flames which no man can control.

I know the spirit of America to be this: We respect other nations, and absolutely respect their rights so long as they respect our rights. We do not claim anything for ourselves which they would not under like circumstances claim for themselves. Every statement of right that we have made is grounded upon the utterances of their own public men and their own judges. There is no dispute about the rights of nations under the understandings of international law. America has drawn no fine point. America has raised no novel issue. America has merely asserted the rights of her citizens and her government upon what is written plain on all the documents of international intercourse. Therefore, America is not selfish in claiming her rights. She is merely standing for the rights of mankind, when the life of mankind is being disturbed by an unprecedented war between the greatest nations of the world. (Applause.) Some of these days we shall be able to call the statesmen of the older nations to witness that it was we who kept the quiet flame of international principle burning upon its altar while the winds of passion were sweeping away every altar in the world. Some of these days they will look back with gratification upon the steadfast allegiance of the United States to those principles of action which every man loves when his temper is not upset and his judgment not disturbed.

I am ready to make every patient allowance for men caught in the storm of national struggle. I am not in a critical frame of mind. I am ready to yield everything but the absolute, final, essential right, because I know how my heart would burn, I know how my mind would be in a whirl, if America were engaged in what seemed a death grapple. I know how I would be inclined to sweep aside the minor impediments of the ordinary transactions of government, and how I would be inclined to say to myself: "Why, we are fighting for our lives. Punctilio has nothing to do with it." So I am ready to make every allowance for both sides, for, having pledged myself, as your chairman has reminded you, to maintain, if it be possible for me to maintain, the peace of the United States, I have thereby pledged myself to think as far as possible from the point of view of the other side as well as from the point of view of America. I want the record of the conduct of this administration to be a record of genuine neutrality and not of pretended neutrality.

You know the circumstances of the time, my fellow citizens. You know how one group of belligerents is practically shut off by circumstances over which we have no control from the ordinary commerce of the world. You know, therefore, how the spirit of America has not been able to express itself adequately in both directions. But I believe the people of America are genuinely neutral. I believe that their desire is to stand in unprejudiced judgment upon what is going on; not that they would arrogate to themselves the right to utter rebuking judgment to any nation, but that they are holding themselves not to assist either side in what is wrong, but to countenance both sides in what they are doing for the legitimate defense of their national honor. (Applause.)

Because the fortunate circumstance of America, my fellow countrymen, is that it desires nothing but a free field and no favor. (Applause.) Our security is in the purity of our motives. The minute we get an impure motive we are going to deserve to be in trouble. The minute we desire what we have no right to, then we are going to get into trouble, and ought to get into trouble. (Applause.) But, my fellow citizens, while we know our own hearts and know our own desires, it does not follow that other nations and other governments understand our purpose and our principle of action. These are days of infinite prejudice and passion, because they are days of war. It is said by an old maxim that amidst war the law is silent. It is also true that amidst war the judgment is silent. Men press forward towards their object with a certain degree of blind recklessness, and they are apt to excite their passions, particularly against those who in any way stand in their way. Therefore, this is the situation that I have come to remind you of, for you need merely to have it stated to see it: The peace of the world, including America, depends upon the aroused passion of other nations, and not upon the motives of the nation itself, and it is for that reason that I have come to call you to a consciousness of the necessity for preparing this country for anything that might happen. (Applause.)

Now, here is the choice, and I do not see how any prudent man could doubt which alternative to take: Either we shall sit still and wait for the necessity for immediate national defense to come and then call for raw volunteers who, probably for the first few months, would be impotent as against a trained and experienced enemy, or we shall adopt the ancient American principle that the men of the country shall be made ready to take care of their own government. (Applause.) You have either got to make the men of this nation in sufficient number ready to defend the nation against initial disaster, or you have to take the risk of initial disaster. Think of the cruelty, think of the stupidity, of putting raw levies of inexperienced men into the modern field of battle! We are not asking for armies; we are asking for a trained citizenry which will act in the spirit of citizenship, and not in the spirit of military establishments. If anybody is afraid of a trained citizenry in America, he is afraid also of the spirit of America itself. I don't want to command a great army under the authority granted me by the Constitution to be commander in chief of the army and navy of the United States. I want to command the confidence and support of my fellow citizens.

Of course you will back me up and come to my assistance if I know you. (Continued applause.) But will you come knowing what you are about, or won't you? (Voices in audience: Yes, yes.) Will you come knowing the character of the arms that you carry in your hands, knowing something of the discipline of organization, knowing something of how to take care of yourselves in camp, knowing something about all those things that it is necessary to know so as not to throw human life away? It is handsome, my fellow citizens, to sacrifice human life intelligently for something greater than life itself, but it is not handsome for any cause whatever to throw human life away.

The plans now laid before the Congress of the United States are merely plans not to throw the life of American youth away. (Applause.) Those plans are going to be adopted. (Applause.) I am not jealous, and you are not jealous, of the details. No man ought to be confident that his judgment is correct about the details. No man ought to say to any legislative body, "You must take my plan or none at all"—that is arrogance and stupidity. But we have the right to insist, and I don't think it will be necessary to insist, that we get the essential thing, that is to say, a principle, a system, by which we can secure a trained citizenship, so that if it becomes necessary to defend the nation the first line of defense on land will be an adequate and intelligent line of defense.

I say "on land," because America apparently has never been jealous of armed men if they are only at sea. And America also knows that you cannot send volunteers to sea unless you want to send them to the bottom. (Applause.) The modern fighting ships, the modern submarine and other instruments of modern naval warfare, must be handled by experts. America has never debated or disputed that proposition, and all that we are asking for is a sufficient number of experts and a sufficient number of vessels at their disposal. The vessels we have are commanded by experts. There is not a better service in the world than that of the American navy. But no matter how skilled and how capable the officers or how devoted the men, they must have ships enough, and we are going to have ships enough. (Applause.) We have been doing it leisurely and good-naturedly, as we are accustomed to do everything in times of peace, but now we must get down to business and do it systematically. We must lay down a program and then steadfastly carry it out and complete it. There are no novelties about the program. All the lines of it are the lines already established, only drawn out to their legitimate conclusion, and drawn out so that they will be completed within a calculable length of time. Do you realize the task of the navy? Have you ever let your imagination dwell upon the enormous stretch of coast from the canal to Alaska—from the canal to the northern coast of Maine? There is no other navy in the world that has to cover so great an area, an area of defense, as the American navy, and it ought, in my judgment, to be incomparably the greatest navy in the world.[2] (Applause.)

But as I say, you have never been jealous of armed force at sea. You have been jealous of armed force on land; and I must say that I share with you the jealousy of a great military establishment. But I never have shared any prejudice against putting arms in the hands of trained citizens whose interest is to defend their homes and their security, and not to serve any political purpose whatever. (Applause.) There is no politics in national defense, ladies and gentlemen. I would be sorry to see men of different parties differ about anything but the details of this great question; and I do not find any essential differences. Some men do not see anything. Some men look right straight in the face of the facts and see nothing but atmospheric air. Some men are so hopelessly and contentedly provincial that they can't see the rest of the world. But they don't constitute a large or influential minority, even. (Applause.) You must listen to them with indulgence, and then absolutely ignore them. They have a right to talk, but they have no right to affect our conduct. (Continued applause.) Indeed, if I were in your place, I would encourage them to talk. Nothing chills folly like exposure to the air, and these gentlemen ought to be encouraged to hire large halls. (Applause and laughter.) And the more people they can get to hear them, the safer the country would be.

The judgment of America is a very hard-headed judgment. The judgment of America is not based upon sentiment; it is based upon facts. And I want to say to you that nothing has encouraged me more, upon this trip that I have been making, than the consciousness that America is awake to the facts. (Applause.) I do not want to say anything disrespectful about any newspaper, but it is astonishing how little some newspaper editors know. (Long applause.) And I would like from some of them a candid expression of the impression they have got from what has happened since I left Washington. They probably will give it their own interpretation, but they will not (and this ought to comfort them if they are moral men), they will not deceive anybody. Because, from the time I left Washington until now, I have had this feeling: The country is up. There is not a man who is not awake. There is not a man who does not realize what the situation is and what we ought to do in order to meet the situation.

The strength of America is in that part of it which is not vocal.

2 In the official text, Wilson changed this to read: "incomparably the most adequate navy in the world." *Addresses of President Wilson*, p. 68.

(Laughter and applause.) The voice of America is a very still but a very powerful voice. (Applause.) My constant endeavor in Washington is to hear that voice. I have often said that it has seemed to me a very fortunate circumstance that all the living rooms of the White House are on the side from which, if you look out of the windows, you cannot see the city of Washington. You see, instead, the broad fields of Virginia across the river. And your imagination has free flight over this scene where the quiet people on the farms and the busy people in the factories and the absorbed men in the offices are realizing and living the life of America. And, therefore, from out those great spaces of the city, where politics is so intense to the square inch, the people in those spaces seem to send in at those southern windows of the Executive Mansion their messages of reassurance. That is where I listen for the still voice of America, and I believe that that voice has brought to me, in unmistaken accents, the resolution of this country to do whatever is necessary and essential to do, in order that no man might question the honor and perfect integrity or disregard the rights of the United States of America.

Printed in the *St. Louis Post-Dispatch*, Feb. 3, 1916, with corrections from the complete texts in the *St. Louis Republic*, Feb. 4, 1916, and *Addresses of President Wilson.*

Remarks from a Rear Platform in East St. Louis

Feb. 3, 1916.

Fellow citizens: I am not accustomed to competing with other hot air that is so audible as that which these engines make, and, of course, you will realize that it is impossible for me to expound, in these circumstances, the important errand upon which I have come. But I feel, after the experiences of the last few days, that it is not necessary for me to expound that errand. You know what it is. You understand it just as well as I do, and I do not entertain the slightest doubt that all American communities are ready to respond in the most intelligent manner to the call for national defense.

The only thing I can do in circumstances like these is to express my very deep wonder, as well as my very deep obligation, that so many of you should have come out to extend your gracious welcome to me, and to say that my wholehearted energy is bearing upon the task of doing everything for you that it is possible for me to do in the great office to which you have exalted me. I want to express my personal interest in this part of the great State of Illinois and to wish you all sorts of good fortune in the days to come, during which we must all cooperate in the most important efforts to maintain the peace and preserve the integrity of the country we all love.

I thank you very much indeed.

T MS (WP, DLC).

To Robert Lansing

Terre Haute Ind [Feb.] 3 [1916]

Please hold message suggested yesterday until I can see you or if it has been sent send word to await further instructions Will explain when I reach Washington   Woodrow Wilson

T telegram (SDR, RG 59, 763.72/29390½, DNA).

Three Letters from Edward Mandell House

Dear Governor: No. 9. Paris, February 3, 1916.

So much has happened since I last wrote that I scarcely know where to begin. I will try not to go into detail leaving that for a personal conference.

I was well received in Germany—better than before if anything. I had many invitations while there, but concluded it would be wiser to see everyone at our Embassy.

I conferred with the Chancellor alone for an hour and a half, and had conferences with von Jagow, Zimmermann and Solf, besides many other important Germans. The Chancellor, for the moment, is in control with the Emperor. When I was there before, von Tirpitz and Falkenhayn were in the ascendancy. The Chancellor's advantage has brought von Tirpitz and von Falkenhayn closer together and the Army is now more favorable to the Navy's contention for an aggressive undersea policy.

I do not believe the Chancellor will be able to hold the first place long, particularly if we do not take measures against the Allies, which, indeed, it would be impossible for us to take in a way that would satisfy Germany.

When they find that this cannot be brought about, and when the pinch of the blockade becomes greater than even now, a revulsion of feeling will probably take place and a sentiment will develop for any measure that promises relief.

The Navy crowd are telling the people that an unrestricted undersea warfare will isolate England. I look, therefore, in any event for troublous times with Germany during the next few months and I am afraid that my suggestion that we remain aloof until the time becomes more propitious for you to intervene and lead them out, is not promising.

The reason I am so anxious that you do not break with Germany over the Lusitania is that any delay may make it possible to carry out the original plan in regard to intervention. And if that cannot be done because of Germany's undersea warfare, then we will be forced in a way that will give us the advantage.

I discussed peace with the Chancellor, with Zimmermann and with Solf. The Chancellor was the most unreasonable, coming back always to the point that he was the only one in power amongst the belligerents that had spoken for peace. He said he felt that the guilt of continuing the conflict was upon their shoulders and not upon his. Time and again, I brought him back to the point that his expression of a desire for peace meant a victorious peace and one which included indemnity from his antagonists.

He admitted this, but wanted to know why that was unreasonable since, indeed, they had been victorious. I told him that the Allies did not admit defeat, but were confident that another year would change conditions in their favor and that the terms then would be in their hands rather than in Germany's. We would then go the round again.[1]

He is an amiable, well meaning man with limited ability. Zimmermann is much abler and my talk with him was more satisfactory.

There are reasons why the officers controlling the army are not pressing for peace. They are directing affairs and it is to their advantage to continue to do so. For instance, Hindenburg received something like $2000. before the war began. He now receives, I am told, something like $25,000. with a palace to live in.

The Prussian junkers formerly paid seventy-five or eighty cents a day for laborers on their farms. They now get Russian prisoners at six cents a day, and their products bring four times as much as they did before the war. They, too, do not desire peace.

I doubt whether internal trouble will come during the war. They have all the discordant elements at the front harnessed to the war machine, impotent for harm. If the war goes against Germany, when the army is disbanded trouble will surely come for the masters. If victory is theirs, the war lords will reign supreme and democratic governments will be imperilled throughout the world   Affectionately yours,   E. M. House

1 Bethmann Hollweg recorded this conversation in "Gespräch mit Oberst House," Jan. 28, 1916, TI memorandum (Der Weltkrieg, No. 2, Vermittelungs-

aktionen, geheim, vol. 15, pp. 127-29, GFO-Ar). According to the Chancellor, House told him that Wilson was determined to continue to champion the freedom of the seas against England during the war, but that the recurring incidents with Germany had always intervened to tie his hands. As to peace negotiations, House said that he had been told in England that Wilson's pro-German attitude had completely disqualified him as a mediator. At any rate, the Entente was at present not interested in peace talks, since Germany, on account of the military situation, would make demands which the Entente would never be willing to concede. Bethmann Hollweg replied that he desired a permanent peace which, however, had to include security for Germany on the Polish and Belgian borders and an indemnity from France. England, the Chancellor concluded, would also have to make up for many things in general before good relations could be re-established between Germany and England.

Dear Governor: No. 10. Paris, February 3, 1916.

Penfield came to Geneva to see me. I thought it best not to go to Vienna and he thought it best not to come to Berlin and both having very much the same reason.

He confirmed our belief that Austria-Hungary and Turkey are now but little more than provinces of Germany. The Central Empire runs from the Baltic to the Dardanelles and beyond. The Germans took charge during the troublous days of last spring when Russia was slowly overrunning Austria and by their efficiency and organization threw the Russians back. The Austrians are consequently grateful.

The Empire, as you know, is made up of many divergent elements, none of which work in harmony and all of which are more distrustful of each other than of Germany.

Food is more plentiful there than in Germany, but the distribution and the leveling of prices is not nearly so well done. The desire for peace is also prevalent, but there again the people are mere cogs in the great German war machine and as helpless to express their desires as the German soldier in the trenches.

Penfield tells me that the feeling against America is stronger than against Russia, France, England or even Italy. He ascribes this to three causes. One is the furnishing of munitions to the Allies. Another the sending of Dumba home and the third the Ancona notes.

The Austrian Empire is the proudest in Europe and they cannot view with complacency such rebuffs from "a crude republic."

Penfield is giving freely to charity and stands well because of this and his relations with the Pope.

There is nothing more to tell of that situation that would be of interest.   Affectionately yours,   E. M. House

Dear Governor: No. 11   Paris, February 3, 1916.

I have seen the Prime Minister and Jules Cambon and have had most interesting and satisfactory talks with them both.

The French press has again treated my coming with cordiality, and I am told on all sides that it has greatly added to the good feeling between the two countries.

I talked to Cambon quite freely outlining the entire situation as it seems to me, and I am hopeful that the result of what I have said will show itself in the immediate future. I took up our shipping troubles with him and he seemed to more readily understand our difficulties than they do in England. I have told them all that what we wanted most was for them to do those things which would help us to help them best.[1]

I am to see Poincare Saturday with Sharp. I saw the other two alone for there was too much of a confidential nature to risk a third person.

I cannot begin to tell you by letter how critical the situation is everywhere, not only as between themselves, but with us as well. In my opinion, hell will break loose in Europe this spring and summer as never before and I see no way to stop it for the moment. I am as sure as I ever am of anything that by the end of the summer you can intervene.

My suspicions regarding Russia have had some confirmation which I had best not write. Thos. Nelson Page sends Richardson,[2] his Second Secretary, with confidential let[t]ers today. Richardson tells me that Italy is tired of the war and that a change of Ministry might occur at any time. The feeling there is strong against England because of her failure to do things that Italy desires. It is stronger, Richardson thinks, against England than it is against Germany.

I am trying to impress upon both England and France the precariousness of the situation and the gamble that a continuance of the war involves. I know I am making an impression in some quarters where reason has not altogether fled.

I am pleased beyond measure to see your efforts to arouse our people to the neces[s]ity for defence. You cannot put it too strongly, for the dangers are greater than even you can realize.

I want to tell you, and Mr. Lansing through you, the importance of not letting notes to and from governments leak. There is complaint of it everywhere and it is a useless cause of friction.

Another thing I will bring to your attention when I return is our Embassy at Petrograd. The German Government is seriously thinking of taking their affairs out of our hands. They claim that more German and Austrian prisoners are dying in Russia from bad treatment than are now being lost on the battlefields, and they attribute it largely to the lack of interest our representatives are giving the matter. From what I can learn from disinterested sources like Gerard and Penfield, Mayre seems totally unfit.

I promised the German Government that I would bring this to your attention promptly upon my return, and I have some data covering the case.

Affectionately yours,   E. M. House

TLS (WP, DLC).

¹ Cambon reported on this conversation in "Conversation du Colonel House avec M. Jules Cambon," Feb. 2, 1916, T memorandum (Guerre 1914-1918, États-Unis, Vol. 498, pp. 174-77, FFM-Ar), our translation. House explained his mission in very general terms and reported on his conversations in Berlin. The French, House went on, had no idea of the strength of American sentiment in favor of the Allies, and of France in particular. It was very necessary for the Allies to understand the necessity of helping the United States to help them. House, Cambon said, went on:

"I would hardly know how to recommend too strongly to you that, in all the initiatives that the Allies take and that might affect neutrals, they be manifestly guided by military necessity. That is essential. America will accept, despite all its reserve and all its more or less formal observations, all measures which meet a military need. Anything that departs from that will stir up complaints and resentments among Americans."

"It seemed essential to Colonel House," Cambon wrote, "to avoid dissatisfactions, because, he added, if you act in that fashion, inevitably America will enter the war, *before the end of the year*, and will align herself on the side of the Allies. However, for that to happen, it would be necessary for an incident to occur that would cause all the American people to rally behind the President."

"This statement from Colonel House astonished me," Cambon wrote. "I had him repeat it and, after having noted it in English, I had him read it. He said to me: 'exactly.'"

Cambon then asked what kind of incident might precipitate American entry into the war, since the Germans seemed to be willing to grant everything that the United States demanded, particularly in the *Lusitania* case. House replied that the Germans would not acknowledge the illegality of their attack on the *Lusitania*. "As a result, any settlement that might be reached in this matter, if one could be reached, will only postpone the conflict, not prevent it."

"For," House continued, "I bring from Germany the conviction that, if the British government takes measures to constrict Germany's trade and food supplies any further, the Germans will wage war without regard for anything or anyone. This is the feeling of Germany. She believes that the war will be decided on the sea; public opinion is convinced that victory will result from submarines and mines. Germany believes that she possesses the most powerful submarines: she will sow unlimited numbers of mines across the ocean to make navigation impossible. She believes that she will thus isolate England. This state of mind will certainly compel Germany to commit the act that will force America's hand."

The conversation now turned to more general aspects of the war. Victory, House said, would strengthen German militarism and reinforce the German feudal system. If, however, Germany was beaten and the Allies avoided all efforts to interfere with Germany's internal affairs, then it was impossible that the general discontent would not produce radical, even revolutionary, changes. Cambon agreed and added that this war was the last war between democracy and what remained of feudalism in the world.

House said that these were his sentiments also. He added that he hoped that, after the war, there would be an alliance among France, the United States, and England—an alliance for peace, not for war. Such an alliance, with the support of other free peoples, could impose peace on the world.

² Norval Richardson.

From William Cox Redfield

PERSONAL AND CONFIDENTIAL.

Dear Mr. President: Washington February 3, 1916.

Mr. Polk tells me information has come from Ambassador Gerard verifying certain statements that German manufacturers in some lines are piling up goods to unload them upon our markets and others when the war shall close. I think there is no doubt as to the facts in certain directions. Nor is there doubt in my mind that the matter can not be covered by a tariff or that if left much longer it may be too late for us to be ready.

Secretary Lansing is familiar with the facts and will speak to you of them, and I now wish to add my earnest plea to his that we do not delay some measure to deal with the dumping question, that we be not deceived by unbelief as to what Germany may do in that respect, and that we take the matter very seriously as one which tariffs will not settle and which needs a remedy of a firmer sort as soon as we can get it.

I am in accord with the tariff board plan as fully outlined by you, but in my judgment it will not do to wait for that board to be created and then to make recommendations respecting dumping and have these recommendations carried out. Should the war close ere that was done harm would be wrought in a few months which years might not replace.

I am no alarmist and have no fears in the matter save that we shall by inaction allow that to come to pass which none desire.

If it is at all possible I beg you to get some legislation started without delay which will forbid unfair foreign competition deliberately intended to destroy some of our industries.

Yours very truly,   William C. Redfield

TLS (WP, DLC).

From Robert Lansing, with Enclosure

PERSONAL AND CONFIDENTIAL:

My dear Mr. President: [Washington] February 4, 1916.

The German Ambassador has just called upon me and left the enclosed memorandum which he gave me to understand was as far as his Government possibly could go in complying with our requests.

I have only analyzed the memorandum very hastily. In the *first* place I think it may be drawn from it that the German Government recognizes that retaliatory acts are not lawful, though justifiable; in the *second* place, it declares that "retaliation must not aim at other than enemy subjects," which means, I think, that it is unlawful so far as neutrals are concerned; and in the *third* place, the German Government assumes liability for the death of citizens of the United States as a result of the sinking of the LUSITANIA. It comes so near meeting all our demands that I wish to study it with care to see if it cannot be considered acceptable.

Of course the word *illegal* and the word *illegality* are omitted, but if we do accept this settlement I believe we could state our understanding of the language in order to show in our acceptance that we consider there is a direct admission of wrong.

Faithfully yours,   Robert Lansing.

TLS (Lansing Letterpress Book, SDR, RG 59, DNA).

ENCLOSURE

Kaiserlich Deutsche Botschaft.   Handed me by the German
Ambassador, Feby 4/16 4 pm RL

The German submarine war against England's commerce at sea, as announced on February 4th, 1915, is conducted in retaliation of England's inhuman war against Germany's commercial and industrial life. It is generally recognized as justifiable that retaliation may be employed against acts committed in contravention of the law of nations. Germany is enacting such retaliation, because it is England's endeavor to cut off all imports from Germany by preventing even legal commerce of the neutrals with her and thereby subjecting the German population to starvation. In answer to these acts Germany is making efforts to destroy England's commerce at sea, at least as far as it is carried on by enemy vessels. If Germany has notwithstanding limited her submarine warfare, this was done in view of her long-standing friendship with the United States and in view of the fact that the sinking of the Lusitania caused the death of citizens of the United States. Thereby the German retaliation affected neutrals which was not the intention, as retaliation must not aim at other than enemy subjects.

The Imperial German Government having subsequent to the event issued to its naval officers the new instructions which are now prevailing, expresses profound regret that citizens of the United States suffered by the sinking of the Lusitania and assuming liability therefor offers to make reparation for the life of the citizens of the United States who were lost by the payment of a suitable indemnity.

In the note of the American Government of July 21st concerning the Lusitania incident the Government of the United States invited the practical cooperation of the Imperial Government in contending for the principle of the freedom of the seas and added that this great object could in some way be accomplished before the present war ends. The Imperial Government will at all times gladly cooperate with the Government of the United States for the purpose of accomplishing this common great object.

T memorandum (SDR, RG 59, 763.72/2611, DNA).

To Robert Lansing

My dear Mr. Secretary,   The White House. 4 February, 1916.

I have just returned and hasten to send the enclosed correspondence from House.[1] I am sure that it will give you food for thought, as it has done me.

The sheets written in this type are the decoded cablegrams. I have just decyphered them, for I did not take my private code with me to the West.

I shall make no comment as yet, but you will understand why I asked you by telegram not to give Gerard further instructions until I could see and talk with you.

I shall seek a conference with you early to-morrow. Do you not think that we could frame a handsome apology from Germany which we could accept without explicit disavowal, and leaving out reference to freedom of the seas. Bernstorff must see that nothing immediate can be done about that.

In haste,   Faithfully Yours,   W.W.
Please return enclosures

WWTLI (WP, DLC).
[1] These were EMH to WW, Jan. 10, 13, 15, 16, and 17, 1916, printed in Vol. 35; and EMH to WW, Jan. 30 and Feb. 1, 1916, printed in this volume.

From Walter Hines Page

Dear Mr. President: [London] Feb. 4. 1916

From the point of view of London, I fear the proposal looking toward the prohibition of Allied merchantmen's carrying defensive guns was a mistake, parallel to the mistake of insisting on the Allies' accepting the whole Declaration of London. The Declaration forbade the putting of copper, rubber and cotton on the contraband list—wh. wd. have worked directly for Germany's advantage. The English saw in the Declaration a German trick and consequently they thought they saw the German effort to use us when we made that proposal. This planted in the British mind a fear lest we shd. not detect or withstand German influences—not from any ill will on our part to the British, but from our remoteness from the war and our natural incredulity about German methods.

Now this new proposal—to disarm merchantmen of defensive guns—links itself in the British mind with our proposal about the Declaration of London—with this added cause of regret: that it wd. be a change of rules made while the war is in progress.

Both these proposals—both these efforts of a neutral Gov't— to secure agreements by the belligerents about the conduct of war —relate to war at sea; and no similar proposals have been made touching war on land. Yet—the British think—there have been quite as serious offenses against humanity on land as on the sea.

The Allies will not agree to this last proposal; but, if they are forced by the United States to submit (so far as our ports are concerned) to such a change of rule made during the progress of the war, they will be embarrassed about their shipping from the United States. They will permit as few British merchantmen to go to our ports as they possibly can. They will forbid them, as far as they can, to bring cargoes except such as are indispensable for the conduct of the war. I fear they will seek other markets, as far as they can, to buy in—not from preference but because of the lessened danger. I telegraphed you[1] the credible rumor that they are preparing to lessen and if need be to discontinue their orders for munitions made in the U. S.—again not from preference but because of the increasing danger of shipment which they think might follow the carrying out of this proposal.

All this fear rests on no feeling of hostility or bitterness to us—no reprisal or punishment—idea: not in the least—but only on the instinct of safety & prudence. They ask themselves, "What may the U. S. not do next? They have so remote and academic a view of the war—they so fail to realize it or to show an understanding of its great issues, that we are afraid of other impossible moves or proposals or embarrassments." Much of this fear is, I think, based on Bernstorff's apparently secure hold. They recall that a British Ambassador was dismissed for advising a man how he shd. vote at an election;[2] and they wonder why a German Ambassador is retained who (by documentary evidence) has paid money to his military attaché which the attaché paid to men who blew up bridges &c. They, unconsciously perhaps, attribute both our proposals to Bernstorff's suggestion or influence.

The relations of our Gov't, therefore, to the British and con-

sequently to all the Allies, seems to be entering on a new phase—
a phase of fear of German influence on our action. I am constantly asked—anxiously and sincerely asked—what the U. S. wd.
have England do (permitting their economic pressure on Germany) to remove our objections—what change in their procedure? Since I have no instructions that enable me to answer such
a question positively, they say they cannot find any positive
answer in our negative objections and protests. Hence the controversy keeps a mere zigzag course. Could it not be settled or at
least mollified? What cd. the British do to enable us to lessen
it—what cd. they do and at the same time continue their pressure
on Germany? For they will not give this up; but I believe they wd.
change their plan if we shd. suggest a change that wd. please us
better & be not less effective.

I fear that under the present conditions the prevalent feeling
is something like this: The Administration showed a popular and
national leadership that was most remarkable and inspiring—the
most remarkable and inspiring in recent history—in securing the
new tariff act, the new banking act and the repeal of the Panama
tolls; but that when the sudden need came, like a clap of thun-
der, of a comprehensive and steady foreign policy, the grasp
shown by the Administration was not so sure. The positive proposals that we have made—about the Declaration of London and
about defensive guns on merchant ships—have, to their minds,
shown an unsteadiness of grasp, a failure to realize the war.

I hear nothing but gratitude for the sympathy of the great
mass of our people; nothing but gratitude for such clear-cut acts
by the Administration as the explanation of the meaning of an
embargo on munitions. Nor do I ever hear any effort to balance
what we have done for the Allies against what we have done for
the Germans. This is not in their minds at all. The two things
that bother them are these:

(1) How can we legitimately use our sea supremacy in its
utmost pressure on Germany and yet keep from offense to the
U.S?

(2) Judging by the two proposals that the U.S. have made to
the belligerents, we fear that they understand the war so imperfectly as to cause apprehension about their general foreign
policy: the U. S. may propose to change—what next?

So much for the British point of view and for my reading of
British opinion now. It is uncertain of us. What wd. we have them
do?   Yours Sincerely,   Walter H. Page

ALS (WP, DLC).

[1] It is missing in WP, DLC; however, Page repeated the telegram as an

enclosure in a later letter: WHP to WW, Jan. 25, 1916, TC telegram, enclosed in WHP to WW, Feb. 23, 1916, ALS (WP, DLC).
    [2] About this, the Sackville-West affair, see S. Low to WW, Sept. 8, 1915, n. 1, Vol. 34.

From Richard Olney

PERSONAL

My dear Mr. President,   Boston, 4 February, 1916
    My warm congratulations upon your triumphal march through the Middle West—a sure omen of a November victory.
    A single track mind surely means a single eye to duty. Yet application, however intense, is both relieved and improved by incidental divertissement—and I am sending you by the same mail as this note a libellum called "Fruitlands"—giving an account of a sequence to the famous Brook Farm experiment in communism.[1] It is at once amusing and pathetic and is a glimpse at some amazing phases of New England life less than three-quarters of a century ago which cannot but interest you.
    With best wishes, and counting upon you not to let your interminable and complicated labors bring about such a national calamity as would be the failure of your health and strength—
    I am—   Sincerely yours,   Richard Olney

TLS (WP, DLC).
    [1] Clara Endicott Sears, comp., *Bronson Alcott's Fruitlands*, with *Transcendental Wild Oats*, by Louisa May Alcott (Boston and New York, 1915). There is a copy of this book in the Wilson Library, DLC.

From Cleveland Hoadley Dodge

My dear President   New York. February 4th, 1916
    Heartiest congratulations on the success of your great trip! I hope the papers are correct in saying that it has done you more good than a week of golf
    With warmest regards to· the one who seems to have contributed as much to the success of the trip as you did[1]
                    Ever aff'ly your's   Cleveland H. Dodge

    Please don't take the trouble of replying to this sign of my irrepressible enthusiasm

ALS (WP, DLC).
    [1] That is, Mrs. Wilson.

From Robert Lansing, with Enclosure

PERSONAL AND CONFIDENTIAL:

My dear Mr. President: Washington February 5, 1916.

I send you copy of a telegram from Sir Edward Grey to Sir Cecil, which he handed to Mr. Phillips this morning. It deals, as you will see, with our suggestion as to a *modus* in regard to submarine warfare.   Faithfully yours,   Robert Lansing.

TLS (WP, DLC).

ENCLOSURE

Handed Mr Phillips by British Amb.
2/5/16 RL

Telegram from Sir E Grey 3. Feb. 1916

I think Secretary of State ought to realize the point of view from which question is naturally regarded here.

Germany having sunk the "Frye" and Dutch ship "Maria" with food for civilian population of Great Britain cynically declared submarine warfare on British and neutral merchant vessels in zone in alleged retaliation for Great Britain's interference with food supply of Germany.

For a year British merchant vessels and in some cases neutral vessels even when bound from one neutral port to another neutral port have been sunk by German submarines without regard for safety of passengers or crew.

United States Government have taken up the case of passengers and have after months of controversy obtained it is understood promise not to sink passenger vessel without warning. It is not clear whether this gives complete protection to British passengers or applies to the so-called war zone but it gives no protection to cargo boats.

United States Government now propose to deprive merchant vessels of defensive armament which was recognized as fair against armed cruisers (? and) is still more necessary when used for defence not only of vessel but of lives of crew against submarine attack.

It appears that the United States Government contemplate altering their regulations as to defensive armament even before an undertaking is obtained from Germany to provide for the safety of crew or any definition of what safety means.

In short after a year of submarine warfare British and allied merchant vessels will be deprived of previously recognised chance of defense and nothing will have been obtained except uncertain and partial mitigation of attacks in the case of passenger vessels only. Net result will be that new development of warfare to suit submarines and ensure their effectiveness will have been recognized to suit Germany. Previously recognised means of defense for merchant vessels will have been taken away to great disadvantage of Great Britain and allies. Any development of old principles of interfering with enemy commerce to suit modern conditions will have been refused Great Britain and allies.

We shall have been deprived of or restricted in the exercise of old rights to enable new German methods to be effective.

Reference to the "Baralong" case[1] is not relevant as no attack was then made on submarine by a merchant vessel but only by an armed cruiser.

I should like Secretary of State to realize that this is how proposed alteration of regulations will appear to us and sense of grievance which we shall feel.

If however you think it inopportune to make this communication while the "Appam" case[2] is occupying attention of State Department you can defer it for a little.

TC telegram (WP, DLC).

[1] About this incident see RL to WW, Aug. 30, 1915, n. 1, printed as an Enclosure with WW to EBG, Aug. 30, 1915 (third letter of that date), Vol. 34.

[2] The British steamship, *Appam*, arrived off Newport News, Va., under German command on February 1. The German prize officer and crew sought to keep the ship in an American port indefinitely and asked the United States to intern the British sailors who had resisted the ship's capture. Bernstorff claimed that the Prussian-American Treaty of 1785, revised in 1799, bound the United States to accede to these requests. The British government, however, appealed to The Hague Convention of 1907, one provision of which stipulated that in such cases the ship should be returned to its owners and the crew freed. While discussions about these rival appeals to international law proceeded, the British owners filed a libel against the ship in the United States district court and thereby tied the ship's fate to judicial settlement under American municipal law. The case dragged on until March 1917, when the Supreme Court of the United States affirmed the decree of the district court awarding *Appam* to her British owners. See *FR-WWS 1916*, pp. 722-45.

From James Hay

Washington, D. C.

My dear Mr. President: February 5th, 1916.

I feel that you would like to know the situation in Congress with regard to Army plans. As I told you in my last interview[1] the Committee is ready and willing to report a bill providing in substance for the increase in the Regular Army which you have recommended.

The Continental Army plan does not meet with the approval of the Committee, and the Committee cannot, in my opinion, be brought to support that plan. But in the place of it, the Committee believes that the organized militia can be federalized and developed in such a way as to supply more men than the most sanguine supporters of the Continental Army can hope for.

You have asked me how this can be done, and since talking with you I have given the subject very careful thought and study, and have come to the conclusion that Congress has the power to prescribe age limits for service and other conditions of the enlistment contract, both as to length of service with the colors and in a reserve, which Congress has the power to create.

Congress also has the power to prescribe the qualifications of officers, those qualifications for appointment to be established by an examination approved by the Secretary of War. It has the power to provide for the total strength and the proportional strength of the organized militia; the power to prescribe who shall constitute the exempt classes to the exclusion of the exercise of state power on the same subject; the power to prescribe uniform organization, armament and di[s]cipline upon such terms as to supersede all conflicting state legislation on the same subject; the power to authorize the President when war is imminent, or, upon a declaration of war, to draft the organized militia immediately into the service of the United States.

The Committee is in favor of having all of these powers exercised by Congress, and it believes that when this is done, together with the compensation which will be proposed, the country will within the next three years have a citizen soldiery of not less than four hundred thousand men and probably five hundred thousand.   Sincerely and cordially yours,   James Hay

TLS (WP, DLC).
    1 Hay had last met with Wilson on this subject on January 11.

Brand Whitlock to Robert Lansing

Brussels via The Hague Dated February 5, 1916.

506. I am deeply sensible of the extraordinary honor the President proposes to me and grateful for this distinguished mark of his consideration but despite a natural ambition I am loath to accept the post in question because of a conviction that my exceedingly narrow personal income would be wholly insufficient to the social demands of a peculiarly susceptible and exacting court and further because of a feeling that my mission here is

unfinished and a fear that the relief work in Belgium would be seriously compromised, if not destroyed, by my departure and that we should thereby lose all the prestige we have gained.

The President knows, I am sure, without protestation on my part, that I am entirely devoted to him and to his administration and that I should be proud to serve our country in any capacity he might designate but the first of the reasons hereinbefore set forth seems to me an insuperable obstacle in the present instance. As to the second point I am writing full details to Colonel House in the conviction that my views will meet with the President's approval. I feel most strongly that some one else possessing the qualifications that I lack should be considered for the post.

Whitlock.

T telegram (SDR, RG 59, 123 W59/48, DNA).

From Alfred Thomas Rogers[1]

Dear Mr. President   Madison, Wisconsin Feby 6, 1916.

The appointment of Mr. Brandeis to the Supreme Bench was a very brave thing to do. It was splendid, and will win the confidence of many millions of people in this country.

We know Brandeis in Wisconsin and therefore are better able to appreciate him.

Success to you always   Alfred T. Rogers

ALS (WP, DLC).
[1] Senator Robert M. La Follette's law partner.

To William Kent

My dear Mr. Kent: The White House February 7, 1916

It has happened, singularly enough, that in the rush that preceded my recent departure from Washington your letter of January twenty-second[1] recommending Mr. Brandeis for appointment to the Supreme Court did not come into my hands. I can now only thank you for it and rejoice that my judgment corresponded with yours in this important matter.

Cordially and sincerely yours,   Woodrow Wilson

TLS (W. Kent Papers, CtY).
[1] *Sic* in the Swem notebook; Wilson probably dictated "twenty-seventh," and Swem misheard him.

To John Sharp Williams

My dear Senator: [The White House] February 7, 1916

Thank you sincerely for yours of January twenty-seventh which I have not earlier had an opportunity to answer. Your reply to your correspondent, Mr. Borcherdt, is most interesting. You interpret my misunderstood utterance just exactly as I should have wished it interpreted, and it is mighty good to have a friend who will do this service for me.

Cordially and faithfully yours,   Woodrow Wilson

TLS (Letterpress Books, WP, DLC).

To Samuel Gompers

My dear Mr. Gompers: The White House February 7, 1916

I realize the great importance of the matter you call to my attention in your letter of January twenty-eighth and thank you very warmly for the letter. I had not heard of the movement to get Secretary Wilson to allow his name to be used as a candidate for the United States Senate in Pennsylvania and my judgment corresponds with your own in the matter so far as I have had time to think about it. I shall, of course, talk it over with the Secretary and see what his own feeling in the matter is. I take it that he feels as we do.

In haste

Cordially and sincerely yours,   Woodrow Wilson

TLS (S. Gompers Corr., AFL-CIO-Ar).

To Robert Latham Owen

My dear Senator: [The White House] February 7, 1916

Your letter of January twenty-ninth from New York City about the nomination of Mr. Brandeis pleased me very deeply and I thank you for it very warmly indeed. I believe the nomination was the wisest that could possibly have been made, and I feel that few things have arisen more important to the country or to the party than the matter of his confirmation.

With warm regard,

Cordially and sincerely yours,   Woodrow Wilson

TLS (Letterpress Books, WP, DLC).

To Richard Olney

My dear Mr. Olney: The White House February 7, 1916

I warmly appreciate your very gracious letter of February fourth. The Western trip was indeed a most interesting and inspiring experience, much fuller of electrical thrills than I had expected.

You are very thoughtful of my pleasure in sending me a copy of "Fruitlands." I shall look forward with the greatest pleasure to reading it.

I hope that everything goes well with you, and I want you to know how cordially and sincerely I value your friendship.

Most sincerely yours,   Woodrow Wilson

TLS (R. Olney Papers, DLC).

To Cleveland Hoadley Dodge

My dear Cleve: The White House February 7, 1916

My love in response to your delightful letter of congratulations on the trip.   Faithfully yours,   Woodrow Wilson

TLS (WC, NjP).

From Edward Mandell House

[Paris, Feb. 7, 1916]

In conference with the French Minister of Foreign Affairs[1] and Cambon to-day I have had a complete and satisfactory understanding.[2] I dare not cable substance further than to say that it was the most important conference I have had in Europe and that it was along the line of my conversation with Lloyd G[eorge]. before leaving London, but much more gratifying. They agreed to help in lessening [minimizing] our shipping troubles. Unless there is a change of government here and in England, the situation is now largely in your hands, provided you do not break with Germany. I strongly advise no positive action upon any of the pending questions between our government and that of the belligerants until I confer with you and the Secretary of State. I leave for England to-morrow, reaching London Wednesday night.

WWT decode of T telegram (WP, DLC).
[1] Aristide Briand.
[2] See EMH to WW, Feb. 9, 1916 (first letter of that date).

From Henry Skillman Breckinridge

Dear Mr. President: Washington. February 7, 1916.

The Secretary of War will return to Washington tonight. I hope that he may see you before any decision is made with reference to what the administration will try to do with reference to the pending Philippine bill.

The bill, as it passed the Senate, directed action contrary to the action advocated by the Secretary of War in his testimony before the Senate Committee and in statements announcing the policy of this administration made heretofore.[1] In other words, it directly reverses the policy which the Secretary of War has heretofore made public as the policy being pursued by this administration. I think therefore, that the importance of seeing the Secretary of War before determining action is a sufficient justification for my molesting you now.

Faithfully yours,   Henry Breckinridge

TLS (WP, DLC).
[1] The Senate had adopted the Clarke amendment to the Jones bill on February 2 by a vote of forty-one to forty-one, with Vice-President Marshall breaking the tie. The Senate approved the amended Jones bill on February 4 by a vote of fifty-two to twenty-four.

From Joel Byron Slocum and Charles Matthias Reed

New London, Conn., Feb. 7-8, 1916.

At the monthly meeting of the Baptist Ministers' Conference of New London and vicinity, representing the pastors of 43 churches, and a membership of 6,600, the following resolution was passed:

While we deplore the necessity which calls for the expenditure of the nation's resources for the purpose of armament, we wish to convey to you our recognition of the principle of police protection, for nation, as well as for city and state, and to further recognize the fact that [as] the chief executive of the nation, you can best know the sufficiency of the national police force, and in further recognition of the fact that while proving yourself a peace loving President, you have, at the same time, deemed the peace of [and] the honor of the country in so great peril from unpreparedness in this time of world wide war, as to leave your official residence at a critical time, and travel many thousand miles to appeal to your countrymen for support of a larger national force for the protection of our country, therefore;

Be it resolved—that it is our belief that your appeal should be heeded by our national legislators, and with this assurance telegraphed you, we also [send] copy of this resolution to the Senators of this state, and to the Congressmen of this district.

Rev. Joel B. Slocum, D.D.;

President; Rev. Chas. M. Reed, Secy

East Lyme Conn.[1]

T telegram (WP, DLC).
[1] Slocum was probably retired; Reed was minister of the Niantic Baptist Church of East Lyme, Conn.

To Joel Byron Slocum

My dear Dr. Slocum: [The White House] February 8, 1916

May I not thank you and Dr. Reed and all for whom you spoke, for the generous assurances of your telegram of February 7th, embodying a resolution passed by the Baptist Ministers' Conference of New London and vicinity? I am indebted to you and your fellow clergymen for your sympathetic interest and support.

Cordially and sincerely yours,   Woodrow Wilson

TLS (Letterpress Books, WP, DLC).

To Arthur Capper

[The White House]

My dear Governor Capper: February 8, 1916

I want to give myself the pleasure of saying to Mrs. Capper[1] and you how thoroughly and entirely Mrs. Wilson and I enjoyed our visit to Topeka and your own gracious and thoughtful hospitality.[2] It will always be a very delightful recollection to us, and Mrs. Wilson wishes to join me in the most cordial good wishes.   Sincerely yours,   Woodrow Wilson

TLS (A. Capper Coll., KHi).
[1] Florence Crawford Capper.
[2] Governor and Mrs. Capper had given a luncheon in honor of the Wilsons at their home on February 2.

To Alfred Thomas Rogers

My dear Mr. Rogers: [The White House] February 8, 1916

May I not thank you warmly for your letter of February 6th? It is, indeed, very gratifying to know that you approve of the selection of Mr. Brandeis.

Cordially and sincerely yours,   Woodrow Wilson

TLS (Letterpress Books, WP, DLC).

From Robert Lansing

LUSITANIA

PERSONAL AND CONFIDENTIAL:

My dear Mr. President: Washington February 8, 1916.

The German Ambassador called upon me at half-past four this afternoon and I talked with him about the suggested changes in his memorandum. He said he would like very much to make the changes himself without consulting his Government, but that he had been so attacked by his enemies at home that he did not dare to do so. He agreed to at once advise Berlin of the changes sought and was satisfied that they would accede to them. He seemed to think there was no doubt about it. I am not at all sure that I share his optimism as I fear they may seek to modify their statements in some way.

It will, therefore, be a few days before anything further can be done, as I assume the Ambassador will not be able to send a telegram until tomorrow morning.

Faithfully yours,   Robert Lansing.

TLS (WP, DLC).

From James Hay

Confidential

Washington, D. C.
My dear Mr. President: February 8th, 1916.

My excuse for writing to you again with regard to Army legislation is that I am profoundly impressed with the imperative necessity of some plan being agreed upon which will be acceptable to you, to Congress and to the country.

Since writing to you on Saturday last I have again canvassed the Committee and find that it will be impossible to obtain a favorable report for the continental army plan. I have also taken great pains to find out the attitude of the House membership, and am forced to the conclusion that the continental army plan will be defeated overwhelmingly in that body.

The plan for the proper organization, disciplining, equipment and development of the militia will receive the support of every man on the Committee, and that of nine thenths [tenths] of the members of the House. Moreover and far more important is the fact that this plan is very popular in the country, while the continental army plan is not.

The continental army plan is considered by all to whom I have talked to be impracticable, and it is firmly believed that the men, for whom it undertakes to provide, cannot be enlisted. This is the opinion not only of members of Congress and other civilians, but is the belief of a large number of Army officers whose private views I have been able to obtain.

The presentation of this plan to the Committee by its advocates has been most unfortunate. The Secretary of War, the Assistant Secretary of War, the Chief of Staff and others connected with the War Department have declared to the Committee that they were in favor of compulsory military service; following these declarations came the resolution of the National Security League declaring in favor of the continental army plan as the first step towards securing compulsory military service. Many southern members fear it because they believe it will be the means of enlisting large numbers of negroes.

The plan for federalizing and developing the militia is feasible. It can be done effectively. It was intended by the framers of the constitution that the militia should be a national force. It was then thought that it was capable of meeting every military exigency of the United States. Washington said in 1795 in a message to Congress on the subject: "In my opinion Congress has the power, by proper organization, disciplining, equipment, and development of the militia to make it a national force, capable of meeting every military exigency of the United States." The Constitution gives full power to Congress to accomplish this: The power is defined in Article 1, section 8, clause 16, of the Constitution, as including the power—

"To provide for organizing, arming, and disciplining the militia and for governing such part of them as may be employed in the service of the United States, reserving to the States respectively the appointment of the officers and the authority of training the militia according to the discipline prescribed by Congress."

It will be observed that Congress has the power to govern such part of the militia as may be employed in the service of the United States and when the United States pays the militia it is certainly employed in their service thus obviating the objection that Congress cannot govern the training of the militia.

As I pointed out to you on Saturday there are powers which Congress has never exercised but which if exercised will accomplish the desired result. It is true that it is contended by some that when Congress exercises these powers the General Government has not the constitutional authority over the states to enforce what it has prescribed. But the mere statement of this argument refutes it. Surely if Congress has the power under the Constitution to prescribe certain things it must have the power to enforce what it prescribes. If it has such powers it also possesses the power to prevent the defeat of its laws enacted in pursuance of those powers.

Under the power to organize, Congress has the unquestioned right to provide for compulsory military training in the militia, according to a system prescribed by Congress; it therefore can enact laws punishing those who fail to comply with the requirements to make effective such training. Having such power Congress can provide that organizations shall not be disbanded, nor the services of officers or men terminated without its consent.

In view of my letter to you on Saturday I will not continue to cite what Congress can do to make the militia effective.

There are some political considerations to which I should call your attention. The people, in such a democracy as ours must be consulted, and I am within the bounds or [of] reason, when I say that the national guard plan is favored by a very large majority of people. Then too, how important it is that we should have a plan which will not only unite our own Party, but which will bring the opposition to the support of your policies, and thus avoid an issue which will inevitably arise if we attempt to force through a plan which will inevitably divide ourselves, and solidify the opposition against us.

It will, if you will permit me to say so, be a very great triumph for you, if the entire Congress shall adopt what you propose.

Mr. Kitchin informed me on Saturday last that he would not oppose the national guard plan and while he might vote against the increase in the Regular Army he would not speak against it.

I hope my dear Mr. President that I have not wearied you by sending you this long letter. My intense interest in the success of your administration, as well as the responsibility which is imposed upon me will I trust excuse me.

Very cordially and sincerely yours,   James Hay

TLS (WP, DLC).

From Lindley Miller Garrison

My dear Mr. President: Washington. February 9, 1916.

Two matters within the jurisdiction of this Department are now of immediate and pressing importance, and I am constrained to declare my position definitely and unmistakably thereon. I refer, of course, to the Philippine question and the matter of national defense.

You know my convictions with respect to each of them.

I consider the principle embodied in the Clark amendment an abandonment of the duty of this nation and a breach of trust toward the Filipinos; so believing, I cannot accept it or acquiesce in its acceptance.

I consider the reliance upon the Militia for national defense an unjustifiable imperiling of the nation's safety. It would not only be a sham in itself, but its enactment into law would prevent if not destroy the opportunity to procure measures of real, genuine national defense. I could not accept it or acquiesce in its acceptance.

I am obliged to make my position known immediately upon each of these questions, in a speech on Thursday afternoon upon the national defense question and in a communication to the House Committee having charge of the Philippine question.

If, with respect to either matter, we are not in agreement upon these fundamental principles, then I could not, with propriety, remain your seeming representative in respect thereto. Our convictions would be manifestly not only divergent but utterly irreconcilable.

You will appreciate the necessity of timely knowledge upon my part of the determination reached by you with respect to each of these matters, so that I may act advisedly in the premises.

Sincerely yours,   Lindley M. Garrison

TLS (WP, DLC).

To Joseph Patrick Tumulty, with Enclosure

Dear T.   [The White House, Feb. 9, 1916]

When you have looked this over will you not have Swem copy it and make a carbon copy? I have only a short-hand copy.[1]

Faithfully,   W.W.

WWTLI (WP, DLC).
[1] It is in WP, DLC.

E N C L O S U R E

To Lindley Miller Garrison

My dear Mr. Secretary,   The White House. 9 February, 1916.

In reply to your letter of to-day let me say,

First, that it is my own judgment that the action embodied in the Clarke amendment to the bill extending further self-government to the Philippines is unwise at this time; but that, in view of the clear pledges of our party in the matter of the independence of the Islands, I should not feel justified in dissenting should both Houses of the Congress adopt that action. I am now, of course, engaged in conference with Mr. Jones and others with regard to the probable action of the House of Representatives, and do not yet know what that action is likely to be.

Second, as I have had occasion to say to you, I am not yet convinced that the measure of preparation for national defense which we deem necessary can be obtained through the instrumentality of the national guard brought under federal control and training, but I feel in duty bound to keep my mind open to conviction on that side and think that it would be most unwise and most unfair to the Committee of Congress, which has such a plan in mind, to say that it cannot be done. We ought to wait and see the details of the plan to be proposed. The bill in which it will be embodied has not yet been drawn, as I learned to-day from Mr. Hay. I should deem it a very serious mistake to shut the door against it.

As you know, I do not at all agree with you in favouring compulsory enlistment for training, and I fear the advocacy of compulsion before the Committee of the House on the part of representatives of the Department of War has greatly prejudiced the House against the proposal for a continental army, little necessary connection as there is between the plan and the opinion of the Chief of Staff in favour of compulsory enlistment.

I owe you this frank repetition of my views and policy in this matter, and am very much obliged to you for your own frank avowal of your convictions with regard to the matter. I think it very important that the distinction should be very carefully drawn in all controverted points between our individual views and the views of the Administration.

Cordially and Sincerely Yours,   Woodrow Wilson[1]

WWTLS (WP, DLC).
[1] For the letter that was sent, see WW to LMG, Feb. 10, 1916 (first letter of that date).

From Joseph Patrick Tumulty

Dear Governor: The White House February 9, 1916.

I have looked over your reply to Garrison and have prepared what I think amply covers the situation. The reply, as corrected, is as follows:

9 February, 1916.

My dear Mr. Secretary:

In reply to your letter of today let me say,

First, that it is my own judgment that the action embodied in the Clarke amendment to the bill extending further self-government to the Philippines is unwise at this time, but that I should dissent from the action of both Houses of the Congress when a bill is presented to me embodying this amendment is a matter that I must consider and withhold judgment upon until the joint action of both Houses reaches me in definite form. What the final action of both Houses will ultimately be no one can at this time determine. I am now, of course, engaged in conference with Mr. Jones and others with regard to the probable action of the House of Representatives in this matter, and do not yet know what that action is likely to be.

(Might you not add this sentence: "The necessity for calm and deliberate action on our part at this time is certainly obvious.")

Second, as I have had occasion to say to you, I am not yet convinced that the measure of preparation for national defense which we deem necessary can be obtained through the instrumentality of the National Guard under federal control and training, but I feel in duty bound to keep my mind open to conviction on that side and think that it would be most unwise and most unfair to the Committee of Congress, which has such a plan in mind, to say that it cannot be done. We ought to wait and see the details of the plan to be proposed before passing final judgment. The bill in which it will be embodied has not yet been drawn, as I learned today from Mr. Hay. I should deem it a very serious mistake to shut the door against it. (Might you not say: "I should deem it a very serious mistake to shut the door against any attempt on the part of the Committee in good faith to meet the terms of the program set forth in my message.")

As you know, I do not at all agree with you in favouring compulsory enlistment for training, and I fear the advocacy of compulsion before the Committee of the House on the part of representatives of the Department of War has greatly prejudiced the House against the proposal for a continental army, little necessary connection as there is between the plan and the opinion of the Chief of Staff in favour of compulsory enlistment.

I owe you this frank repetition of my views and policy in this matter, as we have discussed them on previous occasions in letters that have passed between us. I am very much obliged to you for your frank avowal of your convictions with regard to this matter. I trust that you will feel no hesitancy in expressing your views on both these matters on the two occasions to which you refer, taking care, however, to draw the distinction between your own individual views and the views of the Administration.

Cordially and sincerely yours,

(Might it not be well before concluding the letter to say something like this:

"I am spending every ounce of my energy and every moment of my time with members of the various committees in trying to procure an agreement upon a workable and practicable program. This is a time when a little patience on the part of all of us may help in the consummation of the purpose we all desire, namely, the adequate defense of the Nation. I trust that the friends of the Administration, both in the Cabinet and on the Hill, will never lose sight of this great object, and that they will, therefore, always act accordingly.")

TL (WP, DLC).

Two Letters from Edward Mandell House

Dear Governor: No. 12. Boulogne, France. February 9, 1916.

I shall not go into much detail in regard to my conversation with the French Prime Minister and Cambon, but will give you a drief [brief] outline.

Im [In] the first interview I tried to create a good atmosphere and I was undetermined whether to leave it at that or go further. Up to the present I have been confidential with the British Government alone, and have left to them the bringing into line their Allies.

However, I was never more impressed by their slowness and lack of initiative as upon this trip, and I concluded that we had best take the risk and talk plainly to the French. The result was surprisingly satisfactory.

I outlined the situation to them as I see it, bringing in all the doubtful elements which might throw the balance against them. Their lack of victories, their mistakes, the efficient German organization under an autocracy as against an inefficient organization under democracies, and the danger of separate peace with Russia and Italy. All this I outlined with care. I pictured what was at stake not only for them, but for the world, and while declaring that we felt able to look out for our own interests in our own way, yet I let them see how deeply concerned we were for the future of democratic government.

It was finally understood that in the event the Allies had some notable victories during the spring and summer, you would intervene, and in the event that the tide of war went against them, or remained stationary you would intervene. This conversation is to go no further than between Briand, Cambon and myself and I promised that no one should know of it in America excepting yourself and Lansing.

I told them I had had a similar conversation in England, and that there it would go no further than a group composed of the Prime Minister, Sir Edward Grey, Balfour and Lloyd George. This seemed agreeable to them.

They are to keep in touch with me by letter and messages, and I, in turn, am to do likewise. This was done to give more freedom because of its unofficial character.

Briand and Cambon know and seemed to agree to the advice I gave you concerning the settlement of the Lusitania matter. It is impossible for any unprejudiced person to believe that it would be wise for America to take part in this war unless it comes about by intervention based upon the highest human motives. We are the only nation left on earth with sufficient power to lead them out, and with us once in, the war would have to go on to a finish with all its appalling consequences. It is better for the Central Powers and it is better for the Allies, as indeed, it is better for us to act in this way, and I have not hesitated to say this to the British and French Governments and have intimated it to Germany.[1]

A great opportunity is yours, my friend, the greatest perhaps that has ever come to any man. The way out seems clear to me and when I can lay the facts before you, I believe it will be clear to you also.

In each government I have visited I have found stubbornness, determination, selfishness and cant. One continually hears self-glorification and the highest motives attributed to themselves because of their part in the war. But I may tell you that my observation is that incompetent statesmanship and selfishness is at the bottom of it all. It is not so much a breaking down of civilization as a lack of wisdom in those that govern, and history, I believe, will bring an awful indictment against those who were short-sighted and selfish enough to let such a tragedy happen.   Affectionately yours,   E. M. House

[1] [J. Cambon], "Deuxième Entrevue du Colonel House," Feb. 7, 1916, T MS (Guerre 1914-1918, États-Unis, Vol. 498, pp. 206-208, FFM-Ar), reports the most important parts of their conversation as follows (our translation):
"He [House] assured us anew of the profound sympathies of the United States for the Allies. The intention of the American government is to intervene, either peaceably, or even, according to the circumstances, militarily, in order to procure for the world a peace favorable to the Allied cause. It is especially

France and the energy of which she has given proof which has aroused in American opinion the movement of sympathy which has developed so powerfully for some months, and, Colonel House said, literally, the more the French situation becomes compromised, the stronger will be the friendship of the United States be manifested. (The lower will be the situation of France, the stronger will be the friendship of America.) [English text in the document.]

"Also, you can be assured, Colonel House added, that, if the Allies should have a little success, this spring or summer, the United States will intervene in favor of peace, but if they have a setback, the United States will intervene militarily and take part in the war against Germany.

"In order to facilitate President Wilson's role, it would be very important for the Allies to take care to avoid all little difficulties in matters of shipping. It would be very helpful if we would intervene in this sense with the London cabinet: these difficulties are, by their very nature, bound to dampen spirits in America. It would be supremely important, in Colonel House's view, that President Wilson's intervention in the great conflict which divides Europe not be hindered or prevented by secondary difficulties which our enemies could use in their fight against him in the public arena.

"On his return to America, which will come very soon, Colonel House will urge President Wilson to proceed as quickly as possible to increase the naval and military forces of the United States. In the meantime, he believes that it is preferable that the *Lusitania* affair be settled by agreement between Germany and the United States. According to him, this would cause only a delay in American intervention. But when the occasion for entering the conflict presented itself, America would be better prepared to intervene and decisively determine the outcome of the war.

"Because the Colonel acknowledged in that way the desire of America to be the arbiter of the conflict, we asked him what he thought of Alsace-Lorraine, by pointing out to him the importance of the restitution to France of these two lost provinces. . . .

"I believe, Mr. House replied, that Germany could be led to envisage the restitution of Alsace-Lorraine to France, but in return it would be necessary for her to get compensation, in Asia Minor, for example, where one could award her Anatolia.

"Thus, the Colonel added, Russia, which would take Armenia, would become Germany's neighbor.

"We asked Mr. House what, in his conception, he would do with Turkey. He replied to us that she must disappear.

"Moreover, in the eyes of the Colonel, England and France should act in concert, in a broad and liberal spirit, concerning the conditions of peace that they think possible when the right occasion comes. The United States would support them in their proposals and would enter the conflict if Germany did not accept their terms.

"I pointed out to the Colonel—with the assent of the President of the Council—that the moment for such propositions had not arrived. The situation would not allow an initiative of this sort—neither from the military point of view nor from the point of view of public opinion. I added that England and France were not alone in the cause; they had allies, and they could bring up the question of peace only in agreement with them.

"That is possible, Mr. House replied, but the Government of the United States cannot, in fact, enter into conversation with all of the Allies: it is England and France's business to agree between themselves when it will be wise to them, and at the moment that they judge opportune with their allies, Russia and Italy, and then to approach the American government.

". . . In truth, he considers that only Germany, Russia, and Japan are dangerous to the United States. These three monarchies are, according to him, equally eager for domination and conquest. Concluding, then, as he had in his earlier conversation, he added that the liberal and democratic nations—France, England, and the United States—should be closely united and allied after the war in the interest of the peace of the world.

"Colonel House stressed again Mr. Wilson's determination to act on the side of the Allies, peacefully if possible, and militarily if that should become necessary, stressing also the secrecy which he wanted to surround his statements.

"In closing, he said to the President of the Council that, if we had any communication to address to President Wilson on the subject of all these questions, we would do well to write directly to himself, Colonel House, and to entrust

Mr. Jusserand to send our letters to the White House. He would communicate what we had said to him to President Wilson who, if it was necessary, would bring Mr. Lansing of the State Department into the discussion.

"He would reply to us by the same means."

The importance that Briand and Cambon attached to House's declarations is evident in the telegrams that they sent to their embassies in the following weeks: Foreign Ministry to J. J. Jusserand, Feb. 9, 1916, T telegram (Guerre 1914-1918, États-Unis, Vol. 498, pp. 224-25, FFM-Ar); J. Cambon, "Pour Faire Suite aux Notes sur les Conversations du Colonel House," Feb. 12, 1916, T MS (ibid., p. 252); J. J. Jusserand to the Foreign Ministry, received Feb. 16, 1916, T telegram (ibid., Vol. 499, pp. 2-3); A. Briand to J. J. Jusserand, Feb. 21, 1916, T telegram (ibid., p. 65); A. Briand to P. Cambon, Feb. 21, 1916, T telegram (ibid., p. 64).

Dear Governor: No 13. Boulogne, France. February 9, 1916.

When I reached the station in Paris yesterday I found a beautiful private car had been placed at my disposal by the French Government and in waiting to facilitate our departure the Prefect of Police, the highest railroad officials, etc. etc. I mention this merely as an indication that my conferences with the Government were highly successful. It is these side-lights that sometimes tell the story better than words.

When I reached Boulogne, I found King Albert's Aide waiting to carry me to the front to meet the King. My conversation with him lasted an hour and a half and in a way justified the trip, not so much because of any power that is in his hands to do or not to do, but as an evidence of his state of mind in regard to the war and a possible peace. He was extremely cautious in what he said, but when I left I had the distinct impression that he was anxious for the war to end, and that as far as he was concerned, there would be no obstacles placed in the way by demands that were unreasonable or impossible.

What I wanted to find was whether Belgium would be willing to let Germany purchase the Belgian Congo. This is rather a vital point and has much bearing upon the situation. While he insisted that he could not ask his people to approve such a program, yet again I gathered the impression that it might be done over his head.

He has no illusions in regard to a decisive victory, and I am sure there is no one of the belligerents that would welcome your intervention more sincerely than he.

It may interest you to know that my observation is that the royal houses of Europe, both among the belligerents and neutrals, have a strong pro-German tendancy. This is not altogether brought about by intermarriage, but is largely the sympathy that royalty has for autocracy.

We passed many compliments, I giving messages from you and he sending others in return.

We are crossing the Channel today and I will write again from London.   Affectionately yours,   E. M. House

TLS (WP, DLC).

From Alexander White Gregg[1]

Dear Mr. President: Palestine, Texas, Feby. 9, 1916.

Since the holidays I have been detained at home with my wife[2] who has been and still is, too ill for me to leave her. I don't know when I can get to Washington, but hope to get there in time to support your prepar[e]dness programme, which I will do with great pleasure.   Very truly yours,   A. W. Gregg

TLS (WP, DLC).
[1] Democratic congressman from Texas.
[2] Mary Brooks Gregg.

From Jessie Woodrow Wilson Sayre

Dearest Father,   Williamstown Massachusetts Feb. 9. 1916

We have never gotten over our disappointment at having to leave before you and dear Edith came home again. We saw so *little* of you on this trip that it can hardly be called an entirely satisfactory one, though it was lovely, indeed, to see all the rest of the dear ones; and your presence and love were evident in so many ways that we could not think of you as entirely absent.

When I go down to Philadelphia next month[1] I shall be sorry not to be going further so that I can see you all again. I tried to lure Cousin Helen up here for a week so that I could *hear* of you all in detail, at least, but in vain. She cannot come, and we must be cheerful about it. I shall hope that some excuse can be found to bring you to Philadelphia, so that I can see you there and introduce your new grandchild to you! That would be a happiness, indeed! I long so to see you and hear your dear, dear, voice again, and to have your blessing on our newest happiness.

All goes well with us up here. The Boy is flourishing and gaining in sweetness and strength, and I am delightfully well. Frank is busy as can be, and working very hard, and, therefore, most happy.

We were overjoyed to read of the splendid reception given you on your tour. How I wish I could have been in some of those crowds and heard and seen it all! But I am proud just reading about them!

Give our love to Edith, to all the family and to your sweet self,
Adoringly, your daughter   Jessie.

ALS (WC, NjP).
1 For the delivery of her second child.

An Address to the Chamber of Commerce
of the United States[1]

[Feb. 10, 1916]

Mr. President, ladies and gentlemen: I have been profoundly disturbed by what I have just heard. I am talked to all day long, and this indefinite multiplication and extension of talk is nothing less than appalling. To realize that I cannot only be talked to in my office but from every portion of the continent shows me to what extreme dangers the Chief Executive is exposed.[2] Indeed, I have been talked to so much today, upon many topics of interest and importance, that I find that it is a little difficult to turn the tables and talk myself. Because the field of your activities is so extensive, the number of things that you are legitimately interested in is so great, that it would be a task that no man might undertake—to speak to you about the general duties of the Chamber of Commerce of the United States.

I have recently had occasion to speak to the country upon a topic which is of immediate and pressing importance—the subject of adequate preparation for national defense. But I am not going to speak to you upon that subject tonight, because my thoughts go back of the exigencies of the present moment. And I must say that I think with a great deal of gratification of the preparation we did make for war before we knew that the war was coming—that preparation which we made to be of service to the world in keeping alive some little part of the flame of peace, and of making it possible for the United States to put her thought, her energies and her resources at the disposal of a world swept and

1 At the concluding banquet of the fourth annual convention of the Chamber of Commerce of the United States at the New Willard Hotel in Washington. Among the eight hundred guests were John Henry Fahey, president of the Chamber of Commerce, who introduced Wilson, and several cabinet members and their wives.

2 The American Telephone and Telegraph Company had placed receivers at each plate in order to demonstrate the operation of its new long-distance telephone system. Telephone company officials talked with Governors Hiram Warren Johnson at Sacramento, California, and John Henry Morehead at Lincoln, Nebraska. Wilson, the *New York Times*, February 11, 1916, reported, "applauded that part of the demonstration which recorded the sound of the Pacific Ocean waves beating against the Cliff House near San Francisco."

disturbed by conflict. Because, as I look back, ladies and gentle-men, upon the last three years, I can see how we were guided, I hope, by something superior to our own wisdom in putting at the disposal of the business of the United States the instru-mentalities by which it could make conquest of its opportunities. When you reflect what might have happened if our banking sys-tem had, at the outset of this war, been the clumsy and antiquated thing that it was many years ago, you will realize that, not only might we not have escaped disaster, but that disaster might have been so prolonged that it would have been impossible for the United States to occupy the position she now occupies.

The reason for our neutrality is that it is imperatively neces-sary that the balance should be kept even and some judgments should be kept disengaged and some energies kept alive along the ordinary occupations of industry and of mutual helpfulness, while all the world is torn and distracted by war. It is a cruel thing to have it supposed, as it is in so many quarters, that we have kept out of this war simply because we wanted to keep out of trouble and simply because we wanted to profit by the trouble of others. And yet misunderstandings, for the time being, are not to be reckoned as against the consciousness that we must our-selves have, that we have pursued the right and only serviceable course. I am not afraid, for one, of the slow verdict of history with regard to the neutrality of the United States, and I believe that we are justified in exercising every degree of patience in making it clear what our position is and how sincerely we are determined not to allow this quarrel to become part of ours.

I have only this to say, though, ladies and gentlemen: We hold this trouble at arm's length and keep, or attempt to keep, our own judgments cool, but the rest of the world is hot, and it may be that any time, without our cooperation and without our ability to stop it, then the flame may extend to us. And, therefore, I am glad that the United States has been put in a position to mobilize its financial resources and to get into the position which it must at last get into, whether it wants to or not.

It is amazing to me—it has been amazing ever since I was a thoughtful man—that the businessmen of America have con-cerned themselves so little with the commerce of the world, as distinguished from the commerce of America. They have been doubting and timid; they have not known what they should have known about the opportunities of foreign commerce. And they have been slow to avail themselves of those opportunities when they were known. And now, in the strange turn of events we are called upon to exercise, I believe, in the decades immediately ahead of us, the chief part in those very functions which we have hitherto been avoiding and appearing to fear, America is going to be thrust out into the economic leadership of the world. And it is a matter of congratulation that we have gained the instrumentalities which are necessary for the exercise of this great part. Not only have we the Federal Reserve Banking System, which all objected to who did not understand it, and some feared because they did understand it, but we have other instrumentalities which have been put at the disposal of the businessmen of the country.

I don't think that I need tell you gentlemen that already, although it is of so recent creation, the Federal Trade Commission has begun to be a most interesting and useful intermediary among the business undertakings of the country, in order that they may see how the business of this country can be conducted with the utmost success and yet, not only according to the letter, but according to the spirit of the laws of regulation which Congress has adopted. Some of you have dealt with that commission. You, therefore, know its spirit, which is a spirit of cooperation and of helpfulness. More of you, I hope, from time to time will make use of the assistance of that commission, and you will more and more find that it is, not an instrument to generate friction, but an instrument to avoid friction, an instrument to accommodate all the forces of this country so that they can cooperate with one another with the greatest possible energy and the least possible inconvenience.

It has been the habit of the United States to create a great many excellent instrumentalities and then not know that it had them. One of the instrumentalities which it has been slow to realize the use of, and even the existence of, is that which has been supplied by the great Department of Commerce of the United States. I am glad to say that the present Secretary of Commerce has insisted that you should know what was going on in that department. And while some men are here crying out that we ought to have means by which to ascertain the actual conditions under which the industries of this country were carried on, the Bureau of Foreign and Domestic Commerce has been publishing reports as excellent, I venture to say, as have been published by any governmental instrumentality in the world, giving the most extended, detailed, and authentic information with regard to the things that you are interested to know but allowed to be printed without indulging in reading them. The amount of interesting and important printed matter put out and circulated at the expense of the government is extraordinary, when you consider how small a fraction of it is ever read by anybody. And what we have to congratulate ourselves on is that, in recent years, there has not only been an interesting development of the activities of the Department of Commerce, but an interesting, though slow, extension of the knowledge that it existed and that it was doing very useful and informing work. I commend to you the enterprise of informing our fellow citizens that there is a great deal to be learned in Washington if one cares to learn them, and a great deal to be learned *from* Washington.

Why, ladies and gentlemen, some of the most important and far-reaching scientific work in the world is being done in the quiet government agencies of this city. Anybody who has not visited the Bureau of Standards, for example, has no conception of some of the niceties of exact work which have been going on there. And I want to add that it is not very creditable to the United States that some of the most well-equipped and devoted men of science in this country are conducting patient investigations of the most important kind in this city on a pitifully small compensation—not allowing themselves to be tempted elsewhere by commercial offers, by a great deal more tempting offers, in so far as compensation was concerned, than the government apparently ever will offer. I know men toiling here on $1,800 a year who could give some of the best scientific men in our university faculties points and beat them in their own field of investigation. And I am at once proud of them and sorry that the government does not treat them better. But this is a place where the government exerts itself in an extraordinary degree to supply the country with information and finds a very small market for it.

What I want you to realize is that, while a great many persons have been crying out that we didn't have the scientific instrumentalities for doing business upon an exact foundation, they have long existed and are now being rapidly developed. There never was a time when the means of making conquest of every opportunity in the world were more abundantly open to the businessmen of America than they are now. So that, unconsciously before the war began, and before anybody on this side of the water, at any rate, dreamed that war was imminent, we did make preparation for the tasks, the tasks of peace which fell to us as a neutral nation when that struggle began.

There are some instrumentalities which we still lack and which I believe I can confidently predict we shall get. For example, we do need an instrument which will have a wider scope of power of inquiry in the field which, for lack of a better term, we call the field of foreign exchange, and, therefore, the field which is touched by all matters affecting tariffs. We ought to have a really scientific tariff board, and I think we are going to have one. I want to say that, before the whole face of affairs was changed in the economics of the world by the war, I was not in favor of a tariff board, because the purpose of it then apparently was to keep alive an unprofitable controversy. I am not interested in the doctrine of protection. I am not interested in the doctrine of free trade. I have been a college professor and know why I am not interested—because there is nothing in either doctrine. The only thing that is interesting are the facts of commerce and industry, and the only thing that it is right to deduce from the facts is something that has nothing properly to do with party politics at all. I might be willing to pray that a day might come when that was universally perceived if I was not in the habit of reserving my prayers for things that can be hopefully looked forward to.

I am not sure that God can, overnight, alter human nature. We have got so ingrained in us the passions and the prejudices of this controversy that men think their salvation lies where nothing but controversy lies. But since the whole face of affairs has been changed by the war, and since no man can tell, until the new facts are collected and digested, what the correct details of economic policy are, I am heartily in favor of a tariff board. Only I wish that it were not necessary that it should fall to my lot to choose the men who are to compose it. I look forward to that task with a great deal of trepidation. I know a good many impartial men on a good many subjects, but the impartial men on that subject are so few that, so far, I know only one,[3] and I shall have to institute a very elaborate search for the rest. I don't know how many there are going to be; I hope not many, because I know the difficulty of the task.

Then there is another instrument which we lack, ladies and gentlemen, and which I confidently hope we shall have directly, that we shall make ready to get as soon as possible, and that is a merchant marine. Directly, while all the rest of the world is at war, we can't deliver our goods in other people's ships, and we have hopefully expected that ships would be built by Americans. But there have been no violent symptoms of that prospect being realized, and it is absolutely necessary that we should make a beginning in some way. I think the necessity for this has been more and more perceived in the last eighteen months. A year ago, when the original shipping bill was introduced, I was told that a revolution of some sort was being proposed. I am not afraid, ladies and gentlemen, of any kind of a revolution that is

[3] He undoubtedly referred to his old friend and fellow student, Frank W. Taussig of Harvard University.

useful. I don't care by what honest process the goods are delivered, but they have got to be delivered. We can't hold our whole economic life up stagnant because we are afraid to try to experiment. I am not afraid to try to experiment, provided you put the trying of it into competent hands—the hands of men who understand business and who are truly devoted to the interests of the country. Because, after all, the interest in the new shipping bill centers, in my mind, just as much in the shipping board as in the arrangements which it contemplates for the building of ships. We have needed some guiding minds by which this thing could be worked out and men stimulated to do by private enterprise what the government ought only in the last resort to undertake, but nevertheless capable of guiding governmental effort if private efforts will not suffice. Every American prefers the initiative of private capital, but if private capital will not initiate, then it is necessary that somebody else should do it, and the only other instrumentality by which it can be done is that instrumentality which represents all of us. So I believe that we are presently going to have that means.

So this interesting thing is happening, has happened in the last three years, and is happening still—that the business needs of this country are being met, and they will continue to be met. It is amazing to me how long it took to make a start in these things. The reason I was saying just now that I was appalled by the accumulation of talk is that I remember the recent history of the United States. Nothing was longer discussed, for example, than the banking system of the United States, and everybody said that it was abominably bad, and nobody did anything. I could suggest some of the reasons, but they are not reasons that I care to discuss when everybody is in a good humor. It was not intended in some quarters that anything should be done about the banking system of the United States. But even there the resisting force, while it was a selfish force, was an honest force. I wish that the Lord had made all the stupid men knaves. They would be so much easier to deal with. But when the resisting force consists of honest men, you apparently have first to convince your fellow citizens that the men who are resisting you are not dishonest. Now that is not fair, because the last thing you want to feel is that eminently successful men are stupid. And yet their power of staying still is incredible. Their mere inertia has the majesty of nature itself. And all of that has to be overcome whenever you begin to do a new thing.

Men treat a new thing as they do a strange dish. They not only will not partake of it, but they do not like to look at it. They turn away from it within an instinctive revulsion. I heard of one group of gentlemen, several hundred strong, who vowed that they did not believe in the Federal Reserve Banking System, and it was found that only four of them had read the bill. They had just that attitude. They not only wouldn't partake of the dish, but they would not look at it. They knew beforehand that, because it was strange, it was bad, and it was incredible to them that it should be nutritious as well as palatable.

Now, the thing hasn't proved to be even unpalatable. Not only has nobody been hurt by it, but I challenge you to cite me a time in the past when the resources of the banks of this country have accumulated faster or in more solid fashion than in recent months. The figures speak for themselves, and the United States never was in a condition of such financial strength as she is at present, or in a position to use her financial strength with greater facility than she is at present.

You see, we have instrumentalities of inquiry here which are imperative, and it is perfectly possible to know exactly what is going on in the financial world, and everything that is going on in the financial world just now is extremely wholesome and satisfactory. But that only makes me feel the greater gratification that this inertia has at last been overcome. And the only good thing at present that I can be sure of that is coming out of this war is that it is going to make it absolutely necessary that everybody should get a move on him. You can't do your business after this war is over the way you did it before it began. You can't limit your horizons, when the war is over, as you limited them before it began. You can't limit your activities. All the winds of the world will seem to catch them up and make them parts of the very currents of humanity.

And so it is, if only we can keep this great nation at peace, there is an infinite prospect of happy prosperity before the United States, not because others have suffered, but because the United States is ready to serve the rest of the world with her resources. I believe that she will serve the rest of the world in handsome and gallant fashion, not taking advantage of their necessities, but only taking advantage of the legitimate opportunities which the circumstances have created.

I have followed, with a great deal of interest, gentlemen, the work of this association, and my interest has been chiefly due to the fact to which I called your attention a year ago.[4] You are beginning to know the other parts of the country just as well as you

[4] In his address to the Chamber of Commerce of the United States on February 3, 1915. It is printed at that date in Vol. 32.

know your own part of it; and, better than that, you are beginning to know what the other parts of the country think as well
as what your part of the country thinks. And it will often happen,
I dare say, that you will find that other parts of the country have
an idea or two. One of the best schools that I have attended I am
attending now--the school which brings me into contact with men
of all sorts, of all occupations, from all quarters of the United
States, and brings in more than I can assimilate, of course, but
an infinite deal of instruction and an infinite deal of inspiration
and consciousness that the best function that I can perform is to
register these interesting impressions and to understand, not to
let my own opinions or prejudices stand in the way of understanding, to try and make myself a vehicle by which to interpret
the general life and purpose of the country. And very few instrumentalities are, or will be, more serviceable than yours in this
debate and comparison of views—this frank assessment of the
opinion of the businessmen, at least, of the country, with regard
to what the great matters of public policy are. I congratulate
the country upon having such an instrumentality, and I think
your own committees will testify that they have a broader conception of what this association can do than they had before, and
that they have this as their leading conception—that the life of
this country does not reside even chiefly in any center of population of the United States.

New York knows as much as New York can know. I don't mean
that in a disparaging way at all. But it could not do without what
San Francisco knows; it could not do without what New Orleans
knows; it could not do without the contribution of any part of
the country with regard to the general situation of the nation.

This common impulse is the democratic impulse (I use the word
with a small "d")—the impulse which comes from the general
life and feeling and purpose of the country. For, after all, purpose is the only creative thing in the world, and the only hopeful
purpose, the only serviceable purpose, is that which is justified
in motive.

Patriotism, ladies and gentlemen, is a word to conjure with, but
it is a thing to redeem a nation with. Because if you once get
into your imagination any part of the conception of a great
nation, every individual in which is interested in the welfare
and prosperity of all of it, you find the only means by which
your own motives can be, not only enlightened, but justified—the
only source from which you can draw, as it were, from the common sources of red and pulsating blood that make for energy,
variety of action, and sweep of enterprise. For we ought to have

minds as big as our continent, purposes as great as our historical traditions, and a business that looks out upon all the world to make peaceful conquest of every field of legitimate endeavor.

JRT transcript (WC, NjP) of CLSsh notes (C. L. Swem Coll., NjP).

After-Dinner Remarks to Members of the Grand Army of the Republic[1]

[Feb. 10, 1916]

Mr. Toastmaster and gentlemen: I think I ought to apologize to you for having kept you so long waiting for my coming, but circumstances over which I had no control made that inevitable. I am very glad, indeed, to find myself here with you at last. You will not expect of me, I am sure, an address or any extended speech. But any man, whether in public life or in private life, would be lacking in sensibility who, in a company like this, should not feel some of the deepest things in him move very greatly, indeed. For my own part, having been a close student of the history of our own beloved country, I never stand in the presence of old soldiers that I do not seem, myself, to be standing in the presence of some part of that history and touched very deeply, indeed, by some part of the great tradition of national service.

Therefore, the beauty about a democracy, gentlemen, is that nobody can determine beforehand or predict where its energy is going to come from. It is spontaneous energy. It is energy that seems almost, figuratively, to spring from the soil itself. Nobody knows from what humble dwelling or obscure part of the country the men are going to come who will lead the country or will sacrifice their lives and their fortunes for the country, if it should become necessary to make sacrifices for it. So that you do not have to depend upon a limited class; you do not have to depend upon a group of families; you do not have to depend upon any limited source of supply; but all the energies of a great nation stand ready to be summoned to every task that must be undertaken. And, when I see a body of men like this, it seems to me that they are rendered all the more reverend by the circumstance that the war in which they took part is now so far behind us that all the passion of it has subsided, and all that we read about it now is that two great bodies of Americans honorably met each other in contest for principles which each believed in, and that the outcome was the triumphant preservation of a great Union to continue the energies of a great people.

I remember being very much struck one day. I wanted to recall the dates of the life of General Robert E. Lee, and I turned
to the *Century Cyclopedia of Names* as the readiest reference.
And there I found this interesting entry: "Lee, Robert Edward;
a distinguished American general in the Confederate service." I
looked at the date of the book, and I knew that, not much before
that date, could such an entry have been made. But there was
the record, not only of the man, but of that blessed forgetfulness
of all the points of passion which had come to us in the course of
time, when Americans of all sorts were ready to to be proud of
the American general who, in honorable fashion, had fallen on
the losing side. Isn't that an unconscious tribute on the part
of the editor—I do not know who the editor was—but isn't it an
interesting and unconscious indication on his part of what had
happened to our spirits after that extraordinary and fundamental
struggle? So it seems to me, gentlemen, that all the memories of
that war are now handsome memories.

We are in the presence of war. It does not seem all of it handsome. Passion is more and more deeply engaged. The outcome
no man can predict, and every man must look forward to it with
misgiving. And, yet, when you think of the heroic things that are
happening and of the enormous number of men who have had
to forget their own individual interests in order to be—shall I
use an extravagant expression?—to pool their own blood as a nation, you know that a tremendous, spiritual thing is happening.
No matter what their individual feelings may be, they are
merged, and that merging means that family lines have disappeared, local lines have disappeared, and everything is national
and beats with a great common pulse in each of those countries.
There is something magnificent about that, whatever we may
think about any other aspect of the contest.

And so, in looking about in this room, I feel that here is the
reminiscence of the same thing having happened in America.
And I like to think of those circumstances of the Spanish-American War which brought the men who had fought each other in
the Civil War into the same ranks of a single army, all fighting
for the same national emblem and all feeling the same impulse
of a common patriotism. It makes me believe that the healing
and ennobling influences of a nation are, after all, the permanent
ones, and the separating and dividing influences are the temporary ones, and that the fundamental things of our life are the
common things of our life, which we all share. I don't know many
men in this room, but I venture to say that a very brief conversation with any man in this room would show that we touched at

a thousand points, because we shared the same life, felt an enthusiasm for the same essential things, believed in the same standards of life, had received the same traditions of our national existence. That is the reason that meetings like this take on something more than a mere social character. When we come into contact with each other in bodies like this, or similar bodies, we seem to return to the common springs of suggestion and inspiration which, after all, keep all the finer things in us fresh and young.

So, gentlemen, it is a privilege for me, bearing temporarily great responsibilities, to come and have touch with you of these common memories. Your toastmaster spoke just now of the great powers of the office of President of the United States. I must frankly say that it is not of the power of the office that I often think—even the incumbent of the office feels a bit overwhelmed with the powers of the office. But what I think of more often than the powers is the difficulty of knowing the right use to which to put those powers, and the consciousness that there is only one way to find out, and that is to keep in as wide and intimate touch with the general body of my fellow citizens as possible. In other words, there is one thing which is happily excluded from a popular form of government, and that is the idea that, when you give a man power, he is to use it according to his own sweet will. That is excluded. His will must be harnessed with the general harness of the society of which he constitutes a part, and, while he is given great opportunities, he is also given a great task, a great load to draw, and he must see to it that some little progress is made along the great highway of human advancement while the collar is on his neck.

T MS (WP, DLC).
 1 At the forty-eighth annual banquet of the Department of the Potomac at the New Ebbitt Hotel in Washington. Colonel John McElroy, acting commander of the department, was the toastmaster.

To Lindley Miller Garrison

[The White House]

My dear Mr. Secretary: February 10, 1916

In reply to your letter of today[1] let me say,

First, that it is my own judgment that the action embodied in the Clarke amendment to the bill extending further self-government to the Philippines is unwise at this time, but it would clearly be most inadvisable for me to take the position that I must dissent from that action should both houses of Congress concur in a bill embodying that amendment. That is a matter upon which I must, of course, withhold judgment until the joint action of the two houses reaches me in definite form. What the final action of the houses will be no one can at this time certainly forecast. I am now, of course, engaged in conference with Mr. Jones and others with regard to the probable action of the House of Representatives in this matter and do not yet know what it is likely to be. The one obvious thing, it seems to me, is the necessity for calm and deliberate action on our part at this time when matters of such gravity are to be determined, and not only calm and deliberate action but action which takes into very serious consideration views differing from our own.

Second, as I have had occasion to say to you, I am not yet convinced that the measure of preparation for national defence which we deem necessary can be obtained through the instrumentality of the National Guard under federal control and training, but I feel in duty bound to keep my mind open to conviction on that side and think that it would be most unwise and most unfair to the Committee of the House, which has such a plan in mind, to say that it cannot be done. The bill in which it will be embodied has not yet been drawn, as I learned today from Mr. Hay. I should deem it a very serious mistake to shut the door against this attempt on the part of the Committee in perfect, good faith to meet the essentials of the programme set forth in my message but in a way of their own choosing.

As you know, I do not at all agree with you in favoring compulsory enlistment for training, and I fear the advocacy of compulsion before the Committee of the House on the part of representatives of the Department of War has greatly prejudiced the House against the proposal for a continental army, little necessary connection as there is between the plan and the opinion of the Chief of Staff in favor of compulsory enlistment.

I owe you this frank repetition of my views and policy in this matter, which we have discussed on previous occasions, in the letters which we have exchanged and in conversation. I am very much obliged to you for your own frank avowal of your convictions. I trust that you will feel no hesitation about expressing your personal views on both these subjects on the two occasions to which you refer, but I hope that you will be kind enough to draw very carefully the distinction between your own individual views and the views of the administration.

You will, of course, understand that I am devoting my energy and attention unsparingly in conference with members of the various committees of Congress to an effort to procure an agreement upon a workable and practicable programme. This is a time when it seems to me patience on the part of all of us is of the essence in bringing about a consummation of the purpose we all have in mind.   Very sincerely yours,   Woodrow Wilson

TLS (Letterpress Books, WP, DLC).
1 He meant LMG to WW, Feb. 9, 1916.

From Lindley Miller Garrison

My dear Mr. President: Washington. February 10, 1916.

I am just in receipt of yours of February 10th in reply to mine of February 9th. It is evident that we hopelessly disagree upon what I conceive to be fundamental principles. This makes manifest the impropriety of my longer remaining your seeming representative with respect to these matters.

I hereby tender my resignation as Secretary of War, to take effect at your convenience.
                        Sincerely yours,   Lindley M. Garrison

TLS (WP, DLC).

To Lindley Miller Garrison

                                    [The White House]
My dear Mr. Secretary: February 10, 1916.

I must confess to feeling a very great surprise at your letter of today offering your resignation as Secretary of War. There has been no definite action taken yet in either of the matters to which your letter of yesterday referred. The whole matter is under debate and all the influences that work for clarity and judgment ought to be available at this very time.

But since you have felt obliged to take this action and since it is evident that your feeling in the matter is very great indeed, I feel that I would be only imposing a burden upon you should I urge you to retain the Secretaryship of War while I am endeavoring to find a successor. I ought to relieve you at once and do hereby accept your resignation because it is so evidently your desire that I should do so.

I cannot take this important step, however, without expressing to you my very warm appreciation of the distinguished service you have rendered as Secretary of War, and I am sure that in expressing this appreciation I am only putting into words the judgment of our fellow citizens far and wide.

With sincere regret at the action you have felt constrained to take,   Sincerely yours,   Woodrow Wilson

TLS (Letterpress Books, WP, DLC).

From Henry Skillman Breckinridge

Washington, D. C.
My dear Mr. President: February 10, 1916.

The Secretary of War, Mr. Garrison, has just informed me of the fact that he has submitted his resignation, to take effect at your convenience.

I have been cognizant of each detail of the correspondence between yourself and him leading up to this action on his part. I have subscribed to each statement of principle made by him throughout this correspondence. I share without exception his convictions, and therefore have the honor to tender my resignation, to take effect at your convenience.

Very respectfully,   Henry Breckinridge

TLS (WP, DLC).

To Henry Skillman Breckinridge

[The White House]
My dear Mr. Breckinridge: February 10, 1916.

I can quite understand why you deem it incumbent upon you in loyalty to your chief to follow his example in tendering your resignation, and since I have accepted his resignation I am sure it will be your desire that I accept yours also. I do so with genuine regret because you have in every way fulfilled the highest expectations and rendered the country the most conscientious and efficient service.

It is with genuine sorrow that I see this official relationship between us brought to an end.

Cordially and sincerely yours,   Woodrow Wilson[1]

TLS (Letterpress Books, WP, DLC).
[1] The foregoing correspondence between Wilson and Garrison and Breckinridge and Wilson was published in most newspapers on February 11, 1916.

To Henry Dickinson Lindsley[1]

[The White House] February 10, 1916.

I am much interested to learn from your telegram[2] that the people of Dallas will hold a mass meeting tonight for the discussion of the question of national preparedness. I am confident that this meeting will do much to present in a proper light this very vital question, and I am equally confident that when thus presented it will receive cordial approval. May I not add a word of personal greeting and appreciation?   Woodrow Wilson

T telegram (Letterpress Books, WP, DLC).
  ¹ Mayor of Dallas, Texas, 1915-17.
  ² H. D. Lindsley to WW, Feb. 10, 1916, T telegram (WP, DLC).

A Telegram and a Letter from Edward Mandell House

[London] 10 February, 1916.

Will not agree unless. [After a] Long conference with Sir Edward Grey. He agrees to practically all the programme suggested by me. It is of such vital importance that I dare not cable it. Tomorrow we will bring the substance of our understanding before Asquith and the First Lord of the Admiralty, and if they consent it should mark the beginning of the end of the war. Events are moving rapidly and if nothing is done in Washington to disturb the situation I am hopeful that soon after my arrival home you will be able to initiate the great movement we have in mind. I would appreciate a cable letting me know that my communications have been received.

WWT decode of T telegram (WP, DLC).

No. 14. London, England.

Dear Governor: February 10, 1916.

I arrived here last night and had a conference with Page in which with characteristic pessimism he declared I would not be able to do anything with this Government because of the Lusitania settlement and because of Lansing's proposal in regard to disarming merchantmen.

He told me Sir Edward Grey had said as much to him without telling him exactly to what he referred. I have told Page for the first time something of what we have in mind, and later I shall see that he is brought into the conferences when they broaden sufficiently. I think this is essential because too many now know it and if he should hear of it from anyone excepting me, his sensibilities would be hurt to such an extent that he might resign.

The Lord Chief Justice called early this morning to say that Lloyd George was anxious to see me alone as soon as possible. I asked him to make the engagement.

I had written Sir Edward from Paris and he reserved the entire morning for our conference. I was very frank with him as I always am telling him everything that had happened in both Berlin and Paris. I also told him of my advice to you in regard to the settlement of the Lusitania and why I thought it essential for us to keep out of the war, at least for the present. He disagreed with this as Page intimated he would, but in ten minutes I had brought him around.

After going over the situation with great care and taking up every detail of foreign affairs, we finally agreed that it would be best for you to demand that the belligerents permit you to call a conference for the discussion of peace terms. We concluded this would be better than intervention, and it was understood, though not definitely agreed upon, that you might do this within a very short time, perhaps soon after I returned.

The Allies will agree to the conference and if Germany does not, I have promised for you that we would throw all our weight in order to bring her to terms.

You will see that we have progressed pretty far since I left Paris—further than I had any idea that it was possible to do. I am to meet the Prime Minister, Balfour and Grey tomorrow at lunch to acquaint them of our discussion and to endeavor to get their approval. If this is done there will be a dinner on Monday at which I have requested that Page be present. At this dinner there will be the Prime Minister, Grey, Balfour, Lloyd George and the Lord Chief Justice. There will be no others taken in at any later conference, but what is determined there will be a finality and I can bring you home definite news.

I cannot say with certitude what attitude Asquith and Balfour will take tomorrow, but I doubt whether Grey would have been as positive if he had not been reasonably certain of their cooperation.

I am very happy to be able to write you this and I hope tomorrow I may be able to confirm it by cable. If you can hold the situation at Washington clear of all complications, sending no notes, protests, etc. etc. to any of the belligerents it looks as if something momentous may soon happen.

The discussion of the Lusitania settlement in the public prints has been most unfortunate. Practically the whole controversy has been cabled over from Washington and the papers are commenting upon it which makes the situation exceedingly dangerous. I have asked Grey to undertake to restrain all adverse criticism for the moment and he has promised to do this. I shall also ask the Prime Minister to do the same thing. Grey and I agreed upon a plan by which we thought this could be accomplished.

If I were you I would ask Frank Polk to put the Secret Service on the question of leakage and endeavor to find its source. This seems to me imperative for it may endanger the great work you are trying to do. If decoy messages are given to those that are suspected, it ought not to be difficult to find the guilty party. I cannot impress upon you too strongly how important this is and I hope you will immediately take it in hand.

Affectionately yours,   E. M. House

TLS (WP, DLC).

From John Henry Fahey

Washington, D. C.
My dear Mr. President: February 10, 1916.

I desire to thank you for your consideration of my request for an appointment for a Committee from the Chamber of Commerce of the United States, and to express full appreciation of the unusual demands now being made upon your time.

The Committee for which I asked an appointment desires simply to lay before you the results of a recent referendum in which the business men of America voted their approval of an international court and a joint guarantee of a more lasting peace; an idea to which you made forceful reference in your recent Des Moines address. The specific proposal, of which the Chamber of Commerce of the United States has just voted strong approval, is that the United States should stand ready to do its share in the establishment of an international tribunal supported by a league of nations agreeing to use their concerted force, in the form of commercial and financial nonintercourse, and if necessary as a last resort, military action against any nation refusing to submit its case to the agreed upon tribunal for examination.

Under the by-laws of the organization the directors of the National Chamber are charged with the responsibility of taking such steps as may seem wise to make effective the referendum vote.

The directors and the members of the Committee have been discussing as a possibly wise step, a judiciously planned propaganda for the further strengthening of public opinion in the United States and in the more important states of Latin America, with the hope of crystalizing it into a Pan-American support of such an international program. Before proceeding, however, with any such propaganda we desired to inform you of the trend of our thinking, so that you might be in touch with the entire situation in case you desired to advise one way or the other. It is, of course, our desire to avoid any course that might embarrass you in your handling of the increasingly complex international situation.

As the most convenient memorandum I am enclosing a tabulation of the vote upon the separate proposals.[1]

The Committee desires to thank you for your Des Moines reference to the main principle involved in the program that has just been approved by the referendum vote, and to express its conviction that whatever reference of a like nature you may see fit to make in the future will strike a sympathetic response in the minds of American business men.

Thanking you sincerely for your courtesy, I am,

Very sincerely yours, John H Fahey

TLS (WP, DLC).

[1] The recommendations placed before the members of the Chamber of Commerce of the United States were: (1) Holding conferences of neutral nations to define rules for the protection of life and property on the high seas. (2) The establishment of an international court. (3) The establishment of a council of conciliation. (4) The exertion of economic pressure on nations which resort to military measures without submitting their differences to the international court. (5) The use of concerted military force in the event that economic pressure did not suffice to preserve peace. (6) Frequent international conferences for the progressive amendment of international law.

With the exception of the fifth proposal, which was approved by a vote of 452 to 249, these recommendations were overwhelmingly approved. For example, the first recommendation was approved by a vote of 763 to 29. Chamber of Commerce of the United States, *Referendum Number Eleven: Economic Results of the War and American Business* (Washington, 1916). Fahey enclosed a copy of this bulletin, and it is attached to his letter.

Sir Cecil Arthur Spring Rice to Sir Edward Grey

Washington 10 Feb 1916

No. 446. Your tel No. 256 (of Feb 2)[1] I left copy with S of S who has communicated it to President. S of S made no comment except to say that evidently naval party in Germany were absolutely opposed to any concession on submarine warfare while the politicians were anxious that it should be modified. He thought it possible that Tirpitz would regain power. He did not seem to be hopeful as to serious modification of German methods. I said that his proposal might be very useful as a basis for negotiations after the war. The conversation was vague & unofficial. The decision rests with the President who keeps the matter entirely in his own hands.

Meanwhile Italian ships are allowed to leave with guns

on board. S. of S. made no allusion to any change in treatment of armed merchantmen

Hw telegram (FO 115/2017, p. 98, PRO).
1 Printed as an Enclosure with RL to WW, Feb. 5, 1916.

A Telegram and a Letter from Edward Mandell House

[London] 11 February [1916].

The conference to-day was very satisfactory, but not entirely conclusive. I meet George tonight.

WWT decode of T telegram (WP, DLC).

Dear Governor: No. 15. London, February 11, 1916

The Prime Minister, Grey[,] Balfour and I met at lunch today. We went over very much the same ground as was covered yesterday with Grey. They were not as amenable to the plan as Grey, but adopted it tentatively and I have but little doubt now that when I leave we will have an absolute understanding that you are to propose a peace conference and act as mediator when the time is propitious.

They are to determine the time after consultation with their allies.

They adopted my suggestion as to how this should be done. There are many complications to encounter as you will understand when I explain the matter to you in person.

I feel very happy and I rejoice now that you over-ruled Lansing and me at the time of my visit. The thing I fear most is that Germany will break loose in an unrestricted undersea warfare. If that should happen, all plans will have to be made anew. Nevertheless, what has been done will be of great value.

I am writing hastily in order to catch the pouch which closes within a few minutes.

Affectionately yours,   E. M. House

TLS (WP, DLC).

From James Hay

Washington, D. C.
My dear Mr. President: February 11, 1916.

I have been instructed by the Committee on Military Affairs of the House of Representatives to convey to you the very great appreciation which the committee feels for the confidence which you have shown in its good faith and patriotism; and to assure you of its desire to work in harmony with you in perfecting a plan which would be of the greatest benefit to the country.

Very cordially and sincerely yours,   James Hay

TLS (WP, DLC).

From Hugh Lenox Scott

Washington, D. C.
My dear Mr. President: February 11, 1916.

Very shortly after accession to your present high office, you promoted me to be a Brigadier General, and soon thereafter to be Chief of Staff and a Major General. I have endeavored to carry out your policy not only in the War Department, but also on the Mexican border and in the Indian country, and have received a number of commendatory letters from you, for all of which I am proud and grateful.

I find myself today in this situation. There is no one to act as Secretary of War ad interim, and I am sending you a copy of an order appointing me to the position. I notice, however, in the morning paper what may be construed as a note of dissatisfaction in regard to my testimony about preparedness before Congress in your letter to the Secretary of War, and fearing lest there may be embarrassment in appointing me to act as Secretary of War ad interim and continuing here as Chief of Staff, I place it in your hands to avoid such embarrassment.

Very respectfully yours,   H. L. Scott

TLS (WP, DLC).

From Charles Sumner Hamlin

Dear Mr President: [Washington] Feb. 11, 1916

I have read the morning papers. You are absolutely right in your determination not to foreclose in advance any possible plan for preparedness whether founded upon the State Militia or upon a new National body. Hot heads very likely will attack you but sober minded citizens will sustain you in insisting that the representatives of the people shall discuss this vital question in an orderly, constitutional manner. A President must act as judge as well as Commander in Chief and you can be depended upon to act in both capacities. I have always been for peace,—almost at any price,—but I believe adequate preparation has become necessary in order to *maintain* peace.

When the present war is over the neutral nations must lay down new rules for war. We must have power to warrant us in taking the position that the rights of Neutrals *should* be and *shall* be maintained.

I am for preparedness which will *prevent* war. A man who is inoculated for typhoid fever does not *want* typhoid fever. Nor does the man inoculated for small pox *want* small pox. He wants to prevent both. So far as I can see, the present crisis is between the army and the people of the U. S. The people will sustain you in your final decision as between these contending forces and they will applaud your desire to *think* before *acting* and to give the people first opportunity for debate in the hope that a solution may be found harmonizing apparently irreconcilable views.

In any event, believe me, you are *acting* when you are *thinking* and your leadership will be all the more effective for having reason the motive or the inspiration for your acts.

The people will follow you.
                         Sincerely yours   Charles S. Hamlin.

ALS (WP, DLC).

William A. Kincaid[1] to Joseph Patrick Tumulty

                                        Washington, D. C.,
My dear Mr. Tumulty: February 11, 1916.

In accordance with our understanding, I beg to hand you, herewith inclosed, a communication to the President, which I trust you will call to his attention.[2]

I should be glad if you would endeavor to have it treated as confidential.   Very sincerely yours,   W A Kincaid

TLS (WP, DLC).

[1] Former member of the Texas House of Representatives, appointed in 1901 as one of the judges of the Court of First Instance in the Philippine Islands. He was practicing law in Manila at this time, and his clients included the Roman Catholic Archbishop of Manila and principal Japanese concerns in the islands.

[2] W. A. Kincaid to WW, Feb. 11, 1916, TLS (WP, DLC), enclosing "Bishop Brent on the Philippines," Milwaukee *Wisconsin*, April 24, 1913, and "What of the Philippines?", Columbus, Ohio, *Dispatch*, April 23, 1913, T MSS (WP, DLC). Kincaid warned that the prosperity of the Roman Catholic Church and the protection of its property were essential to "conservative progress" in the Philippines. He had witnessed repeated attempts by various local groups to deprive the church of its property during his fifteen years in the islands. Kincaid feared that the church, and therefore insular prosperity, would be jeopardized if the Filipinos were given control of the government of the islands before they were "thoroughly prepared to assume the responsibilities of government." Furthermore, he thought that the Clarke amendment was "a threat to every Christian church" in the Philippines and "violative of the implied considerations which led to the investment of American capital in the Islands."

To Edward Mandell House

[The White House] 12 February, 1916.

Your cables have been received up to and including that of February tenth and your letters through number seven, ayd [and] deeply appreciated. We are trying to be guided by them and shall await your full report upon your return home before taking any steps that might alter our opportunity, provided the sea operations of the central powers make it possible for us to maintain the status quo. I have not replied to your messages merely because they seemed to need no comment and the situation here in respect of our programme of preparation for national defense required my undivided attention. What you have done seems admirable and gives me lively hope of a development of events that may bring peace.

WWT telegram (WP, DLC).

From Edward Mandell House

[London, Feb. 13, 1916]

The substance of messages and reports February 10th and 11th is that I [had and] am having satisfactory conferences with Asquith, Sir Edward Grey, the First Lord of the Admiralty, and George. I believe that with their consent [a complete] understanding can be had before I leave looking to action by you at the proper time. Is very important that no further notes or protests be sent until I can confer in person with you and the Secretary of State.

T transcript of WWsh decode of T telegram (WP, DLC).

From Benjamin Ryan Tillman

Dear Mr. President: Washington. February 14, 1916.

I wish you would tell me exactly what you want me to say about the size of the Navy. You have been quoted in the newspapers as having said in your speech at St. Louis that you desire the United States to have a Navy "Incomparably the greatest Navy in the world." If you used those words, I think you owe it to yourself, and the Party too, to explain to the country just what you meant by the "Greatest Navy in the world."

You know, of course, that England's very life depends on control of the ocean, because her people would starve except for the food they import; and if the United States sets out to out-strip her, she will necessarily spend money lavishly and finally be compelled to go to war with the United States in order to maintain her supremacy on the ocean. I believe it would be a fatal blunder for the United States to enter on such a race with her; and I also believe it is our solemn duty to have the *second* greatest Navy afloat. I will say this in my speech when the armor plant bill comes up; and I think it is a fine opportunity for me as your spokesman to tell the people just what you did mean by "Greatest." What I have dictated is these words:

"I say now and here that I am not in favor of any such Navy as that; but I do want us to have the second greatest Navy afloat; and by greatest, I mean greatest in efficiency of its officers and in the fighting qualities of its ships of all kinds. With the personnel, from the highest officer to the humblest Jackie in it, I am already well satisfied and believe they are second to none now—not even Britain's."

If you want to change this paragraph in any way, suggest in what way. But I implore you not to take any such stand as the newspapers have said you occupy. You have seen the numerous criticisms of that utterance by friendly and opposition papers too, I know.

Please let me have your answer by the messenger who will wait, because I may have to make the speech in the morning.

Very sincerely yours,   B. R. Tillman

TLS (WP, DLC).

To Benjamin Ryan Tillman

My dear Senator,   The White House. 14 February, 1916.

I hasten to reply to your note of to-day. I was not here when your messenger brought it.

That sentence of mine about "the greatest navy in the world" was an indiscretion uttered in a moment of enthusiasm at the very end of my recent speaking tour, and was not deliberately meant. What I earnestly advocate at the present time is the carrying out of the programme which I proposed to the Congress in my annual message. That is the exact programme I am willing and anxious to stand by, and your utterance, as dictated in the passage quoted in your note of to-day has nothing in it inconsistent with my personal opinion or desire.

Thank you for asking me the question.

After you telephoned me this morning I sent word to Senator

Kern and the others who might be accessible through Senator Pomerene, who was in my office when you telephoned, and who kindly undertook the mission, that I hoped that they would do everything in their power to further the consideration and pass[a]ge of the bill for an armor plant, but I later sent word to them through Tumulty that I did not mean, of course, to ask that anything be done that would prejudice the programme for the passage of any other vital measure. I know that you will agree with me that that was the proper position to take; but I wanted you to know from me direct all that I had done.

Cordially and faithfully Yours,   Woodrow Wilson

WWTLS (B. R. Tillman Papers, ScCleU).

To Alexander White Gregg

My dear Mr. Gregg: [The White House] February 14, 1916

Your letter of February ninth gave me peculiar pleasure. I think that it must be that some of your colleagues of the Texas delegation[1] do not understand the real sentiment of the people at home or they would, like yourself, feel the absolute necessity of sustaining the programme for national defence. It gives me deep gratification that you should feel as you do about that all-important matter.

I am sincerely distressed to hear of your wife's illness and I hope with all my heart that her recovery may now be rapid and complete.

Cordially and sincerely yours,   Woodrow Wilson

TLS (WP, DLC).
[1] Wilson meant especially Representatives Oscar Callaway, James Harvey "Cyclone" Davis, and Martin Dies. For more detailed information on the position of the Texas delegation on the preparedness issue, see Lewis L. Gould, *Progressives and Prohibitionists, Texas Democrats in the Wilson Era* (Austin, Tex., and London, 1973), pp. 160-62.

To Willard Saulsbury

My dear Senator: The White House February 14, 1916

I have been greatly distressed to learn that you and other Senators feel some objection to the promotion of Mr. John van A. MacMurray to the first secretarial rank in the Diplomatic Service.[1] I have known Mr. MacMurray every since he was a boy at college; he was one of my pupils at Princeton; he is a man of some peculiarities which expose him to be easily misunderstood, but his gifts are so unusual and his service in the diplomatic posi-

tions to which he has been assigned has been so unusually satisfactory, that I earnestly hope that it will be possible for you and
our other friends in the Senate to acquiesce in his promotion.
Minister Reinsch particularly commends Mr. MacMurray for his
intellectual capacity, his acumen, his high sense of responsibility,
and the grasp and thoroughness of his methods of work, and I
should esteem it a real detriment to the service if men of this
sort could not receive prompt and generous recognition. It would
be a great pity to have any small failings stand in their way. It is
this feeling that must serve as my reason for sending you this
earnest request.

> Cordially and sincerely yours,   Woodrow Wilson

TLS (W. Saulsbury Papers, DeU).
  [1] Wilson had nominated MacMurray for this rank on November 5, 1915.

To Hugh Lenox Scott

My dear General Scott: The White House February 14, 1916

I am sincerely obliged to you for your letter of the eleventh
because I know that it was prompted by a desire to relieve me of
all embarrassment; but let me assure you that it is my sincere
desire that you should retain your present position and duties.

I did think it regrettable that in the testimony given before the
Committee of the House of Representatives on Military Affairs
your own opinion and the opinion of others in favor of compulsory military training should have been made to seem part
of the judgment of the Department of War in favor of a "continental" reserve; but I fully recognized the fact that you were
merely giving your frank professional opinion and that it was
your undoubted right to do so when questioned by a committee
of the Congress. I meant no personal censure in what I said in
my recent letter to Mr. Garrison, and you may rest assured that
you continue to enjoy, as you have always enjoyed, my trustful
confidence. I am glad to be associated with you in your present
capacity as Acting Secretary of War.

> Cordially and sincerely yours,   Woodrow Wilson[1]

TLS (H. L. Scott Papers, DLC).
  [1] There is a WWT draft of this letter in WP, DLC.

To Frederick A. Duneka

My dear Mr. Duneka: The White House February 14, 1916

I have your letter of February fourth[1] and since receiving it
found time to read the little essay to which you refer, "On Being

Human," and am quite willing that you should republish it in the same form as "When a Man Comes to Himself."

I think you will find that it will not have the same sale. "When a Man Comes to Himself" is a moral homily and appeals to a great many people in a rather obvious way, but the essay "On Being Human" is much more literary and I should say would appeal to a very much more limited class.

If it is published,[2] I should like to reserve, as in the case of the other, the right to republish it in association with other essays in a volume of collected essays at some time.

Cordially and sincerely yours, Woodrow Wilson

TLS (WC, NjP).
[1] F. A. Duneka to WW, Feb. 4, 1916, TLS (WP, DLC).
[2] Harper and Brothers published the essay in 1916.

To Charles Sumner Hamlin

My dear Mr. Hamlin: [The White House] February 14, 1916

May I not thank you very warmly for your letter of February eleventh? You apparently always know when I need cheering and support and you certainly give it in most generous fashion. It is very delightful to have you think of me in such circumstances, and this letter of yours has given me peculiar gratification. Cordially and sincerely yours, Woodrow Wilson

TLS (Letterpress Books, WP, DLC).

From Charles Richard Crane

My dear Mr President [New York] February 14 1916

I have returned from the West and hope to see you before long. There was a general feeling of regret that conditions seemed to prevent Garrison's remaining in office. In his brief public life he had made an excellent impression. However, I think his importance was not exaggerated and there was no bitterness toward the administration shown. I think the incident only served to accentuate your strong position.

I know that you will not mind my telling you of one or two things which occur to me about his successor. I am not saying anything new to you when I only repeat the strong conviction I have of bringing Houston out more into the lime light. He would be very much interested in the Department, as war and war problems have been the main studies of his leisure hours for years. His appointment would also be well accepted. I suppose, however, that the appointment of Goethals would be the one to make the greatest and best impression on the country and would be almost as striking as the nomination of Brandeis.

Your western trip went very well, but you must have gotten out of the control of Dr Grayson. Sometime you must go again and speak to the farmers and to the working people. I should like to arrange two or three meetings of that kind for you. And at one of them you could sell the Mexican story.

With affectionate greetings,

Always sincerely   Charles R. Crane

ALS (WP, DLC).

To James Hay

My dear Mr. Hay: The White House February 15, 1916

I am deeply gratified by the action of the Committee on Military Affairs in instructing you to convey to me their appreciation of the confidence I have shown in the good faith and patriotism of the Committee, and I hope that you will convey to the members of the Committee an expression of my pleasure in their action. I never at any time have had the least reason to doubt the spirit, the knowledge, or the capacity of the Committee and I want to say that it has given me real pleasure to work with it. I hope and believe that amongst us we can work out a thoroughly effective plan for the military defence of the country.

Cordially and sincerely yours,   Woodrow Wilson

TLS (J. Hay Papers, DLC).

To Albert Sidney Burleson

Dear Burleson,   The White House [c. Feb. 15, 1916].

The following seem to me serious omissions from this bill[1] and I would be very much obliged to you if you would kindly call Mr. Hay's attention to them:

See Sect. 42.2

    1. There is no specific provision that the President shall have authority to call the Militia "into the service of the United States" for purposes of manoeuvre and camp drill, or for training in association with units of the federal army. Such a provision, if constitutional, seems to me of the utmost importance. If it is constitutionally impossible, the system seems to me clearly inadequate.

2. So far as I can see, there is no provision by which See Sect. 53 any authority but that of the individual State can initiate discipline by court martial for failure to comply with the federal regulations or to carry out the prescribed discipline. This, too, is a very serious omission.

3. The oath and terms of enlistment prescribed do not See Sect. 15. include any obligation to serve in reserve after service with the colours. Or is this obligation contained in some law to which refer[ence] is made in the references to the Revised Statutes?

I think, however, this was provided for as originally drawn, as it made the enlistment contract the same as that for enlisted men in the Army.[3]

You will see that all these are points which go to the essence, namely, that the federal government should have the directly controlling hand in peace times as well as when war comes over this auxiliary force.[4]   W.W.

WWTLI (WP, DLC).

[1] Wilson was commenting on one of Hay's first drafts of a militia bill, or a provision relating to the militia in an early draft of the army reorganization bill.

[2] ASBhw. Here and below Burleson was referring to a new draft of the bill.

[3] ASBhw at bottom of the page.

[4] All these changes were incorporated into the Hay army reorganization bill that the House adopted on March 23. However, see T. W. Gregory to WW, Feb. 25, 1916, n.2.

To Genevieve Bennett Clark

My dear Mrs. Clark: [The White House] February 15, 1916

I do not know when I have had a harder thing to do than to make up my mind that it was really impossible for me to arrange to meet your wishes respecting the Vinita, Oklahoma, postmastership.[1] I had earnestly hoped to be able to do so and have discussed the matter very thoroughly, not only with the Postmaster General, but also with the Congressman from the Vinita district. I find that to turn away from the Congressman's recommendation with regard to the Vinita postmastership would be so serious a matter for him, and that his choice seems to be so truly the choice of the leading people of the place, that I really could not justify a different choice. It would have gratified me very much indeed to be able to appoint your brother, but I am sure, having always known the exigencies of these matters for the Congressmen concerned, you will understand how I have been prevented.

With warmest regard,

Cordially and sincerely yours,   Woodrow Wilson

TLS (Letterpress Books, WP, DLC).
  ¹ Wilson was replying to Genevieve B. (Mrs. Champ) Clark to WW, Feb. 14, 1916, ALS (WP, DLC).

From Edward Mandell House

[London, Feb. 15, 1916]

After many conferences with Sir Edward Grey and his colleagues, I am satisfied with the result.¹ They cordially accept the suggestion that you preside over the convention when it is held, provided our general understanding is carried out. No action however is to be taken until they signify their readiness.² There is a difference of opinion only as to the time. It would not be wise to cable you more definitely. There is great feeling against disarming merchantmen and I am glad you are holding this in abeyance.   Edward House.

WWT decode of T telegram (WP, DLC).
  ¹ The crucial discussions took place during a dinner at Lord Reading's home on February 14. Present were Reading, House, Asquith, Grey, Balfour, and Lloyd George. For accounts of this meeting see the House diary, Feb. 14, 1916; David Lloyd George, *War Memoirs of David Lloyd George* (6 vols., Boston, 1933-37), II, 137-39; and Arthur S. Link, *Wilson: Confusions and Crises, 1915-1916* (Princeton, N. J., 1964), pp. 131-33.
  ² Grey, on February 22, 1916, initialed the following so-called House-Grey Memorandum:
  "(*Confidential*) Colonel House told me that President Wilson was ready, on hearing from France and England that the moment was opportune, to propose that a Conference should be summoned to put an end to the war. Should the Allies accept this proposal and should Germany refuse it, the United States would probably enter the war against Germany.
  "Colonel House expressed the opinion that, if such a Conference met, it would secure peace on terms not unfavourable to the Allies; and, if it failed to secure peace, the United States would leave the Conference as a belligerent on the side of the Allies, if Germany was unreasonable. Colonel House expressed an opinion decidedly favourable to the restoration of Belgium, the transfer of Alsace and Lorraine to France, and the acquisition by Russia of an outlet to the sea, though he thought that the loss of territory incurred by Germany in one place would have to be compensated by concessions to her in other places outside Europe. If the Allies delayed accepting the offer of President Wilson, and if, later on, the course of the war was so unfavourable to them that the intervention of the United States would not be effective, the United States would probably disinterest themselves in Europe, and look to their own protection in their own way.
  "I said that I felt the statement, coming from the President of the United States, to be a matter of such importance that I must inform the Prime Minister and my Colleagues; but that I could say nothing until it had received their consideration. The British Government could, under no circumstances, accept or make any proposal except in consultation and agreement with the Allies. I thought that the Cabinet would probably feel that the present situation would not justify them in approaching their Allies on this subject at the present moment; but, as Colonel House had had an intimate conversation with M. Briand and M. Jules Cambon in Paris, I should think it right to tell M. Briand privately, through the French Ambassador in London, what Colonel House had said to us; and I should, of course, whenever there was an opportunity, be ready to talk the matter over with M. Briand if he desired it." TI MS (E. M. House Papers, CtY).

From Walter Hines Page

[London] February 15, 1916.

3783. The following is in the Secretary's new private code and is strictly confidential for the President. Please deliver and telegraph me at once that it is without question clearly decipherable.

CONFIDENTIAL TO THE PRESIDENT.

Because of the ever-increasing public feeling against the Administration, the British Government has ordered the censor to suppress as far as he prudently can unfavorable comment on our Government. The LUSITANIA controversy, since it has been continued so long and especially since it is now used by the Germans in their revived submarine programme, has brought British opinion of the Administration to a point where a turn in its tide can be made only by prompt action. My loyalty to you therefore, would not be absolute if I shrank from respectfully sending my solemn conviction of our duty and opportunity.

If you immediately refuse without further parley to yield a jot or tittle of your original LUSITANIA Notes and at once sever diplomatic relations with Germany and follow this action by a rigid embargo against the Central Powers, you will quickly end the war. Economic measures are all that are necessary. German credit will collapse. The wavering Allies, if there be such, will be kept in line. Sweden, Roumania, Greece and other European neutrals will resist further German influences and some of them will join the Allies. The German propaganda throughout the world will be stopped. The moral weight of the United States will be the deciding force in bringing an early peace, for which you will receive immortal credit, even from the people of Germany. I do not believe we should have to fire a gun or risk a man.

This action moreover will settle the whole question of securing permanent peace. It will bring to our side the full and grateful loyalty of the whole British Empire the British fleet and all the Allies. The great English-speaking nations without any formal alliance will control the conditions of permanent peace. The Japanese threat will be silenced. The saving of human life and treasure will be incalculable. Germany can honorably give in with good grace since all the world will be against her and the internal pressure of her bankrupt and blockaded people will hasten her decision.

Such action would also bring the Administration in line with the sympathies of our people.

On the other hand if we settle the LUSITANIA controversy by any compromise of your original demands or permit it to drag on longer, we can have no part in ending the war. Allied opinion will run so strongly against the Administration that no censorship nor other friendly act of any Allied Government can stem the onrushing European distrust of our Government.

Longer delay or any other plan will bring us only a thankless, opulent and dangerous isolation. The LUSITANIA is the turning point and the time for action is come.

Amembassy London.

T telegram (WP, DLC).

From Robert Lansing, with Enclosure

LUSITANIA

PERSONAL AND CONFIDENTIAL:

My dear Mr. President: [Washington] February 16, 1916.

The German Ambassador called on me this noon and left a letter embodying his Government's reply to our official note of July 21st, 1915, a copy of which I herewith enclose.

I told the Ambassador that I would take the matter under consideration, and would give him no opinion on the subject at the present time.

You will perceive that substantially all our suggestions have been accepted, except the change of the last phrase in paragraph 2 which reads—"as retaliation should be confined to enemy subjects." Our suggestion, you will recall, was—"as retaliation must not prevent the exercise of rights of other than enemy subjects." I am not at all sure whether the difference of phraseology is a substantial one.

In view of the recent manifesto from Berlin in regard to armed merchant vessels[1] I do not see how we can now accept this answer as a settlement of the LUSITANIA case. The German Government was fully advised as to our attitude in regard to the legal right to arm merchant vessels. It was, at the time it gave its three several assurances, with full knowledge of the British Admiralty orders to their merchant vessels, yet they gave those assurances without qualification and they became an essential basis for a settlement of the difficulty. The recent declaration, in which it is stated that armed merchant vessels will be treated as auxilliary cruisers is, therefore, contradictory of their former position and would appear to nullify the assurances which they have given.

I believe it would be well for me to see the German Ambassador again, or else write him a note saying that in view of the recent change of policy by his Government the part of the settlement relating to the future conduct of submarine warfare has been materially changed and will require further consideration by this Government before it can accept as satisfactory the enclosed reply.   Faithfully yours,   Robert Lansing

TLS (Lansing Letterpress Book, SDR, RG 59, DNA).
  1 J. W. Gerard to RL, Feb. 10, 1916. FR-WWS 1916, pp. 163-66. The German government, in a memorandum of February 8, announced its intention to treat, "within a short period," armed merchantmen as ships of war. It said that the offensive use of weapons on merchant ships against submarines, along with the British practice of placing gunnery crews, dressed in civilian clothes and trained in antisubmarine tactics deprived armed enemy merchant ships of "any right to be considered as peaceable vessels of commerce."

E N C L O S U R E

Count Johann Heinrich von Bernstorff to Robert Lansing

My dear Mr. Secretary,

Washington, D. C.,
February 16th, 1916.

With refer[e]nce to my letters of September 1st and October 5th, 1915, concerning the "LUSITANIA" and "ARABIC" cases, I beg to transmit to you the following instructions which I have received from my Government in answer to your official note of July 21st, 1915.

"The German submarine war against England's commerce at sea, as announced on February 4th, 1915, is conducted in retaliation of England's inhuman war against Germany's commercial and industrial life. It is generally recognized as justifiable that retaliation may be employed against acts committed in contravention of the law of nations. Germany is enacting such retaliation, because it is England's endeavor to cut off all imports from Germany by preventing even legal commerce of the neutrals with her and thereby subjecting the German population to starvation. In answer to these acts Germany is making efforts to destroy England's commerce at sea, at least as far as it is carried on by enemy vessels. Germany has notwithstanding limited her submarine warfare, because of her long-standing friendship with the United States and because by the sinking of the Lusitania, which caused the death of citizens of the United States, the German retaliation affected neutrals which was not the intention, as retaliation should be confined to enemy subjects.

The Imperial German Government having subsequent to the sinking of the Lusitania issued to its naval officers the new instructions which are now prevailing, expresses profound regret that citizens of the United States suffered by that event and recognizing its liability therefor stands ready to make reparation for the life of the citizens of the United States who were lost by the payment of a suitable indemnity.

In the note of the American Government of July 21st, 1915, concerning the Lusitania-incident, the Government of the United States invited the practical cooperation of the Imperial Government in contending for the principle of the freedom of the seas and added that this great object could in some way be accomplished before the present war ends. The Imperial Government will at all times gladly cooperate with the Government of the United States for the purpose of accomplishing this common great object."

I remain, my dear Mr. Lansing,

Very sincerely yours,   J. Bernstorff

TLS (SDR, RG 59, 763.72/2392½, DNA).

To Robert Lansing

The White House.

My dear Mr. Secretary,   16 February, 1916.

I have no hesitation in saying that, but for the recent announcement of the Central Powers as to the treatment to which they purpose subjecting armed merchantmen and those which they presume to be armed, it would clearly be our duty in the circumstances to accept the accompanying note as satisfactory. But that announcement inevitably throws doubt upon the whole future, and makes it necessary that we should think the situation out afresh.

I would suggest that you have a frank conversation with the German Ambassador and point out to him just our difficulty— the difficulty of interpreting their recent assurances in the light of their new and dangerous policy, and of understanding that new policy in view of the fact that all circumstances upon which they base their adoption of it were known to them at the time of the ARABIC note.

I doubt whether it would be wise to address a note to him. I think that it would be best, all things considered, to make the interchange of explanations oral only, for the present.

Faithfully Yours,   W.W.

WWTLI (SDR, RG 59, 763.72/2393½, DNA).

To Edward Mandell House

The White House [Feb. 16, 1916].

If you deem it wise it would be advantageous to us to present these considerations in your interviews with members of the government: Germany is seeking to find an excuse to throw off all restraints in under-sea warfare. If she is permitted to assume that English steamers are armed she will have found the excuse. If the English will disarm their merchant ships she will be without excuse and the English will have made a capital stroke against her. We are amazed the English do not see this opportunity to gain a great advantage without losing anything.

WWT telegram (WP, DLC).

To David Franklin Houston

My dear Houston: [The White House] February 16, 1916

It must feel queer to be so young as fifty and I congratulate you not only on being no older in this time of extraordinary opportunity, but on having won a place for yourself of unusual influence and usefulness. I want you to know when you think things over tomorrow what genuine pride I have taken in association with you and with what affectionate admiration I have watched the work you have done here and profited by the counsel you have given me.

With the warmest and most affectionate good wishes, this is to hope for you many, many happy returns.

Cordially and faithfully yours,   Woodrow Wilson

TLS (Letterpress Books, WP, DLC).

To Charles Richard Crane

My dear Friend: [The White House] February 16, 1916

Thank you for your letter of February fourteenth. It contains many matters that I shall look forward to discussing with you, I hope, before long.

In haste, with warmest appreciation,

Faithfully yours,   Woodrow Wilson

TLS (Letterpress Books, WP, DLC).

To Louis J. Wortham[1]

My dear Colonel Wortham:

[The White House]
February 16, 1916

My attention has been called to your very strong and interesting editorial entitled, "You May Fire When Ready, Gridley,"[2] and I cannot resist the impulse to send you a line of sincere appreciation of the thoughtful and public-spirited position which the Star Telegram is taking in a matter which is certainly of vital importance to every citizen of the United States.

Cordially and sincerely yours,   Woodrow Wilson

TLS (Letterpress Books, WP, DLC).
  [1] Owner and editor of the *Fort Worth Star-Telegram*.
  [2] Undated clipping from the *Fort Worth Star-Telegram*, WP, DLC. Although the editorial praised Representative Dies as "perhaps the ablest man from Texas" in Congress, it criticized him for his antipreparedness stand and said that he was defying the sentiment of his constituents. The editorial said that the people of Texas, although they did not necessarily support all specific proposals of the Wilson administration, nevertheless approved of a program for "a powerful navy, adequate coast defenses, and a standing army, bulwarked by a reasonable reserve system."

To James Sprunt

My dear Mr. Sprunt: [The White House] February 16, 1916

It was with the deepest sorrow and most genuine and heartfelt sympathy that I learned of the death of Mrs. Sprunt.[1] My heart goes out to you in this bereavement. I hope that you may be sustained by the only sources that avail in such circumstances.

With warmest regard,

Cordially and sincerely yours,   Woodrow Wilson

TLS (Letterpress Books, WP, DLC).
  [1] Luola Murchison Sprunt.

A Memorandum by Joseph Patrick Tumulty

IN RE SPEECH OF SENATOR ELIHU ROOT, NEW YORK CITY
FEBRUARY 15, 1916.

February 16, 1916.

The speech of Root[1] will be ultimately of great aid to the Democratic party. Accepted by the country as it will be as the keynote of the Republican party, it will in the months to come rise like Banquo's ghost to torture and injure, and ultimately destroy Republican hopes of success.

In view of the attitude toward Germany as expressed by Secretary Lansing today,[2] the speech of Root is a word prematurely spoken for it puts the Republican party in the position of advocating war not only against Germany but against Mexico.

Secondly, it will neutralize the German-American opposition to the President. It will throw the middle-of-the-road advocates of preparedness and pacifists into the lap of the President and all decent men will stand back of him in his efforts for peace.

Root's advocacy of war will further embarrass Mr. Bryan and will bring into closer communion Mr. Roosevelt and the regular Republican party because of the similarity of their views with reference to foreign questions.

The unfortunate part of the Root speech, as far as the Republican party is concerned, is this:

It fixes the issues prematurely,—months in advance of both of the campaigns, and in advance of the settlement of the questions about which he says the Administration has made a failure; namely, the LUSITANIA matter and Mexico, so that he runs the risk, if these questions are satisfactorily settled, of leaving the Republican party bereft of an issue.

But in its larger aspects, it means that the Republican party stands for war and the Democratic party for peace with honor.

T memorandum (J. P. Tumulty Papers, DLC).

[1] Senator Elihu Root, former Secretary of State, had addressed a Republican state convention of New York on Wilson's foreign policy at Carnegie Hall on February 15. Root severely criticized the administration for interfering in the internal affairs of Mexico for the purpose of overthrowing Huerta, whose rule Root characterized as "peaceful" and "orderly." "With the occupation of Vera Cruz," he added, "the moral power of the United States in Mexico ended." Now, under Carranza, he continued, American lives and property in Mexico were in constant jeopardy. Turning to the war in Europe, Root strongly denounced the Wilson administration for failing to protest against the German violation of Belgian neutrality and for not being firmer with Germany on the issue of submarine warfare. "No man should draw a pistol who dares not shoot," he said. "The Government which shakes its fist first and its finger afterward falls into contempt. Our diplomacy has lost its authority and influence because we have been brave in words and irresolute in action." *New York Times*, Feb. 16, 1916.

[2] Tumulty referred to Lansing's statement: "Any settlement of the *Lusitania* case must depend on how German submarine warfare will be conducted in the future. The whole question of submarine warfare is again under consideration by our Government. The question is whether the new German declaration of intention to sink armed enemy liners without warning modifies or nullifies the assurances previously given and made public. The new German declaration opens up the question as to how submarine warfare will be conducted in the future, and all this enters into the settlement of the *Lusitania* case." *New York Times*, Feb. 17, 1916.

To Henry A. Barnhart[1]

[The White House]

My dear Mr. Barnhart: February 17, 1916

I thank you sincerely for the frankness of your letter to Mr. Tumulty of February ninth[2] but cannot let it pass without begging that you will reconsider your determination about the resolution you speak of. I can assure you from abundant knowledge of the circumstances that it would be distinctly hurtful to the cause we all have at heart and not helpful. It would be a serious embarrassment just now.

Cordially and sincerely yours,   Woodrow Wilson

TLS (Letterpress Books, WP, DLC).
  [1] Democratic congressman from Indiana.
  [2] This letter is missing in both the Wilson and Tumulty Papers, hence the subject of his proposed resolution is unknown. Barnhart did not introduce his resolution.

To George Thomas Marye

My dear Mr. Marye: [The White House] February 17, 1916

Allow me to acknowledge the receipt of your letter of January twenty-fifth submitting your resignation as Ambassador to Russia.[1] I do not feel at liberty, in view of what you say of your health, to urge a reconsideration of your resignation and, therefore, accept it with assurances of sincere personal regard.

Very sincerely yours,   Woodrow Wilson

TLS (Letterpress Books, WP, DLC).
  [1] G. T. Marye to WW, Jan. 25, 1916, Vol. 35.

To Joseph Campbell Thompson[1]

                                          [The White House]
My dear Mr. Thompson: February 17, 1916

I am very much complimented that you should wish to name the new horse, "Woodrow Wilson," but I must confess to a very considerable disinclination to the use of my name in that way. I am a great lover of horses but I have always felt that they should have names of their own which were more characteristic than any individual's name could possibly be if bestowed upon them.   Sincerely yours,   Woodrow Wilson

TLS (Letterpress Books, WP, DLC).
  [1] Lawyer and well-known horse breeder and exhibitor of Westchester County, N. Y.

From Thomas Watt Gregory

PERSONAL AND CONFIDENTIAL.

Sir: Washington, D. C. February 17, 1916.

On October 7, 1915, you referred to me the request of the Governors of California, Washington, Oregon and Utah for an investigation by the federal government of the alleged activities of members of the organization known as the Industrial Workers of the World, causing abnormal disorders, arson and other crimes in the states above mentioned.[1]

A careful confidential investigation of this matter has been made at Sacramento, San Francisco, Salt Lake City, Butte, Spokane, Seattle, Portland, Los Angeles and San Diego.

The investigation has shown that the membership of the Industrial Workers of the World is made up for the greater part of agitators, men without homes, mostly foreigners, the discontented and unemployed who are not anxious to work, and men of a very low order of intelligence and morals.

The headquarters of the Industrial Workers of the World are in Chicago. The local societies' income is derived from the sale of literature, weekly smokers, dances, etc., one-fifth of the monthly receipts being sent to Chicago for organization and general management.

The membership numbers about 2,000 in each of the states of California and Washington. The movement in Utah and Oregon is receding.

The leaders of the Industrial Workers of the World preach "direct action" and "sabotage." By "direct action" is meant the use of force to accomplish the result desired, and by "sabotage" is meant the wiping out or preventing profits to employers by deliberate inefficiency on the part of employes, as, for instance, working slowly, doing poor work, telling trade secrets, mis-sending packages, giving over weight to customers, etc., etc.

The principal definite statement which alarmed the governors of the states above mentioned, was that of one James McGill, now confined in the penitentiary at San Quentin, California, who told of an elaborate plan to which himself and two other named men were parties to destroy by fire a large number of places which he named.

McGill was examined at the penitentiary by the agent assigned to this investigation at which time he repudiated his previous statements made to state officials. He has been in two reform schools, three times in the State Hospital for the Insane at Howard, R. I., the St. Mary's Industrial Home, Baltimore, Maryland, Blackwell's Island, the United States penitentiary at Leavenworth, the Washington Asylum Hospital, and the Government Hospital for the Insane. He appears to have a mania for confessing crimes with which he had no connection. It is not believed his original confession is true.[2]

A summary of the result of this investigation has been fur-

nished to the Governor of California for the information of himself and the Governors of Oregon, Washington and Utah.[3] It
failed to develop any evidence of violations of the federal statutes
except in the mailing of certain publications and the writing of
obscene and incendiary letters, particularly to the Governor of
the State of California, by individual members of the Industrial
Workers of the World. Unfortunately, with a single exception,[4]
Governor Johnson promptly destroyed these letters. This letter
has been turned over to the Post Office Department which is making a further investigation with respect to it and the publications
issued by the Society or its members and sent through the mail.

Respectfully,   T. W. Gregory

TLS (WP, DLC).
 [1] WW to T. W. Gregory, Oct. 7, 1915, TLS (DJR, RG 60, 150139-48, DNA). The
western governors had sent a telegram to Secretary Lane on October 5, 1915, saying that their states were experiencing "abnormal disorder and incendiarism"
and threats by I.W.W. leaders. They asked Lane to intercede with "the proper
federal authorities" to launch an investigation of the I.W.W. on the ground that
there were "indications of an interstate conspiracy and misuse of mails." F. K.
Lane to WW, Oct. 6, 1915, TLS, enclosing H. W. Johnson *et al.* to F. K. Lane,
Oct. 5, 1915, T telegram (DJR, RG 60, 150139-48, DNA). Lane discussed the matter with Gregory, who thought that Wilson should order such an investigation.
Wilson complied and asked Gregory to begin an inquiry which, as Wilson put
it, seemed "to mean so much to the whole section which it concerns." Wilson
made an identical request of Burleson at the same time. WW to A. S. Burleson,
Oct. 7, 1915, TLS (Letterpress Books, WP, DLC).
 [2] Information about McGill, including the agent's report, is missing. Gregory,
however, had informed Governor Johnson that "information was secured throwing considerable doubt upon the guilt of one James McGill." T. W. Gregory
to H. W. Johnson, Jan. 17, 1916, CCL (DJR, RG 60, 150139-48, DNA).
 [3] It is missing. Assistant Attorney General William Wallace, Jr., explained
to Governor Johnson that the Justice Department had concluded that it would
"not be possible to develop violations of the Federal criminal laws by these
people, unless by use of the mails." W. Wallace, Jr., to H. W. Johnson, Dec.
15, 1916, (DJR, RG 60, 150139-47, DNA). Burleson apparently took no action,
either. In any event, the Editors have not found any documents in the Post Office
Department files, DNA, or in the Burleson Papers, DLC, relating to this matter.
 [4] "I.W.W." to H. W. Johnson, Sept. 14, 1915, TCL (DJR, RG 60, 150139-46,
DNA). It was indeed obscene.

From David Franklin Houston

My dear Mr. President: Washington February 17, 1916.

Kipling once wrote this:

"You are a contemptible lot, over yonder. Some of you are
Commissioners, and some Lieutenant-Governors, and some
have the V.C., and a few are privileged to walk about the
Mall arm in arm with the Viceroy; but I have seen Mark
Twain this golden morning, have shaken his hand, and
smoked a cigar—no, two cigars—with him, and talked with
him for more than two hours! Understand clearly that I do

not despise you; indeed, I don't. I am only very sorry for you, from the Viceroy downward."[1]

I received your note yesterday afternoon. I am trying not to feel sorry for Kipling and the Viceroy and the rest of the lot here and there. I am deeply grateful to you.

I am highly content to "sit in order" in the boat and "to smite the sounding furrows" while you skillfully steer and command.

Faithfully yours,   D. F. Houston

TLS (WP, DLC).
[1] Rudyard Kipling, "An Interview with Mark Twain," in *From Sea to Sea, Letters of Travel* (2 vols., New York, 1899), II, 167.

From Willard Saulsbury

My dear Mr. President: Washington, D. C. February 17, 1916.

Your note of February 14th regarding Mr. MacMurrey reached my office yesterday when I was in Delaware and I reply at the earliest opportunity. I feel of course that you would not desire a man who is not qualified for the position to be placed in one for which he was unfitted and your judgment is so usually correct that I would not venture to differ with it regarding a man unless I had personal knowledge and experience justifying me in forming a rather firm conclusion as to his capacity or qualifications.

I have been able to form such a conclusion regarding Mr. Mac-Murrey from personal observation and if you desire, I should be very glad to tell you of my observation and experiences at Pekin last Summer, where Mr. MacMurrey was acting as Charge in the absence of Minister Reinsch. I hold myself in readiness any time you would care to see me and should be glad to help you check the matter up in any way.[1]

Yours very truly,   Willard Saulsbury

TLS (WP, DLC).
[1] There is no record of a meeting between Wilson and Saulsbury about this matter.

From Charles Richard Crane

Dear Mr President   [New York] February 17, 1916

Your friend Cleveland Dodge is demonstrating his loyalty and devotion to you and your Administration by defending in his usual vigorous way the nomination of Brandeis.

Norman Hapgood has been here to-day and made two interesting suggestions which I pass on with hearty approval. One is George Rublee for Russia. He is in an independant position, is accustomed to large affairs and important negotiations and has the proper temperament (a vital thing in these campaign days) to get along with Russian people who are simple in their modes of thought and the most democratic I know of.

The other suggestion is of Frederick Delano for a cabinet position. I once dwelt at length on this subject with Colonel House and have not changed any opinion of his value in consultations and his relations. He was born and brought up in New England (which is no handicap up around Boston) and his family is greatly respected in that benighted neighborhood. His active life has been spent in the West where he is highly esteemed for his ability, candor and serenity. I believe he would contribute a valuable element to your cabinet and be a most popular appointment in parts of the country where popularity would do no harm even in a campaign year.

I shall be in Washington the latter part of next week and hope to find you as serene as you ought to be after Root's speech.

With warmest greetings,

Always devotedly   Charles R. Crane

ALS (WP, DLC).

Sir Cecil Arthur Spring Rice to Sir Edward Grey

Private.

[Washington] R. 10 a.m., February 17th 1916.

Your telegram of February 16th.[1]

I fear Colonel H. is imperfectly informed as to recent occurrences. Question was not raised by us nor was any publicity given to it till State Department and German Embassy allowed news to transpire. Allies have made no official reply and I have merely communicated your telegram No. 256 unofficially.[2] State Department and German Embassy have issued daily statements in the Press while allies have been silent.

Part of Press took a strong line against United States proposal: an important member of the Cabinet resigned and Mr. Root's speech made to-day was in substance known beforehand to the President while a debate was impending in Congress in the course of which severe criticisms were inevitable.

In the circumstances President is understood to be ready to allow guns to remain if their size is diminished so as to render them inefficient and this concession has been publicly announced.[3]

It has now been stated that change of attitude is due to Colonel House's representations from London.

Belief here is that proposal was part of an arrangement with Germany in order to gain certain advantages, domestic and foreign, and that it was withdrawn in spite of strong campaign in its favour in consequence of strong expressions of disapproval in the country at large and fear among shipping circles of withdrawal of allied shipping from United States ports. From beginning to end we have had nothing whatever to do with the question and I hope we will defer all further communications official or private until allies give their joint official answer.

T telegram (E. Grey Papers, FO 800/86, PRO).
   1 E. Grey to C. A. Spring Rice, Feb. 16, 1916, HwI telegram (E. Grey Papers, FO 800/86, p. 64, PRO). Colonel House, Grey wrote, had told him that he hoped that the American government would leave the question of the arming of merchant vessels open until his return to the United States. In the meantime, House had advised Grey that Britain should let the matter rest and, unless the question of armed ships was discussed in Congress, should avoid giving it unnecessary publicity.
   2 That is, E. Grey to C. A. Spring Rice, Feb. 3, 1916, printed as an Enclosure with RL to WW, Feb. 5, 1916.
   3 On February 15, Wilson and Lansing had agreed that they had made a serious mistake in proposing the *modus vivendi* at this particular time, and in threatening to treat *all* armed ships as warships and intimating that they would warn Americans against traveling on them. Consequently, Lansing announced on the same day that the American government would not insist that the *modus vivendi* be accepted if the Allies should reject it. The Washington government would not classify *defensively* armed merchantmen as warships, but it might well insist that a merchant ship was armed offensively when its armament was superior to that of a submarine. The administration, Lansing concluded, would not warn Americans against traveling on merchantmen armed *solely* for defense, and would take strong measures if American citizens should lose their lives in the event that German submarines sank such vessels without warning. For a detailed account, see Link, *Wilson: Confusions and Crises*, pp. 161-64.

Sir Edward Grey to Sir Cecil Arthur Spring Rice

PERSONAL.

[London] 17 February 1916, 5 p.m.

Colonel House made no complaint whatever and did not suggest that any thing undesirable had been done by me or the Embassy. His remarks to me were pure precaution without faintest hint of reproach as far as you or I are concerned.

Please never suppose that a telegram from me as to precautions in future implies some unspoken criticism of past action.

I told Colonel House, as I had previously told American Ambassador here, of unfavourable impression produced on me by the American communication about defensive armament: he apprehended that views I had already expressed might become known inopportunely and make it more difficult for President to take a strong line. I thought there was reason in this; it agreed with my view; and I telegraphed to you the precaution which I intended to observe myself: it seems from last words of your telegram that you also agree with this view; so happily we all agree.

T telegram (E. Grey Papers, FO 800/86, PRO).

From Robert Lansing, with Enclosure

PERSONAL AND CONFIDENTIAL:

My dear Mr. President: Washington February 18, 1916.
    You are perfectly right in what you stated to me over the telephone in regard to the message from London which I handed you this morning. It is undoubtedly the expression of the Ambassador.
    This message is the same one that was sent to us day before yesterday which we were unable to decipher, and which was repeated in the Green code but read backwards after being interpreted. I am relieved to find that it is not the expression of Colonel House, as I was unable to see any consistency between this dispatch and the dispatches which he had been sending previously.
    I am enclosing herewith a memorandum of the conversation which I had yesterday noon with the German Ambassador.
                    Faithfully yours,   Robert Lansing.

TLS (WP, DLC).

E N C L O S U R E

MEMORANDUM OF A CONVERSATION HAD WITH
THE GERMAN AMBASSADOR AT NOON

February 17, 1916.

    At my request the German Ambassador called upon me today and I told him that his letter of February 16th, relative to the LUSITANIA case I believed would be acceptable to this Government were it not for the fact that Germany had issued a new declaration of policy in regard to submarine warfare. I pointed out to him that there had been in the LUSITANIA controversy two questions—one as to the future conduct of submarine warfare and the other as to proper amends for past conduct; that I had assumed the assurances which had been given by Germany in regard to the future conduct of her submarine commanders settled that branch of the controversy; that in our informal conversations we had only discussed what amends Germany should make for the sinking of the LUSITANIA; and that now, when the branch of the controversy which related to past conduct was substantially settled this declaration of new policy appeared to open up again the part of the controversy which related to the future.

The Ambassador replied that he did not see how this directly affected the assurances which had been given as the assurances related to liners. I told him that the declaration of principle as to submarine warfare in the Mediterranean was not limited in any way, nor was anything said about vessels being armed or unarmed; that that declaration was very comprehensive and would certainly be modified very materially if the present policy was put into effect.

The Ambassador asked me if I thought it would be advisable for Germany to postpone the time for a month at least before putting the policy into operation. I told him that might temporarily relieve apprehension and make easier our future negotiations which he must realize would have to continue, in view of this new departure on the part of his Government.

He asked me if he could say to his Government that otherwise than as to the future of submarine warfare his letter of the 16th was satisfactory. I said no he could not say it was satisfactory, but that he might say in the circumstances that it was acceptable, although I should regret his putting it into formal shape before this other matter was decided.

He said he would communicate the substance of this conversation to his Government and hoped to obtain from them an interpretation or expression which would satisfy our fears as to the new policy.   Robert Lansing

CC MS (WP, DLC).

From Thomas Watt Gregory

Dear Mr. President: Washington, D. C. February 18, 1916.
     You have asked me the following question:
     When may the militia be said to be "in the service of the United States?" May they, for example, be said to be "in the service of the United States" when called into camp for drill in association with units of the regular army and in the pay of the United States?
     One view, of course, is that the militia are "in the service of the United States" only when called forth "to execute the laws of the Union, suppress insurrections, and repel invasions."

Thus, in a case recently decided by the Court of Claims (*Ala. Great Southern R.R. Co.* v. *United States*, 49 Ct. Cl., 522) the view seems to have been taken that the militia are not "in the service of the United States" when they are in camp in association with units of the regular army pursuant to the Act of January 21, 1903 (32 Stat., 775), as amended by the Act of May 27, 1908 (35 Stat., 399), although all that it was necessary to decide in that case was that the militia were not "in the service of the United States" during the transportation to and from the camp.

Again, in *Johnson* v. *Sayre*, 158 U.S., 109, the following statement occurs:

Congress is thus expressly vested with the power to make rules for the government of the whole regular army and navy at all times and to provide for governing such part only of the militia of the several States as, having been called forth to execute the laws of the Union, to suppress insurrections, or to repel invasions, is employed in the service of the United States.

This seems to imply that the militia would not be "in the service of the United States" except where called forth to execute the laws of the Union, to suppress insurrections, or to repel invasions, although a decision on that point does not seem to have been necessary to a disposition of the case before the Court.

Notwithstanding these expressions there seems to me to be ground for taking a broader view, namely, that the militia may be called into camp by the Federal Government at stated times as a necessary or at least expedient means of providing for their proper organization and discipline, and that when so assembled they are "in the service of the United States," as well as when called forth for actual service in war or to preserve domestic peace and order. But whether or not in such case they are "in the service of the United States," I am of the opinion—and, if I understand correctly, that is the point of your inquiry—that Congress has power to call the militia into camp for drill in association with units of the regular army, as a necessary or at least appropriate means of carrying into execution the power to organize and discipline them. (*McCulloch* v. *State of Maryland*, 4 Wheat., 316, 421.)

Very sincerely yours,   T. W. Gregory

TLS (WP, DLC).

From Hugh Lenox Scott

My dear Mr. President: Washington, D. C. February 18, 1916.

Your kind letter of the 14th was duly received. The office of the Chief of Staff of the Army is the greatest to which a soldier may aspire, but it would only be ashes in the mouth without your confidence, and having this I go forward with renewed courage.

I think, however, that some one has told you that the plan for a Continental Army was urged because it would be a step toward conscription. I think you have already seen that this would not be any more true of a "Continental" Army than of one formed from the National Guard or by any plan that fails to produce the requisite number of men voluntarily—as if the number will not come forward for any plan voluntarily the Nation must resort to the draft or go without.

Thanking you very much for your letter, I am

Sincerely yours,   H. L. Scott

TLS (WP, DLC).

From Robert Lansing, with Enclosure

PERSONAL AND CONFIDENTIAL:

My dear Mr. President: Washington February 19, 1916.

I enclose a confidential letter which I have received from Mr. Fletcher in regard to the attitude of the Chilean Government toward the proposed Pan American treaty, and indicating the efforts which are being made by that Government to prevent its being entered into by the three principal powers of South America.

I also enclose a dispatch which I assume you have seen, from Mr. Stimson,[1] showing that Naón is in full sympathy with this Government and that they cannot count on Argentina to assist in the defeat of the treaty.

My own belief is that if they cannot maintain the triple alliance which they have,[2] that Brazil may be persuaded to abandon Chile in her efforts to prevent such a treaty being signed. I have an impression, although I have no evidence to that effect, that there may be some foreign power at work in the countries which seem to be lukewarm, or hostile to the proposed agreement. Of course I may be entirely wrong about this but the more I think of it the stronger my impression grows.

Faithfully yours,   Robert Lansing.

TLS (WP, DLC).
¹ F. J. Stimson to RL, Feb. 18, 1916, T telegram (SDR, RG 59, 710.11/240, DNA).
² See n. 8 to the Enclosure.

ENCLOSURE

Henry Prather Fletcher to Robert Lansing

PERSONAL AND CONFIDENTIAL.

Dear Mr. Secretary: Santiago, Chile January 21, 1916.

Upon receipt of your telegram of the 3rd instant[1] directing me to express to the Minister for Foreign Affairs[2] confidentially and informally your hope that Chile would be willing to accept in principle the four articles of the Pan-American Treaty, the text of which had already been mailed by Suárez, I immediately waited upon Mr. Ramón Subercaseaux, the Minister for Foreign Affairs. Although he had been in office but a short time, he was familiar with the general outline of the treaty and expressed himself as personally favorably impressed by the idea. He explained, however, that inasmuch as the cabinet had resigned and that he was holding office merely until his successor should be selected, it would be impossible for him to endeavor to give an answer within the short time allowed. He also stated that in so grave a matter it would be necessary for the Government to consult with the leading men of the country; that owing to the fierce political struggle which has raged in Chile since last June it had been impossible for the Chilean Ministries, as they passed through the Moneda,[3] to take up a serious international problem such as this one. A few days afterwards the President[4] was able to form, as I have reported in my official despatches, a Ministry in which all parties are represented and for the first time since the Presidential nominations were made last summer has it been possible for this Government to study, with the aid of the Senate and House Committees on Foreign Affairs, this question. Mr. Subercaseaux remained as Minister for Foreign Affairs.

Your announcement at the close of the Pan-American Scientific Congress of the general outline of the proposed treaty was telegraphed to and published in the newspapers here. The Gov-

¹ RL to H. P. Fletcher, Jan. 3, 1916, T telegram (SDR, RG 59, 710.11/218a, DNA). Fletcher had replied summarizing the first portion of his letter (down to "within the short time allowed") in H. P. Fletcher to RL, Jan. 4, 1916, T telegram (SDR, RG 59, 710.11/219, DNA).
² Ramon Subercaseaux Vicuña, who had assumed his post on December 23, 1915.
³ The presidential palace in Santiago.
⁴ Juan Luis Sanfuentes Andonaegui.

ernment called a meeting of the Senate and House Committees on Foreign Relations and laid before them (more particularly the Senate committee) the antecedents and correspondence on the President's plan. The meeting of the Senate committee lasted a number of hours and the proposed treaty was fully discussed in all its bearings, and the conclusion was reached that the treaty as outlined in Mr. Suárez' communication is inacceptable to Chile, especially the article relating to the settlement of territorial disputes, involving as it would the acceptance on the part of Chile of the arbitration of the *Tacna-Arica* dispute.

As I pointed out to you in a former private letter the *Tacna-Arica* difficulty enters into almost every phase of Chile's foreign policy. They have been always unwilling to accept arbitration of this dispute. Their principal objection to the first draft of Mr. Bryan's peace treaty was because it might be construed as a departure from their traditional policy, and it was only when it had been amended to apply to future difficulties that they could be induced to sign it.

It seems that the sentiment of the Government and leading men of Chile is unanimously against the proposed Pan-American treaty as at present drawn. Having decided upon its attitude it was to be expected that Chile would immediately turn to Brazil for support in its opposition to the clause of the article above mentioned. It seems that Müller[5] has always been very keen to have the word 'republican' retained in the article referring to the form of government. Suárez, however, was decidedly opposed. The Chilean Government, not considering the point essential, has instructed Irarrázaval[6] to say to Müller that it will have no difficulty in acceding to his desires in this respect and has appealed to him for support of their objections. According to Irarrázaval's telegrams, (which I have just read at the Foreign Office) Müller immediately promised Brazil's support in the first interview, but asked Irarrázaval to return the following day after he should have had opportunity to consult with the President of Brazil. Subsequently he informed Irarrázaval that he had consulted with the President and could assure him that Chile might count upon the loyal support of Brazil in her objections, and that Brazil would not proceed further with the negotiations until the objections were obviated. In Irarrázaval's presence he dictated to Da Gama a telegram making this clear in indirect but positive language. The Brazilian Minister for Foreign Affairs, according to Irarrázaval, called the Argentine Minister[7] and asked him to find out

---

[5] The Brazilian Foreign Minister, Lauro Müller.
[6] Alfredo Irarrázaval Zañartu, Chilean Ambassador to Brazil.
[7] Lucas Ayarragaray.

what the attitude of his Government would be in view of the Chilean attitude. The Argentine Minister replied to the effect that while Argentine sentiment had hitherto inclined, perhaps, on the side of Peru in the *Tacna-Arica* difficulty, nevertheless the signing of the A.B.C. treaty[8] last May had considerably modified the Argentine position, and that he felt sure his Government would be unwilling to do anything which might embarrass Chile in this or any other of its international relations, and promised to communicate with his Government as requested by Müller. The Chilean Government has also taken steps to sound the Argentine Government as to how far it may count upon its support. Up to this time I have not heard what answer the Argentine Government has made either here or in Brazil.

You know, of course, that Ecuador is closely allied in interest with Chile. Müller in one of his conversations with Irarrázaval, suggested that it might be well to make the Ecuadorian Government acquainted with the Chilean attitude as to the proposed treaty. This suggestion Irarrázaval repeated to the Foreign Office here and it has already been acted upon; the Minister, however, in his telegram to Eastman[9] (Chilean Minister in Quito) was careful to confine himself to a simple statement of the fact that the draft of the proposed treaty had been submitted to the Senate Committee of Foreign Affairs and found inacceptable for the reasons above given, *verbum sap.*

I have been told a number of times, and it was repeated to me yesterday in the confidential interview which I had at the Foreign Office, which is the source of the information embodied in this letter, that Mr. Murature,[10] Argentine Minister for Foreign Affairs, when in Chile with Müller last May stated to Mr. Lira,[11] then Minister for Foreign Affairs, that the Wilson plan was *desestimado* (not highly regarded) in the Argentine. Mr. Naon, however, when here recently as Special Ambassador for the inauguration, seemed extremely keen and very anxious to discuss the matter with the new President of Chile, but was unable to do so. When in view of the statement of Morature I mentioned that this did not seem to harmonize with the almost enthusiastic attitude of Mr. Naon when in Chile recently, I received the reply that the discrepancy might be explained if Naon were exceeding his instructions and going further than his Government, or that

[8] Argentina, Brazil, and Chile had signed a five-year treaty in Buenos Aires on May 25, 1915, in which they agreed to submit any disputes among themselves to neutral investigation and to act in concert on international issues.

[9] Victor Eastman Cox.

[10] José Luis Murature.

[11] Alejandro Lira.

the Argentine Government while not attaching great intrinsic importance to the treaty might be using it to improve its relations with the United States, leaving to Chile and Brazil the onus of objection. I am inclined to think, however, that in view of the new-found A.B.C. formula that Argentine will support Chile in her objections. In fact, unless they are willing to allow the alphabetical lute to expose a rift within less than a year they will be obliged to do so.

Another comment which I have heard is that Chile understood that the treaty was not to be opened out to the other American nations until first agreed upon with the A.B.C. Powers. To this, not knowing definitely the inception of the negotiations, I made no reply.

Since my telegram of September 9th[12] I have not discussed this matter at the Foreign Office, except in a casual way, until the receipt of your telegram of January 3rd. I hesitated somewhat in sending my telegram today and in writing you this long letter, but concluded that the information covered by them might be of interest to you.

Apologizing for the inordinate length of this letter, I am, with highest regard,

Yours very sincerely,   Henry P. Fletcher

TLS (WP, DLC).
    [12] H. P. Fletcher to RL, Sept. 9, 1915, T telegram (SDR, RG 59, 710.11/202, DNA). It reads: "I believe Chilean Government can be brought to accept substantially the President's plan. Minister for Foreign Affairs is ready to open negotiations with me with that end in view. I have read the telegrams exchanged between the Foreign Office and Suarez on the subject and the Minister has offered to place all the papers in my hands. Would the President and the Department like to have me proceed with the negotiations here."

From Albert, King of the Belgians

Monsieur le Président,   La Panne, le 20 février 1916.

J'ai été charmé de recevoir à La Panne la visite du Colonel House et d'avoir un entretien avec lui. Les assurances qu'il m'a données des sentiments d'amitié que vous nourrissez à l'égard de la Belgique et de ma personne m'ont touché infiniment. Je tiens à vous en exprimer mes remerciments les plus sincères et à être en même temps auprès de vous l'interprète de la profonde gratitude du peuple belge pour tout ce que la nation américaine a fait et fait encore tous les jours, en vue de secourir notre malheureuse population et les blessés de notre armée.

J'ai la conviction que votre influence et votre intervention auprès des belligérants auront un heureux effet, quand le moment sera venue de discuter les conditions de la paix, pour assurer le triomphe du droit et établir en Europe un état de chose durable.

A ce moment aussi, la Belgique aura plus que jamais besoin du concours bienveillant des Etats Unis en vue de se relever de ses ruines et de recommencer une nouvelle existence de travail et de progrès.

Croyez, Monsieur le Président, à mes sentiments de haute estime et de sincère amitié   Albert

HwLS (WP, DLC).

TRANSLATION

Mr. President: La Panne, February 20, 1916.

I have been charmed to receive at La Panne the visit from Colonel House and to have an interview with him. The assurances that he gave me of the feelings of friendship that you cherish concerning Belgium and myself, personally, have touched me infinitely. I take this opportunity to express to you my most sincere thanks and, at the same time, to convey to you the profound gratitude of the Belgian people for all that the American nation has done and continues to do in succoring our unhappy population and the wounded of our army.

I am convinced that your influence and your intervention vis-à-vis the belligerents will have a happy effect when the moment will come in sight to discuss the terms of peace, by assuring the triumph of right and by establishing a more lasting state of affairs in Europe. When this time comes, also, Belgium will more than ever need the sustaining support of the United States when it undertakes to reconstruct its ruins and recommence a new existence of work and progress.

Accept, Mr. President, my sentiments of high esteem and of sincere friendship.   Albert

To Charles Richard Crane

My dear Friend: [The White House] February 21, 1916

Thank you for your letter of February seventeenth. It is always delightful to hear from you.

I had understood that you thought the selection of ex-Governor David R. Francis of Missouri[1] an excellent one for Russia, and I had already offered him the place, an offer which he now has under consideration, before your suggestion about Rublee came. I believe in any case that to have put Rublee through the Senate would have been a very difficult undertaking.[2]

As for Delano for a Cabinet position, I had had that suggestion from other quarters as well and you may be sure have been giving it very thoughtful consideration. The choice is a difficult one and I want to be sure to make it the right one.

It is pleasant to know that you will soon be here and I can get a glimpse of you.

In haste

Cordially and faithfully yours,   Woodrow Wilson

TLS (Letterpress Books, WP, DLC).
[1] David Rowland Francis was appointed Ambassador to Russia on March 6, 1916.
[2] The Senate, after much debate, had failed to confirm Rublee's nomination to the Federal Trade Commission on March 2, 1915, and had adjourned on March 4 without taking further action. Wilson thereupon had given Rublee a recess appointment to the commission on March 6, 1915. *New York Times*, Feb. 23 and 27, and March 3, 5, and 7, 1915.

Two Telegrams from Edward Mandell House

London (Received 9:00 a.m., Feb. 21, 1916.)[1]

I have discussed the question of disarming of merchantmen with government and many others, including Bryce, and they are unanimous in opposition to it. I cannot give you a clear understanding of the situation until my return. Everything else is satisfactory and I am eager to report what my visit has accomplished. I am sailing on the Rotterdam February twenty-fifth.

Edward House.

EBWhw decode of T telegram (WP, DLC).
[1] House's copy of this telegram is dated Feb. 20.

[London] 21 February '16.

I have initiated much favorable comment in behalf of your Pan-American policy. I suggested to Sir Edward Grey that he have the question put to the government in Parliament in regard to the time in which he could give a favorable reply. This will be done if it meets the approval of the Canadian Prime Minister. There is a reason for this which I will explain in person.

Edward House.

T transcript of WWsh decode (WC, NjP) of T telegram (WP, DLC).

To William Joel Stone

My dear Senator: [The White House] February 22, 1916

I have been not a little concerned about the matter to which you call my attention in your letter of February twenty-first.[1] A general strike on the railroads just now would be nothing less than a calamity and I am already seeking not only information, but some way to use my good offices.

Cordially and sincerely yours,   Woodrow Wilson

TLS (Letterpress Books, WP, DLC).

[1] W. J. Stone to WW, Feb. 21, 1916, TLS (WP, DLC), enclosing Association of Western Railways, Executive Committee, *Employees Not Asking Real Eight-Hour Day*, dated Feb. 8, 1916; *Average Wage of Enginemen and Trainmen $1253 a Year*, dated Feb. 16, 1916; and *Aristocrats of the Labor World*, dated Feb. 20, 1916, printed leaflets (WP, DLC).

The heads of the Brotherhood of Locomotive Engineers, the Brotherhood of Locomotive Firemen and Enginemen, the Brotherhood of Railroad Trainmen, and the Order of Railway Conductors, representing some 400,000 workers, had agreed at a meeting in Chicago on December 15, 1915, to demand the eight-hour day and time and a half for overtime. They immediately sent out a mail ballot to their respective memberships and soon let it be known that they intended to back up their demands with a nationwide strike and, moreover, that they would not accept arbitration of their demands.

The railroad spokesmen, in the leaflets cited above, claimed that the brotherhoods' real purpose was to increase wages indirectly to the total amount of $100,000,000, which the public would have to pay. The railroad spokesmen added that the brotherhoods' demands were all the more unjustified because railroad workers were already among the best paid in the country. To Senator Stone, the uncompromising attitude of the employers had "an ominous prospect." "Would it not be well," he asked in his letter to Wilson, "if something could be done to bring these opposing interests into harmony and thus prevent a condition that would be exceedingly unfortunate to the country?"

From Clarinda Huntington Pendleton Lamar

My dear Mr. President: Atlanta, Georgia. February 22, 1916.

I cannot tell you how much I appreciate the photograph you have sent me, and the kind expression of friendship which accompanies it.

My sons and I have many priceless legacies from my dear Husband:—his honoured name, the character he bore, the work which he accomplished, and the ideals that he realized,—but first and best of all,—as he expressed it in his will,—"the friendships, many and precious which he left to his family in the hope that they will be continued and cherished."

I cling to these things more and more, as the days go by with no comfort in them.

I am, my dear Mr. President,

Very sincerely and gratefully yours,

Clarinda P. Lamar.

ALS (WP, DLC).

Remarks to a Group of Hungarian Americans[1]

[Feb. 23, 1916]

Mr. Konta: You have thanked me, sir, for receiving you. I do not deserve any thanks; it is a real pleasure to have received you and a privilege to have seen so many of you upon such an errand. I want to say that, so far as my own feelings and opinions are concerned, the errand was unnecessary. I have never myself doubted for a moment, sir, the feeling that gentlemen such as yourselves have towards America. I recognize you as just as much Americans as anybody born in this country.

I have deplored, and I am sure you have united with me in deploring, the spirit which has been manifested by some who have misrepresented those for whom they professed to speak. And my public protests have been against what they said, and against their misrepresentations of what I felt sure was the sentiment of the rank and file of those Americans born on the other side of the water, who have come and enriched America by giving us their talents and their work and their allegiance. So that I welcome this occasion as an opportunity to express my unqualified confidence in those thoughtful citizens like yourselves who have identified themselves in heart as well as in fortune with this great country, which is so dear to all of us, which is compounded of all of us, and which does not belong to any one section or portion of us. I have tried to show, on various occasions, my passion for that equality which ought to obtain amongst all those who profess allegiance to the United States.

I feel highly complimented by this and—I will not say reassured because I did not need the reassurance—but very much cheered by the message you have brought me. I thank you sincerely.

T MS (WP, DLC).

[1] A delegation of Hungarian Americans from New York had come to the White House to express to Wilson their allegiance to the United States. They were led by Alexander Konta, a Hungarian-born businessman and author who had settled in the United States in 1887. In his opening remarks to Wilson, Konta said, in part: "Your Excellency's reception of us today is proof that you believe in our loyalty. You, sir, clothed with the supreme authority of the nation, give us officially in the nation's name, evidence of its trust in us." *New York Times*, Feb. 24, 1916.

To Edward Mandell House

The White House. 23 February, 1916.

I can say positively that all the information which has been given to the press about the LUSITANIA controversy has come directly and deliberately from the German Embassy here for the purpose of affecting public opinion on both sides of the sea.

WWT telegram (WP, DLC).

From William Kent

Dear Mr. President: Washington, D. C. February 23, 1916.

An extremely influential Member on the Republican side of the House, who has always played fair and desires to have things done for the good of the country irrespective of any effect on partisan politics, called to my attention some matters in the Rainey bill which I herewith enclose,[1] that seem to me to be extremely pertinent.

First, we had a lot of discussion in the Sixty-second Congress over the question of the Tariff Commission reporting to the House rather than to the President. Mr. Rainey's bill provides that the proposed Tariff Commission should report to the Ways and Means Committee. My friend seemed to believe that it will be important to provide that the Commission should publish its report and address it to the House as well as to the Ways and Means Committee of the House. The off-hand penciled amendment which you will find in the bill, I believe covers this ground.

A much more important feature which goes direct to the heart of the non-partisan idea that you are so anxious to establish, is suggested by the unfortunate word "effects" found in Sections 3 and 5. My friend seemed to think that this word carried with it a meaning which could only be translated in partisan terms. If the country were prosperous, the Democrats on the Commission might say that it was due to the "effects" of the tariff and if the opposite were the case, the Republicans, under a Democratic Administration, would say that the hardship was an "effect" of the tariff. He laid great stress on this proposition and after having seen the ridiculous emanations of the Progressives in Chicago who called for a non-partisan tariff board to report tariff measures "on a protective theory,"[2] I can see a lot of wisdom in his criticism.

It is his belief that if the bill embodies the suggestions made, it will receive very large support on the Republican side. Republican opponents of the measure would be pretty well gagged if they can find no foundation upon which to raise a charge of partisanship.

I understand that there is considerable Democratic opposition due to the fact that some prominent Democratic Members are anxious to dictate the appointments of Commissioners so as to be sure that the Democratic theory, whatever it may be, will be valorously represented in the Commission.

I have spoken to Mr. Rainey who thoroughly coincides with the suggestions made and believe that he will talk matters over with some of the fair minded people on the Republican side of the House, to the end of securing their support. It is needless for me to say that in my opinion, the open-minded Members on the Republican side greatly prefer that you should make appointments of men who will report fairly the facts and not disfigure their reports by partisan opinion, than that partisans on both sides should be appointed to the end of eternal wrangling. Whether there should be embodied in the bill a prohibition of expressing opinion outside of facts and figures is for the proponents of the bill to determine. For my part, I do not believe that the Tariff Commission should officially express any opinion except when called upon and cross examined by the members of the Ways and Means Committee of the House or the Finance Committee of the Senate.

I wish to thank you for a most delightful entertainment last night.[3] I am not at all musical but Mr. Paderewski's piano playing was the most wonderful thing I have heard in a musical way. It represented disembodied music and I never had any thought that he was playing the piano.

Yours truly, William Kent

TLS (WP, DLC).
    [1] H.R. 10585, 64th Cong., 1st sess. (WP, DLC). Introduced on February 1, 1916, it provided for the creation of a federal tariff commission.
    [2] Kent referred to the tariff plank of the Progressive party's "Declaration of Principles," issued by its preconvention meeting in Chicago on January 11, 1916. *New York Times*, Jan. 12, 1916.
    [3] At a dinner in honor of the Speaker of the House of Representatives. Ignace Jan Paderewski gave a piano concert in the East Room after the dinner and met Wilson for the first time.

From Sir Horace Plunkett

Dear Mr President,   London. 23rd February, 1916.

Colonel House, who to the regret of many besides myself is leaving London to-day, has explained to me your views upon the defensive arming of merchantmen. As I was not able to agree with these views, but am sensible of the motives which inspired them, he suggested that I might write a letter to you giving the grounds of my dissent.

I ought perhaps to say that I am the son of a sailor who was born so long ago that, as he once told me, he could well remember the rejoicing when the news of the battle of Waterloo reached London. So I am naturally obsessed by the British sea psychology. I think, however, that I can look at the matter from a fairly detached point of view.

If I rightly understand the position you take up upon this question, you hold that the submarine, having proved its efficiency, is entitled to be recognised as a legitimate instrument of war on commerce. At the same time the rules of international law relating to war at sea, especially those demanding visit and search, and the safety of passengers and crew, were all made before this new craft was invented. The German naval authorities claim that their submarines cannot take up a position where it is possible to observe the above-mentioned humane provisions without running the risk of being sent to the bottom by a single shot from a (possibly concealed) gun. Therefore you feel that, in the interests of humane warfare, the United States might fairly ask that belligerent merchantmen should carry no guns, on the understanding that all belligerent men-of-war observe the rules of international law.

It seems to me a good answer to the German contention is that they are under an obligation to remedy the defects of their own war vessels, and cannot fairly ask their enemy to disarm his merchantmen. Two considerations from our point of view rather aggravate the unreasonableness of the claim. It is known that the Germans are building, and expect in the near future to put to sea, a new class of submarine which will not be subject to the defect of the older type. Further, it is believed that the real advantage, from the German point of view, of the proposed disarmament of merchant vessels, is that it would enable the submarines to use their guns and save their torpedoes, which can only be carried in very limited numbers, are very costly and, more often than not, miss their mark. I am afraid that, in these circumstances, the abrogation of a universally recognised right—one, moreover, consonant with the fundamental instincts of human nature—to meet a probably passing phase of naval warfare, would provoke rather bitter resentment among the Allied peoples, to whom (in contradistinction to the Central Powers) the maintenance of their seaborne trade and communications in their integrity means so much. May it not be that the future interests of the United States in this matter will shortly prove to be, if indeed they are not already, closely akin to the present interests of the Allies?

There is one argument which I have not seen used, and which seems to me to raise the gravest doubts as to the equity of compelling merchantmen to disarm at the present time. Even if the vulnerability of the submarine be admitted, before special immunity is conceded to these vessels, another quality they possess —their power of self-effacement—must be considered. They are able—indeed it is their common practice—to appear above water, sink a ship without warning, submerge themselves and disappear. No one knows who sunk the "Persia," the Central Powers yielding the honour to the Turks, and the Turks, I presume returning the compliment. We should not know what submarine sunk the "Lusitania" if her commander had not been decorated with the Iron Cross; and many similar cases may be cited. Is it not fair to set what might be called the unrealisable accountability of the submarine, with its power (and apparently irresistable temptation) to murder, against the claim in respect of its alleged vulnerability?

I quite understand that the compromise you suggested was intended to remove all possible excuse for violating the humane principles of international law. For such an object, provided it could be achieved with certainty, and that the sacrifice of existing rights involved were not excessive, the anticipation of what would (you conceived) be the international code of the future, might be accepted. I trust, however, I have shown, even in the somewhat casual and amateur observations I have made, that neither of these saving conditions can be fulfilled.

Believe me, Dear Mr President,

To be yours very respectfully,   Horace Plunkett[1]

TLS (WP, DLC).
[1] House brought this letter back from Europe, along with several other documents, for Wilson.

From William Joel Stone

Dear Mr. President: [Washington] February 24 1916.

Since Senator Kern, Mr. Flood and I talked with you Monday evening,[1] I am more troubled than I have been for many a day. I have not felt authorized to repeat our conversation, but I have attempted, in response to numerous inquiries from my colleagues, to state to them within the confidences that they should observe, my general understanding of your attitude. I have stated my understanding of your attitude to be substantially as follows:

That while you would deeply regret the rejection by Great Britain of Mr. Lansing's proposal for the disarmament of merchant vessels of the Allies with the understanding that Germany and her allies would not fire upon a merchant ship if she hauled to when summoned, not attempting to escape, and that the German warship would only exercise the admitted right of visitation and capture, and would not destroy the captured ship except in circumstances that reasonably assured the safety of passengers and crew, you were of the opinion that if Great Britain and her allies rejected the proposal and insisted upon arming her merchant ships she would be within her right under international law. Also that you would feel disposed to allow armed vessels to be cleared from our ports; also that you were not favorably disposed to the idea of this Government taking any definite steps toward preventing American citizens from embarking upon armed merchant vessels. Furthermore, that you would consider it your duty, if a German war vessel should fire upon an armed merchant vessel of the enemy upon which American citizens were passengers, to hold Germany to strict account.

Numerous Members of the Senate and House have called to discuss this subject with me. I have felt that the Members of the two Houses who are to deal with this grave question were entitled to know the situation we are confronting as I understand it to be. I think I should say to you that the Members of both Houses feel deeply concerned and disturbed by what they read and hear. I have heard of some talk to the effect that some are saying that after all it may be possible that the program of preparedness, so-called, has some relation to just such a situation as we are now called upon to meet. I have counseled all who have talked with me to keep cool; that this whole business is still the subject of diplomacy and that you are striving to the utmost to bring about some peaceable adjustment, and that in the meantime Congress should be careful not to "ball up" a delicate diplomatic situation by any kind of hasty and ill-considered action. However, the situation in Congress is such as to excite a sense of deep concern in the minds of careful and thoughtful men. I have felt that it is due to you to say this much.

I think you understand my personal attitude with respect to this subject. As much and as deeply as I would hate to radically disagree with you, I find it difficult from my sense of duty and responsibility to consent to plunge this nation into the vortex of this world war because of the unreasonable obstinacy of any of the Powers upon the one hand, or, on the other hand, of foolhardiness, amounting to a sort of moral treason against the Republic, of our own people recklessly risking their lives on armed belligerent ships. I cannot escape the conviction that such a thing would be so monstrous as to be indefensible.

I want to be with you and to stand by you, and I mean to do so up to the last limit; and I want to talk with you and Secretary

Lansing with the utmost frankness—to confer with you and have your judgment and counsel—and I want to be kept advised as to the course of events, as it seems to me I am entitled to be. In the meantime I am striving to prevent anything being done by any Senator or Member calculated to embarrass your diplomatic negotiations. Up to the last you should be left free to act diplomatically as you think for the best to settle the questions involved. I need hardly say that my wish is to help, not to hinder you.

With the highest regard and most sympathetic consideration, I have the honor, Mr. President, to be

Very sincerely yours, etc.   Wm J Stone.

TLS (WP, DLC).
[1] For the details of this meeting and the background of the armed ship controversy in Congress, see Link, *Confusions and Crises*, pp. 167-70.

From Joseph Patrick Tumulty

Dear Governor: The White House February 24, 1916.

What I have heard since leaving you this morning confirms me in the belief I have already given expression to that now is the time (before the night passes) to set forth your position in terms that no one can misunderstand on the question of this resolution which has been much discussed in the House.[1]

In the last hour, I have talked with Speaker Clark, Senator Pittman and Mr. Sims and have received impressions from them which lead me to conclude, first, that the consideration of this resolution cannot be postponed much longer, as Speaker Clark so informed me, although Doremus and Pittman say the situation is quieting down. I am firmly convinced that underlying this resolution is a purpose to discredit your leadership for the forces that are lined up for this fight are the anti-preparedness crowd, the Bryan-Kitchin-Clark crowd and some of the anti-British senators like Hoke Smith and Gore. Therefore I cannot urge you too strongly to send *an identical letter to both Flood and Stone*—the letter to embody the following ideas:

First,—Explain in frank fashion just what Secretary Lansing attempted to obtain when he suggested to the Entente nations an agreement on the arming of merchantmen, how this Government was informed by Germany of her intention to destroy armed merchantmen without giving the passengers a moment of warning, and how in order to stave off such a contingency, we tried as the friend and in the interest of humanity to get an agreement between both sides that would bring submarine warfare within the bounds of international law.

Second,—Explain that this is in a process of negotiation right now and that of course while we cannot change sea law of our own initiative, we are still of the hope that some general agreement among belligerents may eventually be obtained. Explain how embarrassing such a resolution as is pending must be while these matters are being threshed out between the executive branches of the Government charged with the conduct of foreign relations, and foreign governments.

Third,—Then say that in the absence of any general agreement, the United States cannot yield one inch of her rights without destroying the whole fabric of international law for in the last analysis this is what is involved,—to yield one right today means another tomorrow. We cannot know where this process of yielding on the ground of convenience or expediency may lead us. These laws are the product of centuries. Our forefathers fought for these principles, obtained them by the loss of blood and treasure. We cannot afford for the sake of convenience when our very life is threatened, to abandon them on the ground of expediency and convenience.

Fourth,—To pass such a resolution at this time will seriously embarrass the Department of State and the Executive in the conduct of these most delicate matters when everything is being done to bring about a peaceful solution of all these problems. You can see what the effect on pending negotiations a resolution of this kind would have,—that the men who are considering voting in favor of this resolution should consider their responsibility co-equal with that of the Executive.

Sixth[2],—Might you not diplomatically suggest that to pass favorably upon a resolution of this kind at this time would be showing a lack of confidence in the Government and *particularly in its chief executive?*

The morning papers have outlined in detail the opposition among the Democrats. The afternoon papers are repeating the same thing with emphasis on the fact that Joe Cannot [Cannon] and Jim Mann and Lodge are going to support you. I would suggest that you place the following in your letter:

"I think that not only would such a vote on this resolution be construed as a lack of confidence in the executive branch of the Government in this most delicate matter but if the division continues as I am informed within the ranks of the Democratic party, it will be difficult for me to consider that the majority party speaks the will of the nation in these circumstances and as between any faction in my party and the interests of the nation, I must always choose the latter, irrespective of what the effect will be on me or my personal fortunes. What we are contending for in this matter is of the very essence of the things that have made America a sovereign nation. She cannot yield them without admitting and conceding her own impotency as a nation and the surrender of her independent position among the nations of the world."   Respectfully,   Tumulty

TLS (WP, DLC).
¹ *H.R. 143*, introduced by Jeff: McLemore of Texas on February 17. It requested the President "to warn all citizens of the United States to refrain from traveling on armed merchant vessels." *Cong. Record*, 64th Cong., 1st sess., p. 2756.
² There was no "Fifth."

To William Joel Stone

My dear Senator: The White House February 24, 1916

I very warmly appreciate your kind and frank letter of today, and feel that it calls for an equally frank reply.

You are right in assuming that I shall do everything in my power to keep the United States out of war. I think the country will feel no uneasiness about my course in that respect. Through many anxious months I have striven for that object, amidst difficulties more manifold than can have been apparent upon the surface; and so far I have succeeded. I do not doubt that I shall continue to succeed. The course which the central European powers have announced their intention of following in the future with regard to undersea warfare seems for the moment to threaten insuperable obstacles, but its apparent meaning is so manifestly inconsistent with explicit assurances recently given us by those powers with regard to their treatment of merchant vessels on the high seas that I must believe that explanations will presently ensue which will put a different aspect upon it. We have had no reason to question their good faith or their fidelity to their promises in the past, and I, for one, feel confident that we shall have none in the future.

But in any event our duty is clear. No nation, no group of nations, has the right while war is in progress to alter or disregard the principles which all nations have agreed upon in mitigation of the horrors and sufferings of war; and if the clear rights of American citizens should ever unhappily be abridged or denied by any such action, we should, it seems to me, have in honour no choice as to what our own course should be.

For my own part, I cannot consent to any abridgement of the

rights of American citizens in any respect. The honour and self-respect of the nation is involved. We covet peace, and shall preserve it at any cost but the loss of honour. To forbid our people to exercise their rights for fear we might be called upon to vindicate them would be a deep humiliation indeed. It would be an implicit, all but an explicit, acquiescence in the violation of the rights of mankind everywhere and of whatever nation or allegiance. It would be a deliberate abdication of our hitherto proud position as spokesmen even amidst the turmoil of war for the law and the right. It would make everything this Government has attempted and everything that it has achieved during this terrible struggle of nations meaningless and futile.

It is important to reflect that if in this instance we allowed expediency to take the place of principle, the door would inevitably be opened to still further concessions. Once accept a single abatement of right and many other humiliations would certainly follow, and the whole fine fabric of international law might crumble under our hands piece by piece. What we are contending for in this matter is of the very essence of the things that have made America a sovereign nation. She cannot yield them without conceding her own impotency as a nation and making virtual surrender of her independent position among the nations of the world.

I am speaking, my dear Senator, in deep solemnity, without heat, with a clear consciousness of the high responsibilities of my office, and as your sincere and devoted friend. If we should unhappily differ, we shall differ as friends; but where issues so momentous as these are involved we must, just because we are friends, speak our minds without reservation.

Faithfully yours,   [Woodrow Wilson][1]

CCL (WP, DLC).
[1] There is a WWsh draft of this letter in WP, DLC, and a WWT draft in the C. L. Swem Coll., NjP. Wilson's letter was widely printed in the newspapers, e.g., the *New York Times*, Feb. 25, 1916.

From Newton Diehl Baker

Cleveland, Ohio, Feb. 24, 1916.

The country is with you. The reported attitude of democrats in Congress is disheartening beyond words. Stand firm. God bless you.   Newton Baker.

T telegram (WP, DLC).

From William Kent

Washington, D. C.

My dear Mr. President: February 24, 1916.

I have no means of knowing your attitude in the matter of armed merchant ships, except what comes to me by rumor or what I see in the press. Without detailed knowledge of the situation, matters appear to me to be about as follows:

Germany has been guilty of barbarous crimes in the sinking of merchant vessels without giving opportunity for passengers to escape, notably in the case of the Lusitania. If I understand the situation, Germany admits the error of such procedure, not to say the wrong, and this incident, I understand, is practically closed without hostilities.

Next, Germany at your suggestion abandoned this practice and has not recently been guilty of it.

Now comes a new contention, namely, the carrying of cannon, on board merchant ships, of sufficient size to be able to sink submarines. This might bring about the following procedure: A submarine halts a merchant ship, gives time for passengers to escape and during this interval is subject to being sunk by the cannon on board the merchantman. Under such a hypothetical case, it would seem to me that the merchantman would be guilty of bad faith and would be taking an unfair advantage of the clemency of the submarine and I can easily see why Germany refuses to accept the risk of having her submarines sunk while carrying out a relatively humane policy.

To me, constitutional law[1] has little weight, because without the power to enforce it, it is practically non-existent and I prefer in every case to try to apply what seems logic and equity rather than precedent.

The fact that merchant ships have carried cannon to protect themselves from pirates is something entirely apart from the present contention. I have always taken the ground and openly expressed the opinion that during such an epidemic of hydrophobia as is occurring in Europe, it behooves our people to keep out of it. A man undoubtedly has a right to walk down a street infested with thugs and take a chance on being beaten up, but it would seem to me a part of wisdom to take another street if possible.

You will recall a story of the Irishman who heard a big row going on in a saloon and went in to see two men rolling around and pummeling and gouging each other, whereupon he politely said, "Mr. Barkeeper, might I ask if this is a private scrap?"

I very much prefer that Europe shall have the benefit of a private scrap, and I do not believe that Uncle Sam should take the Irishman's attitude. From present knowledge, I should deem it my duty to oppose to the utmost any hostile movement on our part that is based on this question of our recognition of armed merchantmen as being other than vessels of war, and I should never advocate asking redress for American citizens who lost their lives while travelling on boats sufficiently armed so as to be able to sink submarine craft.

Yours truly,   William Kent

P.S. As concerns logic as against precedent and non-existent International Law, I enclose a copy of a letter written to the Secretary of State in the matter of the "Appam" case.[2]

WK

TLS (WP, DLC).
  [1] He undoubtedly dictated "international law."
  [2] W. Kent to RL, Feb. 3, 1916, TCL (WP, DLC).

From Robert Lansing

PERSONAL AND PRIVATE:

My dear Mr. President: [Washington] February 25, 1916.

Representative David J. Lewis, of Maryland, called me on the telephone this afternoon and after stating that he was with the Administration in the present difficulty and opposed to any of the resolutions which had been suggested, said that several of the Representatives had been discussing the subject with him and had asked him to communicate with me as to the advisability of proposing arbitration as to the rights of the belligerents in respect to arming of merchantment and the attack upon armed vessels without warning. It is possible, I conclude, that some such suggestion may be made.

I told Mr. Lewis that I could express no opinion on the suggestion at the present time, but would take the matter under consideration.

Personally I do not think that the situation would be helped by any suggestion of this sort. The practical side would be to have Germany relinquish attack until the Court had made a decision which I am convinced the German Government would not consent to. As the proceedings of a tribunal of this sort would undoubtedly take considerable time the immediate relief which is necessary could not be obtained.

It would oblige me if you would give me your views in order

that I may answer Mr. Lewis if he speaks to me again upon the subject.   Faithfully yours,   Robert Lansing

CCL (SDR, RG 59, 763.72/2415½A, DNA).

From Edward Mandell House

London, February 25, 1916.

Yours of twenty-fourth received. I suspected as much. I am sailing to-night and should reach New York March fifth. I have much of great importance to communicate that I dare not cable.
Edward House.

WWT decode of T telegram (WP, DLC).

From Thomas Watt Gregory

Dear Mr. President: Washington February 25, 1916.

I send you herewith a memorandum, in duplicate, relating to the Militia Bill prepared by Representative Hay.[1]

I think we agreed that it would not be well for me to give a formal opinion, but that I should make such general suggestions as occurred to me. On pages 9 and 10 I have put a check mark opposite each of two suggestions which, I think, should be carefully considered by the Committee.[2]

I have been suffering from an attack of grippe and on advice of my physician have remained indoors for the last four days, but expect to be out tomorrow.

If you think it worth while to discuss the matters with me personally, I will call at the White House at any time you may designate.   Faithfully yours,   T. W. Gregory

TLS (WP, DLC).

[1] "MEMORANDUM, February 24, 1916," T MS (WP, DLC). In this long and closely reasoned memorandum, Gregory reviewed all the legal precedents and authorities, and concluded: "Whatever may be the view as to the *policy* of drafting men either into the militia or into the regular army, the nation would be less than sovereign if Congress did not have the *power* to do so in the interest of national security.

"The power to compel military service, either in the regular army or in the militia, seems to be inherent in the power to raise and support armies in the one case and in the power to organize the militia in the other. Neither of these powers would be complete or efficient unless service could be compelled in the event of an insufficient number of volunteers."

[2] Gregory referred to Sections 42 and 66 of the proposed militia bill. Section 42 authorized the President to call "into the service of the United States the organized militia to participate in encampments, maneuvers, etc., in connection with the units of the regular army." Gregory said that of course, for all practical purposes, the militia units would be at such times in the service of the United States. However, he went on, since there was some difference among the authorities on this point, it might be advisable to avoid using the term "in the

service of the United States." The phrase was dropped from the bill that the House adopted on March 23. As to Section 66, which to Gregory seemed to constitute a delegation to the President by Congress of its power to organize and discipline the militia, he suggested that, unless it "was susceptible of a different construction," it would probably violate the principle that Congress could not delegate legislative power to the President.

From Henry Lee Higginson

Boston, Mass., Feb. 25, 1916.

Your letter to Senator Stone is strong clear and right. We Americans wish no quarrel with any nation, but we also have our rights.   Henry L. Higginson.

T telegram (WP, DLC).

Joseph Patrick Tumulty to Edward William Pou

My dear Mr. Pou: The White House February 25, 1916

I have had pleasure in showing your generous letter of February 24th to the President,[1] and he asks me to thank you cordially for your friendly assurances of confidence and approbation. He is glad to know that you so fully endorse his position and course. Your loyal words in these trying days give him strength and encouragement and it was mighty good of you to write.

I hope you are fully recovered from your illness.

With best wishes,   Sincerely yours,   J P Tumulty

TLS (E. W. Pou Papers, Nc-Ar).
[1] It is missing in both the Wilson and Tumulty Papers in DLC. There is no carbon copy in the Pou Papers, Nc-Ar.

A Talk to the Gridiron Club[1]

[[Feb. 26, 1916]]

Mr. Toastmaster and gentlemen: I have very little to say tonight except to express my warm appreciation of the invariable courtesy of this club and of the reception you have so generously accorded me. I find that I am seldom tempted to say anything nowadays unless somebody starts something, and tonight nobody has started anything.

Your talk, Mr. Toastmaster, has been a great deal about candidacy for the presidency. It is not a new feeling on my part, but one which I entertain with a greater intensity than formerly, that a man who seeks the presidency of the United States for anything that it will bring to him is an audacious fool. The responsibilities of the office ought to sober a man even before he approaches it. One of the difficulties of the office seldom appreciated, I dare say, is that it is very difficult to think while so many people are talking, and particularly while so many people are talking in a way that obscures counsel and is entirely off the point.

The point in national affairs, gentlemen, never lies along the lines of expediency. It always rests in the field of principle. The United States was not founded upon any principle of expediency. It was founded upon a profound principle of human liberty and of humanity, and, whenever it bases its policy upon any other foundations than those, it builds on the sand and not upon solid rock. It seems to me that the most enlightening thing a man can do is suggested by something which the Vice-President said tonight. He complained that he found men who, when their attention was called to the signs of spring, did not see the blue heaven, did not see the movement of the free clouds, did not think of the great spaces of the quiet continent, but thought only of some immediate and pressing piece of business. It seems to me that, if you do not think of the things that lie beyond and away from and disconnected from this scene, in which we attempt to think and conclude, you will inevitably be led astray. I would a great deal rather know what they are talking about around quiet firesides all over this country than what they are talking about in the cloakrooms of Congress. I would a great deal rather know what the men on the trains and by the wayside and in the shops and on the farms are thinking about and yearning for than hear any of the vociferous proclamations of policy which it is so easy to hear and so easy to read by picking up any scrap of printed paper. There is only one way to hear these things, and that is constantly to go back to the fountains of American action. Those fountains are not to be found in any recently discovered sources.

Senator Harding[2] was saying just now that we ought to try, when we are a hundred million strong, to act in the same simplicity of principle that our forefathers acted in when we were three million strong. I heard somebody say—I do not know the exact statistics—that the present population of the United States is one hundred and three millions. If there are three million thinking the same things that that original three million thought, the hundred million will be saved for an illustrious future. They were ready to stake everything for an idea, and that idea was not expediency, but justice. And the infinite difficulty of public affairs, gentlemen, is not to discover the signs of the heavens and the directions of the wind, but to square the things you do by the not simple but complicated standards of justice. Justice has nothing to do with expediency. Justice has nothing to do with any temporary standard whatever. It is rooted and grounded in the fundamental instincts of humanity.

America ought to keep out of this war. She ought to keep out of this war at the sacrifice of everything except this single thing upon which her character and history are founded—her sense of humanity and justice. If she sacrifices that, she has ceased to be America; she has ceased to entertain and to love the traditions which have made us proud to be Americans. And, when we go about seeking safety at the expense of humanity, then I, for one, will believe that I have always been mistaken in what I have conceived to be the spirit of American history.

You never can tell your direction except by long measurements. You cannot establish a line by two posts. You have got to have three at least to know whether they are straight with anything, and the longer your line the more certain your measurement. There is only one way in which to determine how the future of the United States is going to be projected, and that is by looking back and seeing which way the lines ran which led up to the present moment of power and of opportunity. There is no doubt about that. There is no question what the roll of honor in America is. The roll of honor consists of the names of men who have squared their conduct by ideals of duty. There is no one else upon the roster. There is no one else whose name we care to remember when we measure things upon a national scale. And I wish that, whenever an impulse of impatience comes upon us, whenever an impulse to settle a thing some short way tempts us, we might close the door and take down some old stories of what American idealists and statesmen did in the past, and not let any counsel in that does not sound in the authentic voice of American tradition. Then we shall be certain what the lines of the future are, because we shall know we are steering by the lines of the past. We shall know that no temporary convenience, no temporary expediency, will lead us either to be rash or to be cowardly. I would be just as much ashamed to be rash as I would to be a coward. Valor is self-respecting. Valor is circumspect. Valor strikes only when it is right to strike. Valor withholds itself from all small implications and entanglements[3] and waits for the great opportunity when the sword will flash as if it carried the light of heaven upon its blade.

Printed in *Address of President Wilson at the Gridiron Dinner. . . .* (Washington, 1919).

[1] At the New Willard Hotel, Washington. Louis William Strayer, Washing-

ton correspondent for the *Pittsburgh Dispatch* and newly elected president of
the club, welcomed the guests at the opening of the dinner.

2 That is, Warren Gamaliel Harding of Ohio.

3 Swem's T transcript (C. L. Swem Coll., NjP), reads "involvements." Wilson
changed it to read "entanglements."

From Paul Oscar Husting

My dear Mr. President: [Washington] Feb. 26, 1916.

May I take the liberty of submitting to you a few observations
on our present difficulty with Germany? I do not presume it is
necessary for me to again assure you that I am now and always
have been in hearty accord with the administration in its handling of our foreign affairs and, for that matter, in the handling
of our domestic affairs and I have no desire to criticise in any
way the attitude of the administration. However, the acute crisis
has brought on considerable discussion between senators and
accordingly I have spoken with a number of senators who are
loyal and friendly toward you and your administration. In discussing the matter with some of them, I presented some views
which some senators thought might not improperly be brought
to your attention. This is neither the place nor the manner in
which to make a long argument. I can only submit to you a bare
outline of some of the thoughts and opinions that have come to
my mind in connection with this important matter.

As I understand the situation, it is briefly something like this:
We are requiring Germany not to torpedo vessels before given
warning for the purpose of enabling such merchantmen to safely
discharge and save their passengers and crews. Merchantmen,
under international law, are permitted to carry guns for defensive
purposes. From certain English admiralty orders, it appears that
England has adopted the policy of fitting out liners and merchantment with guns and ammunition at governmental expense and
of training the crews that man the guns. It is claimed (and these
claims are given color by what purport to be copies of secret
instructions issued to commanders of merchantmen) that they
shoot on sight of enemy. Germany fears or pretends to fear that
in yielding to American demands that she expose herself and
warn such English merchantman, that under the instructions and
orders issued to the commanders, their submarines or their boats
may be fired upon and sunk. Now, the thought suggests itself
to my mind that if we insist that Germany shall *expose herself*
and warn such armed merchantmen before sinking them (something which we do insist upon and rightfully so), then it would
seem to be no more than fair that Germany should receive as-

surances thru us that English boats will not resist or shoot first but will yield to her captors upon such warning.

The mere *presence* of guns on a boat it would seem does not necessarily give a merchantman its character of a warship. The *use* to which the guns on such a boat *are* to be put, the *orders* given to the commander and to the men behind the guns are the factors which in my opinion should really determine the character of a given boat. If a boat is to be used as a warship against the enemy wherever and whenever sighted, then it would seem clear that such a boat does not come within the designation of a merchantman entitled to warning before attack. On the other hand, a boat having guns to be used only for *defensive* purposes would seem clearly to be within the designation of a merchantman and accordingly entitled to such warning.

Now, if I understand public sentiment correctly, it is my opinion that few real Americans want our government to warn people from traveling where they have a right to travel or in any manner to curtail their rights upon the high sea; and contrary-wise, I think very few Americans want our people to travel on auxiliary cruisers and have the government still remain responsible for their safety. Now, it would seem that England, if asked, should be willing to give assurance that her merchantmen are in truth and in fact what they purport to be, viz: merchantmen although carrying guns but with no intent or purpose, however, to use them offensively against the Germans. Then very few of our people would expect or want this government to warn our citizens from traveling on such boats. On the other hand, if England should refuse to give us such assurance, she would thereby confess that she has armed her merchant vessels for the purpose of offense and not defense; in other words, that she has converted them into auxiliary cruisers or privateers, namely, into vessels of a character which does not bring them within that protection which international law accords merchantmen. In this event, it would seem that our citizens should not travel on such boats thus armed and with captain and crew under orders to fire on the enemy's boats at sight. England is not entitled to have her boats protected because of the presence of *our* citizens on them if these are attempting to carry on not only the business of transportation but the business of making war. It would seem to me that England should not be permitted to take advantage of our patriotic desire to protect our citizens by endeavoring to stretch international law to cover and protect vessels under order to attack on sight and therefore no longer entitled to such protection. It is my judgment that our people would overwhelmingly endorse a notice to the public that the pretended character of such English merchantmen is not their true character but, that on the contrary, such boats have been transformed into auxiliary cruisers and have put themselves beyond the protection which merchantmen and their passengers and crews are entitled to under international law and that such notice to our people would be entirely justified and could in no sense be construed as surrendering any of our rights, our dignity or our honor. This position of ours would not in the slightest degree be an abandonment of international law and would not in any sense be a recognition of the contention which is being made so many times by both the English and the Germans "that conditions may change or amend international law." To recognize that a merchantman under orders to fight the enemy on sight and to shoot and sink, if possible, a German submarine which because of *our* requirements must expose herself and warn such merchantman before torpedoing it, is merely to recognize that the character of that vessel is not in truth and in fact a merchantman but that it is in truth and in fact a *warship*. By thus recognizing its altered or converted character we in no wise change international law. We merely recognize that the law pertaining to unarmed merchantmen does not apply to ships whose character has thus been altered. Again, if on the other hand, an armed merchantman is armed purely for defensive purposes with captain and crew ordered to use its guns only in self defense in accordance with its true character and rights as a merchantman, its crew and passengers are entitled to that protection which international law accords such ships and our citizens have a right to travel on them and it would be a pusillanimous act on our part to beg or warn our citizens not to travel on them. If such assurances could be given to Germany she could have no just cause for complaint and the safety of *her* boats would be in no wise jeopardized even tho the vessel warned did in fact carry guns. In the event that England should refuse to give such assurance, I think the people should be fully and duly advised of the real character of their pretended merchantmen; that their captains and crews are under instructions to use them offensively; that her boats are not bonafide merchantmen and that our people should keep off of them.

I might illustrate the point in this way: A man on the street carrying a gun tho subject to arrest is not subject to a murderous assault merely because he carries a gun. On the other hand, a man armed with a gun, who announces his determination to kill his enemy on sight may be shot by that enemy without warning and is not entitled to notice or warning. So a boat manned with a captain and a crew under orders to shoot on sight is not a merchantman but a war-ship and not a proper conveyance for passengers, but a boat even if carrying guns, manned with a captain and a crew who are instructed to shoot only in self defense is clearly a merchantman and a proper converyance [conveyance] for passengers and should not be sunk without notice.

To recapitulate: If we demand that Germany must not without warning sink a British merchantman carrying citizens of the United States, and Germany obeys our demand and in obeying exposes herself to the fire of that ship for whose benefit and safety the warning is required to be given, should we not in the interests of fair play be able to assure Germany that the boat thus warned will not fire upon or attempt to sink such German boat? Should not England in the interest of the safety of her own and our people on merchantmen and in the interests of fair play be willing to give Germany such assurance?

And if England gives such assurances as it would seem in all fairness that she ought to do, then could Germany justly complain because of the mere presence of guns on board such English merchantman?

Now, Mr. President, I have hurriedly and imperfectly reduced these few observations to writing. Of course, it is plain to everybody that our people shrink with instinctive horror from entering into this war and they are indebted to you beyond measures for having kept them thus far out of this awful conflict. If any honorable means can be found now to avert war without humiliation or dishonor on the part of ourselves and on the part of the belligerents, I am sure you will want to seize upon it. The propositions which I am submitting herewith appear to me to be sound. First,—They appear sound to me because they do not involve the abandonment of that which has been at once our compass and sheet-anchor in this perplexing controversy, namely, international law. It is clear that we must maintain undeviatingly our position that international law can not be *altered* by changing conditions but that for the purpose of this war at least and until the nations of the earth again assemble and agree on changes in the law because of changed conditions we can and will continue to recognize international law as it obtains now.

Secondly. These propositions appear to me to be sound because they do not require that either Germany or England should recede from any position they have hitherto taken in the submarine controversy. Germany can not object to guns on board a ship if these guns are not to be used against her when she exposes herself to give the required warning. And England, of course, can not fairly refuse to give assurance that her merchantmen do not propose to try to sink a German boat which in obedience to our demand must expose herself in order to give the warning which we require.

Perhaps this phase of the situation has been gone over fully before by those engaged in these negotiations. In that event, of course, this letter fulfills no office except to express my own personal views upon this subject and I only submit them to you for what they may be worth.

With renewed assurances of my highest personal respect and esteem, I have the honor to remain,

Very sincerely yours,   Paul O Husting

TLS (WP, DLC).

From William Joel Stone

Dear Mr. President: [Washington] February 28, 1916.

I received your very kind letter rather late Thursday night. At that time and since, until now, I have suffered severely from asthma, being subject periodically to spasmodic attacks from that disease. Since that time, until now, I have scarcely been able to be about. I wish especially to thank you for your cordial expressions of friendship and good will, which I assure you are most heartily reciprocated. I have come to have a genuine affection for you, and because of my high respect for you, your opinions on public questions have great weight with me. It has been a source of genuine pleasure to me that I have been able to co-operate with you with so few differences of opinion, and until now with no difference of a vital nature. I have not been able to bring myself into accord with the views you recently expressed to me orally and repeated in your letter—I mean so far as the policy involved is concerned. Although we may not come together in agreement as to this matter, that fact cannot alter my esteem and really affectionate regard for you.

I wish to make a suggestion, which I have more or less discussed with some of our friends at the Capitol, and which I am glad to see in the papers Secretary Lansing already has in mind. It is this: That if nothing more can be done, possibly an agreement might be reached, which would avoid threatened dangers, based on Mr. Lansing's note of September 19, 1914, outlining what might be considered "indications" of defensive armaments.

I desire to call your attention to certain sections of Justice Story's work on the Constitution, Volume 2, Sec. 1566 et seq.;

and John Randolph Tucker's work entitled "Constitution of the United States," Volume 2, Secs. 351, 361, 362, and 363; and especially to the action of former Presidents as set forth in Section 361.[1] While the matter referred to does not directly relate to the severance of diplomatic relations, it does relate to subjects analogous thereto, and to a situation of like character to that which would arise from the severance of diplomatic relations. My idea for calling your attention to these authorities is so manifest that I need not enlarge upon it.

Herewith I am sending you Senate Document No. 332.[2]

This note does not call for a reply.

I am, my dear Mr. President,

Very sincerely yours, etc.   Wm J Stone.

TLS (WP, DLC).

[1] Joseph Story, *Commentaries on the Constitution of the United States: With a Preliminary Review of the Constitutional History of the Colonies and States, Before the Adoption of the Constitution*, 2d edn. (2 vols., Boston, 1851), II, 358-62; and John Randolph Tucker, *The Constitution of the United States: A Critical Discussion of Its Genesis, Development, and Interpretation* (2 vols., Chicago, 1899), II, 715-18, and 744-52. The respective sections mentioned by Stone commented on the delicate balance between the executive and legislative branches of the government with regard to the declaration and execution of war. The authors pointed out that, while only Congress could declare war, and only the President, as commander in chief, could execute it, there were certain instances (such as the recognition or nonrecognition of, or the severance of diplomatic relations with, a foreign government) in which presidential action could put the United States in a position where war would undoubtedly result. Both authorities agreed that, while, by the letter of the Constitution, the President might exercise his powers singlehandedly in these matters, it was nevertheless incumbent upon him to communicate with Congress in order to assure its cooperation. Story especially directed Wilson's attention to times when Presidents had turned problems over to Congress for final decision without, however, abdicating their executive prerogative and without violating the spirit of the Constitution.

[2] 64th Cong., 1st sess., Senate Doc. No. 332, *Armed Merchantmen, International Relations of the United States* (Washington, 1916). This document reprinted, among other things, an article on armed merchantmen, privateers, and the Declaration of Paris from Moore's *Digest of International Law*; three articles by contemporary jurists; and an article in the *North American Review*, May 1915, by George Harvey, which, since it was a defense of Wilson's neutrality policies against the attacks of Theodore Roosevelt, seems to have been included for good measure. One of the contemporary articles—by the Dutch jurist, W. J. M. Eysinga—argued strongly that the British practice of arming merchantmen and training their gunnery crews, begun in May 1914, had created an entirely new situation in which the old rules governing armed merchantmen were no longer applicable.

To William Joel Stone

My dear Senator: [The White House] February 28, 1916

Your generous letter of February twenty-eighth has warmed my heart and I want to send you my affectionate thanks for it. I understand your attitude perfectly and you may be sure have not the sligh[t]est doubt as to the spirit in which you are acting.

I am warmly obliged to you for sending me the compilation with regard to armed merchantmen. I shall take occasion to examine it carefully, because, of course, we are dealing with matters that we ought to deal with only upon the fullest knowledge.

I want you to feel, my dear Senator, that your affection is sincerely reciprocated and that it is a matter of real distress to me to find myself differing with you in any matter of importance. Pray take care of your health and be sure that nothing will ever mar our delightful relationship.

> Cordially and sincerely yours,   Woodrow Wilson

TLS (WP, DLC).

To Newton Diehl Baker

My dear Baker: [The White House] February 28, 1916

Thank you for your telegraphic message of the twenty-fourth. It was like you to send it and it is fine to have such friends.

> Cordially and sincerely yours,   Woodrow Wilson

TLS (Letterpress Books, WP, DLC).

To William Kent

Personal.

My dear Mr. Kent: [The White House] February 28, 1916

I am very much obliged to you for your letter of February twenty-third about the Tariff Commission bill and am inclined to agree with the suggestions it contains. I am glad you have taken them up with Mr. Rainey. I do not think that it was his intention or the intention of any of us to have the Commission report in such a way upon the "effects" of this, that, or the other feature of the tariff as to bring in partisan matters at all, but merely actual facts, whether collateral or otherwise, but if there is any liklihood of the word being construed in a partisan fashion, no doubt a better word can be found.

> Cordially and sincerely yours,   Woodrow Wilson

TLS (Letterpress Books, WP, DLC).

From Robert Lansing, with Enclosure

PERSONAL AND PRIVATE:

My dear Mr. President: Washington February 28, 1916.

I send you herewith copy of a memorandum which the German Ambassador left with me this morning, together with a list of reported offensive acts by armed merchant vessels of the enemy. I am studying the memorandum and am not yet prepared to give any opinion in regard to it.

Faithfully yours,   Robert Lansing

Thank you. Returned for your files   W.W.

TLS (SDR, RG 59, 763.72/2740, DNA).

E N C L O S U R E

Handed me by German Amb. 2/28/16 RL. No discussion took place.

Washington, D. C., February 28, 1916.

The Imperial Government reiterates the pledges given on September 1st and October 5th, 1915, and does not consider that these assurances have been modified by subsequent events. The negotiations conducted between the American and German Governments concerning the Lusitania incident never referred to armed merchant men. In the contrary the note of the American Government of May 13th spoke expressly of "unarmed merchant men." Furthermore the formula agreed upon by both Governments on September 1st contained the proviso "provided that they do not offer resistance." The presence of an armament on board a merchant vessel creates the presumption that the vessel intends "to offer resistance." A submarine commander cannot possibly warn an enemy liner, if the liner has the right to fire upon the submarine. It is obvious that such resistance to the warning by a submarine cannot be the meaning of "armament for defensive purposes," even if it were universally recognized that defensive armament is permitted by international law. This point of view was adopted by the American Government, when it requested assurances from the Italian Ambassador that the armed Italian liners, "Verdi" and "Verona," which entered the port of New York, should not fire on submarines, when warned by them.[1]

The Imperial Government issued its new orders to the German naval commanders after having seen by the secret orders of the

British Admiralty that the armament of British merchant men is to be used for the purposes of attack and that these ships are not merely peaceful traders "armed only for defense." British merchant men have furthermore on several occasions attacked German or Austro-Hungarian submarines. They do, therefore, not conform with the assurances given by the British Government in the note of the British Embassy in Washington of August 25th, 1914, and can even according to the legal point of view adopted by the American Government not be regarded as peaceful traders.

In issuing the new orders to its naval commanders the Imperial Government believed to be entirely in accord with the American Government which expressed similar opinions in the proposals which it submitted to the Entente Powers.

The orders issued to the German naval commanders are so formulated that enemy liners may not be destroyed on account of their armament unless such armament is proved. It is, therefore, obvious that the Imperial Government does not intend to revoke the pledges given on September 1st and October 5th, 1915.

The Imperial Government welcomes the intention of the American Government to bring about a modus vivendi between the belligerents with regard to the disarmament of merchant men, but cannot see its way to change or postpone the new orders to its naval commanders, because the Imperial Government can no longer permit its submarines to be subjected to illegal attacks by armed enemy merchant men.

A list is annexed of cases, in which British merchant men attacked German or Austro-Hungarian submarines.[2]

T memorandum (SDR, RG 59, 763.72/2740, DNA).
[1] About these incidents, see Link, *Confusions and Crises*, pp. 154-55, and the *New York Times*, Jan. 7, 9, 11, 13, and 14, 1916.
[2] "List of cases in which hostile merchantmen fired on German or Austro-Hungarian submarines," T MS (SDR, RG 59, 763.72/2740, DNA). It listed nineteen such instances between April 11, 1915, and January 17, 1916.

From David Lawrence

Personal and Confidential.

My dear Mr. President: [Washington] February 28, 1916

You are going to see the Chilean Ambassador at two o'clock on his farewell call before returning to his country. Confidentially, the Ambassador is not in sympathy with the Pan-American plan recently proposed for the preservation of territorial integrity, etc. He has talked very confidentially to me stating his objections. He is now returning to Chile to lead the opposition party in its campaigns against the government. I wish that before he goes back some of the impressions he has in mind could be removed. He thinks, for example, that our attitude toward Colombia is an evidence of our insincerity and while he has the utmost confidence in you personally, he does not think future Presidents will be as altruistic. His notion that by guaranteeing territorial integrity of the several republics only "under a republican form of government" there is an infringement on the sovereign right of a people to regulate its own kind of government can be removed, I think, by pointing out that this is merely another safeguard against any attempt in the future by foreign *concessionaires* or interests to extend the European system to these continents.

You are, of course, more familiar with the ideals and purposes of the plan than I am but I think that if you will point out to the Ambassador once more that we never intend to annex Mexico or to extend our flag to Panama as has been extravagantly claimed and believed, you will do a great deal toward the ultimate success of the plan, for obviously after the Ambassador's long stay in the United States his judgment will weigh heavily in the counsels of his country on matters of international policy, especially those affecting the United States.

Very sincerely yours,　David Lawrence

TLS (WP, DLC).

From Brand Whitlock

Dear Mr. President:　　　　　　　Brussels. 28 February 1916

My telegram to the Department of State has of course acquainted you with the reasons that seemed to render it inexpedient for me to accept the post at Petrograd, but I have a feeling that I did not adequately express my gratitude and appreciation of the high honor you so generously proposed. I assure you that I was deeply touched by so distinguished a mark of your confidence and consideration; it came to me like a noble decoration of which I am and ever shall be proud. And I should like you to know too, how keen was my regret, not only that a sense of duty impelled me to suggest reasons why I should not avail myself of a promotion I should like to feel that I had earned, but also, and that sentiment was by far the more poignant of the two, that I should ever seem to be reluctant to do anything you might ask. My only consolation is that your fine and imaginative sympathy will cause you to understand and to believe in my entire devotion to you personally and to the great cause that is so happy to have you for its leader in this distracted world.

In the exigency that so suddenly confronted me, here in the midst of a task that is at times so difficult and perplexing that I am not always sure of my ability to envisage situations in that outer world from which we are so isolated, I had two fears; one, that my means were insufficient, and the other that my action in leaving might be construed as a selfish effort to seek an easier post, and these apprehensions prevailed over the natural and, I trust, not unworthy, ambition to be an Ambassador. But, as I have said, I know that you will appreciate my feelings, however inadequately I have expressed them, and know that I do thank you from the depths of a heart that is always with you and asks no higher distinction than to be of some aid to you in the great burden you are bearing, so bravely and so wisely and so patiently, for the sake of our country and of mankind.

In ever high regard, I have the honor to be, dear Mr. President, very gratefully   Your devoted   Brand Whitlock

ALS (WP, DLC).

Two Letters to Edward William Pou

My dear Mr. Pou: The White House February 29, 1916

Your letter of February twenty-fifth to Mr. Tumulty has cheered me mightily. In fact, I am always cheered when I deal with you in any way, because your straightforward manliness about anything reassures me even when others have discouraged me. Your letter brings me assurances which strengthen my heart and I thank you for it most warmly.

Cordially and faithfully yours,   Woodrow Wilson

My dear Mr. Pou: The White House February 29, 1916.

Inasmuch as I learn that Mr. Henry, the Chairman of the Committee on Rules, is absent in Texas, I take the liberty of calling your attention, as ranking member of the Committee, to a matter of grave concern to the country which can, I believe, be handled, under the rules of the House, only by that Committee.

The report that there are divided counsels in Congress in regard to the foreign policy of the Government is being made industrious use of in foreign capitals. I believe that report to be false, but so long as it is anywhere credited it cannot fail to do the greatest harm and expose the country to the most serious risks. I therefore feel justified in asking that your Committee will permit me to urge an early vote upon the resolutions with regard to travel on armed merchantmen which have recently been so much talked about, in order that there may be afforded an immediate opportunity for full public discussion and action upon them and that all doubt and conjectures may be swept away and our foreign relations once more cleared of damaging misunderstandings.

The matter is of so grave importance and lies so clearly within the field of Executive initiative that I venture to hope that your Committee will not think that I am taking an unwarranted liberty in making this suggestion as to the business of the House; and I very earnestly commend it to their immediate consideration.

Cordially and sincerely yours,   Woodrow Wilson[1]

TLS (E. W. Pou Papers, Nc-Ar).
[1] This letter was given to the press.

From Robert Lansing, with Enclosure

PERSONAL AND PRIVATE:

My Dear Mr. President: Washington February 29, 1916.

I enclose for your perusal a letter which I have just received from the German Ambassador, and which you will be good enough to return to me after reading.

Faithfully yours,   Robert Lansing

TLS (SDR, RG 59, 763.72/2538, DNA).

E N C L O S U R E

Count Johann Heinrich von Bernstorff to Robert Lansing

Washington, D. C.,
My dear Mr. Secretary,   February 29, 1916.

With reference to our conversation of yesterday I beg to state that, according to wireless information which I received from my Government, English newspapers amongst others the London "Times" and "Daily Graphic," dealing with the question of armed merchantmen, openly declare that British merchantmen have no intention to conform even to the American viewpoint which permits arming of merchantmen for purposes of defense only.

The naval correspondent of the London "Times" in the edition of February 10th admits that steamers "Kashgar," "City of

Marseille" and the French steamer "Plata" opened fire on submarines after sighting them. The correspondent then, referring
to the episode of the "Clan McTavish" says that it did not meet
deserved success but that it shows the readiness with which merchantmen can "attack."

Likewise "Daily Graphic" in an article of February 12th dealing with the same question says: "Let it be understood that we
shall not limit our action to defensive measures." A similar utterance is reported about the "Daily Telegraph" of February 22nd.

On the other hand the semi-official "North German Gazette"
on February 26th referring to President Wilson's letter to Senator
Stone as viewed by Reuter publishes the following article:

"The principles stated in the German memorandum are by
no means opposed to international law, for secret orders of the
British Admiralty published in the memorandum expressly
instruct armed British merchantmen to not only defend themselves but to attack also. Numerous incidents quoted in the
memorandum give further proof that the ships follow this
instruction. Such vessels according to international law cease
to be peaceful trading ships. On the other hand the precedent
taken by our enemies appears as gross breach of law of nations
since they through merchentmen commit acts of warfare
that only a real manofwar is entitled to. If President Wilson
in his letter to Senator Stone says that announced measures against armed enemy merchant ships are contrary to
express assurances given by Germany and Austro-Hungary
this is apparently caused by misunderstanding. For these
assurances referred only to peaceful liners and not to such
ships whose armament is connected with aggressive purposes.
These misunderstandings were apparently caused by the fact
that the memorandum with annexes is not yet in the hands of
the American Government and that therefore the President is
so far unable to examine both."

I am, my dear Mr. Lansing,
                              very sincerely yours,   J. Bernstorff

TLS (SDR, RG 59, 763.72/2538, DNA).

To Robert Lansing, with Enclosure

My dear Mr. Secretary,   The White House. 1 March, 1916.

The earlier of these two letters seems to me of a great deal of
interest and importance. I am ashamed to say that I have not followed recently the fortunes of the Colombian treaty in our Sen-

ate; but I deem the adoption of the treaty as originally drafted to be of capital importance, especially in view of what Mr. Thompson tells us of the activity of German influences in Colombia and the movement of opinion there.

I would very much like to have your advice and Senator Stone's as to whether I should address a special message to the Senate on this treaty; and I would be very much obliged to you if you would call the Senator's attention to the enclosed letter of February third [second] (not to the subsequent letter,[1] which greatly weakens the force of the first) at the earliest possible moment, at the same time expressing my deep anxiety about the whole situation disclosed.

Do you think it would be serviceable to let Senator Lodge also see it?   Faithfully Yours,   W.W.

WWTLI (SDR, RG 59, 711.21/333½, DNA).

[1] T. A. Thomson to WW, Feb. 11, 1916, TLS (WP, DLC). In this, his second letter, Thomson made no reference to German activities in Colombia and the threat that they constituted to the security of the United States as a reason for ratifying the Colombian treaty. Wilson did not want Senator Stone to see this letter also probably because of the following passage: "Under all the circumstances, would it not be best to make the fight for the Treaty of April 6, 1914, with an expression of mutual regret as the only amendment? Many of the Senators who are opposing the Treaty, represent a class of wealthy merchants, manufacturers, and bankers who will be the chief beneficiaries of a treaty which restores cordial relations with Colombia. I am of the opinion a good deal of bluffing is going on for political vantage, and when the opposition discover that they will have to accept the Treaty of April 6, 1914 (with an expression of mutual regret as the only amendment) or nothing, strong pressure from the constituents of the opposition will force a sufficient number to vote for ratification."

E N C L O S U R E

From Thaddeus Austin Thomson

Mr. President: Bogotá, Colombia, February 2, 1916.

I am sending by this mail to the State Department a despatch about the Treaty and the reported hopes of the Germans here that our Senate will fail to approve it,[1]—some, I am told, saying that when the European war is finished Germany will settle the Panama matter.

I venture therefore to call your attention to the importance of the approval of the Treaty by our Senate from this point of view. I need hardly mention the German wireless station at Cartagena, nor various other German concessions and ambitions in this Hemisphere, but I will mention a confidential report from this Legation of April 30, 1913,[2] that a subordinate of the German Legation here, speaking of the enterprise of the Hamburg-Colombian Banana Company in the Gulf of Darien, said that "the real reason * * * is * * * our desire to possess a coaling station of our own in the Carribean." I desire also to call your special attention to a letter of November 29, 1912, addressed to the President of the United States by my predecessor, Mr. Du Bois, on file in the Department of State.³ Referring to the concession granted by the Colombian Government to this banana company of ten thousand acres, he says: "It is within easy access to coal deposits. The concession includes the widest privileges, railroads, telegraph, pier and wharf construction,—a very liberal banana concession," and he suggests that "Only the future will disclose what there is in this concession and the disclosure may come at a time least expected and least desired." Events since the beginning of the European war have emphasized the apprehension of Mr. Du Bois expressed nearly two years before that conflagration broke out.

On the directorate of the Banana Company appear the names of Herr Ballin,⁴ director of the Hamburg American Line, and of Herr Thomann,⁵ one of the largest stockholders of that line. Mr. Du Bois says that "during the first three months of 1912 the German Minister near the Colombian Government made an inspection along the Atlantic and Pacific Coast lines of Colombia, visiting every port and possible port; made a prolonged staty [stay] in the Gulf of Urabá; and secured statistics and photographs of the improvements being made at Puerto Cesar."

There has never been a doubt in my mind but that the destruction of Admiral Craddock's fleet⁶ was due to information as to its location obtained by the German fleet through the wireless station at either Cartagena or at San Andrés (which, though a Government station, was built by Germans who were still "testing it").

At one time I was under the impression that eighty-five per cent of the Colombian people were pro-allies, but after a careful inquiry within the last few months, my judgment now is that sixty per cent is more nearly correct,—among the pro-Germans being some of the most prominent officials of the Republic. The large pro-German sentiment may be due to two causes: the influence of the Roman Catholic clergy on the extreme conservatives and the intermarriage of the Germans with Colombians; this last has been given as a reason why the Colombians prefer German immigration. There are many Germans engaged in business throughout the Republic, and all whom I have met are above the average in intelligence.

The German activities in the Carribean, it would seem, should be sufficient to emphasize the necessity for having the friendship especially of Colombia and Costa Rica to strengthen our national defenses. I am also reporting by this mail[7] that the attorney who secured a concession for a coaling station in Cartagena Bay (not yet approved by Congress) is also acting as attorney for the German Legation here; and it appears to me certain that the Germans have been making preparations in this country to test the strength of our support of the Monroe Doctrine and extremely probable, in such an event, that if our Senate rejects the Treaty, Colombia will not oppose, if indeed it does not assist, the landing of German troops on its soil for an attack on the Panama Canal.

Without taking into consideration the commercial advantages to be derived from the settlement of a question that has caused so much friction between the two Republics, it occurs to me that the friends of the Treaty might gain a few votes by pressing this argument at the present time when the Nation is aroused to the necessity for preparedness. Most of our national legislators are in total ignorance of what has been transpiring on the Atlantic and Pacific coasts.

One point in the Treaty which seems to meet with some opposition is the expression of regret by the United States; if it should appear that this endangered the entire Treaty, I would suggest that the Senate amend it so as to make the expression of regret mutual on the part of Colombia and the United States. The present Minister for Foreign Affairs[8] informed me confidentially last year that he desired this from the beginning but that the other members of the Commission on Foreign Affairs refused it positively when the negotiations were in progress. I believe that an amendment making the expression of regret mutual would now be accepted by the Colombian Congress.

I have the honor to be, Sir,

Your obedient servant, Thad. A. Thomson

TLS (SDR, RG 59, 711.21/331½, DNA).

[1] T. A. Thomson to RL, Feb. 3, 1916, TLS (SDR, RG 59, 711.21/335, DNA).

[2] L. Harrison to WJB, April 30, 1913, TLS (SDR, RG 59, 821.6156/14, DNA).

[3] J. T. DuBois to P. C. Knox, Sept. 20, 1912, TLS, enclosed in P. C. Knox to W. H. Taft, Nov. 29, 1912, TLS (W. H. Taft Papers, DLC).

[4] That is, Albert Ballin.

[5] Julius Thomann.

[6] Rear Admiral Sir Christopher George Francis Maurice Cradock commanded the North America and West Indies station of the Royal Navy at the outbreak of the war. Late in October 1914, he moved his fleet, the 4th Cruiser Squadron, to the western coast of South America to meet Admiral Maximilian Johannes Maria Hubert von Spee, who had crossed the Pacific with Germany's China Squadron. The two squadrons engaged off Coronel, Chile, on November 1, and Cradock's flagship, H.H.S. Good Hope, was sunk with all souls on board.

[7] The Editors have been unable to find this letter in the State Department files.

[8] Marco Fidel Suárez.

To Robert Lansing

My dear Mr. Secretary,   The White House. 1 March, 1916.

Thank you for letting me see the enclosed.[1] I note what the Ambassador says about my letter to Senator Stone. He leaves no occasion unimproved to put his understanding (his erroneous understanding) of the point at issue forward. I wonder if you have yet drafted your correction of his impressions as a memorandum of the same sort as his?

Faithfully Yours,   W.W.

WWTLI (SDR, RG 59, 763.72/2550½, DNA).
[1] That is, J. H. von Bernstorff to RL, Feb. 29, 1916, just printed.

From Seth Low

Dear Mr. President: New York City, March 1st, 1916.

I am very sorry that I shall not be able to be with Mr. Mills and Mr. Gilday when you receive the Colorado Coal Commission on Thursday. I was under the Doctor's care when I went to Colorado, and I am now, I fear, paying the penalty for going at that particular time. I am not seriously ill, but I am so far disabled as to be obliged to stay at home. I certainly hope that you will feel satisfied with the work of your Colorado Coal Commission, and that our Report[1] will be useful in more ways than one. I hope especially that you will ask the Federal Trade Commission to look into the whole subject of the mining of coal under competitive conditions.[2] The methods are certainly very wasteful, and only the best mines can be profitably worked. The result is, very irregular employment, and great hazard to the working men. I have the impression that the same condition exists in other fields than in Colorado.

I hope the Report will be printed, and that I can have a number of copies for distribution.   Very respectfully,   Seth Low

TCL (RSB Coll., DLC).
[1] *Labor Difficulties in the Coal Fields of Colorado*, 64th Cong., 1st sess., House Doc. No. 859 (Washington, 1916). This report, submitted on February 23, 1916, summarized the impressions that the commissioners had received during their investigation in Colorado in January and February. The report said that recent state legislation establishing an industrial commission with investigatory powers and creating a system of workmen's compensation had materially improved the working conditions of Colorado's miners, mitigated the injurious effects of the strike, and led to less arbitrary control by the operators. The commissioners described conditions in the coal fields as more or less harmonious and said that they were especially impressed by the spirit of "cooperation and conciliation" between employers and employees which had resulted from the so-called Colorado Plan—the company union arrangement of the Colorado Fuel and Iron Co. See S. Low to WW, Dec. 8, 1915, n. 2, Vol. 35. In their conclusion, the commissioners suggested that a study of the entire mining industry be undertaken by the

Federal Trade Commission for the purpose of introducing legislation that would eliminate waste and assure a maximum of safety and steady employment for the workers.

2 The report emphasized that the Colorado operators faced severe problems of competition on account of the lack of a local market and the failure of the railroads to cooperate in distributing their coal.

A Statement

[*March 2, 1916*]

Washington, March 2.—The White House issued this statement tonight: "When the attention of the White House was called to certain statements in Senator Gore's speech this afternoon,[1] the President authorized an unqualified denial of any utterance to which any such meaning could be attached."

Printed in the *New York Times*, March 3, 1916.

1 Senator Thomas P. Gore of Oklahoma had introduced on February 25 a concurrent resolution (S. Con. Res. 14), similar to McLemore's, warning Americans not to travel on armed ships and forbidding them to do so by withholding their passports. *Cong. Record*, 64th Cong., 1st sess., p. 3120. During the debate on his resolution, Gore declared that he had it from "the highest and most responsible authority" that certain senators and representatives, "in a conference with the President of the United States received from the President the intimation, if not the declaration, that if Germany insisted upon her position the United States would insist upon her position; that it would result probably in a breach of diplomatic relations; that a breach of diplomatic relations would probably be followed by a state of war; and that a state of war might not be of itself and of necessity an evil, but that the United States by entering the war now might be able to bring it to a conclusion by midsummer and thus render a great service to civilization." Stone immediately replied that the President had never said to him or in his hearing that "he believed in any way, or in any way entertained the thought, that war between the United States and the central powers would be desirable or would result in good to the United States." *Cong. Record*, 64th Cong., 1st sess., p. 3410.

Actually, Gore was referring to a conversation between Wilson, Speaker Clark, Henry D. Flood, and Claude Kitchin, at what has come to be known as the "Sunrise Conference" at the White House at 9 A.M. on February 25. According to newspaper reports, one of the congressmen asked Wilson what would happen if a German submarine sank an armed merchantman with Americans aboard. Wilson allegedly replied that he believed that the United States should sever diplomatic relations with Germany. What would happen then? Wilson allegedly replied that Von Bernstorff had told Lansing that Germany would declare war if diplomatic relations were broken. What would be the effect of American participation? It might, Wilson is alleged to have said, bring the war to an end much sooner than appeared possible at the present. When one of the congressmen commented that persons were saying that Wilson wanted war with Germany, he is alleged to have replied that his policy was the only one that would preserve peace, and that he had been jeered at, sneered at, and ridiculed for his efforts to maintain peace. "In God's name," Wilson allegedly cried, "could anyone have done more than I to show a desire for peace?" *New York Times*, Feb. 26 and March 3, 1916, and the New York *Evening Post*, cited in the *Springfield*, Mass., *Republican*, March 4, 1916. See also Link, *Confusions and Crises*, pp. 175-76.

A Draft of a Resolution

[c. March 2, 1916]

The Senate of the U. S. will approve no action which abridges the rights of American citizens on the high seas and will support the President of the U. S. in the just maintenance of those rights.[1]

WWhw MS (WP, DLC).
[1] Wilson apparently did not ask any senator to introduce this resolution, as no such resolution was offered.

To William Gibbs McAdoo and Albert Sidney Burleson

My dear Friends,   The White House 2 March, 1916.

You have asked me just what I think necessary to clear up the existing situation and relieve the present embarrassment of the Administration in dealing with the foreign relations of the country. It seems to me absolutely essential that there should be a vote,—an early vote,—on the resolutions introduced by Mr. McLemore, of Texas. No other course would meet the necessities of the case.   Faithfully   Woodrow Wilson

ALS (A. S. Burleson Papers, DLC).

To Robert Lansing

My dear Mr. Secretary: [The White House] March 2, 1916

Here is a letter from Senator Husting which seems to me worth serious discussion. I would be very much obliged if you would read it and let me know how the suggestion strikes you.

Cordially and sincerely yours,   Woodrow Wilson

TLS (Letterpress Books, WP, DLC).

To Paul Oscar Husting

My dear Senator: [The White House] March 2, 1916

I owe you an apology for not having acknowledged sooner your very interesting and important letter of February twenty-sixth about our international situation. The suggestion made in your letter interests me very much indeed and I am going to take the liberty of discussing it with the Secretary of State, who I am sure is as anxious as I am to do everything possible to bring justice out of chaos.

With many apologies for not having sooner acknowledged so important a communication,

Cordially and sincerely yours,   Woodrow Wilson

TLS (Letterpress Books, WP, DLC).

To William Gordon[1]

My dear Mr. Gordon: [The White House] March 2, 1916

Of course, you understood that I spoke in playfulness the other night at the Marshall reception,[2] but I am very much obliged to you for your letter of February twenty-ninth[3] and am glad to have an opportunity of assuring you that the report that you say was current that I was trying in some way to bring on war was too grotesquely false to deserve credence for a moment. If anybody ever strove harder to preserve peace than I have striven and am striving, I wonder who and what he could have been.

Faithfully yours,   Woodrow Wilson

TLS (Letterpress Books, WP, DLC).
   [1] Democratic congressman from Ohio.
   [2] The reception that Vice-President and Mrs. Marshall had given for the President and Mrs. Wilson, the members of the cabinet, the diplomatic corps, congressmen, and army and navy leaders at the New Willard Hotel on January 28, 1916.
   [3] It is missing.

To Thomas Watt Gregory

The White House

My dear Mr. Attorney General: March 2, 1916

May I not thank you very warmly for the carefully considered informal report of the constitutional aspects of the pending militia bill. It contains just the sort of thing I needed and will be most serviceable to me in every way.

Cordially and sincerely yours,   Woodrow Wilson

TLS (T. W. Gregory Papers, DLC).

From John Sharp Williams

My dear Mr. President: [Washington] March 2, 1916.

Enclosed please find an editorial from the Memphis (Tennessee) Commercial-Appeal,[1] (the town where I was born, by the way, although that does not add to its importance). The editorial was written by Mr. C. P. J. Mooney,[2] one of the editors of that paper. I wanted you to see what one of the chief papers in West Tennessee, which is virtually a part of the State of Mississippi, thinks of you and the policy which you have been pursuing and in which I have been aiding and abetting you to a moderate extent.

My friend, Mr. Robert M. Gates, who is the Washington correspondent of the paper, handed me this. I read it with a great deal of gratification and I know that you will. Just take three minutes off while you read it.

I know that Moses never was as glad of anything as he was of having Joshua hold up his hands.

I am, with every expression of regard,

Very truly yours, John S Williams

TLS (WP, DLC).

1 "Get Behind Wilson or Come Home and Stay There," undated clipping (WP, DLC). This editorial denounced as "peace sheep" those congressmen and senators who favored the McLemore and Gore resolutions and lauded Wilson's policy of upholding the right of American citizens to travel on belligerent ships. Wilson, it stated, had "drawn a clear line between national honor and dishonor, national independence and servitude." The United States, it continued, could not permit any abridgement of any right that would interfere with its freedom as a nation. The editorial quoted extensively from Wilson's letter of February 24 to Senator Stone and urged the American people to support the President.

2 Charles Patrick Joseph Mooney, managing editor of the *Commercial Appeal*; member of the committee on resolutions of the Democratic National Convention of 1912.

From Franklin Knight Lane

My dear Mr. President: Washington Mar. 2 1916

Referring to your letter transmitting communication from Mr. Gifford Pinchot,[1] criticising the so-called Shields water-power bill, I have the honor to advise as follows:

The measure as drawn is not, to my mind, entirely satisfactory from the viewpoint of the public interest, and could be greatly improved by amendment. There are several vital changes which I believe should be made, and there are a number of minor amendments which might be desirable, but are perhaps not of sufficient importance to warrant controversy or contention.

You will recall that the matter of development of power upon navigable streams was given extensive consideration by yourself at various conferences, and a measure known as the Adamson bill was agreed upon and passed by the House of Representatives August 4, 1914, H.R. 16053.

(1) The Shields bill now under consideration by the Senate, S. 3331, provides in section 2, page 6, for the use of such lands of the United States as may be required, and specifies that the grantee shall pay to the United States—

such reasonable charges based upon its value as *land* as may be fixed by the Secretary of War; and in fixing such charges consideration shall be taken of the benefits accruing from the use and occupation of such lands to the interests of navigation, as well as to the business of said grantee.

An amendment introduced by Senator Cummins, and adopted by the Senate February 28, 1916, page 3705 of the Congressional Record, amended this provision by striking out all of the original provision in the Shields bill after the word "value" so that it will require that for any lands of the United States used, either public or otherwise,

> the grantee shall pay to the United States such reasonable charges, based upon its value, as may be fixed by the Secretary of War; in ascertaining the value of the land the Secretary of War shall be governed by the rules of the law in force in the State or Territory in which it is situated, applicable to proceedings wherein Government property is sought to be taken for a public use.

The bill as originally drawn was objectionable and inadequate, in that it would have only required the grantee to pay the value as land, which might have been $1.25 per acre or less, where it was of such a character as to be of no value for agriculture or other use as "land"; while as a matter of fact, its value to a water-power company for water-power purposes might be very great, and the land involved might be the very key to the entire development. The so-called Cummins amendment is objectionable, because the method therein provided is so indefinite and uncertain and without provision for carrying it out, as to render the amendment really unworkable. The Secretary of War is charged with the duty of ascertaining the value of the land, but is required to be governed by the rules "of the law in force in the State or Territory * * * applicable to proceedings wherein private property is sought * * * for a public use."

In a State or Territory where private property is sought to be condemned for a public use, it is through proceedings in a court, where evidence is submitted upon both sides, and a determination made by the court, both upon the law and the facts. The Secretary of War will be without power or authority to conduct such a proceeding and his decision, when rendered, would not have the binding effect of a decision by the court. In any event, it is impossible that the Secretary of War shall in each case where a power site is sought undertake to determine just what the proceedings and awards would be under the rules of law in each of the States and Territories of the Union.

The Adamson bill, agreed upon last winter, provided that for any of the lands of the United States used in such a project "the grantee shall pay to the United States such charges as may be fixed by the Secretary of War." The Ferris bill, passed by the House of Representatives January 8, 1916, provides that in case of the use of public lands for the development of electrical power, the lessee shall pay such charges or rentals as may be specified by the Secretary of the Interior in the lease, to be measured "by the power so developed and sold or used by the lessee for any purpose other than the operation of the plant in developing power."

The Senate Committee has reported the Ferris bill, with the following provision with respect to charges for the use of lands and property of the United States:

The Secretary of the Interior is authorized to specify in the lease and to collect charges or rentals for all land leased, which charges or rentals shall be based on the value of the land, to be determined by the amount of horsepower to be developed, and which charge or rental shall not exceed the sum of twenty-five cents per developed horsepower per year sold or used by the lessee for any purpose other than the operation of the plant.

To summarize the foregoing, the original Shields bill provided for an utterly inadequate basis of ascertaining charges, and the Cummins amendment is indefinite and unworkable. Therefore, the Shields bill should be amended so as to conform in substance either to the provision of the Adamson bill, H.R. 16053, or to the terms of the Ferris bill, either as passed by the House or as reported by the Senate Committee.

(2) One vital defect in the Shields bill is that while the grant or lease may be terminated at the end of fifty years, after completion of the initial installment, it can *only* be terminated by the taking over of the plant by the United States. If the United States does not take over the plant, the original grant or lease continues indefinitely upon the original terms and conditions. Therefore, it is an indeterminate lease, subject only to the taking over by the United States, presumably for operation by the United States. The Adamson bill, agreed upon and passed last session by the House of Representatives, provided that at the end of the said term, the property might be taken over upon payment of compensation by the United States "or any person authorized by Congress." This would have permitted of the taking over of such a plant by a State or municipality for public use, upon compensating the original lessee, or have retained in Congress the power to terminate the original lease and grant the property to another under

such terms and conditions as it might deem proper at that time. The Ferris bill, passed by the House of Representatives January 8, 1916, provides that the lease shall run for fifty years, and at the end of that time, upon compensation, may be taken over by the United States, or leased anew to the original party, or to a third party, corporation, or State, upon such terms and conditions as Congress shall then authorize. As stated, this is of vital importance, and the Shields bill should be amended to conform either to the terms of the Adamson bill as agreed upon last year, or to the Ferris bill.

(3) The Shields bill, section 6, page 10, and section 7, page 11, provides that in the event of recapture or in the fixing of rates, no value shall be claimed or allowed for rights granted by the proposed act, but fails to exclude from consideration in those contingencies, as did the Adamson bill, "good will, going value, profit in pending contracts, or other conditions of current or prospective business."

I attach hereto a memorandum[2] discussing more in detail the differences between the Shields bill and the Adamson bill as agreed upon last winter, but, as previously stated, it is my opinion that some of the matters pointed out are of minor importance as compared with those discussed in this letter.

Cordially yours,　Franklin K. Lane

TLS (WP, DLC).
　[1] G. Pinchot to WW, Jan. 29, 1916.
　[2] "Memorandum," undated T MS (WP, DLC).

From Thomas Davies Jones

Chicago, Ills., March 2, 1916.

I hope you will stand immovably upon ground taken toward Congress. In my opinion consequences of yielding will be worse than any possible consequences of firmness. My brother agrees with me.　　　　　　　　　　Thomas D. Jones.

T telegram (WP, DLC).

To Edward Mandell House

The White House, March 3, 1916.

Warmest greeting. Hope you will come at once to Washington.
Wilson

T telegram (E. M. House Papers, CtY).

To Seth Low

My dear Mr. Low: The White House March 3, 1916

Thank you for your letter of March first. I was sorry that you should have been kept away from the conference I had yesterday with Mr. Mills and Mr. Gilday. The report was certainly most gratifying and I congratulate you and the other members of the Commission most warmly on the success of an excellent piece of work.

I note what you say about the competitive conditions in the mining of coal and shall certainly make the suggestion you speak of to the Federal Trade Commission.

Cordially and sincerely yours,   Woodrow Wilson

TLS (S. Low Papers, NNC).

To Thomas Davies Jones

My dear Friend: The White House March 3, 1916

Thank you warmly for your telegram of yesterday. You may be sure I will not budge. It is fine to have such friends thinking of me and counselling me.

In haste, with warmest regard to you all,

Cordially and faithfully yours,   Woodrow Wilson

TLS (Mineral Point, Wisc., Public Library).

From Robert Lansing, with Enclosure

My dear Mr. President: Washington March 3, 1916.

I enclose for your consideration a Note Verbale in answer to the Note Verbale which was handed to me by the German Ambassador on February 28th. Do you think it advisable to send this at once or to wait until the warning of Americans has been determined by Congress?

Faithfully yours,   Robert Lansing[1]

TLS (WP, DLC).

[1] Wilson did not respond in writing to this letter. The enclosure was not sent, obviously because of Wilson's oral instructions.

E N C L O S U R E

Washington, March 2, 1916

In the Note Verbale of the Imperial German Government of February 28, 1916, it is asserted that the Imperial Government does not consider that the assurances given by it on September 1, and October 5, 1915, have been modified by subsequent events.

In view of the statement in the recent declaration of policy as to submarine warfare that "enemy merchantmen armed with guns *no longer* have any right to be considered as peaceable vessels of commerce," and the statement in the Note Verbale of the Imperial Government that it had issued "*new* orders" to its naval commanders, the Government of the United States is unable to harmonize with these statements the assertion that the assurances given by the Imperial Government have not been modified.

The use of the words "no longer" indicates that armed merchantmen had been previously considered peaceful vessels of commerce, but would not thereafter be so considered. Armed merchantmen were, therefore, included in the class of peaceable vessels of commerce, to which the assurances applied until the declaration of policy of February 10th was issued.

As the assurance of October 5, 1915, specifically referred to orders issued to German naval commanders, the "new orders" issued under the declaration, which are referred to in the Note Verbale of February 28th, must relate to the announced withdrawal of armed merchantmen from the application of the assurances and must affect the orders referred to on October 5th.

The Government of the United States in addition to the assurances of the Imperial Government given on September 1st and October 5th, 1915, also relied upon the declaration of principle as to the safety of persons on board a vessel to be sunk contained in the Imperial Government's note of November 29, 1915, and the assurance given January 7, 1916, shortly after the sinking of the s.s.persia which was *known* by Germany, at the time when the assurance was given, to be armed.[2]   ?1

To these assurances, and particularly to the latter which refers specifically to orders given to German submarines, no reference is made in the Note Verbale of the Imperial Government. It is presumed that the "new orders" nullify in large measure the clear and explicit orders[3] of January 7th, which make no distinction between armed and unarmed merchant ships.

Without a more convincing and satisfactory explanation that the assurances of the Imperial Government are immodified[4] by the declaration of February 10th, the Government of the United States is unable to consider the pledges of the Imperial Government to be unbroken by the new orders.

T MS (WP, DLC).

[1] Wilson italicized "known" and wrote the question mark in the margin.

[2] J. H. von Bernstorff to RL, received Jan. 7, 1916, *FR-WWS, 1916*, pp. 144-

45. It stated: (1) German submarines in the Mediterranean, from the beginning of the war, had received orders to conduct cruiser warfare against enemy merchant vessels in accordance with the general principles of international law and had been instructed that measures of reprisal were to be excluded. (2) German submarines were, therefore, permitted to destroy enemy merchant vessels in the Mediterranean only after the safety of passengers and crews had been assured. (3) All cases of destruction of merchant ships by German submarines in the Mediterranean were subjected to official investigations and were submitted to regular prize court proceedings. In the event that American interests were involved, the German government would communicate the results to the American government. (4) Submarine commanders would be punished if they violated their orders, and the German government would make reparation for the injury or death of American citizens.

³ Wilson wrote "assurance" above "orders" and added an "s" to "make."
⁴ Wilson changed this to "unmodified."

From Harry Augustus Garfield

Personal

Dear Mr. President: Williamstown, Mass. March 3, 1916

Your method of dealing with one belligerent at a time has seemed to me eminently wise. You of course are best able to judge when the time is ripe to press our demands upon England, but I am wondering whether the time has not come—for the effect both at home & abroad—when the public should be given to understand that you are determined to deal as firmly with England as with Germany. Perhaps it ought to know this now, but it does not. I find it increasingly difficult to counter the suggestion that the Administration is glad to prolong the controversy with Germany for the sake of postponing that with Great Britain. The intimation was not disquieting until it came from pro-Ally sources.

With warmest regard, as always,

Faithfully Yours,   H. A. Garfield.

ALS (WP, DLC).

From Royal Meeker

My dear Mr. President: Washington March 3, 1916.

I am loath to write you at this time because I know how overburdened you are with communications of all sorts from all parts of the country. However, it does seem to me that you might be glad to hear some of the good things I have heard said of you and your Administration on my recent trips.

I think perhaps I meet with a different class of people from those who write letters or take up your time in other ways. I meet the officials who have to do with the administration of labor laws and with laborers in whose behalf protective legislation has been enacted. Both these classes are almost a unit in supporting you. The sentiment throughout the Middle West, so far as I can judge, is strongly against war. I heard your praises sounded fron [from] every side because you have so successfully kept us clear of the European struggle and yet have maintained our rights and our honor. I have heard many men say within the past week that they did not vote for you for President, but that they intended to do so at the next presidential election. I thought at this time when things look so mixed that you would be glad to know that some of the people keep their senses and stand behind you.

I am, as you know, greatly interested in what has come to be called social insurance. I feel that the compensation legislation in the United States is needlessly backward and that it is necessary for us to forge ahead in this line of social legislation in order to give to the workers of the United States the protection they have a right to expect from the State. European countries are far in advance of us in respect to social insurance, and this is one of the reasons that their people are more united than our people. My own opinion is that the time has come for a bold stand in this matter. I think we should have a model Federal compensation law, covering all employees of the United States Government and of the District of Columbia, which would compensate for injuries due either to industrial accidents or industrial poisons and diseases. All employees engaged in interstate commerce should be protected in like manner either in the same or some other act.

The Federal Government in its legislation providing compensation for its employees and the employees that come within its jurisdiction should create a model for the guidance of the States in enacting their own compensation laws.

I think it is time we should come out boldly and emphatically for a national health insurance act similar to the Health Insurance Act of Great Britain. I believe such an act would be constitutional. I believe further that the advocacy of adequate compensation legislation and health insurance, accompanied by a strong appeal for greater safety in our work shops and factories, would meet with hearty approval of laboring men throughout the country.

The infant mortality rate in the United States is about four times the infant mortality rate in the Australasian countries. Our accident rate is at least two or three times greater than in European countries. We have done much talking about "safety first" and have done little doing. We are utterly careless of life and limb in this country where life and limb should be most precious.

I believe a campaign for the protection of American workmen from injury, disease, and sudden death in our work shops and on our farms would meet with enormous popular success.

I would like very much to see you and talk over these matters personally with you. I feel very strongly on these subjects, and I think I can submit to you facts and opinions which will be of interest and value to you.[1]

Sincerely yours,   Royal Meeker

TLS (WP, DLC).
[1] There is no record of a meeting between Wilson and Meeker on this subject.

Joseph Wright Harriman[1] to Frank Lyon Polk

My dear Frank: New York, 3/3, 1916.

In all this "muss" in Washington, I cannot help sending you a line regarding the Administration's attitude. I think Wilson is the greatest President in our time—yours and mine—and altho' I did not vote for him—did not vote at all in fact (for I couldn't stomach Taft), I am surely going to do so if he runs again. The clever way in which he has turned the tables on Congress is enough to commend him to his countrymen. If Grover Cleveland had done it he would have had less trouble. He is a wonder and I am an enthusiastic supporter from now on. If he is renominated and a man like Whitlock is put on the ticket for V. P., even with the so-called "Democrats" in Congress—Mr. Wilson will sweep the country. You have no idea, the talk in his favor, the firm attitude he has taken and has produced.

Sorry to have missed you when you called.

Expect to be in Washington soon and will drop in on you.

Sincerely yours,   J. W. Harriman.

TCL (WP, DLC).
[1] New York banker and financier; member of the brokerage firm of Harriman and Co.; founder and president of the Harriman National Bank and Trust Co.

From Albert Sidney Burleson

My dear Mr. President: [Washington] March 4, 1916.

In compliance with your request, I am submitting herewith a list of the bills which I think should be voted upon by the Congress at its present session. I feel that the best interest of our Country requires that these bills should be enacted into law:

1. Appropriation Bills, which of course must carry paragraphs necessary to meet Preparedness Program of the Administration.

2. Revenue Bills, which will include Tariff Commission and Anti-dumping paragraphs.

3. The Ship Purchase Bill.

4. The Rural Credits Bill.
   Tariff Bd.[1]

5. The Philippine Bill.
   The Porto Rico bill[2]

6. The Conservation Measures.

7. The Mississippi Relief Measure, which should provide that the work of leveeing and revetment be carried on under a continuing contract system until completed, the annual appropriation for this work to be carried in the Sundry Civil Bill, as was done for the construction of the Panama Canal.

8. Corrupt Practice Act.

Sincerely yours,   A. S. Burleson

TLS (WP, DLC).
[1] WWhw.
[2] WWhw and WWsh. He referred to the Jones bill, which granted territorial status to the island and American citizenship to its inhabitants.

From Henry Lee Higginson

Dear Mr. President,   Boston, March 4th, 1916.

We men & women of this town were much pleased at the vote of the Senate yesterday,[1] for we expected their firm support for the only straight course. We don't wish to fight but we cannot let any nation or man slap the nation's face. Surely you have been patient enough & plenty of quiet & peace loving men would have sent Bernstorff home long ago.

The Germans are foolish to irritate us by their conspiracies & explosions & well-educated spies, who steal plans & papers etc. I heard of a fresh case yesterday—a clever clerk using his time in an office to make plans of forts & harbors & then disappearing. It is dirty work—for the paid spy & for the Government.

One word about Brandeis. I've already given you my views about him, & on this occasion have thought it wiser not to talk or to sign papers. You have heard & seen the opinions about him from the men among whom he has lived, & you may have noted the higher quality of the objections. The sneers & satire of Brandeis supporters, the lies of some of the papers who use this chance to sling mud at decent men injure him. "Save us from our friends."

The whole incident has done harm.

Yours respectfully   H. L. Higginson

ALS (WP, DLC).
¹ That is, the vote on March 3 on the Gore resolution, the preamble of which had been changed to read that the destruction of American lives on armed merchantmen would constitute a *casus belli*. It was tabled by a vote of sixty-eight to fourteen. *Cong. Record*, 64th Cong., 1st sess., p. 3465.

To Newton Diehl Baker

Washington¹ March 5 1916.

Would you accept Secretaryship of War Period Earnestly hope that you can see your way to do so Period It would greatly strengthen my hand.   Woodrow Wilson.

T telegram (photograph in Frederick Palmer, *Newton D. Baker: America at War* [2 vols., New York, 1931], I, facing p. 10).
¹ This telegram was sent from *U.S.S. Mayflower* by radio to Washington and then sent as a telegram to Baker.

To Champ Clark

My dear Mr. Speaker: [The White House] March 6, 1916

Tomorrow will be your birthday and I cannot let the occasion pass without sending you at least a line of warm congratulation and most sincere wishes that you may have many happy returns, in which, as in the past, you will find your usefulness to the country continued and enhanced. I hope that abundant health and strength will continue to be yours as the years go by.

Cordially and sincerely yours,   Woodrow Wilson

TLS (Letterpress Books, WP, DLC).

From Robert Lansing, with Enclosure

PERSONAL AND PRIVATE:

My dear Mr. President: [Washington] March 6, 1916.

I send you a memorandum which I have prepared setting forth clearly, I think, the negotiations and conversations which I have had in regard to the matter of armed merchant vessels, and the recent declaration of February 10th by the Teutonic Powers in regard to submarine warfare.

I suggest, for your consideration, the advisability of reading this memorandum at the Cabinet meeting tomorrow. I feel that the members of the Cabinet ought to know something of the difficulties which we have had to face and particularly the adroit efforts which have been made by the German Ambassador, for I consider Zwiedinek acting more or less under his direction, to cause embarrassment and place this Government in a false light. I assume that when the Ambassador considers the time opportune he will endeavor to show that the recent declaration was instigated by this Government.

Faithfully yours,   Robert Lansing

CCL (SDR, RG 59, 763.72/2479½, DNA).

E N C L O S U R E

MEMORANDUM relative to the NEW DECLARATION OF POLICY
BY GERMANY AND AUSTRIA-HUNGARY IN REGARD TO SUBMARINE
WARFARE. JANUARY-FEBRUARY, 1916.

Read to Cabinet by President Mch. 7/16 RL

March 3, 1916.

The German Government on January 7, 1916, shortly after the sinking of the British steamship PERSIA, made public announcement of the orders which had been issued to its submarine commanders particularly those operating in the Mediterranean. In terms this announcement was generally acceptable but about the same time it came to my knowledge from confidential but reliable sources that the naval party in Berlin were securing the upper hand and that the German Government had under consideration a policy of limiting the class of merchant ships to those which carried no armament. As the orders announced on January 7th made no distinction between armed and unarmed ships, in spite of the fact that the PERSIA was then known to have carried a gun, such a policy would materially affect the assurance of the 7th as well as the assurances previously given, which did not except armed vessels.

At that time the informal negotiations regarding the LUSITANIA were proceeding on the basis that the future conduct of submarine warfare had been satisfactorily settled by the several assurances given by Germany, the subject of discussion being the past conduct of the German naval authorities. It was evident that if the German Government should adopt the policy of eliminating from the benefit of its assurances all merchant vessels carrying guns, the question of the future conduct of Germany would be reopened.

In order to avoid such a situation and also having particularly in mind the humane purpose of preventing as far as possible the loss of life among non-combatants on merchant ships, an identical letter, more or less informal in nature, was on January 18, 1916, addressed to the diplomatic representatives of the Entente Powers at Washington proposing to them that their Governments should disarm all their merchant vessels in consideration of an agreement by Germany to comply strictly with the rules governing the taking and destruction of prizes of war on the high seas.

This letter was not sent to the representatives of Germany and Austria-Hungary at Washington for the reason that the Entente Powers were the only ones asked to modify the established rules of naval warfare. All that was required of the Teutonic Powers was observance of existing law, so that their refusal of the proposed *modus vivendi* would be difficult.

A few days after the letter was sent its substance was published in London and later the full text appeared in a Chicago paper. The Department of State did not give out the letter, which must have been made public by the British Foreign Office or by one of the Embassies in Washington.

On January 26th Baron Zwiedinek, the Austrian Chargé, called upon me and asked me about the letter to the Entente Powers of which he said he had heard. I told him that I could confidentially say to him that we had made proposals to the Entente Powers such as were reported, and that nothing had been said to the Central Powers because they were not asked to change the rules of war but were merely asked to live up to the rules which they were in any event bound to do. I told him further that the United States had two objects in view, one was to avoid a situation which would make very difficult our relations with the Central Powers and the other was the humane purpose of saving the lives of noncombatants.

Baron Zwiedinek then spoke to me of the views of the Central Powers that an armed merchant ship could not be treated as a peaceful trader and added that they were considering issuing an announcement to that effect. He asked me, if they did this, when I thought it would be well to do it.

As this action was in line with the information which I had received and as I felt convinced that it would be done ultimately whatever the express wishes of this Government might be, I considered the matter from the point of view of its effect on the LUSITANIA negotiations and came to the conclusion that, if the announcement was made *after* the LUSITANIA case was settled, and while I was thus advised of the intention of the Central Powers, it could be claimed, and not without reason, that this Government had to all intents acquiesced in limiting the application of the German assurances to unarmed vessels. It would have been difficult to explain the settlement if *before* it was made I was advised of the views of the Central Powers as to armed vessels. There would have been bitter and, I think, justifiable criticism by the American people. The situation was made the more difficult because the disputed points as to the past conduct of Germany in regard to the LUSITANIA were on the verge of settlement, in fact on the day before (January 25th) the German Ambassador and I had agreed on a form of reply by the German Government which he was sending to Berlin for approval, yet I had not been officially notified of the purpose of the German Government to issue a declaration of new policy, although morally sure that Baron Zwiedinek expressed the intention of both Governments. Furthermore, I could not avoid the suspicion that the matter was a clever scheme to commit this Government to the plan of treating only unarmed vessels as merchantmen.

In view of these considerations it was desirable that the proposed declaration should be promulgated before the LUSITANIA negotiations reached their final stage, and so, in reply to Baron Zwiedinek's question as to when I thought it would be well to issue the declaration, I replied to him that I believed that the sooner it was issued the better.

We then discussed whether he should communicate to his Government by wireless through the German Embassy's cipher or by transmission in his own cipher through the Department of State. I told him I disliked very much to transmit cipher messages through the Department and he decided to use the wireless.

The same evening (January 26th) the Telegraph Room at the Department of State read to me over the telephone the translation of Baron Zwiedinek's wireless message to his Government, in which he said that I would "welcome it" if a declaration such as he had proposed was issued. He used the German cipher.

Following the invariable practice of the Department in dealing with cipher messages by wireless I treated the message as a confidential communication to the Austro-Hungarian Government and allowed it to go forward, as there was nothing in the message which was obscure or which conveyed military information, which are the sole subjects of the Department's censorship.

As soon, however, as I authorized the Telegraph Room to send the telegram to the Navy Department for transmission, I made a note in writing to call the attention of Baron Zwiedinek, "if opportunity offered," that is, if he brought the matter officially to my attention, to his erroneous statement that I would "welcome" the issuance of the declaration.

The reason for not correcting erroneous statements in censored wireless messages is manifest. If the Department adopted the practice of correcting all erroneous statements of fact or reports of conversations, the result would be that every message or sentence in a message which was passed without correction would be held to be endorsed by the Department as true. It would be unwise for the Department to assume such responsibility and become the sponsor for the accuracy of all statements passing under its censorship as it would be almost impossible to perform such a service and it would also be a constant source of irritation and dispute.

The opportunity to call the attention of Baron Zwiedinek to the misinformation he had conveyed to his Government came on February 9th, when he called for the first time after January 26th and brought to me a translation of a wireless message from the *German Government*, dated February 6th, but which was stated to be in reply to the Chargé's message of January 26th.

In the message shown me appeared the following: "Germany and Austria-Hungary will publish within a few days declaration welcomed by Mr. Lansing" and applied it to the treatment of all armed merchantmen as auxiliary cruisers.

After reading the message I pointed out to Baron Zwiedinek that the words "welcomed by Mr. Lansing" were unwarranted as I had not intended to convey any such meaning in our previous conversation.

He replied that I had had the opportunity to see the message which he sent to his Government on January 26th and could have corrected it.

I told him that that was so, but that in accordance with our policy I never had censored and would not censor in future the truth of statements in wireless messages, explaining to him our practice.

I told him that my words were "the sooner that it is done the better" referring to the issuance of a declaration as to armed vessels.

He said that my words seemed to warrant his report of our conversation.

I said that I saw how he might have gained that impression, but that I had not intended to convey such a meaning, and I hoped that he would so advise his Government.

Meanwhile on the 8th the German Ambassador had asked me for a copy of my letter to the representatives of the Allies and I had told him that I could not give it to him until replies had been received, as I considered the matter more or less confidential.

Late in the evening of February 9th the Telegraph Room telephoned me the translation of a message by Baron Zwiedinek to his
Government, in which he said that I had called his attention to "a
misunderstanding created by the use of the world 'welcome,'" and
that I "did not wish to imply any initiative."

On the same sheet of paper as the foregoing message was one
from the German Ambassador to his Government which was also
read to me over the telephone. In this message appeared the following: "Mr. Lansing reminded me of fact that from the beginning of controversy with us the American Government always
spoke of unarmed merchant vessels, (American note of May
13th, 1915)."

The statement was absolutely false and manifestly absurd on
the face. The fact was the Ambassador himself had made the
statement calling attention to the note of May 13th, and I had
said to him that it had been used in that connection because of
the charge that the LUSITANIA was alleged to have had guns on
board.

However, following our practice, I directed the Telegraph
Room to permit the message to go forward, but made a note to
call the misstatement to the Ambassador's attention if the
opportunity offered. As the subject has not been brought to my
attention officially I have had no opportunity to speak of it.

I could not but feel that there was an ulterior motive in thus
openly putting words in my mouth, which I never used and could
not have used, knowing that I would see the misstatement when
it was passed for transmission. I suspected and still suspect that
it was believed that, observing this false statement, I would
decline to let the mesage go through until it was corrected, and,
after I had done so, it would be argued that as I had corrected this
message I must have approved since I did not correct the
Zwiedinek message of January 26th, in which it was stated I
would "welcome" the declaration of the Central Powers.

If such was the scheme in sending the statement, and the more
I consider it the stronger grows my conviction that this was the
purpose, it failed because the utterly false report was allowed to
go forward without correction or comment.

Some days after these messages were sent I learned from a
press correspondent that he had heard that, before the declaration of submarine policy had been issued by the Central Powwrs
[Powers] on February 10th, I had informed them that I would
"welcome" such a declaration. It was evident that the source of
this report must have been one of the Teutonic Embassies, so on
February 19th I summoned Baron Zwiedinek to the Department

and informed him that this story had come to me and that in view of my denial of the use of the word or of any intention to convey such a meaning I was greatly surprised that it was in circulation and resented it very much.

The Chargé denied that he had given out the story but said that he was sure I had used the word "welcome." I answered him that in view of what I had said to him ten days before he must realize that I could only deny the truth of his statement, which I told him I should certainly do if the necessity arose.

He again referred to the fact that as a translation had passed through the Department without comment I was bound by the accuracy of the statement. I repeated at some length the explanation of the practice of the Department in regard to the censoring of wireless messages and told him that I had called the misstatement to his attention as soon as the matter came to me officially. I further said that the use of his message by his Government after I had denied its accuracy would be most unjustifiable, and that I hoped that he would not be put in so embarrassing a position.

In order that the matter might be of record I wrote Baron Zwiedinek on the 22d fully detailing the practice of the Department as to the censorship of wireless cipher messages.

On the 24th Baron Zwiedinek replied acknowledging my letter of the 22d and advancing the assertion that before he left me on January 26th he requested me "to carefully look over" the message he was sending before allowing it to pass. He stated that he felt assured that as the message had passed the Department without comment it had been virtually endorsed as correct.

As no request had been made by Baron Zwiedinek at our interview on January 26th I answered him on February 25th that I had no recollection of his having made any such request, but that if he did—and I had to assume that he did because he so stated—I had not understood him and so had followed the usual practice when his message was submitted to me.

Since this last letter was sent, intimations have come from our Embassies at Berlin and Vienna that the Teutonic Governments are beginning to circulate the report that the Declaration of February 10th was directly due to the fact that it would be welcomed by this Government. Our Ambassadors at both capitals have been advised briefly of the truth.   Robert Lansing

TS memorandum (SDR, RG 59, 763.72/2479½, DNA).

From Robert Lansing, with Enclosure

PERSONAL AND CONFIDENTIAL:

My dear Mr. President: Washington March 6, 1916.

I enclose for your perusal a confidential letter which has just come from Mr. Gerard at Berlin. Kindly return the letter to me at your early convenience.

Faithfully yours,   Robert Lansing

TLS (SDR, RG 59, 763.72/2471½, DNA).

ENCLOSURE

James Watson Gerard to Robert Lansing

Dear Mr. Secretary: [Berlin] February 16, 1916.

No great news this week. By this mail you get copies of the Memo regarding armed merchant ships.

There is a fight against the Chancellor—started in the home of the Junkers, the Prussian Chamber. The powerful liberal papers are jumping hard on the disturbers and the Chancellor hit back quite hard. These Junkers are demanding unlimited submarine war and are stirred up by von Tirpitz. It is one of their last kicks; as soon a real suffrage will have to be introduced in Prussia. The Chancellor foreshadowed this in opening this Prussian Chamber: *hinc illae lachrymae.*

The visit of Colonel House here was undoubtedly, from this end, a success; and I am glad that he can give the President and you a fresh and impartial view. After nearly three years my judgment is probably warped.

March 1st we go on a milk and butter card regime. I have put the Polish question (food) up to Zimmermann, and asked informally if proper guarantees against the direct or indirect taking of food and money from Poland will be stopped, if relief is sent; no answer yet.   Yours ever   J.W.G.

TLI (SDR, RG 59, 763.72/2471½, DNA).

From William Joel Stone

Dear Mr. President: [Washington] March 6th, 1916.

I want to see you. I want to have a full and frank personal talk. I gave notice some days ago of an intention to address the Senate on the question of armed merchant ships, so-called, and on subjects related thereto. All along it has been my wish to talk with you before delivering this speech, but I have been so beset with people coming to see me that I have not been able, until now, to prepare the speech I had in mind to make. My desire has been not to make this speech, if at all, until I could talk with you. I will give notice today to postpone this speech to a later date. I want first to talk with you. We should be able to talk with each other, as you said, "with perfect frankness."

Can you so arrange your engagements as to allow me to call on you tomorrow, (Tuesday) afternoon? I say afternoon, because tomorrow is Cabinet day.

Please have me notified this evening at my residence, 3028 Newark Avenue, Telephone Cleveland 664, or at my Committee Rooms tomorrow morning.[1]

Very sincerely yours,   Wm J Stone

TLS (WP, DLC).

[1] Wilson saw Stone at the White House at 8 P.M. on March 7 for about an hour. There is no record of their conversation; however, Stone announced on the following day that he would not give his speech on armed ships. Moreover, he later wrote to Wilson (see W. J. Stone to WW, April 7, 1916) that he had canceled his speech largely because of his talk with Wilson.

From Newton Diehl Baker

Cleveland, Ohio, March 6, 1916.

I accept your judgment and will be in Washington Thursday morning.[1]   Newton D. Baker

T telegram (WP, DLC).

To Newton Diehl Baker

[The White House] March 6, 1916

Your message delights me. My judgment and desire in the matter are clear, and your answer in every way justifies my choice. With your permission I will send in the nomination at once, and shall hope to see you as soon as it is convenient for you to come to Washington for a conference as to your convenience in assuming the duties.   Woodrow Wilson

T telegram (Letterpress Books, WP, DLC).

From Newton Diehl Baker

My dear Mr President: [Cleveland, Ohio] March 6, 1916

Your sudden summons entails so many changes in my plans that I am far from sure that I yet comprehend just how seriously

I have compromised your kindness by allowing it to proceed to the conclusion. But I am very sure that I appreciate the confidence you give me and if I can, by work, cure the defects of inexperience and so relieve you of any part of your burden I shall be very happy.

I shall study to catch not the habit but the wisdom of your voice and so to keep the War Department in step with the high patriotism which marks the whole of your administration

Mrs Baker[1] asks me to send her regards and appreciation

Heartily yours,   Newton D. Baker

ALS (WP, DLC).
[1] Elizabeth Leopold Baker.

From David Benton Jones

My dear Mr. President: Chicago March 6, 1916.

"Not to stir without great argument,
But greatly to find quarrel in a straw
When honor is at stake."[1]

You have not had the above from Shakespeare in your mind when speaking of your present difficulty, but I know of no text that is more fitting or authoritative.

I have no doubt of the outcome, but at the same time we all will be greatly relieved to have these moralists without morality disposed of once and for all, on this issue. Bryan utterly lacks moral perception. He is an evangel of his own fancies and formulas, and not of facts and morals. He could not see that his Sixteen to One formula was immoral. There is a line in Byron telling of Greece which fits the whole crew. It is Byronic in phrasing, but just as true as Shakespeare:

"Self abasement paved the way
To villain bonds and despot sway."[2]

That is just what poor Ford in his ignorance, and Bryan in his hypocrisy and vanity, are trying to prepare for, and would if they were allowed their way. I cannot believe that there is danger in the House when the final vote comes.

I am leaving tomorrow for California. I am sending you this note simply to let you know that we are watching with more impatience than anxiety for the outcome.

Very sincerely yours,   David B. Jones.

TLS (WP, DLC).
[1] *Hamlet*, Act IV, Scene 4, lines 54-56.
[2] Byron, *The Giaour, A Fragment of a Turkish Tale*.

From Walter Hines Page

Dear Mr. President: London, March 6, 1916.

I don't like to burden you with the request to read anything, but if you will read the enclosed copy of a letter that I have written to Mr. Eliot and of the Committee's Programme for the forthcoming Shakespeare celebration,[1] I can make this note to you quite short.

One of the main items—I think that I can say the main item—of the programme that the Committee would have made but for the war would have been an invitation to you, as the political head of the largest body of English-speaking folk in the world and as a scholar and a gentleman besides, to come and deliver the speech of honour on that occasion. That being now impossible, the celebration will be private and not official.

But the Committee will not be content without some word from you—not official—but some private message that may be delivered to the English people about our great common inheritance of Shakespeare. Their wish, as you will see from my letter to Mr. Eliot, is that he may bring it.

I am sure that both you and he will acquit me of discourtesy in writing to you both by the same mail; for the time is short.

I cannot refrain from adding to the Committee's request which they have instructed me to send you for such a message, my personal hope that nothing will stand in the way of your favourable response. It will have an admirable effect.

Yours faithfully   Walter H. Page

TLS (WP, DLC).
[1] WHP to C. W. Eliot, March 6, 1916, TCL (WP, DLC).

From Andrew Clerk Imbrie[1]

My dear Mr. President: New York, March 6th, 1916.

I attach a brief statement of the dyestuff situation[2] which the Hill Bill (H.R. 702)[3] is expected to meet. This statement may be useful to you as a memorandum of our talk on March 8th.

I thank you very cordially for the opportunity to present the facts.[4]   Yours faithfully,   Andrew C Imbrie

TLS (WP, DLC).
[1] Wilson's former student at Princeton, president of the United States Finishing Co. of New York.
[2] [A. C. Imbrie] T Memorandum (WP, DLC). This memorandum pointed out that Germany had traditionally supplied 90 per cent of all dyestuffs used by American manufacturers, and that, since March 1915, no dyestuffs had been imported from Germany. Imbrie went on to urge the importance of developing a strong American dyestuffs industry.

3 A bill introduced on December 6, 1915, by Representative Ebenezer J. Hill, Republican of Connecticut. It imposed duties of 5 per cent ad valorem on all synthetic products made from coal; of three and one-half cents a pound and 15 per cent ad valorem on all "intermediates" made from these synthetic products; and of seven and one-half cents a pound and 30 per cent ad valorem on all colors or dyes derived from coal.

4 See Imbrie's memorandum printed at March 8, 1916.

From the Diary of Colonel House

The White House, Washington, D. C. March 6, 1916.

One of the White House automobiles was waiting at the station. Irving Hoover said he had just received a telephone message from the Navy Yard saying the President and Mrs. Wilson would be up at eight o'clock to breakfast with me.

We did not have much conversation at the breakfast table or afterward, having agreed to leave the important discussion until after lunch.

I saw the Attorney General and Postmaster General and other members of the Cabinet, but nothing of importance passed. They gave a review of the happenings during my absence.

After lunch the President, Mrs. Wilson and I took an automobile ride of something over two hours. During this time I outlined every important detail of my mission. The President, on our return, dropped me at the State Department, and I had an interview of an hour with Lansing, giving him a summary of what I had told the President. I returned to the White House and the President and I went into session again until nearly seven o'clock. I showed him the memorandum which Sir Edward Grey and I had agreed was the substance of my understanding with France and Great Britain. The President accepted it *in toto* only suggesting that the word "probably" be inserted in the ninth line after the word "world" and before the word "leave.["] He also suggested that tomorrow we write out the full text of the reply which I shall send Grey.

I had an engagement to dine with the Postmaster General, and when I arose to leave, the President placed his arm around my shoulders and said: "I cannot adequately express to you my admiration and gratitude for what you have done. It would be impossible to imagine a more difficult task than the one placed in your hands, but you have accomplished it in a way beyond any expectations."

I replied that it made me happy to know he felt satisfied, for I knew he had been criticised for sending me, and I rejoiced that he felt I had justified his action. I spoke of the pride I would feel if the plan could be realized and I could see him sitting at the head of the counsel table at the Hague. He said, "my dear friend, you should be proud of yourself and not of me since you have done it all."

These generous expressions touched me deeply. I shall not go into any general discussion of our conferences for it has all been related before.

I had a pleasant dinner with Burleson who had Gregory for his other guest. I went from there to see McAdoo and had an hour's talk with him, and then returned to the White House.

T MS (E. M. House Papers, CtY).

To Martin Henry Glynn

My dear Governor: [The White House] March 7, 1916

That was an admirable speech you made at the convention in reply to Mr. Root, and I join with the whole country in thinking that the reply was overwhelming and complete.[1] I write these lines merely to express my admiration and to tell you how deeply and sincerely I appreciate your generous attitude in that address towards myself. These are the things that make public service worth while.

Cordially and sincerely yours, Woodrow Wilson

TLS (Letterpress Books, WP, DLC).
[1] In his address at the Democratic state convention in Syracuse on March 1, 1916, Glynn had sounded the keynote of Wilson's campaign for re-election and responded to Senator Root's attack on the administration. After briefly reviewing Wilson's domestic achievements, Glynn turned to the New York Republican convention's censure of the administration's preparedness program. The Republican party alone, Glynn said, was to blame for the present lack of adequate defense. He maintained that Wilson was now trying hard to make up for the derelictions of his Republican predecessors. Glynn then went into a spirited defense of Wilson's policy in Mexico and toward the European belligerents. The Republicans, he charged, were stirring up passions that would plunge the United States into needless war. Wilson, in contrast, was following a wise course of patient negotiations that appealed to reason before it appealed to force. Concluding his eulogy of Wilson, he said: "Mr. Root may beat his drum, and blare his trumpet, but President Wilson will go right on winning the plaudits of the American people by appealing to reason, humanity and common sense and by keeping the United States the uncompromising champion of the neutral world and the undaunted maintainer of the principles which have guided this nation since 1776. . . . No reward, no punishment will make him swerve from what he knows to be his highest duty. He has preserved, strengthened, dignified and uplifted our noblest national traditions and he will continue to do so no matter what the cost or what the penalty." New York Times, March 2, 1916.

To Robert Wickliffe Woolley

My dear Mr. Woolley: The White House March 7, 1916

The desire of the Common Counsel Club to have me come as its guest to the celebration which it is planning for Jefferson's Birthday is very gratifying to me, and the committee you name is certainly a committee I should in any case like to see, but I feel bound in candor to say that it will not be possible for me to accept the invitation[1] simply because I feel that I must not add a feather to the things I am already carrying. The camel has a good back, and so have I, but you know the proverbial straw was too much and a speech is vastly more than a straw to me. It always takes it out of me and my present duty seems in part, at any rate, to be conservation of energy.

I know that all concerned will understand how genuine my regret is that I must come to this decision, and how sincerely I wish that it were otherwise.

Cordially yours,   Woodrow Wilson

TLS (R. W. Woolley Papers, DLC).
[1] It is missing. In fact, Wilson attended the banquet on April 13, 1916, and delivered the principal address. It is printed at that date.

To Harry Augustus Garfield

My dear Garfield: The White House March 7, 1916

Your letters are always welcome and I thank you sincerely for that of March third. Our correspondence with Great Britain is less dramatic than our correspondence with Germany, partly because it moves, so far as the other side are concerned at any rate, as slowly as cold molasses, but it would be a mistake to think that we are not exerting as much pressure in the case of our rights in the one direction as in the other.

In haste, with warm regards to all,

Cordially and faithfully yours,   Woodrow Wilson

TLS (H. A. Garfield Papers, DLC).

To John Sharp Williams

My dear Senator: The White House March 7, 1916

I thank you warmly for having let me see the editorial from the Memphis Commercial Appeal. It has the right red blood in it and is undoubtedly the real voice of America. It is amazing to me that there should be any other sort of voice audible, and I believe that if the real test came all other voices would be drowned. Hurrah for the Commercial Appeal!

Cordially and sincerely yours,   Woodrow Wilson

TLS (J. S. Williams Papers, DLC).

To Henry Lee Higginson

[The White House]
My dear Major Higginson: March 7, 1916
     I have read your letter of March fourth with interest and appreciation and send you just this line to say so.
                    Cordially yours,   Woodrow Wilson

TLS (Letterpress Books, WP, DLC).

From William Kent

My dear Mr. President: Washington, D. C. March 7, 1916.
     I have not the privilege of personal acquaintance with Mr. Baker but from what I can hear about him, I believe he stands with us on the great questions of public rights, as found in policies that represent control and use of our natural resources in the public interest.
     I respectfully suggest that in view of pending water power legislation that he be placed in touch with what is going on with Senator Walsh, Senator Norris, and Representatives Ferris and Lenroot.
     This water power development is something that, under any proposed legislation, will run for at least 50 years and under the Shields bill as it is being fought out in the Senate, will run for an indefinite time, unless upset by revolution or cured by the sovereign power of taxation.
     This bill, as it is being handled in the Senate, will be extremely vicious and whether or not we can secure amendments by conference with the House Committee is extremely dubious. Unless some one in the Administration takes strong ground, there is every chance that nothing at all will be done and that the waters will go to waste simply because some of us feel that a waste for a year or two is better than to sacrifice all public rights practically in perpetuity.
     I know of no greater service that can be immediately rendered by the Secretary of War than in the consideration of control of water power on navigable streams, which comes immediately under his jurisdiction, and it will be my pleasure to put him in touch with the best authorities in this country on this subject.
     We are making a fight against people who thoroughly realize the immense fortunes to be made out of control of these, our common assets. Without fear of contradiction, I again state, as I have often stated before, that for influence and lobbying work,

the water power crowd are the shrewdest and most dangerous people that we have to fight in the country today.

I do not wish to bore you with any long disquisition on this subject, but I wish to express my hope that the new Secretary of War can immediately take up and study this question.

As I have often stated, Senator Norris, of Nebraska, is the soundest man I know in the Senate on this proposition. He is nearly broken down by the contentions of those who disbelieve in public control and he is intensely suspicious of where the Administration stands. I never had any doubt about that matter, since having talked with you, but it is inherently necessary that there should be no doubt about what will happen if a bill goes before you that does not duly protect the public interest and one of such a nature that the injustice may be continued through an indefinite term.　　　　Yours truly,　William Kent

TLS (WP, DLC).

Edward Mandell House to Sir Edward Grey

The White House [March 7, 1916].

I reported to the President the general conclusions of our conference of the fourteenth of February and in the light of those conclusions he authorizes me to say that, so far as he can speak for the future action of the United States, he agrees to the memorandum with which you furnished me with only this correction that the word probably be added at the end of line nine.[1]

WWT telegram (E. M. House Papers, CtY).

[1] House wrote on this document: "After my conference with the President in which I explained to him what was agreed between the Prime Minister, Balfour, Grey, Lloyd George, Reading and myself he confirmed it by typing this cable which he authorized me to send to Grey. E. M. House Washington, Feb. 7, 1916."

From the Diary of Colonel House

March 7, 1916.

The most important happening of today was the writing of the cable to Sir Edward Grey. After some discussion, the President took down in shorthand what he thought was the concensus of our opinion, and then went to his typewriter and typed it off. This document is a part of the diary, and a most important part. The fact that he has approved in writing all I have done, gives me great satisfaction.

I have seen Phillips and Polk of the State Department and

have discussed the diplomatic corps, promotions and demotions in the service being agreed upon. I have also seen members of the Cabinet including McAdoo, Houston, Burleson and Gregory.

In the afternoon the President, Mrs. Wilson and I went to the Mayflower to bid Secretary and Mrs. McAdoo and other members of the Pan-American party goodbye.[1] After that we drove for an hour and the President told of an interview Mr. Bryan had with Lane, which Lane had at once reduced to writing and given him.[2] The President was somewhat worried about it, and wished my judgment as what was best to do. He seems to have come to the parting of the ways with Mr. Bryan. We thought the real cause of Bryan's displeasure was that the President is standing for a second term, and the support of the Administration has not be[en] thrown to Mr. Bryan instead. I recalled Bryan's asking me a year or more ago whether my remark that if he desired to be President he should first become Secretary of State in a Democratic Cabinet and make a record which would inevitably bring about his nomination for President, was the view of the President or entirely my own, and how disappointed he was when I told him it was my view alone.

Mr. Bryan complained to Lane that the President had never given him his confidence. When Lane replied that he had never discussed with any of his Cabinet matters appertaining to other departments, Bryan said, "That is well enough with the balance of the Cabinet, but my position is different. For sixteen years I have been the leader of the Democratic Party, and I am entitled to be consulted upon all matters of importance."

Bryan has told others that I was Secretary of State and not himself, and that the President had never taken him into his confidence. In answer to this the President says he is glad Bryan knows no more of the inside of his mind that he did before they ever met, and if he had been foolish enough to have made him his confident [confidant], the result of Bryan's feelings toward him would not be different, but he would possess an advantage which he does not now hold.

I saw the British Ambassador today for an hour and had a satisfactory talk. Among other things discussed was the reply the Allies should make concerning disarming of merchantmen. The Ambassador said his Government would be willing to put their refusal to accept the proposal in the most advantageous form possible. I promised to advise with the President and let him know what was thought best.

Spring-Rice told me what Lansing said to the Italian Ambassador, an indiscretion of which I am sorry Lansing was guilty.

He told him that his purpose in proposing the disarming of Allied merchantmen was to please Germany and get a favorable settlement of the Lusitania controversy. This is exactly what Lansing and the President have been charged with.

I returned to the White House and discussed the matter with the President. He thought the best reply the Allies could make was a promise that they would strictly adhere to international law, and would not transgress it in any particular, and that their armament would be for defensive and not for offensive purposes. The President took occasion to blame himself and Lansing for allowing this controversy to crop out. I thought it more Lansing's fault than his. Nevertheless, the President insisted upon taking the blame along with Lansing.

I thought the last clause in the Lansing proposal the most dangerous one and was inconsistent.[3] He admitted it was unfortunate, but the only thing to do now was to make the best of a bad situation. The President showed an admirable spirit in refusing to shirk responsibility for an unnecessary blunder.

The President, McAdoo, Burleson and I discussed what was best to do about the McLemore resolution now pending in Congress. Many times yesterday and today I have been in conferences concerning this fight.

There was a large musicale given at the White House tonight.[4] I remained on the outside talking to different members of the Cabinet. When it was over I took the midnight train for New York. Mr. Lamb[5] of the Neutrality Squad had been instructed to remain in Washington until my return and accompany me back.

[1] McAdoo went to Buenos Aires as a member of the American delegation to the International High Commission on Uniformity of Laws Relating to Foreign Trade, which had been created by the Pan American Financial Conference in Washington in May 1915. The delegation included, among others, Senator Duncan Upshaw Fletcher, John Bassett Moore, Samuel Untermyer, Elbert Henry Gary, Paul Moritz Warburg, and John Henry Fahey. The party left Washington on *U.S.S. Mayflower* for Hampton Roads, where it boarded *U.S.S. Tennessee* for Buenos Aires.

[2] It is missing.

[3] It read: "In the event that it is impossible to place a prize crew on board of an enemy merchant vessel or convoy it into port, the vessel may be sunk, provided the crew and passengers have been removed to a place of safety." *FR-WWS 1916*, p. 147.

[4] It took place in the East Room and was the first in a series of musicales at the White House. The program, which had been selected by Margaret Wilson, included works by Schubert and Chopin. The pianist was Enrique Granados, the soprano, Julia Culp. Among the 339 guests were several ambassadors, cabinet members, senators, and congressmen and their wives.

[5] George F. Lamb, clerk in the Customs Service in New York.

Sir Cecil Arthur Spring Rice to Sir Edward Grey

Very confidential.
Your No 580

Washington 7 March 1916.

No. 808. I have received message directly from President to following effect:

(1) He would be glad if blockade note were delayed for a time.

(2) With regard to submarine note (see my desp No 20 Treaty Jan 21) answer might be expedited. It might be short and to the effect that allies prefer to maintain existing practice of international law renewing official assurances that guns would only be used for defensive purposes and offering to discuss questions raised by note after the war is over.

State department suggests that question of interference with mails is the one which excites most feeling and that a settlement of this question is most desirable

Navy department tells me removal of Germans from "China"[1] is causing ill feeling in naval circles and that it would be wise to follow example of French and release them, if possible.

If we can grant some concession on these points and also on matter of wool and cyanide I think blockade question will not be pressed.

Could you suggest to Page without mentioning President that he might ask whether in opinion of U S Govt delay was not advisable in blockade question?

Hw telegram (FO 115/2024, p. 123, PRO).
  [1] On February 18, 1916, *H.M.S. Laurentic* stopped an American ship, *S.S. China*, on the high seas, about ten miles from the mouth of the Yangtze River, and removed at gunpoint twenty-eight Germans, eight Austrians, and two Turks, all civilians. Lansing directed Ambassador Page to lodge a formal protest with the British government and called the action of *Laurentic's* captain "an unwarranted invasion of the sovereignty of American vessels" and a grave "affront to the American flag." RL to WHP, Feb. 23 and April 22, 1916, *FR-WWS 1916*, pp. 632, 637-39. After a long series of exchanges, the British government agreed on May 3, 1916, to release the prisoners. It did so on July 24; however, it never disavowed the action of the captain of *H.M.S. Laurentic*. See *FR-WWS 1916*, pp. 632-35, 637-59, 661-68, 672-73, 678, and 685.

From Robert Lansing, with Enclosure

PERSONAL AND CONFIDENTIAL:

My dear Mr. President: Washington March 8, 1916.

I enclose a memorandum which was handed to me by the German Ambassador this morning, and which contains more or less a historical review of the submarine warfare question, directing particular attention to the shortcomings of Great Britain.

You will note that the Ambassador expresses a desire to give the memorandum publicity and I could not well object to his doing so, as it does not directly affect our negotiations with Germany. I would, however, call your attention to the last paragraph which indicates to me that the memorandum was prepared with the idea of making an appeal to the American people. Please return the memorandum with any suggestions you have as to what treatment we should give it.

Faithfully yours,   Robert Lansing.

TLS (SDR, RG 59, 763.72/2623, DNA).

E N C L O S U R E

Handed to me German Amb. 11:30 am Mch 8/16 RL

The German Amb. asked me if I had objection to making this public as he would like to do so. I told him I could see no objection as it did not affect the negotiations between the two Governments. RL

MEMORANDUM

The Imperial German Government, on account of the friendly relations, which have always existed between the two great nations and earnestly desiring to continue them, wishes to explain the U-Boat question once more to the American Government.

At the outbreak of the war the German Government, acting upon the suggestion of the United States, immediately expressed its readiness to ratify the declaration of London. At that time a German prize code had already been issued, which was entirely —and without modification—based upon the rules of the declaration of London. Germany thereby proved her willingness to recognize fully the existing rules of international law which ensure the freedom of the sea for the legitimate trade of neutral nations not only among themselves but also with belligerent countries.

Great Britain, on the other hand, declined to ratify the declaration of London and, after the outbreak of the war, began to restrict the legitimate trade of the neutrals in order to hit Germany. The contraband provisions were systematically extended on August 5th, 20th, September 21st and October 29th, 1914. On November 3rd, 1914, the order of the British Admiralty followed declaring the whole North Sea a war zone in which commercial shipping would be exposed to most serious dangers from mines and men of war. Protests from Neutrals were of no avail and from that time on the freedom of neutral commerce with Germany was practically destroyed. Under these circumstances, Germany was compelled to resort, in February 1915, to reprisals in order to fight her opponents' measures, which were absolutely contrary to International Law. She chose for this purpose a new weapon the use of which had not yet been regulated by International Law and, in doing so, could and did not violate any existing rules, but only took into account the peculiarity of this new weapon, the submarine boat.

The use of the submarine naturally necessitated a restriction of the free movements of Neutrals and constituted a danger for them which Germany intended to ward off by a special warning analogous to the warning England had given regarding the North Sea.

As both belligerents—Germany in her note of February 17th and Great Britain in those of February 18th and 20th, 1915—claimed that their proceeding was only enacted in retaliation for the violation of International Law by their opponents, the American Government approached both parties for the purpose of trying to reestablish International Law as it had been in force before the war. Germany was asked to adapt the use of her new weapon to the rules which had been existing for the former naval weapons, and England not to interfere with the food supplies intended for the non-combatant German population and to admit their distribution under American supervision. Germany, on March 1st, 1915, declared her willingness to comply with the proposal of the American Government whilst England, on the other hand, declined to do so. By the order in Council of March 11th 1915, Great Britain abolished even what had remained of the freedom of neutral trade with Germany and her neutral neighbors. England's object was to starve Germany into submission by these illegal means.

Germany, after neutral citizens had lost their lives against her wish and intention, nevertheless in the further course of the war complied with the wishes of the American Government regarding the use of her submarines. The rights of Neutrals regarding legal trading were, in fact, nowhere limited by Germany.

Then England made it impossible for submarines to conform with the old rules of International Law by arming nearly all merchant men and by ordering the use of guns on merchant vessels for attack. Photographic reproductions of those instructions have been transmitted to neutral Governments with the memorandum of the German Government of February 8th 1916. These orders are obviously in contradiction with the note delivered by the British Ambassador in Washington to the American Government on August 25th 1914. On account of the proposals, made by the United States on January 23rd 1916, regarding disarmament, the Imperial Government hoped that these facts would enable the neutral Governments to obtain the disarmament of the merchant ships of her opponents. The latter, however, continued with great energy to arm their merchant men with guns.

The principle of the United States Government not to keep their citizens off belligerent merchant ships has been used by Great Britain and her allies to arm merchant ships for offensive purposes. Under these circumstances merchant men can easily destroy submarines, and if their attack fails, still consider themselves in safety by the presence of American citizens on board.

The order to use arms on British merchant men was supplemented by instructions to the masters of such ships to hoist false flags and to ram U-boats. Reports on payments of premiums and bestowals of decorations to successful masters of merchant men show the effects of these orders. England's allies have adopted this position.

Now Germany is facing the following facts:

a) A blockade contrary to International Law (compare American note to England of November 5th, 1915) has for one year been keeping neutral trade from German ports and is making German exports impossible.

b) For eighteen months, through the extending of contraband provisions in violation of International Law (compare American note to England of November 5th 1915) the overseas trade of neighboring neutral countries, so far as Germany is concerned, has been hampered.

c) The interception of mails in violation of International Law (compare American Memorandum to England of January 10th 1916)[1] is meant to stop any intercourse of Germany with Foreign countries.

d) England, by systematically and increasingly oppressing neutral countries, following the principle of "might before right," has prevented neutral trade on land with Germany so as to complete the blockade of the central powers intended to starve their civil population.

e) Germans met by our enemies on the high sea are deprived of their liberty no matter whether they are combatants or non-combatants.

f) Our enemies have armed their merchant vessels for offensive purposes theoretically making it impossible to use our U-boats according to the principles set forth in London declaration (compare American memorandum of February 8th, 1916).

The English white book of January 5th, 1916, on the restriction of German trade, boasts that by British measures Germany's Export Trade has been stopped almost entirely whilst her imports are subject to England's will.

The Imperial Government feels confident that the people of the United States, remembering the friendly relations that for the last hundred years have existed between the two nations, will, in spite of the difficulties, put into the way by our enemies appreciate the German viewpoint as laid down above.

J. Bernstorff.

TS memorandum (SDR, RG 59, 763.72/2623, DNA).
    [1] That is, RL to WHP, Jan. 4, 1916, FR-WWS 1916, pp. 591-92, delivered by Page to the Foreign Office on January 10, 1916.

Two Letters to Robert Lansing

My dear Mr. Secretary,   The White House. 8 March, 1916.

In view of the wording of the last paragraph of this communication, it is evident to me that it is intended not as in any proper sense a memorandum for the information of this Government but as an appeal to American public opinion, and, for my own part, I resent being made use of in this way. Do you not think that it would be well to ask the German Ambassador why, since it is addressed to the American people and makes no reference whatever to a desire to inform the Government of the United States of the subject matter of its contents, it was handed to this Government at all?   Faithfully Yours,   W.W.

WWTLI (SDR, RG 59, 763.72/2635½, DNA).

My dear Mr. Secretary,   The White House. 8 March, 1916.

Thank you very much for having let me see this letter of Gerard's.[1] I return it, as you requested, for your files.

Faithfully Yours,   W.W.

WWTLI (SDR, RG 59, 763.72/2472½, DNA).
    [1] J. W. Gerard to RL, Feb. 16, 1916, printed as an Enclosure with RL to WW, March 6, 1916 (second letter of that date).

To George McLean Harper

My dear Harper: The White House March 8, 1916

I warmly appreciate your thoughtfulness in sending me a copy of your "Life of Wordsworth,"[1] and you may be sure I shall look forward with the greatest pleasure to finding time to read it. I know how much the work has meant to you in the years just gone by and I congratulate you with all my heart on its completion.

Thank you for what you say about my stand for the rights of Americans.[2] It was the obvious and imperative thing to do, but such words from a friend who knows me mean a great deal to me.

With warmest regard to you all,
Cordially and faithfully yours,   Woodrow Wilson

TLS (G. M. Harper Papers, NjP).
[1] George McLean Harper, *William Wordsworth, His Life, Works, and Influence* (New York, 1916). There is a copy of this book in the Wilson Library, DLC.
[2] Harper's letter is missing.

To Joseph Edward Davies

My dear Davies: [The White House] March 8, 1916

Thank you warmly for your letter of Tuesday.[1] It gratifies me deeply always to feel your friendship and approval, and in these days of anxiety and strain the voice of a friend and a true friend at that is indeed grateful and delightful.

I am heartily glad you like the choice of Baker for Secretary of War. I feel confident he will be a great comfort and assistance to all of us. I like to add to the team from time to time.

Always, with real gratitude,
Faithfully yours,   Woodrow Wilson

TLS (Letterpress Books, WP, DLC).
[1] It is missing.

A Memorandum by Andrew Clerk Imbrie

March 8th, 1916

I stated the case substantially as given in the typewritten memorandum which I left with him at the close of the interview.[1]

The President said he was quite familiar with the conditions brought about by the shortage of dyes, and appreciated the importance of the establishment of the industry here. The point about which he was not yet clear was the remedy; and in seeking a remedy, he naturally sought one that was fundamental—which would benefit other industries and not the dyestuff industry alone. He was inclined to believe that whatever increase in duties might be made by Congress, the Germans would overcome by organized price cutting unless prevented by anti-dumping legislation. The President wishes to see price discrimination on the part of foreigners prevented just as it is desired to prevent it as between domestic manufacturers.

I said that the present tariff law, which attached penalties to undervaluation of goods entered at the custom house was, in effect, an "anti-dumping law." The President agreed that this was in a measure true; but regarded the present law as not sufficiently far reaching to accomplish the purposes of a thoroughgoing anti-dumping law.

I told him as far as I knew there was no objection on the part of those who urged the enactment of the Hill Bill,[2] to the passage of an anti-dumping law; but that for the purpose of affording an immediate incentive to capital to develope the dye industry and to meet the present crisis it was necessary to give manufacturers the assurance that they would not be driven out of business when normal times returned. Both dye makers and dye users concur in the belief that the moderate duties proposed by the Hill Bill will give such assurances to manufacturers.

I asked the President especially to consider the testimony of Prof. Charles H. Herty,[3] President of the American Chemical Society at the hearing before the Committee on Ways and Means; testimony that had impressed everyone as a logical and truthful statement of the situation and its remedy; and as showing the correlation of the dyestuff and high explosive industries.

The President said it was planned to establish government plants for the making of high explosives. I called his attention to the letter of General Scott, Acting Secretary of War, to representative Hill (a copy of it accompanying the memorandum I left with him) in which General Scott expressed the opinion that the Government would derive benefit from the establishment by private means of plants that could readily, and almost instantly be made available for a supply of munitions.[4] Furthermore it was seriously to be doubted whether a government plant sufficient to take care of the Country in time of War could be profitably operated in time of peace.

The President said that if, as seemed to him likely, the War should result in an impasse, it would be followed by a tremendous social and political revolution throughout Europe. This would mean further delay in the reestablishment of normal industrial conditions. The destruction of capital, the rise of taxes, and the shortage of labor abroad would make it impossible for Germany to supply materials at anything like the prices prevailing before the War; so that there would be a natural "protection" to the American manufacturer in the enhanced costs of German products—provided an effective anti-dumping law prevents foreign goods being sold here for less than abroad.

I told the President that while there were no doubt many who shared his views as to the events that would follow the War, I was not so sure that enough men had the imagination to see ahead that far, or the courage to invest large capital *immediately* without the more definite assurance that is now within the power of our Government to give them.

The President said he was glad to have a memorandum left with him as a summary of the conversation, and promised to file it for reference when the matter should finally come before him officially.   Andrew C. Imbrie

TS memorandum (RSB Coll., DLC).
    [1] Wilson received him at the White House at 10:30 A.M. on March 8.
    [2] That is, *H.R.702.*
    [3] Charles Holmes Herty, Professor of Chemistry at the University of North Carolina and president of the American Chemical Society.
    [4] H. L. Scott to E. J. Hill, Feb. 16, 1916, TCL (WP, DLC).

To Edward Mandell House

My dear Friend: The White House March 9, 1916

I wonder if it would be possible for you to see the man who wrote the enclosed and give me your judgment about his attitude and intentions, and about the best course for me to pursue?[1]

It was the greatest and deepest pleasure to see you again and I feel that I have very inadequately indeed expressed to you my sense of admiration and obligation. I hope that you can interpret me better than I can interpret myself.

With affectionate regards to you both from us all,
                    Affectionately yours,   Woodrow Wilson

TLS (E. M. House Papers, CtY).
    [1] The enclosure is missing in both the E. M. House Papers, CtY, and in WP, DLC. However, the individual, Edmund Gallauner, was a Hungarian-American leader who had campaigned for Wilson in 1912.

To William Tobias Butler[1]

My dear Mr. Butler: [The White House] March 9, 1916

I have read your letter of March seventh[2] which you were kind enough to send me through Mrs. Wilson, and want to thank you sincerely for its great frankness and the evident sincerity of the views which it presents. As a matter of fact, the balance was never held more scrupulously between parties than it has been held by the State Department, notwithstanding the impression which you seem to have gathered and which seems to prevail among those with whom you have conversed. The whole situation will some day be very clear and I, for one, have no concern as to the ultimate impartial verdict of history. Not that I trust my own judgment always by any means, but that I am dealing with real facts which cannot be mistaken.

You have rightly interpreted my desire to receive the frankest possible counsel and I appreciate most sincerely your friendship.

Sincerely yours, Woodrow Wilson

TLS (Letterpress Books, WP, DLC).
1 Progressive party leader of Brooklyn, former member of the Democratic party.
2 It is missing.

To Franklin Knight Lane

My dear Mr. Secretary: [The White House] March 9, 1916

Thank you very warmly for your full memorandum about the Shields Water Power Bill. The matter is giving me a good deal of anxiety and I am going to ask Mr. Baker to take this question up among the first of those he will have to study when he gets here. I take it for granted you are keeping in touch with Judge Adamson and Mr. Ferris, and I think we ought to have a very definite plan of action when the Shields Bill reaches the House. It is much better to do nothing about the use of water power than to do the wrong thing.

Cordially and sincerely yours, Woodrow Wilson

TLS (Letterpress Books, WP, DLC).

To William Kent

My dear Mr. Kent: The White House March 9, 1916

Thank you for your letter of March seventh. You may be sure that I will call the attention of the new Secretary of War to the water power question at the earliest possible moment, for you know, I am sure, my deep and genuine interest in it. I agree with you that it is better to let the water power run to waste than to settle the question of the use of it in the wrong way. I am watching the progress of legislation with a great deal of anxiety.

Cordially and sincerely yours, Woodrow Wilson

TLS (W. Kent Papers, CtY).

To David Benton Jones

My dear Friend: [The White House] March 9, 1916

Thank you for your letter of March sixth. I am glad you are getting off to California. I envy any man who can take a vacation nowadays, but with such friends as I have it would be unpardonable in me to repine in any way. I count you among my most valued friends and the words of cheer you send me from time to time show how generously and constantly you follow me in your affection. You may be sure that the feeling is warmly reciprocated and that I feel myself constantly your debtor.

May every delightful thing come to you on your vacation!

Cordially and sincerely yours,   Woodrow Wilson

TLS (Letterpress Books, WP, DLC).

From Robert Lansing

PERSONAL AND CONFIDENTIAL:

My dear Mr. President: [Washington] March 9, 1916.

I enclose a memorandum which was handed to me this morning by the Chilean Ambassador[1] in regard to the four articles which were submitted as a basis for a Pan American Treaty.[2] You will observe that the second article of those we proposed is entirely omitted. That article, you will recall, deals with the endeavor to settle as soon as possible all boundary disputes by amicable agreement or by arbitration.

I will be glad to talk with you about this memorandum or, if you prefer, please give me your views in writing as to what comment it would be well to make to the Ambassador.

Faithfully yours,   Robert Lansing

CCL (SDR, RG 59, 710.11/224½B, DNA).
[1] This enclosure is missing in the State Department files and in WP, DLC.
[2] The latest version of the Pan-American Pact, printed at Nov. 11, 1915, Vol. 35.

From Benjamin Ryan Tillman

Dear Mr. President: Washington. March 9, 1916.

Now is the time for you to help me. Please do this: Exert all the influence you have—how great it is has just been demonstrated by the House and Senate both[1]—and impress on the members of the House Naval Committee the vital importance and necessity for having the armor factory bill passed. Get them to do this: There are two or three bills pending before the House on this very question. Let the Committee report one of the bills favorably—no matter which one—and get it on the House calendar. Then when the Senate bill is sent over, as it will be on the 22nd of March, let them substitute the Senate bill for the one on the House calendar and pass it. You can sign it as soon as it is engrossed and sent to you for signature; and the bill ought to become a law between the 25th and 31st of March. Then, we can turn Admiral Harris[2] loose, and he has told me if the red tape is cut in the Navy Department and he is allowed to go ahead, he can have the factory completed and ready to turn out armor in eighteen months; so that by October 1917 we will have the armor problem solved, and the hold-ups to which the Government has had to submit heretofore will no longer exist.

Very sincerely yours,　B. R. Tillman

TLS (WP, DLC).
　[1] The House, on March 7, had voted, 276 to 142, to table the McLemore resolution. The Senate's tabling of the Gore resolution has already been noted.
　[2] Rear Admiral Frederic Robert Harris, U.S.N., a civil engineer, Chief of the Bureau of Yards and Docks.

From Champ Clark

My Dear Mr. President:　　Washington, D. C. March 9, 1916.
　I thank you most cordially for your kind note of felicitation on the anniversary of my birth.
　I am not cocksure that being 66 is really a cause for congratulation; but I am glad that I have lived so long.
　Wishing you length of years & much happiness,
　　　　I am Sincerely Your Friend,　Champ Clark.

ALS (WP, DLC).

To Benjamin Ryan Tillman

My dear Senator:　　The White House March 10, 1916
　I have your letter of March ninth and you may be sure I will take up the matter you suggest at the earliest possible time with Mr. Padgett[1] and see how things lie in the House and what is likely to be possible there.
　In haste
　　　Cordially and sincerely yours,　Woodrow Wilson

TLS (B. R. Tillman Papers, ScCLeU).
　[1] Lemuel Phillips Padgett, Democratic congressman from Tennessee; chairman of the House Committee on Naval Affairs.

To Cleveland Hoadley Dodge

My dear Cleve: The White House March 10, 1916
   It was fine of you to send me that letter of yours of March
eighth.[1] It went straight to my heart. These last days have indeed
been days of strain and anxiety, but apparently all that is necessary when trouble comes is to call their bluff. It is extraordinary
that these things should be necessary.
   With warmest regard to you all from us both,
                        Affectionately yours,   Woodrow Wilson

TLS (WC, NjP).
   [1] C. H. Dodge to WW, March 8, 1916, ALS (WP, DLC).

From Newton Diehl Baker, with Enclosure

My dear Mr. President: Washington. March 10, 1916.
   I inclose herewith copy of a telegram just received from General Funston, dated Fort Sam Houston, Texas, March 10th,
regarding the Mexican situation.[1] This is the last telegram which
the Department has received on this subject, and is the first
authoritative word in full received through General Funston at
the front.
                        Sincerely yours,   Newton D. Baker

TLS (WP, DLC).
   [1] Francisco Villa, on March 9, led a mounted attack force, variously estimated
at from 1,000 to 3,000 men, upon the small town of Columbus, N. M., located
approximately three miles north of the Mexican border and sixty miles directly
west of El Paso. Shouting "Viva Villa" and "Viva México," the raiders galloped
through the settlement indiscriminately shooting, looting, and burning buildings. They were soon engaged by units of the Thirteenth United States Cavalry,
stationed at Columbus, and a six hour-long battle ensued during which the American troops repulsed the *Villistas* and then pursued them five miles into Mexico.
   Villa's motivation for the attack has been the subject of considerable debate.
The reasons most often suggested include: (1) Villa's desire to retaliate against
the United States on account of its recognition of the *de facto* government of
his enemy, Carranza, and Villa's hope of provoking a war between Mexico and
the United States; (2) Villa's partially realized aim of capturing food and arms;
and (3) Villa's hope of securing arms and other forms of support from Germany
in reward for his attack. New documentary evidence, brought to light by
Friedrich Katz in "Pancho Villa and the Attack on Columbus, New Mexico,"
American Historical Review, LXXXIII (Feb. 1978), 101-30, suggests that Villa's
motivation sprang from his belief that Carranza and Wilson had recently reached
an agreement which would have made Mexico a virtual protectorate of the
United States in return for a $500,000,000 loan. For details and other inter-
pretations of the attack, see also Alberto Calzadiaz Berrera, *Por Que Villa atacó
a Columbus* (Mexico City, 1972); Federico Cervantes, *Francisco Villa y la
Revolucion* (Mexico City, 1960); Francis J. Munch, "Villa's Columbus Raid:
Practical Politics or German Design?" *New Mexico Historical Review*, XLIV
(July 1969), 189-214; Link, *Confusions and Crises*, pp. 205-206; James A. Sandos,
"German Involvement in Northern Mexico, 1915-1916: A New Look at the Colum-
bus Raid," *Hispanic American Historical Review*, L (Feb. 1970), 70-89; and Frank
Tompkins, *Chasing Villa* (Harrisburg, Pa., 1934).

Fort Sam Houston, Texas, March 10, 1916.

No. 978. Following received from Colonel Slocum,[1] Columbus, after midnight last night. It was filed at Columbus telegraph office about two P.M., but through failure of operator was not transmitted. Operator assumes full responsibility. This matter will be taken up at once with Western Union officials with view to preventing reoccurence:

Quote: Now two o'clock. When Villa troops fell back just before daylight we followed them with a dismounted line, at same time I sent Major Tompkins[2] with three troops mounted to attack. Tompkins followed them for about five miles into Mexico, having three running fights with them, and finally made a stand with their entire force, stopped Tompkins' advance and he returned here. Had one corporal killed in the pursuit. Mexicans dropped considerable material and loot which they had gotten in town. Am reliably informed it was Villa that made the attack with fifteen hundred men, leaving about one thousand on river east of Boca-Grande. From his spies in Columbus he was informed that there was but four troops here with three machine gun troops. Three of our troops being out, took this opportunity to attack. He intended capturing town, looting bank, killing all Americans. Our casualties five wounded, seven killed, Lieutenant Benson[3] shot in arm, Captain Williams[1] Adjutant slightly wounded in hand, eight civilians killed in town, including one woman. We have already burned twenty-seven Mexican soldiers, most of them killed in camp, some near the bank, and there are many other dead Mexicans on Villa's line of retreat about one mile west not yet collected. Mexican troops under Villa's personal command and by his orders made the charge through camp. Our troops turned out quickly, drove Mexicans out, killing seventeen in or about camp, about ten or twelve Mexicans killed in town. While our people at that time in the morning were surprised, they did their work well. Villa's attempt to capture camp and town was a complete failure. Recommend one battalion infantry, one squadron Eighty [Eighth] Cavalry, be sent here, then take mounted troops to follow up Villa, leaving infantry to protect town. Do not believe Villa will make another attempt here. Several of our families living in town had narrow escapes, as the attack was fierce. All peaceful as summer morning at this writing. Have sent five wounded to Bliss; dead will follow. All troops including machine gun troop now here, Lindsay force in from Gibson.[5] Unquote.   Funston.

T telegram (WP, DLC).
    1 Colonel Herbert Jermain Slocum, commander of the Thirteenth Cavalry at Columbus.
    2 Major Frank Tompkins of the Thirteenth Cavalry, who led the pursuit against Villa.
    3 Second Lieutenant Clarence C. Benson of the Thirteenth Cavalry.
    4 Captain George Williams of the Thirteenth Cavalry.
    5 A detachment of the Thirteenth Cavalry under the command of Major Elmer Lindsley, stationed at a ranch fourteen miles west of Columbus.

From Newton Diehl Baker, with Enclosures

My dear Mr. President: Washington. March 10, 1916.

I am transmitting to you herewith copies of the two latest despatches received from General Funston with reference to the Mexican situation.   Sincerely yours,   Newton D. Baker

TLS (WP, DLC).

Fort Sam Houston, Texas, March 10, 1916.

No. 979. Following telegram received from Colonel Slocum this morning:

Quote: Rumors reach us of suspicious movement Mexican troops west of here. Am having that country patrolled. Have two troops at border gate and will attack Mexican flank if they renew attack tonight. Will send one-half company infantry to Hermanas and one-half to Victoria points on railroad west of Columbus. Expect battalion here about midnight. Am satisfied from further investigation that Villa had his entire force in the attack here this morning, between twenty-five hundred and three thousand men. After being driven out of town and camp here, formed his line about one mile west and was preparing to make second attack which I clearly observed. Our heavy fire on this line from hill near camp, and this together with Tompkins' mounted movement, stopped this second attack of Villa, and he returned across border, followed by Tompkins with three troops as before wired you. If Villa makes another attack tonight, we will give him another whipping. Have town under martial law and disarmed all Mexicans; one troop in control. Hope for some ammunition on train tonight. Further, I find on investigation that my telegram of this morning giving detailed report of attack and pursuit referred to in your telegram, was not sent by telegraph operator through his own error, which he admits and assumes all responsibility. I gave him this telegram in person. Mislaid message is now being sent you. Mr. George C. Carrothers, Special Agent State Department, is now here. Believes Villa will continue attack on Americans and their property on American territory, now that Villa has opened the battle at Columbus. Carrothers knows Villa's frame mind better than we do. If Villa has, as I believe, not less than twenty-five hundred men, he will continue depredations on our territory, raiding with small bands along the border. I should like one squadron Eighth Cavalry sent here so I may leave infantry in control here and cut loose with mounted troops. Three troops of this command did cross the border to pursue Villa for about five miles by my orders. This aggressive move on our part was in my opinion advisable and wholesome. If I had some more mounted troops, the pursuit would have been carried further. Unquote. Funston.

Fort Sam Houston, Tex.,
11:50 a.m., March 10, 1916.

Number nine eight one. Period. Under circumstances, I believe Colonel Slocum entirely justified in violating War Department's order relative to sending troops across border, and am of opinion that had he not thus done so Villa might immediately have returned to attack; after being joined by his men left South of line. Had our force not been so small pursuit would have been continued. Funston.

Fort Sam Houston, Texas, March 10, 1916.

It is opinion of Colonels Dodd[1] and Slocum, in which I concur, that unless Villa is relentlessly pursued and his forces scattered, he will continue raids. As troops of Mexican Government are accomplishing nothing, and as he can consequently make his preparations and concentrations without being disturbed, he can strike at any point on the border, we being unable to obtain advance information as to his whereabout[s]. If we fritter away the whole command guarding towns, ranches and railroads, it will accomplish nothing if he can find safe refuge across the line after every raid. Although probably not more than a thousand took part in Columbus raid, he is believed to have about three thousand. Even if he should not continue raids, he has entered on a policy of merciless killing of Americans in Mexico. To show apathy and gross inefficiency of Mexican Government troops, an American woman held prisoner by Villa for nine days, but who escaped in Columbus fight, states that during all that time he was undisturbed at no great distance from border, collecting a force of about three thousand. The few Carranza troops in the region fled, losing all contact with him and not even informing us as to his whereabouts. If it is proposed to take action suggested, I recommend no information be given out, in order that we may stand chance of surprising. If desired, I shall personally command. It would be desirable to replace as soon as possible from available cavalry in the United States the cavalry taken from the border.   Funston.

(Received 2:20 p.m., March 10, 1916.)

TC telegrams (WP, DLC).
¹ George Allan Dodd.

From Newton Diehl Baker, with Enclosures

My dear Mr. President: Washington. March 10, 1916.

I herewith transmit for your information and files a copy of a newspaper interview which I gave out in form hereto attached this afternoon with regard to the activity of the War Department in connection with the disturbance on the Mexican border; and I also beg leave to say that, some question having been raised among the newspaper men as to the meaning of the word "recruited," I interpreted it to them orally by saying: "The word is not to be taken in any technical sense, but rather means that any and all movements to or along the Mexican border are to be taken as in fulfillment of the intention above expressed, and not as expressing any other intention on the part of the Department."

I beg leave also to attach a written memorandum of authority given by me to the Chief of the General Staff as a basis for his instructions in the execution of the plan outlined in the public statement of the Department, and also containing the limitations which you directed to be contained in the orders.

I also inclose a copy of the telegram sent by the Chief of Staff to General Funston in pursuance of these instructions.

                         Sincerely yours,   Newton D. Baker

TLS (WP, DLC).

E N C L O S U R E   I¹

Statement for the press: Washington. March 10, 1916.

There is no intention of entering Mexico in force. A sufficient body of mobile troops will be sent in to locate and disperse or capture the band or bands that attacked Columbus. So soon as the forces of the de facto government can take control of the situation, any forces of the United States then remaining in Mexico will of course be withdrawn. The forces of the United States now on the border will be immediately recruited, but only for the purpose of safeguarding the territory of the United States from further raids.

[1] For the cabinet's discussion of this matter and Wilson's decision to send troops in pursuit of Villa, see Link, *Confusions and Crises*, pp. 207-208.

ENCLOSURE   II

Washington.

Memorandum for the Chief of Staff: March 10, 1916.

Orders will be issued to General Funston to send in to Mexico a sufficient body of mobile troops to locate and disperse or capture the band or bands that attacked Columbus. He may instruct commanders of troops on the border opposite the States of Chihuahua and Sonora, or, roughly, within the field of possible operations by Villa, and not under the control of the forces of the *de facto* government of Mexico, that the same tactics of defense and pursuit are authorized in the event of similar raids across the border and into the United States by such bands.

General Funston will also be instructed to use the aeroplanes at San Antonio, where possible, for observation. These orders will go confidentially and in cipher, and General Funston will be informed that the President desires them strictly followed.

Newton D. Baker

ENCLOSURE   III

Washington. March 10th, 1916.

MEMORANDUM FOR THE ADJUTANT GENERAL:[1]

The Secretary of War directs that the following telegram be coded without delay and sent to the Commanding General, Southern Department:

You will promptly organize an adequate military force of troops under the command of Brigadier General J. J. Pershing[2] and will direct him to proceed promptly across the border in pursuit of the Mexican band which attacked the town of Columbus and the troops there on the morning of the 9th instant. These troops will be withdrawn to American territory as soon as the de facto Government of Mexico is able to relieve them of this work. In any event the work of these troops will be regarded as finished as soon as Villa's band or bands are known to be broken up. In carrying out these instructions you are authorized to employ whatever guides and interpreters are necessary and you are given general authority to employ such transportation, including motor transportation, with necessary civilian personnel as may be required. The President desires his following instructions to be carefully adhered to and to be kept strictly confidential. You will instruct the commanders of your troops on the border opposite the states of Chihuahua and Sonora, or, roughly, within the field of possible operations by Villa and not under the control of the forces of the de facto government, that they are authorized to use the same tactics of defense and pursuit in the event of similar raids across the border and into the United States by a band or bands such as attacked Columbus yesterday. You are instructed to make all practicable use of the aeroplanes at San Antonio for observation. Telegraph for whatever reenforcements or material you need. Notify this office as to force selected and expedite movement.   H. L. Scott

T MSS (WP, DLC).
  [1] Henry Pinckney McCain, brigadier general, U.S.A.
  [2] John Joseph Pershing, born near Laclede, Mo., on September 13, 1860. At this time, he was a brigadier general in command of all forces at Fort Bliss and nearby areas, including Columbus. General Funston selected him to lead the Punitive Expedition. The best biography is Frank E. Vandiver, *Black Jack, the Life and Times of John J. Pershing* (2 vols., College Station, Tex., and London, 1977); see also Pershing's *My Experiences in the World War* (2 vols., New York, 1931).

ENCLOSURE   IV

MEMORANDUM for the President: March 10, 1916.

As a supplement to the memorandum for the Chief of Staff which I have approved and herewith present, I beg leave to direct your attention to the opinion expressed in conference by the members of the General Staff, to the effect that by reason of the extent and character of the country within which Villa is free to operate, the strong likelihood is that the dispersion of his force will rather result in his taking refuge in inaccessible mountain hiding places and so requiring prolonged operations for his ultimate capture, than that by any sudden stroke his capture could be presently effected. The view, therefore, of the members of the General Staff, is that orders should now be given to General Funston, who is in command of the Southern Department, to act upon discretion in the use of all the forces available to him in prosecuting such a movement as will disperse these brigand bands and drive them to a safe distance from the border, with the capture of Villa as of course the chief objective of the action.

When, however, General Funston shall feel that he has gone as far as his present resources justify, that the dispersion of the Villistas should be regarded as the end of his particular expedition, and that all the post commanders of troops along the frontier be given immediately instruction to follow up any attack or threatened attack by bands from Mexico as far as their strength and resources will permit in each case, with a view to securing from any recurrence of these outbreaks the maximum of advantage in capture and dispersion of the bands, and that these commanders be instructed in their subsequent activities to act without regard to the presence of the international border.

Newton D. Baker

CC MS (WDR, RG 94, AGO Document File, No. 2638774, DNA).

A Press Release

[March 10, 1916]

An adequate force will be sent at once in pursuit of Villa with the single object of capturing him and putting a stop to his forays. This can and will be done in entirely friendly aid of the constituted authorities in Mexico and with scrupulous respect for the sovereignty of that Republic.[1]

WWhw MS (received from T. W. Brahany).
   [1] This press release was issued immediately after the cabinet meeting on March 10 as an official statement from the White House.

From Champ Clark

PERSONAL.

My dear Mr. President: Washington, D. C. March 10, 1916.

I dislike exceedingly to increase your burdens by asking you to take even the little time necessary to read this letter, but my own honor and self-respect as well as the honor and relf [self]-respect of my wife and children compel me so to do.

In the Chicago Herald of Monday, February twenty-eighth, is a remarkable letter dated "Washington, Sunday, February twenty-seventh," written by Honorable John Callan O'Laughlin, at one time Secretary of State.[1]

Ordinarily I would pay no attention to newspaper gossip but Mr. O'Laughlin gives as his authority "close friends of the White House" and "advisers of the President." He declines to divulge the names. Therefore, I come to you to learn if he states your "belief" correctly.

After quoting your opening remarks at the Grid Iron dinner about your preference as to "conversations at the quiet firesides" over "cloakroom conversations," he says:

"The signification of this expression will be realized when it is known that *the administration believes* that a 'cloakroom conspiracy' in which figured Speaker Clark, Representative Flood and Representative Kitchin was responsible for the movement that almost forced the passage of the Bill warning Americans to keep off belligerent armed merchantmen."

Further along he says:

"The administration is convinced that the Presidential bee is still buzzing in Mr. Clark's bonnet, but what astonishes it is that Mr. Flood, who fought for Wilson in Virginia in 1912 should have gone over to the Speaker and that there apparently should be a combination between Clark and Bryan, as evidenced by the action of Congressman Kitchin, the majority leader, an ardent follower of the peerless one.

The mere statement of the situation that exists is sufficient to show the presence of a real split among the leaders of the party. If the test should be made and the President should win, undoubtedly *the administration*'s supporters would agitate for a caucus to take the office of leader away from Kitchin. Whether any move would be made against Mr. Clark is doubtful."

The charge that Messrs. Kitchin and Flood and myself were in a "cloakroom conspiracy" or any other sort of a conspiracy or that we were in any manner responsible for the McLemore resolution or the agitation thereof is untrue.

The charge that Messrs. Flood and Kitchin and myself were conspiring to make me a Presidential Candidate is not only false but absolutely preposterous. Why should I be conspiring with any two Representatives to make me a candidate when for months I have spent considerable time every day declining the requests of people to become a candidate? My position on that question was stated succinctly, clearly and comprehensively in my Tolls Speech.[2] I have adhered to that statement, though belabored by thousands of friends for making it and begged to recant it. Of course I have the same right to change my mind as has every other American citizen, but if I should do so, the change of mind will not be whispered in the cloakroom or in other corners, but stated openly so that all men and women, too, may hear. Just why the New York World and other "close friends of the White House"—including as I believe at least one member of the Cabinet —should be constantly trying to aggravate me into declaring that I am a Presidential Candidate, like the peace of God, passeth all understanding. It seems to me that they would exercise wisdom by acting on the philosophy of "Let Well Enough Alone."

So far as an attempt to remove me from the Speakership is concerned, if any gentleman desires to try that, he need not take the trouble to call a caucus. Let him from the floor of the House move "to declare the Chair vacant" and I will hold his motion in order, rules or no rules.

All this by way of preface.

There is a charge in said article, so detrimental to my character, if it be true, that I desire at your hands a categorical answer and the answer will fix our personal relations for all time to come. The charge is that *"the administration believes* that a 'cloakroom conspiracy' in which figured Speaker Clark, Representative Flood and Representative Kitchin was responsible for the movement that almost forced the passage of the Bill warning Americans to keep off belligerent merchantmen."

As stated before there was no such conspiracy and if there was one neither Messrs. Flood and Kitchin nor myself had anything to do with it.

What I want to know and what it appears to me I have a right to know from you is whether you (the administration) hold any such *belief*. It is a thing incredible because you know that Messrs. Kitchin and Flood and myself spent four days, first at the suggestion of Senator Stone and then at yours, in allaying the excitement in the House so that the action of the German Government stated for the first of March might be postponed until March fifteenth or April first. And, Mr. President, we did allay it until you wrote to Mr. Pou—Messrs. Flood and Kitchin and myself doing our full share in allaying it.

In our last interview, I stated to you that no three men ever kept faith more perfectly with another man than Messrs. Flood and Kitchin and myself had kept it with you. Your reply was, "I know that."

Remembering all these things and more, the statement that *you believe* that I was engaged in plotting a conspiracy came as a bolt from a clear sky. That *belief* on your part, if it exists, means that in your estimation I am both a liar and a double-dealer.

I am neither the one nor the other. If you believe it, you are the only man on earth, who knowing me, does believe it.

No doubt, in the Great Day, I will have many sins to answer for, but lying and double-dealing will not be among them.

I do not intend for my children to live under such a stigma, if I can prevent it. Be kind enough to let me know at your earliest

convenience as to the correctness of the aforementioned statement of your *"belief."*

Your friend,   Champ Clark.[3]

TLS (WP, DLC).
  [1] In fact, O'Laughlin had served as First Assistant Secretary of State from
January 28 to March 5, 1909.
  [2] On March 31, 1914, in which Clark said that he was not a candidate for
President in 1916. Clark added that, if Wilson made a success of his administration, he would be renominated and re-elected; if he failed, the Democratic
nomination would "not be worth having." *Cong. Record,* 63d Cong., 2d sess.,
p. 6056.
  [3] Wilson must have answered this letter on his own typewriter or by hand.
In any event, his reply is missing. He must have completely mollified Clark,
as their friendly relations continued.

From Franklin Knight Lane

My dear Mr. President: Washington March 10, 1916.

    You asked me to draft a bill which would be a condensation of
the Newlands bill. A rough outline of such measure I inclose.[1] It
is a bare skeleton, but I believe it entirely covers the field that the
Newlands bill covers and is more in line with sane legislative
action because less in detail and more of an organic act.

    In this connection let me draw your attention to a proposition
that I have had in the back of my head for several years and
which may be practicable at this time,—that the whole matter of
giving rights of way for dam sites and reservoir sites and other
things pertaining to the development of power plants upon either
the navigable or the non-navigable streams be put in the hands
of a National Waterways Commission. I have the notion that
Congress would be willing to give broader powers to such a commission than it would be to give broad powers to the Secretary
of War or the Secretary of the Interior alone, and possibly many
of the troubles that arise as to the Shields bill and the Ferris bill
might be solved if a board of this high character were to pass upon
the individual permits or franchises that would be asked for. Of
course, the National Waterways Commission would act through
a subordinate board made up of respresentatives [representatives]
of different departments and other outside engineers, but the ultimate decision as to what rules and regulations touching construction, operation charges, etc., would be made by the Commission
itself.

    The idea is prompted by a desire to effect cooperation between
the different Cabinet officers who now act upon their judgment
exclusively, and Congress is loath to give them very large powers.
A large commission would probably be delegated broader powers
by Congress.   Cordially yours,   Franklin K. Lane

TLS (WP, DLC).

¹ T MS (WP, DLC), entitled "A Bill to create a National Waterways Commission, and for other purposes." It created a commission, to be composed of the President and the Secretaries of Agriculture, Commerce, Interior, and War, to study the condition of the nation's waterways and make recommendations to Congress concerning the development of navigation, flood control, irrigation, and other such matters.

From Edward Mandell House

Dear Governor: New York. March 10th, 1916.

It will give me pleasure to see Mr. Gallauner and I shall make an appointment with him at once.

Your kindly and generous commendation of what I have tried to do in Europe fills me with satisfaction. It makes my efforts seem so well worth while and is the greatest reward that could possibly come to me.

I shall always remember those two happy days in the White House with Mrs. Wilson and you.

Affectionately yours, E. M. House

I am delighted with your action in the Mexican trouble. Positive action seems to me now essential.

TLS (WP, DLC).

From Seth Low

Dear Mr. President: New York March 10th, 1916.

I have been so far from well since receiving your letter of March 3rd. that this is my first opportunity to thank you for it. I am glad that you think well of the work which was done by your Commission in Colorado, and I am especially glad that you are proposing to make the suggestion we spoke of to the Federal Trade Commission. The value of such an inquiry will not be limited to Colorado, I am sure.

You do not explicitly say in your letter that you accept the resignations of the members of the Commission as offered in our Report, but I hope I am correct in assuming that you agree with us that our work is finished. Let me thank you again for the confidence you have reposed in me in this connection.

I congratulate you upon the vote in the two Houses of Congress holding up your hands in the matter of our international relations.   Respectfully and sincerely, yours,   Seth Low

TLS (WP, DLC).

From Robert Lansing

PERSONAL AND CONFIDENTIAL:

My dear Mr. President: Washington March 11, 1916.

I enclose for your consideration the draft of a treaty with Denmark, providing for the cession of the Danish West Indies, in consideration of Twenty-five Millions of Dollars.[1] I hope you will find it possible to give this speedy attention, as I think we should close the matter up as promptly as possible, provided you agree with me as to the advisability of this action.

In regard to Article III, Item 3,[2] my suggestion would be to make that conditional upon exhibition of the original documents, and their examination by our Minister at Copenhagen.

Faithfully yours,   Robert Lansing.

TLS (SDR, RG 59, 711.5914/57½A, DNA).

[1] The enclosure, bearing the same file number as the letter, consisted of twelve articles which stipulated the terms of the exchange; the civil, political, and property rights of the island's inhabitants; and the administrative rights and responsibilities of the governments of the United States and Denmark. The treaty also permitted Denmark to proceed with the economic development of Greenland, "provided that such measures are not contrary to the principle of equal opportunity in whatever concerns the commerce and industry of all nations."

[2] A statement in which the United States agreed to assume the contractual obligations which Denmark previously had entered into with a number of enterprises engaged in the development of insular commerce, communications, and finance.

From Wilbur Fisk Sadler, Jr.

My dear Mr. President: Trenton, March 11, 1916.

Permit me to congratulate you upon your appointment of Mr. Newton D. Baker as Secretary of War.

If what I have been told about him is correct, you could have chosen none better to assist you in the very trying situation that you have been and are handling in such a masterful manner.

During the last four months I have been speaking at defense league meetings in various parts of New Jersey, and coming in contact at Washington and elsewhere with the National Guard representatives of nearly all of the states.

If anyone has given you the idea that the splendid course you have been pursuing is not approved by the great mass of the people, he is mistaken.

In my judgment, if you can continue to hold the situation until November, you will be re-elected by an overwhelming majority, and I believe that I have a fair estimate of public sentiment.

I wish you could hear the cries of approval that greet the stories of what you are doing, which, if listened to by some editors, would make them blush with shame.

Before you were inaugurated, I had the temerity to make some suggestions to you relative to the Assistant Secretary of War.

My point was, that unless you named someone who had experience with the War Department, that the newcomer would be surrounded by Regular Army officers, could get only their ideas and views, and would be unable to assist you as he should. Experience has proven whether my contention was correct.

Will you allow me to again suggest that the Assistant Secretary of War should be one who has seen the work of the War Department from the outside and has been forced to leave its ways to get his rights [sights], and should be one who is known to the National Guard of the entire country?

There are a half dozen Adjutants General who have had experience who would loyally support you, and if I am not mistaken, would, within a few weeks, be able to lay data before you that would open even your eyes.

The 9,128 officers and the more than 123,000 men of the Organized Militia would like the Assistant Secretary to be one that knows their many difficulties and shortcomings and who could help to remedy them.

In naming him, won't you consider the citizen soldiers and let them have at least one officer in the War Department? We care not whether he is Jew or Gentile, or what his politics, for that job should not be a political one. Let us have someone to whom we can go that will at least give us a hearing.

Knowing that I acted as your Adjutant General for two years, the National Guard officers from nearly every state have been writing me to call and lay our case before you, but I know that it is almost impossible for you to spare the time to listen to our plaints—hence this letter.

In the days gone by, when the Executive Committee of the Organized Militia met in Washington, they were always invited to shake hands with the President, who professed to be glad to see them, and I have explained that the perplexing situation that you are facing and your many appointments have made it impossible for you to greet them during that visit.

The Committee will again meet in Washington within a few days, and may I suggest that you request Mr. Tumulty to invite them to call upon you for a few minutes?

Those whom they represent yelled themselves hoarse for you three years since and can easily be brought to do so again.

Very respectfully yours, W. F. Sadler Jr.

TLS (WP, DLC).

From Edward Mandell House

Dear Governor: New York. March 12, 1916.

Bernstorff was with me for an hour this morning. As usual I found him reasonable and willing to discuss pending matters quite impartially.

He thinks the best thing that can be done now is to do and say nothing further in regard to the disarming of merchantmen. He intimated that they would drop it if we would. He claims to have gotten into it innocently and at our instigation.

He believes there will be no submarine violations that will embroil our two countries, at least for the present while the Chancellor is in control. I expressed the belief that another outrage of this kind would precipitate war, and I gave him my reasons for believing that it would be the worst thing not only for Germany, but for the Allies as well. That if we became involved there would be no one to lead them out.

He was quite interested in this phase and wanted to know when I thought you might intervene. I told him you had expressed no opinion upon the subject, but that I was advising you to intervene at the proper time. He wished to know when I thought would be the proper time. I replied not until after their Western offensive had been finished and perhaps not until the Allies had made a counter offensive. He wished to know how long I thought this would take. My opinion was it might be several months. He thought Germany would welcome the intervention and asked if I thought the Allies would accept it. My opinion was that the English would resent our interference. This is true,[1] but of course, it was given to him for a purpose.

Grey is away and I merely have a cable from his secretary saying my despatch had been received and would be forwarded.

If things can be held as now I believe that our plan will work out before mid-summer and perhaps much sooner.

Bernstorff said if Roosevelt was nominated you would get the entire German vote. However, if our plan goes through, you will get all the votes.

I gave Bernstorff advice concerning the German propaganda and tried to make it plain to him that the German cause was constantly suffering because of it.

Affectionately yours,   E. M. House

TLS (WP, DLC).
[1] House undoubtedly dictated "This is not true."

From Newton Diehl Baker

My dear Mr. President: Washington. March 12, 1916.

On yesterday, the 11th, General Funston telegraphed that he needed four additional regiments of Cavalry for the purpose of guarding the International Boundary in place of the troops which he was organizing into his "Defense" expedition. The members of the General Staff felt that the request was proper to be complied with, and I, therefore, directed it to be done, asking the General Staff, however, to select regiments as far as possible from the central and southern part of the United States in view of a communication sent me through the Department of Justice to the effect that there was reason to believe that possible disturbances might be expected in New York and along the United States-Canadian frontier. This communication from the Department of Justice might well have been based wholly upon imaginary speculation on the part of the man who informed that Department, but I thought it better, and so directed, that the regiment of cavalry in Vermont be retained there and the additional men requested by General Funston selected from other places.

Today, General Funston requests the militia of the States of Arizona and New Mexico be called out with a view of utilizing them to protect towns along the border from either invasion, or uprising of resident Mexicans. This request General Funston says is due to the fact that in a great many of the border towns on the American side the Mexicans greatly outnumber the American population, and he has been obliged to withdraw troops from some of them to make up his expeditionary force. I consulted with General Bliss[1] on this subject, and he concurred in my view that it would be very much better to move regiments of regular infantry to Arizona and New Mexico for this purpose, since we have such infantry available in sufficient numbers in California, recently returned from the Philippines, and, therefore, in fairly close proximity. My reasons for this view are that it is already known in the country that federal troops are being moved to Arizona and New Mexico to do patrol duty on the border, and calling out the state militia would introduce a new phase to the situation and give rise to speculations either as to the inadequacy of the federal force or greater gravity of the situation than actually exists. The Adjutant General telegraphed General Funston as follows:

"After careful consideration, Secretary of War thinks it most undesirable to call out militia until all resources regular army are exhausted. Wire with minimum delay number additional regular infantry organizations needed. Pending their arrival distribute your present force so as to allay as far as practicable popular apprehension."

On receipt of a reply to this communication available infantry from the nearest points will be despatched at once.

The Mayor of El Paso[2] telegraphed, through Representative Smith,[3] expressing great apprehension in that City due to the removal of some part of the troops previously stationed there. I directed the Chief of Staff to call General Funston's attention to the importance of El Paso and the need for adequate force at that place, both to protect it and give complete feeling of security to the people.

The Secretary of the Navy called my attention to a wireless station in process of erection at Point Isabel, Texas. No naval force being available in the vicinity for its protection, I asked The Adjutant General to call the matter to the attention of General Funston, with directions to provide the necessary safeguards.

I did not feel, during your absence,[1] that any of the matters presented required my reaching you by wireless. The only serious matter arising was with regard to the use of Mexican railroads by General Funston, which he suggested in one of his despatches. I directed him in no way to undertake to control or use Mexican railroad property except as an other person might use it, by tendering his troops and their equipment for ordinary transportation.

General Funston's despatches to the Department have detailed with great particularity the troops, equipment and supplies needed by him. I directed that his requests be met promptly, and as made, feeling that his judgment on the ground is better than any judgment which we could exercise at this distance and that the responsibility for the success of the expedition ought to rest on him. In this view General Scott and the officers of the General Staff have entirely concurred.

Respectfully submitted,   Newton D. Baker

TLS (WP, DLC).

[1] Tasker Howard Bliss, major general, U.S.A., Assistant Chief of Staff.
[2] Tom Lea, mayor of El Paso, 1915-17.
[3] William Robert Smith, Democratic congressman from Texas.
[1] The Wilsons had gone on a weekend cruise in Chesapeake Bay on *U.S.S. Mayflower*.

To Stockton Axson

Dear Stock.,   Hampton Roads, 12 March, 1916.

Edith and I are down here seeking a little rest, on the May-flower—or, rather, a little escape from Washington and, so far as I am personally concerned, a chance to do a little thinking and make a few notes based on the thinking—and my thoughts turn, as they have again and again, to what Lovett has written me about your leaving Houston.[1]

I have little doubt that he is right, my dear fellow, particularly as his judgment is backed by Dercum's,[2] and I am writing just a line to say this: that if there is any way in which I can assist to effect your honorable release by Wesleyan, I am not only ready but anxious to help. Are you willing that I should write to Winchester,[3] and frankly say what I fear with regard to your health and ask if it is too late to let you withdraw? I have not felt at liberty to do anything of the kind without your approval, and, if you do let me do it, I will, if you prefer, omit all reference to your own wishes and take the whole initiative on myself. May I?

I am sure you know why I have not written before. Never, even since the war began, have I been quite so constantly pressed upon by public business as I have been during the anxious weeks just past.

But I am well, surprisingly well. Edith, too, I am happy to say, has stood the fatigue of this first winter of functions famously and seems in fine shape in every way.

Mac. and Nell, as you have doubtless seen in the papers, are off for South America and will be gone for at least six weeks. The baby is at the White House, and in fine fettle. The rest are all well, and I am sure would be joining me in sending messages of warmest love did they know that I was writing. Edith sends you most affectionate greetings. For myself, I am always,

With deepest affection,   Woodrow Wilson

WWTLS (S. Axson Papers, TxHR).

[1] E. O. Lovett to JPT, Jan. 29, 1916, TLS (WP, DLC). Axson had agreed to accept a professorship at Wesleyan University and was now having melancholy second thoughts. Lovett, President of The William Marsh Rice Institute, sought Wilson's advice about Axson's depression over the prospect of leaving Rice to take the position at Wesleyan. Lovett and Axson favored finding an honorable release from Axson's commitment, and Lovett summarized for Wilson the advantages to Axson of staying in Houston, which included great latitude for lecturing outside the Institute, the gift of a house near a golf course, and improved health.

[2] F. X. Dercum, M.D., to S. Axson, Feb. 7, 1916, TCL, enclosed in E. O. Lovett to JPT, Feb. 14, 1916, TLS (WP, DLC). Dr. Dercum, who had treated Axson for many years, seconded Lovett's conclusion that a job at Rice would be far better for Axson's health than a move to Wesleyan.

[3] Wilson's old friend, Caleb Thomas Winchester, Professor of English Literature at Wesleyan University.

To Robert Lansing, with Enclosure

My dear Mr. Secretary,   The White House. 13 March, 1916.

Here is the statement I suggested during our conversation this afternoon. I would be very much obliged if you would issue it at your ea[r]ly convenience.   Faithfully yours,   W.W.

Will you not be kind enough to communicate this immediately to the Secretary of War.

WWTLI (SDR, RG 59, 812.00/17743, DNA).

E N C L O S U R E

In order to remove any apprehensions that may exist either in the United States or in Mexico, the President has authorized me to give in his name the public assurance that the military operations now in contemplation by this Government will be scrupulously confined to the object already announced, and that in no circumstances will they be suffered to trench in any degree upon the sovereignty of Mexico or develop into intervention of any kind in the internal affairs of our sister Republic. On the contrary, what is now being done is deliberately intended to preclude the possibility of intervention.

WWT MS (SDR, RG 59, 812.00/17743, DNA).

Newton Diehl Baker to Frederick Funston

Washington [March 13, 1916].

The President desires that your attention be especially and earnestly called to his determination that the expedition into Mexico is limited to the purposes originally stated, namely the pursuit and dispersion of the band or bands that attacked Columbus. It is of the highest importance that no color of any other possibility or intention be given and therefore while the President desires the force to be adequate to disperse the bands in question and to protect communications, neither in size nor otherwise should the expedition afford the slightest ground of suspicion of any other or larger object.[1]

NDBHw MS (WDR, RG 94, AGO Document File, No. 2377632, DNA).
[1] This was sent as Adjutant General to F. Funston, March 13, 1916.

Two Letters to Franklin Knight Lane

My dear Lane: [The White House] March 13, 1916

Thank you for your draft of the bill about water control. I shall study it with great attention.

Your suggestion about a national waterways commission interests me very much. I wonder if you had thought of the danger which seems to attach to the creation of all sorts of commissions that such commission would take an attitude so aloof and judicial that it might fall out of sympathy with the popular thought at critical times.

       Cordially and sincerely yours,   Woodrow Wilson

My dear Lane: [The White House] March 13, 1916

I do not want to put the least additional burden on you, but knowing that you have been thinking for some time of going to California, I venture to lay before you the very earnest desire of the people interested in the Panama-California International Exposition at San Diego that you should be there to take part in the opening and speak both for yourself and as my representative. The date is March eighteenth, which is very near at hand, but I do not know just what plans you are looking forward to.

It distressed us to hear of Nancy's accident.[1] I hope that she is rapidly getting all right again.

       Cordially and faithfully yours,   Woodrow Wilson

TLS (Letterpress Books, WP, DLC).
[1] Lane's daughter.

To Seth Low

My dear Mr. Low: The White House March 13, 1916

Thank you warmly for your cordial letter of March tenth.

You were right in thinking that I did take it for granted that, since their work was finished, the resignation of the members of the Commission on the Colorado strike was accepted. I would not think of holding them subject to call after their very generous labors.

With renewed assurances of appreciation,

       Cordially and sincerely yours,   Woodrow Wilson

TLS (S. Low Papers, NNC).

To Wilbur Fisk Sadler, Jr.

My dear General: [The White House] March 13, 1916

Thank you for your interesting and important letter of March eleventh. The expressions of approval which it contains gratify me very deeply and the suggestion it makes about the Assistant Secretary of War[1] is one which I intend most seriously to discuss with the new Secretary, who, by the way, deserves all the encomiums of him you have heard. He is a splendid, sterling fellow.

Of course, I will take pleasure in acting on your suggestion about seeing the Executive Committee of the Organized Militia.[2]

In haste

Cordially and sincerely yours,   Woodrow Wilson

TLS (Letterpress Books, WP, DLC).

[1] Wilson, on April 19, 1916, appointed William Moulton Ingraham of Portland, Me., a lawyer, former judge, and Mayor of Portland, 1915-16.

[2] Wilson met with the executive committee of the National Guard Association at the White House on March 16.

From Edward William Pou

Dear Mr. President: Washington Mch 13, 1916.

I am venturing to drop this note to say how heartily I indorse the action you have taken with regard to the attack on Columbus. This morning I made it a point to talk with every member of the House I saw. Without exception they are with you and almost without exception they feel that the matter should be left in the hands of the administration without discussion of any kind on the floor of the House. In my judgment very great harm might result from debate in either the House or the Senate at this time and I am glad to say that, so far as I can judge, there is no disposition to debate the matter in the House.

I hope I may be permitted to say that I very keenly appreciate your personal note of Feby 29th. If I can render any help at all, however small, in aiding you in dealing with the present very delicate situation I shall feel very proud indeed.

Sincerely your friend,   Edwd W. Pou.

ALS (WP, DLC).

From Franklin Knight Lane

My dear Mr. President: Washington March 13, 1916.

If you have no objection I will go West to see my brother[1] tonight.

I have talked with Judge Adamson, who says that the Shields bill will not pass his Committee but that the Committee print bill, which is satisfactory to Lenroot and other conservationists, will be substituted for it in the House. I have also talked with Lenroot, Ferris and Esch,[2] who will do what they can to see that the right kind of a bill comes out of the House. I have asked Mr. Finney,[3] of my office, who is familiar with the history of all of these acts, to call on Secretary Baker, and I have sent the latter all of the data that I have.   Faithfully yours,   Franklin K. Lane

TLS (WP, DLC).

[1] George W. Lane of San Francisco, F. K. Lane's former law partner.

[2] John Jacob Esch, Republican congressman from Wisconsin.

[3] Edward Clingan Finney, member of the Board of Appeals of the Department of the Interior.

From Franklin Knight Lane, with Enclosure

My dear Mr. President: Washington March 13, 1916.

I shall be pleased to go to the San Diego Exposition on my way to San Francisco and say a word as your representative at its opening.

I hope that you may find your way made less difficult than now appears possible as to entering Mexico. My judgment is that to fail in getting Villa would ruin us in the eyes of all Latin-Americans. I do not say that they respect only force, but like children they pile insult upon insult if they are not stopped when the first insult is given. If I can be of any service to you by observation or by carrying any message for you to anybody while I am West, I trust that you will command me. I can return by way of Arizona and New Mexico.

I beg to invite your attention to the inclosed telegram[1] from a man whom I knew well twenty years ago as a newspaper man in California and who has been acting as publicity manager for General Carranza for the last few years. He is an American, and when I saw him recently in this city he was about to start a daily paper in Mexico City in behalf of Carranza. If there is any man who knows Carranza's mind I should say Weeks does. He might serve as an additional conduit to Carranza.

From my talk with Judge Adamson I believe that the water power situation is not as difficult as we had feared. I inclose you a letter just received from Judge Adamson on page 4 of which you will find that his ideas are not radically at variance with ours. I suggest that you transmit this letter to Secretary Baker.

Now for a personal word. I am extremely sorry that we are not to have you and Mrs. Wilson in our house this week. We had looked forward to it as an opportunity to give evidence of our very real personal affection rather than as a quasi official function. We feel, however, that no function is needed to do this. I shall carry your message at noon to Nancy, and I know that it will lighten the pain which she suffers with so much fortitude.

Faithfully yours,   Franklin K Lane

TLS (WP, DLC).

¹ G. F. Weeks to F. K. Lane, March 10, 1916, T telegram (WP, DLC). He asked Lane to assure Wilson that his decision to dispatch American troops to Mexico met with the full approval of all peace-loving Mexicans and foreigners. He added that Villa would have to be eliminated without further ado to assure peace in northern Mexico.

E N C L O S U R E

William Charles Adamson to Franklin Knight Lane

Dear Mr. Secretary: Washington, D. C. March 12, 1916.

Referring to our phone conversation of yesterday, I would be glad to have a talk with you at your convenience. If you are too busy during the day, I will gladly come to your house any evening that will suit your convenience.

I think you and I had better come to a tentative understanding first, before consulting others. I do not profess to know much about the water power situation on public lands and have never interferred with it in any way. My proposition has been to secure hydro-electric development and promote navigation at the same time, on the navigable streams, without expense to the Government. The Government has nothing to sell or give away except the exclusive control of the navigable streams for navigation purposes only, conferred by the Commerce Clause of the Constitution. It seems to me that the material consideration in framing such a bill is simple and easily understood and it is strange to me that they cannot be readily agreed upon.

The first obvious fact is that unless the legislation provides for liberal terms and conditions, such as will promise profit to investors, it will be impossible to induce capital to construct any dams: Second, it is equally obvious and ought not to be disputed that adequate safeguard regulations ought to be provided to insure to the public the use of hydro-electricity where generated for distribution, on terms and conditions that insure fair treatment as to rates and practices.

The two questions on which contention has been rife are first: the Pinchot proposition, providing for an indefinite federal tax that may be changed from time to time at the will of the Secretary of War or other Federal Agencies. Second: the period of life given to the consent of Congress. If the first proposition, to require that uncertain tax, is insisted upon there is no use at all to proceed with the legislation. Capital will not invest on such terms of uncertainty. As to the second proposition, the word "recapture" has found large usage very much to the prejudice of our efforts. Capital regards that as a belligerent term. The word capture is generally used to apply to the apprehension of a criminal or to the subjugation of an enemy, and the word is very unpopular. It may mean something in the public land bill, but it is absolutely meaningless in our bill. The Government has nothing to recapture, it grants nothing to recapture. It never parts, at any time during the transaction with the absolute control of the stream for navigation purposes. The whole question is what privileges will it grant entirely and absolutely consistent with all interest of navigation that will at the same time be liberal enough to induce capital to build the locks and dams in the navigable streams. It occurs to me from a long investigation of the subject and consultation with capatalists and water power promoters that the period is not so importnat [important] as the matter of uncertainty

So far as I have noticed it is not conceded, in any bill by anybody, that the property would be confiscated utterly at the end of the period, unless the grantee was at fault, bucause that condition would carry with it the idea that the grantee would be allowed to amortize the investment during the period, which would mean high rates, utterly inconsistent with the other condition that the public can be assured reasonable and just rates.

So I call your attention to the one consideration that applies to both of these propositions, to wit: that whatever the Government decides it ought to demand it it [sic] should make up its mind and at the time of approving the plans and specifications make clear all the terms and conditions once for all during the life of the grant. If the period of fifty years is adopted as the life of the grant, we should clearly and unequivocally provide that at the end of the period first: the Government may at its option make a new deal with the original grantee. If they fail to agree upon terms the government may second: make a deal with a new grantee providing therein to compensate the original grantee or third: the Government may take over all the property itself, providing in like manner to compensate the original grantee. In both cases the compensation should be the fair and reasonable value of the lands, locks, and dams and all the appertinent works and installation and equipment, provided that in no case shall the compensation exceed the original cost. That would make the investment absolutely secure so as to leave the Government free whether by state or Federal regulation as the case may be to insure fair and reasonable rates of service to the people. In like manner whatever financial demands are made of the grantee ought to be fixed at the time of approval as a part of the terms and conditions to control during the original life of the grant. Even if a Federal tax is required as a condition of consent it ought not to be changed during the life of the grant. It is presumed that we will always have a just man as Secretary of War and he will simply be making the contract for the Government and in that case it is presumed he would make the best terms that the capitalist would agree to. And in addition to many other arguments against deterring capital by requiring a federal tax, the diversity in the size of streams and banks and shoals [and] difference as to possibility of development of water power, render it impossible to fix any uniform scale or standard for such charges.

This letter is rather long, but I tried to make my position plain and I believe you will agree with me on most of it if you will read the letter.

With high regards and best wishes, I remain,

Your friend,   W. C. Adamson.

TLS (WP, DLC).

From William Charles Adamson

Dear Mr. President: Washington, D. C. March 13, 1916.

Of course I take the enclosed clipping from the the [sic] Evening Times[1] cum grano salis, but I wish to call your attention to two matters. First, I do not care to lose sight of the all important question of inducing private capital to develop both navigation and manufacturing on our navigable streams in a fight between the alleged conservationists and what they imagine to be the purposes of my bill. I expect the Committee on Interstate and Foreign Commerce to substitute for the Shields bill the terms of the bill which you approved last Congress. To those terms the gentlemen whom we regarded as responsible for the fight against us agreed in your presence. They kept the letter of the agreement by refraining from offering their contentions in the House in person but by some coincidence more able men did offer them and they voted for them. I am not offering the bill as it passed the House but as it was agreed upon in your presence, and I shall rely upon you at the proper time to do and say what you feel that you can consistently do to help me pass it.

Mr. Kent, mentioned in this clipping, is a good man and I like him and on many subjects he is clear and correct but in common with many so called conservationists he has some very curious misapprehensions, delusions or hallucinations on the water power question. We have been unable to persuade them to differentiate between the Government's proprietary interests on public lands, where it is both owner and sovereign and its sovereignty only for the purposes of navigation on streams where private parties own everything. We have no desire to interfere with the public domain. We have never butted into that. The conflict has been entirely of the seeking of the other crowd resulting, in my judgment, from a misunderstanding on their part of what we are trying to do, and I have never been able to get them to listen long enough to persuade them as to what we are trying to do. There are many thousands of miles of streams in the older parts of the country with water sufficient for navigation and containing so many shoals for water power sites that they can easily pay for their own improvement if permitted to do so by Congress and at the same time generate hydro-electricity sufficient to make all those States prosperous with various kinds of industries and manufacturing.

There are only two things to subserve in framing such legislation. One is, make the terms and conditions of consent liberal enough to entice the investment of capital. Unless you do that it is fruitless to consider the other thing, but that being conceded, the second thing is to safe guard the interests of the public by proper regulation of rates and practices.

An examination of the copy of the committee print bill I send you[2] will disclose the fact that both these things are accomplished in that bill if it is enacted into law.

The second thing I call your attention to is that it was announced in the House today that a program of legislation would soon be formulated and announced. If you are consulted about that program of legislation I do hope you will not permit the most important element of preparedness within the jurisdiction of this committee to be ignored or sidetracked. The renewal of the fleet of Coast Guard cutters is more important than battle ships. Our history of peace and war shows that a cutter is worth more than a battle ship, ship for ship. We have reported a bill for seven new cutters, three large ones and four small ones, all together costing in the neighborhood of a million dollars. The light house service also should be taken care of and the small vessels desired by the Department of Commerce. The two little bills I talked to you about that the Interstate Commerce Commission needs so badly, and the Joint Resolution for a joint committee to investigate the instrumentalities and regulation of commerce recommended by you in your annual message. That was ordered reported at the last meeting of the Committee and should be gotten up in the House immediately, and last but not least the great importance of considering and passing my water power bill is transcending in comparison with some other propositions.

With high regards and best wishes for you and your administration so successful up to this time, I remain,

Your friend,   W. C. Adamson

TLS (WP, DLC).
    [1] "Wilson Promises to Guard Water Power," *Washington Times*, March 13, 1916, clipping (WP, DLC). The story printed the text of Wilson's letter of March 9 to Representative Kent and asserted that that letter intimated "a veto for the Shields bill unless it be radically amended."
    [2] H.R. 3, 64th Cong., 1st sess. (WP, DLC).

From Champ Clark

My dear Mr. President: Washington, D. C. March 13, 1916.

In order to economize your time I am writing you this letter instead of coming to see you. Mr. Kitchin and I had a full and free conference with Brother Mann about the tentative program. He says that we can't put that program through, together with the necessary appropriation bills, by the first of December. Therefore he declines preemptorily to cooperate with us in the expediting of the public business, unless the program is shortened up very materially. We talked with him for a considerable length of time. The first thing that happened this morning after the Chaplain prayed, was that Mr. Garrett of Tennessee, acting Chairman of the Insular Committee, asked for unanimous consent to take up the Porto Rican Bill, which was reported unanimously by the Committee, and consider it at night sessions, beginning tomorrow night at eight o'clock and run until eleven each night until it was finished. Mr. Mann objected, and one objection of course crowded it out. He said that he would help along to shorten up the session so that Members could get home if a *reasonable* program were prepared, but that there was no use in working overtime and wearing everybody out if we were going to stay here all summer anyway.

The trouble about the situation is that as long as Congress is in session with all the troubles that we are in about foreign affairs, any one man, by making a skillful speech on the floor of the House or Senate, can come very near percipitating war, either with Mexico or with some European country—or both.

Your friend,   Champ Clark.

TLS (WP, DLC).

From Robert Lansing

PERSONAL AND CONFIDENTIAL:

My dear Mr. President: Washington March 13, 1916.

I thank you very sincerely for permitting me to see this letter from Senator Husting. I have read it with very much interest.

Faithfully yours,   Robert Lansing

TLS (WP, DLC).

To Frank Lyon Polk,[1] with Enclosure

My dear Mr. Polk: The White House March 14, 1916

Here is a letter from a newspaper man whom I think you know that contains some interesting suggestions. I would be very much obliged if you would prepare such a request as is suggested in the paragraph marked "3" so that we may discuss it together, and, if we finally think it wise, may send for the representatives of the three principal press associations and ask their cooperation.

Cordially and sincerely yours,   Woodrow Wilson

TLS (F. L. Polk Papers, CtY).
[1] Lansing had gone to Pinehurst, N. C., to recover from some kind of a breakdown caused by diabetes from which he suffered chronically; Polk was Acting Secretary of State.

E N C L O S U R E

From David Lawrence

Personal

[Washington]

Dear Mr. President: Monday March 13th [1916]

In the present delicate situation the press can be a helpful as well as a dangerous factor, and I want to draw your attention to some steps that might be taken by you to keep the newspapers from causing trouble.

1. The head of every bureau and news service in Washington, the *head* of each Washington newspaper, and correspondents especially of newspapers published in the border states, should be summoned to the White House and impressed with the fact that the news dispatches they write must be tempered; that they must consider the sensitiveness of the Mexican people and at this time refrain from any unfavorable mention of Carranza or his government, the spread of stories about our relations with the Carranza government that might indicate friction or a likelihood of it; that above all stories hinting at a general invasion or talk of preparations that would give the impression of a large military movement should be avoided.

2. This should be supplemented by a statement from you calling on the press of the United States and especially the newspapers published in border towns and states to refrain at this time from publishing any stories that might inflame public opinion, anatagonize [antagonize] the Carranza government or Mexicans generally, or which might give to the present small expedition the character of a general invasion or intervention.

3. Each of the news services—the Associated Press, the United Press, the International News Service, and the Central News should be asked to send privately to all their clients, both *day* and *night*, a request that stories of troop movements or preparations that might be interpreted as meaning war be withheld, and that the requests made in your public statement be scrupulously observed.

4. Our military commanders at the border points should be instructed to give interviews to the local papers where they are stationed pointing out that there is no intention of invading Mexico but to pursue Villa in accordance with the precedents; that, of course, as soon as the Carranza troops are in control and Villa is captured our forces will be withdrawn and that just now the American government is viewing favorably the request of Gen Carranza for the reciprocal privilege asked for in his communication.[1] (I am satisfied that this privilege was asked for not to be exercised for it need not be if we have sufficient troops alone [along] our boundary but to calm Mexican public opinion).

Much importance is always attached in border towns to interviews given by military commanders. It calms our own people as well.

All these steps may seem to you to be making a mountain out of a molehill but each day that the situation continues as it is increases the danger of a general uprising against our troops the end of which would be a purposeless war. The newspapers have been saying too much about "U S refuses to cooperate with Carranza troops" and have been doing a great deal of damage by giving the impression that we do not want Carranza's help etc. I particularly fear the effect of all this on that garrison at Juarez and I would even advise that special request be made of the two El Paso newspapers to do everything possible to avoid friction.

Very sincerely,   David Lawrence

TLS (F. L. Polk Papers, CtY).

[1] Lansing, in an urgent telegram to Silliman on March 9, had sent a report on the Columbus raid to Carranza and said that, although the American government was suspending judgment, "this appears to be the most serious situation which has confronted this government during the entire period of Mexican unrest," and that the Washington government expected Carranza to do everything within his power to pursue, capture, and exterminate Villa and his band. RL to J. R. Silliman, March 9, 1916, T telegram (SDR, RG 59, 812.00/17382, DNA).

Carranza replied through Foreign Minister Jesús Acuña on March 10. The First Chief said that he had earlier dispatched 2,500 men under the command of General Luis Gutíerrez, Military Governor of the State of Chihuahua, in chase of Villa, but that Villa had escaped by crossing into the territory of the United States. "The government over which the citizen First Chief presides, desiring to exterminate in as little time as possible the horde led by Francisco Villa who was recently outlawed, to capture and inflict upon him the penalty of the law, applies through you Honorable Mr. Confidential Agent, to the Government of the United States and asks the permission necessary to let Mexican forces cross into American territory in pursuit of those bandits acknowledging due reciprocity in regard to forces of the United States crossing into Mexican territory if the raid effected at Columbus should unfortunately be repeated at any other point of the border. The Government of Mexico would highly appreciate a prompt and favorable decision from the Government of the United States." J. R. Silliman to RL, March 10, 1916, T telegram (SDR, RG 59, 812.00/17415, DNA).

To Laura Jenks Shively

My dear Mrs. Shively,   The White House. 14 March, 1916.

I have just learned with the deepest sorrow of the death of your husband.[1] Your own loss is tragical and my heart goes out to you in deep and sincere sympathy; the loss to the country is very great, for he was moved as a public servant by high motives of duty to his State and the nation, and I join with his colleagues in deploring his death, as creating a vacancy in the highest councils of the country which cannot easily be filled. May God sustain you in this moment of your supreme sorrow.

With great respect,   Your friend,   Woodrow Wilson.[2]

TCL (Letterpress Books, WP, DLC).

[1] Senator Benjamin Franklin Shively of Indiana had died a few hours before Wilson wrote this letter.

[2] A notation on the letterpress copy of this letter says that the original was WWhw.

From William Kent

Dear Mr. President: Washington, D. C. March 14, 1916.

I was very glad to get your consent to publish the letter on water power. You may not have noticed how little publicity it obtained, although given out to the papers. This suppression is all part of the general campaign of the water power people. I shall endeavor to put it in the Congressional Record. My only reason for not asking this privilege before, was a desire not to do self-advertising in this connection. It would have been much better if you could have gotten out the statement through some other channel.

When I was a small boy, we had an old coachman whom I used to call "Play Game," which we used to call "S'posin'."[1] We used to take turns in "sposin" all sorts of strange things, and then try to give answers. Here is a "sposin" concerning Mexico, which you may have considered, and which, to my mind, is worthy of most careful consideration.

I have never had the joy of personal acquaintance with Villa. Many of my friends have. He has kept his word with them and has no hatred whatever for Americans. He is simply playing a very shrewd game in the barbarous fashion which might be expected of a man of his bringing up, which barbarous fashion, I think you will admit, is more direct and no worse than the style that prevails in European capitals. He felt extremely sore over the endorsement of Carranza, after he had stood out against war with the United States, and Carranza had seemingly invited it. He despises Carranza as totally inadequate, both from a military and an executive standpoint.

Now to resume our game of "sposin," "sposin" Villa should become the popular hero of Mexico, and that Carranza should go into eclipse except as he joined Villa in the popular move to fight the United States. Then the question would be as to what we were going to do about this new dictator, who would be the man that we would have to reckon with as representing the Republic of Mexico. Would we be justified in sacrificing a great many American lives to destroy a man guilty of murder of American citizens, who had made himself the government of Mexico, and who had back of him all factions?

I am not expressing any opinion, *nor asking any answer*, but in our game of "sposin" the answer will be found difficult.

Yours truly,   William Kent

TLS (WP, DLC).
[1] *Sic!*

From Thomas James Walsh

My dear Mr. President: Washington. March 14, 1916.

I am very much pleased to learn by last evening's paper that your attention has been directed, and perhaps your concern aroused in respect to the pending water power legislation through the letter of Mr. Kent. It is regrettable that the perplexed state of our foreign affairs rendered it impossible for you to give to the subject the consideration which it would otherwise have had from you when the Shields bill was before the Senate. It is scarcely conceivable that it can have the approval of the House without being radically amended. If it is, a dead-lock is not unlikely. If it is not, you may find it, as I believe it to be now, quite unworthy of your sanction. The failure of the legislation for want of executive approval would be deplorable.

Fortunately, the opportunity to incline the Senate to acceptance of the views which have heretofore found expression in the House is at hand. The Ferris bill, which embodies the ideas of Secretary Lane and the heads of the Committees of both houses on Public Lands, and Mines and Mining, was yesterday afternoon made the "unfinished business," without disturbing the order by which the armor plate bill is to be voted on on March twenty-first. This bill, as it came from the House—the Ferris bill— is before the Senate with amendments recommended by the committee which, if adopted, will bring it into substantial conformity with the Shields bill. Unfortunately Secretary Lane has left the city. The fact is that the committee amendments are the contributions of the Republican members, aided by Senator Thomas who, with his colleague, the only Democratic Senators from the West, save Senator Mark Smith, who take that position, are bitterly opposed to the whole program of conservation legislation. In its general features, if not in all details, the Ferris bill has the support not only of Senator Myers and myself, but of Senators Chamberlain and Lane, Newlands and Pittman, Phelan, Ashurst, Hitchcock, Owen, Gore, Thompson and Johnson of South Dakota— all from the public land states, on the Democratic side,[1] as well as of Poindexter, Sterling and Norris, also from the states affected, on the other side of the chamber.[2]

A word from you would go far towards ensuring the rejection of the most objectionable amendments offered by the committee, paving the way for acceptance of any amendments that may be proposed by the House to the Shields bill. Unless some speedy relief comes the committee amendments will be adopted perfunctorily. Senator Myers[3] is, in some measure, as Chairman of the Committee, obligated to champion them, though they do not represent his views. I made myself tedious in an effort to convert members to the principles embodied in the Ferris bill when the navigable waters bill was before the Senate. Most of them sought the seclusion of the cloak rooms or their offices while the debate was in progress, and, appearing in response to the bell, voted with the committee. I am not disposed to make any farther effort unless there is room to hope that some good may result. Indeed, debate must be curtailed if we are to get anywhere on anything.

I am disposed to think that Mr. Kent would not be inconsolable if no legislation on water powers was enacted. I may do him an injustice, but I am led from several conferences had with him to think that he would like to see the pending bills killed either by adverse action in Congress or by a veto. I suspect that Mr. Pinchot would like to have the whole thing deferred until he and his friends get back into power. You may have noticed that that gentleman offers no constructive suggestions in connection with his denunciation of the measures now before us. If the power site bill, as it came from the House, generally known as the Ferris bill, meets your approval, as I was led from conversations with Secretary Lane to believe is the case, I trust you may be moved to let our friends in the Senate know your attitude. In any case, I shall be glad to be advised of how you feel about the bill, if the exacting character of the duties that so engross your attention will permit you to give it even a cursory examination.

Sincerely yours,   T. J. Walsh

TLS (WP, DLC).

[1] That is, George Earle Chamberlain and Harry Lane of Oregon, Francis Griffith Newlands and Key Pittman of Nevada, James Duval Phelan of California, Henry Fountain Ashurst of Arizona, Gilbert Monell Hitchcock of Nebraska, Robert Latham Owen and Thomas Pryor Gore of Oklahoma, William Howard Thompson of Kansas, and Edwin Stockton Johnson of South Dakota.

[2] That is, Miles Poindexter of Washington, Thomas Sterling of South Dakota, and George William Norris of Nebraska.

[3] That is, Henry Lee Myers, Democrat of Montana.

Frederick Funston to Henry Pinckney McCain

Ft. Sam Houston, Texas, March 14, 1916.

Number 1031. Following repeated from General Pershing:

"Consultation with local Car[r]anza commander at Palomas shows that Bertoni[1] has retired south with three hundred men only about one hundred men now at Palomas   Local commander says he will oppose entry unless he receives instructions to the contrary   He has received no orders. He will telegraph his superior(s)   expects reply this afternoon   It seems probable that Carranza troops are going to oppose U. S. This column is ready to move and other column(s) will be ready tomorrow Small force moves across the border not later than noon the fifteenth unless otherwise ordered."   Funston.

CC telegram (F. L. Polk Papers, CtY).
  ¹ Unidentified.

From Newton Diehl Baker, with Enclosure

(CONFIDENTIAL.)

My dear Mr. President: Washington. March 15, 1916.

I hand you herewith a copy of a telegram which I sent to General Funston last night after my conference with you. I will of course send you promptly any response. In the mean time I am to see Mr. Polk this morning. I was not able to reach him until past midnight, and, for reasons which developed in my conversation with him, we determined that he should not try to see Mr. Arredondo until after a further conference I am to have with Mr. Polk this morning, at the end of which it may be necessary for us to see you.   Sincerely yours,   Newton D. Baker

TLS (WP, DLC).

E N C L O S U R E

Washington, March 15, 1916.

The President understands that the de facto Government of Mexico will tolerate the entry of our expedition into Mexico in accordance with the statement of the first chief and the reply of Secretary of State Lansing, which we telegraphed to you.¹ If the military representative of the de facto Government of Mexico refuses to tolerate your crossing the border, wire fully what he says about his instructions before crossing, and await further orders.

TC telegram (WP, DLC).
  ¹ After sending his note of March 10 (through Acuña), Carranza learned that the United States planned to send a large expedition into Mexico. He thereupon issued a stern warning: "I confirmed my message to you transmitting note sent to the American Government and I am awaiting the result of it. There is no reason why on account of the lamentable incident at Columbus we should be carried to a declaration of war between the two countries; but if unfortunately and because of the pressure of our enemies, who have been seeking intervention at all cost, war should be declared, the Constitutionalist Government [over] which I preside, supported by the Mexican people, shall make use of all means possible to repel such an unjust and outrageous war. If the Government of the United States does not take into consideration the mutual permission for American and Mexican forces to cross into the territory of one another in pursuit of bandits and insists in sending an operating army into Mexican soil,

my Government shall consider this act as an invasion of national territory. It is necessary that the Department of State should be caused to understand that it would be unjust to attribute to the Government and people of Mexico the responsibility for the acts committed by a band of brigands, which this Government has placed beyond the law, and that there would be no justification for any invasion of Mexican territory by an armed force of the United States, not even under the pretext of pursuing and capturing Villa to turn him over to the Mexican authorities. It is inconceivable that the Government of the United States should resort to such means to capture Villa, as the only result would be to facilitate his impunity to leave the country and to bring about a war between two countries, with the numberless loss of life and property, without such loss serving to avenge the crimes which the American Government is endeavoring to punish. Such war would be the most unjust which modern history would record and it would also be an evident proof of the lack of sincerity of the American Government, in whose Capital the Pan American Conf[e]rence has just been held and before which President Wilson and the Secretary of State expressed sentiments of fraternity among all the nations of the American Continent. Such war, furthermore, would only serve for the American Government to satisfy the deliberate purpose of Francisco Villa and the reactionaries who have induced him to commit the crimes he did at Columbus, as his only aim was to provoke armed intervention by the United States in Mexico. Francisco Villa and the other traitors who are seeking the above results, will avoid the struggle: and the only ones who would go to it would be honest Mexicans who have in no way provoked it. I will go into further considerations on the matter, as the right and justice of our side is so clear that no other than the reasons hereinbefore given are necessary, which you will set forth in bringing this delicate question to the atention of the Secretary of State. V. Carranza." V. Carranza to E. Arredondo, March 11, 1916, TC telegram (SDR, RG 59, 812.00/17501, DNA). Arredondo read this telegram to Lansing at 4 P.M. on March 12.

Lansing and Wilson met on March 13 and decided not to take the warning seriously in the belief that Carranza had issued it for domestic political reasons. Instead, they agreed to accept his proposed agreement for the reciprocal right of hot pursuit of bandits on both sides of the border and to act as if it applied to the expedition against Villa: "The Government of the United States understands that in view of its agreement to this reciprocal arrangement proposed by the *de facto* Government, the arrangement is now complete and in force and the reciprocal privileges thereunder may accordingly be exercised by either Gov. ernment without further interchange of views."

"It is a matter of sincere gratification to the Government of the United States," the note continued, "that the *de facto* Government of Mexico has evinced so cordial and friendly a spirit of cooperation in the efforts of the authorities of the United States to apprehend and punish the bands of outlaws, who seek refuge beyond the international boundary in the erroneous belief that the constituted authorities will resent any pursuit across the boundary by the forces of the Government whose citizens have suffered by the crimes of the fugitives.

"With the same spirit of cordial friendship the Government of the United States will exercise the privilege granted by the *de facto* Government of Mexico in the hope and confident expectation that by their mutual efforts lawlessness will be eradicated and peace and order maintained in the territories of the United States and Mexico contiguous to the international boundary." RL to J. R. Silliman, March 13, 1916, 3 P.M., T telegram (SDR, RG 59, 812.00/17415, DNA).

To Edward William Pou

My dear Mr. Pou: The White House March 15, 1916

I warmly appreciate your note of the thirteenth which was laid on my table yesterday. It is extremely gratifying to me that the attitude of the members of the House and Senate with regard to the Mexican situation should be what it is. It is a very thorny matter to attempt to deal with and I fear that not all the pitfalls have been disclosed yet, but if I can move independently without trenching upon the powers of Congress, I shall do so with the more confidence because of the fine attitude the members of the two houses are taking.

I want to say again how warmly and deeply I appreciate your own unstinted and disinterested support. It is one of the bright spots amidst many discouragements.

Cordially and sincerely yours,   Woodrow Wilson

TLS (E. W. Pou Papers, Nc-Ar).

To Champ Clark

My dear Mr. Speaker: [The White House] March 15, 1916

Your letter of the thirteenth has given me a great deal of concern. I am very much disappointed at the position taken by Mr. Mann. I am not only disappointed, but genuinely surprised that he should take the position he does. I can conceive of no justification for the deliberate obstruction of the public business or the delay of the consideration of matters of the first consequence to the country. I must believe that he has taken this position under the influence of some passing mood from which he will presently come out and look at things in a wider and more patriotic way.

It is my clear judgment that his position should not affect our action at all. We are under the clearest obligation to the country to go forward in the matters listed on the programme we discussed the other day; our platform pledges leave us no honorable choice; and I for my part am clear that it would be vastly better for the country for Congress to stay here until September bent upon performing its duty, whatever the consequences, than to yield an inch to those who deliberately seek to obstruct and delay action. I take it for granted that there are means within the choice of the majority of the House which can be adopted which will be effective to put the programme through notwithstanding partisan opposition, and my own urgent advice is that the necessary steps be taken.

Cordially and sincerely yours,   Woodrow Wilson

TLS (Letterpress Books, WP, DLC).

To Joseph Edward Davies

My dear Davies: [The White House] March 15, 1916

Tumulty has handed me your note of March sixth to him about the judgeship in Wisconsin.[1] I have sweat blood over this case and feel that in all the circumstances it is really out of the question that we should turn the Senator[2] down with regard to it. The Attorney General and I have discussed it with him repeatedly, at least the Attorney General has discussed it with him repeatedly and I have more than once, and it is perfectly plain that he can never be reconciled to the appointment of Aylward. This is a personal distress to me, as you know, and I have done everything I could, directly and indirectly, to bring him to another view, but since I cannot and have already had an opportunity of showing my confidence in Aylward,[3] the way seems blocked.

I have not yet had laid before me the recommendation of the Attorney General to which you refer and I do not know that he has himself come to any final judgment in the matter.

I need not tell you, my dear Davies, what things of this sort cost me.

Cordially and faithfully yours,   Woodrow Wilson

TLS (Letterpress Books, WP, DLC).
   [1] J. E. Davies to JPT, March 6, 1916, TLS (WP, DLC), in which Davies appealed on behalf of his former law partner, John Arthur Aylward, and requested an appointment with Wilson to discuss the matter.
   [2] That is, Senator Husting.
   [3] He had appointed him United States attorney for the western district of Wisconsin on April 24, 1913.

To Thomas James Walsh

My dear Senator: [The White House] March 15, 1916

In reply to your letter of March fourteenth, for which I sincerely thank you, let me say that the Ferris Bill as it passed the House does meet with my entire approval, and I should be sorry indeed to see any substantial alterations made to it by the Senate. If you would be kind enough to let me have a brief schedule of the changes proposed in the committee amendments, and would indicate any feasible way of cooperating with you in preventing the adoption of amendments which would go to the principle of the bill, I would be very much obliged to you indeed. This is a matter in which I have the greatest interest and in which I wish to be of service in every way.

Cordially and sincerely yours,   Woodrow Wilson

TLS (Letterpress Books, WP, DLC).

To William Kent

My dear Mr. Kent: The White House March 15, 1916

Your game of "S'posin'" puts a very poignant question which has been very much in my mind. The whole problem down there looks very much less simple to me than it seems to appear to some other people, and your question has accentuated my own anxious speculations about the future turn of events down there.

Cordially and sincerely yours, Woodrow Wilson

TLS (W. Kent Papers, CtY).

From Joseph Patrick Tumulty

My dear Governor: The White House March 15, 1916

I have been thinking over what we discussed this morning with reference to the Mexican situation.[1]

I am not acting on impulse and without a full realization, I hope, of everything that is involved. I am convinced that we should pursue to the end the declared purpose announced by you last Friday and endorsed by Congress and the people of the United States of "getting Villa." If the *de facto* government is going to resist the entrance of our troops, a new situation will be presented. I feel that you ought to advise Congress at the earliest possible moment of what the situation really is in order to secure its support and cooperation in whatever action is needed to accomplish the purpose you have in mind. To retrace our steps now would be not only disastrous to our party and humiliating to the country, but would be destructive of our influence in international affairs and make it forever impossible to deal in any effective way with Mexican affairs.

Your appeal to Congress ought to deal with this matter in an affirmative way, asking for the requisite power which you may feel assured will be granted to you in ungrudging fashion.

My apology for writing to you is my distress of mind and my deep interest in everything that affects you and your future and, I hope, the country's welfare. I would not be your friend if I did not tell you frankly how I feel. Faithfully, Tumulty

TLS (WP, DLC).
[1] After the arrival of Pershing's dispatch (F. Funston to H. P. McCain, March 14, 1916), Baker took it to the White House at 11:15 that same evening. Wilson said that, if the report was correct, he would not send troops into Mexico because it would mean intervention and war. See the extract from the House diary, printed at March 17, 1916. As has been revealed, Baker sent new instructions to Pershing early the next morning, directing him, in the event that the *Carrancista* commander refused to permit the Punitive Expedition to enter Mexico, to inform the War Department and to await further orders.

Tumulty related his conversation with Wilson in his *Woodrow Wilson As I Know Him* (Garden City, N. Y., 1921), pp. 157-60, as follows:

"The President sent for me one day to visit with him in his study, and to discuss 'the present situation in Mexico.' As I sat down, he turned to me in the most serious way and said: 'Tumulty, you are Irish, and, therefore, full of fight. I know how deeply you feel about this Columbus affair. Of course, it is tragical and deeply regrettable from every standpoint, but in the last analysis I, and not the Cabinet or you, must bear the responsibility for every action that is to be taken. I have to sleep with my conscience in these matters and I shall be held responsible for every drop of blood that may be spent in the enterprise of intervention. I am seriously considering every phase of this difficult matter, and I can say frankly to you, and you may inform the Cabinet officers who discuss it with you, that *"there won't be any war with Mexico if I can prevent it,"* no matter how loud the gentlemen on the hill yell for it and demand it. It is not a difficult thing for a president to declare war, especially against a weak and defenceless nation like Mexico. In a republic like ours, the man on horseback is always an idol, and were I considering the matter from the standpoint of my own political fortunes, and its influence upon the result of the next election, I should at once grasp this opportunity and invade Mexico, for it would mean the triumph of my administration. But this has never been in my thoughts for a single moment. The thing that daunts me and holds me back is the aftermath of war, with all its tears and tragedies. I came from the South and I know what war is, for I have seen its wreckage and terrible ruin. It is easy for me as President to declare war. I do not have to fight, and neither do the gentlemen on the Hill who now clamour for it. It is some poor farmer's boy, or son of some poor widow away off in some modest community, or perhaps the scion of a great family, who will have to do the fighting and the dying. I will not resort to war against Mexico until I have exhausted every means to keep out of this mess. I know they will call me a coward and a quitter, but that will not disturb me. Time, the great solvent, will, I am sure, vindicate this policy of humanity and forbearance. Men forget what is back of this struggle in Mexico. It is the age-long struggle of a people to come into their own, and while we look upon the incidents in the foreground, let us not forget the tragic reality in the background which towers above this whole sad picture. The gentlemen who criticize me speak as if America were afraid to fight Mexico. Poor Mexico, with its pitiful men, women, and children, fighting to gain a foothold in their own land! They speak of the valour of America. What is true valour? I would be just as much ashamed to be rash as I would to be a coward. Valour is self-respecting. Valour is circumspect. Valour strikes only when it is right to strike. Valour withholds itself from all small implications and entanglements and waits for the great opportunity when the sword will flash as if it carried the light of heaven upon its blade.' "

Tumulty lifted the last sentences relating to "valour" from Wilson's speech to the Gridiron Club printed at February 26, 1916. It is, of course, possible that Wilson said something very much like them to Tumulty.

From Frank Lyon Polk

PERSONAL AND CONFIDENTIAL

My dear Mr. President: Washington March 15th, 1916.

There are no telegrams that are particular[l]y interesting this afternoon except the one I attach, which is a corrected copy of Gen. Carranza's proclamation of the 12th.[1] You will notice that it was published in an extra in La Opinion, the only Mexican paper published at Queretaro, at eleven o'clock P.M., March 12th.

Schmutz,[2] our Vice Consul at Aguascalientes, telegraphed on the 14th instant that he was leaving and had advised all Americans to leave for the border or nearest port. Later, on the same day, he sent another message stating that in view of the favorable news from our representative in Queretaro he had decided to remain to await further developments.

I have directed that an immediate investigation be made to find our [out] whether the messages we have sent in code to our representative near Gen. Carranza are going through.

Faithfully yours,   Frank L Polk

TLS (WP, DLC).

1 This enclosure is missing; however, it was J. W. Belt to the Secretary of State, March 12, 1916, *FR 1916*, p. 487, enclosing a proclamation to the Mexican nation by Carranza, which had appeared in *La Opinión* of Queretaro on March 12 and which read as follows:

"The First Chief of the Revolution issues an appeal to the people to be prepared for any emergency that may arise. I have not yet received any reply from the American Government and, from the reports sent in to the First Chief by the military commanders along the boundary line, I know that forces of the United States are being mobilized to cross into Mexican territory for the purpose, according to President Wilson's declarations published in the American press, to pursue and try to capture Villa and then deliver him up to the Mexican authorities, protesting that the expedition is nothing but punitive in its character and that the sovereignty of Mexico will be respected.

"The Constitutionalist Government has suitably instructed the Confidential Agent of Mexico at Washington immediately to make the pertinent representation, for it will not admit, under any circumstances and whatever may be the reasons advanced and the explanation offered by the Government of the United States about the act it proposes to carry out, that the territory of Mexico be invaded for an instant and the dignity of the Republic outraged.

"I am sure I am voicing the national sentiment and that the Mexican people will worthily perform their duty, no matter what sacrifices they may have to undergo in the defense of their rights and sovereignty.

"If we should unfortunately be plunged into a war which the Government of the United States can never justify, the responsibility for its disastrous consequences will not lie with us but with those who serve as tools for the purposes of treacherous Mexicans who have labored within and without the country to bring about this result but upon whom the inexorable justice of the people will fall.

"As this news might arouse the minds of our fellow-countrymen, I specially recommend that you exercise the utmost prudence and endeavor to maintain order while extending every guaranty to the North American citizens residing in your State.

"With affectionate greetings: V. Carranza"

2 That is, Gaston Schmutz.

From William Joel Stone

Dear Mr. President: [Washington] March 15 1916.

The death of Senator Shively accentuates the situation about which we conversed yesterday morning. If anything can be done, the sooner the better.   Sincerely,   Wm J Stone.

TLS (WP, DLC).

From Edward Mandell House

Dear Governor: New York. March 15, 1916.

A. G. Gardiner sends me today the article he wrote about you the day I left England.

It seems to me he has never done anything better. It is as stirring as an epic poem. Please return it so I may have it republished in the American papers.¹ I also want to suggest it as a campaign document later.   Affectionately yours,   E. M. House

P.S. I saw Mr. Gallauner the other day. I do not think you need worry with him, but let us keep in touch with him and his activities in your behalf.

TLS (WP, DLC).
¹ "Mr. Wilson's Policy and the Pact of Peace," London *Daily News and Leader*, Feb. 26, 1916, clipping (WP, DLC). This eloquent article, directed at Wilson's British critics, showered praise on Wilson and said that his difficulties in waging neutrality were second only to those of Prime Minister Asquith in waging war. Gardiner stressed Wilson's tenacity in opposing submarine warfare and his "dexterity" in contending with American hyphenates, Theodore Roosevelt, and merchants angry over the British blockade. "Through these tumultuous waters," Gardiner continued, "Mr. Wilson has steered with a dexterity all the more admirable because it has never been the dexterity of the mere opportunist. However he changes his course and trims his sails, his eye is always on the stars. His goal is clear before him, and it is always a lofty and disinterested goal. He disappoints everyone in turn. He subjects himself to criticism from every quarter. His handling of events seems weak to this man, wrong-minded to that. He is deafened with advice, tugged at on every side, appealed to, screamed at, traduced, misrepresented, misunderstood. And in the midst of it all he pursues his purpose with an unfaltering constancy that is indifferent to attack and careless of personal ambition."
Gardiner went on: "But behind all these fierce issues of the moment, one sees the true aim towards which this remarkable man is working. It is an aim that has nothing to do with personal ends. No man who ever appeared in public life was more free from the impedimenta of ambition—thought less about elections and more about ideals. 'I used to think,' said a distinguished student of American affairs in this country, 'that for the parallel to Wilson we should have to go back to Lincoln. To-day I think we shall have to go back to Washington.' I might quarrel with the implication. I do not think there is any peak that looks down on that on which Lincoln stands. But let that pass. It is enough for the purpose to express one's view that President Wilson belongs to the strain of Lincoln and Washington."
The emphasis of Gardiner's editorial, however, was upon Wilson's contributions to world peace and unity. He wrote:
"And this world in all its history has produced no greater strain of governing men—practical idealists, breathing the great wind of English liberty, striving with unselfish devotion to
Make this world a better world
For man's brief earthly dwelling.
Each in his turn has contributed his stone to the fabric of human freedom, but until now the range of their vision has been limited to their own land.
"It is President Wilson's part to give that vision a world-wide scope. When Canning invoked 'the new world to redress the balance of the old,' he was anticipating events by a century. The freedom of which the United States dreamed was the freedom of isolation, the freedom of a world geographically and politically divorced from the feudalism, monarchisms and racial rivalries of the ancient world. Behind the great protecting barrier of the Atlantic they would build the new State, where every man was free, where no King reigned, where government of the people for the people by the people should at last solve the troubled problems of human society.

"In that faith President Monroe uttered his great declaration of the immunity of America from European rapacity. The stranger from any and all lands would find a welcome, but America from Labrador to Cape Horn was to be for ever free from the ambitions of European kings, the assaults of hungry States and the fierce racial hates that had their roots in the blood-soaked soil of Europe. Slav and Teuton, Latin and Anglo-Saxon might come, but they must be merged into the peace of a common citizenship. The Highland reaper might still sing on the shores of Huron of those

> Old, unhappy, far-off things
> And battles long ago.

but she would sing then in a new setting where those old barbarisms could never intrude.

"But the war has shown that that ideal is no longer tenable. The barrier of the Atlantic is a barrier no more. The miraculous triumphs of science over matter have brought the distant near and made the whole world one in a measure undreamed of by the fathers of the American Republic. In the presence of these facts the Monroe Doctrine has become less than a scrap of paper. Let Germany win this war, let the British Fleet lose command of the seas, and South America, upon which Prussia has looked so long with a hungry eye, will be ravished from the Latin races that have peopled it. The Western Hemisphere will at last have been absorbed in the maelstrom of European antagonisms and all the hopes with which the founders of the American Republic set up the banner of democracy in the new world will have perished.

"It is this peril with which Mr. Wilson has grappled. He had foreseen it before the outbreak of the war and had set himself as his supreme task the establishment of American unity on a new, larger and enduring basis. It was not only the menace from Europe with which he had to deal. He had to remove the menace of the United States from the mind of the South American republics. They feared the great Republic of the North. What assurance had they that some day, on some wave of public passion, an adventurous President might not set out on a great imperialist crusade against the South American Republics? They had seen with foreboding the 'big stick' politics of Mr. Roosevelt, the absorption of the Philippines, the shady adventure that led to the annexation of Colombian territory. Did these things foreshadow the end of that great principle of liberty for others on which the United States was founded? Was Imperialism to be transplanted into the Western world?

"This fear President Wilson set himself to remove. It was this purpose that inspired his Mexican policy. At all costs he would avoid armed intervention there lest the great hope that he cherished of winning the trust of the South American States should be destroyed. The South Americans watched his patient forbearance with growing confidence. They felt the shadow of their great neighbour passing from their sky, and when Mr. Wilson approached them with his scheme of American federation that was to make the Monroe Doctrine, not merely a protection against Europe, but a protection against the United States, they welcomed it without any fear of what lay behind. That achievement is on the eve of accomplishment. The future will, I believe, find in it one of the greatest and most beneficent events in history. It makes the independence of every State on the whole American continent secure; it gives to the smallest State the guarantees of all the confederation for its liberty, it removed not only the menace of European or Asiatic aggression, but the possibility also of interference from any American Power. In a word it makes all America one on the widest basis of national liberty, common defence, and mutual guarantee.

"But this is not all. There is another phase of the enterprise that extends its operation to the Old World. This country, through the Dominion of Canada, is profoundly concerned in this great scheme for the consolidation of American peace. It is as much our interest to have Canada protected as it is the interest of the Argentine, or Brazil, or Chile, to have those countries protected. I do not think I shall be wrong in assuming that President Wilson has in his mind the idea that we too, through Canada, shall become partners in his scheme to realise that great vision of John Bright, uttered nearly sixty years ago:

> 'I have another and a far brighter vision before my eyes. It may be a vision but I will cherish it. I see one vast confederation, stretching from the frozen north to the glowing south, and from the wild billows of the Atlantic

westward to the calmer waters of the Pacific main; and I see one people and one language, and one law and one faith, and over all that wide continent the home of freedom and a refuge for the oppressed of every race and every clime.'

"Bright was thinking only of North America, but Mr. Wilson's action is bringing all the Americas within the scope of the ideal.

"Is it not possible that in the President's scheme we have the seed of that larger peace that shall encompass the world? With the Americas indissolubly united to preserve their common heritage, and linked up, through Canada, to a reconstructed British Empire, equally committed to the cause of liberty and peace, the victory over the old darkness would be in sight. Nor is this all. We have mingled our tears and our blood with France, Italy, and Russia in a union that can never be severed. They, too, will be drawn inevitably into the great Pact of Peace. And time and the experience of the tragedy through which humanity is passing will bring others who have followed the false gods of Imperialism and Militarism into the shambles of Europe within the orbit of a common deliverance.

"There is one word to be added. These are momentous days for the future of the world. It is in the great Republic of the West that we catch the glow of ideals that can alone rescue humanity from the charnel house of the past. It is the new world that must help the old to find a way out of the wilderness in which it has wandered to this final ruin and misery. Is this not then a time when England should have at Washington the greatest personal force at our disposal? Lord Bryce is old in years, but young in spirit with the undying youth of those ideals that have been the soul of American liberty. He commands, as no one else commands, the admiration, affection, and confidence of the American people and their President. Let him return to Washington, and do the supreme service that his long career and high aims have prepared him to perform not only for his country but for humanity."

For Wilson's reaction to this article, see the entry from the House diary printed at March 29, 1916.

To William Charles Adamson

My dear Judge: [The White House] March 16, 1916

Thank you for your letter accompanying a copy of the bill with regard to the water power in navigable streams. You may certainly count upon me to render any assistance I can render in passing a bill drawn along the principles agreed upon last year.

In suggesting a legislative programme, it was not my thought or purpose in any way to stand in the way of other legislation; I was merely setting forth the major items which I thought ought to constitute a party programme. My interest in the matters you refer to is not abated in the least.

Cordially and sincerely yours,   Woodrow Wilson

TLS (Letterpress Books, WP, DLC).

From Newton Diehl Baker, with Enclosure

PERSONAL AND CONFIDENTIAL.

My dear Mr. President: Washington. March 16, 1916.

Since I sent you the despatch[1] this morning, I re-studied it with General Scott and General Bliss, submitting to them the question as to whether the text of the despatch might, by any possibility, be regarded as tying the hands of our commanders in Mexico in the necessities of emergency situations which might arise.

I inclose you a new copy of the despatch[2] with a memorandum adding a suggestion made by them,[3] which, however, does not go beyond your statement on that subject to me last night, as I have it in my mind.

Respectfully yours,   Newton D. Baker

TLS (WP, DLC).

[1] A memorandum for the Chief of Staff (CC MS dated March 16, 1916, WP, DLC), which Wilson and Baker had prepared at the White House during the evening of March 15.

[2] Baker underlined the only change made in the memorandum.

[3] He referred to the phrase that had been inserted.

E N C L O S U R E

Memorandum for the Chief of Staff: March 16, 1916.

Telegraph in code the following despatch to General Funston, marked urgent, and with a request for acknowledgment of receipt by General Funston and General Pershing, and use every means to expedite its tran[s]mission and delivery:

In view of the great distance between the seat of Government and the forces in the field, the President regards it as of the utmost importance that General Funston and all officers in command of troops of the United States clearly understand the exact nature of the expedition of our forces into Mexico, and he therefore directs obedience in letter and in spirit to the following orders:

ONE. If any organized body of troops of the de facto Government of the Republic of Mexico are met, they are to be treated with courtesy and their cooperation welcomed, if they desire to cooperate in the objects of the expedition.

TWO. Upon no account or pretext, and neither by act, word or attitude of any American commander, shall this expedition become or be given the appearance of being hostile to the integrity or dignity of the Republic of Mexico, by the courtesy of which this expedition is permitted to pursue an aggressor upon the peace of these neighboring Republics.

THREE. Should the attitude of any organized body of troops of the de facto Government of Mexico appear menacing, commanders of the forces of the United States are, of course, authorized to place themselves and their commands in proper situation of defense, *and if actually attacked they will of course defend themselves by all means at their command*, but in no event must they attack or become the aggressor with any such body of troops.

FOUR. Care is to be taken to have in a state of readiness at all times the means of rapid communication from the front to the headquarters of the General commanding the Department, and, through him, to the War Department in Washington; and any evidences of misunderstanding on the part of officials, military or civil, of the de facto Government of Mexico as to the objects, purposes, character or acts of the expedition of the United States, are to be reported to the Department with the utmost expedition, with a view to having them taken up directly with the Government of Mexico through the Department of State.

Paragraph. The definite form of these orders is adopted for explicitness, and is not to be construed as implying any doubt on the part of the President in the discretion of the officers to whom they are directed.   Newton D. Baker

T MS (WP, DLC).

From Thomas James Walsh

My dear Mr. President: [Washington] March 16, 1916.

Replying to your note of March 15th, I have the honor to submit the following:

The Senate Committee reported a substitute for the Ferris bill, as shown by the copy which I am sending you herewith.[1] I shall not trouble you with details. My endeavor will be to call your attention to the essential differences.

(1) The bill as it came from the House provided, in Section 5, that at the expiration of the period of the lease, fifty years, the properties of the lessee, dependent in whole or in part for their usefulness on the continuance of the lease, might be taken over by the Government or some subdivision upon the payment of the *actual cost* of rights of way, water rights and lands, and the reasonable value of all other property. The substitute bill in Section 5 provides that the property may be taken over upon the payment of the *fair value*. There is here presented the direct question of recapture on the basis of *cost* or on the basis of *value of the property fifty years hence*. This question was the subject of earnest debate at the Public Utilities conference lately held in the city

1 H.R. 408, 64th Cong., 1st sess. (WP, DLC).

of Philadelphia.[2] If you feel in need of any further enlightenment upon the subject you will find the papers and debates reported in the last number of the Utilities Magazine. Let me say:

(a) It is useless to provide in any bill that the public may take over the property at the end of fifty years upon paying the "fair value." They have that right already and may exercise it by proceedings in eminent domain.

(b) Rates will be fixed during the fifty-year period on the basis of the actual investment—that is to say, the actual cost. If the lease should be continued after the expiration of the fifty-year period, they will be continued to be fixed on the basis of actual cost. If, however, the Government takes over the property at the end of that time at the "fair value," which value is greater than the actual cost (and in multitudes of instances it will be many times the cost) the rates must be fixed on the basis of the new investment. It will, accordingly, be more profitable to the public not to take the property over. While, therefore, the lease is nominally for fifty years, the re-capture is so restricted as that it is practically perpetual.

In the debate on the Shields bill, Senator Jones,[3] one of its principal supporters, admitted that the permit would be practically perpetual because of the onerous conditions attending re-capture. He added that if he had his way the permit would be granted in perpetuity.

(2) Section 8 of the bill as it came from the House provides that for the use and occupancy of the lands charges or rentals are to be collected, to be measured on the basis of power developed and sold. The substituted bill expresses this idea in somewhat different language, but on Tuesday the Chairman, by the direction of the Committee, reported a number of amendments, one of which provides that the charges "shall be based on the value of the land, to be determined by the amount of horse-power to be developed, and which charge or rental shall not exceed the sum of twenty-five cents per developed horse-power per year for the actual power." The Shields bill contemplated that public lands might be flooded or might even be desired as the site of a dam to be constructed across a navigable stream. It provides that in such case permit to occupy the lands may be granted by the Secretary of War. I tried vainly to prevent this encroach-

[2] A conference on valuation, held November 10-13, 1915. It met under the auspices of the Utilities Bureau, an influential agency devoted to the study of utility problems from the public point of view and to the dissemination of information on standards and policies among American cities. For the proceedings of the conference, see *Utilities Magazine*, I (January 1916).

[3] Wesley Livsey Jones, Republican of Washington.

ment upon the legitimate province of the Department of the Interior. However, the bill provided that for the use of such land the Secretary of War was to fix a charge based on the value of the land taken *as land*. The idea prompting this provision is that under proceedings like those in eminent domain, the present cash value of a power site should be ascertained, and that the Government should receive as compensation for the use of that land a return equivalent to a fair rate of interest upon the value so found. The amendment last above quoted is the result of an attempt to combine that idea with the one represented by the bill as it was originally drawn. The further provision limiting the annual charge to twenty-five cents per horse-power is self-explanatory. It embodies the view that there are some horse-power sites for the use of which a charge of more than twenty-five cents per horse-power would be justified. The excess value will, of course, be a gift to the lessee. I could name for you, however, a dozen sites in Montana, each capable of the production of upwards of 100,000 horse-power, with respect to which investors would gladly offer more than twenty-five cents per horse-power.

It is insisted that whatever amount is paid into the federal treasury will be taken out of the consumers in the territory in which the power is used and must be added by public service commissions and other regulatory bodies to the price that will be charged. This is true to the extent that, generally speaking, the amount paid must come out of the communities in which the power is used, but under the bill the amount thus realized very properly goes into the reclamation fund for use in the very region from which it comes. It is not true, by any means, that all the power developed will be subject to charges by utilities commissions. A company may acquire a site to develop power with which to operate nitrate works and itself use all the power it develops. We cannot control the price at which it sells its product. The Great Northern Railway Company may acquire a power site on the Kootenai River in my state and use all the power developed for the operation of its railroad trains. The regulatory machinery provided by the Federal Government is not so exact and perfect in its operation as to warrant the belief that the reduced cost of power will be reflected in lower freight rates, at least while the favored railroad remains in competition with lines operated by steam power. Moreover, the local public utilities commissions do not act with clock-work precision in fixing rates. It is an intricate problem. Many municipalities prefer to own their own public utilities rather than to be served by private corporations subject to regulation. Who knows but that fifty years hence it may be

The President with the White House Press Corps

President and Mrs. Wilson in St. Louis on the Preparedness Tour

James Hay

Claude Kitchin

Lindley M. Garrison

Newton D. Baker

General Pershing in Mexico

Villa on the Move

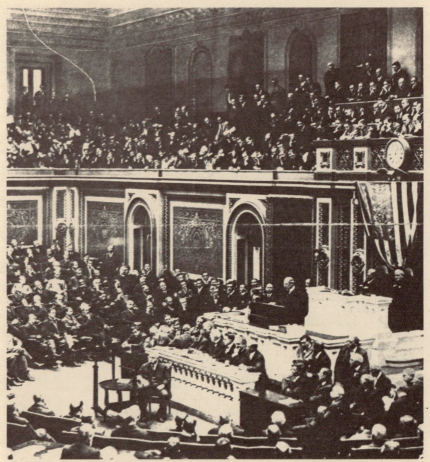

The President Addressing Congress on the Sussex Crisis

the very general view that municipal ownership is the solution of this perplexing problem?

(3) Section 2 of the bill prohibited the lessee from contracting for the delivery to any one consumer of more than fifty per cent. of the energy developed without the consent of the Secretary of War. This is cut out in the substituted bill. (See Section 2 thereof.) I personally make no complaint about this, but thought your attention ought to be called to it.

(4) Section 4 prohibits the sale of energy to a distributing company without the consent of the Secretary of War. This was taken out. (See Section 4 of the substituted bill.) Of this I make no criticism either, though you may deem the provision important.

(5) Section 6 gave to the Government the right to lease its lands at the expiration of the original lease to another lessee. This provision is taken out in the substituted bill, and by one of the later amendments reading "and thereafter until the property is taken over and paid for or a new lease is executed, as provided in Section 6," the lessee remains in possession, notwithstanding the expiration of the fifty-year period, until the dependent property is purchased at its "fair value." This, as explained above, makes the lease practically perpetual.

(6) By Section 7, contracts for the sale of energy extending beyond the life of the lease, but not for more than twenty-five years thereafter, could be entered into with the approval of the Secretary, such contracts to be assumed by the successor of the lessee. The twenty-five year limitation is taken out by one of the new amendments, and the contracts made binding, when approved by a public service commission or similar authority. I think this change is a wise one. You can appreciate that contracts to supply power for pumping water for irrigation ought to be perpetual. One could scarcely venture to improve a farm to the use of which irrigation is essential upon an agreement under which he was to have water only for a limited period.

(7) Section 9 gave to the Secretary authority to regulate rates and service in states having no public service commission. This was cut out. No public land state is in that condition except Utah.

You will understand from the foregoing that the fundamental differences relate almost exclusively to the provisions of Sections 5 and 8 which prescribe, the latter, the charge or basis upon which the charge is to be made for the occupancy of the land, and the former, the terms and conditions upon which the property of the lessee may be taken over at the expiration of the period of the lease. The opposition of Senators Shafroth and

Thomas, however, being of course the most formidable there is, goes far beyond these questions. Their opposition is to any plan of disposition to which the term "lease" may be applied. Though they do not say so directly (perhaps Senator Shafroth does) they want these power sites alienated in fee, granted in perpetuity upon a valuation to be determined at the time the application for the lease is made. They really want these lands turned over to the States with permission to do with them as the States respectively may direct. Senator Shafroth wants to have all the public lands pass from the general government into private hands, regardless of what the Government realizes, in order that the State may subject them to taxation. While governor of Colorado he was doubtless embarrassed in finding revenue with which to meet the necessary expenses of the State. We are all in the same situation. He found a great area in his State not subject to taxation and it occurs to him as a ready solution of that difficulty to pass the title of the public lands into private ownership, every consideration of public policy being made subordinate to the one object—the acquisition of state revenue. We must encounter the continued hostility of the two Senators named, even though the objectionable amendments should be adopted by the Senate.

It is but just to say that all the amendments proposed by the Committee come from enemies of the measure. The committee was dominated by Senators Thomas, Smoot and Clark.[4] None of them will vote for the bill even if their own amendments are adopted. I entertain no doubt that any amendment really objectionable to you could easily be defeated if, in some way, your views could be communicated to the Democratic members. Few of them have given any thought whatever to the subject. They know you have. Most of them would readily, in the clash of views, be glad to be guided by your excellent and informed judgment. Just what is the best method of communicating to them your views you can determine, I am sure, better than I can. It is scarcely fair to ask you to confer with some of the leading Senators on our side about this matter at this time, but if you should care to call in such representative members as Senator Kern, Senator Martin or Senator Swanson, Senator Stone and Senator James, I shall be glad to go with them at any time if you are of the opinion that my presence would be to any extent whatever helpful.

I shall not feel at liberty to make use of your communication of yesterday in any way without your sanction.

[4] That is, Charles Spalding Thomas, Democrat of Colorado; Clarence Don Clark, Republican of Wyoming; and Reed Smoot, Republican of Utah.

It might be advisable to secure from Secretary Baker an expression of opinion to the House Committee on the Shields bill. If the Secretary should concur in the general ideas that find expression in the Ferris bill rather than those exemplified by the Shields bill the embarrassments of the situation will be much relieved.

Very sincerely yours,   T. J. Walsh

P.S. A reprint of the bill as reported by the Committee, with all amendments, is just laid before me. I enclose it rather than the bill as reported and the subsequent amendments severally, as stated above.

TLS (WP, DLC).

From Stockton Axson

My dear Brother Woodrow: Houston, Texas March 16, 1916

I deeply appreciate your taking the time from your busy life to write this long letter. Lovett ought not to have troubled you—*we* ought not, for while it was his doing I passively consented.

As you *have* gone to so much trouble, may I impose on your time for another five minutes to tell you the present situation?

There is nothing now for anybody to do, except the Wesleyan people. I myself have "put it up" to them, and am awaiting their reply—which may be angry.

I wavered temporarily in the idea of asking for my release on general pleas of health—for I have feared the isolation of life in New England, feared the experiment of another transplanting, with that wretched melancholy always lurking in the bush. But when I sat right down to think it out, it seemed a clear case of going on—I should have thought of the dangers before accepting. And so I had reached my decision to go as I had promised.

Then an entirely new element entered into the case. A friend, entirely outside the Institute circle, one day told me of a rather rash remark which one of the trustees had made to him, that the Institute "could afford" to make it financially worth my while to stay. As luck would have it, this conversation came just when I was in despair about Ed and Margaret Elliott—the gloomiest letters from Ed, Margaret in relapse, the law practice experiment a failure, debts and darkness (about which Margaret knows nothing). I had lent all I have, not much, was going to be on a smaller salary next year &c. I went frankly to Lovett with the whole trouble. He was surprised that I had not understood that the Institute was ready to pay me more to keep me. That had not occurred to me. He got the consent of his trustees to offer me

$6,000 (for 5½ months work), a house if I want it, and a pension if I am disabled. I ought to be able to make $2,000 or $3,000 in my "off"-months—if not clear of expenses.

I wrote to President Shanklin and Professor Winchester, asking if they could release me—on this one ground only—the financial advantage and my need of the money. It is just about time to be hearing from them now.

Thank you again for your goodness in the matter, but I am glad you are not to be put to further trouble.

In Texas one hears practically only one opinion about foreign complications, that you have done the best possible thing in circumstances of terrible difficulty. The people seem to be for preparation and the hope that we shall not have to use our increased forces.

With best love for you both, for you all,

Always affectionately yours   Stockton Axson

ALS (WP, DLC).

To Thomas Staples Martin

My dear Senator: [The White House] March 17, 1916

I have been very much disappointed at the action of the subcommittee of the Appropriations Committee of the House in refusing to act favorably upon recommendations which I urgently made to them concerning certain small increases in the provision for our force in the Executive Offices. Recent circumstances have made it really absolutely necessary that we should have two additional messengers, and there are at least two promotions in salary which I do not think can in justice be withheld. I will be very glad to explain the whole matter to you personally if you so desire. We are asking for

One promotion from $1800 to $2500	An increase of $700;
One promotion from $1600 to $2500	An increase of $900;
One messenger at $900	An increase of $900;
One messenger at $840	An increase of $840;
	Making a total increase of $3340.

I hope very earnestly that it will be possible for the Senate to enable me to make these increases, for I deem them essential to the efficiency of the force and the success of the work in the Executive Offices. Either Mr. Tumulty, Mr. Forster, or I will be entirely at your service to explain the matter if you so desire.[1]

Cordially and sincerely yours,   Woodrow Wilson

TLS (Letterpress Books, WP, DLC).

[1] The increases and additions requested by Wilson were included in the ap-

propriations bill passed on May 10, 1916. Compare 38 *Statutes at Large* 1007 and 39 *Statutes at Large* 76.

To John T. Brabner Smith[1]

My dear Mr. Smith: [The White House] March 17, 1916

I have your letter of March fifteenth.[2] I wish sincerely that I could comply with the request it contains but it is literally true that I have not the time to elaborate a letter which would add anything to the mere sentiment (a very earnest sentiment) which I express in the letter you quote from me on the front page of the "Veteran Preacher."[3] The sentiment I there express is very earnestly entertained and I am heartily in sympathy with the work the various denominations are doing to secure endowment funds for the pensioning of aged or infirm ministers of the Gospel. I wish I could write a disquisition on the subject, but it is impossible and you are much better qualified to write it than I am. I can only say Amen.

Cordially and sincerely yours,   Woodrow Wilson

TLS (Letterpress Books, WP, DLC).

[1] Retired Methodist minister of Chicago, editor of *Veteran Preacher*, a periodical published by the Board of Conference Claimants of the Methodist Episcopal Church.

[2] J. T. B. Smith to WW, March 15, 1916, TLS (WP, DLC), requesting that Wilson write a letter on "the pensioning of preachers" to be printed in a special interdenominational issue of *Veteran Preacher* to be published in March 1916.

[3] Smith had enclosed a cover page of the special issue which featured a picture of Wilson and a partial text of WW to J. T. B. Smith, Nov. 18, 1915, TLS (Letterpress Books, WP, DLC). The quoted portion reads as follows: "I take pleasure in expressing my very deep interest in the effort which you represent to obtain an endowment which will supply the means of pensioning aged preachers. This is a matter in which I have long had a great interest, for I have seen so many cases which demonstrated the necessity of such action."

From Frank Lyon Polk, with Enclosure

My dear Mr. President: [Washington] March 17, 1916.

I enclose a rough draft of a notice to be given to the press[1] agencies along the lines suggested in the attached memorandum you sent me.[2] I think something of this kind should be done, or at least you should personally caution the Washington correspondents, as I understand the Mexican Agency here is disturbed over the character of the newspaper stories that are being carried in some of the daily papers.

I have spoken twice to the newspaper men here of the very real danger of carrying rumors of unrest in Mexico. I told them that such stories might indirectly be the cause of the death

of some of our citizens and I felt that they were under obligation to assist. I think most of them saw the point and will try to
help.   Yours faithfully,   Frank L. Polk

TLS (Lansing Letterpress Book, SDR, RG 59, DNA).
    ¹ It is a slightly revised version of the Enclosure. There is a carbon copy
of Polk's draft in the F. L. Polk Papers, CtY. The final version, again slightly
revised, is printed as an Enclosure with F. L. Polk to WW, March 21, 1916.
    ² The Enclosure.

E   N   C   L   O   S   U   R   E

To the Associated Press,
    United Press,
    Int. News Service,
    Central News Service.
    It has been already announced by the President that the pro-
posed expedition of American forces into Mexico is in no sense
an invasion of that Republic nor an infringement of its Sovereignty. It is hoped that the news services will be good enough to
assist the administration in presenting this view of the expedition
to the American people and particularly to the distressed and
sensitive people of our neighboring Republic who are susceptible
to impressions spread by the American press and are prepared to
believe that they represent the views and objects of this Government. Indeed such conclusions are not unnatural when the main,
if not the only, source of their information is the public press of
the United States. To avoid such erroneous impression I call upon
you to use your earnest endeavors not to interpret news stories
regarding the expedition as in any sense meaning war, to withhold stories of troop movements and preparations that might be
given that interpretation, and to refrain from publishing rumors
of unrest in Mexico. On the other hand it is most desirable to impress upon both Americans and Mexicans that the expedition is
simply a punitive measure aimed solely at the elimination of the
bandits who raided Columbus and who infest an unprotected district along the border and use it as a base of operations against
American lives and property in the United States. The whole idea
of the expedition is to cooperate with the forces of General Carranza in removing a cause of irritation to both Governments and
to retire from Mexico so soon as this object is accomplished.

T MS (WP, DLC).

From Frank Lyon Polk

My dear Mr. President: Washington March 17, 1916.

The Argentine Ambassador called here on Wednesday, the 15th, and I took up with him the subject of the treaties with the Central and South American Republics along the line you indicated in our talk on Tuesday.

He quite agreed with you that it would be well to go ahead without Chile and added, for your confidential information, that Chile was objecting to the provisions in regard to the guaranteeing territorial integrity because of its hope to gain territory by force of arms. He suggested that as a possible compromise, the provision in regard to the guaranteeing territorial integrity could be drawn to provide for arbitration in case of disputes arising in the future, and that a clause should be added providing that in cases of existing disputes, these should be settled within a limited period through diplomatic channels. After these disputes were settled, then the treaty should apply to the disputed territory.

He has asked for an interview with you and will probably discuss this matter at that interview.[1] In the meantime it would be worth while considering whether the compromise he suggests has any merit. If, in your opinion, it has no merit, negotiations could be begun for concluding the treaties of the countries that have accepted the original terms.

Yours faithfully,   Frank L Polk

TLS (WP, DLC).
[1] Ambassador Naón saw Wilson at the White House on March 22.

From Joseph Patrick Tumulty

Dear Governor: The White House March 17, 1916.

The Postmaster General has shown me your draft of the platform for use in St. Louis.[1] It is not sufficiently complimentary. Although I dislike to "point with pride or view with alarm," I believe that the Republican policy of iteration and reiteration has some force especially in these days. We should, therefore, I believe, in a spirit of modesty and frankness, point to the following:

First: To the conditions which prevailed when we took over the control of national affairs.

Second: Mention the evidences on all sides of special privileges, namely, in the tariff, in the restriction of credit, and in foreign affairs (dollar diplomacy). Call attention to the broken promises and failures of the Republican party. Although in control of the two branches of Congress, and with a Republican Executive, its failure to keep platform pledges, its impotency as an instrument of progressive government—so impotent and blind to the progressive movements and impulses that a split was made inevitable between the reactionary and progressive groups in the Republican party. All the time special privilege was growing. Even the vital questions of preparedness and defense were woefully neglected.

Under the Democratic party there has come about a new readjustment and dispensation, whose beneficent influences have resulted in the release of the energies of a free people.

Realizing that the period of exclusion and of special favors had passed, the field was made ready for a new growth and cultivation. Into the soil were planted new seeds, whose fructification and benefits our people are beginning to realize. Legislation has been passed whose object has been legitimately to stimulate business—under a Democratic leadership which has neither hesitated nor halted, and in face of obstacles which seemed insurmountable. The legislative axe was applied first to the root of the tree of special privilege, so that the excrescences which have prevented its free and natural growth were destroyed, and business given a new outlet and a new point of view. The operation which was performed was necessary in order that the economic life of the country might be saved.

It was everywhere admitted that this country—which will be called upon to play a great part in the world of business—was living under an archaic system of currency, which in no way responded to the needs and exigencies of legitimate business. The old system concentrated credit in the hands of a few and became a prolific breeder of panics, which were in no way the natural result of business conditions.

This ancient system of selfish control of the credit of our country was destroyed, and in its place there was substituted a system under government control which resulted in the establishment of a democracy of credit which makes the credit of the country accessible to the ordinary man of business. What the Republican party for years had attempted and failed of accomplishment was begun under Democratic initiative and control, and thus, for the first time, supplying American business with one of its urgent needs—a system which has stood the stress and strain of a great European war and which has resulted in the establishment of a prosperity unparalleled in the economic history of this country or any other country.   T.

TLI (WP, DLC).
[1] The Editors have been unable to find this document.

From the Diary of Colonel House

March 17, 1916.

The Attorney General came at six to remain to dinner and go to the theater. I was not well enough to do the latter and Gordon took my place. Gregory telephoned during the day that he had a matter of great importance to tell me—something which could not be told over the telephone. It was this:

He said Tumulty had told Burleson that a despatch had come from El Paso stating that one of Carranza's Colonels had declared he would immediately attack our troops if they crossed the border. In reply to this the President told Tumulty and the Secretary of War that if this were the case he would not send our troops across the border, because it would mean intervention and war with Mexico. Tumulty argued with the President desperately, saying if he did not send our troops after Villa, or if he hesitated a moment to act, he might just as well not contemplate running for the Presidency, since he would not get a single electoral vote. That even such pacifists as Bryan were in favor of the move. It is to be remembered that the President has already issued orders to "catch Villa dead or alive."

Tumulty was unable to convince him or change his determination, so he went post-haste to Burleson. They agreed to call in Houston, and the three of them outlined a letter, which Tumulty signed, telling the President what a mistake he was making. Tumulty sent this letter[1] to the theater where the President happened to be. After it was sent, and before Tumulty saw the President again, it was found that the despatch from El Paso was a fake[2] so the matter ended there.

I am curious to know the truth of the story, for I have some doubts. I cannot believe the President would lack the wisdom and courage, for [to] take drastic action in such circumstances. It is inconceivable that he should not better understand the temper of the American people. It would not only destroy him in the United States, but it would destroy his influence in Europe as well. The world loves boldness and courage and is willing to endorse many actions that are unwise and inexpedient if only they are courageous.

Gregory, Burleson, Houston, Tumulty and others around the President think he lacks courage at critical moments. I am not willing to accept this. His determination not to allow Germany to force him into intervention in Mexico could account for his action. I shall ask him about the matter when I go to Washington.

[1] That is, JPT to WW, March 15, 1916.
[2] The dispatch was not a "fake." However, the threatened crisis proved some-

thing of a fake in that General Pershing soon bought off his putative opponent
by hiring him as a guide for the expedition. See Vandiver, *Black Jack: The Life
and Times of John J. Pershing*, II, 610. Pershing's first contingent of 4,000 men
crossed the border at noon, local time, on March 15.

From Michael Liebel, Jr.[1]

Dear sir: Washington, D. C. March 18, 1916.

I am enclosing, for your perusal, a clipping from the Erie Daily
Times, a Republican newspaper published in Erie, Pa., my
home.[2] This brief item is only one of many published in the congressional district which I have the honor to represent and all of
them take as the basis for their articles the one paramount fact
that, although I was elected on a platform pledged to support you
and your administration I have been ignored in every appointment made in my district, and that every federal appointment
made since my election was given to my political enemies and
to men who openly attacked you and your policies while I have
consistently supported them.

This letter is written because I am convinced that the time
has arrived when I should lay the facts before you so that you
may know the truth concerning conditions in my congressional
district. In my campaign for election I made only one pledge;
that was to give you and your administration loyal support. That
pledge I have kept up to this very moment. Only last Tuesday,
on the McLemore resolution, I supported you and in doing so I
know that I ignored the wishes of the great majority of my constituents. I come from a heavy German district and I am a German myself. Erie, my home city, which I carried by more than
2,000 in the election, is strongly German and I was urged by
many of my constituents to vote against you on the McLemore
resolution. Not one single citizen wrote or asked me to support
you. Yet I did support you because in doing so I kept a pledge. At
the same time I realize that politically it was the worst thing that
I could have done.

I mention this merely to pave the way toward linking up certain circumstances into a homogeneous whole so that you may
better understand the situation and the conditions which have
arisen and which make it seemingly impossible for a Democrat to
be returned to Congress from this particular district. In passing,
I may add in this connection, that I am convinced that it would
be folly for a Democrat to make any real attempt to run and for
this reason I have virtually decided not to be a candidate for re-
election.[3]

From the day that I was elected to the present time I have been completely ignored by the administration. Every appointment made in the district has been made against me and against the Democratic organization which supported you. I am constrained to believe, and I have the proof, that these appointments were made on the advice and at the suggestion of my political enemies, men in whom you had confidence and who took advantage of this fact to lie to you and to misrepresent conditions and to malign me. That these men succeeded is best attested by the fact that they dictated every appointment made and in every case they named men who openly opposed you and in some instances men who are not even Democrats. Every appointment made was with the evident object of breaking up the regular Democratic organization in my congressional district and in discrediting me. To some extent they have succeeded; at any rate they have made it practically impossible to elect a Democrat to congress.

I believe that you wish to know the truth. Take for instance the postmasters named in the enclosed clipping. None of them was the choice of the regular Democratic organization and it was for this reason that I opposed their appointment and their confirmation. All of them without exception opposed you and some of them were bitter in their opposition. Yet they were rewarded through the efforts of one or two men in whom you had confidence and who are my political enemies.

A. D. Colegrove, postmaster at Corry, is the owner and editor of the Corry Journal, a Prohibition newspaper. In my campaign for Congress he openly supported Frank D. Lockwood, the Prohibition-Progressive Republican candidate, who night after night in speeches made the most bitter attacks upon you. He even outdid Mr. Roosevelt in bitterness and Mr. Colegrove editorially applauded him.

D. D. Goshorn,[4] postmaster at Cambridge Springs, was an open and avowed Lockwood supporter. He is at heart a Republican and is not a resident of Cambridge Springs. Further he has not spent more than three or four days in the post office since he was named.

The same applies to Thomas McCobb, postmaster at Cochranton, Preston L. Peters, postmaster at Saegertown and James A. Platt, an aged and infirm man, postmaster at Spartansburg.

All of these men openly opposed you and opposed me. No one thought for a moment that they would be appointed to any office because their opposition was so open. The Democratic organizations in Erie and Crawford counties, which form the twenty-fifth congressional district, were opposed to them.

338 MARCH 19, 1916

Two appointments are now pending in the Senate, those of A. J. Palm,[5] postmaster at Meadville, and A. S. Knepp, postmaster at North East.

Mr. Palm is editor of the Meadville Messenger, a Prohibition newspaper which, during my campaign, was very bitter against me and which urged, day after day, the election of Mr. Lockwood. Mr. Palm is now under charges. He is a feeble man nearly 70 years of age and is wholly unfit for the office.

Mr. Knepp is also under charges. He also opposed my election and even spent his own money in having circulars printed and distributed during the campaign in opposition to me and in favor of Mr. Lockwood, my opponent who spared no words in condemning you.

Up to this minute I have not been asked in a single instance by the Post Office Department or by any other component part of your administration, to recommend anybody for any appointive office. I have been consistently and persistently ignored and virtually insulted. The Democratic organizations in the district have been ignored. I have been misrepresented and maligned. Up to this minute I have given the lie to these misrepresentations. My record in congress will show that I have supported you in every instance although I have reason to believe that you were told that I would not do so. In my campaign I gave my word to the vote[r]s of my district that I would support you. I was elected upon that single pledge and I have kept it.

Believing that you wish to know the truth I am writing you. I have given you the facts and if you wish more details I shall be pleased to give them to you.

Very truly yours,   M. Liebel Jr.

TLS (WP, DLC).

[1] Democratic congressman from Erie, Pa., 1915-17.

[2] "Postmasters Were Confirmed by the Senate," *Erie*, Pa., *Times*, March 10, 1916, (WP, DLC), reporting on postmasters nominated by Wilson on the recommendation of A. Mitchell Palmer and confirmed by the Senate despite Liebel's opposition.

[3] He did not run for re-election in 1916.

[4] Denny D. Goshorn.

[5] Andrew J. Palm.

James Linn Rodgers to the Secretary of State

Queretaro, Mexico, March 19, 1916
Rec'd 20th, 10:15 a.m.

Ten to-night sub-Secretary of State for Foreign Affairs called and presented reply to Department's March 18, 6 p.m. use of railways Chihuahua transportation supplies troops[1] requested transmission the text of the note as follows:

"Queretaro, March 19, 1916.

"Having reported to the citizen First Chief of the Constitutionalist Army in charge of the Executive power of the Union with your note of to-day's date in which you quote the text of a message received by you yesterday from the Department of State of the United States, by order of the said High Functionary, I beg you to transmit to the said Department what follows by way of reply:

"The note referred to has caused great surprise to the Mexican Government for it had not until now received any official notice from the Government of the United States that American troops had crossed into Mexican territory or that they were at or near Casas Grandes, this Government's surprise being made the greater from the fact that negotiations through the proper channels and occasioned by the Columbus incident are under way at this very moment to perfect agreements as to the terms and conditions of the convention that is to govern the passage of troops from one to the other country in the sense of the spirit of the note dated the tenth of this month addressed by the Government over which the citizen First Chief presides to the Government of the United States of America. The Mexican Government cannot but wonder at the fact that the said troops should have crossed the boundary line and entered our territory without previous agreement, official communication, or notice of any kind and reached, as stated in the note referred to a place which, as is Casas Grandes, is much more distant from the boundary line than any other point which under previous treaties have been the extreme limit in cases of pursuits. To the end of maintaining unalterable the good relations that have always existed between the United States and Mexico, the Citizen First Chief of the Constitutionalist Army in charge of the Executive Power of the Union deems it necessary in order to act with full knowledge of the facts of the case in a matter of such great moment that the Department (of State) of the United States of the North be pleased to furnish the Government over which he presides with information as to the circumstances under which the passage of American troops into Mexican territory was affected at El Paso, their number, the branch of the service to which they belong, the name of the officer in command, the place where they are, and the causes which occasioned their crossing.

"Hoping that you will be pleased to transmit the foregoing to the Department of State of the United States and impress it with the necessity of its prompt answer to the points set forth in the note quoted permit me to avail myself of this opportunity to renew to you the assurances of my most courteous and respect[ful] consideration.

"(Signed).   Aguilar,[2] Secretary of Relations."

CONFIDENTIAL.

This unquestionably represents attitude General Carranza himself. As the Foreign Office raised no such question when representation presented and explained this morning, it was stated tonight there is absolutely no official information in War Office here as to presence of American troops Mexico. Unofficial report received stating American troops are in Mexico but whereabouts and destination unknown. Believe representation presented to-day afforded desired opportunity for general query as above.   Rodgers.

T telegram (SDR, RG 59, 812.00/17529, DNA).
  [1] F. L. Polk to J. L. Rodgers, March 18, 1916, T telegram (SDR, RG 59, 812.00/17528a, DNA).
  [2] Cándido Aguilar, new Minister of Foreign Relations.

To Edward Mandell House, with Enclosure

Dear Friend,   The White House. 20 March, 1916.

I would be very much obliged to you if you would give me your early comment and advice on the enclosed despatch from Gerard. What significance do you attach to it, and what reply do you thing [think] we should make to the suggestion about a special ambassador?

There has been nothing to report upon since you were here. All that we knew ourselves (and more than anybody knows, of course) has been in the public despatches, and it was at every turn evident what it was necessary that we should do. But my thoughts have constantly turned towards you; I have felt your kindness in sending me clippings and letters and items of information; and it rejoices me that Mrs. House and you are coming down soon.

All join me in affectionate messages.

Your devoted friend,   Woodrow Wilson

WWTLS (E. M. House Papers, CtY).

Berlin, (via Copenhagen) March 18 1916.

3640. Confidential. Chancellor sent for me yesterday and so had talk of over an hour with him. Could not see that he had anything in particular in view. He asked me how I thought America would take resignation of Tirpitz. I said I thought as guarantee of good relations. He said that Hol[t]zendorf[f] had given very strict orders to submarine commanders. He spoke of sending of special ambassador to America to promote better understanding and asked how the idea was received. He spoke of peace and said he had offered peace in Reichstag but could not give any proposed terms publicly. He said that President Wilson could have played great role as mediator, but that there was a prejudice here against him and America, caused by fact notes to Germany were too rough and exportation of arms and that nothing had been done against England. I said I was sure President was ready to mediate any time he thought his services would be welcomed. On peace terms he said that Germany must have all colonies back and an indemnity to give up northern France. About Belgium he seemed vague, but I think would consent to give most of it up—leaving garrisons for awhile. He said that it was impossible to have a man like Tirpitz in the Government who appealed from the decision of the Government to mob. He said that German losses at Verdun were forty thousand, French losses hundred thousand to date, but what was use of this killing. He said that French killed were nine hundred thousand, German very much less in war to date. He said that he hoped America would do something against England blockade and make better feeling here. I think Chancellor is for good relations with America and a reasonable submarine war but he will have great political trouble here. Am sending in another cable the resolutions regarding submarine war which will come up in Reichstag.[1] I told him that probably public opinion in America did not take much interest in blockade question in comparison with LUSITANIA. He said that sinking of LUSITANIA was a great mistake.

Suggest you cable me about suggestion regarding special ambassador who would see people, etc., as Colonel House did and that you cable me that President is ready to do anything to help peace and that he will be glad to forward confidentially to allies any peace suggestions and to mediate as soon as he thinks his efforts will be welcome. Chancellor also said he hoped that I would not leave Germany so I shall not avail myself of your kind offer of leave.   Gerard, Berlin.

T telegram (E. M. House Papers, CtY).

[1] J. W. Gerard to RL, March 18, 1916, printed in FR-WWS 1916, pp. 208-209,

sending the text of resolutions presented to the Reichstag by the National Liberal party, the Conservative party, and the Center party. The first urged unrestricted use of submarines against all merchantmen except passenger ships. The second expressed dissatisfaction with the German government's present submarine policy. The third declared that full freedom in the use of the submarine should be retained in negotiations with foreign governments.

From Frank Lyon Polk

My dear Mr. President: Washington March 20, 1916.

Mr. Arredondo came in this afternoon. I first called his attention to the note from this Department, dated March 13th, which read as follows:

"The Government of the United States understands that in view of its agreement to this reciprocal arrangement proposed by the *de facto* Government, the arrangement is now complete and in force and the reciprocal privileges thereunder may accordingly be exercised by either Government without further interchange of views."[1]

After some hesitation he said these two recent communications covering the proposed agreement was their reply.[2] I told him I assumed that this proposed agreement would cover future movements of troops and as to the present expedition, we would do everything we could to conform in general to the terms suggested by him. His reply was that the proposed terms were meant to cover this particular expedition and his suggestion was that the agreement should be made at once and that we could then slowly withdraw our troops so as to meet all the terms—that is to say, that there should not be more than one thousand troops over the border and that they should not go more than sixty kilometers from the border into Mexico. I told him that this would be difficult, if not impossible, for obvious reasons. His point is that the chances of catching Villa are slight; that our troops may have to venture a great distance into Mexico; that Villa will hide in the mountains, and it will mean a campaign of months in the heart of Mexico. All this will be very dangerous to existing friendly relations. He thought that our troops could not be secretly withdrawn and the statement then made that Villa had fled into the interior of Mexico. I told him he could tell General Carranza that this Government was most anxious to meet his views in every way possible; that the arrangement proposed would probably be satisfactory to cover all future campaigns, but as to this particular campaign I felt sure that you would wish to have reports showing the progress of this campaign and the chances of success before you could consider reducing the force in Mexico and withdrawing it to the limits suggested. I told him that I would communicate with you and I knew that you would give the matter very careful attention. He said that General Carranza was very anxious for a prompt reply and I told him that we would try to meet his wishes in this connection.

In leaving he again assured me that General Carranza was anxious to do everything he could to maintain friendly relations. This is where the matter now stands.

Yours faithfully,   Frank L Polk

TLS (WP, DLC).

[1] See n. 1 to D. Lawrence to WW, March 13, 1916, enclosed in WW to F. L. Polk, March 14, 1916.

[2] The first was E. Arredondo to F. L. Polk, March 18, 1916, *FR 1916*, pp. 493-94. This was a personal message from Carranza, who protested strongly against the entry of the Punitive Expedition into Mexico without his knowledge and said that the Mexican proposal for mutual hot pursuit of bandits did not apply to the Punitive Expedition. The second was E. Arredondo to F. L. Polk, March 19, 1916, enclosing a draft agreement between Mexico and the United States regarding the crossing of Mexican and American troops over the boundary in pursuit of bandits, *ibid.*, pp. 495-96. The draft agreement stipulated, among other things, that any force in hot pursuit of bandits should be limited to one thousand cavalrymen, should be confined to an area of sixty kilometers on either side of the border, and should not remain in the other nation's territory more than five days.

To James Linn Rodgers

Washington, March 20, 1916.

Your March nineteen, twelve midnight. You will express to General Carranza in the terms of deepest consideration and friendly assurance, the regret felt by this Government over any apprehension he may feel or misunderstanding he may labor under in relation to the specific object of the expedition, the single purpose of which is to pursue and capture Villa, unless his prior capture should be effected by the forces of the *de facto* Government. You will give General Carranza every assurance that immediately upon the accomplishment of this purpose, the forces of this Government will retire from Mexican territory forthwith. From the very inception of the expedition, our troops were given explicit instructions to scrupulously refrain from any act that might cause the slightest friction or the least criticism, and in future operations, insofar as possible, to conform with the suggestions of the de facto government; and this Government confidently assures General Carranza that our forces will not deviate from the directions given them. Therefore, as far as this Government or its troops are concerned, there is no cause for the slightest misapprehension. Paragraph.

You will also say to General Carranza that Señor Arredondo

today submitted the draft for a reciprocal arrangement suggested telegraphically by the Minister of Foreign Relations; that this Government agrees in principle and that, for better adaptability, some modifications are now being given urgent consideration. This Government realizes that such an arrangement will have an immediate and helpful effect and great influence upon the cordial relations of the two Governments, by terminating border out-rages and abating frontier irritation. Paragraph.

General Carranza should be informed, that in the present instance, however, this Government, actuated solely by the in-tention of furthering the amicable relations now existing between the two Governments, accepted, without any hesitation, the proposal made by the Minister of Foreign Affairs, through Mr. Silliman, on March ten. The only hope of success depended upon quick action in the effort to capture Villa, who promises to be a constant menace to the friendship of our countries. Paragraph.

The troops which were sent across the border are under the command of General John Pershing and consists of cavalry, infantry, and artillery. Their location at the present time cannot be stated with preciseness, but is believed to be in the neighbor-hood of San Miguel. From all the advices received by the Depart-ment, the expedition, in accordance with instructions, appears to be cooperating with the forces of the *de facto* Government and they are apparently working together in earnest and friendly endeavor to accomplish the ends so greatly to be desired by our Governments.

You are directed to request General Carranza to issue instruc-tions to the Chihuahua authorities, directing them to give their full cooperation to the expedition. You may also say to General Carranza that the Department will telegraph within the next twenty-four hours, after consultation with Mr. Arredondo, a sug-gestion for greater cooperation of the two forces in the present expedition.   Polk Acting[1]

T telegram (SDR, RG 59, 812.00/17529, DNA).

[1] Polk took Rodgers' telegram of March 19 to the White House at some time, probably in the afternoon, on March 20. Wilson composed the reply, which seems to have been typed by Swem, and Polk, undoubtedly with Wilson's ap-proval, made a few handwritten changes in the telegram. See Link, *Confusions and Crises*, pp. 218-19, and F. L. Polk to R. Lansing, March 21, 1916, CCL (F. L. Polk Papers, CtY).

From David Franklin Houston

My dear Mr. President: Washington March 20, 1916.

At the last Cabinet Meeting, I spoke to you of Mr. Lever's suggestion that instead of having the Military Bill, now pending in the House, merely carry an authorization for the construction of a plant to provide an adequate supply of nitrogen through the fixation of atmospheric nitrogen by the development of water power, or any other means, provision should be made for a commission to investigate the matter and to make a report to the Congress thereon.

I enclose herewith the suggestion which Mr. Lever wishes to have inserted in the bill.[1] You will note that this substitute not only provides for a commission, with an appropriation of $100,-000 for its expenses, but also carries the authorization, in broader terms, that is contained in the Military Bill. The adoption of the amendment would result in the coordination of the activities of the Four Departments principally concerned with the problem and would provide for a thorough investigation of the practicability and best means of producing nitrogen compounds and of obtaining potash. You will observe that the substitute contemplates the production of these substances for agricultural needs. Mr. Lever is of the impression that there will be an economy of effort if the substances are produced for both purposes. Of course, the ultimate determination would be left to the commission and to the Congress, but I can see no good reason why the commission should not consider their production for both purposes.

I understand Mr. Hay believes that this is a good way to handle the matter but feels that he must stand by the provision as presented by the Committee. Mr. Lever wonders whether you would be in a position to write him a letter indicating that in your opinion it would be desirable to have this substitute inserted in the bill.

In the Scientific American of March 18, there is an editorial[2] in which it is stated that the Chairman of the Committee of Physics and Chemistry of the Naval Consulting Board, after an investigation, has suggested that the Secretary of the Navy be requested to urge upon you the coordination of efforts for the production of nitrogen through such a commission as this substitute contemplates. I attach hereto the editorial.

Cordially yours,   D. F. Houston.

TLS (WP, DLC).
[1] T MS (WP, DLC). Houston explains Lever's amendments below.
[2] "War and the Nitrogen Supply," *Scientific American*, CXIV (March 18, 1916), 296, clipping (WP, DLC).

From Edward Mandell House, with Enclosures

Dear Governor: New York. March 20, 1916.

I am enclosing you copies of letters from Mr. Balfour and Sir Horace Plunkett which come this morning.

You will notice the significant sentence in Balfour's letter which I have underscored. Plunkett also writes me another six pages, but it is of no great interest.

Mitchel asked me last night if I had heard from you and I had to tell him no. I know you do not wish to see him and while there is no profit in it, I do not see how it can be avoided.

Affectionately yours,   E. M. House

TLS (WP, DLC).

ENCLOSURE I

Arthur James Balfour to Edward Mandell House

Private.

My dear Colonel House: London. 2nd March, 1916.

I was sorry not to be able personally to say "goodbye" to you and Mrs. House, as I shall always regard our intercourse during your two visits as among my most interesting recollections. *Unless, however, I am making a mistake, it will not be very long before I have again the pleasure of meeting you, and discussing with an open heart some of the great problems raised by the world crisis through which we are living.*

On the subject of Mr. Lansing's Note about the arming of merchant vessels, I have written a draft reply for the Foreign Office; but in all probability they will adopt one prepared by the French. I fancy, however, that this particular point of controversy has lost some of its interest and importance.

As I write, the news from France seems clearly to point to the failure of the Germans before Verdun. Such a conclusion may no doubt be reversed by some unexpected operation there, or elsewhere; but taken by itself, I think it may prove of considerable importance from the point of view of German prestige and the policy of European neutrals.

If anything interesting occurs which I think you will not hear through any other channel, I will make a point of letting you know.

Please remember me to Mrs. House,

And believe me,

Yours sincerely,   Arthur James Balfour.

ENCLOSURE II

Sir Horace Plunkett to Edward Mandell House

My dear Colonel House: London, March 7th, 1916.

I think I ought to let you know by this mail that the stand that the President is taking upon the right of Americans to the benefit of the humane provisions of International Law when they travel on British ships has moved opinion profoundly in this country. At the time of writing I do not know what the attitude of the House of Representatives will be towards him, but his friends here have every confidence that they will behave as did the Senate. Whatever way the vote there may go, you may rely upon it that he stands higher in the regard of the British people than he did when his policy was even less understood over here than it seems to have been in some portions of his own country.

You may be glad to know that the propaganda adumbrated in the penultimate paragraph of my Cabinet document[1] is getting under way. I think you will notice that the only issues it will concern itself with will be those which we believe to be in entire accordance with the views upon International rights the President has given to the world.

I cannot tell you how I rejoice that he is at last getting to be understood, nor how I hope the revulsion of feeling throughout the States will be sufficiently strong to place him in the position which every believer in our ideal of the Pax Anglo-Americana would wish to have conceded to him.

I may have more to write to you by the next mail and possibly may be able to be a little more particular. I can now only speak in generalities.

Yours very sincerely,   Horace Plunkett.

TCL (WP, DLC).

[1] H. Plunkett, "Memorandum on the Anglo-American Situation," T MS (WP, DLC). This document was printed for the British cabinet in February 1916. House brought the typed version to Wilson on March 6. Plunkett sought to explain to British officialdom the attitude of the American people, particularly of Midwesterners, toward the war and the part that Britain was playing in it. He insisted that American opinion was overwhelmingly pro-Ally, or at least opposed to the Central Powers. However, Americans were much less pro-British than pro-French, partly because of the long history of Anglo-American controversies, partly because of present British maritime policies, and partly because of the skillful German propaganda in the Middle West, which, Plunkett said, held the political balance of power in the United States. His only specific suggestion, offered in the penultimate paragraph, was that British policymakers should do what they could to prevent or reduce public expressions of anti-American, and particularly anti-Wilsonian, sentiment in Great Britain because it only exasperated American public opinion.

To David Franklin Houston

My dear Houston: [The White House] March 21, 1916

Thank you for your memorandum of March twentieth about Mr. Lever's proposed amendment to the Hay Bill. I am today writing to Mr. Hay about it.

In haste

Cordially and faithfully yours,   Woodrow Wilson

TLS (Letterpress Books, WP, DLC).

To James Hay

My dear Mr. Hay: The White House March 21, 1916

I wonder what you think of the amendment which Mr. Lever is proposing with regard to the treatment of the subject of obtaining an adequate supply of nitrogen through the fixation of atmospheric nitrogen by the development of water power? It has made a very favorable impression on me and I hope that you will pardon my taking the liberty of saying at least that much to you about it. I think it would be altogether advantageous to the Government and the things we are so much interested in if we were to treat this matter in the broadest possible way.

In haste

Cordially and sincerely yours,   Woodrow Wilson

TLS (J. Hay Papers, DLC).

To Charles Richard Crane

My dear Friend: [The White House] March 21, 1916

There is a rather delicate matter I am going to make bold to ask you if you will not handle for me.

Senator Pittman of Nevada is one of the most valuable and dependable men in the Senate. He has made a delightful impression upon his colleagues not only, but upon all who have dealt with him, and we all agree in feeling that it would be a serious disadvantage, not only to the party but to the country, to lose him. I am informed that there are influences at work in Nevada to combine the Jewish voters of the state in opposition to his re-election, and I am wondering if you would be willing and think it wise to have an interview with Mr. Morgenthau and ask him if he cannot assist us in offsetting these influences. Pittman is worthy of any assistance we can give him and it seems too bad to have anything of this sort, essentially unfair in itself, stand in his way.

If I trespass too far in making this request, I shall understand it perfectly if you say so.

Always

   Cordially and faithfully yours, Woodrow Wilson

TLS (Letterpress Books, WP, DLC).

To Caleb Thomas Winchester

[The White House]

My dear Professor Winchester: March 21, 1916

I hope that you will not think it an unwarranted liberty if I write you a line about Stockton Axson. I think that he made a great mistake in accepting a professorship at Wesleyan and that he did so only out of loyal affection for you and for the college, which I am sure he would be delighted to serve. I think it was a mistake because I think that it would probably be fatal to his health to attempt the duties of a full, unbroken college year. I would not say this if I did not feel that I was speaking with genuine knowledge of the circumstances and of his condition, which, although at present excellent, is liable to yield to strain at any time.

May I not urge upon the authorities of the University some action which will release him?

If I am taking an unwarranted liberty in writing this, pray forgive me. I do so because I believe that Axson's coming to Wesleyan could only lead to breakdown and disappointment.

I hope that you are all well. I very often think of the happy days that I spent at Wesleyan.

   Cordially and sincerely yours, Woodrow Wilson

TLS (Letterpress Books, WP, DLC).

To Hiram Woods, Jr.

My dear Hiram: [The White House] March 21, 1916

Thank you warmly for your note about Charley.[1] It has taken a load off my heart that he should have passed the crisis and appears to be coming out all right. I almost dreaded to hear from you for fear the report might be bad and not good.

   Affectionately yours, Woodrow Wilson

TLS (Letterpress Books, WP, DLC).

¹ H. Woods, Jr., to WW, March 19, 1916, ALS (WP, DLC), informing Wilson that their Princeton classmate, Charles Wellman Mitchell, though seriously ill, was likely to recover.

From Frank Lyon Polk, with Enclosure

PERSONAL & CONFIDENTIAL

My dear Mr. President: Washington March 21, 1916.

The enclosed statement, which you have already seen, was given out to the press associations this afternoon. Special men were very curious, so I took the liberty of giving it to them also, with the distinct understanding that it was not for publication. Several of them suggested that this statement, or one somewhat along its lines, would be very effective if you would give it out for publication. Possibly there is something in the suggestion.¹

I saw Arredondo this afternoon and gave him a draft of the protocol.² He seemed to be much calmer.

I understand the Evening Post of today carried a garbled account of Gerard's confidential cable, which you received yesterday.³ It created no end of excitement among the newspaper men as the article stated that we had been asked to mediate by the Chancellor and that Gerard had been requested to delay his vacation on account of possible peace negotiations. I stated that neither one of these stories were true. I will start an investigation at once to find out how Lawrence got any information on the subject, as the printing of the story made a great deal of hard feeling.

The Secretary will be here Thursday morning.

Yours faithfully,   Frank L. Polk

TLS (WP, DLC).

¹ Wilson's amplified version is printed at March 25, 1916.

² This draft protocol was a counterproposal to the draft agreement enclosed by Arredondo in his letter to Polk of March 19. The counterproposal is printed in E. Arredondo to C. Aguilar, March 21, 1916, Mexican Foreign Office, *Diplomatic Dealings of the Constitutionalist Revolution of Mexico* (Mexico City, n.d.), pp. 155-56. In contrast to the Mexican draft, Polk's proposal set no limits on the distance or number of troops to be involved in hot pursuit and said only: "In no case will the pursuing forces establish themselves or remain in foreign territory for a time longer than is necessary to effect the persecution of the band they went after."

³ That is, J. W. Gerard to the Secretary of State, March 18, 1916, printed as an Enclosure with WW to EMH, March 20, 1916.

ENCLOSURE

Handed to the Representatives of the Press

NOT FOR PUBLICATION   March 21, 1916.

It has already been announced by the President that the proposed expedition of American forces into Mexico is in no sense an invasion of that Republic nor an infringement of its Sovereignty. It is hoped that the press will be good enough to assist the administration in presenting this view of the expedition to the American people and particularly to the distressed and sensitive people of our neighboring Republic who are susceptible to impressions spread by the American Press and are prepared to believe that they represent the view and objects of this Government. Indeed such conclusions are not unnatural when the main, if not the only, source of their information is the public press of the United States. To avoid such erroneous impression he calls upon you to use your earnest endeavors not to interpret news stories regarding the expedition as in any sense meaning war, to withhold stories of troop movements and preparations that might be given that interpretation, and to refrain from publishing rumors of unrest in Mexico. On the other hand it is most desirable to impress upon both Americans and Mexicans that the expedition is simply a punitive measure aimed solely at the elimination of the bandits who raided Columbus and who infest an unprotected district along the border and use it as a base of operations against American lives and property in the United States. The whole idea of the expedition is to cooperate with the forces of General Carranza in removing a cuase [cause] of irritation to both Governments and to retire from Mexico so soon as this object is accomplished.

CC MS (WP, DLC).

To Frank Lyon Polk

Dear Mr. Polk,   [The White House, March 21, 1916]

Pardon this penciled note. I entirely approve of this and thank you for preparing it.   Sincerely,   W.W.

ALI (F. L. Polk Papers, CtY).

Two Telegrams from Frederick Funston
to Henry Pinckney McCain

Received at the War Department, March 21, 1916, 7:20 P.M.

Number 1104. John J. Pershing (Brig. Gen.) advance base now at Casas Grandes, Chihuahua one hundred thirty miles from Columbus, N. M. His troops moving toward Pearson, Chihuahua and Galeana. Will no doubt be two hundred miles from Columbus, N. M. before many days. This great attenuation of our lines of communications and the fact of possible hostile attitude of inhabitants of country to say nothing of possible hostility of organized forces convinces me that there should be sent to Columbus, N. M. one additional regiment of cavalry and regiment of infantry to guard this long line. 6th Infantry and 16th Infantry going forward may be required as a force upon which to assemble this expedition. Without additional regiments asked for above, our line of communications might be severed. A canvass of strength of troops at various border stations shows no point from which I can draw any troops sufficient to meet this requirement. In organizing John J. Pershing I took 7th Cavalry, 10th Calvary and 13th Cavalry from border patrol duty and have replaced them by two depleted regiments 1st Cavalry with ten troops and 12th Cavalry with only eight troops. This reduces strength of border patrols throughout states New Mexico and Arizona which I would not do could I spare troops from other points so as to strengthen this patrol. I am further greatly concerned over reports by Americans coming from Mexico as to growing irritation amongst people and troops relative to presence of our forces in Mexico and am disturbed by undoubted concentration of Mexican soldiers in border towns.

Augustus P. Blocksom (Col. 3rd Cav.) reports arrival at Matamoras, Tamaulipas from south of considerable artillery and new machine guns, and at border towns there have been great quantities of ammunition crossing to Mexico. Regardless of the personal attitude of Carranza I feel we must consider possible independent action by his troops either in opening fire on our towns and garrisons or in attempting raids in force.

In view of your number nine hundred I have requested commanding general Eastern Department and Central Department to send 5th Cavalry to Columbus, N. M. I request a regiment of infantry to be sent to Columbus, N. M. for use on line of communications as stated above and another regiment of infantry to guard towns along that portion of Southern Pacific near border as the repeated calls for assistance indicate the people in that region are bordering on a state of panic. This latter regiment should be sent to San Antonio, Texas. Upon arrival instructions will be given for distribution of companies. Have orfered [ordered] Battery D, 4th Field Artillery from Mercedes to Brownsville, Tex. Funston.

Received at the War Department, March 21, 1916, 8:10 P.M.

Number 1109. Following just received from John J. Pershing (Brig. Gen.) transmitted through base at Columbus.

"Casas Grandes March 20th, 1916, six o'clock message reference camping Casas Grandes report is incorrect   am encamped one mile north of Colonia Dublan. No Mexican town has been or will be occupied by our troops. Mexican authorities were notified to that effect upon my arrival. Aeroplanes squadron left Columbus last night   one of number forty one was disabled below Pearson   the aviator Lieutenant Willis[1] has not yet reported but probably not injured. Machine number forty eight fell this afternoon after a short flight and Lieut. Bowen[2] the aviator had his nose broken and face badly bruised. Machine number fifty two aviator Genelo[3] has not yet arrived and machine No. 42 disabled by breaking axle in landing this morning. Endeavored to obtain communication with moving column vicinity of San Miguel this afternoon altitude fifty two hundred feet and machine No. 44 Captain Dodd[4] driver and Capt. Feulois[5] as observer could not rise to necessary height. Stronger machine will be necessary for work at this altitude. 13th Cavalry arrived today information regarding whereabouts of Villa conflicting. Attitude of natives hereabouts continues friendly."

I am unable to understand difficulties of flying of aeroplanes in view of fact that these machines were flying daily here at great altitudes. The name Genelo reported above is probably meant for Second Lieut. Edgar S. Gorrell. Funston.

T telegrams (WP, DLC).
  [1] Robert H. Willis, Jr., 1st lieutenant, U.S.A.
  [2] Thomas S. Bowen, 1st lieutenant, U.S.A.
  [3] Actually, Edgar Staley Gorrell, as noted below, 1st lieutenant, U.S.A.
  [4] Townsend F. Dodd, captain, U.S.A.
  [5] Benjamin Delahauf Foulois, captain, U.S.A.

From Edward Mandell House

Dear Governor: New York. March 22, 1916.

Thank you for sending me Gerard's cable. If I were in your place I would not express any opinion as to the wisdom of Ger-

many sending a special ambassador, but I would instruct Gerard
to assure them that, if they decided to send a special ambassador,
he would be most welcome.

As to Gerard's suggestion that you offer to forward confidentially to the Allies any peace proposals, I am not so clear. You would
be placing yourself in a position to be refused. We must remember that this is Gerard's suggestion and not the Chancellor's.
Gerard told him that you were "ready to mediate at any time you
thought your services would be welcome" which is saying the
same thing, but is from Gerard and not you.

I do not attach any special significance to the interview further
than an additional proof that Geramny [Germany] desires to cash
in while she is ahead of the game. The Chancellor said to me
just what he has said to Gerard and I repeated it to both Briand
and Grey.

Von Tirpitz' retirement is a triumph for the Chancellor. They
were rivals long before the war began and von Tirpitz has always
wanted to displace von Bethmann-Holwegg.

A special ambassador might make better the feeling between
the two countries. He could be told some of the mistakes that
had been made here in the way of propaganda and he could take
back with him a clearer idea of your purposes.

It would probably lead England to send Bryce, which would
not be a bad thing either.

Sir Edward Grey cables me today as follows:

"Letter of March 10th received. Nothing to cable at present.
Am writing to you this week"

I will send you a copy of his letter when it comes. In my letter to him of March 10th I repeated the cable which it was agreed
to send and told him the matter was now squarely up to them.

Mrs. House and I are looking forward with so much pleasure
to being with Mrs. Wilson and you next Tuesday. There are some
matters in connection with Europe that I want particularly to lay
before you.   Affectionately yours,   E. M. House

TLS (WP, DLC).

From James Hay

My dear Mr. President: Washington, D. C. March 22 1916

I think the amendment, which Mr. Lever is proposing is a very
good one. This committee has taken extensive evidence on the
subject, and was impressed with the importance of providing some means, by which this country could obtain an adequate

supply of nitrogen, and thus render it, independent of the necessity of relying upon the Chilean nitrate birds; hence the provision now in the bill.

The proposition has caused much discussion, and has aroused the antagonism of the extreme conservationists; but the Lever amendment may overcome this.

Very sincerely yours,   James Hay.

ALS (WP, DLC).

From William Joel Stone

Dear Mr. President: [Washington] March 22 1916.

Shortly before the Senate adjourned yesterday evening Senator Shields took me aside, showed me an item in the afternoon Times relating to the conference had at the White House yesterday morning,[1] and asked me about it. He remarked that as there were only two of those present who voted for the so-called Shields Bill he wondered if it was a movement antagonistic to that bill. I told him that I did not know just how the meeting happened to be called, but that I thought you had called it on the suggestion of some Senator or Senators. I told him that naturally you felt a great interest in the subject of the legislation as every one would who gave the subject a moment's consideration. I told him that I understood your wish and purpose to be to confer with Senators and Members of the House from time to time with the object of getting the different points of view, and with the hope of bringing about some greater harmony in thought and purpose so as to secure legislation, etc. I merely suggest that it might be well if at an early day you could have a talk with another group of Senators, including Shields.

After returning to the Capitol yesterday I had a talk with Senator Martin and we have in mind to get Senators, and possibly some leading Members of the House, together and spend two or three evenings if necessary in trying to get upon some common ground—of course keeping in touch with you. I hope this step will have your approval and co-operation.

Sincerely, etc.,   Wm J Stone.

TLS (WP, DLC).
    [1] "Wilson Would Rush Water Power Bill," *Washington Times*, March 21, 1916, a brief article reporting on a conference among Wilson and Senators James, Kern, Martin, Stone, Swanson, Walsh, and Myers on the Shields bill. The article said that Wilson was "out of sympathy" with some provisions of that bill, had discussed with the senators the advisability of framing a new measure, and had urged the passage of a satisfactory bill during the present session.

From Herman Bernstein

New York, March 22, 1916.

On Saturday, March 25th, the Bazar for Relief for Jewish War Sufferers will be opened in New York. The Jews in War Zone are suffering untold agony and direct distress. Their tragedy is sadder even than Belgium's and Poland's. Only the Jews of America can aid them morally and materially. I would deeply appreciate it and the Jewish people would be grateful if you would be generous enough to send a few words as an expression of sentiment on this occasion in your own handwriting. With kind regards and best wishes,   Herman Bernstein

T telegram (WP, DLC).

To Joseph Patrick Tumulty

Dear Tumulty: The White House [c. March 23, 1916].

Will you not be kind enough to answer this telegram? I do not think that Mr. Bernstein can always be trusted to be discreet, and I would be obliged if you would say to him that I have certainly proved in every way my sympathy with the cause he speaks of but am sure that he will understand that it is extremely difficult for me to express sympathy with the sufferers in the war zone without having my words twisted into some sort of significance with regard to the war itself.   The President.

TL (WP, DLC).

From Henry Morgenthau

My dear Mr. President: [New York] March 23, 1916.

When I asked leave to return home after twenty-eight months of service as Ambassador to Turkey, I had no thought of not returning to my post. My desire is to serve where best I may, and without regard to my personal convenience or fortunes.

I have come to the conclusion that my duty lies here for the moment and not in Constantinople. If you will permit me to be the judge as to where I may best serve my country, I beg to offer you herewith my resignation.

I feel free to make this request now because the work in Constantinople is in such shape that my successor can take it up without any difficulty.

Please accept my best thanks for the confidence and support

which you have given me and which enabled me to fulfil my duties in a way which you have been good enough to commend.

With assurances of high esteem, I am, my dear Mr. President,
Yours very sincerely,   Henry Morgenthau

TLS (WP, DLC).

From William Cox Redfield

My dear Mr. President: Washington March 23rd, 1916.

I wonder if it is possible to reconsider the determination not to include the Vocational Education Bill[1] in the legislative program for the present session. I do not speak out of my own great disappointment that this should be deferred but from other and more potent causes. There is a widespread public interest in this measure. Many of the large educational bodies are enthusiastic about it and have so expressed themselves formally as well as by numerous letters to Congress. It is a part of our national platform. The movement has had your expressed public approval. Our hand has therefore been put openly to the plow. In so doing we have had the earnest approval of the American Federation of Labor and of organized labor generally. Can we draw back with safety? Shall we not be open to the charge in the coming campaign that we have in this respect failed to keep faith?

If in a caucus of our party we lay aside a measure to which our platform binds us, which you have approved, which has had the unanimous approval of the House and Senate Committees, and for which labor earnestly calls, how can we meet the criticism of our adversaries that we have left one of our most important duties undone? I am very sure the Republicans will attack us in just this way and I do not see how it is easily possible to meet the attack which may have special weight in the Democratic industrial centers.

Keenly as I feel about the Shipping Bill, I do not think that under present conditions it would be as hurtful to the party to have that rest over as it would be to have the Education Bill. Is there any essential reason why both should not be done? The Democratic caucus is Friday night. If it is known throughout the country Saturday that the Education Bill has been allowed to go over, I feel that there will be widespread disappointment among many who look to us to carry this great reform through.

Yours very truly,   William C. Redfield

TLS (WP, DLC).
[1] The bill, S. 703, introduced by Senator Hoke Smith and Representative Dudley Mays Hughes of Georgia on December 6 and 7, 1915, was the product of

the work of the Commission on National Aid to Vocational Education established by act of Congress in January 1914. It provided for federal grants to the states (ranging from a total of $1,000,000 in the first year of the program to $6,000,000 in the ninth year and afterward) to assist in the payment of salaries of teachers of agricultural, trade, and industrial subjects. It also provided grants to aid in training teachers of these subjects ranging from a total of $500,000 in the first year to $1,000,000 in the fourth year and afterward. In order to participate in the program, the states had to match the federal grants dollar for dollar, pay all other costs of an effective program of vocational education, and establish state boards of vocational education to administer the program. The bill also provided for the creation of a Federal Board for Vocational Education to administer the grants, oversee the work of the state boards, and make detailed reports on various aspects of vocational education for the benefit of the program as a whole. See *Report of the Commission on National Aid to Vocational Education* . . . , 63d Cong., 2d sess., House Doc. No. 1004 (Washington, 1914), especially the text and analysis of the proposed bill on pp. 78-87. For the text of the bill as finally enacted on February 23, 1917, see 39 *Statutes at Large* 929. For a brief history of the movement for federal aid to vocational education, see Dewey W. Grantham, Jr., *Hoke Smith and the Politics of the New South* (Baton Rouge, La., 1958), pp. 264-67.

From Garrett Droppers

Dear Mr. President   Athens, March 23, 1916

I regret more than I can say that I have to bother you about a matter of personal interest. My regret springs from the fact that I am troubling you about myself when it seems to me that you must be overwhelmed with responsibilities such as no President since Lincoln has had to face.

My case is briefly this: So far Williams College has filled the Chair of Economics which I occupied with a temporary instructor. If I return to Williams next fall I go back to my work without change of any kind and Mr. Garfield has been most thoughtful in making all necessary arrangements during my absence. But I doubt whether he can do anything more to extend what is after all tantamount to a very unusual furlough.

Personally I do not think I am bribed, as so many people are, by the glamours of a diplomatic post. I can see the temptations of such a post and I have enjoyed the "rights and privileges pertaining thereto" as they say in conferring honorary degrees. But I am sure that I can lay them aside and return to the work of my profession without a pang of regret.

Ordinarily the post at Athens is one of the least important in Europe. Athens is a place of much show and of rather expensive entertainment. To a certain type of mind the place is fascinating, its social whirl has turned the head of more than one American. While much curtailed on account of the war there is still some of this left. I have tried to do what is necessary without losing my sense of proportion.

If things were normal I think I should ask you to secure a new appointment for this post after next summer. But the truth is the European war is on. Greece is in a critical state and I hate to abandon the place during the continuance of the war, especially after your kind letters to me encouraging me to believe that I am of some use here. I will confess to so much that I can see how a certain type of American could easily lose his head here. Mine at least is mine own.

There is still another point. If I do not return to Williams next fall Mr. Garfield will, as I have hinted, possibly have to provide a permanent man for my place. In that case on my return to America I may be out of my profession for some time to come and then not find what I should like so well. More than that I imperil my chances with the pension fund. This is not a supreme point but it is at least worth considering.

I think I have shown you all the elements in my situation. On the whole I should prefer to return to America yet I doubt whether it is right to do so when I think it really a duty to stay while the war continues. At present I have the strands of the political situation here clearly in my hands and it would be difficult, I am sure, for another to secure them. I am in a quandary and hardly know what to suggest. Perhaps you may be able to find a way out for me.

I remain with best wishes and remembrances

Yours sincerely   Garrett Droppers[1]

P.S. I take the liberty of saying how delighted I am by your appointment of Mr. Brandeis. I knew it would stir the animals up. G.D.

ALS (WP, DLC).

[1] Wilson must have replied in a personal letter. Droppers remained in Athens until 1920.

From Hiram Woods, Jr.

Dear Tommy: Baltimore, March, 23, 1916.

Many thanks for your note. The favorable change of last week in Charlie's condition was not as permanent as we could wish. While his heart, digestion and kidneys—the really vital indicators—are holding out well, there has developed a stubborn, but low grade toxaemia which is upsetting him in various ways. The latest complication is rheumatic trouble in his wrist. The lung is not clearing up as rapidly as we might wish and the muttering delirium continues. However, the good points are still in excess of the bad and we are by no means hopeless of ultimate recovery.

Hastily and affectionately,   Hiram Woods

TLS (WP, DLC).

To James Hay

My dear Mr. Hay: [The White House] March 24, 1916

I cannot let the occasion of the passage of the Army bill through the House by so significant a majority pass[1] without sending you my warm congratulations. The action both of the Committee and of the House must be a source of real gratification to the country as the first step towards adequate preparation for national defense. May I not say how much I have admired the energy and capacity by which the action of the House has been conducted under your leadership?

Cordially and sincerely yours,   Woodrow Wilson

TLS (Letterpress Books, WP, DLC).
[1] By a vote of 403 to 2.

To William Joel Stone

My dear Senator: [The White House] March 24, 1916

Thank you for your letter of March twenty-second. As a matter of fact, the conference we had the other day was held at the suggestion of Senator Walsh and was arranged for by him. I am warmly obliged to you for representing the matter as you did to Senator Shields, for you put it in just the right light.

I am very much interested in the plan that you and Senator Martin have in mind to get some leading members of both houses together for the purpose of planning cooperative and harmonious action about this all-important matter of conservation. I have no doubt that you feel as I do, that the matter has many sides to it and that one of the important sides is the very strong opinion there is in the country back of men like Mr. Gifford Pinchot, for example, in favor of the most careful and provident legislation in this great field. We cannot be too careful to do the right thing, for a mistake made now cannot easily be undone.

Cordially and faithfully yours,   Woodrow Wilson

TLS (Letterpress Books, WP, DLC).

From Robert Lansing, with Enclosure

My dear Mr. President: Washington March 24, 1916.

I submit a draft of a letter to the German Ambassador which follows, I believe, your views as to the attitude we should take in regard to the memorandum which he delivered on March 8th, and which was given to the press on the same day.

I should like to send this letter as soon as possible.[1]

Faithfully yours,   Robert Lansing

TLS (WP, DLC).

[1] The letter was not sent. Wilson put Lansing's letter and its enclosure in his confidential file. He must have told Lansing orally that he thought that it would be inexpedient to send the letter because it would only exacerbate German-American tension.

E N C L O S U R E

My dear Mr. Ambassador: Draft March 24, 1916.

On account of absence from Washington I have delayed commenting on the Memorandum explanatory of "the U-Boat question," which you handed me on March 8th. Meanwhile the memorandum has received the careful consideration of the President and myself, and he directs me to call your attention particularly to the wording of the last paragraph which escaped my attention during our conversation on the 8th when it was agreed that it should be made public. Upon consideration, however, the Government is constrained to the belief that it was the intention of the Imperial Government to appeal to the American people and to submit the case before the bar of public opinion, rather than to this Government. This belief is confirmed by your earnest desire to furnish the Memorandum to the press for publication immediately upon its delivery.

This unusual, if not unprecedented, procedure, which gives the impression of having been adopted for the purpose of securing popular support in the United States for the German position without regard to the attitude of this Government, cannot be passed over without comment, especially as it was employed in relation to a subject, which, at the time, was being considered by the Congress of the United States.

As the subject of the Memorandum was a matter of diplomatic discussion between the two Governments, the Government of the United States must express its disapproval of the course of the Imperial Government in appealing directly to the American people in support of its position on a pending question between the two Governments. Not only does this Government disapprove this action but it resents the delivery to it by your Excellency as the diplomatic representative of Germany of a document which on its face is intended to influence public opinion in the United States and possibly to arouse directly or indirectly opposition in the Congress to the policy of the President in dealing with the question of submarine warfare.

I am reluctant to believe that your Government fully considered the consequences before permitting you to become the medium of transmitting this appeal to the people of the United States, though in form addressed to this Government. Without exceeding the bounds of diplomatic propriety this Government cannot permit a diplomatic representative to address the people of this country through the press or otherwise on a controversy pending between the Government of the United States and the Government which he represents.

I would be wanting in duty to my Government and in justice to yours, if I did not thus candidly state the unfavorable impression which has been made by the Memorandum of March 8th and by the way in which it was laid before the American public.

T MS (WP, DLC).

From Charles Herbert Levermore,[1] with Enclosure

My dear Wilson: Boston March 24, 1916

Might not our present national defense policies be coupled in some judicious manner with an international pledge of our desire to co-operate, as soon as our neighbors will join us, in the discussion of plans for a better organization of the world than we have hitherto possessed? For a long time it has been in my mind that such a declaration might unite pacifists and militarists in support of the Administration measures for greater military and naval preparations. Within the Democratic party the general statement of foreign policy, thus outlined, would surely go far to mitigate the opposition of the representatives of rural constituencies to the increase of our national forces and consequent taxation: increases which international statesmanship might eventually render unnecessary.

With this end in view I drew up the memoranda, which I enclose herewith, sent them to a Congressman with whom I happen to have some acquaintance, and asked his opinion. I have learned that in the House Committee on Naval Affairs, Messrs. Hensley, Callaway, Butler and Britten[2] all approve of this proposition, and that Congressmen Kitchin and Slayden are also in favor of it.

If you should see no objection to the recognition of this wider outlook upon the future in connection with current defensive measures, and felt that you could, as opportunity permits, safely indicate such a view, I believe that the interests of reasonable preparedness and of Democratic unity would both be promoted.

With cordial greetings and best wishes, I am,

Yours very sincerely, Charles H. Levermore

TLS (WP, DLC).

[1] A fellow graduate student of Wilson's at The Johns Hopkins University; at this time director of the College and University Bureau of the World Peace Foundation.

[2] Walter Lewis Hensley, Democrat of Missouri; Oscar Callaway, Democrat of Texas; Thomas Stalker Butler, Republican of Pennsylvania; and Frederick Albert Britten, Republican of Illinois.

E N C L O S U R E

A Declaration of Policy, that might accompany
defensive enactments in Congress.

In connection with any appropriation bill, authorizing a material increase of the military and naval forces of the United States, there should be joined a statement, indicating a possible and preferable policy of constructive statesmanship, of the following character:

If, at any time before the total sum or sums hereby appropriated shall have been expended or placed under contract, there shall have been established with the co-operation of the United States of America a league of nations to insure the establishment and maintenance of international peace, with provision for international courts and conciliation and for the development of international law, the United States will gladly unite with such nations in considering agreements for the international limitation of armaments and for the adaptation of national forces to the needs of the international organization.

In case such agreements are mutually acceptable, the plans for defense adopted by the United States will be changed, as it may be necessary, in order to secure conformity with the aforesaid agreements and with the new international conditions.

Whenever appropriation bills, such as are above referred to, are enacted into law, it would become the duty of the President to transmit the conditional pledges, herein outlined, to the Governments of all States represented in the second Hague Conference.[1]

T MS (WP, DLC).
¹ He enclosed, in addition, "Memorandum in support of a Declaration, suggested as a possible Amendment to the Military and Naval Appropriation Bills," T MS (WP, DLC).

A List

The White House [c. March 25, 1916]

AMERICAN PLOTTERS AND LIARS IN MEXICO¹

Dr. Sidney Ulfelder,   William A. McLaren,
Samuel W. Rider,   K. M. VanZandt,
George W. Cook,   Eman L. Beck,
Burton W. Wilson,   Dr. P. W. Monroe,
William F. Layer,   Ralph Smith,
William L. Vail,   I. H. Jacobs,
James Carson,   Dr. S. C. Griffen,
Charles A. Hopkins,   Clinton G. Ray,
Robert M. Raymond,   E. M. Funston,
Charles E. Cummings,   J. D. Helm,
Victor M. Braschi,   J. E. Dennison,
                 E. E. Darnielle.

E. N. Brown

WWT MS (WP, DLC).
¹ The only persons on this list who can be identified are James S. Carson, chief of the Associated Press Bureau in Mexico City; Edward Norphelt Brown, of Mexico City, former president of the National Railways of Mexico; William Augustus McLaren, lawyer of Mexico City; Khleber Miller Van Zandt, Jr., vice-president and manager of the Mercantile Banking Co. of Mexico City; and Emanual L. Beck, proprietor of the Mexico City *Mexican Herald*. "Ralph Smith" was probably Randolph Wellford Smith, a journalist, who was about to publish a book entitled *Benighted Mexico* (New York, 1916), a strong attack on the Mexican Revolution and its leaders and on Wilson's Mexican policies.

To Joseph Patrick Tumulty

Dear Tumulty   [The White House, March 25, 1916]
    Will you please let the newspaper men have this for release on Monday morning? Do you not think that better than *Sunday*?
                                                    W.W.

ALI (WP, DLC).

A Statement and Warning

[*March 25, 1916*]

    As has already been announced, the expedition into Mexico was ordered under an agreement with the de facto Government of Mexico for the single purpose of taking the bandit Villa, whose forces had actually invaded the territory of the United States, and is in no sense intended as an invasion of the republic or as an infringement of its sovereignty.

I have, therefore, asked the several news services to be good enough to assist the Administration in keeping this view of the expedition constantly before both the people of this country and the distressed and sensitive people of Mexico, who are very susceptible, indeed, to impressions received from the American press, not only, but also very ready to believe that those impressions proceed from the views and objects of our Government itself. Such conclusions, it must be said, are not unnatural, because the main, if not the only, source of information for the people on both sides of the border is the public press of the United States.

In order to avoid the creation of erroneous and dangerous impressions in this way I have called upon the several news agencies to use the utmost care not to give news stories regarding this expedition the color of war, to withhold stories of troop movements and military preparations which might be given that interpretation, and to refrain from publishing unverified rumors of unrest in Mexico.

I feel that it is most desirable to impress upon both our own people and the people of Mexico the fact that the expedition is simply a necessary punitive measure, aimed solely at the elimination of the marauders, who raided Columbus and who infest an unprotected district near the border, which they use as a base in making attacks upon the lives and property of our citizens within our own territory. It is the purpose of our commanders to co-operate in every possible way with the forces of General Carranza in removing this cause of irritation to both Governments, and retire from Mexican territory so soon as that object is accomplished.

It is my duty to warn the people of the United States that there are persons all along the border who are actively engaged in originating and giving as wide currency as they can to rumors of the most sensational and disturbing sort, which are wholly unjustified by the facts. The object of this traffic in falsehood is obvious. It is to create intolerable friction between the Government of the United States and the de facto Government of Mexico for the purpose of bringing about intervention in the interest of certain American owners of Mexican properties. This object can not be attained so long as sane and honorable men are in control of this Government, but very serious conditions may be

created, unnecessary bloodshed may result, and the relations between the two republics may be very much embarrassed.

The people of the United States should know the sinister and
unscrupulous influences that are afoot, and should be on their
guard against accepting any story coming from the border; and
those who disseminate the news should make it a matter of
patriotism and of conscience to test the source and authenticity
of every report they receive from that quarter.

Woodrow Wilson.[1]

Printed in the *New York Times*, March 26, 1916.
 [1] The only surviving document relating to this statement is a TC, with WWhw
and WWsh changes and additions, in WP, DLC, of the Enclosure printed with
F. L. Polk to WW, March 17, 1916.

From William Joel Stone

Personal.

Dear Mr. President: [Washington] March 25 1916.

I am going to bore you with another letter. I write you for the
reason that it takes less of your time and mine for me to write
what I have in mind to say and for you to read it than to consume
the time necessary for an intelligent discussion of the various
matters that occur to me as important. About all I can do in any
event is to seek to rivet your attention for a little while to my
thought.

In this morning's papers I read that a legislative program has
been announced in the House, which is said to have your approval.[1] Every item of this program is of course important, but
some items are of more pressing importance than others.

To my thinking, looking to the future, the most important
thing we have to deal with at this time, and the one to which we
should devote special attention, relates to the commercial and
industrial conditions we will have to confront at the close of the
European War. It seems to me—although as to this, of course,
I may well be mistaken—that because of the overwhelming superiority of the Entente Allies in fighting power on both land and
sea, and because of the vast superiority of their collective
resources, that inevitably the ultimate end will be the defeat of
the Central Powers. The probable effect of this end will be a
practical disappearance of Germany as a naval and commercial
maritime power, at least for many years. Germany is the only
European rival of Great Britain, and if that rivalry is crushed by
the war, Great Britain will stand forth as the undisputed mistress
of the seas in naval war strength and in commercial strength.

This seems so perfectly plain that it is not worth while to elaborate it.

Assuming what I have said to be true, what will be the effect on the industrial and commercial activities of this country? As the result of the war we have gained something in international commerce, but it does not seem to me that our gains in this behalf have been commensurate with our opportunities, and I fear that what gains we have made will not prove to be permanent.

I present this view of the situation: Whatever gains we have made, or might have made, in Europe I would not consider as definitely permanent. I separate Europe from the balance of the world, especially from Central and South America. Great Britain has seriously obstructed and hampered our European trade during the war. This has been done at least in large degree in violation of our neutral rights under international law. You are too familiar with these details to make it necessary for me to deal with particulars. Indeed it is not my purpose to discuss the international law questions involved. I refer to the subject at this time merely to have you as the President, looking solely to the welfare of our own country, to consider not only the possible, but the probable reasons influencing the British policy. Did those reasons relate only to the war? were the restrictions on neutral trade, against which you protested, intended merely to aid the Entente Allies as a whole in waging war against their enemies, or did this course also contemplate the ultimate commercial aspects of the question? While the excuse advanced for the course taken was advanced as a war measure, did the policy adopted have a deeper meaning also, and did it have a wise, far-reaching commercial significance? I do not argue this question; I merely suggest it.

I turn now to other countries outside of Europe, especially South America. I will condense what I have to say, and so will speak only of South America. We have made a great effort, and in its way a wise effort, to promote what we call the Pan American Entente. But what substantial thing have we done, and are we doing, to promote this movement? The two great congresses recently held in Washington[2] were very good in their way; but in a practical way what, Mr. President, do you think will come of it? Secretary McAdoo and his confreres are now in Buenos Aires, hoping at the conference there to arrange banking, exchange, and general financial relations between those countries and this country that will redound to our benefit. I have no doubt that some general agreements will be had along this line. But we cannot do business on paper alone. We must ship our goods to

South America, and the South American countries must ship their goods to us. In other words, we must have actual commercial exchanges—and we must have commercial exchanges if we are to have money exchanges. What will be our position at the end of the war, and what will be the position of Great Britain who will be by a thousand fold the chief beneficiary of the war, assuming that the Entente Allies are successful?

That brings me to the point where I wish to impress upon your attention the attitude of the British Government as recently announced by Mr. Walter Runciman, President of the British Board of Trade. On March 17th it was given out in London that by order in council it had been determined to prohibit importation into the United Kingdom and into all countries subject to British authority, including Canada, of a large number of articles defined by this order to be luxuries. Among these "luxuries" thus placed under the ban are such articles as automobiles for private use, cutlery of all kinds, hardware, soap, yarns, chinaware, fancy goods, etc. etc. Mr. Runciman spoke to the Associated Press as follows:

"American traders and manufacturers, must prepare for a rigid, though friendly, British commercial competition in neutral markets after the war."

He also declared that because of a shortage of tonnage the British Government would be compelled to limit the shipment of bulky "luxuries" in order to provide room on ships for necessaries.

All this seems very significant to me. When the war is over what means will we have for transporting our foreign commerce? What boots it that we exploit a commercial propoganda with a view to enlarging our commercial dealing with South America or any other country, if we are without means at hand to keep our engagements and conduct our business?

Mr. President, it surely must be that this view has been the subject of your consideration. Because of this situation it seems to me that the most important thing of immediate concern with which we have to deal concerns "preparedness" to meet what under present conditions will be an overmastering rivalry in the commercial world. I do not underestimate the importance of the other things referred to in this published program. But as I see it the one thing of all others upon which we should now fasten our thought is to provide some way of furnishing adequate, or at least comparatively adequate, facilities for the transportation of our exports.

This is enough to say to a man like you—with your wide comprehension of current questions—but this much I felt impelled to say.   Your friend,   sincerely,   Wm J Stone.

TLS (WP, DLC).

[1] Speaker Clark, in a caucus of House Democrats during the evening of March 25, presented a memorandum from President Wilson which recommended a legislative program of ten items: appropriation bills, including those necessary for the preparedness program; revenue bills, including an antidumping provision; and bills for a tariff commission, a federal shipping board, rural credits, the Philippines, Porto Rico, conservation, flood control on the Mississippi River, and prevention of corrupt practices in federal elections. *Washington Post*, March 25, 1916.

[2] That is, the Pan American Financial Congress and the Pan American Scientific Congress, about which see, respectively, n. 1 to Wilson's remarks to the financial conference printed at May 24, 1915, Vol. 33, and n. 3 to the extract from the diary of Colonel House printed at Dec. 15, 1915, Vol. 35.

From Walter Hines Page[1]

London, March 26, 1916.

4032 March 26, 4 p.m. The following is personal and confidential for the President only:

Thoughtful men here in public and private life agree on two propositions.

First. That a break in American-German diplomatic relations would quickly end the war. This is, in English opinion, the one practical and effective move to bring an early peace, to save perhaps a million lives and incalculable suffering.

Second. Nobody believes that a diplomatic break would lead to war between the United States and Germany. It would be merely such a threat of war as would convince the Germans that their cause is lost. For commercial and financial reasons after the war they will not provoke open hostilities. Kitchener holds these two opinions and openly expresses them.

A *third* proposition would follow namely that such a breach of diplomatic relations would prepare a practical basis for an enduring peace which it will be exceedingly difficult otherwise to arrange. And this is the only plan where the moral influence of the United States can be exerted for peace.

Ambassador London.

T telegram (SDR, RG 59, 763.72/2637½, DNA).

[1] This telegram was undoubtedly inspired by the *Sussex* incident, about which see RL to WW, March 27, 1916.

To William Cox Redfield

My dear Mr. Secretary: [The White House] March 27, 1916

I appreciate to the full the importance of the vocational education bill, but in considering a programme for the session it was a mere question of what is *possible* and I put in the things which I felt must be dealt with without any delay. There is always something of capital importance from which we must turn away and it is always an effort to do so, but surely we shall have filled the time at our disposal so full of action that we cannot be exposed to just criticism.[1]

                    Cordially and sincerely yours,   Woodrow Wilson

TLS (Letterpress Books, WP, DLC).
    [1] The Senate did consider the Smith-Hughes bill in July and passed it on July 31. However, the House did not act upon it until January 9, 1917. After a conference committee had reconciled the differences in the House and Senate versions, Wilson signed the bill on February 23, 1917.

To Claude Kitchin

My dear Mr. Kitchin: [The White House] March 27, 1916

In considering the programme of the session there are two matters which seem to me to stand out more prominently than the rest as matters in which time presses, even though they should not be deemed to take precedence in intrinsic importance. It would seem as if the whole movement of our trade and industry waited on satisfactory solutions of our problems of transportation. That is the reason why it seems to me that the shipping bill should be pressed to an early passage, and I write today to express the hope that the Senate Joint Resolution No. 60, for the investigation of the conditions of transportation by railway, may find an early opening in the business of the House for its consideration. I did not put this on the list of legislation which I suggested because it did not in my mind fall under the head of legislation at all but only of incidental action for the purpose of laying the groundwork for future legislation at another session of the Congress.

The railways of the country are becoming more and more the key to its successful industry and it seems to me of capital importance that we should lay a new groundwork of actual fact for the necessary future regulation. I know that we all want to be absolutely fair to the railroads, and it seems to me that the proposed investigation is the first step towards the fulfillment of that desire.

I hope that you will agree with me that this important matter can be dispensed of without putting any spoke in the wheels that we are now trying to make go around in the matter of legislation.

                    Cordially and sincerely yours,   Woodrow Wilson

TLS (Letterpress Books, WP, DLC).

A Tribute

March 27, 1916.

The death of Tom Pence[1] has brought to all who knew him, and to all whom he so loyally and earnestly served, not only the deepest grief but a sense of irreparable loss. Few finer spirits have ever connected themselves with public service. He had very great ability and he devoted that ability to the promotion of the things he thought were right with a singular devotion and self-forgetfulness. I feel that every man who desired the public good has lost a partner, and that the Democratic party in losing him as Secretary of its National Committee has suffered a loss which it may not be possible to repair at all.

T MS (WP, DLC).
[1] Pence had died at 3:30 A.M. on March 27. Wilson visited his apartment to extend condolences to his family at 7:45 P.M.

To Thornton Whaling[1]

My dear Doctor Whaling: [The White House] March 27, 1916

I am sorry to say you have been misinformed as to the possibility of my visiting Columbia in the near future.[2] I wish that such a pleasure were in store for me, but my duties here are too exacting and too uninterrupted.

I would be very much pleased if you would let me know when you are about to come North. I should enjoy seeing you for a little while as you pass through.

In haste
        Cordially and sincerely yours,   Woodrow Wilson

TLS (Letterpress Books, WP, DLC).
[1] President of Columbia Theological Seminary.
[2] Whaling's letter is missing.

From Robert Lansing

PERSONAL AND CONFIDENTIAL:

My dear Mr. President: Washington March 27, 1916.

All the information which we are receiving in regard to the sinking of the SUSSEX in the English Channel, by which several Americans were injured and some undoubtedly killed, indicates that the vessel was torpedoed by a German submarine.[1] If this information is corroborated as the investigation proceeds it will present a very serious situation in our relations with Germany.

I think we should determine what course should be taken in the event that the evidence points very strongly to the culpability of the Germans.

Every effort undoubtedly will be made by the Allies to prove that the vessel was torpedoed, and I believe that they will make a strong case, judging from the telegrams we have thus far received. On the other hand, I feel sure that the German Government will deny the charge and assert that a floating mine of English origin caused the disaster. There will be thus a flat contradiction of statements as to the facts.

I do not believe that the Government can remain inactive because of this contradictory evidence. There will be a strong demand that something should be done and, personally, I would be disposed to view such a demand as justifiable.

The argument which will meet with general favor will be that the sinking of the SUSSEX is similar to that of the sinking of other vessels in the last few days, and is a direct result of the greater activity of submarines, in accordance with the new German policy which went into effect March first; and that even if the evidence of torpedoing was absent the presumption raised by the announced policy of Germany and the submarine attacks of the past ten days makes it almost certain that the vessel was torpedoed.

Assuming that Germany will fail to establish conclusively the innocence of her submarine commanders I do not see how we can avoid taking some decisive steps. We can no longer temporize in the matter of submarine warfare when Americans are being killed, wounded, or endangered by the illegal and inhuman conduct of the Germans.

Of one thing I am firmly convinced and that is that the time for writing notes discussing the subject has passed. Whatever we determine to do must be in the line of action and it must indicate in no uncertain terms that the present method of submarine warfare can no longer be tolerated.

Proceeding on the assumption that the SUSSEX was torpedoed the action which seems to me the most practicable would be to demand the immediate recall of Count Bernstorff and the severence of diplomatic relations with Germany. This action might be made conditional upon the German Government unequivocally admitting the illegality of submarine warfare in general, paying a just indemnity for the Americans killed and injured, and guaranteeing that the present method of warfare will cease. Such a conditional admission would be in the nature of an ultimatum which could very properly include a time limit at the expiration of which, in case of failure to comply with the conditions, Count von Bernstorff could be given his passports.

I realize that this action is drastic but I believe that to be patient longer would be misconstrued both at home and abroad. We have already shown in the case of the LUSITANIA an earnest desire to avoid trouble with Germany and now, after ten months of negotiations and on the eve of an amicable settlement, Germany has renewed the method of warfare against which we so strongly protested. In these circumstances I do not see how we can avoid the issue and remain inactive. The honor of the United States and the duty of the Government to its citizens require firm and decisive action.

While I have advanced these views on an assumption as to the sinking of the SUSSEX I think that the assumption will be justified. Doubtless the German Government would view the breaking off of diplomatic relations as an unfriendly act and might possibly go so far as to declare war against the United States, yet, with the probable consequences fully in mind, I can see no other course open to us. The case arises at a most unfortunate time in view of the state of our Mexican affairs and also in view of the proposed treaty which is receiving the consideration of the Danish Government. If we could, consistently with the dignity of the United States and our duty as a Government, delay action I would favor delay, but, in view of all the facts, if the assumption of German responsibility is established, I do not believe a long delay is possible.

Faithfully yours,   Robert Lansing.

TLS (WP, DLC).
¹ *Sussex*, a Channel packet, British-owned but flying the French flag, was torpedoed by *UB29*, Commander Pustkuchen, on March 24. *Sussex* did not sink. About eighty passengers were killed or injured. Four Americans were injured, none killed. Among the passengers was the late Samuel Flagg Bemis, Sterling Professor of History at Yale University for many years, and one of the first members of the Editorial Advisory Committee of *The Papers of Woodrow Wilson*.

From Edward Parker Davis

My dear Woodrow   [Philadelphia] March 27 1916

Eleanor Sayre weighed 7 lbs. 12 ounces. She is a beautifully formed baby, and vigorous. Soon after her arrival she looked around for her Grandfather! and hopes to see you soon.

Mother and Baby are doing well today.

I am doing what I can for Mrs. Howe: she is fairly well.

Affectionately Yours,   E P Davis.

ALS (WP, DLC).

To Charles Herbert Levermore

My dear Levermore: [The White House] March 28, 1916

Thank you for your letter of March twenty-fourth. I need not tell you my own personal attitude towards the suggestion made in the declaration you submitted to a member of Congress, but I am bound to tell you that I think it would be a mistake at this time to make any such declaration; a mistake, not because it would misinterpret the attitude of the country, but because one of the things that the belligerents are most resentful of at present is systematic suggestion from this side of the water as to what shall follow the war. It would not set forward, but rather delay, the objects you have in mind.[1]

Always   Faithfully yours,   Woodrow Wilson

TLS (Letterpress Books, WP, DLC).

[1] Actually, much of the substance of Levermore's "Declaration of Policy" was embodied in a rider to the naval appropriations bill known as the Hensley Resolution. Hensley first offered it to the House Committee on Naval Affairs on May 18, 1916, which approved it in order to appease the "small navy" members of that committee. In its final form, the rider declared that it was the policy of the United States to settle international disputes through mediation or arbitration, to the end that war might be honorably avoided. The United States also looked "with apprehension and disfavor" upon the general increase of armaments throughout the world, but it realized that no nation could unilaterally disarm. The rider then went on to authorize and request the President, "at an appropriate time, not later than the close of the war in Europe," to invite all the great governments of the world to send delegates to a conference which should be charged with the duty of formulating a plan for a "court of arbitration or other tribunal," to which disputed questions between nations should be referred for adjudication and peaceful settlement, and "to consider the question of disarmament." The Hensley rider authorized the President to appoint nine persons to the conference and appropriated $200,000 for their salaries and expenses. The rider concluded:

"If at any time before the construction authorized by this Act shall have been contracted for there shall have been established, with the cooperation of the United States of America, an international tribunal or tribunals competent to secure peaceful determinations of all international disputes, and which shall render unnecessary the maintenance of competitive armaments, then and in that case such naval expenditures as may be inconsistent with the engagements made in the establishment of such tribunal or tribunals may be suspended, when so ordered by the President of the United States." 39 *Statutes at Large*, 618.

To William Joel Stone

My dear Senator: [The White House] March 28, 1916

I have read your letter of March twenty-fifth with the greatest interest and feel very keenly the point of it all.

The present moral seems to me to be that we should push forward with the greatest zeal such action as is involved in the pending shipping bill, and that we should seek every opportunity to correct the mistakes that we have made in the past in absolutely neglecting the machinery of international commerce both in the fields of shipping and international credit. These things once arranged, our business men ought to organize their wits in such a way as to take possession of foreign markets with the same degree of intelligence and persistency that have marked their German and English rivals.

I do not mean to imply that this is the whole of the story but it is, at any rate, the beginning of it.

Cordially and faithfully yours,   Woodrow Wilson

TLS (Letterpress Books, WP, DLC).

From the Diary of Colonel House

The White House, Washington [March 28, 1916]

When we arrived at the White House the President was golfing, but I had an immediate conference with Frank Polk. We discussed the foreign situation and also the domestic as far as it bears upon other countries. He cautioned me about Lansing. He said Lansing has a high regard for me, but he saw some evidence of pique the last time I was over, because I was attending to matters which were entirely within his province. Lansing said the President should consult him more or, at least, let him know in advance of decisions.

It seems when the President wrote the letter to Senator Stone, Chairman of the Foreign Relations Committee, the first Lansing knew of it was when he read it in the papers. I spoke to the President about this and asked him to be careful. He was not inclined to pay any attention to it, and said Lansing must understand that he, himself, was conducting foreign affairs, and he would do it in the way he thought best.

In connection with the President's request that I button up the South American Pact, which has been allowed to drag interminably, I thought Lansing would resent it, but the President was determined that I should do it anyway. We had only a few minutes before dinner, and agreed to postpone a more detailed discussion of affairs until tomorrow. We talked enough, however, for me to fathom what was in his mind, and from the way he looked at me, I am inclined to believe that he intends making excuses for not acting promptly in this new submarine crisis forced upon him by the sinking of the Sussex. He evidently does not wish to back up his former notes to Germany upon this subject. He does not seem to realize that one of the main points of criticism against him is that he talks boldly but acts weakly. It would be better to talk weakly and act boldly.

The President had to go to a Press banquet[1] at half past seven o'clock and return later to attend the musicale which was being given at the White House. I started to bed at half past nine, when the musicale began, but before I could succeed in getting under cover, Burleson came to my room and was followed later by Gregory and they remained until half past eleven. The President had told Burleson he would not appoint Johnson Postmaster of New York until after he discussed it with me again, and Burleson was trying to convince me it was the best thing that could be done. I did not argue with him because Burleson could never understand the reasons why Johnson should not be appointed.

¹ Wilson went to the Raleigh Hotel for the annual dinner of the Evening Star Club, an organization of newspapermen.

From Benjamin Ryan Tillman

My dear Mr. President: [Washington] March 29, 1916.

I believe, and I have reason for that belief, that if you will write Claude Kitchin a letter expressing the wish that he expedite the armor bill as much as possible, and as an *independent proposition*, he will move actively and get the Rules Committee to bring in a special rule for its consideration and induce the Naval Committee in the House to report it so that it can be considered.

There is a fearful fight against it, you know, and having passed the Senate so promptly and with such an overwhelming majority, it would be a pity—I would consider it a crime almost— if it doesn't become a law. Promptness will save much money.

You asked me to tell you "How." I have found that this is the way to "turn the trick."

Yours faithfully and sincerely,   B. R. Tillman

TLS (WP, DLC).

From Wesley Norwood Jones¹

My dear Mr. President: Raleigh, N. C. March 29, 1916.

I desire to express to you for my family and myself our grateful appreciation of your kindness to my late nephew, Thos. J. Pence, during the past three or four years, and especially during the period of his illness; and also to thank you for the tribute you paid to him upon his death.

I am sure that Tom loved you with the love of a genuine affection; and that in health he found in you the source of inspiration to the larger aims and endeavors of his life, while in sickness your gracious attentions gave him much comfort and consolation.

It is good to reflect, now that he is gone, that he knew what it was to have so many friends and that amongst them he found such an one as yourself.

Assuring you that my family and myself shall ever hold in grateful remembrance what you were to Tom, and what you have done for him, I beg, Mr. President, to remain,

Very truly yours,   W. N. Jones.

TLS (WP, DLC).
   [1] Lawyer of Raleigh, N.C.

From Hiram Woods, Jr.

Dear Tommy: Baltimore, March 29, 1916.

I was very sorry to be away from Charlie's house when you called there last Saturday.[1] I arrived a few minutes after you had gone. It is a great pleasure to say that we are again quite confident of his ultimate recovery, unless some more complication ensues.

I hate bothering you with official matters, but it is practically impossible to avoid sending the enclosed.[2] I have never heard of the young man who wants the Consular appointment, but feel his Uncle's judgment of his ability is probably correct and sincere: all of which may or may not appeal to you.

Affectionately Yours,   Hiram Woods

ALS (WP, DLC).
   [1] Wilson had driven to Baltimore during the afternoon of March 25.
   [2] It is missing, but it was a letter from Philemon H. Tuck to Woods concerning the appointment of Somerville Pinkney Tuck, Jr., to the consular service. See W. Phillips to WW, April 5, 1916, TLS (WP, DLC).

From the Diary of Colonel House

March 29, 1916.

The President, Cleve Dodge and I talked for about a half hour after breakfast mainly upon general topics. The President and I agreed to have an executive session at six o'clock and to continue after dinner as long as necessary. This gave me the day fairly free.

I saw Burleson again in the morning. With him it was the inevitable postmastership of New York and his version of the Mexican crisis which I recorded when Gregory told me of it last week.

Frank Polk came and remained for nearly an hour. The President asked me this morning whether I still thought of Polk for National Chairman. I said I had not changed my mind as to his availability, but I hoped he would say nothing of [it] to anyone for if he did, there would be much confusion and disagreement. Polk is not keen to accept the undertaking but is willing to do so if my judgment approves. I convinced him that he and McAdoo thought more alike than he and some of the others around the President and with whom he was far more likely to clash.

Neither the President, Lansing, Polk nor I can understand the new submarine activity by the Germans. Bernstorff has not come near the State Department, and from all we can learn, he is not worried in the slightest. . . .

Immediately after lunch, Lansing and I went into executive session. We first took up the New York situation and found that we did not disagree at all as to men or measures. I had suggested to the President this morning that ex-Governor Glynn should be made Temporary Chairman of the Saint Louis Convention.[1] The President brought up the subject by saying that Burleson had suggested Champ Clark, and he wished to know what I thought of it. I did not think well of it. Clark is not amenable to suggestions and the man who makes the keynote speech should be one for whom it could be written, either in part or in whole.

After we finished the New York situation we took up foreign affairs. He showed me the latest despatches regarding submarine attacks upon the Sussex, Englishman[2] and other boats. He read a letter he had written the President concerning the controversy in which he strongly advised sending Bernstorff home and breaking relations with Germany. His letter was calm and met with my approval, provided the subsequent facts justified his desires.

We both believe the President will be exceedingly reluctant to back up his own threats.

Lansing drove me to the White House where I had some minor engagements. At six o'clock the President and I went into another session. We discussed the coming campaign as to men and measures. We decided upon Morganthau's resignation and his substitute.[3] I favored Brand Whitlock but feared his health was not up to it. The President gave his estimate of Willard.[4] He does not think as well of him as I do. He said Willard always

[1] The Democratic National Convention of 1916.

[2] *Englishman*, a Dominion Line horse ship bound for Portland, Me., was torpedoed after leaving Avonmouth, England, on March 21. Several Americans among the crew were killed.

[3] Abram Isaac Elkus, lawyer of New York. He was nominated on July 21, 1916, and confirmed by the Senate on the same day.

[4] That is, Joseph Edward Willard, Ambassador to Spain.

seemed to regard the perfectly obvious as something new, which no mind had hitherto worked out.

We then took up the foreign situation. I explained what I had planned regarding the membership of the proposed peace conference, that is, the prime minister and foreign minister to be the only ones to attend from belligerent countries, and that members from neutral nations should be confined to ministers for foreign affairs. In other words, the belligerents should have two representatives and the neutrals should have one member each.

The President asked how this could be regulated since we would have nothing to do with arrangements for the peace conference. I expressed a belief that if he would let me undertake it, I could bring it about. I suggested himself as the only member from the United States. No other I thought would be necessary. I outlined what I wrote in the diary the other day concerning the staff we should have around us.[5] This seemed to please him, and make him more comfortable over the situation.

He is determined not to intervene in Mexico. He even goes so far as to say that he will address Congress demanding that in no circumstances shall we intervene at this particular time, because of the foreign situation, and because the enemies of the United States so ardently desire it.

I was glad to hear him say that he was pleased with Newton Baker. I had heard some pleasant things from other members of the administration concerning him and these I repeated to the President. Polk, who has considerable to do with the War Department, gave it as his opinion that Baker would make a better Secretary of War than Garrison, since Garrison was away so much of his time and depended almost wholly upon his staff for advice.

No one outside the family were at dinner. After dinner we went into the sitting-room upstairs and I asked the President if he had read A. G. Gardiner's sketch of him in the London News which I had sent him about a week ago.[6] I asked him to get it and read it aloud. When he finished, everybody commented upon the brilliancy with which Gardiner had written, and of the complimentary way in which he had brought forth the best features of the President's policy. The President smiled and said:

[5] "I shall try to have an effective organization to help influence members of the conference toward proper solutions of the problems before them, urging this country to give way here, and that country to give way there. I have this force pretty well picked out in my mind now. I should want to have information just as available as if I were in a library with every book at my command, excepting the information would be immediately obtainable through people instead of through books." The Diary of Colonel House, March 19, 1916.

[6] See EMH to WW, March 15, 1916, n. 1.

"I seem to see something of the Colonel's fine Italian hand in this article."

We finished this and went into his study and again took up our work and continued it until half past nine o'clock, when he had to leave for a Red Cross function[7] which he had promised to attend.

I asked him what had been done about the Pan-American Pact. He said he was continually prodding Lansing, but somehow or other he could not get him to move with celerity. I suggested that the Germans and others interested in keeping the pact from materializing had something to do with the delay. He admitted this, but thought it should be pressed to a conclusion, even if Chile and Brazil should not at the moment consent.

Chile, it seems, does not wish to subscribe to the clause "guaranteeing republican form of government" alleging that it restricts her to what form of government she shall have. The President and Lansing thought and suggested to Chile that a clause could be inserted by which, if she desired to adopt a monarchical form of government, she could withdraw from the pact. I did not approve this. I thought we should insist on their agreeing to the clause as it is. In my opinion, it is better for Chile to remain out than to have the entire pact spoiled by a tacit admission that any republic in the Western Hemisphere might at some future time desire a monarchical form of government.

The President again insisted upon my taking hold of the matter regardless of Lansing's sensibilities. He said no man's feelings must stand in the way of such important work. Gardiner's eulogy of him for having put this Pan-American Pact into motion, evidently stirred him. As a matter of fact, Gardiner had merely repeated in that part of his article what I had told him, and had given my estima[t]e of its importance.

The President does not seem to me to be up to the mark. In discussing the New York Postmastership, he surprised me by frankly confessing that he would like to appoint Johnson because it would please Murphy, and Murphy could help him carry out some beneficent legislation and help in other directions where he thought needful. For instance, he said, he thought it desirable that Fitzgerald should not be re-elected to Congress, as he was detrimental to the public service. Murphy could accomplish this if he desired. I was silent, and he knew I disapproved. He therefore asked me the direct question whether I thought his reasoning sound. I replied that I did not; that he could accomplish Fitzgerald's defeat himself without the help of Tammany. I told

[7] A ball sponsored by the Red Cross at Rauscher's restaurant.

him Tammany was not to be trusted; that they had no desire whatever for his re-election; that they were playing for position in order to re-elect a Tammany man Mayor of New York in Mitchel's place a year from now; that the national and state situations were unimportant to them in comparison with the City, for it was there that the loot lay.

He still clung to the belief that it was wise to appoint Johnson, affirming Burleson declared he was the best man that had been brought before him. Johnson was honest, he was able, he was not a Catholic, which was desired by the Protestants.

The President appeared almost more interested and absorbed in these local situations than by the foreign crisis. I myself am so little interested in them that I talk of them with reluctance, and it is immaterial to me whom he appoints. Ordinarily, I should insist that he should not appoint one of Murphy's henchmen, but it seems so insignificant compared with the vital questions now on the boards, that I find myself not caring what he does so he drops it from our discussions.

There is another thing I cannot bring the President to realize, and that is the importance of making ready to meet the crisis which may fall upon him any day. He was compelled to go into Mexico at a moment's notice. The same will happen in the European situation, and yet, we are as inert as if it were a remote possibility of some future age. I have urged him ever since the war began to make ready, and we are no more ready today than we were two years ago. For the first time the depletion of the army is beginning to be filled, and this only because of the chase after Villa, and the consequent realization that we have no army worth speaking of. I tried to get him to do this last summer, and I tried to get him almost a year before the war began to pay attention to the army as this diary will show.

To Robert Lansing

My dear Mr. Secretary,   The White House. 30 March, 1916.
        I have your letter of the twenty-seventh in which you state your preliminary impressions about the SUSSEX Case. My impressions are not quite the same. The proof that the disaster was caused by a torpedo seems to me by no means satisfactory or conclusive. And, if it was caused by a torpedo, there are many particulars to be considered about the course we should pursue as well as the principle of it. The steps we take and the way we take them will, it seems to me, be of the essence of the mat-

ter if we are to keep clearly and indisputably within the lines we have already set ourselves.

But in this, as in other matters referred to in the papers I am now sending back to you, a personal conference is much the best means of reaching conclusions. We must have one very soon.

Faithfully Yours,   W.W.

WWTLI (SDR, RG 59, 851.857 SU 8/54½, DNA).

To Robert Lansing

My dear Mr. Secretary,   The White House. 30 March, 1916.

I have read these proposals[1] with a great deal of interest, of course. We must have an oral conference about them. Perhaps there are concessions in line with their suggestions which we could make, always assuming that it were agreed that they should not apply to the present expedition.[2]

I shall try to make an early appointment to confer with you.

Faithfully Yours,   W.W.

WWTLI (SDR, RG 59, 812.00/17713½, DNA).

[1] A slightly different version of the draft protocol summarized in F. L. Polk to WW, March 20, 1916, n. 2. E. Arredondo to RL, March 27, 1916, TLS (SDR, RG 59, 812.00/17650½, DNA).

[2] Lansing prepared a revision of Arredondo's draft protocol which repeated many of Arredondo's provisions. However, Lansing's version eliminated Arredondo's provision limiting the stay of the pursuing force to eight days, "unless its aid be solicited," and substituted the following: "In no case shall the pursuing force establish itself or remain in foreign territory for any time longer than is necessary to enable it to pursue the band which it is following." CC MS (SDR, RG 59, 812.00/17713½, DNA).

Lansing sent his revised draft to Arredondo on April 4. RL to E. Arredondo, April 4, 1916, CCL (SDR, RG 59, 812.00/17650½, DNA). Lansing included a second letter (RL to E. Arredondo, April 3, 1916, FR 1916, pp. 507- 508), which Wilson had undoubtedly seen and approved and which reads as follows:

"The Government of the United States, in entering into the reciprocal agreement with the de facto Government of Mexico relative to the pursuit of lawless bands across the international boundary by the military forces of the respective Governments, does so on the understanding that the conditions imposed by that agreement are not to be applied to the forces of the United States now in Mexico in pursuit of Villa and his bandits who attacked and burned Columbus, New Mexico, killing a number of American citizens, the said forces having in good faith entered Mexico under a previous agreement which arose out of the outrage perpetrated by outlaws at Columbus on March 9th.

"The Government of the United States assures the de facto Government of Mexico that, in exercising the privilege of entry upon Mexican territory, it will confine the operations of its military forces to the sole object of the present pursuit, and that immediately upon its accomplishment they will be withdrawn across the international boundary.

"The Government of the United States takes this opportunity to express its gratification at the consideration and friendliness shown by the de facto Government in entering into the previous agreement by which military forces of the United States are permitted to pursue Villa and his band into Mexican territory, and desires to assure the de facto Government that the Government of the United States will respect the confidence thus exhibited and in no way violate the sovereignty of Mexico or abuse the privilege so generously and freely granted by the de facto Government."

From Robert Lansing, with Enclosure

PERSONAL AND CONFIDENTIAL:

My dear Mr. President: [Washington] March 30, 1916.

I send you herewith the translation of an identical memorandum which was received a few days ago by this Government from the Ambassadors of France, Great Britain, Italy and Russia, and the Minister of Belgium.[1] The memorandum is in reply to the letter of January 18 in reference to the disarmament of merchant vessels.

I also enclose a proposed answer to be sent to each of the Ambassadors and the Minister. I would be obliged if you would let me know if this answer meets with your approval. I assume that it will close the incident.

Faithfully yours,   Robert Lansing

CCL (SDR, RG 59, 763.72/2522, DNA).
    [1] It is printed as C. A. Spring Rice to RL, March 23, 1916, in *FR-WWS 1916*, pp. 211-12.

E N C L O S U R E

Robert Lansing to Jean Jules Jusserand

My dear Mr. Ambassador: [Washington] April 7, 1916.

I have received your courteous letter of the 22d ultimo and given careful consideration to the Memorandum enclosed relating to the proposal for an agreement to disarm merchant vessels by the Entente Powers, which I unofficially submitted to you in my letter of January 18, 1916.

The proposal was made with the humane purpose of removing the principal reason given by the German and Austro-Hungarian Governments for the failure of their submarines to comply strictly with the rules of naval warfare in intercepting the merchant vessels of their enemies on the high seas, a practice which has resulted in an appalling loff [loss] of life among the passengers and crews of vessels which have been attacked without warning.

Believing that an arrangement, such as I had the honor to propose, would have resulted in the discontinuance by Germany and Austria-Hungary of a method of attack on merchant vessels which puts in jeopardy the lives of hundreds of men, women and children of neutral as well as belligerent nationality, I cannot but regret that the Governments of the Entente Powers could not see their way to accede to the proposal.

The Entente Governments having, however, reached a decision

to decline the proposed arrangement, it becomes my duty to accept their decision as final, and in the spirit in which they have made it.

I am, my dear Mr. Ambassador,

Very sincerely yours,   Robert Lansing

CCL (SDR, RG 59, 763.72/2522, DNA).

To Robert Lansing

My dear Mr. Secretary,   The White House. 30 March, 1916.

There are several reasons why I think it would not be wise to send a reply of exactly this sort to these governments; but it would be very unsatisfactory to set them forth in a letter. I would like the pleasure of an early conference with you, on this an[d] one or two other pending matters. No doubt we can agree upon a time when I see you at the meeting of the Cabinet to-morrow.

Faithfully Yours,   W.W.

WWTLI (SDR, RG 59, 763.72/2638½, DNA).

To Edward Parker Davis

My dear E. P.:   [The White House] March 30, 1916

Thank you for the little note about Eleanor Sayre. It is fine to know that Jessie is in such hands and that everything is going well. I long to see the dear girl and the little baby and wish with all my heart that things would let up here a little so that I might run over. Please give my love to the dear girl, and believe me

Gratefully yours,   Woodrow Wilson

TLS (Letterpress Books, WP, DLC).

From Walter Hines Page

Dear Mr. President: London, March 30, 1916

I write under the shadow of the "Sussex" disaster, and I have telegraphed you and the Department so fully that there is left little to write. Nor do I take it that there is need to restate again the condition of public feeling towards us here—certainly not at any great length.

But I could not exaggerate its ominous quality for the future. I hope that I have made it plain that *primarily* English opinion does not show any eagerness for us to come into the war for the

help we shd. give the Allies, great as that help wd. be and gratefully as it wd. be received. It isn't their need of help that rests on
their minds, for they rightly feel assured of victory and they
believe that the beginning of the end has come. But they feel a
deep disappointment in us—that we took a righteous stand in the
Lusitania controversy and have (as they see it) been inveigled
into inaction for well-nigh a year; that the Germans have caused
us to submit to delay so long that delay is equivalent to surrender;
that, tho' Bernstorff has outdone all ambassadors on record in the
extent and impropriety of his activities, he is still tolerated—in a
word, as the English think, we are become a peace-at-any-price
conglomeration of folk—no longer a people with the English love
of freedom and a willingness to fight for it. They have, therefore,
made up their minds that we can be of no use for any virile action
—the bringing of peace, or the maintaining of it, because we are
so divided and so "soft" that, when action is required, we do not
even keep our own pledge, made of our own volition.

I believe that this is a fair (and surely a moderate) statement
of English feeling—a feeling of profound disappointment. We
continue to regard the German Gov't as an honorable gov't; we
(*i.e.* the Administration) permit its Ambassador to do with impunity what no other Ambassador was ever permitted to do. They
think that the real "stuff" has gone out of us, and that in time
both Japan and Germany will put this nation to a test. And the
English regard our possible usefulness as a champion of right or
freedom as gone: they can't depend on us. In some minds this
feeling takes the form of bitterness. In most minds, it takes the
form of disappointment or of pity. Instead of regarding us as
partners in the furthering of civilization, as they did two years
ago, they regard us as having fallen aside.

The story is going about London that the editor of the *Providence Journal*[1] has information about Bernstorff, which would
inflame the public and compel his dimissal and that he has withheld it because the Administration requested him to withhold it.
I do not know who is meant by "the Administration." I am afraid
that this story will get into print, for some of the journalists here
surely know it. I think the King had heard it; for, when I took
luncheon with him a few weeks ago, he began to talk of Bernstorff
and he said: "He wishd. to be sent here as Ambassador but we
declined to receive him."

The *Sussex* outrage has raised the silent hope among our best
friends here that Bernstorff will be dismissed. But nobody, I
think, believes that the breaking off of diplomatic relations wd.
lead to war. They regard that threat as a bit of German bluff.

But, if it shd. lead to war, the war wd. probably end before we cd. put a man in the field. The feeling here is that Germany will go to the extreme limit to avoid war with us, because she wishes, when peace comes, to have the U. S. as a friendly financial and commercial field. She'll have no such large friendly field in Europe.

If diplomatic relations are cut off because of the *Sussex*, of course there will be some revision of this dismal, disappointed, and disappointing opinion of us.

I fear, Mr. President, that this whole letter is a dismal one. But you may be sure that it is a true one. I especially commend to you for a report of what he found here, a very able and honest man—Mr. Strong, the President of the Reserve Bank in New York, who is going home, I think, on the ship that will carry this letter. He has done a remarkable piece of work here, and he has discovered English opinion with unusual accuracy. Of course the British Government continues to treat me with the utmost courtesy. Sir Edward Grey, who understands our difficulties as few Englishmen do, is unchanging in his friendly and sympathetic attitude. But I am afraid that indications are not lacking that other parts of the Government (and surely the public) regard us less and less. There is a persistent rumor that Sir Edw. will give way to Lord Hardinge[2] as soon as Lord Hardinge can get home from India. I do not know him; but I cannot contemplate such a change without some misgiving. Sir Edw. as Foreign Secretary has been a providential kindness to us. It is sometimes rumored, too, that Curzon may become Foreign Secretary. God deliver us! I do know *him*.

But if it shd. be possible and you shd. think it wise to sever relations with Germany and if the Germans shd. take the next step and bring a real breach, we shd. thereby make the greatest contribution to peace that any nation ever made in any war. We shd. probably save 1,000,000 lives and immeasurable treasure, and we shd. put ourselves in the position of being the savior of Europe in the hour of Europe's greatest stress and need—provided such a succession of events come quickly.

If my memory of the American Fathers be correct—over a good many years since I read them—they had high hopes that Europe wd., nation after nation, long before this, follow our example and uncrown their Kings and dispossess their hereditary privileged classes—become real democracies. In spite of the growth of liberalism, this hope has been disappointed. No real Democrat can come to know even this Kingdom, to say nothing of most continental countries, without a deep sadness at the slowness of the change. Jefferson wd. not believe his own senses if he cd. see how little change has come—anywhere.

In Germany he wd. see a sterner and more ruthless absolutism that [than] Frederick's, because the docile people have, by the most curious reversion in all history, accepted absolutism as freedom. So much for the slow pace of democracy in the past—so slow that it is now engaged in the hardest fight it ever had, for its very existence. One wd. say that its pace, after this war, will be quickened: it is the people rather than their masters who are winning it. But much will depend for the good credit of democracy, upon where *we* stand when the war closes. As matters now are, Allied Europe has a gathering fear that an absolute democracy, such as ours, permits the sense of nationality to be dissipated and national virility to decay.

God grant it may not be so!

Yours, my dear Mr. President,

Always faithfully   Walter H. Page

ALS (WP, DLC).
  [1] That is, John R. Rathom.
  [2] Charles Hardinge, Baron Hardinge of Penshurst, Viceroy of India, 1910-16.

From the Diary of Colonel House

March 30, 1916.

I called for E. S. Martin and took him to the Department of Agriculture where we had some talk with Secretary Houston. Senator Newlands was there and it was agreed that Newlands, Houston, Senator Stone and I should get together upon my next visit to Washington and talk of foreign affairs. They are all deeply interested in them and desire to hear something of my trip.

From there I went to call on Senator Culberson at his apartment. I feel I should see Culberson each time I go to Washington on account of his physical condition. I took him to the Senate and then drove to the French Embassy.

Jusserand and I talked for nearly an hour. He was gratified at having received from his Government a memorandum of what I had done in Paris, and my estimate of him. Jusserand believes if our plan is carried out it will be under great difficulties. He does not believe the American people will quite rise to the occasion. He thinks, however, it would be a mistake if the United States should fail to actively take part, or at least cooperate, with the Allies for the purposes we have in mind.[1]

And this reminds me that in the recent conferences of the Allies in Paris,[2] the French used their best endeavor toward getting concessions for the American position in regard to certain trade matters. This is in line with what they promised when I was in France.[3]

I returned to the White House at five minutes of one o'clock to find the Director of the Mint[4] and Thompson[5] of the Department of Justice waiting for me. I had gotten the President to consent to speak at the banquet which the Common Council Club is to give on Jefferson's birthday,[6] and they desired an additional concession from the President that he would talk over the telephone to the banquets to be given by democrats throughout the Nation.

After lunch the President and I went into executive session again. I put the matter of our controversy with Germany quite strongly to him. He was afraid if we broke off relations the war would go on indefinitely and there would be no one to lead the way out. He was repeating the argument I have been giving him for the last six months and somewhat to my embarrassment. I told him, however, I had thought of another way by which we could lead them out even though we were in.

I suggested that when he sent von Bernstorff home, he should make a dispassionate statement of the cause of the war and what the Allies were fighting for. I suggested that he should say nothing unkind of the German people but should strike at the system which had caused this world tragedy, and contend, when that was righted, the quarrel with Germany, as far as we were concerned, would be ended. Then I thought at the right time, which would perhaps be by mid-summer, I could go to Holland and after a conference with the Allies, and with their consent, I could open negotiations directly with Berlin, telling them upon what terms we were ready to end the war.

I thought the same arrangement could then be carried out I had planned; that is, he should preside over the conference and we should take part. This would make our participation more effective than as a neutral, and we could do greater and better work in this way than we could in the way we planned.

He was visibly pleased at my suggestion and I believe will now be more inclined to act. What I tried to impress upon him was, that he would soon lose the confidence of the American people, and also of the Allies, and would fail to have any influence at the peace conference. I tried to make him see that we would lose the respect of the world unless he lived up to the demands he has made of Germany regarding her undersea warfare.

He promised to come to New York April 15th to make a short

talk to the Young Men's Democratic Club,[7] an invitation extended through me. I did this at Gordon's insistence.

Mrs. Wilson told Loulie that she wished we would come to Washington to live, and said she was sorry I did not remain longer and be with the President more. She also expressed to me her lack of confidence in Lansing's judgment, saying he had gotten the President into two or three bad situations. I excused him as best I could by saying the times were so critical that it was difficult not to make mistakes.

Frank Polk and Dudley Malone were waiting when the President and I finished. The President desired me to see Bernstorff and say to him that we were at the breaking point and that we would surely go into the war unless some decisive change was made in their submarine policy.[8]

Polk said Bernstorff had returned to Washington, but he would let me know when he was going to New York again. He was doubtful as to the expediency of my seeing him. He read me some letters and reports of conversations of some of the German Embassy staff with their lady friends, which have been obtained through our Secret Service. It seems that from the Ambassador down they have affinities, and with the tapped wires, the Secret Service Corps keep in touch with all their activities. I have never approved of such methods of obtaining information even in wartime.

[1] Jusserand's report of this conversation (J. J. Jusserand to A. Briand, No. 261, March 31, 1916, TLS [La Guerre, 1914-1918, États-Unis, Vol. 500, pp. 44-46, FFM-Ar]) follows (our translation):

"During the brief visit he just made to Washington, Colonel House wished to see me, and I received a long visit from him at the embassy. He expressed to me emphatically the views he had already expressed in the presence of Your Excellency and Mr. Jules Cambon, and which, consequently, it is not necessary to repeat here. He added that, upon his return, he had rendered a faithful account of them to the President, who had fully approved and ratified his statements, including his assertion that the United States, in perhaps the not too distant future, would take an active part in the war.

"In my responses, I elaborated two sets of ideas. First, that it would be in the interest of the United States itself, as well as of the world, if things turned out as he said. The moment of anguish will come one day for the United States, as it has come for other countries. If it happens at that moment that it has taken no one's side in the present great crisis, no one will take its side then. There is an opportunity now, which will not be repeated, for the United States to make friends for itself, and it can do so without taking risks in any way comparable to those that we run. That hypothesis aside, filled as we are with gratitude for the sympathies we have encountered here, we will show ours in like manner: supplies of arms, loans, etc. But otherwise the Allies would remain spectators in case of a crisis in the New World which, besides, could not have the same importance as the present crisis for the future of humanity; it is the survival of liberalism in the world which is at stake. Should we lose, it would not survive, not even here.

"But then, again, is this country really disposed to intervene? The national spirit, once so strong in the United States, has attenuated greatly under the enormous influx of immigration. No longer does the bell peal forth a pure sound, so much has its metal been alloyed. The other day, it was only thanks to a parliamentary finesse that a bill, contrary to the views of the President, was defeated which would have forbidden Americans to travel on armed merchant vessels. What is more, the country is getting used to German crimes. Its violent indignations at the beginning of the war not having been followed by results, it is less and less moved by renewed attempts which are without result; pursuits are undertaken but slowly carried out; the country is gradually becoming immune. Furthermore, the Mexican affair has made manifest to the people their military weakness. But should assistance be postponed to a date when a military organization would be effective, it would be too late. We are ready and determined to struggle indefinitely; but we have to have the power to end the war without too long delay. Neither the soldier returning from the front, nor his long-suffering family, hoping like him for *détente*, must be subjected to new hardships and unbearable taxes, which would impede that *détente* by hindering efforts at reconstruction.

"Mr. House declared his agreement with the first point. With tranquil assurance and surprising candor, he stated that it was indeed in the interest of the United States to act as I had said, and that it was resolved to do so. The effect will manifest itself in the way which shall seem most useful in the circumstances: arms, credits, use of the fleet, etc. The date may coincide with the general advance which the meeting which has just taken place in Paris will doubtless have determined. [See n. 2 below.]

"As for the state of mind here, he acknowledges that there is a lot of truth in what I said about the diminution of the national spirit. But, according to him, there is still enough for the country to be able to act. It is not, he claims, becoming immune to German crimes but is becoming more and more aroused about them. He claims that he is well informed and that, should the President decide to move forward, he would be followed.

"Everyone, he added, comprehends the danger to liberalism of a German victory, which must be avoided at all cost. But, if, on the other hand, the Allies were to win, no throne, except that of England, would be secure; the Russian would hardly be any more stable than the German. This is a sobering hypothesis. The Czar's entourage is worried by it, and this worry is a bad counselor. It could give rise to surprising rapprochements.

"It is perfectly obvious, as he has already made clear in his conversations with Your Excellency and Mr. Cambon, that, among the Allies, it is the liberal union of France, England, and Belgium which must, according to Mr. House, especially appeal to the United States.

"He made no allusion whatsoever to any peace terms. He congratulated himself enormously on the courteous welcome he had received in Paris, the cordiality and openness shown him, and the way in which Your Excellency was kind enough to receive him.

"I cannot help but retain my first impressions. Given his so firm assertions, which we have every reason to believe authorized, we should not believe it absolutely impossible that this supplementary aid will be supplied. But the role of chance is too great for us to bank on this hypothesis without having seen more."

2 A conference of political and military leaders of the Allies met in Paris on March 27 and 28, 1916. The chief purposes of the meeting were to make arrangements to tighten the blockade against the Central Powers and to increase economic cooperation among the Allies themselves. This meeting was a prelude to the Allied Economic Conference which was to meet in June in Paris. See the *New York Times*, March 28 and 29, 1916, and Marion C. Siney, *The Allied Blockade of Germany, 1914-1916* (Ann Arbor, Mich., 1957), pp. 175-76.

3 House's remark to the contrary notwithstanding, there is no evidence that the French attempted to gain concessions for any American position on trade matters at the Paris conference. The reader will recall that House had told Jules Cambon in Paris that the United States would accept all Allied measures affecting neutral trade which conformed to "a military necessity." See EMH to WW, Feb. 3, 1916 (third letter of that date), n. 1.

4 That is, Robert W. Woolley.

5 Samuel Huston Thompson, Jr., Assistant Attorney General.

6 Wilson's speech is printed at April 13, 1916.

7 This appearance was canceled. See WW to EMH, April 13, 1916.

8 House conveyed the essence of Wilson's words to Bernstorff on April 8. Bernstorff immediately sent the following telegram to Berlin (our translation):

"House gave me a very gloomy view of the situation regarding the *Sussex*. At the White House, the situation is considered hopeless because the view there is that, in spite of Tirpitz's resignation, the German government, with the best will in the world, cannot curb the submarine campaign. It has hitherto been merely due to good luck that no American has lost his life, and any moment might precipitate a crisis which would inevitably lead to a break. The American government is convinced that the *Sussex* was torpedoed by a German submarine. A repetition of such mistakes would inevitably drive the United States into war with us. Wilson would greatly regret this because he wants—as I have already reported—to make peace in a few months. If the United States were to be drawn into the war, all hope of an early peace would be lost." J. von Bernstorff to the Foreign Office, received April 11, 1916, T telegram (Der Weltkrieg, No. 18, geheim, Unterseebootkrieg gegen England, Vol. 12, pp. 5-6, GFO-Ar).

An Address on Francis Asbury[1]

March 31, 1916.

Mr. President, ladies and gentlemen: I have found it always, in the course of my acquaintance with him, so safe to follow Bishop Cranston's example that I have asked his permission to read Washington's reply:[2]

"To the Bishops of the Methodist Episcopal Church in the United States of America.

"Gentlemen: I return to you, individually, and, through you, to your society collectively in the United States, my thanks for the demonstrations of affection and the expressions of joy offered in their behalf on my late appointment. It shall be my endeavor to manifest the purity of my intentions for promoting the happiness of mankind, as well as the sincerity of my desire to contribute whatever may be in my power toward the civil and religious liberties of the American people. In pursuing this line of conduct, I hope, by the assistance of Divine Providence, not altogether to disappoint the confidence which you have been pleased to repose in me. It always affords me satisfaction when I find a concurrence of sentiment and practice between all conscientious men in acknowledgements of homage to the great Governor of the universe and in professions of support to a just civil government. After mentioning

[1] Wilson spoke at a special session of the Baltimore Conference of the Methodist Episcopal Church, held in the Foundry Methodist Church in Washington, to celebrate the centennial of the death of Bishop Francis Asbury. Wilson was introduced by Bishop Earl Cranston. Josephus Daniels and Bishop Theodore Sommers Henderson of Tennessee also spoke. "Mr. President" was probably John T. Stone, president of the lay electoral conference, also represented at the meeting.

[2] In introducing Wilson, Bishop Cranston had quoted the address of the bishops of the Methodist Episcopal Church to President Washington, which Asbury had read aloud in Washington's presence in New York on May 29, 1789. Washington responded with the reply which Wilson quotes below. For the texts of both, see Elmer T. Clark, J. Manning Potts, and Jacob S. Payton, eds., *The Journal and Letters of Francis Asbury* (3 vols., London and Nashville, Tenn., 1958), III, 70-72.

that I trust the people of every denomination who demean themselves as good citizens will have occasion to be convinced that I shall always strive to prove a faithful and impartial patron of genuine vital religion, I must assure you in particular that I take in the kindest part the promise you make of presenting your prayers at the throne of Grace for me, and that I likewise implore the divine benediction on yourselves and your religious community."

I must admit, ladies and gentlemen, that I came to this celebration with unaffected hesitation, because I knew only too well that I did not have the time to prepare such things as I would have liked to say to you about the great character whose memory we are trying to recall tonight in such vivid fashion that it shall mean something to us. And, yet, I was drawn to this occasion by the irresistible attraction which such examples and characters exert upon us.

One of the most interesting things to me is the unchanging character of human nature. There is a little bit of discouragement about it. You do not have to probe very deep in any generation, however remote, to find the characteristics and the needs and the impulses and the aspirations which we ourselves feel, and it would sometimes seem as if nothing differed from generation to generation except the external setting of our lives. Man is just the same in one generation as in another. He wears a different costume; he follows a different custom of life, it may be. He speaks this, that, or the other language; he professes this, that, or the other creed. But his heart is just the same that is to be found in any other generation and in any other man. And the touching thing about it is that, in every generation, you see the hearts of men on the same quest—an unending quest for the satisfaction of their spirits. They do not get that satisfaction out of the material circumstances of their lives. On the contrary, they feel hampered and burdened and sometimes crushed by those material circumstances. It is sometimes a very troubling thought that, in the rush of our modern life and in the imperious demand made upon us by hourly duties, we scarcely have time to think of our individual souls.

I think it is fortunate we do not have time to think of our individual *characters*. I have no patience with the principle that a man's chief business in life is to cultivate his character. That means that his chief business is to think about himself. That is the last person he ought ever to think about. I believe that character is essentially a by-product. If you try to make it directly, you make a prig; but if you do your duty to mankind and your God,

you make a character. And perhaps we are relieved of some elements of discouragement by the fact that the rush of circumstance makes it seldom possible to think about ourselves and
always necessary to think about the duty immediately in hand;
because, if that is well done, the character will take care of itself.
But it is a serious thing that there are so few minutes in the
twenty-four hours when we can pause to think of God and the
eternal issues of the life that we are living, for the thing that we
call civilization sometimes absorbs and hurries whole populations
to such an extent that they are constantly aware that they are not
breathing the air of spiritual inspiration which is necessary for
the expansion of their hearts and the salvation of their souls.

And so, in every generation, most of all in generations like
our own—crowded with events of the most startling and serious
character—man is bent upon this eternal quest for some rest and
satisfaction for his spirit, and, occasionally, there arises a figure
like that of Francis Asbury, a knight-errant bent upon the errand
of rescuing the soul from this absorption in its physical environment and bringing it out where it can breathe the pure air of
the uplands, where the spirit of God moves upon us—men of no
nativity, men of no citizenship, men who feel that they are not
locally rooted anywhere, but that their errand and their home is
wherever they are needed, and that they are needed wherever
it is necessary to speak to a man something that will reveal to him
the mission with which his spirit has been sent into the world—
men riding tirelessly over mile upon mile of many a tedious
journey with uplifted eyes and eager spirit, knowing what they
are in quest of and finding it at every turn of the road where they
meet a fellow man!

Bishop Henderson has just been speaking of how some rugged
men of our generation have broken down in the mountains of
our southern country following the same trails that Francis
Asbury followed without breaking down. I do not know—I have
never read—whether Francis Asbury was physically robust or
not, but it does not make any difference. The only thing that is
indomitable is the human spirit, and not the human body. And, if
the spirit is indomitable, if it has the power to lift over every
obstacle and barrier, the body in which it dwells apparently can,
by the Providence of God, stand anything. I have known frail
men who could carry burdens that robust men could not carry.
I have known men so ill that apparently they could not carry any
burden at all, work with exquisite spirit and vision through a
long generation, weaving their health and their vitality out of
some invisible stuff which other men did not know how to use

or live upon. It was the *spirit* of Asbury that survived these hardships and traveled these roads. His body accompanied him only as an impediment.

I once told a doubting pupil of mine, when I was trying to teach, that there was no such thing as a dry subject; that the only thing that was dry was the mind it came in contact with, and that if that mind perceived the significance of the subject, it yielded all the sap that was necessary for the most intense interest. And that is true of everything in life. The thing that makes it worthwhile is your comprehension of it and your enthusiasm for it, and the thing that makes it endurable, and upon occasion delightful, is your confidence in the result of what you are going to do. There is no more delightful picture in the world than the picture of these knights-errant of the spirit going up and down, rescuing men from the dungeons and distresses of their own sins.

So that I was drawn here, as I have admitted to you, by the irresistible attraction of this man who did this thing. No man ought to refuse to come and render tribute to a man who has done all men disinterested and devoted service. His is a stimulating example for anybody who is susceptible to being stimulated. A very witty gentleman who preceded me in the presidency of Princeton University[3] once said to a mother who brought her son to him, personally, when she entered him in the university and committed him to his individual care, forgetting how many others there were, "Madam, we guarantee satisfaction or return the boy." Very often it is necessary to return the boy. And very often it is necessary to return the man when you are trying to communicate enthusiasm, because you find him noncombustible. He will not burn; he will not even glow, he is not even incandescent. He will not receive heat. He will not transmit heat; particularly will he not transmit it into power. And, yet, if any man is susceptible of being stimulated, it is by examples, self-forgetting examples, such as this of Asbury's. And, while I share the hope that, in the City of Washington, some worthy monument of Asbury may be erected, it does not make any difference whether it is done or not, for he does not need the monument. His fame is imperishable. The monument would be an evidence of it, not an addition to it. The monument would be merely our admission that the princes among us are those who forget themselves and serve God and mankind.

T MS (WP, DLC).
3 Francis L. Patton.

To Thomas Nelson Page

My dear Mr. Ambassador: The White House March 31, 1916

I have your two letters of March fourth[1] which I have read with the greatest interest and with the sincerest appreciation of your kindness in writing and keeping me posted.

May I not particularly thank you for your comment upon the foreign policy of the administration and for your desire to see it set in the right light and vindicated in the right way? I quite agree with you that there is nothing to defend and everything to make an aggressive fight for, and I believe that that will be the point of view and policy of most of the friends of the administration in the coming campaign. I shall look forward with the greatest interest to reading the article which you have so generously prepared, and thank you for thinking of it and writing it.[2]

Everything goes here moderately well in respect of domestic matters. The German submarine policy is making an extremely complicated and difficult situation for us, and sometimes there seems to be little prospect of extricating ourselves from it without serious conflict, but we are still hoping that it will be possible.

With the warmest regard and appreciation,

Cordially and sincerely yours,   Woodrow Wilson

TLS (T. N. Page Papers, NcD).
[1] T. N. Page to WW, March 4, 1916 (two letters), TLS (WP, DLC).
[2] In one of his letters to Wilson of March 4, Page wrote that the article was entitled "The President and his Critics: Not a defense; but a challenge," and that he intended to revise it and then submit it to Lansing and House for their approval. House noted in his diary on April 18, 1916, that Lansing had sent the article to him and that, while he, House, had not read it, he believed that it was not "in the best of taste" for an incumbent ambassador to write in defense of a President, particularly on the eve of a presidential campaign. Although there is no further mention of the article in House's diary, it seems reasonable to assume that he recommended that it not be published. In any event, no published version has been found.

To Newton Diehl Baker

My dear Mr. Secretary: The White House March 31, 1916

Thank you for letting me see the enclosed.[1] I would trust Senator Gallinger to try to tell the truth but I do not think that Senator Fall even tries. It was very thoughtful of you, nevertheless, to send me these letters. I shall be curious to know whether the statements that Senator Fall makes are corroborated by your own dispatches.

Cordially and sincerely yours,   Woodrow Wilson

TLS (N. D. Baker Papers, DLC).
[1] A. B. Fall to J. H. Gallinger, March 27, 1916, TC telegram, and J. H. Gallinger

to NDB, March 28, 1916, TLS, both in WDR, RG 94, AGO Document File, No. 2638774, DNA. Fall's telegram asserted that Pershing was unable to obtain supplies because of the opposition of the regional *Carrancista* authorities and that both Pershing's army and American border communities, such as El Paso, were in serious danger of attack from *Carrancista* and/or *Villista* forces. He concluded: "We must in my judgment provide additional forces and immediate supplies for those in Mexico and handle situation firmly or withdraw immediately or else meet disaster." In transmitting Fall's telegram to Baker, Gallinger wrote that, while he and his Republican colleagues in the Senate did not want to embarrass the President in his handling of Mexican affairs, he believed that the present situation called for "prompt and more efficient action."

Two Letters to Benjamin Ryan Tillman

My dear Senator: The White House March 31, 1916

Thank you for your letter of March twenty-ninth. I am keeping tab on the armor plate bill and you may be sure will do everything I can for it. I understand the action of the House caucus night before last was quite in line with your suggestion.[1]

In haste

Cordially and sincerely yours,   Woodrow Wilson

[1] The House Democratic caucus, on March 29, unanimously adopted a resolution requesting the House Rules Committee to report a rule permitting amendments to all military, naval, and sundry civil bills having as their object the establishment of an armor-plate plant to be owned and operated by the government. In this way, the armor-plate bill, presently bottled up in committee, could be brought on the floor of the House as an amendment to other preparedness measures. *Washington Post*, March 30, 1916.

Personal.

My dear Senator: The White House March 31, 1916

Thank you sincerely for your letter of the twenty-seventh with its enclosures, which I am returning.[1] The conclusions seem as plain to me as they do to you. I think there is every evidence that the most sinister influences are at work and we shall have to expose them thoroughly before we can overcome them.

Cordially and sincerely yours,   Woodrow Wilson

TLS (B. R. Tillman Papers, ScCleU).

[1] Actually, Wilson sent the letter and its enclosures to the Attorney General. A White House memorandum about Tillman's letter reads: "Re Mexican situation. States it is evident to every intelligent man that some powerful interest is financing Villa. Refers to the oil fields of Mexico as the stakes on the table. Believes the secret service would be able to get proof." T MS (WP, DLC).

To Hiram Woods, Jr.

My dear Hiram: [The White House] March 31, 1916

Thank you for your news of Charlie. It cheers me very much.[1]

I am taking up the matter of Mr. Tuck's letter with the State Department and will see what can be done, if anything.

In haste   Affectionately yours,   Woodrow Wilson

TLS (Letterpress Books, WP, DLC).
[1] Mitchell lived until December 28, 1917.

From Newton Diehl Baker, with Enclosure

CONFIDENTIAL AND URGENT.

My dear Mr. President: Washington. March 31, 1916.

I am sure you will be glad to see the full text of our latest important despatch from General Funston.

I have directed that the thanks of the Department be immediately conveyed to Colonel Dodd and his command for this fine exploit.   Sincerely yours,   Newton D. Baker

TLS (WP, DLC).

E N C L O S U R E

Fort Sam Houston, Texas, March 31, 1916.

Following just received.

"San Geronimo Ranch March thirtieth nineteen sixteen. Dodd struck Villa's command, consisting five hundred six o'clock March twenty-ninth at Guerrero. Villa who is suffering from a broken leg and lame hip was not present. Number Villa's dead known to be thirty, probably others carried away dead. Dodd captured two machine guns, large number horses, saddles and arms. Our casualties four enlisted men wounded, none seriously. Attack was surprise, the Villa troops being driven in a ten mile running fight, and retreated to mountains, northwest of Railroad, where they separated into small bands. May assemble upper part Santa Maria Valley. Large number Carranzista prisoners who were being held for execution were liberated during the fight. In order to reach Guerrero, Dodd marched fifty five miles in seventeen hours and carried carried [sic] on fight for five hours. Now endeavoring to run down Villa's whereabouts. Elizio Hernandez,[1] who commanded Villa's troops was killed in fight. With Villa permanently disabled, Lopez[2] wounded, and Hernandez dead, the blow administered is a serious one to Villa's band. Am sending forces tonight in endeavor to cut off retreat Villa's forces. Pershing."

T telegram (WP, DLC).
  [1] General Eliseo Hernandez.
  [2] Pablo López, the perpetrator of the Santa Ysabel massacre, about which see C. H. Dodge to WW, Jan. 14, 1916, n. 1, Vol. 35.

From Edward Mandell House

Dear Governor: New York. March 31st, 1916.

Fletcher is here. I have taken up the Pan American Peace Pact with him and now have the Chilian sentiment in regard to it.

I would suggest that you tell Lansing that now Fletcher is here, you would like the matter closed before he leaves for Mexico, and you would appreciate it if he would write me a letter asking me to work with Fletcher and give him what knowledge I have concerning it.

I asked Fletcher if there was any reason it could not be closed within ten days. He said there was none. He is to forget that I have said anything to him and the first he is to know of it will come from Lansing.

If you will let Lansing send for Fletcher and have him in Washington Monday I believe the matter can soon be closed. I have told him exactly what I think should be done and he is willing to devote his entire time to it, referring everything to Lansing as it progresses. He will also keep me advised so I can really direct it.

This, I think, is the wisest course and if you agree with me we will work it that way.

Bernstorff is not here. Polk will be here tomorrow and we will discuss again the best method of procedure. Yesterday just before leaving in talking to Polk he thought it would be a mistake to send for Bernstorff. Bernstorff has always sought me and it may be that I can arrange through Morganthau to have him do it now. What do you think of this?

                    Affectionately yours,   E. M. House

My visit to you has put me on my feet again. Thank you both so much.

The Young Men's Democratic Club are very happy over the thought of your coming over on the 15th and looking in on them after the theatre.

TLS (WP, DLC).

From James Woodrow

My dear Cousin Woodrow: Columbia, S. C. Mch. 31, 1916.

All of us here have been keeping up, as well as is possible through the columns of the newspapers, with all of your wonderful work. My grandmother[1] reads every word she can find about you, and if there is ever an uncomplimentary remark, she starts on a little tirade of her own against those who should even *think* anything uncomplimentary.

I know your time is too filled with work—with troubles, pleasures, worries—to spend any of it reading purely a personal letter. Therefore I have refrained writing for some time. However, to-night I feel as though I must write to one who has been so kind to me, so helpful, such an example, such a friend, whether there be time for any interest or not on your part. This is simply to tell you of my good fortune. I am to be married the early part of the summer (28th of June) to Miss Blanche Powers of Riverside, California. Sometime ago I wrote Nell, but after mailing the letter I saw where she had sailed for South America, so I do not suppose she has received it. The wedding will be rather a quiet one as I am not financially able to take anyone out with me, so only announcements will be sent out. But I wanted you & that dear family to know.

I know nothing of my plans for next year, as I am not certain whether I shall continue in my present position or take a position which is offered me in California. I thought for the three months this summer I might probably get a position in the campaign with the Committee in the West, if I am to be out there next winter, or in the East, if here, so I wrote Tom Pence. But old Tom is gone now—& in his going *you* have lost a staunch friend. I am sure no one knows that better than you. He was a big, lovable chap, & all of us who knew him sorrow over his death.

Please pardon this lengthy letter but, believe me, it is prompted only by my love for you & yours.

My grandmother has been wonderfully well during the past few months, & seems quite happy. She has been suffering today, however, from a slight cold.

With kindest regards, the very best of wishes, & the deepest sympathy in all of your trials, troubles & worries.

Ever Sincerely & Affectionately yours,　"Jimmie."

ALS (WP, DLC).
[1] That is, Wilson's Aunt "Felie," Felexiana Shepherd Baker Woodrow.

From Caleb Thomas Winchester

Middletown, Conn.,
My dear President Wilson:　　　　　　March 31, 1916.

I received your letter with reference to Professor Axson some days ago; but delayed acknowledging it partly because I was confined to my rooms some days by illness, and partly because I wished first to confer with President Shanklin, who returned last night from a tendays absence from town.

I need not say that the letter of Professor Axson requesting a release from his engagement here was a great disappointment to me. I had not, I believe, urged him to come to us against his own deliberate wishes; but I was extremely gratified by his decision to take the chair. As you know, there is no one I could prefer for a colleague and a successor; and I felt a profound satisfaction in the certainty that I could, in a few years at fartherst, leave the department in better hands than my own.

But however pronounced my own disappointment, I certainly should not wish Professor Axson to come here under any sense of constraint. We neither of us should enjoy that. It seems to me, therefore, that if he is convinced that his own best interests and his obligations to others demand his release, the college authorities should certainly release him—as I have no doubt they will. The consideration you mention in your letter—the uncertainty of his health—had not occurred to me, as he had not himself mentioned it; but that would be an additional reason for his release.

I am sure I need not assure you, as I have already assured him, that however deep my disappointment at his decision, there can be no change in my long continued friendship for Axson, or of my high estimate of his work and ability.

May I venture, my dear President Wilson, to express, with the added emphasis of personal friendship, my profound gratitude that in these days of danger and difficulty Woodrow Wilson is President of the United States. No man since Abraham Lincoln—if I read history aright—has held the position in such a time of crisis; and no one could have held it with more wisdom and firmness.   Very sincerely yours,   C. T. Winchester

TLS (WP, DLC).

To Albert Sidney Burleson

My dear Burleson,   [*U.S.S. Mayflower*] 2 April, 1916.

I have a chance while I am on these little trips down the river on the MAYFLOWER to think things over which the daily tasks that chowd [crowd] upon me while I am in Washington seem to leave no room for.

I have been thinking on this trip of various matters concerning transportation and the regulation of the railways, and I would very much like your opinion, in view of a certain vexed question which persists in cropping up again and again, on this inquiry: Would it not be right and fair to let the Interstate Commerce Commission dertermine [determine] the rates at which the railroads should carry the mails,—that is, try questions where the Government is shipper as well as those where private individuals are the shippers? What do you think?

Faithfully Yours,   Woodrow Wilson

WWTLS (A. S. Burleson Papers, DLC).

To Joseph Edward Davies

My dear Davies,   [*U.S.S. Mayflower*] 2 April, 1916.

When I am on these little trips down the river on the MAYFLOWER I have a chance to think about a lot of things which the routine of the days I spend in Washington seems to crowd out.

I understand that the Trade Commission is investigating, or is about to investigate, the cost of gasoline. May I take the liberty of suggesting that in the course of that inquiry you keep in close touch with the Department of Justice? You know the Department has had the best reasons for being entirely dissatisfied with the decree against the Standard Oil Company. It would be of great assistance to it if it might have the benefit of what you learn in the course of investigation; and I feel confident that it could, in its turn, be of great assistance to the Commission. I hope you will think favourably of my suggestion.

Cordially and faithfully Yours,   Woodrow Wilson

TCL (RSB Coll., DLC).

To William Bauchop Wilson

[U.S.S. Mayflower] 4/2/16

My warmest congratulations on your birthday   May you have many another in which to continue the fine work you are doing work in which I feel it a privelege to be associated with you.

Woodrow Wilson

T radiogram (received from Mary A. Strohecker).

From the Diary of Colonel House

April 2, 1916.

Chas. R. Crane telephoned this morning to say that David L [R]. Francis was with him and wished to see me. I have invited them to lunch on Tuesday. Francis sails for his new post Thursday and there are some things I would like to say to him before he goes to Russia.

We lunched with Mr. and Mrs. Sidney Brooks. The other guests were Mr. and Mrs. Burke Cochran[1] and Mr. and Mrs. James Byrne. I had to leave before coffee was served in order to meet William Phillips, who was leaving on an early afternoon train for Washington.

Phillips is much disturbed, as indeed are all the President's friends, regarding his lack of action in the present crisis. They are afraid he will allow Germany to do pretty much as she pleases, despite all his notes of protest. Phillips begs me to come to Washington and see if I cannot move him to action. I half-way promised to go, ostensibly on other matters.

Grayson followed Phillips and he, too, is worried. He says the Saturday Evening Post is about to turn against the President because of his inaction, both as to Mexico and Germany. Grayson thinks the President is a man of unusually narrow prejudices and is intolerant of advice. I did not argue the matter with him as I feel that while the President is not unwilling to accept advice from me, Grayson's general characterization of him is correct. Grayson says if one urges Wilson to do something contrary to his own conviction, he ceases to have any liking for that person. He does not like to meet people and isolates himself as much as anyone I have ever known.

Grayson realizes that a great crisis is impending and the President's place in history is at stake. The President's penchant for inaction makes him hesitate to take the plunge, but if he once takes it, I have every confidence he will go through with it in a creditable manner. Anyway, his immediate entourage, from the Secretary of State down, are having an unhappy time just now. He is consulting none of them and they are as ignorant of his intentions as the man in the street. I believe he will follow the advice I gave him last week, but even to me, he has not expressed his intentions. This, however, is not unusual as he seldom or never says what he will do. I merely know from past experience.

1 [William] Bourke Cockran, New York lawyer, celebrated orator, and former Democratic congressman, and Anne Ide Cockran.

To Robert Lansing

My dear Mr. Secretary: The White House April 3, 1916

I understand that Fletcher has arrived to make ready to go to Mexico. It occurs to me that he will know more familiarly than any of the rest of us do the exact sentiment of the Government of Chile with regard to the Pan-American agreement. It occurs to me that he ought to learn from House all that House originally ascertained when he began the negotiations about this agreement at my request, while Mr. Bryan was Secretary. I would appreciate it very much if you would write Mr. House a letter asking him to work with Fletcher and give him what knowledge he has concerning the matter. It is probable that Fletcher may be of real service to us in this matter of dealing with the Latin-American countries because of his long familiarity with the political atmosphere of the southern continent. Perhaps it would be well, also, to send for Fletcher and have him down here as soon as he has seen House.

Cordially and faithfully yours,   Woodrow Wilson

TLS (SDR, RG 59, 710.11/225½, DNA).

To Thomas Nelson Page

My dear Mr. Ambassador: The White House April 3, 1916

Your letters[1] are very illuminating. They often come, as you realize, after the dispatches of a later date have somewhat altered the complexion of the situation, but they none the less afford me a glimpse behind the situation which is very valuable to me indeed.

I wish I could do you a corresponding service in return by writing you such letters as I should like to write, reciting in some detail the movements of events and politics on this side of the water, but, of course, you understand why I cannot. I hardly have time to send a line now and again to members of my own family. I hope that there is some friend on this side of the water who is performing this service for you.

This is just a general acknowledgement of your series of letters and of your personal kindness.

Cordially and sincerely yours,   Woodrow Wilson

TLS (T. N. Page Papers, NcD).
[1] His most recent ones received by Wilson were T. N. Page to WW. Jan. 20, Feb. 14, and March 4, 1916 (2), TLS (WP, DLC).

To Pleasant Alexander Stovall

My dear Stovall: [The White House] April 3, 1916

Your letters are always very welcome and I must beg that you will forgive me for not having acknowledged sooner your letter of November twenty-ninth and your letter of March first.[1] I am sure you are generous enough to understand what has made it practically impossible for me to write. Even now I can only send you a few lines to say how genuinely I appreciate your thought of me and your desire to keep me informed as to the impressions you are forming on the other side of the water with regard to the matters which so deeply concern us all and the world itself. My thoughts very often turn to you and always with a feeling of sincere gratification that I had the opportunity of putting you in a place in which you have fulfilled every expectation.

Cordially and sincerely yours,   Woodrow Wilson

TLS (Letterpress Books, WP, DLC).
[1] P. A. Stovall to WW, Nov. 29, 1915, and March 1, 1916, TLS (WP, DLC).

To Wesley Norwood Jones

My dear Mr. Jones: [The White House] April 3, 1916

I was touched by your letter of March twenty-ninth. I feel that in the death of Tom Pence, your nephew, I have lost a personal friend whom I peculiarly valued, and that the country itself has lost an invaluable servant who was moved by the highest motives and did his work in a fashion that any man might have been proud of.

I appreciate your letter very highly and join with you and all the rest of the family in your grief at the loss of this splendid man.   Cordially and sincerely yours,   Woodrow Wilson

TLS (Letterpress Books, WP, DLC).

From Robert Lansing

PERSONAL AND CONFIDENTIAL:
RE: MODUS VIVENDI.

My dear Mr. President: [Washington] April 3, 1916.

I enclose a proposed letter[1] in reply to the rejection of our proposal of January 18th, relative to the disarming of merchant vessels.

I have already sent you a draft of a letter on this subject, and in the enclosed I have sought to meet your views on the previous draft.   Faithfully yours,   Robert Lansing

TLS (Lansing Letterpress Book, SDR, RG 59, DNA).
[1] It is printed as an Enclosure with WW to RL, April 7, 1916 (first letter of that date).

From Edward Mandell House, with Enclosure

Dear Governor: New York. April 3, 1916.

I am enclosing you a copy of a letter which has come from Bernstorff. I shall see him on Saturday unless you advise my doing so sooner.

Unless the Germans discontinue their present policy a break seems inevitable. Before it comes do you not think it would be well to cable Grey telling him the status of affairs and asking him whether or not it would not be wise to intervene now rather than to permit the break to come?

Our becoming a belligerent would not be without its advantages in as much as it would strengthen your position at home and with the Allies. It would eliminate the necessity for calling in the conference any neutral because the only purpose in calling them in was to include ourselves.

Your influence at the peace congress would be enormously enhanced instead of lessened, for we would be the only nation at the conference desiring nothing except the ultimate good of mankind.

We could still be the force to stop the war when the proper time came, and in the way I outlined to you when I was in Washington.   Affectionately yours,   E. M. House

TLS (WP, DLC).

E N C L O S U R E

Count Johann Heinrich von Bernstorff
to Edward Mandell House

My dear Colonel House: Washington, D. C. March 31, 1916.

I had heard that you were in Washington, but for obvious reasons I did not try to see you, as our friend Hugh Wallace was not here to arrange a meeting.

If you had the opportunity here to discuss the German situation and wish to speak to me about it, I will gladly come to New York at any time you may appoint. I do, however, not wish to trouble you, unless you think it advisable to talk matters over.

Anyway I shall be in New York on Saturday and Sunday, April 8th and 9th, and could give myself the pleasure of calling on you one of those two mornings.

With many thanks in advance for a kind answer,
                    Very sincerely yours,   J. Bernstorff.

TCL (WP, DLC).

From William Cox Redfield

My dear Mr. President: Washington April 3, 1916.

I understand that you are to have a conference with Mr. Kitchin to-day with reference to the dyestuffs situation. This is just a line to let you know that I have been in touch with the recent developments in the situation and that I heartily approve of the suggestions made by Mr. Kitchin to a committee of the manufacturers and consumers of dyestuffs in his office on Friday evening.

I believe that the proposals suggested on that occasion would solve a difficult and perplexing situation. These proposals, as I understand them, are (1) to enact legislation to prevent unfair competition on an international scale, either by giving the Federal Trade Commission the power to prevent international unfair competition, and to extend the provisions of the present anti-trust laws. (2) To reorganize the present tariff schedule on dyestuffs so that there will be three classes, namely, (a) crudes, (b) intermediates, (c) finished dyestuffs. The first to be admitted free of duty, the second at the rate of 15% ad valorem, and the third at the rate of 30% ad valorem. This is essentially the present scale of duties. (3) That an additional temporary and emergency surtax be levied either in an ad valorem or specific form, which should be graduated in some way so that it will be entirely eliminated at the end of ten years.

I think the provision that there must be a considerable proportion of the domestic consumption manufactured in this country at the end of some stated period, as suggested by Mr. Kitchin, would be a happy addition.

I understand that all of the consumers and manufacturers of dyestuffs have agreed on these proposals and will support them. I understand further that they have definitely decided to withdraw their support from the so-called Hill bill.[1]

Very truly yours,   William C. Redfield

TLS (WP, DLC).

[1] That is, H.R. 702, about which see A. C. Imbrie to WW, March 6, 1916, n. 3.

From William Bauchop Wilson

My dear Mr. President: Washington April 3rd, 1916.

I have been thrilled and exalted by your words of congratulation and commendation on the occasion of my fifty-fourth birthday. In whatever I have sought to accomplish through the agency of the department over which you have selected me to preside, I have been inspired and encouraged by your sympathetic support, your comprehensive grasp of the problems involved, and the high standards and ideals you have impressed upon every phase of your administration.   Faithfully yours,   W B Wilson

TLS (WP, DLC).

John Hall Stephens to Joseph Patrick Tumulty, with Enclosure

Dear Mr. Secretary: Washington. April 3, 1916.

I enclose you herewith a letter from Mr. J. D. Short of Albuquerque, New Mexico,[1] and I hope you will see that the President gets it. Mr. Short is personally known to me and is a good man and good citizen.

I am, Most Respectfully,   Jno. H Stephens

TLS (WP, DLC).
[1] Jefferson D. Short, a broker of Albuquerque who dealt in mines and mining, ranches, timberland, etc.

ENCLOSURE

Jefferson D. Short to John Hall Stephens

Dear Mr. Stephens: Albuquerque, New Mexico March 30, 1916.

Not having what I consider any representatives in Congress from this State, I am still compelled to write to you concerning any matters that I believe to be for the good of the Country.

I am enclosing herewith some clippings from our local papers concerning the activities of our Senator (?) Albert B. Fall in the matter of the Mexican Expedition.[1]

Our President has never said a more truthful word than that there were insidious influences at work trying to bring about war between this country and Mexico. And the headquarters of these influences is in El Paso, Texas,[2] and possibly, also, in the offices of a certain Senator in Washington.

It goes without saying that the rank and file of the sound citizenship of this state as well as that of all of the other states, is with the President, but there is an element who will stop at nothing in their power to bring about trouble of any nature in order that they may carry out their aims, which are personal profits and personal advertising.

I believe that the President can do a very great deal to stop the work of these people by placing this matter in the hands of the secret service (which I would suppose had already been done) with instructions to keep a strong force at work in El Paso, and also to keep a very close watch on certain men in Washington, no matter how prominent these men may consider they are.

These clippings state that the Senator is down getting information at first hand. What he is really doing is loading his popgun, and, if I am not very much mistaken, you will find that when he gets back to Washington, he will make all the noise possible.

I do not suppose that there will be but little attention paid to him by people who are well advised, but he can play to the galleries and get some advertising for himself and can do a good deal to cause distrust among the Mexican people who have been downtrodden so long and imposed upon so much that they are by nature very suspicious and easily influenced.

A reading of the larger of the enclosed clippings will show that this Senator considers the Election of President Wilson was a very great crime imposed upon the people of the United States. The crime of the President consists mainly in the fact that this Senator has extensive mining interests in the northern part of the Republic of Mexico, and he (the President) refuses to annex the northern tier of the Mexican States to the United States for the especial pecuniary benefit of this Senator.

As to the crimes of democracy, this Senator was a democrat until he learned that it was not profitable to be one in this state.[3] I have been informed, and reliably, I believe, that the slow plodding Cleveland, when he was President, removed this gentleman from the Federal Court Bench by wire; not waiting for the relatively slow process of the mails.

The reason that I am writing this letter is that I believe the President should know some of the facts from the view point of the people of this section, and for the further reason that I am utterly disgusted with these self-seeking patriots who would cause untold bloodshed and the sacrifice of thousands of the lives of American boys for the aggrandizement and personal selfish interests of a coterie of self seekers who have not yet learned that there is such a word as patriotism.

I wish you would go to the President personally and discuss this matter with him, for I am sure that if the facts in this matter are dug up and spread before the public, it will go a very long way toward ending the distrust along the border and will make a certain element very careful about how they put a certain class of reports in the press.

With best regards to yourself and family, I am

Yours very truly,   J D Short.

TLS (WP, DLC).
1 Two unidentified newspaper clippings, dated March 27 and March 30, 1916. The longer clipping, of March 27, reported that Fall was making his own "quiet investigation" of the Mexican situation. It quoted the Senator as saying that Wilson had refused to see any American living along the border who really understood the situation and declared that, if the administration failed to "redeem itself by bringing about the extermination of Villa in Mexico," he would lead a strong Republican attack on its policy in the Senate. In the clipping of March 30, Fall was reported as saying that the *Carrancista* forces were doing nothing to assist Pershing in the pursuit of Villa.
2 While Fall maintained his voting residence in Three Rivers, N. M., he practiced law mainly in El Paso.
3 Fall officially switched to the Republican party in 1908, when he became a delegate to its national convention.

To Joseph Patrick Tumulty

Dear Tumulty: [The White House, c. April 3, 1916]

I wish you would call the attention of the Department of Justice and of the State Department to the matters here referred to and to the clippings. I think we should go to the bottom of this thing.   The President.
Done 4/12/16[1]

TL (WP, DLC).
1 JPThw.

To Brand Whitlock

My dear Mr. Whitlock: [The White House] April 4, 1916

Thank you very warmly for your letter of February twenty-eighth which reached me only yesterday. I do not know by what devious routes such letters travel.

You may be sure that I understood perfectly why you declined the Russian post. I greatly regretted your inability to accept it, because I felt that you were so peculiarly fitted for the work now waiting to be done there and because I have such a complete faith in your character and devotion to the best interests of the country, as well as in your ability, but even if you had not given me the reasons for declining, you may be sure I would have either divined them or at least known that they were sufficient and altogether compatible with my estimate of you.

I sincerely hope that the burden of your present duties is not growing heavier but that, on the contrary, you feel that the splendid position you have established for yourself in Belgium has made your path easier than it was for a while. Pray take care of your health and remember always how many sincere and loyal friends you have here at home.

Cordially and sincerely yours,   Woodrow Wilson

TLS (Letterpress Books, WP, DLC).

To William Cox Redfield

My dear Mr. Secretary: [The White House] April 4, 1916

Thank you for your letter of April third about the dyestuffs. I am sincerely glad to learn that you think the provisions Chairman Kitchin has in mind will meet the situation. I found him very clear on the subject and believe that something satisfactory will come out of the work we have done.

I suggested to Mr. Kitchin that he confer with Mr. Davis[1] and with yourself or Doctor Pratt[2] in this important matter.

Cordially and sincerely yours,   Woodrow Wilson

TLS (Letterpress Books, WP, DLC).

[1] Wilson dictated "Davies," that is, Joseph E. Davies, who had written numerous reports on industries at least somewhat related to dyestuffs while Commissioner of the Bureau of Corporations.

[2] Edward Ewing Pratt, chief of the Bureau of Foreign and Domestic Commerce, Department of Commerce.

To James Woodrow

My dear James: [The White House] April 4, 1916

We all unite in congratulating you very heartily and sincerely on your engagement and hope that it will not be very long before we can see the young lady.

I am sorry that your plans are in any way unsettled but I dare say they will straighten out promptly enough.

Please give our love to Aunt Felie and to all. This is just a hasty line but our sincere best wishes go with it.

Faithfully yours,   Woodrow Wilson

TLS (Letterpress Books, WP, DLC).

To Caleb Thomas Winchester

[The White House]

My dear Professor Winchester: April 4, 1916

Your letter of March thirty-first is characteristic of you in its thoughtfulness and generosity, and I thank you for it most warmly. In what you say of myself I recognize the voice of an old friend who, I hope, understands me better than some others do, and you may be sure that the approval is particularly grateful to me.   Cordially and sincerely yours,   Woodrow Wilson

TLS (Letterpress Books, WP, DLC).

From Robert Lansing, with Enclosure

PERSONAL AND CONFIDENTIAL:

My dear Mr. President: Washington April 4, 1916.

I enclose a confidential letter which I have just received from Ambassador Page at London in regard to the Chino-Japanese situation. It confirms the information which we already have in regard to the matter. Faithfully yours, Robert Lansing

TLS (SDR, RG 59, 793.94/514½, DNA).

ENCLOSURE

Walter Hines Page to Robert Lansing

Personal and *Confidential*

Dear Mr. Secretary: London. 23d March 1916

I reported to you by telegraph the result of my interview with Sir Edw. Grey concerning the rumours of Japan's activity towards China.[1] I now add the following—

The Chinese Minister in London[2] was educated in the U. S. where he spent the formative years of his life. He is an able, occidental-minded man whom I know quite well & for whom & for whose judgment I have a high respect. I had a confidential conversation with him on this subject, in which I gave him an opportunity to tell me whatever he would. He was quite frank and, of course, very confidential.

He confirmed what Sir Edw. Grey had told me—that there are now, in his belief, no definite proposals from Japan before His Majesty's Gov't. But Mr. Sze very freely made known his fears. He is convinced that Japan will use her utmost power and influence to drive a hard bargain with her Allies when the war ends —with an eye on as many and as onerous concessions from China as she can possibly force. That is the substance of what I got from the Chinese Minister.

He was very appreciative of our interest in the subject and he promised to keep me informed of all that he may learn.

Yours Sincerely, Walter H. Page

ALS (SDR, RG 59, 793.94/514½, DNA).
   1 WHP to RL, March 23, 1916, T telegram (SDR, RG 59, 893.00/2383½, DNA), which reads as follows: "Sir Edward Grey tells me that his information from China is that the rebellion is very serious and that this fact causes him some apprehension. A violent civil war would probably open the door to all sorts of undesirable influences and events."
   2 Sao-Ke Alfred Sze.

From Robert Lansing, with Enclosure

PERSONAL AND PRIVATE:
RE: PAN-AMERICAN TREATY

My dear Mr. President: Washington April 4, 1916.

I enclose a draft of a proposed Pan American Treaty, together with a suggestion for the second article made by Mr. Mueller, the Brazilian Minister of Foreign Affairs, which was handed to me by Mr. Naón on March 30th.

My own impression is that the suggested second article might be accepted as it is in substance the principle of settlement of disputes as to territory, as contained in the original draft.

Please indicate your wishes in this matter, and I will then take it up with the Argentine Ambassador at once.

     Faithfully yours,   Robert Lansing.

TLS (WP, DLC).

E N C L O S U R E

ARTICLE I.

That the high contracting parties to this solemn covenant and agreement hereby join one another in a common and mutual guarantee of territorial integrity and of political independence under republican forms of government.

ARTICLE II.

To give definitive application to the guarantee set forth in Article I. the high contracting parties severally covenant to endeavor forthwith to reach a settlement of all disputes as to boundaries or territory now pending between them by amicable agreement or by means of international arbitration.

ARTICLE III.

That the high contracting parties further agree, First, that all questions, of whatever character, arising between any two or more of them which cannot be settled by the ordinary means of diplomatic correspondence shall, before any declaration of war or beginning of hostilities, be first submitted to a permanent international commission for investigation, one year being allowed for such investigation; and, Second, that if the dispute is not settled by investigation, to submit the same to arbitration, provided the question in dispute does not affect the honour, independence, or vital interests of the nations concerned or the interests of third parties.

ARTICLE IV.

To the end that domestic tranquility may prevail within their territories the high contracting parties further severally covenant and agree that they will not permit the departure from their respective jurisdictions of any military or naval expedition hostile to the established government of any of the high contracting parties, and that they will prevent the exportation from their respective jurisdictions of arms, ammunition or other munitions of war destined to or for the use of any person or persons notified to be in insurrection or revolt against the established government of any of the high contracting parties.

T MS (SDR, RG 59, 710.11/225½B, DNA).

From Robert Lansing, with Enclosure

PERSONAL AND CONFIDENTIAL:

My dear Mr. President: Washington April 4, 1916.

I enclose a personal letter which I have just received from Ambassador Gerard and which I think will interest you.

I would call particular attention to the next to the last paragraph on page two, which appears to require an answer, although I hesitate to make one in view of the present situation.

Faithfully yours,   Robert Lansing

TLS (SDR, RG 59, 763.72/2552½, DNA).

E N C L O S U R E

James Watson Gerard to Robert Lansing

Personal.

My dear Mr. Secretary,   [Berlin] Tuesday, March 14th, 1916.

As I cabled you, I read your Zwiedenck memorandum to von Jägow.[1] He said it was too long to remember and asked for a copy. Government people here are convinced that you *were* in favor of the German side of the armed merchantmen controversy but say that the President came home from a trip and ordered you to switch. I dont think however they are going to start any controversy with you on the matter.

The "illness" of von Tirpitz is announced. I think it means his resignation, and have just so cabled you, although it is possible that his resignation may never be publicly announced.

For one thing, the K___[2]. and army people began to think it was a bad principle to introduce to have *any* officer or official appealing to cheap newspapers and the "man in the street" in a conflict with superior authority.

I heard that at Charleville conference both the Chancellor and von Jägow said they would resign if von Tirpitz's policy of unlimited submarine war on England was adopted.

Verdun is still being attacked and will be anyway until the 22nd. when the subscriptions to the War Loan close.

The Catholic or Centrum party is very much against the U. S. A., and the President. It is said the cause for this is that the Catholics in America are against the President's Mexican policy.

The food question becoming really acute—the village people are about starving in some sections and are not as well off as the people in the big towns; it being the policy to keep the people in the cities as satisfied as possible in order to prevent riots, demonstrations, etc.

Some Germans have asked me if the sending of a German Colonel House to America would be agreeable to the President. Probably the Envoy would be Solf, and he could informally talk to President and prominent people. How about this? If sent he would require a safe conduct from England and France.

I hear the submarines now are mostly engaged in mine laying, at the Thames mouth, etc.   Yours ever   J.W.G.

TLI (SDR, RG 59, 763.72/2552½, DNA).
    [1] Lansing's original memorandum, dated March 3, 1916, is printed as an Enclosure with RL to WW, March 6, 1916 (first letter of that date). The slightly altered version, which he sent to Gerard on March 9, 1916, is printed in *FR-WWS 1916*, pp. 202-204.
    [2] The Kaiser.

From Newton Diehl Baker

My dear Mr. President: Washington. April 4, 1916.

Under date of April 3rd Governor-General Harrison cables as follows:

    "Reported here that American papers state Filipinos opposed to Clarke amendment. My observation from declarations of Assembly, all three political parties, and from personal conversations in Manila and in the provinces convince me that although Filipino people would prefer temporary guarantee of independence as at first proposed, the great majority, including all classes, are in favor of Clarke amendment as it passed the Senate and earnestly desire immediate settlement of Philippine question."

          Very sincerely,   Newton D. Baker

TLS (WP, DLC).

From William Charles Adamson

Dear Mr. President: Washington, D. C. April 4, 1916.

It looks like danger is brewing in the railroad situation. We are casting about to find some way to avert the universal strike which seems eminent.[1]

I presume you have also been thinking over the situation. We would like to have the benefit of any suggestions you might make if you have time to see me and talk a few minutes about it.

I am to have an interview with the Interstate Commerce Commission to-morrow morning. After that time I would like to see you at your convenience.

With high regards and best wishes, I remain,

Your friend,   W. C. Adamson

TLS (WP, DLC).
[1] The heads of the four brotherhoods had announced on March 9 that their members had voted overwhelmingly in favor of their leaders' demands, and that these demands be placed immediately before the railroad presidents. See WW to W. J. Stone, Feb. 22, 1916, n. 1.

Walter Hines Page to Joseph Patrick Tumulty

Dear Mr. Tumulty: London, April 4, 1916.

Jo Davidson[1] is a sculptor whom I have known for a good many years in New York and in London, for he works on both sides of the ocean. He is a man of a good deal of ability and sometimes he has done admirable work. At other times he has missed his likenesses somewhat. Lately he has done a bust of Lord Northcliffe, of Joseph Conrad and of other men of influence and importance here.

He is now going to the United States and is consumed with the hope of making a bust of the President. I told him that I would write you this letter. That's all I have told him and I don't put into it any request that you should get him an audience with the President, but I do go so far as to say this—that he is a man of sufficient attainments to deserve consideration if by any chance the President wants anybody to make a bust of him. He will call to see you before long.

Yours sincerely,   Walter H. Page

TLS (WP, DLC).
[1] Born in New York in 1883, Davidson had studied at the Art Students League and at Yale University before going to Paris in 1907 for further training. Most recently, he had been working in England and, in addition to the works mentioned by Page, had executed portrait busts of Rabindranath Tagore, Frank Harris, Havelock Ellis, and Page himself. By the time of his death in 1952, he had sculpted busts of many of the important political and literary figures of his era. See Jo Davidson, *Between Sittings: An Informal Autobiography* (New York, 1951).

Two Letters from Newton Diehl Baker

My dear Mr. President: Washington. April 5, 1916.

I have had made a parallel comparison of the telegram from Senator Fall to Senator Gallinger with the reports on file in this Department from all sources.[1] It would not justify the use of your time to read this entire document, but it is clear that Senator Fall's telegram is a confused jumble of rumors, some of which have slight foundation, some of which have none, and none of which appear to have been wholly justified by any facts yet brought to notice. I am supplying this so that it can be put in your private files under an appropriate alphabetical head and to be available if you are ever called upon to comment upon the degree to which Senator Fall has not helped the Mexican situation.

Very truly yours,   Newton D. Baker

TLS (WP, DLC).
[1] T MS (WP, DLC).

(CONFIDENTIAL)

My dear Mr. President: Washington. April 5, 1916.

I inclose for your confidential information a detailed statement of the several commands and their strength on the Mexican border and in Mexico.[1] These facts have not been made public, as it seemed to me that any discussion of the number of troops located at different places might give rise to comparisons in the degree of protection afforded to different points on the border, and embarrass General Funston with further demands upon his limited resources.   Sincerely yours,   Newton D. Baker

TLS (WP, DLC).
[1] T MS (WP, DLC).

From the Diary of Colonel House

The White House, Washington [April 5, 1916].

Gordon and I arrived at 4.30 and were met by a motor from the White House. The President insisted upon Gordon remaining as his guest with me. The President and I had only a few minutes conversation. Lansing came at six o'clock and we talked for nearly an hour. After the President received my letter of April 3rd, he evidently made up his mind to follow my advice and take more vigorous action, for he told Lansing to prepare a memorandum for Gerard to present to the German Government. Lansing showed me what he had drawn up.[1] It is an exceedingly vigorous paper and one which I think the President will modify greatly before he sends it. It was well written and very much to the point. It recalls Gerard and notifies the Imperial German Government that Count von Bernstorff will be given his passports.

Lansing was so full of our troubles with Germany that I could hardly bring him down to the Pan-American Peace Pact. I finally did this, and he gave me what memoranda he had upon the subject to look over and we are to confer again tomorrow. I promised to get the President to arrange a conference for the three of us tomorrow.

Gordon, Miss Bones and I went to the theater. When we returned the President had gone to bed.

[1] It is printed as an Enclosure with RL to WW, April 10, 1916 (first letter of that date). As the extract from the House diary printed at April 11 reveals, Wilson suffered a severe digestive disorder for at least four days after reading Lansing's draft note.

An Address Celebrating the Centennial of the United States Coast and Geodetic Survey[1]

April 6, 1916.

Mr. Minister, Mr. Superintendent, ladies and gentlemen: I had another reason for asking to come last. I remember reading with appreciation in the preface of a volume of essays written by a very witty English writer a passage to this effect: The pleasure with which a man reads his own books is largely dependent upon how much of them has been written by somebody else. And I have found that my enjoyment of making speeches after dinner is almost directly in proportion to the amount of inspiration that I can derive from others.

It was manifestly impossible for me to make such preparation for addressing you tonight as I should have wished to make in order to show my very great respect and admiration for this service of the government. I can only say that I have come here for the purpose of expressing that admiration. I have been very much interested in the speeches that I have heard tonight, not only because of what they contained, but also because of many of the implications which were to be drawn from them. I was very much interested, indeed, in the excellent address of the representative of the free and admirable Republic of Switzerland. He reminded

[1] At a banquet at the New Willard Hotel. The Superintendent of the Survey, Ernest Lester Jones, presided. The other speakers were Paul Ritter, Swiss Minister to the United States; William C. Redfield; Josephus Daniels; and Thomas Corwin Mendenhall, a former Superintendent of the Survey.

us of what we must constantly remember—our very great intellectual debt to Switzerland—as well as to the many other countries from which we draw so much of our vitality and so much of the scientific work which has been accomplished in America.

As he was speaking, I was reminded (if there are Pennsylvanians present, I hope they will forgive this story) of a toast mischievously offered at a banquet in Philadelphia by a gentleman who was not himself a Pennsylvanian. He said he proposed the memory of the three most distinguished Pennsylvanians, Benjamin Franklin, of Massachusetts; James Wilson, of Scotland, and Albert Gallatin of Switzerland. I dare say that in many American communities similar toasts could very truly and with historical truth be offered. And I, myself, had the privilege of sitting under one of the distinguished Swiss scholars to whom reference was made, Doctor Arnold Guyot, under whom I pretended to study geology. Doctor Guyot was not responsible for its not being carried beyond the stage of pretense.

I feel myself in a certain sense in familiar company tonight, because a very great part of my life has been spent in association with men of science. I have often wished, particularly since I entered public life, that there was some moral process parallel to the process of triangulation, so that the whereabouts, intellectually and spiritually, of some persons could be discovered with more particularity. Yet, as I listened to the Secretary of Commerce, I suspected that he was priding himself upon the discovery of a process by which he had discovered the whereabouts of a great many committees of Congress and a great many other persons connected with the process of appropriating public monies. I have a certain sympathy with those committees of Congress which, in investigating the Coast and Geodetic Survey, have found that the Superintendent had the great advantage of knowing all about the service and they the great disadvantage of knowing nothing about it. Because, as I have said, I have spent a great part of my life in association with men of science and, never having been a man of science, I have at least learned the discretion of keeping my opinions on scientific subjects to myself.

I have had association particularly with the very exact and singularly well informed brother of a distinguished gentleman present. General Scott has a brother who is a member of the faculty of Princeton University, and Professor William B. Scott is one of the most provoking men I have ever known. He not only asserts opinions and delivers himself of information upon almost every subject, but the provoking thing about him is he generally knows what he is talking about. A good talker, who volunteers opinions on all subjects, ought to be expected in fairness to his fellow men to make a certain large and generous portion of mistakes, because you can at least catch him napping. But Professor Scott is one of those men who successfully—I have sometimes told him I suspected adroitly—avoided the pitfalls of eminent conversationalists like himself. But association with such men has taught me a very great degree of discretion and, therefore, I am not going to express any opinion whatever about the work of the Coast and Geodetic Survey. But I am going to give myself the privilege, for it is a real privilege, of saying this:

This is one of the few branches of the public service in which the motives of those who are engaged cannot be questioned. There is something very intensely appealing to the imagination in the intellectual ardor which men bestow upon scientific inquiry. No social advantage can be gained by it. No pecuniary advantage can be gained by it. In most cases, no personal distinction can be gained by it. It is one of the few pursuits in life which gets all its momentum from pure intellectual ardor, from a love of finding out what the truth is, regardless of all human circumstances—as if the mind wished to put itself into intimate communication with the mind of the Almighty itself. There is something in scientific inquiry which is eminently spiritual in its nature. It is the spirit of man wishing to square himself accurately with his environment, not only, but also wishing to get at the intimate interpretations of his relationship to his environment. And when you think of what the Geodetic Survey has been attempting to do—to make a sort of profile picture, a sort of profile sketch, of the life of a nation, so far as that life is physically sustained—you can see that what we have been doing has been, so to say, to test and outline the whole underpinning of a great civilization. And just as the finding of all the outlines of the earth's surface that underly the sea is a process of making the pathways for the great intercourse which has bound nations together, so the work that we do upon the continent itself is the work of interpreting and outlining the conditions which surround the life of a great nation.

I can illustrate it in this way—the way in which it appeals to my imagination: I have always maintained that it was a great mistake to begin a history of the United States intended for beginners by putting at the front of the book a topographical map of this continent, or at any rate of that portion of it which is occupied by the United States, because if you begin with that, you seem to begin to deal with children when you deal with the first settlers. They knew nothing about it. They expected to find the

Pacific over the slope of the Alleghenies. They expected to find some Eldorado at the sources of the first great river whose mouth they entered upon the coast. They went groping for the outlines of the continent like blind men feeling their way through a jungle. They were as big men as we, as intelligent. They had as full a grasp upon the knowledge of their time as we have upon the knowledge of ours. But set the youngster in the school to watch these men groping, and he will get the impression that they were children and pigmies. That is not the way to begin the history of the United States. You will understand it only if you comprehend how little of what the work of this department of the government, for example, has since disclosed, was known to those then engaged in this great romantic enterprise of peopling a new continent and building up a new civilization in a new world.

So that you have the picture of a service like this lifting the curtain that, before that time, rested upon all the great spaces of nature. You remember how, in the early history of Virginia, a little company of gentlemen, moved by a sort of scientific curiosity, and yet moved by a spirit of adventure still more, penetrated no further than to some of the unknown fastnesses of the Allegheny Mountains and were thereafter known as the Knights of the Golden Horseshoe—given a sort of knighthood of adventure because they went a little way upon the same quest upon which you gentlemen have gone a great way.

So when I stand in the presence of scientific men, I seem to stand in the presence of those who are given the privilege, the singular privilege, the almost contradictory privilege, of following a vision of the mind with open, physical eyes; making real the things that have been conjectural; making substantial the things that have been intangible.

And, as the Secretary of Commerce has said, there is a great human side to the things that you are doing. You are making it safe to bind the world together with those great shuttles that we call ships that move in and out and weave the fabric of international intercourse. You are providing the machinery by which the web of humanity is woven. It is only by these imaginative conceptions, it is only by visions of the mind, that we are inspired. If we thought about each other too much—our little jealousies, our rivalries, our smallnesses, our weaknesses—there would be no courage left in our hearts.

Sometimes, when the day is done and the consciousness of the sordid struggle is upon you, you go to bed wondering if the sun will seem bright in the morning, the day worthwhile. But you have only to sweep these temporary things away and to look back and see mankind working its way, though never so slowly, up the slow steps which it has climbed to know itself and to know nature and nature's God, and to know the destiny of mankind— to have all these little things seem like the mere mists that creep along the ground and have all the courage come back to you by lifting your eyes to those blue heavens where rests the serenity of thought.

T MS (WP, DLC).

To Sir Edward Grey

The White House [April 6, 1916].

Since it now seems probable that this country must break with Germany on the submarine question unless the unexpected happens and since if this country should once ⟨get its teeth in⟩ become a belligerant the war would undoubtedly be prolonged I beg to suggest that if you had any thought of acting at an early date on the plan we agreed upon you might wish now to consult with your allies with a view to acting immediately.[1]

WWT telegram (E. M. House Papers, CtY).
    [1] House noted at the bottom of the page: "This is a joint composition of the President and my own. I suggested elimination 'get its teeth in' and substituting 'become a belligerent.' " This telegram was sent as EMH to E. Grey, April 6, 1916, T telegram (E. M. House Papers, CtY).

From the Diary of Colonel House

April 6, 1916.

Before the President started his dictation, we held a conference where we met in the hall just outside my room, and it lasted so long that he gave up all thought of his mail and dismissed his stenographer so we might finish.

I told him, it seemed to me, a break with Germany was inevitable. They were torpedoing boats without warning contrary to their solemn pledge not to do so, and that the Sussex case was in a way as bad or worse than the Lusitania. I thought he ought to definitely make up his mind what he intended to do and if he agreed with me that a break was inevitable, then he should prepare for it from today in order to give us the advantage of two or three weeks time to get ready before the Germans knew of our purpose.

We discussed whether it would be advisable to give the Allies a last chance to accept our offer of intervention. There were many arguments for and against it. The suggestion was originally mine, made in my letter of April 3rd, but I was uncertain as to the advisability of doing so. He thought, too, it might cause them to think we wished them to act in order to save us. The President did not wish to indicate any weakness in this direction. And yet he thought they should know that, in our opinion, the war would last longer with us as a belligerent than as a neutral.

The President asked me to frame the despatch to Sir Edward Grey, but I yielded to him and insisted that he do it. My reasons for this have been explained before. The despatch as finally drafted by him in his own handwriting, as we call his little type-writer, is as follows:

"Since it seems probably [probable] that this country must break with Germany on the submarine question unless the un-expected happens, and since, if this country should once become a belligerent the war would undoubtedly be prolonged, I beg to suggest that if you had any thought of acting at an early date on the plan we agreed upon, you might wish now to consult with your allies with a view of acting immediately."

He wrote first, "and since if this country should once 'get its teeth in,' to which I objected because in a cable it would not read smoothly without proper punctuation, and I suggested us-ing the words 'become a belligerent.'["]

I gave this cable to Gordon and had him take it to New York on the Congressional Limited for my Secretary, Miss Denton, to code and send.

The President telephoned Lansing to come to the White House at two o'clock for a conference.

Polk came and remained for an hour and a half. I will not go into the details of our conversation for it would be something of repetition. He was telling how unsatisfactory the London Embassy was in presenting protests, or business of any kind, to the Foreign Office. He thought Page and his staff went to the Foreign Office and said, "Here is another damn fool request from our Government which you need not pay any attention to."

I told Polk in confidence, which he promised to keep, how Page felt about the State Department, and how he suggested that they should all be discharged and, for fear the new force might be contaminated by going into the same offices, a tent should be erected south of the White House and they should be broken in there. Polk seemed to find less humor in this than in other things I told him.

I took a short motor drive with my friend Alfred Millard of

Omaha[1] who is visiting Washington, and then I returned to the White House for luncheon.

At two o'clock the President, Lansing and I went into conference. We first took up the Pan-American Peace Pact and it was agreed, as the President and I had planned, to have Fletcher go immediately to work upon it after first conferring with me. This plan, as I have stated before, is a concession to Lansing, since Fletcher and I have already had our conference in New York.

We then took up the foreign situation which the President tried to evade, but which Lansing and I rather forced upon him. I did this for Lansing's sake for, as a matter of fact, I should have preferred talking to the President alone about it. Lansing showed him the draft of the letter he had shown me.[2] The President merely glanced at it, and said he would look it over later. He caught enough of it, however, to see that it was to be our last word to the Imperial German Government.

We went over pretty much the same ground as Lansing and I did last night, Lansing doing most of the talking. Before finishing with the Pan-American Pact they began to argue about certain minor clauses, and asked my opinion as to one of them. I thought it was of no consequence and the main thing was to get Clause 2 adopted, and get it adopted quickly, and let the other clauses take care of themselves. The President replied, "I believe you are right and suppose we let it go that way."

When the President left, Lansing and I had a few minutes conversation alone. After he left, I drove for an hour with the Secretary of War. I like Baker and we got along famously. I wished to see him so as to tell him just how critical our relations with Germany are and to suggest that he find out at once what troops would be available for the protection of New York, Chicago and the larger centers, and whether we had sufficient without withdrawing troops from Mexico. If there were not sufficient, I thought the pursuit of Villa should be abandoned and our forces be properly distributed.

I asked him to please treat my information as confidential, and to use it merely in the way indicated. After some discussion, he decided he would go to New York tomorrow and confer with General Wood, and later have the Commanding General in Chicago meet him at Cleveland so as to get the situation in the West. I urged Baker to use a firm hand in the event trouble should ma[n]ifest itself in any way. I thought it was mistaken

---

[1] A banker.
[2] A draft of a *Sussex* note, printed as an Enclosure with RL to WW, April 10, 1916 (first letter of that date).

mercy to temporize with troubles of this sort; that such a policy would merely cause it to grow and in the end much suffering would ensue.

He cordially agreed to this and promised to use the iron hand. He was in favor of giving up the Villa chase and bringing the troops back from Mexico. He thought the purpose had been accomplished, that is, the Villistas had already been dispersed and it was foolish to chase a single bandit all over Mexico.

I cautioned Baker, too, about mentioning General Wood to the President, telling him the President did not like Wood. I thought in this crisis Wood should be used conspicuously, for he was known to be unfriendly to the Administration and close to Roosevelt and republican leaders, and if the President passed him by and trouble followed, it would invite criticism of the administration. Baker said it was his purpose to put pronounced Roosevelt men to the front. We went over every phase of the situation from a military viewpoint, including the militia, the police forces of different cities, etc. etc. I believe Baker is an abler man than Garrison and that time will prove him so.

I had to return to the White House at 4.15 in order to meet Secretary Houston[.] I put the problems confronting the administration to Houston so as to get the benefit of his judgment. He knew nothing of what was going on. He thought we were moving in the right direction with Germany, but he was much opposed to withdrawing our troops from Mexico. His argument was that we had better take a gamble upon rioting than to receive the certain abuse which the bringing the troops back would entail. He thought too, that the "hyphenates" would have just cause for resentment if they saw plans were being made for their suppression. His argument was that if the troops were withdrawn from Mexico, Villa would come back and make further raids and we would have to go in again and thus indicate a weak and vacillating policy.

Secretary Lane followed Houston and gave exactly the reverse opinion. He thought Villa should not be chased any further, and that the troops should be recalled. He thought that eighty percent of the American people wanted peace at almost any price, and he doubted whether Congress or the people would sustain the President in breaking with Germany. He was very pessimistic. He thought I should be in Washington more. He said it was generally known that I was the only man to whom the President gave his inner thoughts, or in whose counsel he had any confidence. He said the Cabinet never knew anything except what they read in the newspapers, and that Lansing was considered merely a clerk.

I tried to bring him to a more cheerful frame of mind, but he was determined to see things darkly. I had to leave him to dress for dinner and meet the President a few minutes before it was ready.

I told the President of my conversations with Houston and Lane. Here are two of the ablest men in the United States—admittedly so—and yet their views are totally at variance. It wearies me to have consultations where I get nothing but confusion of thought. The President was sympathetic to this view, as I knew he would be.

I told him of my conversations with Baker, Lansing, Polk, Lane and Houston, and we summed up by ma[r]king Lane, Polk, Baker and Lansing for withdrawing the troops, and Houston against it. Strangely enough, just after dinner, Lane telephoned to change his views. I remembered that Houston was taking dinner with him so there was not much difficulty in finding the reason. The President had gone, but I gave this information to Mrs. Wilson to tell him when he returned.

Gregory's opinion, whom I saw later, coincided with Houston's, so the sum total was there was Lansing, Baker and Polk on the one side, and Houston, Lane and Gregory on the other. As a matter of fact, I believe it is a question of chance and either may be right. If the troops are not withdrawn and a conflict with all Mexico should come about because of their presence there, the President would be censured for permitting war with Mexico at the moment when a break with Germany was contemplated.

I spoke to the President about Morganthau and he asked me to tell him he had definitely decided to accept his resignation, and would so confirm it in writing in a few days. He did not think well of the idea of Brandeis resigning from the Supreme Court if he was once confirmed. He said it would smack too much of Hughes.[3] This amused me.

[3] House recorded in his diary on March 31: "Morganthau has a great idea. He wants Brandeis to be confirmed by the Senate and then decline to serve as Justice of the Supreme Court and run for the Senate against Henry Cabot Lodge. Before approaching Brandeis, he wished my approval. I gave it provided he did not mention my name to Brandeis. It would be far more profitable to the President to have Brandeis in the campaign. He would make an effective force, and his resignation would be dramatic. Morganthau is planning to meet him tomorrow and make the proposal." House noted in his diary on April 1 that Morgenthau had telephoned and reported that he had conferred with Brandeis for three hours in New London, Connecticut. "Brandeis," according to House, "did not decide whether he would act upon his [Morgenthau's] suggestion, but did not absolutely decline to consider it."

There is no further comment on the subject in House's diary.

Morgenthau's own account of this affair, written some five years after the event, differs considerably from House's. Morgenthau wrote that he had suggested that Brandeis, after being confirmed, should run for the Massachusetts senatorship without resigning from the Supreme Court. He had argued that Brandeis had a good chance to unseat Lodge and that, in doing so, he would not only add a vital Democratic vote in the Senate, but also swing Massachusetts,

The President had to go to another banquet, and Mrs. Wilson and I had a talk of an hour or more. We decided that the most helpful things that could be done for the President at this time, would be the elimination of good Josephus Daniels and Joseph Tumulty. She undertakes to eliminate Tumulty if I can manage the Daniels change. I do not know which is the more difficult feat, but I shall approach it with some enthusiasm and see what can be done.

Mrs. Wilson said the President felt somewhat less disturbed over the foreign situation, now that he had practically made up his mind. This is as I thought; it was the indecision which was giving him the worry. She spoke of the threatening letters she was constantly receiving, and she wondered whether it was increasingly dangerous to go to New York. I thought it was, and yet we arranged for them to come over on the 14th to be our guests for Friday, Saturday and Sunday.

Henry P. Fletcher called at half past nine. I read him the riot act in a few words. I told him I was entirely responsible for his having charge of the Pan-American Pact, and that I had affirmed he could close it in ten days. He rather winced at this, but thought he could make good progress in ten days. I outlined the method I considered it best to adopt, and told him to send cables in unrestricted volume if necessary, both for our Government and for the smaller republics, so that correspondence might be avoided. I requested him to do this in Lansing's name, and to keep the Secretary in touch with what he was doing, but to confer with me frequently by letter and telephone. I promised to return to Washington Tuesday to see what progress he had made, and expressed the hope we would not be disappointed. Fletcher was eager to do this work when I first spoke to him about it in New York, but I think he has some doubts now. I told the President it would take longer than ten days, but that was the limit set for Fletcher.

---

and probably Connecticut and Rhode Island also, into the Democratic column in the presidential election. Moreover, he had told Brandeis that this was the best way to vindicate himself against the charges made by the two Massachusetts senators in the confirmation hearings.

Brandeis was not very receptive to Morgenthau's plan. "He objected," Morgenthau recalled, "that it would be 'undignified' for him to run for office while holding a seat on the Supreme Bench, but finally said that he would take the matter under 'prayerful consideration.' I feared this meant that nothing would come of it, and nothing did." Henry Morgenthau, "All in a Life-Time . . . : The Campaign of 1916," *World's Work*, XLIII (Dec. 1921), 141-42. Morgenthau did not include this account in his *All in a Life-Time* (Garden City, N. Y., 1922).

To Robert Lansing, with Enclosure

My dear Mr. Secretary,   The White House. 7 April, 1916.

I have taken the liberty of altering the enclosed a little, for the reasons I expressed to you the other day at Cabinet. I think that we should be as non-commit[t]al on this subject now as possible, in view of the use the German representatives have tried to make of the proposal referred to, and have sought to make the letter as colourless as possible. I hope that you will not think that I have altered it too much.   Faithfully Yours,   W.W.

WWTLI (SDR, RG 59, 763.72/2640½, DNA).

E N C L O S U R E[1]

Robert Lansing to Sir Cecil Arthur Spring Rice

My dear Mr. Ambassador: Washington March 31, 1916.

I have received your courteous letter of the 23d instant and given careful consideration to the Memorandum enclosed relating to the proposal for an agreement to disarm merchant vessels by the Entente Powers, which I unofficially submitted to you in my letter of January 18, 1916.

The proposal was made with the humane purpose of removing the principal reason given by the German and Austro-Hungarian Governments for the failure of their submarines to comply strictly with the rules of naval warfare in intercepting the merchant vessels of their enemies on the high seas, a practice which has resulted in an appalling loss of life among the passengers and crews of vessels which have been attacked without warning.

Believing that an arrangement, such as I had the honor to propose, would have resulted in the discontinuance by Germany and Austria-Hungary of a method of attack on merchant vessels which puts in jeopardy the lives of hundreds of men, women and children of neutral as well as belligerent nationality, I cannot but regret that the Governments of the Entente Powers ⟨have rejected⟩ *could not see their way to accede* the proposal ⟨and have declared their unwillingness to agree to refrain from the use of armament in protecting their property on the high seas.⟩

The Entente Governments having, however, reached a decision to decline the proposed arrangement, it becomes my duty to accept their decision as final, ⟨although I can assure your Excellency that I do so with the greatest reluctance and with grave apprehension for the future.⟩ *and in the spirit in which they have made it.*

I am, my dear Mr. Ambassador,

Very sincerely yours,[2]

TL (SDR, RG 59, 763.72/2525, DNA).
  [1] Text in angle brackets deleted by Wilson; text in italics added by him.
  [2] This letter was sent in its revised form as RL to C. A. Spring Rice, April 7, 1916. It is printed in *FR-WWS 1916*, pp. 223-24. It was also sent, *mutatis mutandis*, to the ambassadors in Washington of the other Entente powers.

Two Letters to Robert Lansing

My dear Mr. Secretary,   The White House. 7 April, 1916.

Thank you for letting me see the enclosed.

It is probably too late now to answer Gerard's question about the advisability of sending a special representative of the German Government here (a "German Colonel House"), but if there should be a renewal of the suggestion or Gerard should for any reason remind us of it I think we should say that we would of course welcome any messenger of friendly counsel the Emperor might think it desirable to send—without indicating any judgment or desire of our own about the matter.

Faithfully Yours,   W.W.

WWTLI (SDR, RG 59, 763.72/2615½, DNA).

My dear Mr. Secretary,   The White House. 7 April, 1916.

Thank you for this.

This matter between China and Japan is the trouble that gives me in a way deepest concern just now, because I do not see what is to be done. I have not had time to study Reinsch's despatches enough to derive any suggestion from them. Had they given you a clue to any definite course of action?

Faithfully Yours,   W.W.

TCL (RSB Coll., DLC).

To William Charles Adamson

My dear Judge: [The White House] April 7, 1916

I am only too keenly aware of the trouble that is impending in the railroad world and I have been casting about to see if there is anything that I could do. I will seek an early interview with you, and in the meantime would be obliged if you would make

any suggestions that occur to you. We must all do what we can.
Cordially and sincerely yours, Woodrow Wilson

TLS (Letterpress Books, WP, DLC).

From Robert Lansing, with Enclosure

PERSONAL AND CONFIDENTIAL:

My dear Mr. President: Washington April 7, 1916.

I enclose a flimsy just received from The Hague giving the detail of the sinking of the Dutch steamships TUBANTIA and PALEMBANG, and the Dutch schooner ELZINA. I think that the features which are of particular interest are that both steamships were enroute to neutral ports from ports in The Netherlands; that they were both large—one being fourteen thousand tons and the other ten thousand tons; and that both were distinctly marked in large letters, which were illuminated at night.

While there were no American citizens on board any one of the three vessels torpedoed, the fact is indicative of the general policy which is now being pursued by the German naval authorities.
Faithfully yours, Robert Lansing

TLS (WP, DLC).

E N C L O S U R E

The Hague, April 6, 1916.

547. Department's circular instruction April 3rd, 4 p.m., received April 5th.

Dutch passenger liner TUBANTIA, fourteen thousand tons, proceeding from Amsterdam to South America, March 16th, two a.m., weather misty, moonlight, sea moderate. Ship about to anchor near North Hinder Lightship, was heavily struck below water line without warning by torpedo, wake of which was seen by lookout and two officers. Ship sank in about three hours, no lives lost except one Russian passenger missing. Fragments of bronze afterwards found in one of the lifeboats, carefully examined, belong to air chamber of Schwarz Kopf torpedo, made only in Germany. Above particulars brought out in official investigation under oath.

Dutch freighter PALEMBANG, ten thousand tons, proceeding from Amsterdam to Java, near North Galloper buoy, off English coast, about noon, March 18th, weather fair, sea smooth, felt heavy shock on starboard and immediately stopped engine. Ship not under headway but drifting slightly to larboard [starboard], two other heavy explosions followed on starboard side. First mate and two sailors saw tracks of these torpedoes approaching athwart the bow of an English destroyer lying parallel. Life boats were launched after second explosion, one boat was blown out of the water by third explosion and several sailors wounded, one Javanese boy missing. No warning was given, ship sank in about ten minutes.

Dutch schooner ELZINA from Norway to England with cargo of lumber. Off English coast German submarine[s] U-30 U-thirty-first attempted to burn then torpedoed schooner, April 3rd, three p.m., weather fair, crew escaped in schooner's boat towed by submarine to North Hinder Lightship.

Both steamers distinctly marked in large letters, illuminated at night. Schooner was marked and carried Dutch flag. No United States citizens were on any of these ships but a number of South Americans on TUBANTIA.   Van Dyke.

T telegram (WP, DLC).

From William Joel Stone

Dear Mr. President: [Washington] April 7 1916.

You will recall the conversation we had some weeks since in which I told you of the speech I had prepared to deliver on the subject of armed merchant ships and correlated subjects. Largely because of that talk, but partly also because of an apparent change in the international situation, making it less acute, I deemed it the part of wisdom to withhold any further agitation of the subject at that time. In view of recent occurrences, however, I have concluded to have a small number of so much of that speech printed as related especially to the question of armed ships and submarine warfare, for submission to and examination by a few men whose opinions I value—especially for your consideration and that of Secretary Lansing and Attorney General Gregory. I hope that you and they may find time to examine it.

I have sought to draw a line between warships and merchant ships, and to define their relative rights. My contention is that any armed enemy ship must be considered to be a warship, and cannot as a matter of law, and should not as a matter either of national or international policy, be treated as a merchant ship. On the other hand I maintain that a legitimate—that is an un-armed—merchant ship must be absolutely immune from attack except in strict accord with the formalities prescribed by international law. This view I have emphasized under the last sub-head of the printed document.

I am sending you this document[1] in the hope that you will consider it of sufficient value to attract your attention as expressive of the views of one you know is interested only in establishing correct principles of law, as well as of one who is deeply interested in the success of your administration.

I do not wish you to reply to this note—I only wish you would read the document I enclose.

Very sincerely, Wm J Stone.

TLS (WP, DLC).
[1] *Extract from Speech of Hon. William J. Stone . . . on Armed Merchant Ships and Other Related Questions, Prepared March 1916 . . .* (WP, DLC).

From Newton Diehl Baker

CONFIDENTIAL.

From: The Secretary of War.   Washington. April 7, 1916.
To: The President.

MEMORANDUM ON PREPAREDNESS AS A POLICY.

The European war has brought into sharp relief the fact that under modern conditions a great war involves three elements of national preparedness:

1st: An army which may be mobilized speedily, adequately trained and adequately officered.

2nd: A navy adequate in equipment and personnel to the needs of the particular nation.

3rd: Such an organization of the industrial, commercial, financial and social resources of the nation as will enable them to be mobilized, both to support the military arm and to continue the life of the nation during the struggle.

In the United States a widespread agitation on the subject of "preparedness" has taken place. The sources of this agitation are, some of them interested, some of them disinterested. Many causes have contributed to the movement, and it has taken many forms. As a whole, it constitutes a great enthusiasm, and sound political policy would seem to suggest that this enthusiasm ought not to be allowed to cool and pass away as a fruitless agitation, but rather should be captured and capitalized into a policy tending to strengthen and consolidate our national life. In other words, it is suggested for your consideration that in a statement you undertake to lead the emotion for preparedness into definite lines and to make of it a national policy.

So far as the cry for preparedness affects either the Army or the Navy, nothing need here be set down. The fact that the mobilization of the industrial, commercial, financial and social resources of the country is as important as the mobilization of either the Army or the Navy in the event of a crisis, is the pivotal point in the suggestion. No one of the European combatants would be able to go forward in the military struggle but for an intensive, almost military, organization of its industries; and in those European countries in which the least forethought had been given to this subject, the most laggard military preparation resulted.

It is to be remembered, too, that under modern conditions the mere manufacture of munitions and supplies for fighting units requires long preparation. England's difficulty in turning her industries to this use is an illustration in point; and our American industries, splendid as they are, have found it very difficult to respond to the enticement of war profits, because of the lack of training and lack of special preparation for munition-making in our industrial establishments. Should the United States be called suddenly into war, the disorganization which would result to our industry by a calling out of the State Militia and the acceptance of volunteers who would come out of industrial life without regard to the question as to whether their real value was not greater as industrial workers, would be profound.

Considerations of this kind have led to such work as is being done by Mr. Coffin,[1] a survey of the industrial resources of the country being undertaken to determine where and under what conditions of time and expense the various supplies needed for military operations could be secured. Other studies are being made by highly trained men of the whole industrial field of the United States, having in view the determination of the weak points of supply, cataloguing the resources of the country in raw material, manufacturing capacity, and labor, and pointing out too the places of our dependence upon other countries for raw material, with suggested substitutes or possible alternative sources of supply. The body of this work is extensive, but it is all a present survey of existing conditions. When made, its makers are through and their work begins to lose value at once with the constant change of our industrial condition. All of this work ought, therefore, to be brought to some national agency which could coordinate it, prevent duplication, and provide for its continuation. To this end a certain amount of new national machinery is necessary. The minimum would seem to be the creation of a council of national strength, which would have under its control a staff of industrial mobilization, the council itself to consist of certain appropriate officers of Cabinet rank and certain captains of industry and commerce who would bring to the council the highest expert acquaintance with the industrial, commercial, financial and social resources of the nation. Membership in such a council would be a distinction, and its creation would secure for the country a patriotic attitude on the part of the great business interests of the nation.

Such a council might well provide a plan whereby the enumerated, catalogued and known industrial resources of the nation could be given a minimum of peace-time work under contracts which would just pay for the labor and material involved in keeping them ready to turn their energies from ordinary industry to those special branches of industry needed in a national emergency. It could be provided, under suitable contracts, that in the event of war, industrial plants so prepared should become Government plants on the basis of a retention of all of their employees as enlisted men and a payment made by retention for the plant which would insure merely a continuance of normal dividends and deny the possibility of war profits, thus destroying the danger of a profit interest in war at the very beginning.

It could be provided that Government arsenals should become largely experimental stations for the purpose of keeping our information abreast of the development of the art of munitions and also training an adequate company of men to be used to reinforce the workers in industrial plants temporarily converted into Government plants for manufacturing purposes. Such a plan, in addition to providing in advance for a rapid if not instantaneous adaptation of the industry of the country to the needs of the country in a crisis, would also have the effect of enlisting the sympathetic and voluntary cooperation of the industrial interests of the country in defense, and the plan being made in advance of the crisis, would solve automatically many of the problems of labor and war profit which have proved embarrassing in some of the European countries.

The Government arsenals might also be made the assembling plants, so that constituent elements of war materials, manufactured in plants predetermined to be specially adapted to such production, could in these Government central depots be assembled into completed munitions and shipped where needed.

In other words, the plan here suggested provides for the creation of a national council as the third element of preparedness, having as its function a continuous survey of the industrial, commercial, financial and social resources of the nation, and the making of such plans, contracts and laws, all in advance, as shall be necessary or appropriate, in the event of danger, to make the calling out and mobilizing of the industrial resources of the nation as automatic as the mobilization of its army, and this through sympathetic cooperation between the Government and the business interests of the country, rather than by coercive action on the part of the Government when the hour of need comes.

This memorandum has been considered with the Secretary of the Navy, and he and I have made a tentative draft of a bill which would provide for the creation of such a coordinating council as is here suggested. If you desire to consider the matter any further, either as to the wisdom of present discussion of the subject by you or any details of the plan which the Secretary of the Navy and I have so far matured, we would of course be very happy to respond to any suggestion as to time for discussing the matter with you.

Respectfully submitted,   Newton D. Baker

TLS (WP, DLC).
¹ Howard Earle Coffin, vice-president of the Hudson Motor Car Co. and member of the Naval Consulting Board (about which see n. 1 to remarks to the Naval Consulting Board, printed at Oct. 6, 1915, Vol. 35). Coffin served as chairman of the Naval Consulting Board's Committee on Industrial Preparedness and in that capacity was directing a nationwide inventory of industrial plants capable of producing war materials. See Robert D. Cuff, *The War Industries Board: Business-Government Relations during World War I* (Baltimore, 1973), pp. 16-27.

From Edward Mandell House

Dear Governor: New York. April 7, 1916.

I have asked a good many of our friends with whom I could talk with some degree of freedom, concerning Mexico and the concensus of opinion is almost entirely against withdrawing the troops.

I have not, of course, given any indication of why it should be done further than to say that the foreign situation seemed to justify extreme caution in this direction.

It is contended that a withdrawal from Mexico at this time would be an evidence of weakness not only to Villa and Carranza but to the Germans as well. It is thought they would feel that a nation so powerful as this was impotent indeed if it could not maintain a few thousand men in Mexico no matter what the situation was abroad.

I think there is a general feeling here that the militia could take care of any disturbance that might arise.

I am merely giving you this opinion for your information.

Affectionately yours,   E. M. House

TLS (WP, DLC).

From Robert Lansing, with Enclosure

CONFIDENTIAL:

My dear Mr. President: Washington April 7, 1916.

I have just received the enclosed letter from Mr. Thomas J. Anketell, of Detroit,[1] who was introduced to me at Pinehurst by a letter from Mr. Tumulty.

Knowing the intense loyalty of Mr. Anketell to you, I thought you would be interested to see his point of view on the present German situation.

Faithfully yours,   Robert Lansing.

TLS (R. Lansing Papers, DLC).

[1] Thomas Jackson Anketell, proprietor of a lumber and coal company in Detroit.

E N C L O S U R E

Thomas Jackson Anketell to Robert Lansing

My dear Secretary Lansing: Atlantic City, N. J. April 6, 1916.

Referring to our conversation in regard to the tides of political opinion, I would like to relate a little incident which occurred at Pinehurst.

You will remember at the Carolina[1] news bulletins are read in the office after dinner. The other evening one was read as follows:

"Wilson is losing faith in German pledges; says he cannot rely on promises."

The spontaneous laugh of derision which greeted this bulletin was significant, particularly as heretofore all over the country the President's words have at least been treated with respect.

As a devoted friend of the President, and as one who feels deeply that the Democrat party has a mission to perform, I believe that unless diplomatic relations are broken off with Germany, and broken off by the President without shifting the responsibility to Congress, it will be many years before our party is again given the confidence of the American people.

From the conversation I had the honor to have with you, I also feel that your position is correct, that the American people are

not willing to give up one single right. I would go further, however, and say: While the American people love peace and prefer
not to have war, our countrymen are not cowards (as our German brethren now seem to think), they expect their executives
to uphold the honor and dignity of the country at all hazards.

Please present my compliments to Mrs. Lansing. Trusting your
visit to Pinehurst did you both a world of good,

Sincerely yours,   Thos. J. Anketell

TLS (R. Lansing Papers, DLC).
¹ That is, at the Carolina Hotel in Pinehurst, N. C.

From Walter Hines Page, with Enclosure

Dear Mr. President: London. 7 April 1916

Mr. Benj. Strong and Mr. Cameron Forbes were invited by
Lord Kitchener to call to see him. Lord Kitchener evidently wishd.
to give expression to his views to some unofficial Americans—not
for publication, of course, but (I think) with the hope that they
wd. privately make them known at home. Messrs. Strong and
Forbes gave me a copy of the report of the conversation, a copy of
wh. I enclose to you. I had a conversation about it with the Prime
Minister, with whom I took luncheon to-day. He hoped I wd. send
it to you, but (as usual) he refrained from himself expressing
any opinion. He can be silent in more languages than any other
man I know.   Very heartily Yours,   Walter H. Page

ALS (WP, DLC).

E N C L O S U R E

Interview with Lord Kitchener London, March 24, 1916

On Friday, March 24, 1916, on the invitation of Lord Kitchener, Mr. Strong, of the Federal Reserve Bank, New York, and
Mr. Forbes, Receiver of the Brazil Railway Company, presented
themselves at the War Department and were shortly after received. Lord Kitchener was cordial in his greeting and throughout the interview, which lasted nearly an hour, showed no
evidence of the reticence he is reputed to observe, talking steadily,
fluently and somewhat intensely. The topic of the interview was
mainly the relations between the United States and Great Britain,
the attitude of the United States toward the war, and the effect
that action by the United States in regard to the atrocities, particularly terminating diplomatic relations with Germany, would

have in terminating the war. We discussed no military aspects of the war and only incidentally did Lord Kitchener give any idea as to the probable duration of the war, always referring to the war as likely to be of long duration, speaking always of years, and on one occasion speaking of the coming of peace as "say three years hence," except in the case the United States should take this action, which he felt would shorten the period of the war.

In preparing these notes no effort has been made to quote the exact language used but to give a general sketch of the purport of the conversation as recalled afterward.

Speaking of a visit to Australia, Lord Kitchener remarked that it was extremely lucky he had made that trip at that time, because he had started the movement which had led to a sort of compulsion, as he called it, which had served an extremely useful purpose in training Australia for preparedness in this war, besides which he had brought about the creation of a military school modelled upon West Point. He said there was no school in England where the discipline was so sharp and severe as it was at West Point and that it took a democratic country to be really stern in its disciplinary measures; that the Australian school which had been accordingly established was stricter than any other school in the British Empire.

Coming to the question of present and future relations between our countries, Lord Kitchener expressed the hope that the United States would change its attitude and break off diplomatic relations with Germany, in that way publicly taking up the position of being Anti-German. He seemed to think it was wholly unnecessary that the United States should become sufficiently Pro-Ally as to take an active participation in the war, merely that we should officially and authoritatively express our condemnation of Germany's barbarism and methods, thus putting ourselves squarely on the side of the great fundamental principle of right for which the Allies were fighting, which was really the principle of freedom of the individual. He felt that this action of the United States would make the Germans feel that they had practically the whole world against them and this would bring about a sense of the helplessness of their position which would have most potent effects.

He stated that in his judgment there would be no real and satisfactory end to the war until the military control of Germany was terminated; that such termination and really the only satisfactory termination of the war would be brought about by an internal revolution in Germany; that there was within Germany now a great dissatisfaction, a strong feeling against the domination of the military caste, but the Germans had no tangible method of knowing that their policies and methods were abhorrent to other countries. The effect of England's condemnation of them was offset by the fact that England was considered their hereditary enemy. France they felt had a grievance and Russia also was a natural enemy. The United States was a great powerful country, with one hundred million people and unlimited resources, whose standing and opinion could have a controlling weight on the people of Germany. If the United States were to come out and declare themselves as no longer friendly he believed it would stimulate the unrest in Germany to a point that would set the German people to thinking whether they were really right; whether they hadn't been misled; whether after all their rulers hadn't led them into violating the fundamental principles of justice and right. The control exercised by the military caste was so complete that most information was withheld and only some fact of supreme importance, like breaking off relations with the United States, which could not be suppressed, would reach them in convincing form. Consciousness that they had been misled he felt would be the controlling factor in leading them to bring about that internal revolution which he felt necessary to end the war and he expressed it as his opinion that this action by the United States would serve to be the last straw and bring about an early termination of the war. He didn't give a period within which this would come about but left us with the impression that he thought it would come about within six months.

He took occasion to express great admiration for the United States. When Mr. Strong suggested that our people hadn't yet become entirely assimilated he replied "Oh, what a country it will be when that time comes."

He said that peace would not be signed in Berlin. He thought that when peace came the armies would still be in the trenches and probably not very far from their present locations.

Lord Kitchener was very interesting and very positive about the unfortunate effects of a premature peace or an unsatisfactory or indeterminate conclusion to the war. Unless an end were made to this military spirit and control of Germany he felt peace would only last at the outside seven years, at which time Germany would start again and it was reasonable to suppose that they would be more successful in their diplomacy a second time and succeed in catching the Allies disunited. He expressed the difficulty of obtaining and maintaining a satisfactory concert by the Allies. That this had been done in the present instance was most fortunate and he expressed confidence in the power of the Allies to continue these relations, but it was an intensely difficult thing to do and it would hardly do to count on it in the future. If the war dragged on until the Allies got fearfully tired of it they might disagree as to the necessity for exacting terms that would assure a durable peace and some of the Allies might assent to letting up. He gave the impression that the influence of the United States having broken off relations with Germany and sided squarely for the establishment and maintenance of a durable peace would be of incalculable advantage toward bringing about a condition that would do away with this menace hanging over the world. If this menace were still left the United States would be one of the countries concerned. The Germans had shown wonderful ingenuity and great persistence in worming their way into the heart of the financial systems of neighboring countries, like some cancer or disease or worm; they found their way close to the heart's blood of the commercial life and got a strangle hold, as it were, upon the intimate financial workings of the country. He instanced Italy, which even now hadn't declared war on Germany because of the German strength in their financial institutions. He spoke of Russia, where their influence, he said, in lines of finance was paramount, and even England and France, he said, were honeycombed with German financiers and German influence in their financial structure. He said after the war they would be clever enough to see that the United States was the place where the greatest amount of money could be found and that was the place where they would lay their plans for the strongest intervention.

He told us of the extraordinarily subtle way in which the Germans had obtained control of the manufacture of explosives. He himself had been out of the country for thirty or forty years; his service has been all foreign; he didn't know until the war broke out home conditions. He was astonished, when he called the manufacturers of explosives in, to find that they were all Germans; many of them couldn't even speak English, and although the companies had made contracts and agreements for delivery, they were constantly falling short. The whole thing had to be purged of German influence before they could begin with efficiency. It took time to train men up to handle this business and do it properly. The Germans had even taken the factory for the manufacture of benzoine bodily to Holland; there was none manufactured in the United Kingdom, and they were compelled to take necessary measures to return it. This had been accomplished and England is not only supplying herself but also her Allies with this necessary ingredient for explosives.

Mr. Strong mentioned the growth of a certain irritation respecting the attitude of the United States. Lord Kitchener interrupted to disclaim the existence of such an irritation. He said it was rather a misunderstanding or lack of appreciation of the policy of our Government. Mr. Strong then said that if it was not irritation it might become irritation as the result of the aggressive and rather boastful attitude of the American press regarding our financial strength on the one hand and on the other hand of the propaganda now being undertaken by the British press to promote the continuance of the war commercially after the military war had ended. Mr. Strong said that nothing would so surely establish a basis for future wars as attempts to interfere between the commercial relations of nations by unnatural means, such for instance as protective tariffs, preferential treatment of Allies, etc. Lord Kitchener said that this movement was not directed toward the United States but against Germany, to which Mr. Strong replied that he understood that to be the case now but that possibly if the United States held aloof until peace was discussed it would nevertheless come to apply to the United States. Mr. Strong went on to explain the situation as to American public opinion in regard to these matters. The United States had never had a foreign policy in the sense that European nations had. The sole interests of the United States in foreign matters consisted (first) of a certain respect for Washington's advice in regard to foreign entanglements which might involve them in the European political system and (second) their respect for the Monroe Doctrine, both of which were designed to protect the integrity of the United States, and (third) the more recently developed and still but little understood policy of the open door in China as developed by Mr. Hay. That the same situation prevailed as to the financial relations of the United States with the rest of the world. The development of our resources required the use of all the funds we could raise at home and in the cheaper money markets of Europe. We had been borrowers abroad and not lenders, consequently had not acquainted ourselves with financial conditions abroad or with the credit of Governments or institutions. In other words, the people of the United States were not conscious of any international responsibilities and had not regarded themselves as of any importance in international affairs. Now, suddenly, a war broke out which involved the whole of Europe and it developed that the United States was of very great, possibly of deciding importance, both politically and financially, on account of their large population and wealth. It could not be expected that one hundred million people would, in the short period of this war, abandon the ideas so deeply planted in their minds in regard to foreign affairs and suddenly reverse their former view of what the country's position should be. Recognizing, however, the importance of our position, as many people now do, it would be deplorable if misunderstandings arose in regard to commercial and financial matters which would make the United States and Great Britain bitter commercial rivals at the conclusion of the war. The solution, Lord Kitchener felt, was an alliance between the great English speaking peoples, namely, the United States and England. Mr. Forbes expressed the hope that some day we would come to some such understanding. Mr. Strong said that in his opinion the tradition of the people of the United States against what Washington cautioned them as being entangling alliances would prevent the approval by the United States Senate of any treaty of offensive and defensive military alliance; that such an agreement could not be expected to meet with the approval of the United States in the reasonably near future. Lord Kitchener, without defining the exact nature of the agreement, expressed the hope that England and the United States would enter into some relation that would result in bringing all English speaking people together in a determination to prevent recurrence of Germany's aggression and make it impossible for the German military spirit ever again to become formidable in influencing world development or bringing about general war.

Lord Kitchener spoke with great earnestness in regard to America's hope that it might act as mediator. He said that if the Allies won the war, and he expressed his confidence in their determination and power to do so, the mediation of the United States would not be sought or welcomed; there would be no need of a mediator. It was only if the war went against them that any mediation could be considered. By "going against them" it is presumed he includes some such condition as a stale-mate, in which case mediation might be profitable.

Mr. Forbes put the direct question as to what steps were necessary to bring about peace. Mr. Strong suggested that perhaps the Allies might announce the terms upon which they would accept peace and let Germany come to them when they saw the hopelessness of obtaining anything better. Lord Kitchener said the announcement of terms was a sign of weakness; it seemed to be somewhat like throwing up the sponge; the fact of terms being announced would put heart into the other side and stiffen their determination. He said that is what England was hoping Germany would do, but they would not consider doing it. (Note: apropos of this, it is interesting to observe that the British Prime Minister already, at the beginning of the war, has done something of this sort. This indicated exactly what England is fighting for and what it proposes to get, including a very general statement of terms.)

Lord Kitchener emphasized the extremely improved position that the United States would have in influencing the situation after the war if she had ranged herself squarely on the side of the Allies by breaking off terms with Germany in case the Allies, as he expects, are victorious, an expectation which would be much more likely to be realized were the United States to take this step.

Lord Kitchener, as we were saying goodby, spoke very bitterly of the German atrocities, their duplicity and their thoroughly underhand manner of conducting the war. He characterized their policy as foul play of the most dastardly sort; in comparison he said the Dervishes, the Boers and the Turks, with all of whom he had conducted warfare, were gentlemen; that they fought each with their code of honor. He told us that the Turkish soldiers refused to do the dirty underhand things ordered by their German officers. He said that after fighting with any of the others he was glad to be friends with them; that he would shake the hand of his enemy, and made special mention in a most complimentary manner of General Smuts, who is commanding a campaign under his orders now and with whom he had fought over an important part of a continent, but he said that he never wanted to shake hands with a German foe.

Messrs. Strong and Forbes came away with a feeling that Lord Kitchener had brought about the interview with the particular purpose of convincing representative Americans and having them bring back to their own people their conviction that no permanent peace in Europe could be expected except as a result of some effective arrangement between Great Britain and the United States; that now was the time to prepare the foundations for this; that public opinion in England would welcome any such movement, and it would be most effective in assuring a world peace. Great Britain will undoubtedly have similar close relations with her present Allies but their nearness to Germany and the heavy burden of debt which they must carry after the war will bring it about that the assistance and the cordial cooperation of the United States will be necessary to give the arrangement the greatest degree of efficiency.

CC MS (W. H. Page Papers, MH).

From Edward Mandell House, with Enclosures

Dear Governor: New York. April 8, 1916.

Here are two letters from Sir Edward Grey which have just come.

I think I see quite clearly his desire to have us communicate directly with the French. He has some hesitation in doing so himself. When I was in London, he expressed particular satisfaction that I had approached the French directly when I was in Paris. He said it had relieved him of some embarrassment.

His government feel that the suffering in England has been so small in comparison with that in France that they dislike to be the first to suggest a halt. It is this thought that runs through his letter, and it was continually present in all our conversations.

What do you think of my talking to Jusserand when I am in Washington Tuesday and letting him communicate with his government practically what we cabled Sir Edward?

Affectionately yours,   E. M. House

TLS (WP, DLC).

ENCLOSURE   I

Sir Edward Grey to Edward Mandell House

Private.

Dear Colonel House: London. March 24, 1916.

After receiving your telegram I told those colleagues of it who had already seen the report of our conversation to which your telegram referred.

We all feel that we cannot at this moment take the initiative in asking the French to consider a conference.

I have had no indication since I gave M. Cambon the record that the French are more prepared to consider a conference now than they were then. The fighting for Verdun is still in doubt (though the French are said to be very confident) and I do not suppose the French could take any important decision, until that is settled.

My own feeling is that the moment they express any desire to bring this struggle to an end by a conference, we should and must defer to their views. Owing to the occupation of their territory and the treatment of their population in it by the Germans their sufferings, like those of Belgium, have been greater than ours (though our material contributions to the war all told may be greater) and we cannot urge them to make greater sacrifices than they are themselves prepared to make.

On the other hand to urge a conference on them before they desire it would lead them to suppose that we were not prepared to support them, when they wished to go on. To give such an impression would be most repugnant to our views or feelings, besides having a disastrous political effect.

I propose therefore 1st to let M. Briand know that since you left I have heard if France and England were willing President Wilson would on his own initative summon a conference to end the war on the terms and in the spirit indicated by you at Paris and London.

I will say (2) that we could not put the matter before any of the other Allies unless after consultation with and in concert with the French Government and do not therefore propose to mention this subject at the Conference of Allies in Paris next week.

(3) That if M. Briand has any views to express on the subject he will no doubt let me know them either himself or through M. Jules Cambon, while we are in Paris.

The Prime Minister and I go there on Thursday evening. Of course there is nothing in this to prevent your making any communication to the French that you think opportune.

Yours sincerely,   E. Grey

TCL (WP, DLC).

E N C L O S U R E   I I

[London] April 8, 1916.

I acted as proposed in my letter of March 24th to you but neither Briand nor Cambon mentioned the subject at Paris. Feeling there was that war must yet continue to have any chance of securing satisfactory terms from Germany. We felt it was not a time when we could ask the French Government to consider a conference and put the matter before the other allies.

German Chancellor's speech[1] will now harden opinion here and in allied countries.

Am sending letter by Lord E. Percy who is going to Washington tomorrow.

E. Grey.

This cable has just come. 7 P.M. E.M.H.

TC telegram (WP, DLC).

[1] In a speech to the Reichstag on April 5, Bethmann Hollweg strongly defended Germany's conduct of the war and declared that the German people would never permit the destruction of German military and economic power. He indicated

that Germany would demand some undefined new status for both Belgium and Poland in any peace settlement. He denied reports that Germany would invade North America after the conclusion of the European conflict. But his most significant statement concerned submarine warfare. "No fair-minded neutral," he declared, "no matter whether he favors us or not, can doubt our right to defend ourselves against this war of starvation, which is contrary to international law. No one can ask us to permit our arms of defense to be wrested from our hands. We use them, and must use them. We respect legitimate rights of neutral trade and commerce, but we have a right to expect that this will be appreciated, and that our right and our duty be recognized—to use all means against this policy of starvation, which is a jeering insult not only to all laws of nations, but also to the plainest duties of humanity." *New York Times*, April 6, 1916. See also J. W. Gerard to RL, April 5, 1916, *FR-WWS 1916*, p. 23.

E N C L O S U R E   I I I

Sir Edward Grey to Edward Mandell House

Dear Colonel House: London. March 23rd, 1916.

Soon after you left the Chilean Minister[1] volunteered a statement to Sir M. de Bunsen[2] of his conversation with you about the Pan-American proposal.

In consequence of what Sir M. de Bunsen told me I thought it desirable to see the Chilean Minister before saying anything in public. I found him pleased with what you had said to him but insisting very carefully that the idea of partnership must be emphasised and that of tutelage suppressed.

He admitted that you had done this but he made it clear that if I made any public statement it must be evident that I was founding myself not only on what President Wilson had said but on the feelings of the A.B.C. countries in South America as well.

I asked him to send me a statement which he said the President of Chile had made favourable to the idea so that if I had to say anything in public I might refer to it as well as to what President Wilson had said.

The Canadian Government were quite willing that I should say what I thought of saying in favour of it but finding I should be on rather delicate ground as regards the A.B.C. countries, I think I will wait till the matter comes up in the Press again before making any public utterance.

I made it clear to the Chilean Minister that we were favourable to the plan as put before him by you, and that you had spoken to me in exactly the same way as to him, but I said nothing of having discussed with you the question of a public statement here.

Yours sincerely,   E. Grey.

TCL (WP, DLC).
  [1] Agustin Edwards.
  [2] Sir Maurice William Ernest de Bunsen, former British Ambassador to Spain (1906-13) and to Austria-Hungary (1913-14), at this time an Assistant Undersecretary of State in the Foreign Office.

From Edward Mandell House

Dear Governor: New York. April 8, 1916.

Bernstorff was with me for an hour this morning. I outlined the situation to him just as we had planned. He expressed his inability to understand matters any better than we do.

He said a break must not occur and that he would immediately get busy. Asking for suggestions, I thought he should cable his government that you felt completely discouraged. That it had been only by the grace of God that American lives had not been lost upon ships torpedoed without warning. That it might happen today, tomorrow or next week, but it would surely come unless they renounced their submarine policy and a break was inevitable.

Bernstorff admitted that if passenger ships were torpedoed without warning and American lives lost, you had no alternative excepting a severance of relations with Germany. He said he had communicated this to his government, but that he had cried wolf so many times, perhaps it did not have as much effect as it should.

I let him know that the most distressing feature of the break was our inability to lead the belligerents out. He said he had hoped you were ready to do this now and wished to know when I thought the time would be opportune. I explained that it seemed necessary to let them try out their offensive plans on both sides during the spring and early summer. That Germany had begun with Verdun and had seemingly failed. That when she had finished, the Allies would probably make their attempt and if they were no more successful, it would be evident then to everybody that the deadlock was unbreakable and you could then intervene with success.

I asked him if he had any information in regard to Hughes' views upon foreign affairs. That I, myself, had not been able to find just what he thought. Bernstorff replied that the only light he had on the subject was that *on October 9th, 1914, Justice Hughes called upon him to express his sympathy* and that he, Bernstorff, not only appreciated the unusual courtesy, but gathered from it that the Justice's sympathies were not against Germany.[1]

This is significant and is to be remembered in the event Hughes is the republican nominee.

Affectionately yours, E. M. House

TLS (WP, DLC).

[1] Bernstorff reported his conversation with House in J. H. von Bernstorff to the Foreign Office, received April 11, 1916, T telegram (Der Weltkrieg, No. 18,

geheim, Unterseebootkrieg gegen England, Vol. 12, pp. 5-6, GFO-Ar). It follows in part (our translation): "House described the atmosphere in very gloomy terms on account of the *Sussex*. In the White House, the situation is regarded as hopeless, because it is believed there that the German government, in spite of Tirpitz' resignation, cannot check its submarine warfare, even if it genuinely intended to do so. So far, it has merely been due to chance that no American has lost his life, but each moment could bring a crisis which would necessarily precipitate a break. The American government is convinced that the *Sussex* was torpedoed by a German submarine. A repetition of such mistakes would have to drive the United States into war with us. Wilson would greatly regret this, because, as I already reported, he wants to bring about peace in a few months. If the United States would be drawn into the war, all hope for an early peace would be lost."

From Robert Lansing, with Enclosure

PERSONAL AND CONFIDENTIAL:

My dear Mr. President:　　　　　　Washington April 10, 1916.

I enclose a suggested insertion in the draft of instructions to the American Ambassador at Berlin, which I handed to you at the White House on the 6th instant.

The suggestion is due to Mr. Gerard's telegram #3713 of April 6th.[1] I have just this moment received another telegram from Mr. Gerard saying that he expected to receive today the German reply in the SUSSEX case.[2] I am, however, sending forward this suggestion for insertion because I assume the German answer will deny the presence of one of their submarines in the vicinity of the SUSSEX at the time she was wrecked—which will not materially affect our position as I see it.

I also enclose a flimsy of Mr. Gerard's 3713 and also a statement of the facts in the case of the SUSSEX based on the evidence which we now have in hand.[3] My idea is that this statement should accompany the proposed instructions, together with the evidence upon which it is based.

In case that course is followed it will be necessary to insert on page one of the draft of instructions a parenthetical clause at the end of the third paragraph, reading: "(A statement of the facts in the case is enclosed.)"

In spite of the dispatches we are receiving from Berlin I am still of the same opinion which I have by letter and orally expressed to you—that the course of action of this Government should be decided upon as soon as possible.

Faithfully yours,　Robert Lansing.

TLS (SDR, RG 59, 851.857 SU 8/54½A, DNA).

[1] J. W. Gerard to RL, April 6, 1915, T telegram (SDR, RG 59, 851.857 Su 8/42, DNA), printed in *FR-WWS 1916*, p. 225. Gerard transmitted a note from Von Jagow to himself of April 5 in which the Foreign Secretary stated that the German Admiralty's investigation of the *Sussex* affair had thus far been inconclusive. He assured Gerard that, should further investigation prove that *Sussex* had been attacked by a German submarine contrary to the assurances given to the

American government, the German government would "as a matter of course . . .
immediately order the necessary redress . . . to take place." In order to "facilitate
and accellerate" the investigation, Von Jagow asked the American government to
forward full details on the *Sussex* incident as soon as possible. Gerard added
his own impression that the German government did wish to "adjust matter with
America."

2 J. W. Gerard to RL, April 8, 1916, T telegram (SDR, RG 59, 851.857 Su
8/43, DNA).

3 Lansing's revised version of this document is cited in RL to WW, April 15,
1916 (second letter of that date), n. 1.

E N C L O S U R E

Drafted on account of
Gerard's #3713 of April
6, 1916.

Suggested insertion at the beginning
of DRAFT OF INSTRUCTIONS TO AMERICAN
AMBASSADOR AT BERLIN (April 6, 1916)
Robert Lansing.

I did not fail to transmit immediately by telegraph to my Government your Excellency's note of the 5th instant in regard to the
disasterous explosion, which on March 24th wrecked the French
steamship SUSSEX in the English Channel. I have now the honor
to deliver, under instructions from my Government the following
reply to your Excellency:

The Government of the United States, after careful consideration of the Imperial Government's note of April 5, 1916, regrets
to state that it appears from the statements and requests contained in the note that the Imperial Government fails to appreciate the gravity of the situation which has resulted not alone
from the attack on the SUSSEX but from the submarine warfare
as waged by the German naval authorities, which without apparent discrimination has been directed against neutral merchant
vessels as well as those of Germany's enemies.

If the SUSSEX had been an isolated case, the Government of the
United States might consider that the officer responsible for the
deed had wilfully violated his orders and that the ends of justice
would be satisfied by imposing upon him an adequate punishment and by a formal disavowal of the act by the Imperial Government. But the SUSSEX is not an isolated case, though the attack
was so utterly indefensible and caused a loss of life so appalling
that it stands forth today as one of the most terrible examples of
the inhumanity of submarine warfare as it is now being waged
by Germany.[1]

1 Wilson drew a line alongside the right side of the paragraph above.

Even if the SUSSEX was torpedoed by mistake or in deliberate disobedience of orders, the fact remains that the act is in accord with the spirit manifested by the German naval authorities in their general policy and practice of submarine warfare. In view of this fact no apology, no disavowal, no admission of wrongdoing, no punishment of a guilty officer, and no payment of indemnity will satisfy the Government of the United States. Furthermore, the question of submarine warfare, which has for so many months been under discussion, is no longer debateable. The evidence of the determined purpose of the Imperial Government in the employment of submarines against peaceable merchant vessels is too certain and too plain to require explanation, and it is too manifestly lawless to admit of argument.

Thoroughly convinced that the attack on the SUSSEX was directly due to the German policy, though there may possibly have been a technical violation of orders by the commander of the submarine who torpedoed the vessel, the Government of the United States, while communicating to the Imperial Government the facts in the case of the SUSSEX, is constrained to go further and to announce the course of action which it has determined to follow and the reasons for such action.

A[2]

Draft of Instructions to the
AMERICAN AMBASSADOR—BERLIN
April 6, 1916.

You are instructed to deliver to the Secretary of Foreign Affairs a note reading as follows:

On March 24, 1916, at two-fifty p.m. the unarmed steamer SUSSEX, with three hundred and fifty to four hundred passengers on board, among whom were a number of American citizens, was torpedoed in the English Channel enroute from Folkestone to Dieppe. Eighty of the passengers, which consisted of non-combatants of all ages and sexes, were killed or injured.

A searching and impartial investigation by officers of the United States has established conclusively that the vessel was torpedoed without warning or summons to surrender, and that the torpedo was launched by a German submarine.[3]

The attack upon the SUSSEX, like the attacks made upon the ENGLISHMAN, MANCHESTER ENGINEER, EAGLE POINT and other steamers of belligerent and neutral nationalities, was contrary to

---

[2] WWhw.

[3] Here Wilson wrote in shorthand: "(full statement of the facts is enclosed)."

the rules of civilized warfare and in violation of those principles of humanity which enlightened nations respect in conducting hostile operations on the high seas.

The Government of the United States has been forced to the conclusion, by evidence of the most convincing character, either that the explicit assurances heretofore given to it by the Imperial Government as to the employment of undersea craft in intercepting enemy and neutral commerce have been violated by German submarine commanders with the knowledge and acquiescence of the Imperial Government, or that that Government in recently issuing orders to its submarines to renew their activities did so with the intention of ignoring the assurances given.

Whichever of these alternatives is the fact is immaterial, for in either case the Imperial Government has, through its naval authorities, broken its solemn pledge to the Government of the United States and resorted to a method of warfare which invites the condemnation of the civilized world. The Government and the people of the United States have viewed with abhorrence this policy of wanton and indiscriminate slaughter of helpless men, women and children traversing the high seas in the enjoyment of their recognized rights, and it justly resents the breach of faith, of which the Imperial Government is guilty in thus renewing an inhuman and illegal practice which it had expressly agreed to abandon.

For a century the tendency of the nations has been to ameliorate the human suffering which is the inevitable consequence of war. By treaties, by declarations, and by common usage non-combatants have been more and more protected in their lives and property from the horrors incidental to conflicts between nations. The spirit of modern civilization revolts against needless cruelty and the wanton destruction of human life. The present conduct of submarine warfare by Germany is hostile to this spirit; it is a reversion to that barbarism which took no thought for human life and which caused the innocent and defenseless to suffer even more grievously than those who bore arms.

In its first note in regard to the sinking of the LUSITANIA, the Government of the United States expressed the opinion that it was impossible for a submarine to conduct operations against the commerce of an enemy and conform to the laws of naval warfare and to the principles of humanity. The Government of the United States, though subject to the greatest provocation to adopt severe measures against the Government which had permitted and which defended the lawless act of its submarine commander, conducted its negotiations with a restraint and patience which evinced its earnest desire to obtain by amicable means a settlement which would make amends for the past and guarantee humane conduct for the future. As the negotiations progressed, the Government of the United States becamse [became] increasingly hopeful that the Imperial Government would recognize the illegality of the sinking of the LUSITANIA and prevent a repetition of the outrage by its submarine commanders. The recent operations of German submarines, which have been carried on with the same brutal indifference to the right of life as was exhibited in the case of the LUSITANIA, has destroyed this hope and proved that the patience and restraint of the Government of the United States have been in vain, while the moderation shown appears to have been misconstrued by the Imperial Government.

The opinion, which the Government of the United States expressed in the note, to which reference has been made, as to the impossibility of legally and humanely employing submarines as commerce destroyers, has become a settled conviction. The course, upon which Germany has now entered, can no longer be tolerated, and a Government, which permits such practices, is no longer entitled to continue its intercourse with other Governments which regard the rules of international law and the principles of humanity as binding upon all belligerents.

In view of the manifest intention of the Imperial Government to continue this lawless and inhuman method of warfare it becomes, therefore, my solemn duty to inform your Excellency that the Government of the United States is compelled to sever diplomatic relations with the Imperial German Government until such time as that Government shall announce its purpose to discontinue and shall actually discontinue the employment of submarines against commercial vessels of belligerent as well as of neutral nationality.

I am, therefore, instructed to request my passports and directed to depart from Germany without delay; and I am further instructed to announce to your Excellency that the German Ambassador at Washington will forthwith be handed his passports and requested to take his immediate departure from the United States.

❖

In view of the manifest purpose of the Imperial Government to prosecute relentlessly submarine warfare against commercial vessels, without regard to legal right or the dictates of humanity, the

Government of the United States is compelled to announce its intention to sever diplomatic relations with Germany unless the Imperial Government declares unconditionally that it will abandon its purpose and no longer employ its submarines against vessels of commerce.

T MS (SDR, RG 59, 851.857 SU 8/54½A, DNA).

From Robert Lansing

PERSONAL AND CONFIDENTIAL:

My dear Mr. President: [Washington] April 10, 1916.

In view of the fact that you are studying the present German situation, I enclose you a memorandum prepared by Mr. L. H. Woolsey, First Assistant Solicitor of the Department, on GERMAN SUBMARINE WARFARE, which you may find useful.[1]

I am sending you the original draft in order that there may be no delay as a result of copying it in better form.

Faithfully yours,   Robert Lansing

TCL (SDR, RG 59, 763.72/2647½, DNA).
[1] L. H. Woolsey, "German Submarine Warfare," April 10, 1916, TS MS (SDR, RG 59, 763.72/2647½, DNA). This sixteen-page memorandum reviewed the history of German submarine warfare since February 1915 and of the correspondence between the American and German governments about it. Woolsey reached a devastating conclusion: "It is impossible either to accept the assurances of the German Government or to rely on its instructions to its commanders to carry them out—the result of either is the continued slaughter of citizens of the United States."

A Draft of a *Sussex* Note[1]

[April 10, 1916]

You are instructed to deliver to the Secretary of Foreign Affairs a communication reading as follows:

I did not fail to transmit immediately, by telegraph, to my Government Your Excellency's note of the fifth instant in regard to the disastrous explosion which on March twenty-fourth last wrecked the French steamship SUSSEX in the English Channel. I have now the honour to deliver, under instructions from my Government, the following reply to Your Excellency:

The facts in this destressing case, as they have now been established to the satisfaction of the Government of the United States, are these: On the twenty-fourth of March, 1916, at about two-fifty o'clock in the afternoon, the unarmed steamer SUSSEX,

[1] There is an undated WWsh draft of the following document in WP, DLC.

with some three hundred and fifty to four hundred passengers on board, among whom were a number of American citizens, was torpedoed while crossing from Folkestone to Dieppe. The SUSSEX had never been armed; was a vessel known to be habitually used only for the conveyance of passengers across the English Channel; and was not following the route taken by troop ships or supply ships. Eighty of her passengers, non-combatants of all ages and sexes, were killed or injured.

A careful, detailed, and scrupulously impartial investigation by officers of the United States has conclusively established the fact that the SUSSEX was torpedoed without warning or summons to surrender and that the torpedo by which she was struck was of German manufacture. The Government of the United States does not think that the plain inference that the torpedo was fired from a German submarine can, all the attendant circumstances being taken into consideration, be avoided. A full statement of the facts upon which the Gov't of the U. S. has based its conclusions is enclosed.

The Government of the United States, after having given careful consideration to the note of the Imperial Government of the fifth of April, regrets to state that the impression made upon it by the statements and requests contained in that note is that the Imperial Government has failed to appreciate the gravity of the situation which has resulted, not alone from the attack on the SUSSEX, but from the whole method and character of submarine warfare as disclosed by the unrestrained practice of the commanders of German undersea craft during the past twelvemonth and more in the indiscriminate destruction of merchant vessels of all sorts, nationalities, and destinations. If the sinking of the SUSSEX had been an isolated case, the Government of the United States might find it possible to hope that the officer who was responsible for that act had wilfully violated his orders and that the ends of justice might be satisfied by imposing upon him an adequate punishment, coupled with a formal disavowal of the act by the Imperial Government. But, though the attack upon the SUSSEX was manifestly utterly indefensible and caused a loss of life so appalling as to make it stand forth as one of the most terrible examples of the inhumanity of submarine warfare as the commanders of German vessels are conducting it, it unhappily does not stand alone.

On the contrary, the Government of the United States is forced by recent events to conclude that it is only one instance, even though one of the most extreme and distressing incidents, of a deliberate method and spirit of indiscriminate destruction which have become more and more unmistakable as the activity of German undersea vessels of war has in recent months been quickened and extended.

The Imperial Government will recall that when, in February, 1915, it announced its intention of treating the waters round about Great Britain as a closed zone and seat of war and of destroying all merchant ships owned by its enemies that might be found within that area of the seas, and warned all vessels, neutral as well as belligerent, to keep out of the waters thus proscribed, or enter them at their peril, the Government of the United States earnestly protested and took the position that such a policy could not be pursued without constant gross and palpable violations of the accepted law of nations, particularly if submarine craft were to be employed as its instruments, inasmuch as the rules of visit and search prescribed by that law and the strict principles of protection which it had carefully thrown around the lives of non-combatants at sea could not in the nature of the case be observed by such vessels; because vessels of neutral ownership would thereby be exposed to extreme and intolerable risks; and because no right to close any part of the high seas could lawfully be asserted by the Imperial Government in the circumstances then existing. The law of nations in these matters upon which the Government of the United States based its protest were not of recent origin or founded upon merely arbitrary principles set up by convention. They are based, on the contrary, upon manifest principles of humanity and have long been established with the approval and by the express assent of all civilized nations. The Imperial Government, notwithstanding the protests of the Government of the United States, persisted in its policy, expressing the hope that the dangers involved, at any rate to neutral vessels, would be reduced to a minimum by the instructions which it had issued to the commanders of its submarines, and assuring the Government of the United States that it would take every possible precaution both to respect the rights of neutrals and to safeguard the lives of non-combatants.

In pursuance of this policy of submarine warfare against the commerce of its adversaries, thus announced and thus entered upon in despite of the solemn protest of the Government of the United States, the commanders of the Imperial Government's undersea vessels have carried on practices of ruthless destruction which have made it more and more evident as the months have gone by that the Imperial Government had found it impracticable to put any such restraints upon them as it had hoped and promised. Vessels of neutral ownership, even vessels of neutral ownership bound from neutral port to neutral port, have been destroyed along with vessels of belligerant ownership in constantly increasing numbers. Sometimes the merchantmen attacked have been warned and summoned to surrender before being fired on; sometimes their passengers and crews have been vouchsafed the poor security of being allowed to take to the ship's boats before the ship was sent to the bottom. But quite as often no warning has been given, no escape even to the ship's boats allowed to those on board. Great liners like the LUSITANIA and mere passenger boats like the SUSSEX have been sunk without a moment's warning, before they have even become aware that they were in the presence of an armed ship of the enemy, and the lives of non-combatants, passengers and crew, have been destroyed wholesale and in a manner which the Government of the United States cannot but regard as wanton and without the slightest colour of justification.

Again and again the Imperial Government has given its solemn assurances to the Government of the United States that at least passenger ships would not be thus dealt with, and yet it has as often permitted its undersea commanders to disregard those assurances with entire impunity. In February last it gave notice that it would regard all armed merchantmen owned by its enemies as part of the armed naval forces of its adversaries and deal with them as with men of war, thus, at least by implication, pledging itself to give warning to vessels which were not armed and security of life to their passengers and crews; but even that limitation their submarine commanders have recklessly ignored. No limit of any kind has in fact been set to their indiscriminate pursuit and destruction of merchantmen of all kinds and nationalities within the waters which it has chosen to designate as lying within the seat of war. The roll of Americans who have lost their lives upon ships thus attacked and destroyed has grown month by month until the ominous toll has mounted into the hundreds. The Government of the United States has been very patient. At every stage of this distressing experience it has sought to be governed by principles of the utmost consideration for the extraordinary circumstances of an unprecedented war and to be guided by sentiments of very genuine friendship for the people and Government of Germany. It has accepted the successive explanations and assurances of the Imperial Government as of course given in entire sincerity and good faith and has hoped, even against hope, that it would prove to be possible for the Imperial Government so to order and control the acts of its naval commanders as to square its policy with the recognized principles of humanity as embodied in the law of nations. It has made every allowance for unprecedented conditions and has been willing to wait until the facts became unmistakable and susceptible of only one interpretation.

It now owes it to a just regard for its own rights to say to the Imperial Government that that time has come. It has become painfully evident to it that the position which it took at the very outset is inevitable, namely that the use of submarines for the destruction of an enemy's commerce is of necessity, because of the very character of the vessels employed and the very methods of attack which their employment of course involves, utterly incompatible with the principles of humanity, the long established and incontrovertible rights of neutrals, and the sacred immunities of non-combatants.

If it is still the purpose of the Imperial Government to prosecute relentless and indiscriminate warfare against vessels of commerce by the use of submarines without regard to what the Government of the United States must consider the sacred and indisputable rules of international law and the universally recognized dictates of humanity, the Government of the United States is at last forced to the conclusion that there is but one course it can pursue. Unless the Imperial Government should now immediately declare its intention to abandon its present practices of submarine warfare and return to a scrupulous observance of the practices clearly prescribed by the law of nations, the Government of the United States can have no choice but to sever diplomatic relations with the German Empire altogether. ⟨It will await an early announcement of the future policy of the Imperial Government in the earnest hope that this unwelcome course will not be forced upon it.⟩[2]

WWT MS (WP, DLC).
[2] Wilson struck out the final sentence printed in angle brackets.

From Newton Diehl Baker

Confidential

My dear Mr. President: Washington. April 10, 1916.

As I shall be away tomorrow, I place this memorandum in your hands to bring your information up to date with regard to the situation in Mexico:

1. On last Saturday, while I was testifying before the Military Committee of the House, newspapermen asked General Scott whether it was true that Carranza had assembled 15,000 men and given our soldiers four days to depart from Mexico. General

Scott said there was nothing in it. They then asked him how long our troops were going to stay there, to which he replied that they would doubtless retire as soon as they had accomplished their object, and pointed out to them the language of the despatch to General Funston, written March 10th and in verbal accord with the statements issued by me at that time, defining the objects of the expedition. The newspapermen thereupon proceeded to discuss the despatch as though it were a new contribution and disregarded the fact that its date was coincident with the beginning of the undertaking. I have been much embarrassed and distressed at the incident, but the origin of the story was really in El Paso, and General Scott's comment added nothing new to a situation already known to the newspapermen.

2. Today I have had a full telegram, through General Funston, from General Pershing to the effect that General Herrera[1] and staff had called upon him at his (Pershing's) headquarters and offered full cooperation. General Pershing sent a message to General Guitterrez[2] at Chihuahua by aeroplane. As the aeroplane landed some boys threw stones at it and a couple of by-standers shot at it. Our aviators evidently exercised commendable self-restraint. The incident passed over, and General Guitterrez expressed regret. He later sent back by the same aviator a cordial message offering cooperation to General Pershing. Today (Monday) a conference was scheduled to take place between General Pershing, General Herrera and General Guitterrez. General Pershing's comment is that, apparently, the Carranzista Generals are cooperating to the full extent of their ability.

We are now using the Mexican railroads for the shipment of commissary supplies, and the question of providing our expedition with such supplies seems, temporarily, solved.

I have had no despatches since yesterday as to the whereabouts of Villa. It seems, however, persistently reported that he is in the neighborhood of Parral, and General Pershing reports quite definitely that Villa was shot in the right knee and seriously wounded. If, as a result of the conference today, such cooperation was arranged as will enable the Carranzista Generals to close one side of the country to Villa's further progress our men ought to be able to catch up with him.

I have directed General Scott in my absence to give to the newspapers no comment of any kind on any transaction, past or present, and to limit his giving out of news to such reports of facts from General Funston as could with propriety be published. I have further asked him to send to you at once, under confidential cover, any despatch from General Funston of importance, either as showing the progress of our expedition or any change in the present cordial attitude of the Carranzista people.

Respectfully submitted,   Newton D. Baker

TLS (WP, DLC).
  1 Luis Herrera, former Military Governor of the State of Chihuahua.
  2 That is, General Luis Gutiérrez, *Carrancista* commander in Chihuahua.

From William Church Osborn

Kindness of Mr. Henry Morgenthau.

My dear Mr. President: New York. April 10th 1916.

I think I should tell you that a movement is on foot here to elect Mr. Edward S. Harris[2] Chairman of the State Committee in my place. Mr. Harris's selection is regarded as a serious political mistake by all classes of up-state Democrats. It will be considered the result of an understanding between representatives of the administration and Mr. C. F. Murphy and a complete turning over of the State organization to Murphy. I think this extremely prejudicial to the Presidential campaign and should be stopped, but I must advise you that apparently some of the Washington people have agreed to it. The Tammany people are giving out that Harris is selected because he was chosen by the administration's influence. In common with most up-state Democrats I think it very detrimental to the interests of the party in this State to turn the Chairmanship over to Murphy and if the matter goes through without disavowal on the part of the administration, I may feel it necessary to make a public statement on the subject. I trust however, that with the good advice of Mr. Morgenthau and your own assistance in the matter this serious injury to the campaign may be averted.

Believe me with respect,

Very truly yours,   Wm. Church Osborn

TLS (WP, DLC).
  1 Edwin, not Edward, S. Harris, of Schuylerville, N. Y., former Deputy State Controller of New York and a protégé of Charles F. Murphy, boss of Tammany Hall. Harris was elected chairman at a meeting of the state committee in New York on April 14.

From William Howard Taft

My dear Mr. President: [New Haven, Conn.] April 11th, 1916.

On behalf of the members and friends of the League to Enforce Peace, I write to ask you to address the League on the occasion of its first annual meeting, to be held in Washington, Friday and

Saturday, May 26th and 27th. In your speech at Des Moines, on February 1st, you said:

"I pray God that if this contest have no other result, it will at least have the result of creating an international tribunal and producing some sort of joint guaranty of peace on the part of the great nations of the world."

The declared principles and aims of the League to Enforce Peace seem to be in accord with the hope you thus expressed. The banquet on Saturday evening at the New Willard, with which the meeting closes, offers the most favorable occasion to secure the close attention which we desire for the expression and expansion of the keynote you struck so aptly in the phrase I have quoted. A subject which would embody your thought and the League's principles, would be "National and International Preparedness and Permanent Peace," and would give an opportunity for most valuable constructive suggestions. May we shop [hope] that you will do us the honor of being present and speaking on that occasion.

Sincerely yours, Wm. H. Taft
President, League to Enforce Peace.

CCL (W. H. Taft Papers, DLC).

From the Diary of Colonel House

The White House. Washington, April 11, 1916.

I was met by one of the White House motors. I took breakfast alone, the President being indisposed.

At nine o'clock he came to my room and we went to his study to take under consideration a note which he wrote last night to Germany on the submarine issue. He had discarded Lansing's note entirely and had written a much abler one covering all the facts from the beginning and arguing against the use of submarines on merchantmen. I could see that the data I brought back from England, which included a very able presentation of the case by A. H. Pollen,[1] and also one from Sir Horace Plunkett,[2] had had their effect.

The President's voice was weak, and he seemed not at all well,

[1] Arthur Joseph Hungerford Pollen, "Private and Confidential. Memorandum," n.d., T MS (WP, DLC). Pollen, a British writer on naval affairs, discussed in some detail the problems raised by submarine warfare against merchantmen. His principal conclusions were that submarines, by their very nature, could not be used in accordance with international law and that belligerent merchant ships had a right to be armed for defense. House left the memorandum with Wilson on March 6, 1916.

[2] That is, H. Plunkett to WW, February 23, 1916.

having not recovered from the digestive spell which seized him a few days ago. I objected to the last page of the note as being inconclusive, and as opening up the entire question for more argument. The President did not agree with me, but at my suggestion, cut out the last paragraph[3] which strengthened the note somewhat. He also inserted the word "immediately"[4] which strengthened it further. Mrs. Wilson declared it weak and unsatisfactory at the end. He patiently argued the matter with her, but refused to admit any sort of weakness in it.

His contention was that if he did as we advised, it would mean a declaration of war, and he could not declare war without the consent of Congress. I thought if he left it as it was, it would place him in a bad position, for the reason it would give Germany a chance to come back with another note asserting she was willing to make the concessions he demanded, provided Great Britain obeyed the letter of the law as well. This seeming willingness of Germany to be fair would make a large part of the American public believe the German people were being treated unfairly, and that the President was unduly insistent. He saw the danger of this, but contended that he was helpless. I urged him to keep the note as he had written it and after eliminating the entire last clause, which he did, to say if Germany declined to agree immediately to cease her submarine warfare, that Ambassador Gerard was instructed to ask for his passports. This, I told the President, would come nearer preserving the peace than this plan, because the alternative of peace or war would be placed directly up to Germany in this single note, whereas, the other wording would still leave room for argument and in the end, war would probably follow anyway.

Another point we discussed at much length was his promise to Senator Stone that he would not break off diplomatic relations with Germany without first notifying Congress. The President spoke with much contrition for having foolishly made such a promise, but having made it, he was determined to live up to it, both in form and spirit. This makes the situation awkward. In going before Congress and explaining the matter before he has taken any action, [he] makes a weak statement a necessity. What I should like is for him to go before Congress after the break is made, and deliver a philippic against Germany, not indeed against the German people, but against the cult that has made this calamity possible. No one as yet has brought the indictment

---

3 That is, the last sentence, as has been noted.
4 In the sentence which reads: "Unless the Imperial Government should now immediately declare. . . ." Wilson inserted the "immediately" by hand.

of civilization against them as strongly as it might be done, and I would like the President to do this in a masterly way.

We were in conference for two hours, or indeed, until the President had to leave for an eleven o'clock Cabinet meeting. He was undecided whether to read the note to the Cabinet. He said he did not care for their opinion and was afraid to trust them with it; that the contents would be in the afternoon papers if he did so. He finally decided to read them the note almost in its entirety, but as an argument he had in his own mind against submarine warfare, and not as a note which he had prepared to present Germany.

As soon as the President left, I got in touch with Ambassador Fletcher to find what progress he had been making in the South American Pact. I was disappointed to find it had gone no further [than] when I was here last week. The Chileans are contending for this, that or the other. They want us to practically guarantee the validity of the their [sic] territorial disputes with both Peru and Bolivia.

I took this feature up later with the President at lunch and he asked me to instruct Fletcher to see the Brazilian and Argentine Ambassadors and ascertain whether they were ready to sign without Chile, and if they were, to proceed to have them do so. Fletcher reported later in the afternoon that Ambassador Naon was ready to sign for Argentine, but da Gama wanted instruction from Rio before acting.

In discussing this with the President I suggested that Lansing supplement da Gama's cable and send one direct to the Minister for Foreign Affairs. Also that he cable to Chile direct to ascertain whether they are willing to proceed, provided we make some concessions in the wording of the convention. This met with the President's approval and I telephoned Lansing who promised to send both despatches tonight.

I had some doubts about giving these instructions of the President to Lansing, but I have been so busy and my time is so limited that I took the risk. Polk tells me that the Secretary is in great good humor with me at present. This will not last long, however, unless I use care. I have not be[en] able to see him today, which is in itself a mistake, but there has been no real necessity for it.

I asked Lansing what he thought of the President's note about the submarine controversy. He liked it excepting the last page. He objected to the same things I do. He hoped the tone might be strengthened. At that time he thought the President would be in New York Saturday and Sunday, but in discussing this with the President later, he put it squarely whether I considered it advisable for him to come to New York on a semi-pleasure jaunt while such a momentous decision was pending. Much as I wished him to come, I could not advise him to do so, for it seemed patent he ought to remain in Washington for the present. It was therefore practically decided that way.

The President had a dinner engagement and I dined with Senator Newlands who asked me to name the other guests. Secretary Houston, Senator Stone of the Senate Foreign Relations Committee, and Flood of the House Committee on Foreign Affairs were the ones I wished to meet. My purpose in seeing them was to disabuse their minds as to my activities as exploited in the newspapers. I did this without actually bringing up the subject, but by letting the conversation drift into certain channels where I could turn it in the direction I wished. My idea was that it might save me some trouble in the future if Stone and Flood knew more of my endeavors in Europe, and were informed that those accredited to me were false, and could spread the truth in Congress.

We had a delightful evening. The talk was general but was confined largely to foreign affairs.

I returned to the White House by 10.30 in order to meet the President. On our way back, Houston told me of the Cabinet meeting and of how Burleson drooled along for nearly an hour advising the President to bring our troops out of Mexico. The President finally said, "Burleson I hardly know what to say to you in answer." Lane spoke up and said, "Mr. President, I would suggest that you say to him just what the Postmaster General said to you at the last Cabinet meeting upon the same subject." This brought general laughter, for Burleson then objected just as strongly to withdrawing our troops as he does now to keeping them there.

The President in speaking to me about the Cabinet meeting said he had been bored for two hours with a lot of childish talk. I replied that he evidently did not have a very high regard for his official family, and did not enjoy assembling with them. It reminded me of a tale of Lord Salisbury who so seldom attended Cabinet meetings when he was Prime Minister that he had difficulty in recalling the names of the different members. At one meeting, Salisbury learned over to the man sitting next to him and asked, "Who is that fellow at the other end of the table with the disagreeable face?" His colleague replied, "that is your Chancellor of the Exchequer."

Before dinner, the President, Mrs. Wilson and I went to the Executive Office and remained for nearly two hours, the President signing accumulated mail, commissions, acts of Congress, etc. etc. Mrs. Wilson and I helped him in the mechanical part of it as far as we could. This work had accumulated during the last four days while he has been ill. He tells me he signs his name on an average of about 1000 times a month. Some way should be devised by which the President could be spared this unimportant detail.

The President came to my room while I changed from my evening clothes and made ready for the train. He thanked me for coming over, and for the help I had been to him. He said we had cleaned up much accumulated matter.

He asked again about the New York Postmastership and whether the independent democrats were more reconciled to Johnson. I replied that their objections were irreconcilable.

We discussed whether it would be advisable to send some such message to the French Government as we had sent to the British, since it was evident Grey preferred our going to them direct rather than through him. We decided to do nothing in that direction because it would have to be done through Ambassador Jusserand since I neglected while in Paris to arrange any direct means of communication.

The President wondered whether the South American countries would be willing to sign a peace pact with us, guaranteeing our political and territorial integrity in the event we broke with Germany. We both thought this might halt proceedings, and yet it is possible it might accelerate them for the reason that if our existence is menanced, theirs will be likewise.

Dr. Grayson came to the train with me. I told him I was disturbed by the many complimentary articles appearing about me in the press, and I was afraid they might get on the nerves of the President. Grayson said he did not believe anything could shake the President's affection and confidence in me. He said Mrs. Wilson told Miss Bones the other day that Grayson and I were the only two friends the President had who were serving him without a selfish motive.

To Newton Diehl Baker

My dear Mr. Secretary,   The White House. 12 April, 1916.

I received your letter of the tenth about the conversations General Scott had had with the newspaper men during your last absence. I had divined the explanation before you made it, but I none the less warmly thank you for it.

Now I fear that he has not been as discreet as he should have been while you were away this week. He seems to have, consciously or unconsciously, given full particulars as to the number of troops with or supporting Pershing, the number on the border, the remaining number available in continental America, and all the rest. I dare say this seems to you as unwise as it does to me, in view of the fact, particularly, that we had declined to tell Carranza himself the figures notwithstanding the fact that it was in a way his reasonable right to know.

Am I right in the inferences I draw from the newspapers items?   Faithfully Yours,   W. W.

WWTLI (N. D. Baker Papers, DLC).

To Robert Lansing

My dear Mr. Secretary,   The White House. 12 April, 1916.

Mr. Anketell is, I know, a sincere friend of the Administration, and I am obliged to you for letting me see this letter from him. I have no doubt it represents in the anecdote it tells, a very common feeling. For ourselves, we dare not be guided by feeling, least of all by feeling about ourselves.

Faithfully Yours,   W.W.

WWTLI (R. Lansing Papers, DLC).

To John Worth Kern

My dear Senator: The White House April 12, 1916

May I not express the earnest hope that the general development bill[1] which has been reported out of the Public Lands Committee of the Senate may get its place on the calendar of the Senate? There has always been a strong sentiment in the country that our undeveloped resources should be freed under such safeguards and restrictions as were necessary to secure them against waste, and in recent months this sentiment has grown very powerfully and with a new stimulus. The shortage of gasoline has made the development of the oil resources very important; the potash is very much needed because of our dependence hitherto upon Germany for that product; and the phosphates are required as fertilizers for our western lands. The release of these resources would seem a necessary part of our plan of preparedness and I sincerely hope that it will be possible for this bill to be given a chance to pass at this session. It would really be a very serious detriment to the nation if it did not.

Cordially and sincerely yours,   Woodrow Wilson

TLS (C. Bowers Coll., InU).

¹ Wilson referred to H.R. 406 (a bill to authorize exploration for and disposition of certain minerals on the public lands of the United States), usually referred to as the "general leasing bill," introduced by Scott Ferris of Oklahoma on December 6, 1915. This measure, very similar to one which had failed in the last hours of the Sixty-third Congress when the House and Senate were unable to agree on Senate amendments, provided for the leasing to private interests of the mineral rights on the public lands of the United States with suitable safeguards of the public interest and the payment of royalties to the federal government. This legislation had been inspired by the controversies aroused by President Taft's withdrawal, by Executive Orders, in 1909 and 1910 of some three million acres of oil land from the public domain. These withdrawals, which had the effect of preventing private individuals and firms from entering these lands for prospecting or any other purpose, affected the interests of those who had made entry before the withdrawals, as well as many who did so subsequently in defiance of the Executive Orders. The House passed H.R. 406 with some amendments on January 15, 1916. The Senate Committee on Public Lands, on March 31, reported out a new bill which retained only the enacting clause and the number "H.R. 406." Senators Paul Oscar Husting of Wisconsin and William Howard Thompson of Kansas, in a minority report filed on May 31, charged that the Senate version of the bill was in effect a sell-out to the oil interests. Wilson, obviously, simply wanted to get the bill on the floor of the Senate. See 64th Cong., 1st sess., House Report No. 17, Parts 1 and 2, and Senate Report No. 319, Parts 1 and 2; Arthur S. Link, *Wilson: The New Freedom* (Princeton, N. J., 1956), pp. 132-33; John Ise, *The United States Oil Policy* (New Haven, Conn., 1926), pp. 309-41 *passim*; and J. Leonard Bates, *The Origins of Teapot Dome: Progressives, Parties, and Petroleum, 1909-1921* (Urbana, Ill., 1963), pp. 1-96 *passim*.

To John Fox

My dear Doctor Fox: [The White House] April 12, 1916

No, I am sorry to say I have not the heart to speak to Pitney and urge him to make a speech.¹ I ought not to make one myself; I am carrying a killing load and I have the most intense human sympathy for other men who are doing the same. I know you will understand, though I sometimes wonder if anybody outside of this place knows what the load is.

In haste

Cordially and sincerely yours,   Woodrow Wilson

TLS (Letterpress Books, WP, DLC).

¹ Wilson had promised Fox, a corresponding secretary of the American Bible Society, to speak to that organization on May 7. Fox, in J. Fox to WW, April 6, 1916, TLS (WP, DLC), had asked Wilson to "speak favorably" to Supreme Court Justice Mahlon Pitney about Pitney's making brief remarks on the same occasion.

From Robert Lansing, with Enclosure

I *First* redraft W.W.[1]

PERSONAL AND CONFIDENTIAL:

My dear Mr. President: Washington April 12, 1916.

I am very heartily in accord with the proposed redraft of an instruction to Ambassador Gerard, (though I have suggested certain alterations in the text which do not change the spirit or sense), except as to one thing and that is the closing part which defines our action.

It seems to me to say that we must sever relations *unless* Germany ceases her submarine practices weakens the communication very much. The impression I get is this, that we say we will wait and see if you sink another vessel with Americans on board. If you do we will recall our Ambassador. Why should we postpone to the happening of another outrage action which I feel will do much to prevent such outrage? It impresses me we are actually endangering the lives of our citizens by such a course.

I do not see that we gain anything strategically by postponing an action which I believe, and I think you agree with me, we will have to take in the end.

On the other hand, I think that vigorous and uncompromising action will be far more effective and may accomplish the purpose we desire. I am afraid that the ending as it reads will be construed as indefinite as to time and as giving an opening for discussion.

I have taken the liberty to put down the ending, which I would very much prefer. If they intend to submit at all they will have time to do so before his passports are handed to Gerard. If they do not intend to give up their practices, we are far better off than if we waited till they killed some more Americans.

Of course there is another way and that is to fix a time limit for a favorable answer, say, forty-eight hours; but to me that seems more offensive and more like an *ultimatum* than to break off diplomatic relations without delay or opportunity for parley.

I feel strongly in favor of the action I have proposed, as I think that it would have a profound effect on Germany, on this country and on other neutral nations.

Faithfully yours,   Robert Lansing.

TLS (SDR, RG 59, 851.857 SU 8/55½A, DNA).
[1] WWhw.

ENCLOSURE

Draft April 12, 1916
Additions *underlined*
Omissions bracketed ( )

You are instructed to deliver to the Secretary of Foreign Affairs a communication reading as follows:

(1) I did not fail to transmit immediately, by telegraph, to my Government Your Excellency's note of the fifth instant in regard to the disastrous explosion which on March twenty-fourth last wrecked the French steamship SUSSEX in the English Channel. I have now the honour to deliver, under instructions from my Government, the following reply to Your Excellency:

(2) The facts in this distressing case, as they have now been established to the satisfaction of the Government of the United States, are these: On the twenty-fourth of March, 1916, at about two-fifty o'clock in the afternoon, the unarmed steamer SUSSEX, with some three hundred and fifty to four hundred passengers on board, among whom were a number of American citizens, was torpedoed while crossing from Folkestone to Dieppe. The SUSSEX had never been armed; was a vessel known to be habitually used only for the conveyance of passengers across the English Channel; and was not following the route taken by troop ships or supply ships. *About* eighty of her passengers, non-combatants of all ages and sexes, *including citizens of the United States*, were killed or injured.

(3) A careful, detailed, and scrupulously impartial investigation by officers of the United States has conclusively established (the fact) that the SUSSEX was torpedoed without warning or summons to surrender and that the torpedo by which she was struck was of German manufacture. The Government of the United States does not think that the plain inference that the torpedo was fired from a German submarine can, all the attendant circumstances being taken into consideration, be avoided. A full statement of the facts upon which the Government of the United States has based its conclusions is enclosed.

(4) (The Government of the United States, after having given careful consideration to the note of the Imperial Government of the fifth of April, regrets to state that the impression made upon it by the statements and requests contained in that note is that the Imperial Government has failed to appreciate the gravity of the situation which has resulted, not alone from the attack on the SUSSEX, but from the whole method and character of submarine warfare as disclosed by the unrestrained practice of

the commanders of German undersea craft during the past twelve months and more in the indiscriminate destruction of merchant vessels of all sorts, nationalities, and destinations.) If the sinking of the sussex had been an isolated case, the Government of the United States might find it possible to hope that the officer who was responsible for the act had wilfully violated his orders and that the ends of justice might be satisfied by imposing upon him an adequate punishment, coupled with a formal disavowal of the act *and payment of a suitable indemnity* by the Imperial Government. But, though the attack upon the sussex was manifestly utterly indefensible and caused a loss of life so appalling as to make it stand forth as one of the most terrible examples of the inhumanity of submarine warfare as the commanders of German vessels are conducting it, it unhappily does not stand alone.

(5) On the contrary, the Government of the United States is forced by recent events to conclude that it is only one instance, (even) though (one of the most) *an* extreme and *most* distressing (incidents of a) *one, of the* deliberate method and spirit of indiscriminate destruction *of merchant vessels of all sorts, nationalities and destinations—the method and spirit of* which have become more and more unmistakable (as the activity) *in the practice of the commanders* of German undersea (vessels of war has in recent months been quickened and extended) *craft during the past twelve-month or more.*

(6) The Imperial Government will recall that, when, in February, 1915, it announced its intention of treating the waters (round about) *surrounding* Great Britain *and Ireland* as (a closed zone and) *within the* seat of war and of destroying all merchant ships owned by its enemies that might be found within that (area of the seas) *zone of danger*, and warned all vessels, neutrals as well as belligerent, to keep out of the waters thus proscribed or *to* enter them at their peril, the Government of the United States earnestly protested (and). *It* took the position that such a policy could not be pursued without constant gross and palpable violations of the accepted law of nations, particularly if submarine craft were to be employed as its instruments, inasmuch as the rules (of visit and search) prescribed by that law (and the strict) *and founded on the* principles of *humanity for the* protection (which it had carefully thrown around) *of the* lives of non-combatants at sea could not in the nature of the case be observed by such vessels (because). *It further urged this protest on the ground that persons of neutral nationality and* vessels of neutral ownership would (thereby) be exposed to extreme and intolerable risks; and (because) *that* no right to close any

part of the high seas could lawfully be asserted by the Imperial Government in the circumstances then existing. (The law of nations in these matters, upon which the Government of the United States based its protest, (were) *are* not of recent origin or founded upon merely arbitrary principles set up by convention. They are based, on the contrary, upon manifest principles of humanity and have long been established with the approval and by the express assent of all civilized nations.)

(7) The Imperial Government, notwithstanding the protests of the Government of the United States, persisted in its policy, expressing the hope that the dangers involved, at any rate to neutral vessels, would be reduced to a minimum by the instructions which it had issued to the commanders of its submarines, and assuring the Government of the United States that it would take every possible precaution both to respect the rights of neutrals and to safeguard the lives of non-combatants.

(8) (In pursuance of this policy of submarine warfare against the commerce of its adversaries, thus announced and thus entered upon in despite of the solemn protest of the Government of the United States,) *Nevertheless* the commanders of the Imperial Government's undersea vessels *in carrying out this policy* have (carried on practices of) *practiced such* ruthless destruction (which have made it) *that it has become* more and more evident as the months have gone by that the Imperial Government (had) *has* found it impracticable to put any such restraints upon them as it had (hoped and) promised *to do.* Again and again the Imperial Government has given its solemn assurances to the Government of the United States that at least passenger ships would not be thus dealt with, and yet it has as often permitted its undersea commanders to disregard those assurances with entire impunity. (In) *Even as recently as* February last it gave notice that it would regard all armed merchantmen owned by its enemies as part of the armed naval forces of its adversaries and deal with them as with men of war, thus, at least, by implication, pledging itself to give warning to vessels which were not armed and *to accord* security of life to their passengers and crews; but (even that) *this* limitation (their submarine commanders have) *has been* recklessly ignored.

(9) Vessels of neutral ownership, even vessels of neutral ownership bound from neutral port to neutral port, have been destroyed along with vessels of belligerent ownership in constantly increasing numbers. Sometimes the merchantmen attacked have been warned and summoned to surrender before being fired on *or torpedoed*; sometimes their passengers and crews have been

vouchsafed the poor security of being allowed to take to the ship's boats before the ship was sent to the bottom. But quite as often no warning has been given, no escape even to the ship's boats allowed to those on board. Great liners like the LUSITANIA *and* ARABIC and mere passenger boats like the SUSSEX have been sunk without a moment's warning, before they have even become aware that they were in the presence of an armed ship of the enemy, and the lives of non-combatants, passengers and crew, have been destroyed wholesale and in a manner which the Government of the United States cannot but regard as wanton and without the slightest color of justification.

(No limit of any kind has in fact been set to their indiscriminate pursuit and destruction of merchantmen of all kinds and nationalities within the waters which it has chosen to designate as lying within the seat of war.) The roll of Americans who have lost their lives upon ships thus attacked and destroyed has grown month by month until the ominous toll has mounted into the hundreds.

(10) The Government of the United States has been very patient. At every stage of this (distressing) experience *of tragedy after tragedy* it has sought to be governed by (principles of) the utmost consideration for the extraordinary circumstances of an unprecedented war and to be guided by sentiments of very genuine friendship for the people and Government of Germany. It has (accepted) *received* the successive explanations and assurances of the Imperial Government as (of course) given in entire (sincerity and) good faith, and has hoped, even against hope, that it would prove to be possible for the Imperial Government so to order and control the acts of its naval commanders as to (square) *conform* its policy (with) *to* the recognized principles of humanity as embodied in the law of nations. (It has made) *But making* every allowance for unprecedented conditions and (has been willing to wait until the facts became unmistakable and) *sincerity of purpose the deeds committed are* susceptible of only one interpretation,

(It now owes it to a just regard for its own rights to say to the Imperial Government that that time has come. It has become painfully evident to it that the position which it took at the very outset is inevitable,) namely that, *as indicated at the very outset,* the use of submarines for the destruction of an enemy's commerce is (of necessity), because of the very character of the vessels employed and the very methods of attack which their employment (of course) involves, utterly incompatible with the principles of humanity, the long-established and incontrovertible rights of neutrals, and the sacred immunities of non-combatants.

(11) *The Government of the United States now owes it to a just regard for its own rights to declare that,* if it is still the purpose of the Imperial Government to prosecute relentless and indiscriminate warfare against vessels of commerce by the use of submarines without regard to what the Government of the United States must consider the (sacred and) indisputable rules of international law and the universally recognized dictates of humanity, the Government of the United States is at last forced to the conclusion that there is but one course it can pursue. (Unless the Imperial Government should now immediately declare its intention to abandon its present practices of submarine warfare and return to a scrupulous observance of the practices clearly prescribed by the law of nations, the Government of the United States) *It* can have no choice but to sever diplomatic relations with the German Empire (altogether) *until such time as the Imperial Government shall declare its purpose to abandon and shall abandon its present practices of submarine warfare, return to a scrupulous observance of the rules of naval warfare prescribed by the law of nations, and agree to make amends so far as is possible for the deaths and injuries suffered by citizens of the United States through the wanton attacks of German naval commanders on vessels of commerce.*

I have the honor to inform your Excellency that I am further instructed to request my passports and to depart from the German Empire as soon as possible, and to state that the Imperial German Ambassador at Washington will be requested to take his immediate departure from the United States.

T MS (SDR, RG 59, 851.857 SU 8/55½A, DNA).

From Martin Henry Glynn

My Dear Mr. President: Albany, N. Y. April 12, 1916

Absence in Porto Rico and some trouble with my eyes, brought on by excessive reading in the tropical sun during my vacation, accounts for my delay in acknowled[g]ing your kind and gracious letter of March 6.[1] I have been back home for two weeks, but this is the first letter the doctor has allowed me to write since my return and I wanted to answer your letter with my own hand.

I am glad you liked my reply to Root. I wish I could have done fuller justice to the subject, but my heart was in the work and whatever the speech may have lacked in ability and consummation was atoned for in purpose and intention, I hope. Root's attack was outrageous and I tried to hand him back a Roland for every Oliver he sent.

You can hardly appreciate what a treasure your commendation of my speech has become in the Glynn household. Like a peacock spreading its feathers, Mrs. Glynn[2] parades forth your letter every time one of our relatives visit the house, just to show "What the President thinks of Martin's speech." I am sure you would enjoy a little humorous satisfaction if you could see how carefully "My Lady" guards the letter lest it be misplaced. As for myself, your commendation of the speech is rich compensation for the work I put on it. Your work as President deserves far better praise than my poor pen can bestow. You deserve to be reelected to continue your good work and I believe you will be. I am at your service anywhere and anyhow that I can serve in the good fight.   Most Respectfully Yours   Martin H Glynn

ALS (WP, DLC).
  [1] He meant Wilson's letter to him of March 7, 1916.
  [2] Mary Magrane Glynn.

A Jefferson Day Address[1]

April 13, 1916.

Mr. Toastmaster, ladies and gentlemen: It is a spirit that we assemble to render honor to tonight, and the only way we can render honor to a spirit is by showing that we are, ourselves, prepared to exemplify it. The immortality of Thomas Jefferson does not lie in any one of his achievements, or in the series of his achievements, but in his attitude towards mankind and the conception which he sought to realize in action of the service owed by America to the rest of the world.

One of the things that has seemed to me most to limit the usefulness of the Republican party has been its provincial spirit, and one of the things which has immortalized the influence of Thomas Jefferson has been that his was the spirit of humanity exemplified upon the field of America. Thomas Jefferson was a great leader of men because he understood and interpreted the spirits of men. Some men can be led by their interest; all men can be led by their affections. Some men can be led by covetousness; all men can be led by the visions of the mind. It is not a circumstance without significance that Jefferson felt, perhaps more than any other American of his time, except Benjamin

  [1] At a banquet sponsored by the Common Counsel Club, a Democratic organization, at the New Willard Hotel in Washington. The toastmaster was Robert W. Woolley; the other speakers were Senators Henry F. Hollis, Thomas J. Walsh, and Representative Carter Glass.

Franklin, his close kinship with like thinking spirits everywhere else in the civilized world. His comradeship was as intimate with the thinkers of France as with the frontiersmen of America, and this rather awkward, rather diffident man carried about with him a sort of type of what all men should wish to be who love liberty and seek to lead their fellow men along those difficult paths of achievement.

The only way we can honor Thomas Jefferson is by illumining his spirit and following his example. His example was an example of organization and concerted action for the rights of men, first in America and, then, by America's example, everywhere in the world. And the thing that interested Jefferson is the only thing that ought to interest us. No American who has caught the true historic enthusiasm of this great country that we love can be proud of it merely because it has accumulated great material wealth and power. The pride comes in when we conceive how that power ought to be used.

As I have listened to some of the speeches tonight, the great feeling has come into my heart that we are better prepared than we ever were before to show how America can lead the way along the paths of light. Take the single matter of the financial statistics, of which we have only recently become precisely informed. The mere increase in the resources of the national banks of this country in the last twelvemonth exceeds the total resources of the Deutscher Reichsbank; and the aggregate resources of the national banks of the United States exceed by three thousand millions the aggregate resources of the Bank of England, the Bank of France, the Bank of Russia, the Reichsbank of Berlin, the Bank of the Netherlands, the Bank of Switzerland, and the Bank of Japan. Under the provincial conceptions of the Republican party, this would have been impossible. Under the world conceptions of those of us who are proud to follow the traditions of Thomas Jefferson, it has been realized in fact. And the question we have to put to ourselves is this: How are we going to use this power?

There are only two theories of government, my fellow citizens. The one is that power should be centered in the control of trustees who should determine the administration of all economic and political affairs. That is the theory of the Republican party. A carefully hand picked body of trustees! The other theory is government by responsible and responsive servants of the great body of citizens, able to understand the common interests because in direct and sympathetic touch with the common desire and the common need. The peculiarity of those who think in the terms of trusteeship is that their thinking always squares with the preferences of the powerful and never squares with the lessons of history.

I was talking one day with a gentleman who was expounding to me the very familiar idea that somebody (I dare say he would have preferred to name the persons) should act as guardians and trustees for the people of the neighboring Republic of Mexico. I said, "I defy you to show a single example in history in which liberty and prosperity were ever handed down from above." Prosperity for the great masses of mankind has never sprung out of the soil of privilege. Prosperity for the great masses of mankind has never been created by the beneficence of privilege. Prosperity and right, prosperity and liberty, have never come by favor; they have always come by right. And the only competent expounders of right are the men who covet the opportunity to serve the right. When I see the crust even so much as slightly broken over the heads of a population, which has always been directed by a board of trustees, I make up my mind that I will thrust, not only my arm, but my heart, in the aperture, and that, only by crushing every ounce of power that I can, shall any man ever close that opening up again. Whenever we use our power, we must use it with this conception always in mind—that we are using it for the benefit of the persons who are chiefly interested, and not for our own benefit.

So, by such processes, and by such processes alone, can we illumine and honor the spirit of Thomas Jefferson. You cannot draw example from the *deeds* of Thomas Jefferson, who presided over a little nation only just then struggling for recognition among the nations of the world—without material power, without the respect of foreign nations, without the opportunities of wealth, without the experiences of long periods of trial. There is no parallel in the circumstances of the time of Thomas Jefferson with the circumstances of the time in which we live. My pride is that, in the three years in which we have been privileged to serve this great and trustful people, we have devoted ourselves to the constructive execution of the promises we so solemnly made. Mr. Glass, with the pleasing modesty which has always characterized him, sought to show that his was not the statesmanlike mind that conceived one of the great achievements of the last three years. There is not going to be any quarrel as to where the credit belongs. The thing that is going to strike the imagination of the country is that the Democratic party, without picking out the men or discriminating the praise, produced the constructive statesmanship which the Republican party has not in long generations produced. It has spent its time harking back to a single outworn economic error to which its intellectual armory apparently is limited, while we have gone forward in the spirit of a new age to conceive the methods by which the new necessities of civilization shall be met. We have conceived it in such spirit and in such method that, for the first time since the Republican party and their predecessors destroyed the merchant marine of the United States, we have turned the thoughts and the energies and the conquering genius of the businessmen of America to the great field of the business of the world at large. We have struck the trammels of provincialism away from them, and they are beginning to see that great world in which their genius shall henceforth play the part that other nations have hitherto usurped and monopolized.

Frankly, gentlemen, I am not interested in personal ambitions. May I not admit, even in this company, that I am not enthusiastic over mere party success? I like to see men, generations strong, take fire of great progressive ideas and, banding themselves together like a body of thoughtful brothers, put their shoulders together and lift some part of the great load that has depressed humanity. This country has not the time, it is not now in the temper, to listen to the violent, to the passionate, to the ambitious. This country demands service which is essentially and fundamentally nonpartisan. Some gentlemen will learn this soon, some will learn it late, but they will all learn it so thoroughly that it will be digested. This country demands at this time, as it never did before, absolutely disinterested and nonpartisan service. And I do not now refer merely to foreign affairs, where everybody professes to be nonpartisan. I refer just as much to domestic affairs, for, in saying "nonpartisan," I do not mean merely as between parties and political organizations, but also, and more fundamentally, as between classes and interests.

One of the things that it has been just as interesting to prove as anything else that we have proved in the last three years is that we are not partisan as against any legitimate business interest, no matter how great; that we are not fighting anybody who is doing legitimate business, but that we are fighting *for* everybody who wants to do legitimate business. And we are not partisans as between the rich and the poor, as between the employer and the employee, but, if it be possible, we are partisans of both and would, if we could in our thinking, draw them together to see the interests of the country in the same terms and express them in the same concerted purposes. Any man who fights for any class in this country is now fighting against the interest of America and the welfare of the world. We are nonpartisans as between classes, as between interests, as between political ambitions, as between those who desire power and those who have it. For power will never again in America, if I know anything of its temper, long be entrusted to those who use it in their own behoof.

Gentlemen, are you ready for the test? God forbid that we should ever become directly or indirectly embroiled in quarrels not of our own choosing and that do not affect what we feel responsible to defend. But if we should ever be drawn in, are you ready to go in only where the interests of America are coincident with the interests of mankind and to draw out the moment the interest centers in America and is narrowed from the wide circle of humanity? Are you ready for the test? Have you the courage to go in? Have you the courage to come out according as the balance is disturbed or readjusted for the interests of humanity? If you are ready, you have inherited the spirit of Jefferson, who recognized the men in France and the men in Germany who were doing the liberal thinking of their day as just as much citizens of the great world of liberty as he was himself, and who was ready in every conception he had to join hands across the water or across any other barrier with those who held those high conceptions of liberty which had brought the United States into existence. When we lose that sympathy, we lose the titles of our own heritage. So long as we keep them, we can go through the world with lifted heads and with the consciousness of those who do not serve themselves except as they conceive that they have purified their hearts for the service of mankind.

These are days that search men's hearts. These are days that discredit selfish speech. These are days that ought to quiet ill considered counsel. These are solemn days, when all the moral standards of mankind are about to be finally tried out. And the responsibility is with us, gentlemen, with us Democrats, because the power for the time being is ours, to say whether America, under our leadership, shall hold those eternal balances even, or shall let some malign influence depress one balance and lift the other, till we shall look around and say, "Who stands for the old visions of liberty, and whose eyes are still open to those spiritual images conceived at our birth?"

T MS (WP, DLC), with many corrections from the complete text printed in the *Washintgon Post*, April 14, 1916.

To Edward Mandell House

The White House April 13th. 1916

Am confirmed in opinion it would not be wise to carry out our plan for Saturday.[1]   Woodrow Wilson.

T telegram (E. M. House Papers, CtY).
[1] That is, for the Wilsons to visit the Houses and for Wilson to speak to the Young Men's Democratic Club in New York.

To Walter Hines Page

My dear Page: The White House April 13, 1916

It must be a pretty dreary thing to you to send me letter after letter, upon which you spend so much thoughtful energy and in which you so conscientiously convey to me the things that it is useful for me to know in a way that enables me really to know them, and yet receive no adequate response from me, not only, but only now and then at very long intervals a scant line of acknowledgment like this. But I know that you have both the knowledge and the imagination to understand. There is no reply I can make in kind. Even if I had the time, I could not give you the inside of things here as you give me the inside of things there in a way that would really serve to guide and enlighten you, and I am sure that you know how genuine and sincere my appreciation is of your own admirable letters. My task every day is to go breathlessly through innumerable tasks whose pace constantly makes me fear that I am going too fast to exercise wise and deliberate judgment.

I note what you said in your letter of March sixth about the Shakespeare celebration, and, to tell you the truth, I have hesitated to back up your invitation to Doctor Eliot because of the extreme dangers of travel on the sea just now. It would be such a tragedy to have the fine old man's life end in the going down of a torpedoed ship, and I have not had the heart to say anything to him. Since you wrote your letter of March sixth this terrible business has developed so much and so fast as to seem to me to change the whole aspect of such a thing as this. I know that you will understand and I hope that you will approve.

House has brought me back the most interesting and sympathetic reports of your activities and I am sure he would join with me in warm regards if he were here.

Cordially and faithfully yours,   Woodrow Wilson

TLS (W. H. Page Papers, MH).

To Wallace Buttrick[1]

My dear Doctor Buttrick: [The White House] April 13, 1916

Having heard that the General Education Board has it in contemplation to establish a school in the South to do work along the same lines as have already been undertaken and so admirably developed by my friend, Miss Martha Berry, of Mount Berry, near Rome, Georgia, I write to beg that you will suggest to the Board that before doing this it send a committee to examine the Berry School. It is a school whose development I have watched for a great many years. It is thoroughly worth looking into and I sincerely hope that the Board will show its interest in what has already been accomplished by giving it personal inspection.

Cordially and sincerely yours,   Woodrow Wilson

TLS (Letterpress Books, WP, DLC).
[1] Secretary of the General Education Board, a philanthropic organization sponsored by the Rockefeller family.

To William Berryman Scott

My dear Wick: [The White House] April 13, 1916

I am sincerely glad to know that you are going to be in Washington again soon and I shall look forward with genuine pleasure to seeing you. Please get in touch with the office when you get here and let us make some definite arrangement.[1]

In haste

Cordially and faithfully yours,   Woodrow Wilson

TLS (Letterpress Books, WP, DLC).
[1] Scott had a brief visit with Wilson at the White House on April 17. Scott relates in his autobiography that he called upon Wilson every spring from 1915 to 1917 while attending the annual meeting of the National Academy of Sciences. William Berryman Scott, *Some Memories of a Paleontologist* (Princeton, N. J., 1939), p. 302.

From Edward Mandell House, with Enclosure

Dear Governor: New York. April 13, 1916.

Here are some extracts from a letter which comes from Fletcher this morning.

There is something in his contention and I think we ought to consider it carefully before going ahead too quickly.

I hope you are feeling yourself again. It worries me to have you feel as you did when I was there.

Affectionately yours,   E. M. House

TLS (WP, DLC).

E N C L O S U R E

Washington, April 12, 1916.

"The Brazilian Ambassador telegraphed his government this morning to find out its views as to the next step in view of Chile's attitude. It will place Brazil in an awkward dilemma—they will not on the one hand care to desert the United States and the Argentine nor on the other to leave Chile.

The Chilean Brazilian friendship is traditional and unbroken. Argentine has had questions with both Chile and Brazil, but Chile and Brazil have always walked hand in hand.

I rather think Muller will try to temporize and evade a definite decision, so when da Gama receives his reply I think the President and Mr. Lansing should receive him, hear what he has to say and get a definite idea of Brazil's position.

I think the Treaty would lose the greater part of its force and effect if concluded without Brazil and Chile and might easily have a disturbing effect on the present very cordial and satisfactory state of affairs.

If Chile alone remains out it will of course not be so bad but I fear that in that case the A.B.C.[1] may be considered broken up and we shall be blamed for doing it. Chile will naturally feel peaved, but until we know definitely of Brazil's attitude it is perhaps better to wait."

T MS (WP, DLC).
  [1] That is, the A.B.C. treaty of friendship of May 25, 1915, about which see H. P. Fletcher to RL, Jan. 21, 1916, n. 8, printed as an Enclosure with RL to WW, Feb. 19, 1916.

From Edward Mandell House

Dear Governor: New York. April 13, 1916.

For sometime past I have been discussing McCombs with Baruch with a view of getting him out amicably. Baruch tells me that this has come about and that McCombs is ready to announce that he will not be a candidate to succeed himself because of some business connections he has just made and which will occupy his entire time.

He promises to say to the public that his best endeavors will be used to further your re-election. In other words, he gets out and you let him out gracefully. He is ready to go to Washington and tell you about it and have the necessary formalities gone through with whenever you indicate you are ready.

Affectionately yours,   E. M. House

TLS (WP, DLC).

From William Frank McCombs

My dear Mr President: New York April 13 1916

I am informed you are to be here on the evening of the 15th to speak at the Hotel Knickerbocker.

It has occurred to me that it might be of advantage if, while you are here, we discussed some party matters.

I shall be very glad to call on you at your convenience.

The matter of the selection of a temporary secretary of the National Committee is pressing. There is much work to be done and in my view campaign organizing should proceed without delay. The general feeling of the Committee as I gather it would indicate the temporary selection of one of its members as secretary as soon as possible.

I should be very glad indeed to have your advices.

Sincerely Yours   Wm. F McCombs

ALS (WP, DLC).

From Robert Lansing

PERSONAL AND CONFIDENTIAL:

My dear Mr. President: Washington April 13, 1916.

I enclose translations of two despatches[1] which were handed to me today by Mr. Arredondo relating to the Parral affair—of which I presume you have received the reports from Letcher and Cobb, but the flimsies of which[2] I am enclosing in order that you may have all the information we have received on the subject.

It seems to me a most unfortunate affair and emphasizes the increasing difficulties of the present situation. I will have copies of these two despatches sent at once to the Secretary of War.

Faithfully yours,   Robert Lansing

TLS (SDR, RG 59, 812.00/17866, DNA).

[1] C. Aguilar to E. Arredondo and V. Carranza to E. Arredondo, both dated April 12, 1916, *FR 1916*, pp. 513-14, giving details of a clash in Parral, in which two American soldiers and between forty and one hundred Mexicans had been killed. See also Link, *Confusions and Crises*, pp. 282-83.

[2] Z. L. Cobb to RL, April 12, 1916, *FR 1916*, pp. 514-15; Z. L. Cobb to RL, April 13, 1916, T telegram (SDR, RG 59, 812.00/17833, DNA); and Z. L. Cobb to RL, April 13, 1916, T telegram (SDR, RG 59, 812.00/17834, DNA). The first two telegrams relayed messages from Marion Letcher. All three gave details of the Parral incident.

From John Fox

My dear Mr. President: New York April 13, 1916.

I have your favor of April 12th. Justice Pitney has declined and also Justice Van Devanter,[1] and today President Alderman, of the University of Virginia. I am distressed to know how our appointment burdens you. Our prayers will be offered that God may strengthen you for your heavy duties.

We have one difficult corner to turn—the color question. You know the difficulties which seem peculiarly accentuated in Washington. As a national organization, having an Agency among colored people with a colored minister at its head, we have certain obligations which we cannot avoid. There is a bishop of one of the colored Methodist Churches not resident in Washington on one of our co-operating committees.[2] Would you think it unwise for us to ask him to take a minor part in the religious service at the meeting at which you will speak—say to read a hymn or a passage of Scripture? This is not fixed, but would relieve strain.

I shall be in Washington on Monday to meet the committee of which Mrs. Wilson is honorary chairman, and you can reach me at the New Willard Hotel. If you wish to reach me here you had better wire me tomorrow.

With much appreciation,   Sincerely yours,   John Fox

TLS (WP, DLC).
[1] Willis Van Devanter, Associate Justice of the United States Supreme Court.
[2] Alexander Walters, Bishop of the African Methodist Episcopal Zion Church.

To William Howard Taft

My dear Mr. Taft: The White House April 14, 1916

I am very much complimented that the members and friends of the League to Enforce Peace should desire me to address the League on the occasion of its first annual meeting to be held in Washington, Friday and Saturday, May twenty-sixth and twenty-seventh, and I wish most unaffectedly that I could look forward to accepting the invitation. The truth is, however, as you will readily imagine, that my preoccupation with public duties is such that it seems literally impossible for me to do justice to a great theme such as I would have an opportunity to speak upon at such a meeting. It is practically impossible for me to prepare an address nowadays, and I have no choice but to hope merely that some other way may disclose itself in which I can show my earnest sympathy with the cause of organized peace.

Cordially and sincerely yours,   Woodrow Wilson

TLS (W. H. Taft Papers, DLC).

To Benjamin Franklin Battin

My dear Professor Battin: [The White House] April 14, 1916

I thank you for the friendly suggestion of your letter of April twelfth[1] and wish most sincerely that I could avail myself of it. The truth is that what with the reports Mr. Gerard makes and the repeated interviews Mr. House has had with the representatives of the Foreign Office, the point of view of all parties in Germany is very clear to us here. The difficulty is not with what they think, but with what is done. That is the matter upon which we must form our conclusions and our action. Our desire for peace I need not expound to you.

Cordially and sincerely yours,   Woodrow Wilson

TLS (Letterpress Books, WP, DLC).
  [1] It is missing.

To Joseph Edward Davies

My dear Davies: [The White House] April 14, 1916

Thank you for having let me read this letter again.[1]

There is one thing that distresses me. The implication of Mr. Aylward's letter is (or would seem to one who did not know the circumstances to be) that I had not shown my gratitude for all the generous things he did in promoting my candidacy. Surely he does not feel that. Is it not true that I have appointed him to the office he now holds? that I did so with the greatest pleasure as gratifying his own personal wish, and that the office itself has afforded him an opportunity of showing his real quality and mettle to the people of his state in the performance of duties for which he is eminently qualified? And have I not tried, my dear Davies, in every possible way to show my warm and sincere appreciation and my loyal friendship both to you and to him? It distresses me to find any other implication even latent between the lines, and the inference left to be drawn is that if I should not appoint him to the federal bench, it would be virtually an act of ingratitude on my part. I am sure he cannot soberly mean that, for it is so far from just.

It seems to me my clear duty to do in this case, as in all others, the thing which commends itself to my judgment after the most careful consideration as the wisest and best thing, both for the interests of the bench and the interests of the party.

Always, with real affection,

Faithfully yours,   Woodrow Wilson

TLS (Letterpress Books, WP, DLC).
¹ It is missing.

From Ambrose White Vernon

Brookline, Massachusetts

My dear Mr. Wilson: April 14, 1916

Emboldened by the gracious friendliness you have shown me in the old days, I am venturing to say to you how earnestly I hope, should von Jagow's explanation of the doings of the German submarines be unsatisfactory, that it may be possible for you to accept his offer of arbitration.¹ I am well aware that this offer may not have been made in good faith, but whatever the motive of the German government may be, Germany would be compelled to abide by the judgment of the court she herself invokes. And no matter how complete an array of facts or of asseverations may have been gathered by our government, still the Hague tribunal would be, from the very nature of the case, more likely to reach an absolutely just decision. It seems to me that there is here presented to you such a marvellous epoch-making opportunity to show that great nations are at last willing to submit cases of the highest honor to the judgment of trustworthy and eminent men, even in the midst of war and heat, that one can think of no chance that is greater to advance the welfare of human kind. With such a prospect, I am sure we should be too proud and too grateful to fight.

I know the popular clamor about you, but I believe that you will do at this crisis only what you see to be the highest and the best. It may not be what I think it is, but I felt I wanted to write you. I remember Mr. Lincoln's saying that God is more likely to reveal a man's duty to himself than to his friends. And it is in full belief in that saying that I write.

With deepest gratitude for all that you have done for the country believe me,   Ever affectionately Yours   A W Vernon

TLS (WP, DLC).
¹ Vernon referred to G. von Jagow to J. W. Gerard, April 10, 1916 (conveyed in J. W. Gerard to RL, April 11, 1916, T telegram [WP, DLC], printed in *FR-WWS 1916*, pp. 227-29), which had just been published in full in many American newspapers. Jagow first disposed of the *Berwindvale, Englishman, Manchester Engineer*, and *Eagle Point* cases by saying (1) that a ship resembling *Berwindvale* had tried to escape after being warned, but that her crew were permitted to evacuate the ship before *Berwindvale* was sunk; (2) that *Englishman* and *Eagle Point* had been sunk in similar circumstances; and (3) that the case of *Manchester Engineer* was still under investigation. As for *Sussex*, Jagow said that a submarine commander had torpedoed a ship in the English Channel at the time that *Sussex* had been attacked, and on the same course. However, the commander had submitted a sketch of the ship that he had attacked. This sketch indicated that the ship was a minelayer of the *Arabic* class. Moreover, the

sketch did not resemble the picture of *Sussex* obtained from an English news-paper. Jagow said that, on a basis of its own evidence, the German government had to conclude that a German submarine had not torpedoed *Sussex*. Perhaps she had struck a mine. Should the American government have additional evidence, the German government would be glad to consider it. "In the event of differences of opinion arising between the two Governments in this connection," Jagow concluded, "the German Government declares at this time its readiness to permit the facts to be ascertained by a mixed committee of investigation pursuant to the third title of The Hague Convention of October eighteenth nineteen naught seven for the pacific settlement of international disputes."

Ironically, it later turned out that the newspaper photograph had been made before the war, and that *Sussex* had since undergone alterations that made her look like a warship. Arno Spindler, *La Guerre Sous-Marine* (3 vols., Paris, 1933-35), III, 205-206.

From Jennie Bradley Roessing,[1] with Enclosure

My dear Mr. President: Washington, D. C., April 14, 1916.

As you will be the undisputed candidate for President of the Democratic party at the coming election, the platform makers for your party will undoubtedly desire your views on the important issues of the day. Recognizing the influence which your views will and should have, I am enclosing two suggestions for a plank in the Democratic platform endorsing woman suffrage.

The National American Woman Suffrage Association will appeal to the National Democratic Convention at St. Louis in June for the inclusion of a plank endorsing the principle of woman suffrage, and will be glad to accept either one of these tentative planks or such other endorsement as may be drafted by the Platform Committee. If either of our drafts meet with your approval, may we ask that you refer it to those leaders of your party whose work it will be to formulate the Democratic platform?

In submitting these planks may I call to your attention that they ask merely for the endorsement of our principle. If you so desire, I should be glad to call upon you to give further information with regard to our request, or to discuss any phase of the situation.   Sincerely yours,   Jennie Bradley Roessing

TLS (WP, DLC).

[1] Mrs. Frank M. Roessing of Pittsburgh and Washington, first vice-president of the National American Woman Suffrage Association.

E N C L O S U R E

SUGGESTED PLANKS FOR DEMOCRATIC PARTY, 1916.

Believing that in a true democracy all citizens are entitled to participate in the government on equal terms, we favor the enfranchisement of women.

OR.

Believing that just governments derive their power from the consent of the governed, we acknowledge the right of women to participation in our government and favor their enfranchisement.

T MS (WP, DLC).

To Edward Mandell House

The White House. April 15, 1916.

Would like your opinion of the following action which I am seriously considering. To send to the Senate the name of State Senator Wagner for Postmaster in New York without asking anybody's advice or assent or giving anybody notice except the Postmaster General.   Wilson.

T decode (E. M. House Papers, CtY) of T telegram (WP, DLC).

From Edward Mandell House

[New York, April 15, 1916]

I heartily congratulate you upon having thought of the best way out of a disagreeable and hopeless situation. It should satisfy everybody.   Edward House.

EBWhw decode of T telegram (WP, DLC).

Two Letters from Robert Lansing

My dear Mr. President: Washington April 15, 1916.

In accordance with your request yesterday at Cabinet meeting, I herewith return the redraft of the instruction to Gerard in the submarine matter.[1]   Faithfully yours,   Robert Lansing

TLS (WP, DLC).
    [1] It is printed as an Enclosure with WW to RL, April 17, 1916.

PERSONAL AND CONFIDENTIAL:
    RE: SUSSEX

My dear Mr. President: Washington April 15, 1916.

I have been through the affidavits which were taken in France in the case of the SUSSEX, and also some that were taken in England. They do not add materially to our fund of knowledge in regard to the case, although they do furnish three additional witnesses who saw the wake of the torpedo as it approached the vessel.

I am enclosing a redraft of the statement of facts, giving the authorities.[1]   Faithfully yours,   Robert Lansing.

TLS (SDR, RG 59, 851.857 SU 8/82½, DNA).
   [1] "FACTS IN THE SUSSEX CASE," T Memorandum, n.d. (SDR, RG 59, 851. 857 SU 8/82½, DNA). This was the document which accompanied the *Sussex* note sent by wire to Berlin on April 18, 1916. "FACTS IN THE SUSSEX CASE" is printed in *FR-WWS 1916*, pp. 234-37.

From Edward Mandell House, with Enclosure

Dear Governor: New York. April 15, 1916.

I herewith enclose for your information a copy of a letter which has just come from Bernstorff.

I do not believe we can get anywhere through him for he does not seem to know much more about what is in the minds of his government than we do.

                    Affectionately yours,   E. M. House

TLS (WP, DLC).

E N C L O S U R E

Count Johann Heinrich von Bernstorff to Edward Mandell House

My dear Colonel House: Washington, D. C. April 14, 1916.

With regard to our last confidential conversation I beg to add the following remarks based upon instructions just received from Berlin.

Careful investigation showed, that no German submarine was responsible for the attack on the "Sussex," but my Government is willing to examine any evidence the American Government may have. In case of disagreement my Government suggests decision by a mixed commission of inquiry according to the Hague Convention. My Government will, of course, assume the consequences of such a decision and considers this sufficient proof of our bona fides.

The steamers "Englishman," "Eagle Point" and "Berwindvale" all tried to escape, regardless of warning, but were not destroyed until the crews were saved in life boats. The investigation about the "Manchester Engineer" has so far not had any result and my Government has requested more details from the American Government.

My Government is willing to conduct the submarine warfare with due regard to neutral rights. It stands by our assurances given to the United States and has issued such precise instructions regarding this matter that, according to human foresight, errors are excluded.

If contrary to expectation any mistakes should happen, my Government is willing to remedy them in every way. Germany in face of daily increasing violations of International Law by England cannot give up our submarine war altogether and regrets that England apparently succeeds in hiring a few American citizens for freight ships in the war zone and thus tries to cause a break between Germany and the United States.

There can be no doubt in the bona fides of my Government, since the Chancellor for the second time announced before the whole world that Germany is ready to conclude peace and pointed out that we have only defensive aims. Our enemies, however, sneeringly refused our outstretched hand and are still preaching Germany's lasting military and economic annihilation. My Government entirely shares your wish to bring about peace and hopes that the relations between the United States and Germany will remain so friendly that both Governments can work together for the purpose of achieving this object so desirable in the interest of humanity and of all nations.

The foregoing statements as I said before, are entirely based on instructions from my Government. For my own part, I venture to suggest that it might be advisable to refrain from a further exchange of official notes, the publication of which always causes irritation.

At your suggestion, I called on Mr. Lansing the other day and put myself at his disposal in case he wished me to take up any phase of the matter. Experience has proved, again in the question of exportation of dyestuffs from Berlin, that we always obtain better results if I take up matters confidentially with my Government. Otherwise, they do not, in Berlin, get the right impression of the state of affairs in this country.

I shall give myself the pleasure of calling on you the next time I visit New York which will probably be during the Easter Holidays.

I remain, my dear Colonel House.

Yours very sincerely,   J. Bernstorff.

TCL (WP, DLC).

From Robert Lansing

My dear Mr. President: Washington April 15, 1916.

Yesterday afternoon the French Ambassador called upon me and left me the enclosed clipping from the New York Times[1] in which it is stated that it was announced at Berlin on April 12th that Lieutenant Steinbrinck had received the Prussian Order of Merit in recognition of his exceptional merit in military and naval matters, and that he was the commander of a submarine. Undoubtedly this officer was the commander of a submarine which torpedoed the SUSSEX,[2] and the decoration was conferred apparently after it was known that he was charged with this offense.

I do not think that this can be used in any way at the present time, but I think you should know the attitude of the German Government in regard to the incident.

Kindly return the papers after reading them.

Faithfully yours,   Robert Lansing.

TLS (SDR, RG 59, 851.857 SU 8/81B, DNA).
  [1] Of April 13, 1916.
  [2] As has been noted, one Pustkuchen commanded UB29.

To John Fox

My dear Doctor: [The White House] April 16, 1916

In reply to your letter of April thirteenth, I wish to send only a hasty line but it is to the effect that I do not think it would be wise for you to ask the bishop you referred to to attend the meeting in which I will speak.

In haste

Cordially and sincerely yours,   Woodrow Wilson

TLS (Letterpress Books, WP, DLC).

From Edward Mandell House

Dear Governor: New York. April 16, 1916.

Unless you give the Senator[1] some notification of what you intend doing he will be deeply offended and may be able to get the proposed appointee to decline.

Would it not be well to tell the Senator at ten o'clock in the morning of your intention and let him do the notifying? It could all be done within the space of two hours and would perhaps avoid some complications.

I can see the objections to this, but they seem less than the other way.   Affectionately yours,   E. M. House

TLS (WP, DLC).
  1 That is, Senator O'Gorman.

A Welcome to the Daughters of the American Revolution[1]

April 17, 1916.

Madam President, ladies and gentlemen: I esteem it a real privilege to act as your nominal host again and welcome you to this city where you have just as much right to be as I have. I have always told you, upon more than one occasion, of the sentiments which are chiefly stirred in me by looking upon a company like this. I was thinking today that, if this organization had been formed in the very early years of our republic, it would have been looked upon with a good deal of disfavor, because you would then have been suspected of setting up some sort of aristocratic class. It would have been thought that you were acting in a spirit contrary to the democratic spirit professed by the founders of the republic itself.

You will remember that that sort of criticism was stirred by the foundation of the Society of the Cincinnati. It was supposed that they were setting up an organization which, because its membership was handed on by primogeniture, was an organization entirely contrary to the spirit of American institutions. But a very interesting thing has happened. The proportion of those who can derive their lineage from officers who took part in the American Revolution is a constantly decreasing proportion. You cannot be suspected of trying to build up an organization which will control the country. On the contrary, the spirit in which you have formed this organization was from the first manifest. It was not a spirit of caste or of privilege, but a spirit of reverence for a great tradition. And, for my part, I believe that the chief service of a great organization like this is to keep a certain beautiful sentiment warm and vital in the consciousness of the American people.

Tradition is a handsome thing in proportion as we live up to it. If we fall away from the tradition of the fathers, we have dishonored them. If we forget the tradition of the fathers, we have changed our character; we have lost an old impulse; we have become unconscious of the principles in which the life of the nation itself is rooted and grounded. Therefore, this organization undertook to keep those who fell under its influence constantly reminded of the circumstances of the birth of this nation and of the significance of the birth of this nation. That significance was a very singular significance. No other nation was ever born into the world with the purpose of serving the rest of the world just as much as it served itself. The purpose of this nation was, in one sense, to afford an asylum to men of all classes and kinds who desired to be free and to take part in the administration of a self-governed commonwealth. It was founded in order that men of every sort should have proof given that a commonwealth of that sort was practicable, not only, but could win its standing of distinction and power among the nations of the world. And America will have forgotten her traditions whenever, upon any occasion, she fights merely for herself under such circumstances as will show that she has forgotten to fight for all mankind. The only excuse that America can ever have for the assertion of her physical force is that she asserts it in behalf of the interests of humanity.

What a splendid thing it is to have so singular a tradition—a tradition of unselfishness! When America ceases to be unselfish, she will cease to be America. When she forgets the traditions of devotion to human rights in general, which gave spirit and impulse to her founders, she will have lost her title deeds to her own nationality.

So it is to my mind a very happy circumstance that, here in the capital of the nation, in this home of your own building, you should meet every year in order to keep bright the fires that have always burned upon this altar of devotion to human rights. That is the title of this society to distinction and to immortality, and, therefore, I feel that I am greeting you as if come to a renewal of all the pledges of our national life when I greet and welcome you, as I so warmly do, to this, our common capital.

T MS (WP, DLC).
    1 Wilson spoke at Memorial Continental Hall at the opening session of the twenty-fifth annual continental congress of the Daughters of the American Revolution. Daisy Allen (Mrs. William Cumming) Story, the president general of the organization, presided. *Washington Post*, April 18, 1916.

To Robert Lansing, with Enclosure

My dear Mr. Secretary,   The White House. 17 April, 1916.

Here is the draft of our communication to the Imperial German Government as I think it should go to Berlin.

I have gone over it again and again, and believe now that it is sound at every point. I will see you to-morrow and agree with you as to the exact time at which it shall be sent. Will you not, in the meantime have it put in code and made ready to send?

May I not add this earnest caution? So soon as copies of your suggested revision of this paper were made at the State Department (or was it only a single copy,—the one I am now returning with my own final handling of it?) the newspapers became aware of its contents. Will you not use extraordinary precautions in having this final draft copied and make it *absolutely* safe against the newspaper men both in the transcription and in the coding? This seems to me of the essence of wisdom just at this juncture. I hope that you will make absolutely sure how it is handled and by whom, and hold each individual to the strictest responsibility, upon pain of immediate dismissal. The draft you sent me was undoubtedly given out from the Department (I mean the substance of it), for no one here saw it in the form in which I had written it or in your first redraft except myself.

Faithfully Yours,   W.W.

T MS (SDR, RG 59, 763.72/2596½, DNA).

E N C L O S U R E[1]

II *Final* redraft W.W.   Draft April 12, 1916
                                           Additions *underlined*
                                           Omissions bracketed ( )

You are instructed to deliver to the Secretary of Foreign Affairs a communication reading as follows:

(1) I did not fail to transmit immediately, by telegraph, to my Government Your Excellency's note of the fifth[2] instant in regard to certain attacks by German submarines and particularly in regard to the disastrous explosion which on March twenty-fourth last wrecked the French steamship SUSSEX in the English Channel. I have now the honour to deliver, under instructions from my Government, the following reply to Your Excellency:

[1] This enclosure is Wilson's revision of the same document (Lansing's revision of Wilson's draft) that Lansing sent to Wilson on April 12—what Wilson called the "*first* redraft." The reader will please ignore Lansing's explanations in the upper right hand corner of the page of this "final redraft." In reproducing this document, the Editors have removed Lansing's "brackets" and deleted text when Wilson accepted Lansing's deletions. The Editors have also printed in roman text those additions and substitutions by Lansing that Wilson accepted. Wilson's deletions in the "final redraft" are printed in angle brackets, his additions and restorations of his earlier text, in italics.

[2] Lansing changed this to "tenth" to make the note responsive to Von Jagow's note to Gerard of April 10, as he did in another instance below.

⟨(2) The facts in this distressing case, as they have now been established to the satisfaction of the Government of the United States, are these:⟩

(2) *Information now in the possession of the Government of the United States fully establishes the facts in the case of the* SUSSEX, *and the inferences which my Government has drawn from that information it regards as confirmed by the circumstances set forth in Your Excellency's note of the tenth instant.* On the twenty-fourth of March, 1916, at about two-fifty o'clock in the afternoon, the unarmed steamer SUSSEX, with some three hundred and fifty to four hundred passengers[3] on board, among whom were a number of American citizens, was torpedoed while crossing from Folkestone to Dieppe. The SUSSEX had never been armed; was a vessel known to be habitually used only for the conveyance of passengers across the English Channel; and was not following the route taken by troop ships or supply ships. About eighty of her passengers, non-combatants of all ages and sexes, including citizens of the United States, were killed or injured.

(3) A careful, detailed, and scrupulously impartial investigation by[4] officers of the United States has conclusively established *the fact* that the SUSSEX was torpedoed without warning or summons to surrender and that the torpedo by which she was struck was of German manufacture. ⟨The Government of the United States does not think that the plain inference that the torpedo was fired from a German submarine can, all the attendant circumstances being taken into consideration, be avoided.⟩ *In the view of the Government of the United States these facts from the first made the conclusion that the torpedo was fired by a German submarine unavoidable. It now considers that conclusion substantiated by the statements of Your Excellency's note.* A full statement of the facts upon which the Government of the United States has based its conclusions is enclosed.

(4) *The Government of the United States, after having given careful consideration to the note of the Imperial Government of the fifth of April, regrets to state that the impression made upon it by the statements and requests contained in that note is that the Imperial Government has failed to appreciate the gravity of the situation which has resulted, not alone from the attack on the* SUSSEX, *but from the whole method and character of submarine warfare as disclosed by the unrestrained practice of the commanders of German undersea craft during the past twelve-*

---

[3] Lansing later changed this to read: "three hundred and 25 or more . . ."
[4] Lansing later added "naval and military" following "by."

month and more in the indiscriminate destruction of merchant vessels of all sorts, nationalities, and destinations. If the sinking of the sussex had been an isolated case, the Government of the United States might find it possible to hope that the officer who was responsible for that act had wilfully violated his orders[5] *taking none of the precautions they prescribed,* and that the ends of justice might be satisfied by imposing upon him an adequate punishment, coupled with a formal disavowal of the act and payment of a suitable indemnity by the Imperial Government. But, though the attack upon the sussex was manifestly ⟨utterly⟩ indefensible and caused a loss of life so ⟨appalling⟩ *tragical* as to make it stand forth as one of the most terrible examples of the inhumanity of submarine warfare as the commanders of German vessels are conducting it, it unhappily does not stand alone.

(5) On the contrary, the Government of the United States is forced by recent events to conclude that it is only one instance, *even* though *one of the most* ⟨an⟩ extreme and most distressing ⟨one⟩ *instances,* of the deliberate method and spirit of indiscriminate destruction of merchant vessels of all sorts, nationalities and destinations ⟨the method and spirit⟩ which have become more and more unmistakable as the activity ⟨in the practice of the commanders of⟩ *of* German undersea ⟨craft during the past twelve-month or more.⟩ vessels of war has in recent months been quickened and extended.

(6) The Imperial Government will recall that, when, in February, 1915, it announced its intention of treating the waters surrounding Great Britain and Ireland as ⟨a closed zone and⟩ *embraced* within the seat of war and of destroying all merchant ships owned by its enemies that might be found within that zone of danger, and warned all vessels, neutrals as well as belligerent, to keep out of the waters thus proscribed or to enter them at their peril, the Government of the United States earnestly protested. It took the position that such a policy could not be pursued without constant gross and palpable violations of the accepted law of nations particularly if submarine craft were to be employed as its instruments, inasmuch as the rules prescribed by that law, ⟨and⟩ *rules* founded on the principles of humanity *and established* for the protection of the lives of non-combatants at sea, could not in the nature of the case be observed by such vessels. It ⟨further urged this⟩ *based its* protest on the ground that persons of neutral nationality and vessels of neutral ownership would be exposed to extreme and intolerable risks; and that no right to close any part of the high seas could lawfully be asserted by the Imperial

---

[5] Lansing later added "or had been criminally negligent in."

Government in the circumstances then existing. *The law of nations in these matters, upon which the Government of the United States based that protest, is not of recent origin or founded upon merely arbitrary principles set up by convention. It is based, on the contrary, upon manifest principles of humanity and has long been established with the approval and by the express assent of all civilized nations.*

(7) The Imperial Government⟨,⟩ notwithstanding ⟨the protests of the Government of the United States,⟩ persisted in ⟨its policy,⟩ *carrying out the policy announced*, expressing the hope that the dangers involved, at any rate to neutral vessels, would be reduced to a minimum by the instructions which it had issued to the commanders of its submarines, and assuring the Government of the United States that it would take every possible precaution both to respect the rights of neutrals and to safeguard the lives of non-combatants.

(8) ⟨Nevertheless⟩ *In pursuance of this policy of submarine warfare against the commerce of its adversaries, thus announced and thus entered upon in despite of the solemn protest of the Government of the United States*, the commanders of the Imperial Government's undersea vessels ⟨in carrying out this policy⟩ have ⟨practiced⟩ *carried on practices of* such ruthless destruction ⟨that it has become⟩ *which have made it* more and more evident as the months have gone by that the Imperial Government has found it impracticable to put any such restraints upon them as it had *hoped and* promised to ⟨do⟩ *put*. Again and again the Imperial Government has given its solemn assurances to the Government of the United States that at least passenger ships would not be thus dealt with, and yet it has ⟨as often⟩ *repeatedly* permitted its undersea commanders to disregard those assurances with entire impunity. ⟨Even⟩ *As* recently as February last it gave notice that it would regard all armed merchantmen owned by its enemies as part of the armed naval forces of its adversaries and deal with them as with men of war, thus, at least⟨,⟩ by implication, pledging itself to give warning to vessels which were not armed and to accord security of life to their passengers and crews; but *even* this limitation ⟨has been⟩ *their submarine commanders have* recklessly ignored.

(9) Vessels of neutral ownership, even vessels of neutral ownership bound from neutral port to neutral port, have been destroyed along with vessels of belligerent ownership in constantly increasing numbers. Sometimes the merchantmen attacked have been warned and summoned to surrender before being fired on or torpedoed; sometimes their passengers and

crews have been vouchsafed the poor security of being allowed to take to the ship's boats before the ship was sent to the bottom. But ⟨quite as often⟩ *again and again* no warning has been given, no escape even to the ship's boats allowed to those on board. Great liners like the LUSITANIA and ARABIC and mere passenger boats like the SUSSEX have been ⟨sunk⟩ *attacked* without a moment's warning, *often* before they have even become aware that they were in the presence of an armed ship of the enemy, and the lives of non-combatants, passengers and crew, have been destroyed wholesale and in a manner which the Government of the United States cannot but regard as wanton and without the slightest color of justification.

No limit of any kind has in fact been set to their indiscriminate pursuit and destruction of merchantmen of all kinds and nationalities within the waters which the Imperial Government has chosen to designate as lying within the seat of war. The roll of Americans who have lost their lives upon ships thus attacked and destroyed has grown month by month until the ominous toll has mounted into the hundreds.

(10) The Government of the United States has been very patient. At every stage of this *distressing* experience of tragedy after tragedy it has sought to be governed by the ⟨utmost⟩ *most thoughtful* consideration ⟨for⟩ *of* the extraordinary circumstances of an unprecedented war and to be guided by sentiments of very genuine friendship for the people and Government of Germany. It has ⟨received⟩ *accepted* the successive explanations and assurances of the Imperial Government as *of course* given in entire ⟨and⟩ *sincerity and* good faith, and has hoped, even against hope, that it would prove to be possible for the Imperial Government so to order and control the acts of its naval commanders as to ⟨conform⟩ *square* its policy ⟨to⟩ *with* the recognized principles of humanity as embodied in the law of nations. ⟨But making⟩ *It has made* every allowance for unprecedented conditions and ⟨sincerity of purpose the deeds committed are⟩ *has been willing to wait until the facts became unmistakable and were* susceptible of only one interpretation.

It now owes it to a just regard for its own rights to say to the Imperial Government that that time has come. It has become painfully evident to it that the position which it took at the very outset is inevitable, namely that, ⟨as indicated at the very outset;⟩ the use of submarines for the destruction of an enemy's commerce is *of necessity*, because of the very character of the vessels employed and the very methods of attack which their employment *of course* involves, utterly incompatible with the principles of humanity, the long-established and incontrovertible rights of neutrals, and the sacred immunities of non-combatants.

(11) ⟨The Government of the United States now owes it to a just regard for its own rights to declare that, if it is still the purpose of the Imperial⟩ *If it is still the purpose of the Imperial* Government to prosecute relentless and indiscriminate warfare against vessels of commerce by the use of submarines without regard to what the Government of the United States must consider the *sacred and* indisputable rules of international law and the universally recognized dictates of humanity, the Government of the United States is at last forced to the conclusion that there is but one course it can pursue. ⟨Unless the Imperial Government should now immediately declare its intention to abandon its present practices of submarine warfare and return to a scrupulous observance of the practices clearly prescribed by the law of nations,⟩ *Unless the Imperial Government should now immediately declare its purpose to abandon its present methods of submarine warfare[6] against passenger and freight-carrying vessels,* ⟨It⟩ *the Government of the United States* can have no choice but to sever diplomatic relations with the German Empire ⟨until such time as the⟩ *altogether.[7] This action the Government of the United States contemplates with the greatest reluctance but feels constrained to take in behalf of humanity and the rights of neutral nations.[8]*

WWTLI (SDR, RG 59, 763.72/2596½, DNA).

[6] At some point later, this phrase was made to read: "should now immediately declare and effect an abandonment of its present methods . . ."

[7] Here Wilson excised Lansing's text on this page (p. 9) beginning "until such time"; he then deleted Lansing's closing paragraphs on the following page by tearing the page off the document.

[8] This note was sent as RL to J. W. Gerard, April 18, 1916. It is printed in *FR-WWS 1916*, pp. 232-34. It was accompanied by a statement of facts, printed in *ibid.*, pp. 234-37.

Three Letters to Robert Lansing

My dear Mr. Secretary,   The White House. 17 April, 1916.

Apparently this was, after all, far from being the correct version of the affair.[1] The Mexican authorities, if they are frank with us, are as ill informed, and as tardily informed, as we are.

Faithfully Yours,   W.W.

WWTLI (SDR, RG 59, 812.00/17921½, DNA).

[1] Wilson referred to C. Aguilar to E. Arredondo, April 12, 1916, T telegram (SDR, RG 59, 812.00/17865, DNA), an early and incorrect report on the Parral incident. This telegram is printed in *FR 1916*, pp. 513-14, and *Diplomatic Dealings of the Constitutionalist Revolution*, p. 173.

My dear Mr. Secretary,   The White House. 17 April, 1916.
Circumstances of this sort are of course very disturbing; but I did not know that we had learned the name of the submarine which attacked the SUSSEX.   Faithfully Yours,   W.W.

WWTLI (SDR, RG 59, 851.857 SU 8/81½, DNA).

My dear Mr. Secretary,   The White House. 17 April, 1916.
Thank you for letting me see this statement of fact which is to accompany our communication to the Imperial German Government. It seems to me quite complete enough.
I understood you to say that the affidavits received by mail will necessitate only one or two alterations of detail in the statement.   Faithfully Yours,   W.W.

WWTLI (SDR, RG 59, 851.857 SU 8/83½, DNA).

To Martin Henry Glynn

My dear Governor: [The White House] April 17, 1916
I am distressed to hear that you had trouble with your eyes and beg that you will take good care of yourself.
Thank you with all my heart for your letter of April twelfth. It is delightful to think that anything that I have written you should be treasured and appreciated, even though so much beyond its merits.
Cordially and sincerely yours,   Woodrow Wilson

TLS (Letterpress Books, WP, DLC).

To John L. Golden[1]

My dear Mr. Golden: [The White House] April 17, 1916
Mrs. Wilson and I were greatly pleased to see you and to hear the march,[2] and I am writing to say how sincerely I hope you will have great success in launching it. It quickens the blood and carries a spur which only music, apparently, can use, and I am sincerely complimented that you should have chosen the words from[3] the song from my speeches. I envy those who can make any great impulse, particularly the great impulse of patriotism, move in such strains and accents as will quicken the pulse of a whole people.
Cordially and sincerely yours,   Woodrow Wilson

TLS (Letterpress Books, WP, DLC).
    [1] New York theatrical producer and prolific author of popular songs, musical comedies, and plays.
    [2] *Fall in, for Your Mother Land*, words by Woodrow Wilson, music by Dr. Frank Black and John Golden. There is a copy of this sheet music in WC, NjP. The White House and Executive Office diaries do not reveal the date when the Wilsons saw Golden. However, as J. L. Golden to WW, March 31, 1916, ALS (WP, DLC) reveals, Golden was at the White House near the end of March. He wrote to thank Wilson for giving him "the greatest moment of his life."
    [3] Wilson dictated "for."

To Florenz Ziegfeld, Jr.[1]

My dear Mr. Ziegfeld: [The White House] April 17, 1916

Dudley Malone had sent me your letter of April first to him[2] in which you express the wish to devote the finale of the new Follies to the preparedness idea. I am greatly gratified that you should have this wish and purpose, and I will take great pleasure in talking the matter over with Malone so that I may render any assistance that is possible.

Cordially and sincerely yours,   Woodrow Wilson

TLS (Letterpress Books, WP, DLC).
    [1] Theatrical producer, best known for his musical revues called the Ziegfeld Follies.
    [2] F. Ziegfeld, Jr., to D. F. Malone, April 1, 1916, TLS (WP, DLC).

From Robert Lansing, with Enclosure

PERSONAL AND CONFIDENTIAL

My dear Mr. President: Washington April 17, 1916.

I have just received from the Navy Department an incoming radiogram from Berlin via Tuckerton for the German Ambassador, which appears to contain his latest instructions in regard to the SUSSEX case. This telegram (copy enclosed) will probably be delivered to the Ambassador by the radio service tonight.

Faithfully yours,   Robert Lansing

TLS (SDR, RG 59, 851.857 SU 8/84½ A, DNA).

ENCLOSURE

17 April 1916.
From Radio Station Tuckerton N. Y.

22016 Radicode Herewith copy message quote German Embassy Washington Columbia 140, April 15th 9972. I suggest that you talk over submarine question once ask [more] with Mr. Lansing in following outline: We are now conducting submarine war now absolutely in accordance with general principles of international law. Only exception is commercial war against enemy freight ships in English war zone. This [is][1] only [aimed] at destruction of ships but we try to save human lives as far as possible. This retaliatory step against English starvation policy does not touch interests of neutrals as neutral passengers on enemy freight ships manifestly try to render futile German war measure and as neutral members of crew are brought into relation of dependents on state whose flag ship flies; consequently both neutral passengers and crew on enemy freight ships lose neutral character. We therefore never gave any promises regarding enemy freight ships in war zone. Continued Foreign Jagow unquote.

Quote Germany Embassy Washington Columbia. 141 April 15th in pursuance of wireless No. 140. Instructions to submarine commanders regarding their proceeding and observance of all our assurances are so precise that according [to] human foresight errors are excluded and certainly not more possible than in ordinary naval war; furthermore submarine commanders are instructed not to attack ships when in [doubt]. Ruthless submarine war would [certainly have] greatly increased loss in enemy ships; for this reason alone all doubts whether our instructions are meant seriously and strictly carried out bona fide are without foundation. We have modified submarine war to maintain friendly relations with America recognising [sacrificing] important military advantages and in contradicting [contradiction] to excited public opinion here. We therefore trust that American Government will appreciate this and not put forward new demands which might [bring] us into an impossible situation. In order to correct errors apparently existing in American press I state that we have not suggested arbitration SUSSEX case but commission of inquiry to establish facts which are different. End. Acknowledge receipt. Jagow unquote.

09017 Officer in Charge.

TC radiogram (SDR, RG 59, 851.857 SU 8/84½A, DNA).

[1] This and following corrections and additions in square brackets from German Foreign Office to J. H. von Bernstorff, April 18, 1916, T telegram (SDR, RG 59, 763.72/2650½, DNA).

From William Joel Stone

Dear Mr President: [Washington] April 17, 1916.

I want you to read the marked part of the enclosed speech.[1] I will feel complimented if you will—and besides I [think] the view suggested is worthy of serious consideration.

Your friend &c   Wm J Stone

ALS (WP, DLC).
[1] Delivered in the Senate on April 13, 1916, during a general debate over preparedness. The full text is printed in *Cong. Record*, 64th Cong., 1st sess., pp. 6023-26. In the portion of the speech that he marked, Stone said that he abhorred equally German militarism and British navalism. However, he went on, on account of American isolation from Europe, German military power posed little threat to the United States, while British control of the seas was a real danger: "A supreme dominance of the seas by any single power on earth is something which comes immediately home to us." He would, therefore, support any plan to secure protection to the American people "and make the honor of our Nation safe beyond peradventure anywhere in the world." Printed tear sheets (WP, DLC).

From Joseph Edward Davies

My dear Mr. President: Washington April 17, 1916.

I can not refrain from dropping you a line in connection with your letter returning Aylward's letter because I fear that you may be doing an injustice in your thought to Aylward.

The Aylward letter was dated February 3rd, and was received before your previous letter to me had been sent. It was in no sense prompted by your letter, but was elicited by my statement, made theretofore, that the fact that he had bitter enemies in Wisconsin had been mentioned by the Department of Justice in connection with his name. The suggestion contained in the first paragraph was directed entirely to those who were administrative officers, and who did not always appear to appreciate the factor of past service to a cause when other considerations were equal.

Neither Aylward nor myself went into the fight in Wisconsin because of hope of reward; that I know positively. We did it because of what you stood for, and because of your preeminent typification of what we believed and tried to stand for in Democracy.

My reason in urging Aylward's candidacy was not because of any service that he had rendered. It was because of Aylward's character and ability and exceptional qualifications for the Federal bench. It was a happy coincidence in my mind that this appointment should be entirely consonant with rewarding him for the fight for the principles for which he had stood.

Aylward does feel rather strongly in the situation, and feels that he has been unjustly dealt with by Husting, and he is desirous of having you know all the facts. That was the purpose of the letter. I have talked with him a great deal, and he has never suggested by word or innuendo that there was the remotest suggestion in his mind of ingratitude on the part of the President if he should not receive this appointment. Indeed, he said, only the last time I talked with him, that nothing could affect his attitude toward you or toward your administration. He did say that he would like to have the issue made, however, clear that it was not the Administration but the Senator from Wisconsin who made his appointment impossible. And, of course, he understands that the opposition of the Senator would be conclusive on confirmation.

Believe me, my dear Mr. President, did I believe otherwise, or did I have the slightest ground for the belief that there was any suggestion of a hostile or ungracious spirit in this matter of my friend Aylward—which I am sure there is not—I should not have been a party to it to the slightest degree. No one would dare to say to me that in any of your relations with men, and particularly with me or with my friends, that there has been any suggestion of ingratitude. I know too well the quality of large generosity and wisdom with which you have dealt not only with me but with all matters that I have presented to you, to permit of any such suggestion.

Anything that you do in this or any other matter I know is actuated only by what you consider your highest obligation to the country and the usefulness of the organization which you are the head of in serving the people of the United States.

Indeed, the suggestion in your letter that you might perhaps believe that any such idea might have come into my mind has rather hurt. And I therefore feel that I must try to make this situation clear by letter, fearful that my effort to explain last evening at the White House was not entirely clear.

With great respect and with devoted loyalty and affection, believe me to be,   Faithfully yours,   Joseph E. Davies

TLS (WP, DLC).

Frederick Funston to Henry Pinckney McCain

Ft. Sam Houston, Texas, April 17, 1916.

Following just received from Pershing, Quote: Namiquipa, April 17, 1916, Number 115 Replying your 106 following resume of attitude Mexican people and recommend. There have been apparent attempts by de facto Government forces to cooperate in efforts to capture Villa. In some instances efforts cooperate possibly sincere efforts to capture Villa. My opinion is general attitude Carranza has been one of obstruction. This also universal opinion Army officers this expedition. Carranza forces falsely report all acts against Villa forces and death of Villa leaders. Activity Carranza force in territory through which we have operated probably intentionally obstructive. Marked example obstruction refusal allow our use of railroads. Captious criticisms by local officials against troops passing through town prompted by obstructive spirit. Colum[n]s often delayed this reason when continuous pursuit was very important. Guerrero fight would have been complete success but for treachery of Mexican guide. The populace at every critical stage this campaign have circulated misleading information regarding whereabouts Villa band and assisted in escape. Inconceivable that notorious character like Villa could remain in country with people ignorant his general direction and approximate location. Since Guerrero fight it is practically impossible obtain guides even from one town to another except by coercion. Small bands Carranza troops under guise Villistas have often fired upon our columns. The further we advance south the less friendly the people have become. The centres population and among members various factions deep seated sentiment against presence of troops exists. No opportunities lost by our officers explain conditions protocol. At first people exhibited only passive disapproval American entry into country. Lately sentiment has changed to hostile position. The movement of Government troops through Sonora towards our line of communication must be regarded with grave suspicion. Recent outbreak in Parral against troops undoubtedly premeditated. Believe this generally represents attitude of both Carranza and Villistas. Little difference between them. Carranza Government may express regret at treacherous indignity inflicted upon our troops at Parral but Government impotent prevent recurrence should we continue pursuit Villa. National control over local Government cannot be said to exist this section. Protection to individuals from pillage by both factions not in any sense afforded. In fact anarchy reigns supreme in all sections through which we have operated. In view these facts future promises Government could not be depended upon. In order to prosecute our mission with any promise of success it is therefore absolutely necessary for us to assume complete possession for time being of country through which we must operate and established control of the railroads as means of supplying forces *required*. Therefore recommend immediate capture by this command of city and state of Chihuahua also the seizure of all railroads therein as preliminary to further necessary blank Unquote.[1]

Funston.

T telegram (SDR, RG 59, 812.00/17903, DNA).

[1] Pershing gave copies of this dispatch to reporters on April 18, 1916. It was printed in full, e.g., in the *New York Times*, April 21, 1916.

Upon receipt of this telegram, Wilson and Baker decided to send General Scott immediately to confer with General Funston at Fort Sam Houston.

An Unknown Person
to Count Johann Heinrich von Bernstorff

VERY SECRET

New York, April 17, 1916.

No. 335/16 Judge Cohalan[1] requests the transmission the following remarks:

The Revolution in Ireland can only be successful if supported from Germany. Otherwise, England will be able to suppress it, even though it be only after hard struggles. Therefore, help is necessary. This should consist primarily of aerial attacks in England and a diversion of the fleet simultaneously with Irish revolution. Then, if possible, a landing of troops, arms, and ammunition in Ireland, and possibly some officers from Zeppelins. This would enable ·the Irish ports be closed against England and the establishment of stations for submarines on the Irish coast, and the cutting off of the supply of food for England. The success of the revolution may therefore decide the war.

He asks that a telegram to this effect be sent to Berlin.

5132 8167 0230

T telegram (photostat in C. L. Swem Coll., NjP).

[1] Daniel Florence Cohalan, New York Supreme Court justice. As this telegram indicates, Cohalan was deeply involved in Irish revolutionary activities and in close touch with the German embassy in Washington. See, particularly, Reinhard R. Dorries, "Die Mission Sir Roger Casements im Deutschen Reich, 1914-1916," *Historische Zeitschrift*, CCXXII (1976), 578-625.

To Charles Manly Stedman[1]

My dear Major: [The White House] April 18, 1916

I know you must have wondered why your letter of February twenty-fifth about Miss Phillips has remained so long unanswered,[2] but I am sure you will understand when I say that I feel obliged in all such cases to make a reference of the matter to the

Civil Service Commission and get their judgment concerning it. I beg that you will pardon any apparent neglect on my part. It was only apparent.

I do not know anything that gives me greater searchings of conscience than these questions of executive orders. They arise more frequently, I dare say, than you have any realization of and I feel obliged to observe the greatest care, not only, but to act as if the presumption were against the issuance of such orders. They slowly eat away the whole principle of the Civil Service system and I have sought to confine them to really extraordinary cases.

I need not tell you how hard it goes with me to be obliged to conclude that Miss Phillips's case is not one of those in which I can make an exception to the severe rule I have set myself, because everything pulls my heart in the direction of acquiescing in your suggestion, but I know that you will understand and honor a point of conscience.

Cordially and sincerely yours,　Woodrow Wilson

TLS (Letterpress Books, WP, DLC).
  1 Confederate veteran, Democratic congressman from North Carolina since 1911.
  2 C. M. Stedman to WW, Feb. 25, 1916, TLS (WP, DLC), enclosing L. Craig to C. M. Stedman, Feb. 18, 1916, TLS (WP, DLC). Stedman and Locke Craig, Governor of North Carolina, urged Wilson to issue an Executive Order appointing Nora Phillips to "one of the Government offices." Miss Phillips, described as "a woman in middle life, unusually capable," was the daughter of the late Samuel Field Phillips, sometime Solicitor General of the United States and Professor of Law at the University of North Carolina. The Civil Service Commission reported (John A. McIlhenny et al. to WW, March 4, 1916, TLS, WP, DLC), that Miss Phillips had never taken a civil service examination and declared that it could not recommend an Executive Order in her favor.

To William Libbey

My dear William:　　　　　[The White House] April 18, 1916

I have your letter of April thirteenth,[1] but I am sorry to say that I don't think it would be of the least use to tell the many people who are now acting and talking indiscreetly about the great question of preparedness to get together. After all, the number of those who are playing mischief is not very great and they are only bringing themselves into contempt, not the great question we are so much concerned with.

In haste, with warm regard,

Cordially and sincerely yours,　Woodrow Wilson

TLS (Letterpress Books, WP, DLC).
  1 It is missing.

From John Van Antwerp MacMurray

Personal

Dear Mr President,   Peking, April 18th, 1916

Now that word has come of my confirmation as a Secretary of Class One, I feel free, as I did not before, to thank you for what you did in removing the opposition that had arisen in the Senate. I need not assure you that I am more than sorry that the question arose, and that it became necessary for you, among all your preoccupations, to take my part against objections that were the harder to meet because they rested not so much upon particular acts which might be explained or justified as upon a general conviction, on Senator Saulsbury's part, of my unfitness to represent our Government properly and becomingly. But since the incident did come up, I feel proud that you had enough confidence in me to warrant you in taking up the matter in my behalf, and am more than grateful to you for interesting yourself in my cause.

It was a very keen disappointment to me that I failed to see you during my leave of absence at home. I called one morning, and failed to find the opportunity to see you before you had to leave town: and while you were still away, I learned of Senator Saulsbury's objection to my confirmation and of your having the matter under consideration, so that I hesitated to thrust myself upon you lest I should seem to be importuning you. In the end, a letter is the only means of expressing to you my appreciation of your action in my behalf; but I feel sure that you will understand my feeling and realize how genuinely and heartily I thank you.

With respect and cordial good wishes to you and to all your family, I remain, my dear Mr President,

Yours, very sincerely,   J. V. A. MacMurray

TLS (WP, DLC).

From Richard Victor Oulahan

Dear Mr. President: [Washington] April 18, 1916.

I thank you from my heart for the kindly and thoughtful sympathy symbolized in the exquisite wreath that came from you as a tribute to the one who was nearest and dearest to my boy and me.[1] In her name I wish to express our deep appreciation to you for whose welfare and guidance in this time of crisis we have prayed so often. Let me hope that the prayers have helped you, as your sympathy has helped us in this greatest sorrow.

Most gratefully yours,   Richard V. Oulahan

ALS (WP, DLC).

[1] Anne McGowan Oulahan had died at her home in Washington on April 12. She had been in poor health for some two years. *New York Times*, April 13, 1916.

An Address to a Joint Session of Congress

19 April, 1916.

Gentlemen of the Congress: A situation has arisen in the foreign relations of the country of which it is my plain duty to inform you very frankly.

It will be recalled that in February, 1915, the Imperial German Government announced its intention to treat the waters surrounding Great Britain and Ireland as embraced within the seat of war and to destroy all merchant ships owned by its enemies that might be found within any part of that portion of the high seas, and that it warned all vessels, of neutral as well as of belligerent ownership, to keep out of the waters it had thus proscribed or else enter them at their peril. The Government of the United States earnestly protested. It took the position that such a policy could not be pursued without the practical certainty of gross and palpable violations of the law of nations, particularly if submarine craft were to be employed as its instruments, inasmuch as the rules prescribed by that law, rules founded upon principles of humanity and established for the protection of the lives of non-combatants at sea, could not in the nature of the case be observed by such vessels. It based its protest on the ground that persons of neutral nationality and vessels of neutral ownership would be exposed to extreme and intolerable risks, and that no right to close any part of the high seas against their use or to expose them to such risks could lawfully be asserted by any belligerent government. The law of nations in these matters, upon which the Government of the United States based its protest, is not of recent origin or founded upon merely arbitrary principles set up by convention. It is based, on the contrary, upon manifest and imperative principles of humanity and has long been established with the approval and by the express assent of all civilized nations.

Notwithstanding the earnest protest of our Government, the Imperial German Government at once proceeded to carry out the policy it had announced. It expressed the hope that the dangers involved, at any rate the dangers to neutral vessels, would be reduced to a minimum by the instructions which it had issued to its submarine commanders, and assured the Government of the United States that it would take every possible precaution both to respect the rights of neutrals and to safeguard the lives of non-combatants.

What has actually happened in the year which has since elapsed has shown that those hopes were not justified, those assurances insusceptible of being fulfilled. In pursuance of the policy of submarine warfare against the commerce of its adversaries, thus announced and entered upon by the Imperial German Government in despite of the solemn protest of this Government, the commanders of German undersea vessels have attacked merchant ships with greater and greater activity, not only upon the high seas surrounding Great Britain and Ireland but wherever they could encounter them, in a way that has grown more and more ruthless, more and more indiscriminate as the months have gone by, less and less observant of restraints of any kind; and have delivered their attacks without compunction against vessels of every nationality and bound upon every sort of errand. Vessels of neutral ownership, even vessels of neutral ownership bound from neutral port to neutral port, have been destroyed along with vessels of belligerent ownership in constantly increasing numbers. Sometimes the merchantman attacked has been warned and summoned to surrender before being fired on or torpedoed; sometimes passengers or crews have been vouchsafed the poor security of being allowed to take to the ship's boats before she was sent to the bottom. But again and again no warning has been given, no escape even to the ship's boats allowed to those on board. What this Government foresaw must happen has happened. Tragedy has followed tragedy on the seas in such fashion, with such attendant circumstances, as to make it grossly evident that warfare of such a sort, if warfare it be, cannot be carried on without the most palpable violation of the dictates alike of right and of humanity. Whatever the disposition and intention of the Imperial German Government, it has manifestly proved impossible for it to keep such methods of attack upon the commerce of its enemies within the bounds set by either the reason or the heart of mankind.

In February of the present year the Imperial German Government informed this Government and the other neutral governments of the world that it had reason to believe that the Government of Great Britain had armed all merchant vessels of British ownership and had given them secret orders to attack any submarine of the enemy they might encounter upon the seas, and that the Imperial German Government felt justified in the circumstances in treating all armed merchantmen of belligerent ownership as auxiliary vessels of war, which it would have the right to destroy without warning. The law of nations has long recognized the right of merchantmen to carry arms for protection and to use them to repel attack, though to use them, in such circumstances, at their own risk; but the Imperial German Government claimed the right to set these understandings aside in circumstances which it deemed extraordinary. Even the terms in which it announced its purpose thus still further to relax the restraints it had previously professed its willingness and desire to put upon the operations of its submarines carried the plain implication that at least vessels which were not armed would still be exempt from destruction without warning and that personal safety would be accorded their passengers and crews; but even that limitation, if it was ever practicable to observe it, has in fact constituted no check at all upon the destruction of ships of every sort.

Again and again the Imperial German Government has given this Government its solemn assurances that at least passenger ships would not be thus dealt with, and yet it has again and again permitted its undersea commanders to disregard those assurances with entire impunity. Great liners like the LUSITANIA and the ARABIC and mere ferryboats like the SUSSEX have been attacked without a moment's warning, sometimes before they had even become aware that they were in the presence of an armed vessel of the enemy, and the lives of non-combatants, passengers and crew have been sacrificed wholesale, in a manner which the Government of the United States cannot but regard as wanton and without the slightest colour of justification. No limit of any kind has in fact been set to the indiscriminate pursuit and destruction of merchantmen of all kinds and nationalities within the waters, constantly extending in area, where these operations have been carried on; and the roll of Americans who have lost their lives on ships thus attacked and destroyed has grown month by month until the ominous toll has mounted into the hundreds.

One of the latest and most shocking instances of this method of warfare was that of the destruction of the French cross-Channel steamer SUSSEX. It must stand forth, as the sinking of the steamer LUSITANIA did, as so singularly tragical and unjustifiable as to constitute a truly terrible example of the inhumanity of submarine warfare as the commanders of German vessels have for the past twelvemonth been conducting it. If this instance stood alone, some explanation, some disavowal by the German Government, some evidence of criminal mistake or wilful disobedience on the part of the commander of the vessel that fired the torpedo might be sought or entertained; but unhappily it does not stand alone. Recent events make the conclusion inevitable that it is only one instance, even though it be one of the most extreme and distressing instances, of the spirit and method of warfare which the Imperial German Government has mistakenly adopted, and which from the first exposed that Government to the reproach of thrusting all neutral rights aside in pursuit of its immediate objects.

The Government of the United States has been very patient. At every stage of this distressing experience of tragedy after tragedy in which its own citizens were involved it has sought to be restrained from any extreme course of action or of protest by a thoughtful consideration of the extraordinary circumstances of this unprecedented war, and actuated in all that it said or did by the sentiments of genuine friendship which the people of the United States have always entertained and continue to entertain towards the German nation. It has of course accepted the successive explanations and assurances of the Imperial German Government as given in entire sincerity and good faith, and has hoped, even against hope, that it would prove to be possible for the German Government so to order and control the acts of its naval commanders as to square its policy with the principles of humanity as embodied in the law of nations. It has been willing to wait until the significance of the facts became absolutely unmistakable and susceptible of but one interpretation.

That point has now unhappily been reached. The facts are susceptible of but one interpretation. The Imperial German Government has been unable to put any limits or restraints upon its warfare against either freight or passenger ships. It has therefore become painfully evident that the position which this Government took at the very outset is inevitable, namely, that the use of submarines for the destruction of an enemy's commerce is of necessity, because of the very character of the vessels employed and the very methods of attack which their employment of course involves, incompatible with the principles of humanity, the long established and incontrovertible rights of neutrals, and the sacred immunities of non-combatants.

I have deemed it my duty, therefore, to say to the Imperial German Government that if it is still its purpose to prosecute relentless and indiscriminate warfare against vessels of commerce by the use of submarines, notwithstanding the now demonstrated impossibility of conducting that warfare in accordance with what the Government of the United States must consider the sacred and indisputable rules of international law and the universally recognized dictates of humanity, the Government of the United States is at last forced to the conclusion that there is but one course it can pursue; and that unless the Imperial German Government should now immediately declare and effect an abandonment of its present methods of warfare against passenger and freight carrying vessels this Government can have no choice but to sever diplomatic relations with the Government of the German Empire altogether.

This decision I have arrived at with the keenest regret; the possibility of the action contemplated I am sure all thoughtful Americans will look forward to with unaffected reluctance. But we cannot forget that we are in some sort and by the force of circumstances the responsible spokesmen of the rights of humanity, and that we cannot remain silent while those rights seem in process of being swept utterly away in the maelstrom of this terrible war. We owe it to a due regard for our own rights as a nation, to our sense of duty as a representative of the rights of neutrals the world over, and to a just conception of the rights of mankind to take this stand now with the utmost solemnity and firmness.

I have taken it, and taken it in the confidence that it will meet with your approval and support. All sober-minded men must unite in hoping that the Imperial German Government, which has in other circumstances stood as the champion of all that we are now contending for in the interest of humanity, may recognize the justice of our demands and meet them in the spirit in which they are made.[1]

WWT MS (WP, DLC).

[1] There is a WWsh draft of this address, dated April 16, 1916, in WP, DLC. Wilson, obviously for reasons of security, used his WWT manuscript as his reading copy. The Editors have corrected Wilson's misspelling of belligerent and disobedience.

To Joseph Edward Davies

My dear Davies: [The White House] April 19, 1916

Thank you very warmly indeed for your letter of April seventeenth. I am sorry if my last letter caused you any distress. You may be sure that I did not mean to imply by it anything at all like a challenge to Mr. Aylward's attitude, while I meant my letter rather to be understood as an affectionate reminder to you merely of the difficulties I was laboring under in making the appointment in the Wisconsin district. Please dismiss the whole matter from your mind and be sure that I understand perfectly.

Cordially and sincerely yours, Woodrow Wilson

TLS (Letterpress Books, WP, DLC).

To William Joel Stone

My dear Senator: [The White House] April 19, 1916

Thank you for your letter of April seventeenth with its enclosure. I have read the passages you marked with the greatest interest and am glad you called my attention to them. I am always interested in everything that you say.

Cordially and sincerely yours, Woodrow Wilson

TLS (Letterpress Books, WP, DLC).

From Edward Mandell House, with Enclosure

Dear Governor: New York. April 19, 1916.

I have just received another autograph letter from Sir Edward a copy of which I enclose.

You will notice that he makes the point that we saw was inevitable, that is if Germany is permitted to continue her submarine policy unrebuked, we would lose the friendship and respect of the Allies to such an extent that they would not have confidence in our acting with a sufficiently strong hand in the peace councils.

Your action today, I believe, will meet with the approval of the best opinion in this country and in Europe. It marks an epoch in American history. With deep affection, E. M. House

TLS (WP, DLC).

ENCLOSURE

Sir Edward Grey to Edward Mandell House

Private.

Dear Colonel House: London, April 7th, 1916.

I sent to M. Briand through the French Embassy here before I went to Paris the message proposed in my letter of the 24th of March to you.[1]

The conference itself was a huge affair confined to generalities, but the Prime Minister and I discussed some matters separately with M. Briand and M. Cambon and neither of them mentioned the subject.

The French Press was full of the German failure at Verdun and the sinking of the Sussex and it was very clear from the whole feeling at Paris that the French Government could not take up the idea of a conference then.

I am bound to say that I think feeling here is the same. Everybody feels there must be more German failure and some Allied success before anything but an inconclusive peace could be obtained. The German Chancellor's speech reported today will harden that feelings.[2]

I cannot think that the entry of the United States into the war would prolong it, whether it came about over the Sussex or over a conference and conditions of peace—indeed I feel it must shorten it; but I remember you expressed the apprehension that Germany would force a rupture by some violent act and you preferred that it should not come about that way.

I understood and understand that but there is no doubt that this case of the Sussex and the ruthless torpedoing of neutral ships, Norwegian, Dutch and Spanish (though I do not know all the circumstances) has created a dilemma.

If the United States Government takes a strong line about these acts it must I suppose become more difficult for it to propose a conference to Germany; if on the other hand it passes them over the Allies will not believe that the United States Government will at a conference take a line strong enough to ensure more than a patched up and insecure peace.

My personal touch with you and through you with the President makes me more hopeful, but amid such tremendous forces an individual opinion formed in private knowledge can count for little.   Yours sincerely,   E. Grey.

TCL (WP, DLC).

[1] It is printed as an Enclosure with EMH to WW, April 8, 1916.

[2] See E. Grey to EMH, April 8, 1916, n. 1, printed as an Enclosure with EMH to WW, April 8, 1916.

From Wallace Buttrick

Dear Mr. President: New York April 19, 1916

Your letter of April 13 addressed to me at my home in White Plains was received last evening on my return from a visit to Mississippi.

I have long known Miss Martha Berry and have visited her

school. I am directing that when one of my associates shall next visit Georgia he shall endeavor to call on Miss Berry and see her work.

The General Education Board does not contemplate establishing a school in the South of any sort. Hitherto our Board has done its work through existing schools and other educational agencies. I am of the opinion that Miss Berry has been reading a paper recently put out by this Board which Dr. Abraham Flexner wrote, entitled "A Modern School,"[1] and that she has inferred that we were contemplating founding such a school somewhere in the South. I am directing that a copy of this paper shall be sent to your address, although I cannot hope that with your many cares and great responsibilities you will find time to read it.

With great respect, I am

Faithfully yours,   Wallace Buttrick

TLS (WP, DLC).
[1] Abraham Flexner, *A Modern School* (New York, 1916).

To Albert Sidney Burleson, with Enclosures

MEM.   The White House [c. April 20, 1916].

I think Mr. Hay will agree with me that the situation of the country in regard to its foreign relations has changed so much since the House Bill was passed as to make it admissible to reconsider the question of the numerical strength of the army.

The *peace* strength provided for in the Senate Bill seems to me much too large;[1] but I [am] not sure that it would not be wise to come somewhere very near its figures in the number of units its [it] creates. (Mr. Hay will remember that I have all along been keen on this point of the number of nuits [units], and have desired, in particular, as many officers as I could get authorization for). The number of engineering units seems to me especially important, and the number of units of field artil[l]ery more important than the number of units of infantry.

What I hope is, that the measure can be so framed as to give us an ample skeleton and unmistakable authority to fill it out at any time that the public safety may be deemed to require it.

W.W.

WWTLI (J. Hay Papers, DLC).
[1] About this, see Hay's memorandum, printed below.

ENCLOSURE I

From James Hay

My dear Mr. President: Washington, D. C. April 19th, 1916.

At the suggestion of Mr. Burleson I am sending you a memorandum showing the salient points of difference between the House and Senate preparedness bills. I am also enclosing comments on the Senate Bill which may be of some interest and which I will ask you to regard as confidential.

Very sincerely yours,   James Hay

TLS (J. Hay Papers, DLC).

ENCLOSURE II

House Bill Provides for minimum strength of enlisted men of the line of the Army in time of peace 140000, the Senate Bill provides for 250000.

House Bill provides for forty Regiments of Infantry.
Senate Bill provides for sixty four Regiments of Infantry.
House Bill provides for 108 betteries of field artillery
Senate Bill provides for 126 batteries of field artillery.
House Bill provides for 222 Companies of Coast Artillery
Senate Bill provides for 263 Companies of Coast Artillery.

See attached mem.[1]

House Bill provides for 15 Regiments of Cavalry
Senate Bill provides for 25 Regiments of Cavalry
House Bill provides for 23 Companies of Engineers
Senate Bill provides for sixty Companies of Engineers.
War strength of House Bill including all enlisted men 207000.
War strength of Senate Bill 254000.
Commissioned Officers under House Bill 7669
Commissioned Officers under Senate Bill 10561.

The Senate Bill carries a provision for raising a Volunteer Army in time of peace under the act of April 25th 1914, and provides for training these volunteers for thirty days each year.

There is nothing like this in the House Bill.

House[2]

The Senate Bill provides for federalization of the National Guard but does not provide in a constitutional way for the use by the United States of the National Guard outside of the United States. The House Bill provides for this in a manner about which there is no difference of opinion. The House Bill provides for a complete system for training the National Guard.

The House Bill provides for summer camps.

The House Bill provides for the utilization of industries in time of war.

The Senate Bill contains neither of these provisions.

The Senate Bill contains a provision for a nitrate plant, a similar provision was contained in the House Bill, but was stricken out by the House.[3]

The Senate Bill contains a provision giving preference to discharged soldiers to positions in the civil service of the Government. No![4]

The House Bill so far as the National Guard feature of it is concerned is drawn strictly in accordance with the views expressed by the President, and gives him absolute authority to train the National Guard in time of peace, while the Senate Bill makes it doubtful as to the power of the President in this regard. House[5]

The House Bill provides for an enlistment period of seven years three with the colors, four in the reserve, and also provides that at the end of one year an enlisted man upon the recommendation of his company commander, and with the approval of the Secretary of War may be furloughed to the reserve. But do not regard this as a point to stick on.[6]

The Senate Bill provides for a five year period, two years with the colors and three with the reserve.

T memorandum (J. Hay Papers, DLC).
    1 WWhw and large bracket.
    2 WWhw.
    3 Senator Ellison D. Smith of South Carolina on April 7 proposed an amendment to the Senate version of the army bill (*H.R.* 12766) which authorized the Secretary of War to recommend one or more water power sites for withdrawal and to construct on these sites the plants and facilities necessary to produce both electric power and nitrates. The President was authorized to make the necessary site withdrawals. The nitrates were to be used for military purposes, but any surplus beyond military needs might be sold or otherwise disposed of for fertilizers under the direction of the Secretary of Agriculture. All plants and facilities constructed for these purposes were to be operated solely by the federal government. The sum of $15,000,000 was to be appropriated to carry out the provisions of the amendment. The Senate adopted this amendment on April 14. *Cong. Record*, 64th Cong., 1st sess., pp. 5637, 6125.
    4 WWhw.
    5 WWhw.
    6 WWhw.

To William Bauchop Wilson

My dear Mr. Secretary: The White House April 20, 1916

I feel every confidence, after having read the enclosed copy of your letter to Mr. Clemens Horst,[1] representing the San Francisco Chamber of Commerce, that you have given the most careful consideration to the representations he made about the treatment of Chinese merchants entering the country. But I take the liberty of writing you concerning this matter, because it occurs to me that something might be done, perhaps, to change the attitude of mind of the immigration officials at San Francisco towards cases of the sort referred to. The prejudice on the Pacific Coast against the Chinese is so intense and so touched almost with passion that I can readily believe the officials of the immigration service when dealing with Chinese citizens can be very severe and even unjust without being conscious of it or without intending to do anything but enforce the law in its true construction. Perhaps if you would have a talk with Mr. Caminetti, you might impress him with the importance and true wisdom of treating such applicants for admission to the country with punctilious consideration. Every item of this sort nowadays, great or small, has assumed a new significance.

Cordially and sincerely yours,   Woodrow Wilson

TLS (received from Mary A. Strohecker).
 1 It is missing, but see E. C. Horst to WW, April 17, 1916, TLS (WP, DLC), and W. B. Wilson to WW, April 25, 1916.

To Richard Victor Oulahan

My dear Mr. Oulahan: [The White House] April 20, 1916

Thank you for your little note of the eighteenth. You may be sure that my heart has gone out to you in your tragical loss. The flowers did not call for any personal acknowledgment. They were merely a token of how personal our feeling is towards you when anything, like this, touches you at the very heart of all that you hold dear.

Cordially and sincerely yours,   Woodrow Wilson

TLS (Letterpress Books, WP, DLC).

To Edward Mandell House

Dearest Friend: The White House April 20, 1916

Mr. F. A. Duneka, Vice President of Harper & Brothers, a man who has always impressed me as being of rather fine quality, came down to see me the other day to ask this question, whether I thought you would be willing to write for Harper's Magazine, to be published after the conventions, an article on "President Wilson's Policies," "Accomplishments of the Administration," "Some Observations of the Administration," or some similar title.

I told him I would put the matter up to you. Of course, I rely very much more on your judgment in matters of this kind than on my own. I am sure that you could do this particular thing, if it ought to be done at this time, better than anybody else could do it, and I am now just putting it to you to see what you think about it.

In haste   Affectionately yours,   Woodrow Wilson

TLS (E. M. House Papers, CtY).

From William Joel Stone

Dear Mr. President: [Washington] April 20 1916.

Yesterday forenoon when four of us whom you had requested to confer with you at the White House were present and heard your statement,[1] you will recall that I remarked "I presume that is all for the present," and you said in a half humorous way that you had not heard anything from me. That observation was true, of course. It was true because in the circumstances of the moment I preferred not to discuss the subject under consideration. But I do want to talk with you about this grave matter, but to talk just with you. You did not ask my opinion about your message to Congress or your note to Germany before the message was written or the note dispatched; but I am going to follow a different course with you with respect to my attitude. You know how deeply distressed I am that I have not been able to put myself in accord with your views on this question, and you know how anxious I am for many reasons to maintain the utmost harmony of thought and purpose between us. I want to discuss this whole situation with you. I do not want to discuss it as a Senator with the President. I want to talk about it as one sincere man, one Democrat, one friend may talk with another sincere man, Democrat and friend—just a plain, frank, heart-to-heart talk, so that each may fully understand the feeling and attitude of the other. You are bound to know not only the esteem in which I hold you as a public official, but the affection I have for you as a man. Out of this situation to which I refer has grown the only serious difference of opinion between us on great questions of national policy. I fear we have not discussed this great question with that fullness and frankness that should have characterized either our personal or official relations to each other.

I want you to arrange your affairs so that I may have a talk with you alone, without the restraint of having others present. I have engagements for this evening and Friday evening. Having that in view I would be glad to have you so arrange your affairs as to make an appointment of the kind and for the purposes indicated.   Your friend, sincerely,   Wm J Stone.

TLS (WP, DLC).

1 Wilson conferred with Senators Stone and Lodge and Representative Flood and Henry Allen Cooper, ranking Democratic and Republican members of the Senate and House committees on foreign affairs, at the White House, at 10 A.M., about his forthcoming address to the joint session. Wilson left for the Capitol at 12:45 P.M.

From Edward Mandell House

Dear Governor: New York. April 20, 1916.

I have been working on the McCombs matter for several days along with Baruch and Morganthau.

Baruch tells me that he will have the letter from McCombs today. He was to have had it yesterday and I am sceptical. We can only hope.

Morganthau wants to secure quarters for the National Committee now. Dodge, Crane and I looked at them with him yesterday and approved. They will be in the 42nd Street Building opposite the Manhattan Hotel. McCombs also approves and unless you object it will be decided that way.

Unless these quarters are taken now they cannot be had and that is Morganthau's reason for immediate action. Hollister[1] can come over and things can be gotten ready to start after the St Louis Convention and without the confusion usually incident to opening up.   Affectionately yours,   E. M. House

TLS (WP, DLC).

1 W. R. Hollister of New York, assistant secretary of the Democratic National Committee.

From Franklin Knight Lane

My dear Mr. President: Washington April 20, 1916.

I have written to a number of senators regarding our conservation bills, asking that these bills be taken up by the Steering Committee and given a place. We stepped aside for the Chamberlain bill[1] and now are put aside for the Rural Credits bill. The best response that I have received is from Senator Walsh, and I enclose his letter.[2] I believe that if you would write a letter to Senator Kern, saying that you would like to have the Myers Water Power and the Ferris Leasing Bill[3] taken up immediately after the Rural Credits bill, this would be done. You see if we could get any kind of bills through the Senate, we could get them whipped into proper shape in conference.

Faithfully yours,   Franklin K Lane

TLS (WP, DLC).

[1] That is, the Senate army reorganization bill.

[2] Wilson returned this letter.

[3] About the Myers bill reported out of the Senate Committee on Public Lands on March 14 as a substitute for the Ferris water power bill, see T. J. Walsh to WW, March 16, 1916, and n. 1 thereto. About the Ferris leasing bill, see WW to J. W. Kern, April 12, 1916, n. 1.

From Newton Diehl Baker

PERSONAL AND CONFIDENTIAL.

My dear Mr. President: Washington. April 20, 1916.

I have delayed any report to you on the suggestion about our forces in Mexico because of the statement of the Secretary of State that he wanted to take up some phases of the situation with me today in the light of information which he expected to receive today before any action of any kind was planned.

I am told that General Funston is sending me tonight a long message, but for the last day or two little information of any kind has come.

You will be interested to know that General Wood, who came here yesterday by my direction to talk with me about the Training Camp situation, in an incidental discussion about Mexican affairs, made exactly your suggestion[1] as being the soundest military plan and also better in its effect than the maintenance of our present extended formation there.

Sincerely yours,   Newton D. Baker

TLS (WP, DLC).

[1] Wilson's "suggestion" was to withdraw Pershing's expedition to a more defensible position in northern Chihuahua. This was what the administration did in the next few days. See Link, *Confusions and Crises*, pp. 284-86.

Sir Horace Plunkett to Edward Mandell House

London, April 20, 1916.

Copy of Cablegram sent through Admiralty cypher.

Sir Horace Plunkett desires the following to be delivered to Colonel House.

"Mr. Balfour fears you may think that the British Government is indifferent to American intervention.

The desire to prevent any suggestion of attempting to influence opinion in the United States opposed to the Government may have caused this erroneous impression.

The Cabinet unanimously believe your intervention would be immensely helpful and probably decisive.

Should this come to pass The President may rely on a cordial welcome as an ally and on the full appreciation of the high motives which determined his action." Nicholson.[1]

T telegram (WP, DLC).
[1] Walter Frederic Nicholson, Principal Clerk of the Admiralty.

To William Joel Stone

My dear Senator: [The White House] April 21, 1916

Of course I will be glad to have a talk with you just as man to man about our foreign relations. I will welcome the opportunity.

I wonder if it would be convenient for you to come to the house at eight o'clock on Monday evening next?[1]

Cordially and sincerely yours,   Woodrow Wilson

TLS (Letterpress Books, WP, DLC).
[1] Wilson conferred with Stone at the White House at 6 P.M. on Wednesday, April 26.

Two Telegrams to Edward Mandell House

The White House [April 21, 1916]

Referring to my recent telegram may I count on you to secure the consent of our friend[1] to the appointment I mean to offer him

Woodrow Wilson

[1] Robert F. Wagner.

The White House [April 21, 1916].

In pursuance of our telephone conversation of this afternoon I think it right to discuss with the German Government any accommodation it may suggest provided their maritime warfare is entirely stopped during the discussion. Secy of State Lansing is sending you for your private guidance in talking with Walter [Bernstorff] a statement of what we hold we have a right to demand.

WWT telegrams (WP, DLC).

To James Aloysius O'Gorman

My dear Senator O'Gorman: [The White House] April 21, 1916

I do not know any appointment which has caused me more perplexity than the appointment of a postmaster in New York. I know, I think, the many perplexities which surround the situation and after a great deal of careful thought about the whole matter I have come to the conclusion that the wise and right thing for me to do was to make a personal choice in this case and send it in for the consideration of the Senate. I did not feel at liberty to do this, however, without letting you first know of my purpose and I am writing to say that in my own judgment State Senator Robert F. Wagner is the man best qualified for the place, and that I am intending to send in his name to the Senate.

I am sure that you know how full a consideration I have given to your own suggestion as to this appointment and how difficult it has been for me to solve this unusually complicated problem.

Very sincerely yours, [Woodrow Wilson]

CCL (WP, DLC).

To Franklin Knight Lane

My dear Lane: [The White House] April 21, 1916

Thank you for calling my attention to the matter referred to in Senator Walsh's letter which I return.

I will of course write to Senator Kern, as you suggest, not so much to express a wish as to express my interest and see what is possible.

In haste .

Cordially and sincerely yours, [Woodrow Wilson]

CCL (WP, DLC).

To John Worth Kern

My dear Senator: The White House April 21, 1916

I think you know how deeply I am concerned to see the Myers Water Power and Ferris Leasing Bills taken up in time to assure their passage at this session of the Congress. It seems to me that this is not only necessary from the point of view of the credit of the party, but, as I have, I believe, said to you before, from the point of view of the preparation of the country to use its resources as freely as possible, and for the general development in which we are, of course, so much concerned. I drop you this line to plead for as early a place on the calendar for these bills as is possible. I understand that the present plan is to take up the Rural

Credits Bill immediately. Would you be kind enough to let me know what the Steering Committee have in mind after that?

I know that you will pardon my insistent interest in these vital matters.

Cordially and sincerely yours,　　Woodrow Wilson

TLS (C. Bowers Coll., InU).

To Henry Morgenthau

[The White House] April 21, 1916

Referring to our recent conversation may I count on you to secure the consent of our friend to the appointment I mean to offer him.　　　　　　　　　　　　　Woodrow Wilson.

T telegram (Letterpress Books, WP, DLC).

To Wallace Buttrick

My dear Mr. Buttrick:　　　　　[The White House] April 21, 1916

Thank you warmly for your letter of April nineteenth. I am very much obliged to you for it and sincerely hope that your re-examination of the Berry School will commend it to you as much as it has been commended to me by what I have learned of it.

No doubt Miss Berry did understand[1] Doctor Flexner's paper. I am relieved to hear that there is no intention of founding a school in the South, because there is so much danger down there of duplication and dispersion of effort.

Cordially and sincerely yours,　　Woodrow Wilson

TLS (Letterpress Books, WP, DLC).
[1] Wilson dictated "misunderstand."

To Martha Berry

My dear Miss Berry:　　　　　[The White House] April 21, 1916

After receiving your letter of April sixth, I wrote to Doctor Buttrick, the Secretary of the General Education Board, and want you to see the enclosed reply which I have just received from him.

In haste

Cordially and sincerely yours,　　Woodrow Wilson

TLS (Letterpress Books, WP, DLC).

Three Letters from Edward Mandell House

Dear Governor: New York. April 21, 1916.

I saw Senator Wagner immediately upon receipt of your telegram.

He was deeply appreciative, but said that his ambition lay along other lines and that he could not possibly accept. He indicated that he thought Johnson a bad selection. I asked him to make a suggestion himself and he will do this on Monday.

He promised upon his honor not to mention to anyone the offer you made him or to mention the matter either directly or indirectly in any way.

Affectionately yours,   E. M. House

Morgantau says Johnson has asked him to employ him in the campaign saying it would satisfy him and his friends and that he would withdraw his name from consideration. M. has consented.

Dear Governor: New York. April 21, 1916.

After wrestling with McCombs two days Baruch got the letter from him. Here is a copy of it.[1]

Baruch is holding the original expecting me to go to Washington and take it in person which does not seem to me necessary. We both regard it as important that you clinch the matter by accepting his offer to eliminate himself from the situation. If you will write McCombs upon receipt of this and send the letter to me I will make the exchange.

McCombs wants to make the announcement of his change of firm on Monday and along with it he would like to publish his letter to you and your reply.

He says he hopes you will express appreciation of his services and regret that he cannot continue. He hopes, too, that you may be able to say that you are aware of the sacrifices he has made and wish him success in his new venture.

It is a good way to get rid of an ugly situation and eliminate McCombs for all time.

Baruch is anxious for you to write as cordially to McCombs as you feel that you can believing that it will have a good effect all round.

Will you not write the letter tomorrow and send it by special delivery so the McCombs incident may be closed for good and all on Sunday. This will give him time to make his announcement on Monday.   Affectionately yours,   E. M. House

¹ He enclosed a TCL. The TLS is printed as an Enclosure with EMH to WW, April 24, 1916 (third letter of that date).

Dear Governor: New York. April 21, 1916.

For fear you did not understand what I said over the telephone about Bernstorff I will repeat it here.

He is suggesting to his Government that they agree to suspend temporarily their submarine activities in order to negotiate with us for the purpose of seeing whether or not activities cannot be taken up later upon a basis that would satisfy neutrals.

He wants to know what you think of this and whether it will satisfy you. His idea is that if they agree to do this it will save their faces at home and that it will lead to a complete abandonment of their activities.

He tells me they are eager for you to make an end of the war. I told him I thought this could be done before the summer was over.

He believes he cannot get an answer from his Government before Thursday.   Affectionately yours,   E. M. House

TLS (WP, DLC).

From Lillian D. Wald

My dear Mr. President: Washington, D. C. April 21, 1916.

Your invitation, made recently in St. Louis, to the people who differ with you regarding the need for unusual expenditures for national defence at this time, to "hire large halls" and state their views, has been accepted—not without due appreciation of its humor—by the Anti "Preparedness" Committee. We have hired the largest halls we could find in New York, Buffalo, Cleveland, Detroit, Chicago, Minneapolis, Des Moines, Kansas City, St. Louis, Cincinnati and Pittsburg and stated to very large audiences the reasons why we feel opposed to some of the features of the pending army and navy programs.

Among the speakers who helped us on that tour were Rabbi Stephen S. Wise, Amos Pinchot, Rev. John Haynes Holmes and Hamilton Holt of New York City; Rev. A. A. Berle of Cambridge, Massachusetts; Herbert S. Bigelow of Cincinnati; John A. Mc-Sparran of the National Grange; Professor Scott Nearing of Toledo University; and President James H. Maurer of the Pennsylvania State Federation of Labor.¹ These gentlemen gave their services night after night without compensation. While they were of widely different political views, they were very nearly a unit in their attitude toward the so-called "preparedness" program.

We feel that we received an extraordinary response from the country, a response which the press has done its best to ignore. In some cities the meetings were almost spontaneous, so anxious were the people to hear the other side. We learned more about the sentiment of the country than we had known before.

We should like the privilege, Mr. President, of having our speakers appear before you to tell you briefly what they learned on their tour of the country, and to present the resolutions which they received from audiences in the various cities they visited.

Very sincerely yours, Lillian D. Wald.

TLS (WP, DLC).
[1] All persons in this sentence, hitherto unidentified, are identified in the notes to the memorial and colloquy printed at May 8, 1916.

To Edward Mandell House, with Enclosure

My dearest Friend, The White House. 22 April, 1916.

This is just a hasty line to accompany the enclosed for McCombs. I hope that what I wil[l] have written will seem to you the right thing.

Could you not prevail on Wagner to accept temporarily, as Mitchell did the Collectorship? I wish with all my heart he would.

I think my telegram and the letter from the State Department fully covered the Bernstorff matter.

In great haste, to get this off,

Affectionately Yours, W.W.

WWTLI (E. M. House Papers, CtY).

E N C L O S U R E

To William Frank McCombs

My dear McCombs, The White House. 22 April, 1916.

I have your letter of the twentieth of April apprising me of your inability to retain the chairmanship of the Democratic National Committee for the approaching campaign.

I fully appreciate the necessity you feel yourself to be under to resign after the convention shall have been held in June; I know that you would not have reached such a decision had not your new business obligations made it unavoidable. I do not feel at liberty, therefore, to urge you to make the sacrifice that a retention of the chairmanship would in the circumstances involve. You have made many and great sacrifices already for the party, and I know that I am speaking the sentiment of all loyal Democrats when I express the very deep appreciation I have felt of the great services you have rendered. I am sure that the greatest regret will be felt at your retirement and that a host of friends will join me in the hope that your new business connections will bring you continued abundant success.

With the best Wishes,

Sincerely Yours,   Woodrow Wilson[1]

WWTLS (WP, DLC).

[1] There is a WWsh draft of this letter in WP, DLC.

From Edward Mandell House

Dear Governor: New York. April 22, 1916.

Bernstorff was in again this morning and I read him the first sentence of your code message.

I made it clear to him that if you did not take a strong stand in regard to submarine warfare as conducted by Germany you would not have the slightest influence in bringing about peace. The Allies would consider this country impotent to either help or hurt, and they would look upon us as they look upon the South American republics.

I expressed the hope that his Government would be wise enough to immediately discontinue their submarine activities and come to terms with you. If they did I thought it would be a helpful aid to peace and would perhaps be its fore-runner.

All this impressed him and he accepted it as true and will try to bring his Government to the same way of thinking.[1]

The State Department will send over tomorrow the memoranda you desired me to have and with it before me I will have another talk with Bernstorff Monday morning.

If the German Government have not gone entirely mad we should be able to find a way out.

Affectionately yours,   E. M. House

TLS (WP, DLC).

[1] J. H. von Bernstorff to the Foreign Office, April 23, 1916, T telegram (Der Weltkrieg, No. 18, geheim, Unterseebootkrieg gegen England, Vol. 14, pp. 3-4, GFO-Ar) reports the most important parts of this conversation as follows (our translation): "At Wilson's request, I am negotiating confidentially with House in order to avoid a break. Wrong as it may seem to us, the notion is nevertheless prevalent here that we violated our pledges, since we either did not want to or could not check our submarines. I always insisted that a complete abandonment of our submarine warfare was impossible, if only for the reason that public opinion in Germany would not accept it. I cannot determine from here

whether it is feasible, on the other hand, to take up my earlier suggestion for a temporary suspension of submarine warfare against commerce in order to enter into negotiations. This proposal, however, would eliminate the tension here. Wilson would accept it, and he would then also be willing to take measures against England and to make peace overtures. He believes that, backed by our concession of a temporary suspension of submarine warfare, he will be strong enough to force our enemies to enter into peace negotiations. . . . In any event, Wilson's desire is not, as is repeatedly claimed, to help England, but to bring about peace and to be re-elected. He believes, however, that, at the moment, the British would simply laugh at him and his peace proposals, if he had not achieved anything with us by all his notes."

The Ambassador repeated his advice for a suspension of the submarine war in J. H. von Bernstorff to the Foreign Office, April 26, 1916, T telegram (*ibid.*, pp. 139-40). He reiterated that Wilson would then take steps against England, and added (our translation): "However, he is of the opinion, as he assures me through House, that it will be easier to bring about peace than to force England to give up its blockade. The latter could only be achieved by war, and for this, as is well known, the United States is not sufficiently prepared. It would also be impossible to threaten England with an embargo on American exports. American public opinion would not support it, as it would have adverse effects on the prosperity of the country. According to House, however, Wilson believes that our enemies will agree to peace."

From Robert Lansing

PERSONAL AND CONFIDENTIAL:

My dear Mr. President: Washington April 22, 1916.

I send you a letter which I have just received from the Attorney General[1] in regard to the seized papers in the Von Igel case[2] and would like to have your views at the earliest possible moment in regard to the disposition which should be made of them.

I do not believe that these papers can be claimed as archives of the Embassy as they were unsealed and were taken from a room which was rented by an individual as an advertising agency. Von Igel, as I understand it, rented this room before he was notified to us as an Attaché of the Embassy.

I believe that there are two things that a Government should respect in regard to the papers of a foreign government in its territory: First, papers that are on the premises of the Embassy; and, second, papers that are under seal of the Government. I think that the immunity of even official documents attaches solely from the immunity which applies to the premises of the Embassy or the official seal.

If this is a correct interpretation of the rule I do not see that the Von Igel papers are covered by it. My impression is that the Department of Justice can retain them all.

I would also call your attention to that portion of the Attorney General's letter which points out that these papers in no way pertain to the legitimate purposes of an Embassy—that is, to its relations with the Government to which the Ambassador is accredited, with a few exceptions.

Faithfully yours,   Robert Lansing.

TLS (SDR, RG 59, 701.6211/370½, DNA).

¹ It is missing.

² Wolf von Igel, a military attaché of the German embassy, was arrested at his office in New York on April 18, 1916, by agents of the Department of Justice on charges of violating the neutrality laws of the United States. The agents seized a sizable quantity of papers, many of which implicated Von Igel and other German subjects in various espionage and sabotage activities in the United States and Canada. Some of the papers were later used in trials of several German agents. Von Igel himself was immediately released on bail and his case, repeatedly postponed, never came to trial. He returned to Germany with the embassy staff following the severance of diplomatic relations in February 1917. See *FR-WWS 1916*, pp. 807-15; *FR-LP*, I, 95-97; *New York Times*, April 19-June 25, 1916, *passim; ibid.*, Feb. 7 and 14, 1917; and Henry Landau, *The Enemy Within: The Inside Story of German Sabotage in America* (New York, 1937), pp. 70-71.

Hugh Lenox Scott to Newton Diehl Baker

Fort Sam Houston, Texas, April 22, 1916.

Whereabouts Villa unknown period Variously reported in different directions period He is no longer being trailed period Pershing has been obliged to withdraw Colonel Brown's¹ force to Satevo account lack food and forage period Animals much run down by little food and long swift marching period. It is evident Carranza troops concentrating to oppose our southward advance period There are three courses open comma one to drive our way through by force after recuperation and seizure of railroad to supply large reenforcements that would be necessary for this purpose period It is believed that this will not result in capture of Villa who can go clear to Yucatan period Second course open is for Pershing to concentrate forces some where near Colonia Dublan where water rations to include May fifteenth and considerable forage are now on hand period At this point road from Columbus strikes Mexican North-Western railroad and protection can be given Mormon colonists period These troops can be maintained here indefinitely as an incentive to Carranza forces to kill or capture Villa if we have use of Mexican Northwestern Railroad period Only other course open to remove our troops from Mexico as it is felt that longer they stay south Casas Grandes more acute will be present situation period With Villa in hiding very small chance exists of finding him in a population friendly to him and daily becoming more hostile to us period Realizing that first course cannot be considered General Funston and I recommend second course period Approach of rainy season

which will make Columbus road impassable will make it necessary for us to have use of Mexican North Western Railroad from
Juarez to Casas Grandes.   Scott

T telegram (H. L. Scott Papers, DLC).
¹ William Carey Brown, 10th Cavalry.

To Robert Lansing

The White House.
My dear Mr. Ambassador,¹   23 April, 1916.

This is certainly an unfortunate time for these questions to
have arisen. It is, of course, merely fortuitous that this arrest and
seizure of papers should have come at about the same time as
our last communication to the German Foreign Office, but it can
be made to appear, by those whose interest and plan it is to disregard the truth, that we have already begun to cooperate with
the Allies in breaking up conspiracies against them, as if we
intended something more than a mere execution of our own laws
and a mere protection of the United States against violations of
her neutrality. But, however unfortunate the coincidence, we
must insist upon our rights and exercise them.

I think you took the right course in calling upon the German
Ambassador to examine the seized papers and declare which of
them he claims as official. Probably it would be well to let him
retain those which he thus designates. The rest should be retained.

It seems to me clear that no immunity can be claimed for von
Igel for acts committed prior to his designation to the Department
as an attaché of the Embassy.

A full statement of the circumstances of this case to the German Foreign Office ought surely to be conclusive of our rights in
the premises; and I think that it would probably be wise to send
such a statement to Gerard so that they may not get all their information and impressions from Bernstorff.

Faithfully Yours,   W.W.

WWTLI (SDR, RG 59, 701.6211/372½, DNA).
¹ Sic!

To Robert Ferdinand Wagner

[The White House] April 23, 1916
Sincerely hope you will accept Post Office appointment. It
would be a real service to the party.   Woodrow Wilson

T telegram (Letterpress Books, WP, DLC).

From Robert Ferdinand Wagner

My dear President Wilson: Albany April twenty-third, 1916.

I cannot adequately express to you my gratitude in selecting me for the high office of Postmaster of New York, especially as it was not sought by me. Your kindness in this matter makes it doubly difficult for me to decline the appointment.

I received your telegram urging me to accept, and thus render a real service to the Party. I feel sure, however, that I can be of greater service to the people, as well as to my Party, in my present position. Besides being leader of the Democratic Party in the State Senate, I am Chairman of the New York County Committee and a delegate to the Democratic Convention at St. Louis. These offices will enable me to take an active part in the coming political campaign in which I confidently expect to see the Democratic Party supreme, not only in the nation, but also in this state.

I have never accepted or sought political office for my personal or financial advancement, but I have only been attracted by the opportunities for constructive work. In consideration of this, I know that you will not press me to accept this position, dignified and important as it is, but still not offering the opportunities for the betterment of civic conditions which attract me to public life.

Please accept my sincere good wishes during these, the most trying times in the history of our Country. I am one of those Americans who rejoices that our nation is at peace with the world, and at the same time has maintained its national honor.

I expect to be in Washington this week, when I hope I shall have the honor of meeting you again.

                    Very sincerely yours,   Robert F. Wagner

TLS (WP, DLC).

From Edward Mandell House

                                        [New York, April 23, 1916]

Damon (McCombs) requests that your letter and his be given out at Washington tomorrow morning. Please ask Tumulty to do it in time for the afternoon papers. Morganthau is working on the postmaster matter with some hopes of success. The proposed appointee wrote you this afternoon declining but you need not pay any attention to it. He will probably either accept or make a suggestion that will be satisfactory. A definite decision will be made by Tuesday.   Edward House.

CC telegram (E. M. House Papers, CtY).

From Melancthon Williams Jacobus

Hartford, Connecticut
My dear President Wilson: Easter Sunday April 23, 1916

Americans today should support you not with words alone, but with deeds—and they will, no matter what may be the solemn issues to which they may be summoned.

But Congress must understand that it rests with it whether we shall do this well or ill. If we are to fight again for the liberty and freedom for which our fathers fought, and are compelled by it to do the fighting with nothing better than poor munitions and ill prepared men, we will do it, but the blood of the slaughter and disaster will be upon the heads of the men who, at the Capitol, are wasting time with political discussions and partisan debates.

Perhaps this is the calamity through which our Nation is to go, in order that the democracy we have produced be changed for something better.

We are learning lessons from this War, and one lesson is coming to us swift and sure. Theoretically we are a government of the people; administratively we are a government by the people; but with the hopeless individualism into which we have allowed our democracy to drift we have not been and never will be a government for the people.

And so we have produced in politics the individual political boss, and in business the individual high financier, and in society the individual social faddist. Even when we have seemed to legislate for the people, we have done little better than array one individualistically conscious class in hostility against another class equally conscious of its individualism.

Surely between the imperialistic autocracy of Germany, which nobody wants, and the individualistic democracy of America, which everyone wants—for himself—there must be something to mark the future way of real democracy.

Long since the Church has ceased to think and act alone for the individual within its walls, and has moved out with its message and its mission to the community around it. It would seem that the time had come for the State to follow in that way.

If democracy is so to hold to the rights of the individual that there can be no rights for the people at large; if we have become so insistent upon our own rights that we will allow no curbing of them for the rights of others; if our individual liberty has made us so selfish of freedom that we have become essentially a lawless nation, then we can make no better sacrifice for our day and generation than to abandon the democracy we have produced

Historically all democracies have failed, and the hundred and thirty years of our democracy should not blind us to the fact that we are still on trial and that there is no inherent reason that we should succeed.

The issues at stake in Europe are making us all think. We were asleep in our prosperity when the crash came, but we are awake now to those issues as they are affecting us, and if we too must take our place in the struggle, it will be with a solemn consciousness of what our action may mean for the political institutions of which we have been so proud, but upon which we have builded to such mortification and shame Whatever may be the crisis through which we are to go, no true lover of his Country but will support you as you lead us out to a democracy in which a selfish individualism shall be curbed for the common good. Behind such a leading stands a mighty moral tide which is beating against the individualistic politics and commercialism and materialism that has warped our democracy to its present impotence of thought and life.

With the sincerest best wishes, and with a true American loyalty   Faithfully yours   Melancthon W. Jacobus

ALS (WP, DLC).

From Richard Heath Dabney

Dear Woodrow: Charlottesville 23 April, 1916.

Although I know you have been flooded with letters and telegrams commending your last note to the German Government, yet, since I also know that you have been snarled and snorted at both for your milk & mush cowardice and for your ferocious thirst for German gore, I cannot but tell you that I am one of those who thoroughly approves of your resolute determination to submit no longer to the hypocrisy & barbarism of the German Government.

From the very beginning I have put no faith whatever in the promises of a Government which, after assuring the Belgian Foreign Minister through its Ambassador at Brussels on July 31, 1914, that Belgian neutrality would be respected, proceeded in a few days to attempt the brutal assassination of that little nation. As a private individual you have probably put no more faith in German promises than I have. But I can appreciate thoroughly why, as Chief Magistrate of a hundred millions of men, you have so strongly maintained official neutrality and have officially accepted the German assurances at their face value. Your patience has been wonderful—far greater, I believe, than I could possibly have displayed—but I do not wonder that it has been exhausted at last, and that you have in clear, though diplomatic language, accused the Imperial Government not only of barbarism but of deliberate breach of faith.

In accordance with your publicly expressed wish, I tried hard to maintain a neutral attitude during the early part of the war, but it has been a long time now since there was a neutral bone in my body. For, in spite of my admiration for many German qualities, and in spite of my personal gratitude for what I have learned from the Germans & for the happy days that I spent in Germany, I have become profoundly convinced that the Prussian Spirit is the enemy of the human race, and that the complete triumph of Prussianism in this war would mean the death of liberty throughout the world.

Such being my conviction, I not only back you up in your present stand, but go further. I do not, like you, regret that it has come to this. The cause of American rights and the sacred cause of humanity are both at stake, and I wish to do my part in defending those causes. I do not desire further friendship with Prussianism. On the contrary, I fervently hope that Germany will flatly refuse your demands, that you will sever diplomatic relations with her, and that she will then declare war. I want my country to help shorten this infernal war, to save thousands of lives, and to help make such wars impossible in future. By the moral effect of our stand for humanity and by the billions of dollars that we could pour into the coffers of the Allies, we can be of incalculable benefit to all mankind.

With sincerest sympathy, I remain

Faithfully your friend,   R. H. Dabney.

ALS (WP, DLC).

From Robert Lansing

PERSONAL AND PRIVATE:

My dear Mr. President: [Washington] April 24, 1916.

I enclose a memorandum on the *status* of armed merchant vessels, which I prepared a month ago.

It is possible that Germany may abandon submarine war against merchant vessels, and then attack vessels with armaments, claiming that they are not merchant vessels. I think that we should be prepared to meet this move at the very outset, otherwise they will appeal to the letter of January 18th as an expression of the ideas of this Government.

The memorandum was prepared to show the consistency of the statements in the letter of January 18th with the accepted rules as to the arming of merchant vessels.

I would be obliged if you could let me know at Cabinet tomorrow whether you approve of the memorandum as I may have to use the substance orally in interviews with Count Bernstorff.

Faithfully yours,   Robert Lansing

CCL (SDR, RG 59, 763.72/2634½, DNA).

To Robert Lansing, with Enclosure

My dear Mr. Secretary,   The White House. 24 April, 1916.

I have looked this memorandum through with a good deal of care, and think that it covers the whole question comprehensively and with great clearness.

I take it that paragraph #13, on page 9, is the one which really defines what we must maintain to be the law with regard to the particular question raised in the German orders of February last with regard to armed merchantmen. It shows that they have left out some of the most necessary elements of their case, namely, orders to attack in all circumstances, right to prize money, and liability to discipline if orders are not carried out.

Is it not law, and might it not be well to bring sharply out, that vessels bound on normal errands of trade are never transformed into war vessels by attacking everything that threatens them on their way, when the purpose is protection?

Faithfully Yours,   W.W.

WWTLI (SDR, RG 59, 763.72/2634½, DNA).

ENCLOSURE

March 25, 1916.

MEMORANDUM ON THE STATUS OF ARMED MERCHANT VESSELS.

I.

The *status* of an armed merchant vessel of a belligerent is to be considered from two points of view: *First*, from that of a neutral when the vessel enters its ports; and, *second*, from that of an enemy when the vessel is on the high seas.

First: An armed Merchant Vessel in Neutral Ports.

(1) It is necessary for a neutral government to determine the

status of an armed merchant vessel of belligerent nationality which enters its jurisdiction in order that the Government may protect itself from responsibility for the destruction of life and property by permitting its ports to be used as bases of hostile operations by a belligerent warship.

(2) If the vessel carries a commission or orders issued by a belligerent government and directing it under penalty to conduct aggressive operations, or if it is conclusively shown to have conducted such operations, it should be regarded and treated as a warship.

(3) If sufficient evidence is wanting, a neutral government, in order to safeguard itself from liability for failure to preserve its neutrality, may reasonably presume from the facts the *status* of an armed merchant vessel which frequents its waters. There is no settled rule of International Law, as to the sufficiency of evidence to establish such presumption. As a result a neutral government must decide for itself the sufficiency of the evidence which it requires to determine the character of the vessel. For the guidance of its port officers and other officials a neutral government may therefore declare a standard of evidence, but such standard may be changed on account of the general conditions of naval warfare or modified on account of the circumstances of a particular case. These changes and modifications may be made at any time during the progress of the war, since the determination of the *status* of an armed merchant vessel in neutral waters may affect the liability of a neutral government.

Second: An Armed Merchant Vessel on the High Seas.

(1) It is necessary for a belligerent warship to determine the *status* of an armed merchant vessel of an enemy encountered on the high seas, since the rights of life and property of belligerents and neutrals on board the vessel are impaired if its *status* is that of an enemy warship.

(2) The determination of warlike character must rest in no case upon presumption but upon conclusive evidence, because the responsibility for the destruction of life and property depends on the actual facts of the case, and can not be avoided or lessened by a standard of evidence which a belligerent may announce as creating a presumption of hostile character. On the other hand, to safeguard himself from possible liability for unwarranted destruction of life and property the belligerent should, in the absence of conclusive evidence, act on the presumption that an armed merchantman is of peaceful character.

(3) A presumption, based solely on the presence of an arma-

ment on a merchant vessel of an enemy is not a sufficient reason for a belligerent to declare it to be a warship and proceed to attack it without regard to the rights of the persons on board. Conclusive evidence of a purpose to use the armament for aggression is essential. Consequently an armament, which a neutral government seeking to perform its neutral duties may presume to be intended for aggression, might in fact on the high seas be used solely for protection. A neutral government has no opportunity to determine the purpose of an armament on a merchant vessel, unless there is evidence in the ship's papers or other proof as to its previous use, so that the Government is justified in substituting an arbitrary rule of presumption in arriving at the *status* of the merchant vessel. On the other hand, a belligerent warship can on the high seas test by actual experience the purpose of an armament on an enemy merchant vessel, and so determine by direct evidence the *status* of the vessel.

Summary.

The *status* of an armed merchant vessel as a warship in neutral waters may be determined, in the absence of documentary proof or conclusive evidence of previous aggressive conduct, by presumption derived from all the circumstances of the case.

The *status* of such vessel as a warship on the high seas must be determined only upon conclusive evidence of aggressive purpose, in the absence of which it is to be presumed that the vessel has a private and peaceable character and it should be so treated by an enemy warship.

In brief, a neutral government may proceed upon the presumption that an armed merchant vessel of belligerent nationality is armed for aggression, while a belligerent should proceed on the presumption that the vessel is armed for protection. Both of these presumptions may be overcome by evidence—the first by secondary or collateral evidence, since the fact to be established is negative in character; the second by primary and direct evidence, since the fact to be established is positive in character.

II.

The character of the evidence, upon which the *status* of an armed merchant vessel of belligerent nationality is to be determined when visiting neutral waters and when traversing the high seas, having been stated, it is important to consider the rights and duties of neutrals and belligerents as affected by the *status* of armed merchant vessels in neutral ports and on the high seas.

First: The Relations of Belligerents and Neutrals as Affected by the Status of Armed Merchant Vessels in Neutral Ports.

1. It appears to be the established rule of International Law that warships of a belligerent may enter neutral ports and accept hospitality there upon condition that they leave within twenty-four hours, or as soon as repairs necessitated by sea damage have been completed.

2. Belligerent warships are also entitled to take on coal once in three months in ports of a neutral country.

3. As a mode of enforcing these rules a neutral has the right to cause belligerent warships failing to comply with them, together with their officers and crews, to be interned during the remainder of the war.

4. Merchantmen of belligerent nationality, armed only for purposes of protection against the enemy, are entitled to enter and leave neutral ports without hinderance in the course of legitimate trade.

5. Armed merchantmen of belligerent nationality under a commission or orders of their government to use under penalty their armament for aggressive purposes or merchantmen which, without such commission or orders, have used their armaments for aggressive purposes, are not entitled to the same hospitality in neutral ports as peaceable armed merchantmen.

Second: *The Relations of Belligerents and Neutrals as Affected by the Status of Armed Merchant Vessels on the High Seas.*

1. Innocent neutral property on the high seas can not legally be confiscated, but is subject to inspection by a belligerent. Resistance to inspection removes this immunity and subjects the property to condemnation by a prize court, which is charged with the preservation of the legal rights of the owners of neutral property.

2. Neutral property engaged in contraband trade, of blockade or unneutral service obtains the character of enemy property, and is subject to seizure and condemnation by a belligerent.

3. When hostile and innocent property is mixed, as in a neutral ship carrying a cargo which is entirely or partly contraband, this fact can only be determined by inspection. Such innocent property may be uncertain character as it has been frequently held that it is more or less contaminated by association with hostile property. For example, under the Declaration of London (which, so far as the provisions covering this subject are concerned, has been adopted by all the belligerents) the presence of a cargo, which in bulk or value consists of fifty per cent contraband

articles, impresses the ship with enemy character and subjects it to seizure and condemnation by a prize court.

4. Enemy property, including ships and cargoes, is always subject to seizure and condemnation. Any enemy property taken by a belligerent on the high seas is a total loss to the owners. There is no redress in a prize court. The only means of avoiding loss is by flight or successful resistence. Enemy merchant ships have, therefore, the right to arm for the purpose of self-protection.

5. A belligerent warship is any vessel which, under commission or orders of its Government, imposing penalties is armed for the purpose of seeking and capturing or destroying enemy property or hostile neutral property on the seas. The size of the vessel, strength of armament, and its defensive or offensive force are immaterial.

6. A belligerent warship has, incidental to the right of seizure, the right to visit and search all vessels on the high seas for the purpose of determining the hostile or innocent character of the vessels and their cargoes. If the hostile character of the property is known, however, the belligerent warship may seize the property without exercising the right of visit and search which is solely for the purpose of obtaining knowledge as to the character of the property.

7. When a belligerent warship meets a merchantman on the high seas, which is known to be enemy owned, and attempts to capture the vessel, the latter may exercise its right of self-protection either by flight or by resistance. The right to capture and the right to prevent capture are recognized as equally justifiable.

8. The exercise of the right of capture is limited, nevertheless, by certain accepted rules of conduct based on the principles of humanity and regard for innocent property, even if there is definite knowledge that some of the property, cargo as well as the vessel, is of enemy character. As a consequence of these limitations, it has become the established practice for warships to give merchant vessels an opportunity to surrender or submit to visit and search before attempting to seize them by force. The observance of this rule of naval warfare tends to prevent the loss of life of non-combatants and the destruction of innocent neutral property which would result from sudden attack.

9. If, however, before a summons to surrender is given, a merchantman of belligerent nationality, aware of the approach of an enemy warship, uses its armament to keep the enemy at a distance, or after it has been summoned to surrender it resists or flees, the warship may properly exercise force to compel surrender.

10. If the merchantman finally surrenders, the belligerent warship may release it, take it into custody or sink it under certain conditions, which according to the general rules are as to a belligerent merchantman that the prize is unseaworthy, that no prize crew is available or that rescue is imminent, and provided always that the persons on board the prize are put in a place of safety, while, as to a neutral merchantman the right to sink it in any circumstances is doubtful.

11. A merchantman, entitled to exercise the rights of self-protection, may do so when certain of attack by an enemy warship, otherwise the exercise of the right would be so restricted as to render it ineffectual. There is a distinct difference however between the exercise of the right of self-protection and the act of cruising the seas in an armed vessel for the purpose of attacking enemy naval vessels.

12. In the event that merchant ships of belligerent nationality are armed and under commission or orders to attack in all circumstances certain classes of enemy naval vessels for the purpose of destroying them, and are entitled to receive prize money for such service from their Government or are liable to a penalty for failure to obey the orders given, such merchant ships lose their *status* as peaceable merchant ships and are to a limited extent incorporated in the naval forces of their government, even though it is not their sole occupation to conduct hostile operations.

13. A vessel, engaged intermittently in commerce and under a commission or orders of its government imposing a penalty, in pursuing and attacking enemy naval craft, possesses a *status* tainted with hostile purpose which it can not throw aside or assume at will. It should, therefore, be considered as an armed public vessel and receive the treatment of a warship by an enemy and by neutrals. Any person taking passage on such a vessel can not expect immunity other than that accorded persons who are on board a warship. A private vessel, engaged in seeking enemy naval craft, without such a commission or orders from its Government, stands in a relation to the enemy similar to that of a civilian who fires upon the organized military forces of a belligerent and is entitled to no more considerate treatment.

T memorandum (SDR, RG 59, 763.72/2634½, DNA).

From Robert Lansing, with Enclosures

PERSONAL AND CONFIDENTIAL:

My dear Mr. President: Washington April 24, 1916.

Señor Arredondo called upon me this afternoon and read to me a message which he had received from General Carranza, indicating that his Government was desirous of General Obregon conferring with General Scott.[1] I am delivering a copy to Secretary Baker.   Faithfully yours,   Robert Lansing.

TLS (WP, DLC).

[1] Aguilar, on April 12, had addressed a long note to Lansing. It reviewed in detail the Mexican-American negotiations since the Columbus incident and made the point, very emphatically, that the Mexican proposition of March 10 for mutual hot pursuit of bandits applied only to *future* incidents and was never meant to be retroactive. Since no agreement for the reciprocal passage of troops across the border had been concluded, Aguilar said, Carranza considered "that it is now time to treat with the Government of the United States upon the subject of the withdrawal of its forces from our territory." E. Arredondo to RL, April 13, 1916, TCL (SDR, RG 59, 812.00/17867, DNA), printed in *FR 1916*, pp. 515-17.

Wilson discussed this note with the cabinet on April 14. That same day Lansing instructed James Linn Rodgers, special representative in Mexico, to reply that American troops would remain in Mexico to hunt for Villa, and that the best way to hasten the withdrawal of the Punitive Expedition would be for the *de facto* government to throw enough of its troops into the region where Villa was hiding to insure his speedy capture. RL to J. L. Rodgers, April 14, 1916, *ibid.*, pp. 518-19. Carranza replied that he desired a formal reply to Aguilar's note. J. L. Rodgers to RL, received April 17, 1916, *ibid.*, p. 522. Then, following the receipt of Pershing's dispatch of April 17 (see F. Funston to H. P. McCain, April 17, 1916), Wilson and Baker decided to send General Scott immediately to confer with General Funston at Fort Sam Houston. Moreover on April 22, they suggested to Carranza that it would be well if General Scott and General Obregón conferred at some place near the border in order to eliminate misunderstandings and make possible real cooperation between the two governments. RL to J. L. Rodgers, April 22, 1916, *ibid.*, pp. 527-28.

E N C L O S U R E   I

General H. L. Scott, Fort Sam Houston, Texas.

Number * * * *   Washington, D. C. April 23, 1916.

Your important cipher telegram of last night received. Second course is approved except no present seizure of railroad. Further provisioning will leave that question open you for the present. Publicity here is limited to following statement. General Funston recommends a redistribution of the forces in Mexico for the purpose of recuperation and pending opportunity for further cooperation with the de facto Government. His recommendation is approved and its execution is left entirely to his discretion.

McCain.

E N C L O S U R E   I I

Mexico City, April 24, 1916.

In accordance with the contents of your cipher message of

yesterday, General Obregon left last night for Chihuahua. See Secretary Lansing in order that his Government may instruct General Scott to the end that they hold the conference in El Paso or Juarez, and it would be convenient that General Funston should be present.   V Carranza.

TC telegrams (WP, DLC).

From Edward Mandell House, with Enclosure

Dear Governor: New York. April 24, 1916.

Bernstorff telephoned today but I did not see him since he said he had nothing to communicate, and it did not seem to me wise to break in with the memorandum sent from the State Department upon what had already been done.

I am sending you a copy of the memorandum for your information in the event you have not looked it over.

It means a submarine must conform to all the rules governing other warships. This, I think, is right but it would be useless to go into such detail with Bernstorff at this moment. It is much better for us and much better for them to accept his proposal to discontinue their submarine warfare entirely until an agreement can be reached as to how it should be conducted. When that time comes, if at all, we could take up with them this memorandum.

If you disagree in any way with this conclusion please let me know by code telegram.[1]

Bernstorff is remaining over until Tuesday awaiting developments.   Affectionately yours,   E. M. House

TLS (WP, DLC).
[1] Wilson replied, in code, on April 25, as follows: "Think it would be best if opportunity offers to communicate to Bernstorff substance of State Department memorandum." Decode in House diary, April 26, 1916.

E N C L O S U R E

1. A belligerent warship can directly attack if a merchant vessel resists or continues to flee after a summons to surrender.
2. An attacking vessel must display its colors before exercising belligerent rights.
3. If a merchant vessel surrenders, the attack must immediately cease and the rule as to visit and search must be applied—
   (a) By a visit to the vessel by an officer and men of the attacking ship; or
   (b) By a visit to the attacking ship by an officer of the vessel attacked, with the ship's papers.

4. An attacking vessel must disclose its identity and name of commander when exercising visit and search.

5. If visit and search disclose that the vessel is of belligerent nationality, the vessel may be sunk only if it is impossible to take it into port, provided that the persons on board are put in a place of safety and loss of neutral property is indemnified.

Note—(a) A place of safety is not an open boat out of sight of land.

(b) A place of safety is not an open boat, if the wind is strong, the sea rough, or the weather thick, or if it is very cold.

(c) A place of safety is not an open boat which is over-crowded or is small or unseaworthy or insufficiently manned.

If, however, visit and search disclose that the vessel is of neutral nationality, it must not be sunk in any circumstances, except of gravest importance to the captor's state, and then only in accordance with the above provisos and notes.[1]

T memorandum (WP, DLC).

[1] The original of this document in the State Department archives in DNA bears the file number 763.72/2630.

From Edward Mandell House

Dear Governor: New York. April 24, 1916

If I were you I would not over persuade Wagner. He has been accused of saying what this clippings states[1] and whether he did or not, a large part of the people will always believe he did so.

It is evident that Tammany is looking to next year's City election and they will only be satisfied with an appointment that has a direct bearing upon it.

They wanted Johnson because his nomination would be a direct slap at Mitchel and they thought it might cause a break between Washington and New York.

They will probably suggest Robert Dowling in the event Wagner declines, and Dowling is grooming himself for Mayor next year. Dowling is not an Irish Catholic, is not too close to Tammany Hall, would have the support of many of the Independents and would be considered a good appointment.

Affectionately yours,   E. M. House

TLS (WP, DLC).

[1] "Wagner Refuses Wilson's Plea He Be Postmaster," New York *World*, April 24, 1916. The portion of the article which House enclosed included a translation from the *New Yorker Staats-Zeitung* which reported Wagner as saying: "How can I accept a post from a President who has so unjustly treated the land of my birth and who draws into uncertainty the loyalty of Americans who were born in Germany or are of German-American extraction?" When a *World* reporter asked Wagner if he had made this remark, he replied that there was "absolutely no truth in the quotations."

From Edward Mandell House, with Enclosure

Dear Governor: New York, April 24, 1916.

Here is the original McCombs letter which you may want for your files.

I have not replied to your letter concerning Mr. Duneka's proposal for the reason that I thought it would be wise for us to discuss it together the next time I am in Washington. There is nothing that would please me so much as to do this if it is considered advisable.   Affectionately yours,   E. M. House

TLS (WP, DLC).

ENCLOSURE

From William Frank McCombs

My dear Mr. President: New York April 20, 1916.

I have just formed a new partnership for the practice of law which will become effective on the first of May. The change will necessitate my devoting substantially all of my time to my profession. My political activities must be largely curtailed. My arrangements however, will justify my proceeding through to the end of the Convention at St. Louis.

In view of the Party precedent that the nominee for the Presidency is requested to indicate his preference for the Chairmanship of the National Committee, and in view of the unity of sentiment for your renomination, I am writing you at the earliest moment to let you know that I could not, under any circumstances assume the leadership of the coming Democratic campaign. I am happy in the thought however, that there are hosts of able and true men who can very readily take my place.

The Democratic organization is loyal to your policies and purposes. We all feel assured of a triumphant result for you and for the Party nominees throughout the Country, in November. For five years now I have been in the active service of the Party and it is with a keen feeling of regret that I am forced to conclude that my activities are of necessity to be more limited. If within the limits of my time I can be of assistance, be assured that I am always available.

With assurance of high regard, I am,
                        Sincerely yours,   William F. McCombs[1]

TLS (WP, DLC).
    [1] This letter and Wilson's reply, printed as an Enclosure with EMH to WW, April 22, 1916, were published in the newspapers on April 24 and 25.

Bernard Mannes Baruch to Edward Mandell House

My dear Colonel: New York April 24, 1916.

After investigation, and after mature deliberation, I believe that there can be placed at the disposal and command of the U. S. Government, an organization that could vie with, if not surpass, the much vaunted German efficiency.

Already the necessities of the warring nations has given to manufacturers here an experience in the manufacture and production of the things necessary for the continuance of the war that would be of invaluable assistance to the various Departments of this Government in case of need.

I feel satisfied that these organizations would give the experience of their men trained in large affairs with an idea alone of showing zeal and patriotism for the country. The Government would in this way obtain experienced, earnest and efficient workers that could not be duplicated anywhere.

I outlined last summer in a paper which I left with the President more in detail my views on this subject.[1]

Although I am not looking for any work, I would be glad to open the way for such an organization, or even if it were found necessary, to help continue its work.

To our Army and Navy great economy in time and money would result.   Very sincerely yours,   Bernard M Baruch

TLS (WP, DLC).
[1] Baruch left a copy of his memorandum when he visited him at the White House on September 8, 1915. It was, apparently, their first meeting. Baruch's memorandum is missing in all collections. However, a digest of it appeared in the *New York Times*, September 9, 1915. Baruch suggested appointment of an unpaid civilian commission of leading businessmen to "plan for mobilizing the business of the country for effective use in time of war."

From Harry Augustus Garfield

Personal

Dear Mr. President;   Williamstown, Mass. April 24, 1916

While the multitude applaud & Mr. Roosevelt roars valiantly,[1] may I venture to speak a word in your ear,—as a friend, as one who believes that you will be able to avoid the catastrophe which would involve us in war. Unquestionably the United States has been deeply stirred by Germany's submarine warfare. Its results are immediate, tangible, shocking; but, questions of international law aside, can we really distinguish between the inhumanity of submarine warfare & the inhumanity of starvation warfare. I admit that I cannot. Moreover, can we,—the people as distinguished from the government,—come into the court of humanity with clean hands. Again I think not. The people of the country may emulate the Colonel & roar like lions, but they do not want war. If we go to war, we must do so because our sovereign rights are violated, & on this ground I cannot believe we would be justified, having in view the larger interests of Western Civilization. As always, with warmest regard,

Faithfully Yours,   H. A. Garfield.

ALS (WP, DLC).

[1] Theodore Roosevelt issued a statement on April 19 in which he attacked Wilson's policies toward Germany and his failure to do more to prepare the nation for war. If Wilson had consistently stood by his "strict accountability" note of fourteen months before, the present crisis would never have arisen. Moreover, it was unpardonable to have permitted fourteen months to go by without instituting the strong measures of preparation for war necessary to back up the brave words of the *Sussex* note. *New York Times*, April 20, 1916.

To William Howard Taft

My dear Mr. Taft: The White House April 25, 1916

I am sure you must instinctively know how warmly I appreciate your attitude in the present crisis,[1] but I want to give myself the pleasure of sending you at least this line of genuine appreciation.

Cordially and sincerely yours,   Woodrow Wilson

TLS (W. H. Taft Papers, DLC).

[1] In a speech to the Mystic Athletic Club in Chicago on April 21, Taft endorsed Wilson's *Sussex* note. "He is right," Taft declared, "and we must all stand by him. . . . In view of the critical nature of the issue . . . , is there anything for a clear-headed, patriotic American to do but to back up our President, who is our chosen constitutional leader? This is no time to point out mistakes of the past." *New York Times*, April 22, 1916.

To Benjamin Ryan Tillman

My dear Senator: The White House April 25, 1916

I have your letter of April twenty-first[1] and hope you will pardon me for not having replied to it sooner. I think you will understand how I have been rushed.

I am sure I do not need to prove to you, my dear Senator, my deep interest in the armor plant bill, but I dare not comply with the suggestion of your letter. I am so definitely pledged to the support of a particular programme and sequence of action by the House with regard to the Philippine and Shipping Bills that I could not in fairness to the men I have been dealing with there propose now an alteration of plans.

I know the influences that are being brought to bear to defeat the armor plant bill, and I know how powerful and persistent they are, but I believe that the purpose and character of the bill are now so clear that it will be feasible to resist those influences successfully. I shall do everything in my power to accomplish that end.[2]

Cordially and sincerely yours, Woodrow Wilson

TLS (B. R. Tillman Papers, ScCleU).
  [1] B. R. Tillman to WW, April 21, 1916, TLS (WP, DLC), urging Wilson to put pressure on leaders of the House of Representatives to speed passage of the armor plant bill.
  [2] Representative Padgett reintroduced Tillman's armor plant bill on May 31 as an amendment to the pending naval appropriations bill. The House approved the amendment on June 2 and it became part of the Naval Appropriations Act of 1916. It provided for the purchase or construction of a factory, to be operated by the Navy Department, with an annual capacity of not less than 20,000 tons of armor plate, and appropriated $11,000,000 for this purpose. *Cong. Record*, 64th Cong., 1st sess., pp. 8959-60; 9187; 39 *Statutes at Large* 563.

To William Kent

My dear Mr. Kent: The White House April 25, 1916

Thank you sincerely for your courtesy in consulting me about the wisdom of introducing a bill for the purpose of creating a commission consisting of representatives from China, Japan, and the United States, to consider Oriental relations and promote mutual understanding.[1] My own impression is that this is not an opportune time to do this. The world is peculiarly weakened in counsel by all sorts of international suspicions and, while I think that candid conference is generally the best solvent of such things, I fear that the temper of dispassionate conference is hardly to be found now. I know that I should be at a loss to suggest the commissioners whom the bill would authorize.

Cordially and sincerely yours,   Woodrow Wilson

TLS (W. Kent Papers, CtY).
  [1] W. Kent to WW, April 24, 1916, TLS (WP, DLC).

From Robert Lansing, with Enclosure

PERSONAL AND CONFIDENTIAL:

My dear Mr. President: Washington April 25, 1916.

In view of the press despatches which are coming from Berlin —although we have received nothing of an official nature indicating the course which the German Government will pursue—I am convinced that there will be an attempt to compromise in the declaration, if they do make any declaration in regard to the abandonment of submarine warfare. Any conditions which they may advance will undoubtedly be based upon their position as to armed and unarmed merchant vessels.

It would seem to me a decided strategic advantage to have made known clearly our position in regard to armed vessels before Germany presents her reply. To do that it will be necessary for us to make public in some way the memorandum which I sent you Monday morning, and which you returned to me with your general approval. It could be done by a formal statement issued from the Department; by sending the memorandum to the various belligerents; or by sending it to the Committees on Foreign Relations and Foreign Affairs in Congress. If it seems advisable to you to do this it seems to me that the time to do it is at once, before we receive Germany's reply.

Faithfully yours,   Robert Lansing

P.S. Since writing the foregoing Mr. Polk has just handed me the enclosed memorandum of a conversation over the telephone with Colonel House this afternoon.   RL

TLS (WP, DLC).

ENCLOSURE

MEMORANDUM, April 25, 1916.
For the Secretary

Colonel House called me up this afternoon shortly after four and said he had just had a conversation with the German Ambassador who had heard from his Government. His Government is most anxious to avoid a break and asked him what was the best course to pursue. They also asked him what was meant by "illegal method of submarine warfare." These two questions will be answered by the Ambassador without going to the Department of State.

His Government also wanted to know if they gave up submarine warfare what the United States would do about the blockade.

Colonel House advised him to tell his Government not to send a note suggesting a compromise, and, above all, not to raise any question in regard to the blockade. He stated the only safe course to pursue would be to advise the German Government to agree to discontinue submarine warfare pending negotiations.

This the Ambassador said he would do at once, and also said

he would warn them not to send anything in the nature of a note. In regard to the blockade, Colonel House pointed out that our relations, as far as Great Britain is concerned, are quite different from our relations with Germany; that war with Germany would be possible, whereas, war with Great Britain was more or less out of the question. This the Ambassador said he understood.

Colonel House thought it advisable to issue at the earliest possible moment the memorandum on armed merchant vessels, a copy of which he had seen. He suggested that it be issued tonight for the morning papers, but I told him in the absence of the President that was impossible. He urged that the matter be presented to the President with the suggestion that the memorandum be given out not later than in time for the afternoon papers Wednesday.

He suggested one or two changes in the wording of the memorandum. These changes have been called to your attention and have been made.

T memorandum (WP, DLC).

From Robert Lansing

PERSONAL AND CONFIDENTIAL:

My dear Mr. President: Washington April 25, 1916.

I have information from an absolutely reliable source that the German Ambassador is not particularly worried over the Von Igel case. The submarine question is absorbing all his attention, and the fact that he is not pressing the Von Igel matter is indicated by the fact that he did not return Monday to Washington as he had planned to do and I have heard nothing for two days about the papers in that case.

        Faithfully yours,   Robert Lansing

TSL (WP, DLC).

From Edward Mandell House

Dear Governor: New York. April 25, 1916.

Bernstorff has just left me. He has a cable from his Government saying in substance:

"We wish to avoid war. Please suggest how this may be done. What is meant in the Note by 'illegal submarine warfare'[?] If we accede to their demands will they bring pressure upon Great Britain in regard to the blockade?"

Bernstorff thinks they have not received the cable he sent after our conference last Friday which was transmitted Saturday.

I advised his sending another despatch warning them not to suggest any compromise. That if they really desired to avoid a break, it was essential for them to discontinue their submarine warfare entirely, and immediately, pending negotiations.

He sees the difficulty in "forcing Great Britain to make concessions in her blockade." He sees, too, that war between England and this country would be quite different from war between this country and Germany and he will impress upon his Government the impossibility of our forcing Great Britain to modify her blockade.

He is advising his Government that the position we take regarding submarine warfare is a fore-runner to the freedom of the seas which Germany so much desires for it looks to the protection of commerce.

As a matter of fact, it is the freedom of the seas for England, and as far as I can see, not freedom for Germany, for it would merely restrict depredations by submarines, and the nation that controlled the seas would destroy commerce with their other war ships.

He asked if he could say to his government that I thought acquiescence to your demands would bring peace nearer. I told him he could.

The State Department has sent me over Lansing's memorandum regarding the disarming of merchantmen and they ask my opinion as to the advisability of giving it out now.

There are arguments for and against it. It seems to me it should have been done before, but on the whole, I think it might as well go out now. Germany will not like it, but she might as well get the whole story at once so she may know what to expect. They say they will bring this before you tomorrow for your decision.   Affectionately yours,   E. M. House

TLS (WP, DLC).

From William Bauchop Wilson

My dear Mr. President: Washington April 25, 1916.

Concerning your letter of April 20th relative to the treatment of Chinese entering the United States, of which Mr. Clemens Horst, representing the San Francisco Chamber of Commerce, complains, I have given a great deal of attention to the subject matter during the past three years and have freely consulted with Assistant Secretary Post, Solicitor Densmore,[1] Commissioner-General Caminetti, and other officials of the Department in an effort to devise methods by which the Chinese exclusion law could be administered with the least cause for complaint. I have realized and understood from the beginning the intense opposition to Chinese coolies existing on the Pacific Coast, and have sought to impress upon the Bureau of Immigration the idea that local sentiment must not be permitted to sway us in the administration of the Chinese exclusion law or any other immigration law or agreement. Chinese coolies successfully smuggled into the United States are reputed to be worth $500. to $1,-000. to the smugglers. This seems to be verified by the fact that numbers of them enter Canada, paying the $500. head tax, and are immediately smuggled over the border into the United States. As a result of this condition many attempts are made to bring boys and young men illegally into the country as students, sons of merchants, or sons of native American Chinese. This is our greatest difficulty. We have practically no difficulty with the real merchant or the native American. Our naturalization laws are paradoxical. They specify that a child born in this country of alien parents is a citizen of the United States. By this means Chinese children born in the United States of parents who are ineligible to citizenship become citizens by virtue of their place of birth. They also specify that children born abroad of American parentage are citizens of the United States. Many Chinese born in the United States go to China and take unto themselves wives according to the Chinese custom. They return to the United States leaving their wives behind them, and from time to time make trips to China. When their male children have reached the age when they can be useful to them in the United States, they send for them to come. In administering the law it becomes necessary for us, on the arrival of the boy or young man, to determine the citizenship of the father and the relationship of the alleged son. This means investigation which takes some time, and if the decision of the officials at the port is adverse, appeal is had to the Bureau and Department and the case presented in every way known to astute lawyers. These processes take time, and hence the protest of Mr. Horst.

The Supreme Court has held that Chinese merchants in the United States are entitled to have their wives and children with them, if they so desire. The same motives for misrepresentation exist in these cases as in the others, and the same need exists to investigate the mercantile status of the alleged father and the relationship existing between him and the applicant for admission, with the same conditions arising which result in delay.

We have made a number of changes with a view to removing embarrassment from those entitled to admission and facilitating the proper administration of the law. Under former administrations Chinese students were taken to our immigration stations upon their arrival and held there pending an investigation of the validity of their certificate. That method has been changed, and, by direction of this office, students holding certificates are landed immediately when the vessel reaches the pier.

Several months ago we made some changes in the official staff at the immigration station at San Francisco solely for the purpose of improving the service, and I am not at all sure that the interest manifested by the San Francisco Chamber of Commerce is not instigated by some of the former officials who are no longer in the service. The subject was first brought to the attention of the Chamber of Commerce through the Chinese Consul-General at San Francisco[2] in a communication in which he impugned the motives and integrity of the Bureau of Immigration and of this Department. However, that does not change the merits of the complaints, although I have presented the matter to the Secretary of State and have asked him to request the removal of the Chinese Consul-General at San Francisco.

Upon the recommendation of a committee appointed by me some six months ago to investigate the San Francisco office and report such improvements as it found the service needed, I increased the number of inspectors and other employes at that station in order to facilitate the handling of the work. To avoid the necessity of delay in making the investigations after applicants have arrived at our ports, I have, in cooperation with the Secretary of State, stationed inspectors at certain ports in China to investigate the claims of applicants so that their certificates might be accepted at their face value when they arrive in the United States. To reduce the possibility of fraud, I have made arrangements with the Secretary of State by which only those native American Chinese will have their citizenship investigated before leaving the United States, who make application to the State Department for passports. In all of these changes I have had the hearty cooperation of Assistant Secretary Post, Solicitor Densmore and Commissioner-General Caminetti.

In a service so extensive that it takes in all of the land and water boundaries of the country, all of the interior and all of our insular possessions except Guam and the Philippines, and which by virtue of the law under which it operates must inspect millions of people annually, it would be extraordinary if some just cause for complaint did not occasionally occur, but I assure you that it has been my purpose and the purpose of the Bureau under my jurisdiction to enforce the provisions of the Chinese exclusion and immigration laws and agreements with as little hardship and embarrassment to the applicants as possible.

Faithfully yours, W B Wilson

TLS (WP, DLC).
1 John B. Densmore.
2 Hsu Shan Ching.

From Francis Bowes Sayre

Williamstown
Dearest Father, Massachusetts April 25, 1916.

It was such a disappointment to miss seeing you in Philadelphia on Friday. Jessie told me all the delight of your visit. It meant more to her to have you come all the way from Washington to see her and the little girl than you can realize. It was a visit that will always live in her memory.

Dr. Mohler,[1] the head of the hospital, said that we were not to pay the remaining half of the hospital bill because you had arranged to pay it. Dear father, how loving and big your generosity! We have decided to use the money, which we had set aside for this purpose before Jessie went to the hospital, for future expenses of the little one, so that it will be a continuing gift from you to her. It seems too big a gift to take except when we think of the love with which it was given. Dear father, your thoughtful kindness will always stand out in our memories.

The journey home was comfortable and happy; and you can imagine the thankfulness of our hearts on Easter Sunday. I wish you could have seen little Frank when he first saw his sister. He was awed and silent and full of wonder.

Both Jessie and the little girl are gaining splendidly. We are looking forward now to the time when you and Edith can share the happiness of our little home, and see the two babies together.

With hearts full of love and appreciation,

Ever devotedly Jessie and Frank

ALS (WC, NjP).
1 Henry Keller Mohler, M.D., medical director of Jefferson Medical College Hospital.

To Hugh Lenox Scott

Washington April 26, 1916.

Number 1172. You will meet General Obregon and discuss with him the future military operations of our forces in Mexico on the following basis: The Government of the United States earnestly desires to avoid anything which has the appearance of intervention in the domestic affairs of the Republic of Mexico. It desires to cooperate with the de facto Government of that Republic, and its pursuit of the bandit Villa and his bands is for the sole purpose of removing a menace to the common security and the friendly relations of the two Republics. So long as he remains at large and is able to mislead numbers of his fellow citizens into attacks like that at Columbus, the danger exists of American public opinion being irritated to the point of requiring general intervention. For, of course, depredations on American soil and the loss of lives of American citizens cannot be tolerated, and one other such experience would make it difficult to restrain public opinion here. The Government of the United States realizes that the de facto Government of the Republic of Mexico is equally anxious to avoid occasions of conflict and misunderstanding. It likewise realizes that public opinion in the Republic of Mexico must be taken into consideration. It, therefore, has instructed its military commanders to observe the most considerate sense of all the proprieties, to recognize in every way the dignity of the Republic of Mexico and its de facto Government, and to proceed with its operations in harmonious cooperation with the military forces of Mexico towards an object which is, of course, of common concern and of even greater importance to the Government of Mexico than to that of the United States, since the major portion of the depredations and lawlessness committed by the bandit Villa is upon Mexican soil. Suggest to General Obregon that the presence of American troops in Mexico, if welcomed by Mexican authorities, can have no other appearance than that of friendly cooperation of two governments to suppress a cause of irritation to their common peace and their friendly relations. The American military commanders will respond instantly to all invitations for cooperation with forces of the Mexican Government. The Mexican Government has the means of locating more or less definitely the present whereabouts of Villa. Upon that fact being determined American military commanders will be glad to aid Mexican commanders in surrounding and capturing him and by such cordial cooperation the permanent friendly relations of the two governments would be demonstrated to their respective peoples. If it be deemed better American troops can be detained in the northern part of the State of Chihuahua while the forces of the Mexican Government drive Villa and his associates towards the north, in this way enabling the American troops to aid in his ultimate capture. The Government of the United States has no pride involved in who makes the capture, and its only interest is that it should be done expeditiously so that American troops can be withdrawn and the peace of its borders assured. If General Obregon shows a spirit of cooperation, it should be met fully and generously.

If, on the other hand, his attitude should be a preemptory command for the immediate withdrawal of the American troops across the border, General Scott and General Funston should say that that question is a diplomatic question and should be worked out through the agency of the respective department of foreign affairs of the two republics. Generals Scott and Funston will, of course, treat with General Obregon on the basis of high military representatives of their respective governments and emphasize the friendly attitude of the Government of the United States toward the Government and people of Mexico, but will insist that so long as the possibility of further depredations by Villa exists the withdrawal of American troops would increase the dangers and in any event be very difficult. It is possible that General Obregon may meet you with definitely stated objects on which alone he is authorized by the de facto government to confer with you. If so, the limitations thus imposed on the conference may result in embarassment in reaching a thoroughly satisfactory conclusion. It is, therefore, desired that, without interfering with or delaying your conference with him you advise the Secretary of War and the Secretary of State at once on the bases presented by General Obregon for negotiations. This will enable further instructions to be promptly communicated to you. Meanwhile, in your conference, you will proceed with full powers to discuss and agree upon all points raised by either of the conferees which relate purely to the military situation including questions of lines of supply and use of railways. All doubtful matters, and all matters which evidently concern the Department of State, will be referred by you to Washington for instructions. It is assumed that General Obregon may follow this course with his own government in respect of matters on which he is not authorized to confer.   McCain.

T telegram (SDR, RG 59, 812.00/18003, DNA).

To Williams Atkinson Jones

My dear Mr. Jones: [The White House] April 26, 1916

My attention has been called to a statement in one of the New York papers to the effect that I did not favor the passage of the Senate bill known as the Philippine Bill, now pending in the House. I think it important to correct this misapprehension. After giving careful consideration to the bill as it came from the Senate, it has seemed to me highly necessary to the public interest that it should be adopted, and I sincerely hope for its early adoption by the House.

Cordially and sincerely yours,   [Woodrow Wilson][1]

CCL (WP, DLC).

[1] Jones read this letter to the House Democratic caucus during the evening of April 26. It was summarized in the newspapers on the next day. *New York Times*, April 27, 1916.

To Melancthon Williams Jacobus

My dear Friend: The White House April 26, 1916

Your letter of Easter Sunday has come to me like a blessing, the blessing of clear thinking and high feeling in the midst of confused counsels and many petty things which obscure the whole face of policy. I thank you for it with all my heart.

Cordially and sincerely yours,   Woodrow Wilson

TLS (WP, DLC).

To Richard Heath Dabney

My dear Heath: The White House April 26, 1916

Thank you with all my heart for your letter of April twenty-third. I have not the time to do more than send you a line, but it is a line full of affection and of gratitude that you should feel as you do about what I have been attempting. These are certainly times that try men's souls and I hope that the fire will purify the whole nation.   Affectionately yours,   Woodrow Wilson

TLS (Wilson-Dabney Corr., ViU).

From Robert Lansing, with Enclosure

PERSONAL AND PRIVATE:

My dear Mr. President: [Washington] April 26, 1916.

I enclose a proposed telegram to Mr. Gerard. While I am not disposed to unduly press the German Government for an answer to our note, I feel that we should let that Government know that we are becoming impatient at the delay, which would seem to indicate that they intend to avoid a frank declaration. I also thought it would be well to furnish Gerard with our idea as to the rules which should govern the conduct of naval operations against merchant vessels.

I would be very much pleased for any changes or suggestions which you may desire to make, and also your views as to the advisability of sending a telegram·like the enclosed.

Faithfully yours,   Robert Lansing

CCL (SDR, RG 59, 763.72/2630, DNA).

E   N   C   L   O   S   U   R   E

[Washington] April 26, 1916.

951 Your 3799, April twenty-fourth, 11 p.m.[1]

You will realize and I hope you will be able to make the Foreign Office realize that this Government looks for as prompt a declaration as possible from the Imperial Government in the sense of our last communication. If Secretary von Jagow asks you as to the methods of warfare which this Government considers to be legal you may hand to him a memorandum reading as follows: Quote— (Memorandum in *Blue*)

MEMORANDUM ON CONDUCT OF NAVAL VESSELS
TOWARD MERCHANT SHIPS.

One. A belligerent warship can directly attack if a merchant vessel resists or continues to flee after a summons to surrender.

Two. An attacking vessel must display its colors before exercising belligerent rights.

Three. If a merchant vessel surrenders, the attack must immediately cease and the rule as to visit and search must be applied—

(a) by a visit to the vessel by an officer and men of the attacking ship; or

(b) by a visit to the attacking ship by an officer of the vessel attacked, with the ship's papers.

Four. An attacking vessel must disclose its identity and name of commander when exercising visit and search.

Five. If visit and search disclose that the vessel is of belligerent nationality, the vessel may be sunk only if it is impossible to take it into port, *provided* that the persons on board are put in a place of safety and loss of neutral property is indemnified.

Note—(a) A place of safety is not an open boat out of sight of land.

(b) A place of safety is not an open boat, if the wind is strong, the sea rough, or the weather thick, or if it is very cold.

(c) A place of safety is not an open boat which is overcrowded or is small or unseaworthy or insufficiently manned.

Sixth—If, however, visit and search disclose that the vessel is of neutral nationality, it must not be sunk in any circumstances, except of gravest importance to the captor's state, and then only in accordance with the above provisos and notes. Unquote.

You may further state that this Government is unwilling and cannot consent to have the illegal conduct of Germany's enemies toward neutrals on the high seas made a subject of discussion in connection with the abandonment of illegal methods of submarine warfare.

Delay of the declaration of such abandonment is causing this Government grave concern lest the Imperial Government attempt to introduce subjects of discussion before the declaration, a course which would be entirely unacceptable to this Government and cause a critical situation by compelling action on the part of this Government. You will, therefore, present these views to the Minister of Foreign Affairs and urge that a very early answer be given this Government in order that it may not be forced to take the action which would now be unavoidable should the Imperial Government fail to declare and effect at once the abandonment of illegal submarine warfare. Lansing[2]

T telegram (SDR, RG 59, 763.72/2630, DNA).

[1] J. W. Gerard to RL, April 24, 1916, *FR-WWS 1916*, pp. 242-43. In response to a request from Lansing (RL to J. W. Gerard, April 22, 1916, *ibid.*, p. 239), Gerard attempted to recall Von Jagow's exact words when Gerard presented the *Sussex* note to him on April 20. As Gerard remembered it, the Foreign Secretary said: "You know we cannot give up sinking ships without notice in the war zone so it (looks like?) a break, but of course I have to consult with Chancellor who is at General Headquarters." Von Jagow had also asked if the United States Government could not do something against the British blockade. Gerard had responded that the United States could never agree, in return for any promise from Germany, to "do anything" to England.

[2] This telegram was sent verbatim to Berlin on April 28. It is printed in *FR-WWS 1916*, p. 252.

From Martha Berry

Dear Mr. President: Mount Berry Georgia April 26, 1916.

I am re-enclosing the letter from Doctor Buttrick, and I want to thank you very gratefully for the interest which prompted you to write him in our behalf.

Their representative, Doctor Sage,[1] has just visited the Berry School, and I do hope and pray that the Board will be so impressed by his report as to both endorse our work and make an appropriation to help it forward.

Always deeply appreciating your kindness toward the work of the Berry school, I am, with great respect,

Sincerely yours,   Martha Berry

TLS (WP, DLC).
  [1] The Rev. Dr. Eben Charles Sage, assistant secretary of the General Education Board.

Johann Heinrich von Bernstorff to Edward Mandell House

My dear Colonel House: Washington, April 26, 16.

I just received my first message from Berlin, which is rather disappointing to me, as it seems, that a temporary complete abandonment of submarine warfare for the purpose of negotiating would be unacceptable to public opinion in Germany.

I have once more urged my proposal, and will continue to do so, but I am afraid that my Government will not be able to put it through. Their idea seems to be to conduct *all* submarine warfare in future according to the rules of international law for cruiser warfare, as they were laid down in our notes and memoranda concerning the cases of the "Frye" and the "Persia."

The chief thing for the moment is to know whether a declaration of my Government in this sense would avert a break, as this is the object I want to attain.

I should be very much obliged for a kind answer to this question, which I would transmit to Berlin immediately. If this letter does not make the matter sufficiently clear, I am ready to go to New York immediately to talk things over with you. In this case please send me a wire.

With many thanks in advance,

Very sincerely yours,   J. Bernstorff.

Dear Governor,   [New York] Thursday 1 p.m. April 27

I have just rec'd this. Will you not telephone me or send me a code message what to answer? Shall I get B. over here or shall I come there on the midnight and see him on some neutral ground. If they will conduct their submarine warfare according to the rules laid down in the memo. sent me by Lansing is it not all we can ask?   Affectionately yours,   E. M. House[1]

TCL (WP, DLC).
[1] EMHhw at the bottom of Von Bernstorff's letter.

Karl Edwin Harriman to Joseph Patrick Tumulty

                                   Philadelphia April twenty-sixth
My dear Mr. Secretary: Nineteen hundred and sixteen

In accordance with the suggestion made by you on the occasion of my call on you in Washington last Monday I am very glad to present herewith the proposal made you at that time, which was to the following effect:

Approximately four million women will vote at the coming presidential election—many of them for the first time. It seems to us that we could do nothing better in the way of serving the vast number of those women, who, we have reason to believe, are readers of The Ladies' Home Journal, than to present in the October or November issue of the magazine an article by President Wilson, directed specifically to women and explaining for their benefit the platform upon which he will stand as the candidate of the Democratic Party. Obviously, the value of such an article to the women who read The Ladies' Home Journal would be greatest were it written for the magazine by President Wilson himself. Were it deemed by him for any reason undesirable to do this, may I suggest the alternative of securing with him, by any journalist of his selection, an interview in which the purpose of the desired article would be carried out?

The suggestion made by yourself when you were good enough to let me explain the proposal to you last Monday, to the effect that a certain gentleman now in Washington write the article, does not seem to us on consideration to be desirable from our editorial point of view, since it would not in any degree carry the interest that would be possessed by an article from President Wilson himself or an authorized interview with him.

In view of the fact that the mechanical requirements of Journal publication make it necessary for us to have editorial material in hand long in advance of its actual use, may I suggest that either the article or interview should be in The Home Journal office by July 1, 1916? Furthermore, it gives us very great pleasure to say that this article or interview might appear in either the October number, published September 20th, or the November number, published October 20th. The choice is left entirely with President Wilson.

It seems to me that the points made in the brief talk we had on Monday are completely covered in this letter, but if there are any here obscure or that have not been touched upon, please let me know.

Anticipating your favorable reply on behalf of President Wilson,[1] and with personal compliments, I remain

Very cordially yours,   Karl Edwin Harriman

TLS (WP, DLC).
[1] Wilson wrote an article, "The Mexican Question," which appeared in *Ladies' Home Journal*, XXXIII (Oct. 1916), 9. It is printed at its composition date, Aug. 1, 1916.

Draft of After-Dinner Remarks to the American Newspaper Publishers' Association[1]

[c. April 27, 1916]

We have witnessed in our day an extraordinary multiplication of journals of all sorts and an extraordinary increase in the amount of printed matter of every kind. Printing has become so cheap that it has become almost a commonplace medium of speech. There was a time when anything we saw in print seemed very serious and deliberate. It had an extraordinary adventitious dignity, and we attached to it a corresponding weight and significance. Journals were comparatively few in number. The utterances of their editors and contributors attracted a great deal of attention, and there was much more time than there is now to give them a deliberate and serious reading. But in our own time there has been an unmistakable falling off in the influence of printed opinion. The power of the editorial is certainly not what it once was.

The telegraph and the telephone, moreover, have drawn the world together into something like a single community. It is just as easy and natural to read the news of yesterday from Rome as the news of yesterday from the neighboring town. And with the news comes the comment—comment from every quarter, not only from our neighbors, but from editors and correspondents all over the world. And, so, what we read begins to have for us only the significance of what we hear. Printed opinions are coming to take their rank with casual spoken opinions, and editorial comment has very little more weight than conversational comment.

A very interesting thing has happened, therefore, involving an entirely new assessment of what we read. We are beginning to judge what we read as we judge what we hear—by the character of the person who utters it. It is becoming a matter of common knowledge who own certain journals, for example, and that the opinions of those journals are the opinions of the owners, and that they may not be at all the individual opinions of the editor who penned them. In other instances, the whole country knows the character and antecedents of the chief editorial writer of a particular paper. If his character is high, his opinions carry great weight. If it is not, they are merely among the negligible comments of the day.

The same thing is going on, therefore, in respect of our attitude towards what we read, that is going on upon so wide a scale and at so tremendous a pace with regard to our attitude towards public affairs. We are engaged in nothing less than a grand reassessment of character and motive. The close contacts of the world are bringing men's individualities clearly into view. The court of public opinion has direct sight of the men whom it is assessing— to whom it is according its praise or its blame, its faith or its condemnation. Back of everything lies a man and a motive, and it is to that that our judgment is penetrating. It goes very far beneath the surface.

All politics, all industry, all literature, must accept the drastic revaluation, and, for my part, I think it very heartening to live in such a time. I believe that the time is full of the beginnings of great things, of great readjustments, great simplifications of responsibility, great clarifications of the bases of judgment, great readjustments of organization. No newspaper, no corporation, no organization of any kind will much longer serve any man as a mask or covert. Opinion calls him forth. He stands for himself. And the final verdict with regard to him will be based upon the answer to this question: Is he serving himself alone, or is he serving the public interest? Has he private and sinister purposes to serve, or does he indeed wish to clarify common counsel and bring the country to better things?[2]

T MS (WP, DLC).

[1] Wilson did not deliver this speech. Newton D. Baker spoke in his stead at the banquet held in the Waldorf-Astoria Hotel in New York on April 27. *New York Times*, April 28, 1916.

[2] There is a WWsh outline of these remarks, entitled, "The Power of the Editorial," in WP, DLC.

Two Letters to Joseph Patrick Tumulty

Dear Tumulty: [The White House, April 27, 1916]

What do you think of this?[1] It seems to me literally impossible for me to have these people come and make speeches to me.

The President. C.L.S.

The Secretary does not see how the President can turn Miss Wald down. W.F.J.[2]

[1] Lillian D. Wald to WW, April 21, 1916.
[2] Warren F. Johnson, Tumulty's secretary.

Dear Tumulty: [The White House, April 27, 1916]

Will you not express to Miss Wald my appreciation of this letter and ask her how much time they would need, and say that I will be glad to give it to them as early as possible.

The President. C.L.S.

TL (WP, DLC).

To Harry Augustus Garfield

My dear Garfield: The White House April 27, 1916

Your letter of April twenty-fourth has reached me and you may be sure I understand just the spirit that prompted it. But I am afraid I cannot take the same view of the matter that you do. I have been through all the intricacies of our controversies regarding neutrality with the several belligerent powers, and it seems to me that the blockade and the submarine matter stand on different grounds.

But the comfort of having a friend like yourself is that I know you will comprehend even when we differ.

In haste

Cordially and sincerely yours, Woodrow Wilson

TLS (H. A. Garfield Papers, DLC).

To Robert Ferdinand Wagner

My dear Senator Wagner: [The White House] April 27, 1916

Allow me to acknowledge the receipt of your letter of April twenty-third. Of course, I am deeply sorry that you cannot accept the appointment as Postmaster at New York, but I appreciate to the full the reasons you give for declining. They are based on considerations of public duty which are beyond challenge, and I sincerely hope that you may have many opportunities of realizing your purposes of service to the party.

Cordially and sincerely yours,   Woodrow Wilson

TLS (Letterpress Books, WP, DLC).

From Robert Lansing, with Enclosure

PERSONAL AND PRIVATE:

My dear Mr. President: Washington April 27, 1916.

I send you a letter which I have received from Mr. Gerard, and in which you may be interested.

Faithfully yours,   Robert Lansing

Thank you very much   W.W.

TLS (SDR, RG 59, 763.72/2663½, DNA).

ENCLOSURE

James Watson Gerard to Robert Lansing

Personal.

My dear Mr. Secretary.   [Berlin] April, 11th. 1916

The recent sessions of the Reichstag have been lively. Liebknecht caused a row on several ocassions. Once by interrupting the the [sic] Chancellor to imply that the Germans were not free, next to deny that the Germans had NOT wished the war, and another time by calling attention to the attempts of the Germans to induce Mohammedan and Irish prisoners of war to desert to the German arms. The Irish being attacked through the notorious Sir Roger Casemate.[1] Liebknecht finally enraged the Government by calling out that the loan subscription was a swindle.

The German-American spies and traitors are hard at work, Gaffney, Emerson,[2] and others, work at 48 Potsdammer Strasse and Emerson also at the Oversea News Service; a convern [concern] paid for by Krupps. Gaffney in addition gains money by getting permits for goods to go out of Germany. Capitalizing his "pull" as it were. Emerson and a man named Martin[3] claim that they are paid by the Republican National Committee to "collect" evidence against the President, and the Embassy. They claim they have private letters of the President, but I am sure and positive that if they have them they amount to nothing. They already have published the letter to Joline re. Bryan and a cocked hat.[4] Some of the money for their dirty work is given them by Roselius Breman, the proprietor of "Caffee Hag."[5] Aubrey Stanhope[6] a dirty traitor, who writes against the President, also works with the gang.

This cry in America that German babies have not sufficient milk is all rot. Enclosed is a report of one of our Doctors on the subject. The cry is only raised to get a hole in the British blockade.

The Germans probably will take Verdun in the end. They are going at it carefully, and an imitation of each French position or trench they wish to take—planned from airmens' and spies' reports—is constructed behind the German lines and the German soldiers practise at taking it until they are judged letter perfect and are put to work to capture the original.

It is said the Germans have developed a submarine periscope so small as to be almost invisible and which works up and down so that only at intervals for a second does it appear above the water. Also it is said the wireless vibrations by means of copper plates at each end are transmitted through the boat, and every member of the crew learns the wireless code, and no matter when working can catch the vibrations.

Sussex and other four ships' note just received—that we treat by cable. I think Germany is now determined to keep peace with America as the plain people are convinced that otherwise the war will be lengthened, a contingency abhorrent to all.

Yours ever   J.W.G.

Enclosures go in letter to President.[7]

TLI (SDR, RG 59, 763.72/2663½, DNA).

[1] Sir Roger David Casement (1864-1916), who had been knighted in 1911 for his investigations and exposures of atrocities by Belgians against natives in the Congo Free State and of even worse atrocities in the rubber-growing regions of Peru. Casement, a romantic Irish nationalist obsessed by the idea of Irish independence, had gone to Germany in 1914 to organize an Irish brigade among Irish prisoners of war. He had hoped to prevent, for the moment, what is known as the Irish Easter Rebellion and had sailed from Germany for Ireland aboard a German submarine loaded with arms on April 12. All of Casement's plans went awry. He was captured soon after landing by local authorities near Tralee, Ireland. He was taken to London on April 23, and his arrest was made public on April 25. See Brian Inglis, Roger Casement (London, 1973), and Benjamin Lawrence Reid, The Lives of Roger Casement (New Haven, Conn., 1976).

[2] Thomas St. John Gaffney, Irish-born United States Consul-General in Dresden (1905-1913) and Munich (1913-1915). Long active in the Irish nationalist cause, he was dismissed from his consular post in 1915 for unneutral activities. He became a close friend of Casement during the latter's sojourn in Germany. Edwin Emerson, Jr., born in Dresden of American parents, was for many years a foreign and war correspondent, author of numerous books, and was at this time associated with the Berlin Continental Times, a German propaganda newspaper published in English and distributed throughout the world.

[3] Unidentified

[4] WW to A. H. Joline, April 29, 1907, Vol. 17.

⁵ Roselius Breman, or Braeman, proprietor of a famous coffee house in Berlin.
⁶ English-born journalist, for many years a foreign correspondent of the *New York Herald*.
⁷ This letter is missing.

Ralph Pulitzer to Joseph Patrick Tumulty, with Enclosure

My dear Mr. Tumulty: New York April 27, 1916.

Mr. Jo Davidson, who already has a card of introduction to you from Ambassador Page, is very anxious to have the pleasure of meeting the President. My admiration for Mr. Davidson and his extraordinarily able work would at any other time lead me with the greatest promptness to give him a letter of introduction directly to the President. In these exceptional days, however, when I know under what a terrible pressure the President is living, I feel that it is wiser to leave to your judgment the question as to whether my letter of introduction should be presented to the President. Personally, I believe that a conversation with Mr. Davidson would afford the President a refreshing, artistic interlude between all his very practical cares. This, however, as I said before, I think can most safely be left to your own discretion. If, as I hope, you think that this interview, unlike most interviews, instead of being a strain on the President's energies would be a relaxation, I would appreciate your bringing to the President's attention my letter to him which I have given Mr. Davidson herewith.

With kind regards,   Faithfully yours,   Ralph Pulitzer

TLS (WP, DLC).

E N C L O S U R E

From Ralph Pulitzer

My dear Mr. President,   New York. April 27th [1916]

Knowing, as I well do, the terrible pressure of labor and responsibility under which [you] are at this time living, I have felt that I should leave it entirely to the discretion of Mr. Tumulty whether or not this letter may wisely at this moment be brought to your attention. If you receive it, it will serve to introduce to you a man who I feel sure will afford you an exceedingly stimulating and refreshing break away from Statesmanship to Sculpture.

Mr. Davidson's work is of such really extraordinary artistic interest and excellence, and he himself is such an interesting personality that my letter of introduction needs no apologies.

I am sure you will enjoy meeting Mr. Davidson. I can only hope most sincerely that having met him, you will be able to see your way clear to granting him the few sittings he would require to make a portrait bust of you. Being a man of vigorous convictions he feels that this would be not only a favor to him but a duty to the country. And I am inclined to agree with him.

With kindest regards

Faithfully yours   Ralph Pulitzer.

ALS (WP, DLC).

From Michael Francis Doyle[1]

Philadelphia, Pennsylvania, April 28, 1916.

Mrs. Agnes Newman, widowed sister of Sir Roger Casement, residing in New York, has retained me as counsel[2] and has earnestly requested me to see you and if possible to enlist your interest on his behalf on the grounds of humanity. Could you kindly make an appointment so I could see you in reference to this matter?   Michael Francis Doyle.

T telegram (WP, DLC).
  [1] Lawyer of Philadelphia.
  [2] Although Casement had not yet been arraigned, it was obvious that he would be tried for high treason.

From Edward Charles Wade, Jr.[1]

Santa Fe, N. M., April 28, 1916.

Six citizens of Mexico have been sentenced by state district court to to [sic] hang, May nineteenth, for participation Villa's raid at Columbus, after trial in border county. These men maintain their innocence of intentional wrong-doing; that they were forced to accompany Villa to Columbus against their will, under threat of death, should they refuse. They are ignorant illiterate, and like children mentally; one is seriously wounded. They were, I am informed, taken prisoners in Mexico by Pershing's expedition and were brought out of Mexico without extradition proceedings and turned over to the state authorities for punishment. They contend they are military prisoners, entitled to the protection of the United States. They have no friends, are in a strange country and have no financial means to assert their innocence in higher court or to urge their contention that they are prisoners of war and should be so treated. In view of the broad international questions involved and probable effect on the minds of people of Mexico which might lead to revengeful reprisals against our citizens in that country and the further fact that these men are strangers in a strange country without friends or means, their cases should be further passed upon before sentence is carried into effect. Many citizens believing that these poor ignorant unhappy creatures should not be hanged, join me in appealing to you, in name of humanity, to urge Governor of New Mexico to grant respite to these men where thorough investigations can be had by federal authorities on law and facts.

Edward C. Wade, jr.

T telegram (WP, DLC).
1 Lawyer of Santa Fe.

Joshua Willis Alexander to Joseph Patrick Tumulty

Dear Mr. Tumulty: Washington, D. C. April 28, 1916.

I am enclosing herewith tentative drafts of the proposed shipping bill,[1] and would suggest that you call same to the attention of the President.   Yours very truly,   J. W. Alexander

TLS (WP, DLC).
1 A new draft (T MS, WP, DLC) of the shipping bill described in WGM to WW, Jan. 10, 1916, n. 1, Vol. 35. The new bill differed from the earlier draft significantly in the following respects: (1) Its announced objective was to encourage and develop an American merchant marine, without any reference to developing a "naval auxiliary and naval reserve." (2) The new version cut out any reference to the coastwise trade and to the chartering of vessels. (3) It also provided for the creation of a corporation with capital stock not specified, which might be offered for public sale.

To Edward Mandell House

The White House April 29, 1916

Your confidential letter with enclosure from Walter [Bernstorff] received   information   requested   already   sent   direct   to   youth [Gerard][1]   Woodrow Wilson

T telegram (E. M. House Papers, CtY).
1 That is, RL to J. W. Gerard, April 26 [28], 1916, printed as an Enclosure with RL to WW, April 26, 1916.

From Samuel Gompers

Sir: Washington, D. C., April 29, 1916.

In a letter from the representative of the American Federation of Labor in Porto Rico I received a copy of a report made to the Chairman of the House of Delegates of Porto Rico by a commission that had been authorized to investigate charges that the government had suspended the constitutional rights of citizens in Arecibo.

This statement of the commission contains an explanation of its failure to make a full, comprehensive report, but the workers of Porto Rico, those whose rights were denied, feel that the real explanation of the failure to make a comprehensive report is political rather than mere lack of time.

The statement made by the commission is of such significance that I wish to bring it to your personal attention. It is an official confirmation of the claims of the workers that they have been denied constitutional rights. A copy of the report is enclosed.[1]

It has fallen to me as my duty on several occasions to call to your attention unwarranted acts of several of the officers of the government of Porto Rico—denial of justice to the workers, denial to them of rights guaranteed by the constitution of the United States, guaranteed to them by every law of honor, justice and decency.

It may not be amiss to say that when on March 6, 1916,[2] I submitted a complaint as to the action of government agents which denied the workers the fundamental rights of free citizens, you stated in your reply of March 20th that you were referring my letter to the Governor of Porto Rico, in whom you had great confidence.[3]

I have long been under the impression, as a result of my own observation, that in so far as the Governor's policy and course affect the interests, the welfare and the rights of the people of Porto Rico, Governor Yager is not deserving of the confidence that you feel toward him.

I am fully appreciative of the great duties and responsibilities that devolve upon you particularly at the present time, but I hope that this matter which I now bring to your attention will also receive your sympathetic and favorable action.

Very respectfully,   Saml. Gompers.

TLS (WP, DLC).

[1] Hermogenes Vargas to House of Delegates of Porto Rico, April 13, 1916, (WP, DLC), stating that there had been insufficient time for the commission to prepare a comprehensive report before the adjournment of the House of Delegates. However, the commission, after examining the evidence, was prepared to say that there was no necessity or justification for the action taken by the police in Arecibo in suspending the rights of the people to hold peaceable public meetings.

[2] It is missing.

[3] WW to S. Gompers, March 20, 1916, TLS (S. Gompers Corr., AFL-CIO-Ar).

From Sir Cecil Arthur Spring Rice

Dear Mr President   Washington April 29 1916

Sir Edward Grey has just heard of the incident which occurred at Trinidad. He directs me to deliver to you at once a personal message expressing his great regret. An inquiry will be at once made. He has heard with astonishment and regret that the Governor of Trinidad[1] did not extend to the Secretary of the Treasury on his recent visit to Trinidad the cordial and courteous reception which it was certainly the desire of the King's Government should be given him. Sir Edward feels it all the more as the Secretary was accompanied on his journey by his wife, the President's daughter. He is most sincerely grieved if anything has occurred to give an impression of discourtesy and I am to request the honour of an audience in order to deliver his message personally.

I should be very grateful for an intimation as to when I could be received.

I have the honour to be with profound respect dear Mr President

your most obedient humble servant   Cecil Spring Rice

ALS (WP, DLC).
[1] Samuel William Knaggs, at this time Acting Governor of Trinidad.

To Joseph Patrick Tumulty

Dear Tumulty: [The White House, c. April 30, 1916]

I must frankly admit I don't know how to answer this letter. I am convinced that very prejudiced reports have been sent Mr. Gompers and that the authorities in Porto Rico have not gone beyond what was justified by the circumstances, so that it is an issue of fact and that is the hardest of all issues to know how to manage courteously. Does anything occur to you?

The President.

TL (WP, DLC).

From Joseph Patrick Tumulty

Dear Governor: [The White House, c. April 30, 1916]

I have had many talks with people from Porto Rico who have given the impression that Governor Yager, in his sympathies, is inclined to favor the sugar interests. I do not mean by this to convey the impression that there is anything dishonest but his point of view, my informants believe, is the view of the upper classes. I would like to talk with you about this matter.[1]

> The Secretary.

TL (WP, DLC).

[1] Wilson finally replied to Gompers' letter in WW to S. Gompers, June 8, 1916.

To the Shakespeare Tercentenary Committee

Washington, April 30, 1916

I join with all lovers of great literature in unqualified admiration of the great genius which spoke the human spirit in fuller measure and more authentic tones than any other man of any race or age.   Woodrow Wilson.

T telegram (SDR, RG 59, 841.415, DNA).

From John Worth Kern

Dear Mr President   Washington. Apr 30 1916

Your letters requesting early consideration of Water Power, and leasing bills have been received. The Steering Committee will meet on Tuesday, and I have no doubt will give these measures a place on the Senate legislative program.

The trouble about the Water Power bill is a lack of interest. The Senators from the Rocky Mountain States are the only ones manifesting any interest in the subject, and they are divided in sentiment—the Colorado Senators being unalterably opposed to the principle of the pending bill

You may be sure that it will be a pleasure to me to do every thing I can to carry out your wishes in the matter

> Very Sincerely   Jno W Kern

ALS (WP, DLC).

Hugh Lenox Scott and Frederick Funston to Robert Lansing

El Paso, Texas Apr. 30, 1916 2 am

We received General Obregon and party on their official call this morning with every courtesy and arranged for conference this afternoon. Mexicans made quite a point of having conference in Juarez which request was acceded to at once. We gave the views of the Department as laid down in instructions and

endeavored to get full cooperation and use of railway. The conference was most amicable throughout but Mexicans contending always for immediate withdrawal of troops from Mexico, saying that Villa is dead or if alive innocuous. Two hundred of his followers killed, remainder dispersed and there is no one now to seek for. Obregon claims that continued presence of American troops in Mexico makes his task most difficult, as no satisfactory explanation can be made to Mexican people. He made no threats. We evidently came to discuss one question, Obregon another. He would not discuss cooperation as he several times put aside politely request for cooperation and use of railway, declining to discuss anything but withdrawal of troops. Conference lasted two hours with dead lock imminent, when conference was amicably broken off saying the Mexican position would be telegraphed our Government. Conference will be resumed on receipt of reply. General Funston and I think our approved proposition should be adhered to, viz. to hold our present position until our Government is satisfied that Villa is killed or captured, under no circumstances to retire north of Casas Grandes, Chihuahua, until this is accomplished. Very few Mexicans are in the Santa Maria and Casas Grandes valleys and should be controllable if desire is sincere. We warned Obregon of collection of bandits near Victoria to invade lower Rio Grande river section of United States, which might bring on a condition in Tamaulipas similar to that now in Chihuahua. Obregon promised to investigate. Nothing has been given out to the press. Request early reply. Copy sent Secretary of War.   Scott
                                                                Funston

T telegram (WP, DLC).

To Hugh Lenox Scott

[Washington] April 30, 1916.

Your cipher telegram signed Scott and Funston received four fifty this morning Period. In reply the following instructions of the Secretary of War are communicated for your guidance Quote We desire to make all possible concessions to General Obregon and to the de facto Government of Mexico comma and concede the probable elimination of Villa comma but urge that it is not yet certain and that the formation of similar bands or further activities by undispersed remnants of his followers is not only possible but probable as our most recent reports continue to show attacks upon our people by bands disposed to Villa Period We recognize the reasonableness of General Obregon's suggestions and appreciate the hospitality of the Government and people of Mexico but General Obregon will recall that our difficulty arose from an actual hostile aggression upon American soil and that while we are willing to comply with his suggestions so far as we can without again exposing our border comma we must safeguard our people especially along that portion of the border where there is little Mexican population and where it is most difficult for the de facto Government of Mexico to afford us protection Period. Suggest willingness comma therefore comma on our part to retire our forces comma in a convenient number of days to permit unhurried removal of supplies et cetera comma to a place nearer the border than our present advanced positions to be agreed upon by you with General Obregon comma from which place should further trouble appear we can act promptly and effectively in cooperation with the forces of the de facto Government or independently if the need be urgent Period. It being understood that complete withdrawal will of course take place so soon as we are assured of the safety of our borders from further aggression Period In selecting the place for retirement you should have in mind questions of supply comma of ease of operation in case of danger to the border and presence of populations of Americans in Mexico upon whom attack would cause fresh exasperation of opinion in the United States Period If General Obregon will agree to the selection of such a place and assure us railroad facilities for supply the presence and activities of our present motor supply system will be removed and one of the most obvious signs of our being there will be removed as a cause of misunderstanding to Mexican people while use of railroads will show the de facto Government understands temporary character of our presence and approves it as furthering the common object of the two Governments Unquote.   McCain.

T telegram (SDR, RG 59, 812.00/18030, DNA).

Remarks at the National Service School for Women[1]

May 1, 1916.

Mrs. Fahnestock,[2] ladies of the camp, ladies and gentlemen: It is with unaffected pleasure that I come to greet you as you have assembled for the interesting things you are going to do. I have always felt that there was very much more inspiration in things that were voluntarily done than in things that were done under official direction and by official summons. You have volunteered to come together without official suggestion in order to study some things which, while they are characteristic of the sort of comfort and assistance which women have been accustomed to offer, are nevertheless, in this instance associated with a very great national conception and duty.

We, of course, are living in the presence of conditions which we cannot yet assess, because they are unprecedented. The world never witnessed such a war as is now convulsing almost every part of the world except this part which we particularly love and would seek to safeguard. And the very foundations of the ordinary life of nations have been disturbed, so deeply disturbed that no man can predict what the final settlement will be. And if this war has done nothing else, it has at least done this: It has made America aware of dangers which most of us had deemed unreal, and has made us aware that the danger of our own time is nothing less than the unsettlement of the foundations of civilization.

Civilization does not rest upon war. It rests upon peace. It rests upon those things which men achieve by cooperation and mutual interest in one another. It does not flourish in the soil of hostility and antagonism, and a world war is a war in the presence of which civilization holds its breath and wonders if it will itself survive. As we see these great issues joined, we on this side of the water are done this great service: We are reminded of our spiritual relation, not only to this great struggle, but, particularly, to this great nation of which we constitute parts, and our spiritual relation to the rest of the world is determined by our spiritual relation to America.

You have come together to be prepared for any unusual duty which America may call upon you to perform, but what has moved you to do this? Your duty to your country. But what is the foundation of that duty? What do you conceive America to be? When you come to the last, searching analysis, we do not owe any duty except to those things that we believe in. And the glory of performing our duty towards America is that we believe in America. And we believe in America because—I venture to say it with entire respect for other peoples and other governments—this government was established with a special purpose such as no other government ever avowed. This government was established in order that justice and liberty might belong to every man whom our institutions could touch, and, not only that justice and liberty should belong to America, but that, so far as America was concerned, and her influence involved, they should be extended to mankind everywhere. So the inspiration of serving America is a very profound inspiration.

Have you not thought what might be the outcome of this great struggle, so far as the nations already engaged are concerned? Can you not imagine the great awakening that has come to a country like France, for example, how much more intensely every Frenchman and every German feels the national compulsion than he ever felt it before? How much more he feels himself, not an individual, but a fraction in a great whole? How much more his blood springs to the challenge of patriotic suggestion? He is not fighting for his own life. He is sacrificing his own life, or willing to sacrifice it, in order that a greater life than his might persist— the life of his nation. So, in America we are getting already the indirect benefit of that suggestion. We are beginning to realize how a nation is a unit, and that any individual of it who does not feel the impulse of the whole does not belong to it and does not belong in it. We have heard a great deal about divided allegiance in this country, but, before we discuss divided allegiance in its political aspect, we ought to let our thoughts run back to what were perhaps our divided allegiances in respect to our relations to each other. America had been brought to such a point of diversification of interest, of occupation, of objects sought, that she was in danger of losing the consciousness of her singleness and solidarity. There were men pulling at cross-purposes in regard to their private interests and their public endeavors in this country long before the war came to remind us that we were a single nation, with a single duty and a single ideal. And the first thing that has happened to us is that we have all been pulled together by a great tug at the heart in respect of our individual interests. We have all been reminded with an emphasis for which I, for one, thank God—that we are first of all Americans, and only after that at liberty to seek our individual interest. And, then, those of our fellow citizens, who may, for a little while, have been tempted to think rather of the lands of their origin than of the land of their present allegiance, have been reminded that there is, politically speaking, only one allegiance conceivable and possible.

You have heard a great deal about the hyphen. I, for one, have never been deceived. The number of persons of really divided allegiance in this country is very small. And if I had been born in some other country, I would, for one, resent the representations which have been made by those who were not the spokesmen of those for whom they pretended to speak in suggesting a divided allegiance. I have never had the slightest doubt of what would happen when America called upon those of her citizens born in other countries to come to the support of the flag. Why, they will come with cheers, they will come with a momentum which will make us realize that America has once more been cried awake out of every sort of distemper and dream and distraction, and that any man who dares tamper with the spirit of America will be cast out of the confidence of a great nation upon the instant.

I believe that a certain spiritual regeneration is going to come out of this thing. We have been thinking too much about our individual selves and too little about the country of which we constitute a part. And one of the services which you ladies are going to render is to show how, upon no summons at all, upon the mere offering of the opportunity, women will come together to render those inestimable services which are necessary if the country should get into any sort of trouble.

God forbid that we should be drawn into war, but if we should be, America would seem once more to shake herself out of a dream to say, "Did any man deem that we were asleep? Did any man deem that we had forgotten the traditions of America? Did any man deem that he could tamper with the honor or integrity of the United States?" And, in the great voice of national enthusiasm which would be raised, all the world would stand once more thrilled to hear the voice of the new world asserting the standards of justice and of liberty.

T MS (WP, DLC).

¹ A preparedness camp for young women, sponsored by the Navy League of the United States. Approximately two hundred women were resident in the camp at Chevy Chase, Maryland, and some four hundred more commuted from Washington and vicinity during each of two two-week training periods during the month of May. They studied first aid and care of the sick, practiced various forms of signal communications, and participated in military drill and calisthenics. In addition, they attended lectures on such subjects as national defense, good citizenship, food conservation, American history, and "Americanization of the Foreign Born." Wilson spoke at the opening exercises of the camp. *New York Times*, April 26, 1916, and *Washington Post*, May 2, 1916.

² Carolyn Andrews (Mrs. Gibson) Fahnestock of Washington.

To Joshua Willis Alexander

My dear Judge: The White House May 1, 1916

Thank you for your great courtesy in leaving me drafts of the proposed shipping bill. I shall look them over most attentively and with the greatest interest.

I hope most sincerely that it will be possible for the committee to report the bill out at a very early date. The necessity for action in this matter grows daily more evident and more pressing, and the labors of the committee have certainly been fruitful in improving the bill in many important particulars.

Cordially and sincerely yours,   Woodrow Wilson

TLS (photostat in RSB Coll., DLC).

To Paul Oscar Husting

My dear Senator: [The White House] May 1, 1916

This is just a line to say how deeply I have admired your courageous, manly, and loyal course of action.[1] I think it will elicit the admiration of the whole country.

Cordially and sincerely yours,   Woodrow Wilson

TLS (Letterpress Books, WP, DLC).
[1] Husting had delivered a speech in the Senate on April 27 calling attention to the thousands of telegrams which had been sent to senators and congressmen on April 26, all demanding that the United States stay out of the European conflict and all appearing to derive from a limited number of form telegrams. Husting charged that these communications were inspired by and either had been or would be paid for by a Chicago organization, the American Embargo Conference. He demanded an investigation of this group and, while stopping short of calling it a pro-German organization, suggested that a flood of telegrams of this nature, at this particular time, could have no other logical purpose than to convince the German government that the American people would not stand behind President Wilson. Husting also pointed out that it was Wilson who had kept the peace during Congress's long adjournment in 1915 and said that he strongly resented the insinuation of the telegrams that it was Wilson who now wanted to plunge the nation into war. *Cong. Record*, 64th Cong., 1st sess., pp. 6888-94.

To William Bauchop Wilson

My dear Mr. Secretary: The White House May 1, 1916

Thank you sincerely for your very full letter concerning the difficulties of handling Chinese immigration at the Port of San Francisco. I warmly appreciate the care you have taken in doing this for me.

Cordially and sincerely yours,   Woodrow Wilson

TLS (received from Mary A. Strohecker).

From James Hamilton Lewis

                                    Washington In bed,
Dear Mr President: Monday [May 1, 1916]

I have fallen ill. The doctors say I must be sent away for some days. I have suffered so very much over the insults and humilia-

tion put upon me in Chicago, as a result of the post office mat-
ter.¹ Pardon this reference. I write this note not to complain, as I
know you will not allow me to be destroyed in usefulness. I know
you will remedy this unintentional injustice. I write to assure you
that I will get a *union* of all leaders on a new man. Sir, *if you have
any need for me send for me. I'll come at once, sick or well, to
serve you.* Mr Tumulty has my address.

Your faithful servant   Jas. Hamilton Lewis.

ALS (WP, DLC).
¹ Wilson, on April 24, had nominated Dixon C. Williams, a Chicago indus-
trialist, to be Postmaster of Chicago.

From Robert Lansing, with Enclosure

My dear Mr. President: Washington May 1, 1916.

I have received a reply from the German Ambassador to my
letter of the 24th ultimo, in the von Igel case, and I enclose a copy
for your information. I am studying it with a view to preparing an
answer in the next few days.

Faithfully yours,   Robert Lansing

TLS (WP, DLC).

E N C L O S U R E

Count Johann Heinrich von Bernstorff
to Robert Lansing

My dear Mr. Secretary,   Washington, D. C., April 27, 1916.

I hereby acknowledge the receipt of your letter of 24th instant.
I appreciate most fully the good will towards my Government
which animated you in writing that letter. In the absence of any
instructions from my Government in regard to the von Igel situation my individual views as to the respective rights and obligations presented by and arising from what has occurred differ very
radically from those suggestions in your letter. Primarily we are
not agreed on the facts.

First as to Mr. von Igel's status. He had been prior to his arrest
notified to your department as attached to this Embassy and
entrusted with the continuance of the office of the former Military
Attaché at New York and you thereafter placed his name upon
the list of the officials of this Embassy. Prior to such notification
he was Secretary to the Military Attaché having come to this
country on August 27th, 1914, for such purpose. The crime is

charged as committed on August 1st, 1914. He was then in Germany. It seems clear that under universally accepted rules of international law he was on April 18, 1916, immune from criminal prosecution or arrest at the hands by your Government for any offence committed by him while he was in Germany or after his arrival here.

As to the papers, my information is that they were physically taken from the possession of Mr. von Igel at the time of his arrest and that the seizure was attempted to be justified because of that fact by the local officials. The situation is therefore not that which might have arisen had the papers been taken from premises in the absence of a duly accepted official of the Embassy's staff. Moreover, the lease was in the name of Mr. von Igel whose official status I have already referred to. In addition the papers had been on the day of the arrest in a safe in the office which safe bore the seal of the Embassy. The papers had been temporarily taken from the safe by Mr. von Igel.

It seems clear to me that the seizure of the papers cannot be sustained as legal and that they should be returned together with all copies and notes taken therefrom.

In the absence of instructions from my Government I cannot accede to your suggestion that I should inspect the documents and make a declaration upon such inspection as to what I regard as official and what, if any, I do not so regard.

I am in accord with your view that if any crime has been committed by an official under the protection of the Embassy he should be punished. I must respectfully add, however, that such punishment should be meated out by his own Government upon presentation to that Government of the facts.

As I have not yet received instructions in this matter from my Government and as your department has not finally acted in the matter, I would respectfully request that pending or until a final conclusion has been reached the local officials should be asked not to proceed with the prosecution.

I am, my dear Mr. Lansing,

Very sincerely yours,   J. Bernstorff.

TCL (WP, DLC).

From William Howard Taft

My dear Mr. President: New Haven, Conn May 1st, 1916.

I have your kind note of April 25th, and I am very glad if anything I have said in the present crisis with Germany meets your approval. I am earnestly praying that Germany will not be so foolish as to array this country among her enemies. Your reasonable demand and warning I sincerely hope will bring her to her senses.

Sincerely yours,   Wm H Taft

TLS (WP, DLC).

Hugh Lenox Scott and Frederick Funston to Robert Lansing

El Paso, Texas. May 1, 1916.

Your telegram of Seven fifty and eleven fifty nine p.m. April 30th received and carefully considered.

Practically every subject in telegram seven fifty p.m. was considered at last conference except conceding Villa's elimination which was strongly denied as at variance with the facts. Other subjects were politely rejected. We feel that an ultimatum to retire immediately from Mexican soil was only avoided by diplomatic adjournment. Your telegram eleven fifty nine p.m. instructs that if deadlock seems imminent another adjournment should be attempted for further instructions from department. We feel certain that deadlock will result. General Funston last night suggested to General Pershing a closer concentration warning him and every border commander of tenseness of situation and directing precautions.

Every source of information leads us to believe that Mexican generals are certain of our entire lack of preparedness, feeling that they can cope successfully with the United States and propose to attempt it unless we retire at once. General Calles and Gutierrez have left hurriedly for their stations probably to prepare for an overt act if we do not withdraw.

We expect accurate information of their instructions from inside source about 11 o'clock May 1st. An American correspondent reported to us that he showed to Obregon afternoon April 30th press forecast from Washington, D. C. of our instructions. Obregon turned at once to Trevino and said in substance that one mile or five hundred across the border was the same thing so far as it affected the sovereignty of Mexico. We feel that last conference covered so much of latest instructions which have been rejected that in present temper of Mexicans no good will result from proposing them again and we expect a flat ultimatum to get out of Mexico at once or take the consequences. If acceded to this will be a complete victory for Mexicans over the United States in

the eyes of the Mexican people already arrogant and encourage further aggressions. Therefore in order to comply with directions in telegram of 11:59 P.M. no conference will be called until department sends further instructions. We feel that the border should be greatly strengthened at once to allow concentration of regular troops to most expected eventualities in Mexico, repel invasion at many border points and cause Mexicans to feel that the United States is able and willing to repel attacks and we believe that if attacks can be prevented at all this prevention will be best accomplished by show of strength. It is common belief that Carranza and Obregon have had a break. Carranza's name was not mentioned *once* at the conference by any Mexican which indicates that Carranza will have no influence on Obregon's course of action.   Scott.
                                                                 Funston.

T telegram (SDR, RG 59, 812.00/18033, DNA).

To Joseph Patrick Tumulty

Dear Tumulty: [The White House, May 2, 1916]
    We have no choice in a matter of this sort. It is absolutely necessary to say that I could take no action of any kind regarding it.[1]   The President.

TL (WP, DLC).
    [1] See M. F. Doyle to WW, April 28, 1916.

To Sir Cecil Arthur Spring Rice

My dear Mr. Ambassador: [The White House] May 2, 1916
    I am really sorry that Sir Edward Grey should be distressed about the incident at Trinidad which, after all, was negligible, but you may be sure that I shall be very glad to make it an occasion for seeing you, and would be pleased if you would call at two o'clock on the afternoon of Thursday, the fourth.
    With sincere regard,
                              Cordially yours,   Woodrow Wilson

TLS (Letterpress Books, WP, DLC).

To John Wesley Wescott

My dear Judge: [The White House] May 2, 1916
    I am a little embarrassed to express such a preference before the event, but on the assumption that I am to be nominated again

for the Presidency, I want you to know how earnestly desirous I am that you should again nominate me in the convention. It does my heart good to think how loyal and generous a friend you have been and I should consider it a great honor if you would renew the endorsement you gave me in your first nominating speech. When I get the opportunity, I shall, of course, express this preference to others.

Affectionately yours,   [Woodrow Wilson]

CCL (WP, DLC).

To Henry Jones Ford

My dear Ford: [The White House] May 2, 1916

I had no idea you had written a book about me.[1] I am deeply complimented that you should have undertaken it and shall read it with the greatest interest, because I am sure you know how sincerely I value your critical opinions upon public affairs, and I feel sure, without having read either the article in the Atlantic[2] yet or the book, that you have spoken as a judicial critic, as well as a generous friend.[3] Thank you with all my heart.

Cordially and faithfully yours,   Woodrow Wilson

TLS (Letterpress Books, WP, DLC).
[1] Henry Jones Ford, *Woodrow Wilson, the Man and His Work: A Biographical Study* (New York, 1916).
[2] Henry Jones Ford, "The Record of the Administration," *Atlantic Monthly,* CXVII (May 1916), 577-90.
[3] Both were highly complimentary.

From Robert Lansing, with Enclosure

PERSONAL AND PRIVATE:

My dear Mr. President: Washington May 2, 1916.

I enclose a letter which I have received from Mr. Arredondo embodying the contents of a telegram from Mr. Carranza which he read to me yesterday afternoon. You will notice that the communication is entirely unofficial as Mr. Arredondo was not instructed to deliver it to me.

I thought you might wish to see this letter before Cabinet meeting today.   Faithfully yours,   Robert Lansing.

E N C L O S U R E

Eliseo Arredondo to Robert Lansing

Personal and confidential.

My dear Mr. Lansing: Washington, D. C. May 1st, 1916.

Complying with Your Excellency's desire that I furnish you a copy of the telegram I received from Mr. Carranza, which I read to you confidentially, directing me to insist on the urgency that American troops be withdrawn from Mexican territory, I beg leave to give you herein the substance of the aforesaid message.

Mr. Carranza informs me that it would seem inconceivable that the Government of the United States should insist on maintaining its troops in our soil, there being no reason or even a pretext under which they should remain there now that the band headed by Villa has been completely routed and Villa himself appears to be dead, because nothing has been heard of him since the last encounter, which occurred over a month ago; that the argument adduced by Your Excellency, that American public opinion should be borne in mind in withdrawing the troops from Mexico, cannot be taken into consideration, because public opinion ought not to prevail over the integrity and honesty of a government in whose hands the people have confided their power and that the best proof President Wilson can give of the confidence reposed in him should be his honest adherence to duty against the opinion of his enemies, as it can hardly be a fact that the whole nation would disapprove his acting in accordance with justice [in] ordering the withdrawal of American troops from our country, unless the United States has decided to wage an unjustifiable war against us, the only purpose of which would be to favor private interests of American citizens residing in Mexico or who have interests in that country; that the conferences between Generals Obregon and Scott can have no other result than the one which the American Government may wish them to have, as General Obregon can prove to General Scott that the presence of American troops in Mexico is in every way unjustifiable and that it is a matter of urgent necessity that they should be withdrawn immediately.

As I said to your Excellency during our short interview, I brought this message to your attention as a sincere expression of the serious situation which is developing in my country on account of the presence there of American troops.

With the assurance of my highest consideration, I have the honor to be,

Your Excellency's most obedient servant,

E. Arredondo

TLS (WP, DLC).

From Newton Diehl Baker

Dear Mr. President: Washington. May 3, 1916.

I beg to inclose a copy of a letter and its inclosure which I am sending to Mr. Jones with reference to the pending Philippine bill.[1]

The differences between the administrative features of the bill as it passed the Senate and as it passed the House are by no means so great as is usual in the case of such important measures. It would, therefore, seem that the adjustment of these differences in conference should create no difficulty. In fact, the House Committee showed in reporting the Senate bill without amendment that it did not regard the acceptance of the administrative provisions of the Senate bill to be seriously objectionable.

You will observe that I do not make any suggestion looking to the adjustment of the differences between the House preamble and Senate Section 34 (the Clarke amendment). I refrain from doing this for obvious reasons. I do not, however, believe that there will be great difficulty in compromising even this difference, for it must be remembered that the Senate Committee reported to the Senate a bill with a preamble not differing in its intent so much from the apparent intent of the present House preamble.

In laying before you what I have tried to do I also desire to urge that you do all that is possible to bring about a prompt agreement and the early passage of a bill. This is earnestly desired by our officials in the Philippine Islands. In fact, Governor-General Harrison has shown a disposition to accept with good grace any bill so long as it contained the progressive steps embodied in both of these slightly conflicting measures.

Senator Hitchcock is absent from the city and I am informed will be back Friday. I hope that it may be possible for you to see Senator Hitchcock and Mr. Jones to impress on them our deep interest in the early passage of the Philippine bill.

I have written to Senator Hitchcock to the same effect as to Mr. Jones.   Faithfully yours,   Newton D. Baker

TLS (WP, DLC).

¹ The copy of the letter is missing. The enclosure was a T memorandum (WP, DLC), dated May 2, 1916, which had been prepared by the Bureau of Insular Affairs, probably by General McIntyre. It reviewed the history of the Jones bill since its introduction in the House of Representatives on July 11, 1914, compared the House and Senate versions just approved by the two houses, and made certain recommendations concerning their differences.

From Newton Diehl Baker, with Enclosure

My dear Mr. President: Washington. May 3, 1916.

I have had made for you a fair copy of the first full report made by General Pershing. It brings his explanation up to April 14th, and seems to me a very interesting and keen comment on the general attitude of the Mexicans, official and otherwise, towards his expedition. The paper is sent only for your information.

Sincerely yours,   Newton D. Baker

TLS (WP, DLC).

E N C L O S U R E

HEADQUARTERS PUNITIVE EXPEDITION, U. S. ARMY,
In the field, Mexico, April 14, 1916.

From: The Commanding General, Punitive Expedition, U. S. Army.
To: The Commanding General, Southern Department, Fort Sam Houston, Texas.
Subject: Report on General Situation.

ATTITUDE OF THE DIFFERENT FACTIONS.

1. The attitude of those Carranza factions with whom we have come in contact, so far, has been, generally speaking, one of friendliness, coupled with an apparent desire to be considered as cooperating with us toward the attainment of the same end. On the contrary, while there have been no positive acts deserving of serious criticism, there have been incidents and rumors that might be suggestive of their possible ultimate attitude. Considering the numbers of Carranza troops moving about in this part of the country under various leaders there has been a notable lack of actual accomplishment on their part.

2. The rumor recently circulated and previously reported on, that General Herrera had become disaffected and that he was moving westward from the Mexican Central Railroad in command of 2,000 men with hostile intent toward our line of com-

munications, has proved to be unfounded, both as to numbers and as to purpose.

He visited my camp at San Geronimo on the 7th instant and, while rather formal and reticent, he was not at all haughty or aloof. It soon developed that he was an uneducated man, unable to read or understand a map. He was unfamiliar with the country and did not know the location of his own troops, neither did he possess any information regarding the movements of Villista bands. The short visit was confined to a general conversation and a brief exchange of courtesies concerning cooperation.

Two days later at Guerrero, General Herrera openly objected to a movement south of a column under Colonel Dodd, claiming that the appearance there of our troops would interfere with his plans. Major Ryan[1] was sent from San Antonio to Guerrero to explain our operations. After a short conversation it developed that General Herrera had no definite plans of his own. A diplomatic representation of my message by Major Ryan resulted in the endorsement by General Herrera of my plans and the withdrawal of his objections. General Herrera undoubtedly made boasts before leaving Chihuahua as to what he was going to do against Americans, but he has not yet shown actual hostility. On the other hand, current gossip in some of the villages through which we have recently passed suggests the probability that either he or his officers have been spreading word through the country that he would stop the American advance at three hundred miles from the border. That there is in this some idle talk is almost certain, but it leaves one in doubt as to just what stand he and his followers will take eventually.

3. General Gutierrez is in command of all the troops in the State of Chihuahua and is also in charge of operations against the Villistas. When Captain Foulouis visited Chihuahua by aeroplane on the 7th instant he was very politely received at the quartel general. General Gutierrez sent me a cordial message regarding his desire to cooperate with us. He offered me the free use of the telegraph line for official purposes, and discussed the possibilities of our use of the railroad to ship supplies evincing no objection to such use. He sent word to me that he would be in Pedernales the following Monday and would pay me a visit at San Antonio. Consul Letcher informed me on the 11th instant, by telephone at Santa Ysabel, that General Gutierrez's visit had been indefinitely postponed. In the meantime I found it advisable to move south, and must of necessity defer meeting him for the

---

[1] James Augustine Ryan, 13th Cavalry.

present. All his acts hitherto have seemed to indicate a friendly attitude.

4. General Acosta,[2] a former Villista officer, is said to be in the hills back of Guerrero having renounced Villa and declared himself neutral. He says he does not want to fight with the Americans, but that he will not ally himself with the de facto government. He did not participate in the Columbus raid nor the fight at Guerrero.

General Cavazos[3] recently declared at Cusi that he did not intend to allow the American forces to enter his territory. He even went so far as to object to Colonel Brown's[1] column passing through Cusi, and also to Major Tompkins' column passing through San Borja, although they were in hot pursuit of Villa. Through the diplomatic action of both of these officers an amicable understanding was reached in each case and after considerable delay they continued on their journey. Notwithstanding the objections of General Cavazos on these occasions, he is known to favor American intervention as the only hope for Mexico.

5. A brief report was made a few days ago regarding the mutiny of several members of the Carranza garrison stationed at Matachic. It appears that these men heard that other commands had turned against the Americans, so they concluded that it was time for them to place themselves on record with the others. After they learned that the commands referred to had made no such declaration, it was reported that they came back and joined their proper command. There now seems to be some doubt about this. On the 9th instant, Captain Kendrick, 7th Cavalry,[5] who had been sent to Matachic, with two troops of the 7th Cavalry, to investigate the situation, heard firing near the town early in the morning and soon learned that it was an attack by these mutineers against their former comrades. Prompt action by Captain Kendrick drove them off, and incidentally doubtless saved the lives of two Americans residing there.

The reported Carranza movement from Sonora against our communications would be rather disturbing if it should eventually prove to be true. The Mexican military men surely realize that our line is already very long and they probably know that our forces are relatively small. From this they conclude that a well organized command of moderate size could seriously interfere with us. If the Mexicans on their own part have not already grasped this fact, the numerous suggestions of our newspapers at

[2] Julio Acosta, a veteran revolutionary.
[3] José Cavazos.
[4] William Carey Brown, 10th Cavalry.
[5] William J. Kendrick.

home have undoubtedly presented to their minds the possibilities of the situation. Only one rumor has reached here from Mexican sources that there was a suspicious movement of troops toward the eastern boundary of Sonora. Information just received from Douglas, dated 9th instant, indicates suspicious movements of troops south.

6. The other day while Colonel Allen's[6] squadron was marching through a small town in the vicinity of Bachineva, his pack train was fired upon. Colonel Allen sent back a troop of cavalry to investigate the firing, and arrested two of the leading men of the town, one of whom, it appears certain, participated in the incident. That section is a hot bed of Villistas, one of his leaders, General Rios,[7] being a resident of Bachineva. Unless we can obtain proof against these two men, they must, of course, be released.

Another incident of this sort was an attack on the Aero Squadron trucks on the night of the 12th instant about fifteen miles north of here by a small band of so-called Villistas. The officer in charge of the trucks stopped his column and very promptly returned the fire killing one man and wounding others. In the excitement a recruit auto driver disabled his automobile by jamming it into the rear end of a truck. As it was impossible, late at night, to ascertain the extent of injury to the car, it was left behind under previous instructions issued to cover such cases, and the next morning was found destroyed. The people living in the small village in the vicinity cleared themselves of participation in the attack, and declared that it was the work of Villista bandits. Hostile acts of this sort are naturally to be expected of Villistas.

ATTITUDE AND CONDITION OF THE PEOPLE.

7. The official class of Mexicans seem to lay considerable stress upon the importance of their government's action regarding our use of their railroads. They claim to see in such concession the first step to actual intervention. One can readily appreciate their views when it is realized that the Mexican official of today was yesterday perhaps a peon, and that American occupation would end his opportunity to live without work.

The common people have few opinions and rarely express themselves on any subject. They meet us with every evidence of approval and occasionally one is brave enough to hope that we are here to stay. Those of the agricultural class are generally

[6] Henry Tureman Allen, 11th Cavalry.
[7] Either Ernesto or Juan José Rios.

cowed beyond the point of openly having opinions. Feeling that we are here temporarily they have not as yet given us their full confidence, fearing the penalty after we leave. If assured that we were more or less permanent there would be little difficulty in enlisting their aid and assistance.

The people have been ground to death between the upper and nether mill stone. A state of anarchy exists that has not yet been actually depicted. The Villista brigand of last month is the carrancista soldier of to-day, who robs and steals just as he has done for years under one flag or another. The peaceful countryman is shamefully treated by both sides, and he can see no difference between them. Each faction, under its local brigand, and there are many such, represents quite as much as any other to the average pacifico, who fully realizes that none could ever establish or maintain a stable government unaided even though they wished to do so.

Stripped of all visible wealth, this country is in desolation; its people are in rags and poverty; they have few cattle and no horses to cultivate the land; the despondent pacifico has no incentive even to attempt it. After years of revolution upon revolution he has learned the lesson that it is wisest to accept a situation he cannot alter and he sits and [w]aits in hopeless despair.

8. When our troops enter a new district, some people regard us much as they do the revolutionists, but when they find we pay our way, they bring out their eggs and chickens, their burros loaded with wood hastily collected, some corn, a few beans and what little else they have cached away to sell. One man in the mountains near Bachineva came out to meet the troops and said he thanked God the Americans had at last arrived, and refused to take pay for his produce. Others meet us and say we have come too late, that there is now nothing left to save.

PURSUIT OF VILLA BANDITS.

9. It is very probable that the real object of our mission to Mexico can only be attained after an arduous campaign of considerable length. It is possible that the truth of this statement may not be fully appreciated. But it should be realized that the country through which our cavalry is now operating is unfamiliar to every member of the command; very few white men of any class know it in the interior; it is sparsely settled by ignorant people usually unreliable, and almost wholly terrorized by roving bands of robbers and bandits; much of the country is barren and mountainous and, except for the grazing on the plains and the few small farms in the valleys, it is generally unproductive.

Under such conditions, our various forces have had to rely for their guidance upon the inaccurate knowledge of untried American employees, or else upon the uncertain information of frightened or unwilling natives. Thus have well laid plans often miscarried and the goal has moved further and further into the future. While this is all true as to ourselves, almost the exact contrary is true as to Villa and his men. Villa is entirely familiar with every foot of Chihuahua, and the Mexican people, through friendship or fear, have always kept him advised of our every movement. He carries little food, lives off the country, rides his mounts hard and replaces them with fresh stock taken wherever found. Thus he has had the advantage since the end of the first twenty-four hours after the Columbus raid occurred.

As to the Carranza troops even the little reliance we have placed upon their cooperation has failed us. They did not offer serious opposition to Villa's progress south in the Santa Maria Valley, and, although making every pretense at aiding us, they have offered no *active* resistance to his farther advance southward. They [Their] half-hearted and unorganized efforts to overtake Villa themselves have been futile. They have not only neglected or have been unable to give us timely information which might have led to his capture and destruction, but by captious objections and protests have delayed our advance when haste was imperative.

10. If unmolested, there is little doubt that this command will succeed in its mission. There will be need, of course, of plenty of men, horses and supplies. But it is scarcely possible that any one with even an inconsiderable number of followers would be able long to evade continuous, perisistent, systematic pursuit provided the assistance of the natives themselves could be obtained. At present the native feels that our stay in his country may be brief, and he is therefore loathe to commit himself to our cause and take the chance of the certain punishment that would be his after our departure.

Success then will depend (a) Upon our continuing occupation of as many distinct localities as possible in the territory to be covered; (b) the establishment of intimate relations with a sufficient number of reliable inhabitants in each locality to insure their assistance in obtaining trustworthy information; (c) a very full and accurate knowledge of the country through which we may operate, to be obtained by careful study and reconnaissance; (d) the maintenance of ample and regular lines of supply, especially through the large extent of unproductive or mountainous territory; and a sufficient number of men and animals to occupy localities and keep fresh columns constantly at work. As long as Villa remains at the head of an organized band and moves about there is a possibility of overtaking him or of cutting him off, but when his forces divide into smaller detachments that scatter to different localities to become part and parcel of the people then the problem becomes more difficult. The execution of the general plan has already been begun and will be pushed to completion as fast as possible, consistent with vigorous pursuit of organized bands of considerable size.

CONDITION OF FORCES OF DE FACTO GOVERNMENT.

11. In previous correspondence both by letter and wire, brief reference has been made to the general state of the military forces of the de facto government. From what I have personally seen and from the reports that come from other officers, these forces must be considered as very inferior in every respect. The soldiers are mainly young, ignorant, immature boys without any military training. They are led by almost equally ignorant and untrained officers, mostly of the peon class. They are all poorly fed, half clad and poorly armed, and live almost entirely upon the people. The officers are a conceited lot and assume a superior attitude because they have driven the land owners and the educated classes from the country, have destroyed the prestige of the Catholic church and have overthrown the Mexican Government. This so-called army lacks not only organization of the smaller units, but the officers no doubt lack the ability to organize large commands. As to modern tactics they are entirely ignorant.

ATTACK ON OUR FORCES AT PARRAL.

12. The unprovoked outrageous attack by Mexicans upon our soldiers sent into Parral to purchase supplies is indicative of the feeling against us among certain classes. It is an act for which immediate reparation should be insisted upon, by force if necessary. As reported today by telegraph, General Gutierrez has suggested the withdrawal of our troops from Parral, basing his action on the assumption that the cause of the attack was that the command had occupied the plaza. While I have not yet received the details of the incident, I am very sure that the plaza of Parral has not been occupied. The men simply entered the town to purchase supplies and were attacked. I can but feel that it was an unwarranted and premeditated attack, as people have had ample time to receive notice of the protocol regulating our entry into Mexico. It is possible that the de facto government has been unable to prevent the demonstration but that does not lessen its responsibility. It is very clear that the necessary steps were not

taken and it may develop that the attack was made by the Government's forces.

All our detachments in that section, consisting of Major Howze's[8] column of 175 men, Major Tompkins' column 90 men and Colonel Allen's column of 90 men have been ordered to unite at Parral unless the affair has been satisfactorily adjusted. The command has been directed to remain in the vicinity of Parral, at least temporarily, and to take necessary measures for protection. Two pack trains with supplies and ammunition will be ordered from San Antonio to Parral at once. I have endeavored to arrange for the transportation of commissary supplies and forage by rail from Chihuahua both to Parral and San Antonio, but have little hope that such an arrangement can be depended upon. For the present our troops should not be moved one inch backward if it can be avoided, because such a move is certain to be construed as a retreat and would possibly bring upon us the combined attack of all factions. Copies of the letter sent to Consul Letcher by General Gutierrez and forwarded to me together with my letter addressed direct to General Guiterrez are enclosed herewith.[9] No reply has been received to my letter

RECOMMENDATIONS.

13 (a) Regardless of whether the Parral incident be satisfactorily settled, it has now become important that the strength of this command be increased. It is recommended that all regiments connected with this Expedition be raised to the maximum limit authorized by law, and that one additional regiment of infantry and another of cavalry be ordered here.

(b) Should it be at all indicated that the Parral incident is likely to lead to complications, then the immediate capture of Chihuahua and the seizure of both railroads leading thereto is recommended as a preliminary military move that would secure a tenable line of communication and otherwise give a very great advantage in the conduct of further operations. A rapid concentration of a sufficiently large force of this command could be made at some point on the Northwestern Railroad and still leave ample protection to the line of communications from Columbus.   John J. Pershing

TC memorandum (WP, DLC).

[8] Robert Lee Howze, 11th Cavalry.

[9] The letter from L. Gutiérrez to M. Letcher is missing. The second letter is J. J. Pershing to L. Gutiérrez, April 14, 1916, TCL (WP, DLC). Pershing said that the American troops involved in the Parral incident had done nothing to incite the Mexicans and concluded that there had been "an unprovoked attack upon American troops by irresponsible Mexicans at Parral." He demanded that "the necessary steps be taken to apprehend and punish the offenders, to the end that there may not be a recurrence of such a deplorable incident."

Hugh Lenox Scott and Frederick Funston
to Newton Diehl Baker

El Paso, Texas. Received at the War Department, May 3, 1916.

Number 6. May 2d. It has been impossible so far to accomplish satisfactorily diplomatic results meeting in a formal way before a hostile audience which General Obregon must satisfy and carry with him period. So long as this condition existed such results have been despaired of. From time to time however mutual friends have gone to General Obregon privately, entirely unknown to each other and apparently independent of us, who have assured General Obregon of the complete sincerety of the President in his friendship for Mexico upon which he might implicitly rely. They have pointed out coming entirely from themselves the deplorable consequences of an attack upon our troops which could only result in destruction of his Government and loss of his country, of our intense personal desire to carry this through in a manner which will insure the welfare and dignity of both countries. This propaganda has now borne fruit in so far that a mutual friend A. J. McQuatters[1] President Alvarado Mining Company, Parral, former employee of General H. L. Scott's son[2] at Parral notified me last night that General Obregon had requested him to find out if he could meet General Scott privately and secretly in McQuatters room in hotel to discuss situation alone. This has been answered affirmatively with General Funston's cordial approval and we are waiting now for notification of the time for meeting. General Scott met General Obregon at the Paso del Norte hotel about 12 M May second with a J. H. McQuatters,[3] one interpreter, and one stenographer, only persons present during conference. An agreement was reached this morning after a continuous struggle of twelve hours duration which was not equaled by any similar struggle with the wildest and most exasperated Indian heretofore encountered. Conference was unusually amicable throughout. Papers were drawn up in English and Spanish, agreed and disagreed to, changed again and again, hours being expended in apparent interminable argument on every subject, the main object being to have a time limit placed upon our stay in Mexico. This was amicably thwarted with great difficulty. McQuatters drew the papers in order to permit General Scott to keep General Obregon from going away and falling under hostile influence waiting in hallway. The agreement is not altogether satisfactory but if circumstances are considered it will be recognized that it has not been easy to avert a war with Mexico which all believed was imminent. The agreement is submitted for approval. The President has it still in his hands for final determination and may yet reject if unsatisfactory. It is however the best that General Scott has been able to accomplish and is thought to be within the scope of instructions inasmuch as President has announced that he does not desire American troops to stay in Mexico indefinitely and he has their rate of progress toward the border in his own hands. General Obregon has promised in case of approval of agreement by both Governments to withdraw his Sonora troops which threaten General Pershing's line of communications west and away from Pulpito pass and to granting use of the Casas Grandes railroad for transportation of food forage and many other uses but excepting munitions of war. Obregon requests our stay here until both Governments are heard from to adjust differences if thought necessary will be done subject to the approval of the department.

El Paso Texas, May 2, 1916. Memorandum of conference between General Alvaro Obregon, Secretary of War of the Republic of Mexico, Major General Hugh L. Scott, United States Army, and Major General Frederick Funston, United States Army, to which they all subscribe, and transmit to their respective Governments with their recommendations for approval. In view of the fact that the American punitive expeditionary force destroyed or dispersed many of the lawless elements and bandits who committed the recent outrage upon American territorial officials at and near Columbus, N. M., or have driven them far into the interior of the Republic of Mexico. And in view of the further fact that the Constitutionalist Government declares to the United States Government that they are carrying on a vigorous pursuit of such small numbers of bandits or lawless elements as may have escaped. And in view further of the full assurance of the Constitutional Government that their forces are, at the present time, being augmented and strengthened to such an extent that they will be able to prevent any disorders occurring in Mexico that would in any way endanger American territorial officials. And in view of the further assurances of the Constitutional Government that they will continue to diligently pursue capture or destroy any lawless bands or bandits that may still exist or hereafter exist in the Northern part of Mexico. The Government of the United States has decided to gradually withdraw the forces of the punitive expedition from Mexico, commencing the withdrawal immediately. In fact, the American Government has already withdrawn small bodies of troops for a distance of approximately one hundred miles from most southerly point penetrated by them, in order to more conveniently supply the ex-

peditionary forces with food and forage which are almost wholly lacking in that particular part of Mexico. The Constitutional Government of Mexico will make proper distribution of such of its forces as may be necessary to prevent the possibility of invasion of American territory from Mexico. The decision of the American Government to continue the gradual withdrawal of the troops of the punitive expedition from Mexico was inspired by the belief that the Mexican Government is now in a position and will omit no effort to prevent the recurrences of invasion of American territory and the completion of the withdrawal of American troops will only be prevented by occurrences arising in Mexico tending to prove that such belief was wrongly founded. The conferees representing both Governments express satisfaction at the friendly settlement of the questions discussed at the conference, and believe that this will solidify the good relations existing between their respective countries.   Scott
                                                          Funston

T telegram (WP, DLC).
   1 Arthur J. McQuatters, also president of the Mine Owners' Association, a group representing foreign mine operators in Mexico. See the reports of the conference in the *New York Herald*, May 3 and 4, 1916.
   2 Lewis Merrill Scott, a mining engineer who had worked in Parral.
   3 An error in decoding. They meant Arthur J. McQuatters.

From Robert Lansing, with Enclosure

MOST CONFIDENTIAL:

My dear Mr. President: Washington May 3, 1916.
    Enclosed is a most confidential message just received from Gerard. I am a little puzzled as to the real purpose of introducing the subject at the present time. It would look to me like an attempted diversion on Germany's part in order to create here a sympathetic feeling which would prevent radical action on our part. Of course I may be in error as to the motive of the German official who undoubtedly inspired this telegram but I confess to be very skeptical as to the bona fides of the suggestion.
                          Faithfully yours,   Robert Lansing.

TLS (WP, DLC).

E N C L O S U R E

                          Berlin (via Copenhagen) May 2, 1916
    3834. Have best reason to believe Germany will welcome mediation of presentments (President ?) and any steps he may

take looking to peace. Colonel House will be very welcome here.

Gerard, Berlin

CC telegram (WP, DLC).

James Watson Gerard to Edward Mandell House

My dear Colonel: [Berlin] May 3rd. 1916

I got back from three days at the Great Headquarters, last night and am so busy today & so tired that I cannot write a long account.

The Germans, if the note makes the concessions demanded, will be greatly disappointed if the President does not strictly enforce international law against England.

Of course a big party in Germany still wants war with the U. S.

The Chancellor also says that Germany is strong enough & has won enough in war to be able to talk about peace and the hope is that the President will force a peace which Germany is willing to make reasonable. . . .

I am very careful to impress on everybody that in return for any concessions from Germany there could be no agreement by the U. S. to enforce the law against England.

The Chancellor said he hoped the President would be great enough, if our dispute was settled, to make peace, that Germany could make peace as she had won so much etc. . . .

Yours ever   JWG

The Chancellor said he hoped you would come over under the President's direction & *make peace*

ALS (WP, DLC).

A Draft of the Pan-American Pact

Brazilian (Chilean) draft as amended by the President[1] and Secretary of State. To be submitted unofficially to Brazilian Embassy
May 3, 1916

TRANSLATION.

ARTICLE I.

The High Contracting Parties will guarantee to one another their present *undisputed* territorial possessions in America and political independence under republican forms of government.

ARTICLE II.

The High Contracting Parties undertake to settle by arbitration or other amicable process the territorial questions that may arise in the future between two or more of them and declare, in this instrument, their purpose to settle those that are now pending or those that may flow from these, by friendly means and without resort to violence.

ARTICLE III.

The High Contracting Parties undertake not to permit the organization and departure of military or naval expeditions hostile to *American* governments already established. They therefore undertake to prohibit the exportation of arms and munitions of war intended for insurgents against established American Governments *unless such insurgents have been recognized as belligerents.*

T MS (SDR, RG 59, 710.11/282½, DNA).
    [1] The original document that Wilson emended has not survived. However, its text follows, with Wilson's emendations printed in italics. For our knowledge of the emendations, see H. P. Fletcher to RL, June 16, 1916, printed as an Enclosure with RL to WW, June 17, 1916.

From the Diary of Colonel House

The White House, Washington. May 3, 1916.

I arrived at the White House by half-past seven and breakfasted alone at eight o'clock. The President came to my room soon after, and we began our talks which continued on and off during the entire day until 10.15 at night. We both had the feeling that this would perhaps be my last trip to Washington until cool weather, and we talked of matters of interest at the moment, and of prospective happenings.

The first subject that held our attention was the Pan-American Peace Pact. Fletcher had sent me a copy of what the Brazilian and Chileans [Chilean] Governments would agree to. We went over this and made such changes in the verbiage as we thought necessary, the President writing them in with his own hand, the copy of which I retained. Later, Fletcher added the word "present" to the first paragraph.

It took some time to thresh this out sufficiently because of its many bearings. For instance, Chile desired to leave the question in doubt as to whether we should guarantee the territory in dispute between herself and Peru which is now in her "possession." The President said he would prefer the Pact to fail rather than do such an injustice to one of the smaller nations; since the whole pact was based upon mutual good will and justice he did not wish to start it with a palpable injustice. I like to bring out these characteristics of the President, for it shows him at his best.

I found him set in his determination to make Germany recede from her position regarding submarines. He spoke with much feeling concerning Germany's responsibility for this world-wide calamity, and thought those guilty should have personal punishment.

I believe I have more influence over the President than I realize. For instance, the last time I was here he was so disinclined to be firm with Germany that I feared he might destroy his influence. I therefore did all I could to make him stand firm. I evidently overdid it for I now find him unyielding and belligerent, and not caring as much as he ought to avert war.

After our conference I sent for Fletcher, had him take a copy of the changes made by the President in the peace pact covenant, and asked him to see both the Brazilian and Chileans Ambassadors at once and report later in the day. I advised what he should say when making the suggestion that they accept the text as we now have it. I thought there was much in the manner in which it was presented to them.

He returned in about an hour to report that the Brazilian Ambassador was in New York and would not return for several days. This makes another unavoidable delay. I requested him to send a copy to the Ambassador and to get an answer as soon as he could. I first suggested that he go to New York and see Da Gama. He was willing to do this if I thought best, but he did not feel it was dignified for one ambassador to chase another around the country. I laughingly apologised and told him I was so eager to close matters that ambassadorial dignity failed to enter my thought.

Frank Polk called and spent nearly two hours. We discussed the Mexican and European questions, and took up matters relating to the coming campaign. I have gotten the President so thoroughly imbued with the idea that Polk is the right man for Chairman that I cannot shake him lose. This is another evidence of having overdone it. Polk and I have come to the conclusion that he should remain in the State Department during these critical times, if it is possible to secure another man for National Chairman. Lansing is not over-well and must have a vacation, and it would not be advisable to have a new man entirely unfamiliar with what has happened, become acting Secretary of State during Lansing's absence.

Polk mentioned several men whom he thought might do. I told him the President would not take any of them because he knew them. Polk asked why the President was willing to take him, but added, "I have only seen the President two or three times to talk with him." I smilingly replied, "If you had seen more of him he would probably not want you any more than the others. He is taking you on the faith I have in you—a faith he would probably lose if he knew you better." Polk took this as good-naturedly as it was meant. As a matter of fact, there is much truth in what I said.

The President and I lunched alone and I took up with him several of the names of men Polk and I thought might do for National Chairman. None of them suited him. I told him it would inconvenience Lansing too much to lose Polk. He thought the contrary. Lansing's convenience was not as important as it was to have a proper man for National Chairman. He declared he did not desire to be President any longer, and it would be a delightful relief if he could conscienciously retire. He said he felt it his duty toward his country and his party to continue. He believes a second term may be anti-climax.

The reason I wanted Polk as National Chairman, and the arguments I gave the President for wishing him are that he has good judgment and is absolutely clean in purpose and thought. He would never "go to sleep at the switch," and the President need never have a moment's worry concerning the manner in which the campaign was being conducted. There could be no scandal or anything approaching one with Polk at the helm.

I discussed with the President the plan which Fred Lynch and others have to assess office holders for campaign purposes. I told him I thoroughly disapproved, and had expressed myself as being sure he would also. He was emphatic in his disapproval and was sorry such a move was contemplated, and authorized me to stop it.

I advised him to let the New York postmastership alone. I advised this in the beginning, in the interim and again now. I am inclined to think he will regard it. I never tell the President "I told you so," but he looks at me sometimes in a way that makes me know he is thinking this himself.

We desired to find a particular word and its different shadings as to meaning. The President went into another room, procured a Century Dictionary, and came back with it balanced on his head very much as the Negroes in the South balance pails of water. Mrs. Wilson and I laughed to see him walk along in the grotesque way necessary to keep the book balanced. I said to her, "you see we have reason to be proud of him in more ways than one." The President took this in good humor, but removed the book from his head.

Mrs. Wilson's portrait painted by Muller-Ury[1] which I gave them as a wedding present, has been hung above the mantel in the rose sitting-room. The President stood with one arm around me and one around Mrs. Wilson and thanked me for having thought to give it to him.

He apologized for leaving me in order to play golf and expressed a willingness to remain if I thought necessary. I insisted that he go for I had much to do in the meanwhile.

I found Secretary Houston out of town. The President desired me to see him and ask the loan of Solicitor Caffey during the time Polk was absent from the State Department in the event he became National Chairman.

Polk came over for another conference. I told him none of the men mentioned were acceptable to the President and it looked as if he would have to serve. In the circumstance, I thought he had better speak to Lansing. He did this later in the afternoon and said Lansing was terribly upset over it.

I persuaded the President to ask Lansing for a conference, not that a conference is needful, but I thought it would be well to have him feel he was being consulted. The President named eight o'clock, but as Lansing was giving a dinner I changed the hour to 6.30, trusting it would be agreeable to the President who was not at the moment available.

Today Polk told me of additional conversations caught by our Secret Service. Some of them related to me. The German Ambassador guardedly referred to me as being the one to be reckoned with in the settlement of the submarine dispute. They now call me by various names, but always something relating to a house. It is palace one time, column another etc.

A despatch came from Gerard today not relating to the submarine controversy, but stating he thought Germany would be willing to accept the President as mediator, and that "Colonel House would be very welcome here now."

The German Ambassador sent a letter to the White House asking if I could see him within the next day or two. I had Phillips telephone that I would see him in New York tomorrow morning. I did this for two reasons. The first was that I wished to leave tonight, the second, I thought it better to see Bernstorff immediately rather than defer it a few days.

[1] Adolfo Muller-Ury, Swiss-born portrait painter who came to the United States in 1886. He specialized in portraits of famous people, such as Pius X, William McKinley, J. Pierpont Morgan, and William II.

I asked Phillips to come to the White House to discuss matters relating to his particular sphere. I desired to know what had been done about some readjustments in the Diplomatic and Consular Services.

The President came in from golf and took me for a short motor ride before Lansing arrived. I have been urging the President from time to time today not to allow the war to continue beyond the Autumn. I am certain he can end it whether the belligerents desire it or not. He can so word a demand for a conference that the people of each nation will compel their governments to consent. He asked me to give my views in detail, and I outlined what was in my mind as to how and when it should be done. I thought during May, June and July, certainly by August, the Allies would have had sufficient time to demonstrate their ability or inability to make a dent in the German lines. After two months' constant effort the Germans have shown their inability to break through at Verdun, and it is not likely that a greater or more successful effort can be made anywhere on the western front by either side.

Our conference with Lansing was more or less a formal affair. We told him of the changes in the Pan-American Pact which Fletcher had already shown him, and in which Lansing had made an additional suggestion in the third clause regarding the shipment of munitions of war to revolutionists who had been recognized as belligerents.[2] The clause if left as it was, Lansing thought, would prevent any of the republics from shipping arms to revolutionists, even when their cause was thought to be just. For instance, Madero would not have had any assistance of this kind from the outside in his effort to overthrow the Diaz tyranny.

We discussed the German and Mexican situations, but there was nothing said or done that I have not already outlined elsewhere.

There were no outside guests at dinner. After dinner we sat for awhile in the second floor sitting room, and then we adjourned to the study for a two hour and a half conference.

The President was so insistent that I write an article about him for Harper's Magazine that I concluded to do so, provided I have the time and can work out something worth while. I told him I could either do it quickly or not at all. I advised getting a journal of wider circulation, such as Collier's or the Saturday Evening Post. He approved of this, provided it could be done with propriety, but Duneke [Duneka] of Harper's had made the

[2] According to Fletcher's letter, just cited in the preceding document, Wilson made this addition himself.

suggestion and he did not think it fair to publish the article in some other journal. I relieved his mind in this by telling him the suggestion was not new, that I had been asked many times by many different magazines and periodicals to write of him He left the matter in my hands.[3]

We definitely decided on Governor Glynn for Temporary Chairman of the Saint Louis Convention, and the President and I will aid him in preparing the keynote speech. I agreed to take charge of it and after the speech is finished, I am to send it to the President for criticism.

We discussed the question of appointing a commission to mobilize industrial resources in the event of war, and I spoke of my conference with Dr. Crampton and Dr. Hollis Godfrey.[4] He asked me to express his appreciation to them for the work they have so unselfishly carried on for more than ten months and at much personal sacrifice.

I asked him to make a list of the men I thought should form the Executive Committee to run the campaign. He objected to some; agreed to others, and we got it into shape. I explained if Polk ran the campaign we would have a private wire from headquarters to wherever I spent the summer, and when Polk did not care to take the responsibility, I would do so.

I thought the republicans were holding their convention a week before ours because they intended to put something in their platform concerning the war, its settlement and its aftermath in order to forestall the democrats. I felt so certain of this that I advised him to make a speech prior to the Republican Convention outlining our policy in such a manner that they could not appropriate it. The President was keen about this and will do so. In outlining this policy we agreed that I should either write or cable Sir Edward Grey and get his approval of the policy, and when the President announced it as his own, the approval of Great Britain would follow.

We talked of the time when Grey should announce that Great Britain was in accord with our Pan-American Peace Pact, of which Great Britain would like to become a party as far as her American possessions are concerned. We discussed this a little while Lansing was present in the afternoon, and we later took

---

3 House never wrote the article.

4 Henry Edward Crampton, Professor of Zoölogy at Columbia University, and Hollis Godfrey, President of the Drexel Institute in Philadelphia. Godfrey had been concerned about the problem of American military and economic preparedness since 1906 and, at this time, he and Crampton were quietly collecting information about materials and personnel that would be critical in a national emergency. They were also promoting the concept of a "Council of National Defense." See Cuff, *War Industries Board*, pp. 27-30.

it up more in detail. The President thought if the North and South American States guaranteed each other territorial integrity under republican forms of government, England could not sign such a pact because the British Government was not a republic. We wondered how we could overcome this obstacle. I shall take it up with Grey and try to think a way out. I began to get my traps together at 10.15 so as to go by the Department of Justice where I had an engagement with the Attorney General. Gregory and Grayson went with me to the station around midnight.

Gregory was concerned over some anticipated trouble with McAdoo about the employment of Samuel Untermyer in the Riggs Bank criminal prosecution case. Gregory will refuse to employ Untermyer even through [though] it should cause a break in his relations with McAdoo. I suggested a plan by which he could throw the burden upon the President, believing if this were done, hard feeling between the two Secretaries might be averted. I know the President's feeling is the same as Gregory's, and it would be better to have him tell McAdoo than to have Gregory do so.

The President read me a draft of the platform he has written for the St Louis Convention. He has done it well. but it is too verbose according to my taste and ideas, and he, himself, wondered if he had not erred in that direction. He had left out one or two things which I thought should be embodied and he made a memorandum to insert them.

To James Hamilton Lewis

My dear Senator: [The White House] May 4, 1916

I need not assure you that the matter of the appointment to the post office in Chicago has been giving me a great deal of concern, particularly because of your distress about the matter which I certainly did not for a moment intend to create. I only intended to solve a difficult case. I hope most sincerely, my dear Senator, that your mind has been relieved of all thought of humiliation in the matter. I cannot see that there is any ground for that, because I have only exercised my clear constitutional right to make a personal selection in a case where the selection was very difficult indeed and where it was hard to come to a concurrence of judgment. If there should be any public impression remaining that your judgment had been ignored in the matter, I hope that you will feel at liberty to publish my letters to you about it, which ought entirely to remove that impression.

I do not feel that I can withdraw the nomination of Mr. Williams. The more I look into his qualifications, the more I am convinced that I was justified both by his ability and by his character in making the nomination. I would not have made it if I had not been convinced upon these points, and I do not feel that I am making any unreasonable request of you when I beg that you will consider the nomination as made upon my full constitutional responsibility and, of course, without the least thought of embarrassing you in any way.[1]

Cordially and sincerely yours,   Woodrow Wilson

TLS (Letterpress Books, WP, DLC).
[1] The Senate rejected Williams's nomination on September 6.

To John Worth Kern

My dear Senator: [The White House] May 4, 1916

Thank you heartily for your letter of April thirtieth about the conservation measures. I realize the difficulties lying in your way and all the more appreciate your generous interest.

Cordially and sincerely yours,   Woodrow Wilson

TLS (Letterpress Books, WP, DLC).

From Newton Diehl Baker, with Enclosure

(CONFIDENTIAL.)

My dear Mr. President: [Washington] May 4, 1916.

I inclose a statement which I submit for you to give to the press this afternoon with regard to the Scott-Obregon conference.

The Secretary of State has gone over the despatch and approves it, and makes the further suggestion that he thinks it would be wise, in your later publicity when you come to give out the terms of the agreement, to add that in view of the removal of all outstanding questions between the two governments, you are directing Mr. Fletcher to proceed to Mexico City and will receive Mr. Arredondo officially.

I am preparing a statement for submission to you, to be given out to the press when we are notified that General Carranza has approved the tentative agreement.

Respectfully yours,   Newton D. Baker

CCL (WDR, RG 94, AGO Document File, No. 2638774, DNA).

ENCLOSURE

Statement for the Press by the President:

I have examined with the Secretary of War the report made by General Hugh L. Scott of the conference between him and General Obregon, Secretary of War of the Republic of Mexico.

The report includes a tentative agreement covering the future operations of both the American and Mexican military forces, and evidences cordial cooperation between the two governments in their common purpose.

As this agreement is being submitted to the *de facto* government of Mexico, it would not be proper for me to permit its publication until that government has had an opportunity to examine and consider its provisions. The full text of the proposed agreement will be given out immediately upon its acceptance by both governments. In general I may say that it provides a basis of cooperation which promises to prevent misunderstanding and strengthens the cordial relations of the two Republics.[1]

CC MS (WDR, RG 94, AGO Doc. File, No. 2638774, DNA).
    [1] This statement was published verbatim in the newspapers (e.g., the *New York Times*) on May 5, except that "covering" in line 1, paragraph 2, had been changed to "regarding."

From Robert Lansing

PERSONAL AND PRIVATE:

My dear Mr. President: Washington May 4, 1916.

Secretary Baker, this noon, read over to me the full report of General Scott and the terms of agreement which had been arranged between him and General Obregon. While I have not the text of the agreement before me I felt on its being read that it was in general satisfactory and that if General Carranza accepted it there was no especial reason why we should decline to do so.

In case the matter is arranged satisfactorily do you not think it would be well to have Mr. Fletcher proceed at once to his post and present his credentials, and, at the same time, have Mr. Arredondo received here, in order that we may establish full diplomatic relations between the two Governments?

I believe that this would be an advisable course and would very strongly impress the Mexican Government with the friendship and honesty of purpose of this Government. Furthermore, the real problem of stabilizing the Mexican Government must be met and solved within a short time. I think I have said to you that I thought it was largely a financial problem and that if the *de facto* Government could be financed there would be little reason why it would not succeed in the pacification of the country. In order to handle the fiscal question it seems to me important that Mr. Fletcher should be in Mexico.

I make this suggestion and hope you will be willing to give me your views in regard to it.

Faithfully yours,   Robert Lansing.

TLS (WP, DLC).

Henry Prather Fletcher to Edward Mandell House

Dear Colonel House: Washington, D. C. May 4, 1916.

I called on the Argentine Ambassador, M. Naon, today and gave him copies of the Brazil-Chile counter proposal and of the President's modifications of same. He seemed disappointed that we had not held out for the original draft and said he intended telegraphing to his Government recommending that the original draft be insisted upon.

I suggested that in that case his Government should try to convince Chile to go the whole way as originally planned—that Brazil had succeeded in getting her well over half way etc. and that we had no objections, but that three quarters of a loaf was better than no bread—and we wished to hold what we had gained.

I am quite sure that if Brazil and Chile accept the President's amendments, Argentine will come along, and if they step out because it does not go far enough, then if Chile and Brazil hang back and refuse to accede to the President's amendments we have lost nothing and the President will be free to go with Argentine alone, though I am inclined to think this will not be necessary.

The Brazilian Ambassador has not yet returned—is expected tomorrow, but I have left the draft with the First Secretary who promised to telegraph him. I have not seen the Chilean Chargé but will do so as soon as I have seen da Gama.

I think it is very useful to have Naon insisting on the original plan—it is what I hoped would happen.

I shall keep you posted.   Sincerely,   H. P. Fletcher.

TCL (WP, DLC).

William Calhoun McDonald to Joseph Patrick Tumulty

Santa Fe, N. M., May 4, 1916.

You may say to the President that nothing official has ever come to me concerning the cases of the seven men convicted of complicity in the Columbus murders and sentenced by our district court to be hanged May nineteenth. They were tried the same as any other prisoner, having been defended by counsel appointed by the court. They are now confined in the State Penitentiary for safe keeping. These cases will be given the most careful and thoughtful consideration. After as thorough and complete an investigation shall have been made, is [as] possible under the circumstances, I shall be glad then to communicate further touching the facts that may be disclosed.

W. C. McDonald,   Governor.

T telegram (WP, DLC).

Norman Hapgood to Cary Travers Grayson

Dear Dr. Grayson: New York May 4, 1916.

I have not communicated with you for some time, partly because I knew you were busy and partly because my information in the Brandeis case was only such as was available to several men close to the Administration. At last, however, I think my information is absolute, and so I want you to have it. In spite of his talk with the President, Senator Shields would vote No today if a vote were taken in the Judiciary Committee. So would O'Gorman. So would Hoke Smith, in spite of some statements of his to the contrary. Overmann I do not absolutely know about. Outside of the Committee Underwood, Clarke and Hardwick would vote No. In other words we have very distinctly lost ground recently. By insiders, notably by certain members of the Committee, this loss is attributed to lack of leadership in behalf of the Administration. Senator Chilton has been in Virginia[1] looking after his own affairs. Senator Fletcher has been in South America. Senator Walsh is admirable, but not exactly in a position to make effective the full force of an Administration policy.

I have strong hopes that when Mr. McAdoo gets back this situation may be changed. Meantime, one of the strongest arguments being used by those on the fence is that the Administration does not care, and this charge has even been made public by the Boston Herald. Of course, it is grossly unjust, but it takes the form of supporting the absurd charge that the appointment was made for political purposes and that those political purposes have already been accomplished. We know how despicably unjust this statement is, but it is growing in force. It is even said that a most influential Democrat,[2] very high in the councils of the administration, would rather see the confirmation fail than succeed, but I know that man very intimately and cannot believe it.

I have also exact information about the Republicans who will support the confirmation, but that is another story. Obviously if the Administration cannot hold the party together on this critical matter, the effect on the laboring classes and on liberal opinion generally through the country is going to be extremely serious.

I get back to Washington tonight and expect to remain there practically all the time for several weeks.

Yours sincerely,   Norman Hapgood.

TLS (WP, DLC).
  [1] Where he owned extensive coal properties.
  [2] He undoubtedly referred to Colonel House.

Sir Cecil Arthur Spring Rice to Sir Edward Grey

Washington. May 4th 1916.

Personal.

Your telegram of May 3rd.

President was much obliged for your message and will be very glad to see new Governor[1] on his way through. Nothing else passed.

T telegram (E. Grey Papers, FO 800/86, PRO).
  [1] Major Sir John Robert Chancellor.

A Draft of a Statement

May 5, 1916.

The *de facto* government of Mexico and this government have approved the agreement drawn up by General Scott, General Funston and General Obregon. The principal point at issue in these conferences was the time of the withdrawal of the American expedition into Mexico, the object of which from the first was to disperse the bands which made the Columbus raid and, if possible, to capture Villa, the leader, and, secondly, to prevent further depredations upon American soil by these irregular groups of bandits from Mexico.

General Obregon contended that either Villa is dead or else that his adherents are so far scattered that further trouble could not be expected. We did not feel safe, however, in the absence of definite information as to Villa's present whereabouts, in assuming his death or that the present withdrawal of our armed forces might not be followed by fresh outrages upon American men, women and children on our side of the border.

The agreement drawn up and approved by both governments contemplates the gradual retirement of the American force toward the border, the prosecution of the search for Villa, and the dispersal of his remaining following by the Mexican forces, and the entire withdrawal of the American expedition so soon as either Villa shall have been captured or the Mexican forces shall have secured such complete control of the country in northern Mexico as to render us safe from any fresh outbreaks by bandits or partisan groups opposed alike to the *de facto* government of Mexico and to the maintenance of order on the frontier of the United States.

This agreement happily provides for cordial cooperation between the two governments and, ultimately, for the complete accomplishment of the purposes for which our expedition was undertaken. Our advices from General Pershing show that there are now no large bodies of Villa followers anywhere within 400 miles of our border, and that further pursuit would have to be by small parties of soldiers, over very wide areas, rounding up mere remnants of these original bodies. This policing work, the forces of the *de facto* government can accomplish, and have undertaken. Should there be any fresh organized activity, the American forces will be in a position from which they can cooperate effectively with those of the *de facto* Government of Mexico for its suppression.

The ratification of this agreement by the two governments removes all controversy from their relations, and I have therefore decided officially to receive Mr. Arredondo, Ambassador-designate of Mexico, and shall direct Mr. Fletcher presently to proceed to Mexico City as the representative of the United States to that Republic.

T MS (WP, DLC).

To Edward Mandell House

The White House. May 5, 1916.

What do you think of the German answer and advise as to our attitude and action? Official version not yet received but assume press report is correct.[1]   Wilson.

T decode (E. M. House Papers, CtY) of T telegram (WP, DLC).
    1 The official version came into the State Department between 7:30 and 10:30
P.M. on May 5. It is printed as an Enclosure with RL to WW, May 6, 1916.

To Charles Allen Culberson

My dear Senator: The White House May 5, 1916

I am very much obliged to you for giving me an opportunity to make clear to the Judiciary Committee my reasons for nominating Mr. Louis D. Brandeis to fill the vacancy in the Supreme Court of the United States created by the death of Mr. Justice Lamar, for I am profoundly interested in the confirmation of the appointment by the Senate.

There is probably no more important duty imposed upon the President in connection with the general administration of the Government than that of naming members of the Supreme Court; and I need hardly tell you that I named Mr. Brandeis as a member of that great tribunal only because I knew him to be singularly qualified by learning, by gifts, and by character for the position.

Many charges have been made against Mr. Brandeis: the report of your sub-committee[1] has already made it plain to you and to the country at large how unfounded those charges were. They threw a great deal more light upon the character and motives of those with whom they originated than upon the qualifications of Mr. Brandeis. I myself looked into them three years ago when I desired to make Mr. Brandeis a member of my Cabinet and found that they proceeded for the most part from those who hated Mr. Brandeis because he had refused to be serviceable to them in the promotion of their own selfish interests, and from those whom they had prejudiced and misled. The propaganda in this matter has been very extraordinary and very distressing to those who love fairness and value the dignity of the great professions.

I perceived from the first that the charges were intrinsically incredible by anyone who had really known Mr. Brandeis. I have known him. I have tested him by seeking his advice upon some of the most difficult and perplexing public questions about which it was necessary for me to form a judgment. I have dealt with him in matters where nice questions of honor and fair play, as well as large questions of justice and the public benefit, were involved. In every matter in which I have made test of his judgment and point of view I have received from him counsel singularly enlightening, singularly clear-sighted and judicial, and, above all, full of moral stimulation. He is a friend of all just men and a lover of the right; and he knows more than how to talk about the right,—he knows how to set it forward in the face of its enemies. I knew from direct personal knowledge of the man what I was doing when I named him for the highest and most responsible tribunal of the nation.

Of his extraordinary ability as a lawyer no man who is competent to judge can speak with anything but the highest admiration. You will remember that in the opinion of the late Chief Justice Fuller[2] he was the ablest man who ever appeared before the Supreme Court of the United States. "He is also," the Chief Justice added, "absolutely fearless in the discharge of his duties."

Those who have resorted to him for assistance in settling great industrial disputes can testify to his fairness and love of justice. In the troublesome controversies between the garment workers and manufacturers of New York City, for example, he gave a truly remarkable proof of his judicial temperament and had what must have been the great satisfaction of rendering decisions which both sides were willing to accept as disinterested and even-handed.

Mr. Brandeis has rendered many notable services to the city and state with which his professional life has been identified. He successfully directed the difficult campaign which resulted in obtaining cheaper gas for the City of Boston. It was chiefly under his guidance and through his efforts that legislation was secured in Massachusetts which authorized savings banks to issue insurance policies for small sums at much reduced rates. And some gentlemen who tried very hard to obtain control by the Boston Elevated Railway Company of the subways of the city for a period of ninety-nine years can probably testify as to his ability as the people's advocate when public interests call for an effective champion. He rendered these services without compensation and earned, whether he got it or not, the gratitude of every citizen of the state and city he served. These are but a few of the services of this kind he has freely rendered. It will hearten friends of community and public rights throughout the country to see his quality signally recognized by his elevation to the Supreme Bench. For the whole country is aware of his quality and is interested in this appointment.

I did not in making choice of Mr. Brandeis ask for or depend upon "endorsements." I acted upon public knowledge and personal acquaintance with the man, and preferred to name a lawyer for this great office whose abilities and character were so widely recognized that he needed no endorsement. I did, however, personally consult many men in whose judgment I had great confidence, and am happy to say was supported in my selection by the voluntary recommendation of the Attorney General of the United States, who urged Mr. Brandeis upon my consideration independently of any suggestion from me.

Let me say by way of summing up, my dear Senator, that I nominated Mr. Brandeis for the Supreme Court because it was, and is, my deliberate judgment that, of all the men now at the bar whom it has been my privilege to observe, test, and know, he is exceptionally qualified. I cannot speak too highly of his impartial, impersonal, orderly, and constructive mind, his rare analytical powers, his deep human sympathy, his profound acquaintance with the historical roots of our institutions and insight into their spirit, or of the many evidences he has given of being imbued to the very heart with our American ideals of justice and equality of opportunity; of his knowledge of modern economic conditions and of the way they bear upon the masses of the people, or of his genius in getting persons to unite in common and harmonious action and look with frank and kindly eyes into each other's minds, who had before been heated antagonists. This friend of justice and of men will ornament the high court of which we are all so justly proud. I am glad to have had the opportunity to pay him this tribute of admiration and of confidence; and I beg that your Committee will accept this nomination as coming from me quick with a sense of public obligation and responsibility.

With warmest regard,

Cordially and sincerely yours,   Woodrow Wilson[3]

TLS (American Jewish Archives).

[1] *Nomination of Louis D. Brandeis: Hearings before the Subcommittee of the Committee on the Judiciary, United States Senate . . . Together with the Report of the Subcommittee . . .* , 64th Cong., 1st sess., Senate Doc. No. 409 (2 vols., Washington, 1916), II, 175-235, 297-371.

[2] Melville Weston Fuller, Chief Justice of the United States, 1888-1910.

[3] There is an undated WWsh draft of this letter in WP, DLC. Wilson drew the opinions attributed to Fuller and the information about Brandeis's activities as "the people's advocate" from an undated and unsigned T memorandum in WP, DLC. Alpheus T. Mason, *Brandeis: A Free Man's Life* (New York, 1946), pp. 498-99, argues convincingly that Gregory wrote this memorandum. The Attorney General in turn drew upon letters of George Weston Anderson, United States Attorney for Massachusetts, and a leader in the fight to secure Brandeis's confirmation. Wilson's letter was given to the press.

To Bernard Mannes Baruch

My dear Mr. Baruch: The White House May 5, 1916

Mr. House has handed me your letter to him of April twenty-fourth about what I may briefly call industrial efficiency in case of need to mobilize all the resources of the nation. I remember the stimulation I received from our conversation about the matter and it has ever since been at the front of my thoughts. We are now trying to give shape to the matter and I heartily value your generous interest and cooperation.

Cordially and sincerely yours, Woodrow Wilson

TLS (B. M. Baruch Papers, NjP).

To Newton Diehl Baker

My dear Mr. Secretary: The White House May 5, 1916

Here is a letter from one of the best friends we have, Bernard M. Baruch, which speaks for itself.

Some weeks ago Mr. Baruch came down here with a plan for a "council of executive information," to use the name you have chosen for it, and he is so full of sincere enthusiasm and intelligent ideas about the whole thing that I think it might serve us, as well as compliment him, if you would ask him to come down for a talk with you.

Cordially and sincerely yours, Woodrow Wilson

TLS (WDR, RG 94, AGO Document File, No. 2638801, DNA).

To Oscar Wilder Underwood

My dear Senator: [The White House] May 5, 1916

I am very much concerned to see the proposed legislation adopted for the increase in the Interstate Commerce Commission.[1] It does not seem to me to conflict in the least with the investigation which I hope we are going to have in compliance with the very useful suggestion you made to me and which I embodied in my message to Congress, and it is from every point of view, whatever is done in the future with regard to the powers of the Commission, so pressing a necessity from the standpoint of administrative efficiency. I hope very much that this legislation may have your support, and I very earnestly ask that you assist in getting it through without its being encumbered with additional provisions with regard to the powers of the Commission.

I am so sure that you know my way of thinking about these matters so well that you will understand this appeal on a matter which has for a long time seemed to me to require action.

Cordially and sincerely yours, Woodrow Wilson

TLS (Letterpress Books, WP, DLC).
  [1] *H.R. 308*, introduced in the House by William C. Adamson on December 6, 1915. It increased the membership of the Interstate Commerce Commission from seven to nine and permitted the commission to divide itself into sections to expedite its business. The House passed the bill on April 17, 1916. It was debated briefly in the Senate on June 2, 1916, and again on February 19 and 20, 1917, but it failed to come to a vote before the end of the Sixty-fourth Congress on March 4, 1917. The text of the bill appears in *Cong. Record*, 64th Cong., 1st sess., pp. 6310-11.

From Robert Lansing, with Enclosure

PERSONAL AND CONFIDENTIAL:

My dear Mr. President: Washington May 5, 1916.

I enclose herewith Gerard's report of his interview with the Kaiser. It seems to me that taken altogether he handled the matter very well and assumed a position very much in accord with this Government. He does not mention whether or not he used the definite rules which were sent him, as to visit and search, and I have therefore wired him to ask whether he brought them to the attention of the Secretary of Foreign Affairs before the German note was delivered to him. I think it is important we should know this before drafting any answer or deciding what course should be taken.

Faithfully yours,   Robert Lansing

TLS (WP, DLC).

ENCLOSURE

Berlin (via Copenhagen) May 3, 1916.

3839. I returned last night from General Headquarters, having been there from seven p.m., Friday, to eleven thirty p.m., Monday. Grew[1] went with me. We were accompanied by a gentleman from the Foreign Office. In Charleville we were given small villa and dined each day with the Chancellor and lunched there Sunday. I had numerous conversations with the Chancellor and others of the Foreign Office as well as von Treutler,[2] Prussian Minister to Munich, who represents the Foreign Office and is always with the Emperor. In all these conversations the Chancellor laid great stress on the fact that we had done nothing to England. I said that we could never agree to do anything to another country as a price of obtaining something from Germany but I did state that I honestly believed both that the President was absolutely neutral and that he intended to enforce international law whenever its violation interfered with the rights of Americans, that however if some one murdered my sister I would probably pursue him first in preference to a small boy who had stepped on my flower beds. All agreed that the President's memorandum about armed merchantmen would seem to mean that he intended in cases where English gave ships orders to fire immediately to either keep such ships out of American ports or warn Americans off. We had general discussion as to what America could do if she came into the war, the SUSSEX case, et cetera. In talk of the British blockade I cited the German FRYE note which stated that food bound for an enemy fortified port was presumably bound for the enemy army and therefore contraband. Monday morning I was notified that the Chancellor would call for me to take me to the Emperor at twelve thirty and that there would be lunch with the Emperor at one. I also received a copy of the log of a submarine. When the Chancellor came he (#) [asked], have you read the log of that submarine. I said, yes. He said, you see how careful the submarine commanders are, this one did not sink a ship because he would not put the crew in boats one hundred and twenty miles from land. I said, one swallow does not make a summer and anyway today's papers speak of a crew being put in boats at exactly this distance from land. We went to the chateau where the Emperor lives; he received us in the garden; although lunch was at one we talked until one thirty, about three quarters hour in all. The Emperor said smilingly, do you come like a Roman Pro-Consul bringing peace in one hand and war (in the other?). I said, no Your Majesty, only hoping that the differences between two friendly countries may be satisfactorily adjusted. The Emperor then began a sort of speech; he spoke first of the rather rough and uncourteous tone of our note as he considered it; he said that the German notes had spoken of the friendship of the two countries since the days of Frederick the Great. He said that we had charged the Germans with being barbarous in warfare; that at first as Emperor and christian and head of the church of his country he had wished to carry on war in a knightly manner; he referred to his speech to the Reichstag members, but he said that the opponents of Germany had used weapons and means which had compelled him to resort to similar means. He said that the French were not at all like the French of 1870 and did not have the same noble feelings and officers but that the officers came from one did not know where. He then spoke of the English blockade and the effort of the English to starve out the Germans and keep even milk and Red Cross supplies out and other instances of breaches of international law by England. He said that this justified any

means of submarine war and that before he would permit his
wife and little grand children to die of hunger he would utterly
destroy England and even the whole English royal family. He said
that the submarine was a weapon used by all nations including
America, that he had lately seen with great interest the plans
of a battle submarine of large size in an American paper, that the
submarine had come to stay and law must be changed to meet
this condition and then both he and the Chancellor said that there
was no international law anyway. He said that if an American
travels on a cart behind the battle lines and is hurt by a shell
what right has his nation to complain. I said that first I did not
believe the note charged the Germans with general barbarity in
war but referred only to the use of submarines; that we could
never promise to do anything to one country in return for a
concession from another, that if we made it a condition that
he should do something to Great Britain that he would of course
refuse; that the President only desired to enforce international
law; that an American on the battlefield was a far different
case from an American on an enemy ship at sea; that the battlefield was in some hostile territory but that outside of the three
mile limit the sea was free and no one could declare it war territory; that as for the British blockade we want first to settle cases
where the lives of Americans were involved; that the President
was not acting as a referee for the world in breaches of international law but was engaged in protecting Americans in their
rights; that he had sent me some dumdum bullets alleged to
have been used by the French but that the President had refused
to investigate and that many friends of Germany thought the
President had thereby helped Germany as otherwise for days
the White House would have been filled with waiting Belgians
exhibiting mutilated women and children alleged to have been
mistreated by the Germans. I said that the American ships
CARIB and GREEN BRIAR coming to Germany with cotton had been
blown up by German mines; that I had heard of a food ship
called the WILHELMINA destined for Germany being taken into
an English port, that I believed the cargo had been bought by
the English before any decision in the English Prize Court. The
Emperor then spoke of the DACIA and I said the DACIA was captured because she was a German ship transferred after the war
and therefore subject to capture and the Chancellor said, that
is right. I also referred to the German FRYE note as above. I
said that President Wilson was violently attacked in Germany
but that he stood for peace and the speeches of Roosevelt and
Root showed that their parties were for war even about Belgium;

that it was not as he had said a case of sending a note after two years of war demanding that the Germans give up a legal weapon, but that the President had stood a great deal as representing America from the LUSITANIA case on. He said that there was ample warning given in the LUSITANIA case. I said if the Chancellor warns me that if I go on the Wilhelm Platz he will kill me and I go and he kills me the fact that he gave me warning does not excuse the killing if I had the right to go on Wilhelm Platz. I said we specify the ARABIC where the ship was westward bound and therefore there was no question of munitions as well as the ANCONIA where we knew that everything about the submarine was German except the flag; that it was not the case of coming in late in the war with a note asking Germany to give up a lawful means of war but of American patience at last coming to an end. We had some pleasant general conversation. The emperor said, are the German troops not splendid and it takes some courage to remain six hours under vexing fire from American ammunition. At lunch I sat next to the Emperor. We talked of Henry Ford, the female suffrage, et cetera. After lunch he referred to the submarine log and I said the same thing as to the Chancellor. He said that the TUBANTIA was sunk by an English torpedo fired on purpose to make trouble but that a German torpedo which had been fired and missed some days previously and which was floating in the North Sea happened to run against the TUBANTIA at the same time. He said that Holland and its Corvette Captain in Berlin were convinced of this and that Holland had sent a note to England demanding payment. In the evening the Chancellor said he hoped the President would be great enough to take up peace, that Germany had won enough to be able to talk of peace without suspicion of weakness and that this awful loss of life should cease. He said that he hoped Colonel House would take up the question and shall perhaps come here, under the President's direction.   Gerard, Berlin.

T telegram (WP, DLC).
¹ Joseph Clark Grew, Secretary of Embassy at Berlin.
² Karl Georg von Treutler.

From Edward Mandell House

Dear Governor,   [New York] 10.30 P.M. May 5, 1916.

Your code message has just come. I would advise saying (or having Lansing say) that you are glad that "the German government feels that responsibility could not be borne before the forum of mankind and in history if after twenty-one months of the war's duration the submarine question under discussion between the German government and the government of the U. S. were to take a turn seriously threatening maintenance of peace between the two nations.["] (2.) That you were pleased that "the German government is prepaired to do its utmost to confine operations of the war for the rest of its duration to the *fighting forces of the belligerents.*" (3.) That it was gratifying to know that new orders had been given German naval forces to conduct future operations in accordance with recognized international law. (4) That this government would exercise its own judgement in regard to negotiations with other belligerents who infringe upon our rights.

These are the points I would bring out in a way that you know so well how to do. I would let Bernsto[r]ff and Gerard know and let our public have an intimation that the first infraction would bring on immediate severance of relations. I will write you tomorrow of my conversations with Bernsto[r]ff.

Affectionately yours, E. M. House

ALS (WP, DLC).

From Paul Oscar Husting, with Enclosure

Dear Mr. President: Washington, D. C. May 5, 1916.

Please pardon me for my belated acknowledgment of your letter of May 1, in which you were kind enough to commend my actions in the Senate concerning the present crisis with Germany. I beg to assure you that I appreciate and most highly prize your very cordial approval of my humble efforts in the premises.

May I also, at this time, enclose for your perusal and consideration a copy of Section 5335, Revised Statutes of the United States, entitled "Criminal correspondence with foreign governments," which would seem to be applicable to at least some of the activities in connection with the pro-German propaganda now being carried on so extensively in this country. I send this to you in response to the suggestion you made at our last conference. Of course, I do not want to be understood as claiming that this is the only statute that might apply but merely submit it as one which I think might cover some phases of the situation.

I am also calling the attention of the Attorney General to this section.

With assurances of my highest respect and esteem, believe me,

Sincerely yours, Paul O Husting

TLS (WP, DLC).

E N C L O S U R E

Criminal correspondence with foreign governments.

"Sec. 5335. Every citizen of the United States, whether actually resident or abiding within the same, or in any foreign country, who, without the permission or authority of the Government, directly or indirectly, commences or carries on any verbal or written correspondence or intercourse with any foreign government, or any officer or agent thereof, with an intent to influence the measures or conduct of any foreign government, or of any officer or agent thereof, in relation to any disputes or controversies with the United States, or to defeat the measures of the Government of the United States; and every person, being a citizen of, or resident within, the United States, and not duly authorized, who counsels, advises, or assists in any such correspondence, with such intent, shall be punished by a fine of not more than five thousand dollars, and by imprisonment during a term not less than six months, nor more than three years; but nothing in this section shall be construed to abridge the right of a citizen to apply, himself or his agent, to any foreign government or the agents thereof for redress of any injury which he may have sustained from such government, or any of its agents or subjects."

T MS (WP, DLC).

From Newton Diehl Baker

My dear Mr. President: Washington. May 5, 1916.

I have asked General Bliss to send you, under confidential cover, any telegram received by him from General Scott in my absence, showing the completion of the Scott-Obregon arrangement, for as yet we have not had any official word of the consent of the *de facto* Government of Mexico to the agreement. The suggested newspaper publicity, which I left with you this morning, is of course to be considered by you only in the event of the *de facto* Government of Mexico authorizing the formal execution of that agreement. I have notified General Scott that he is authorized to execute it for this government.

Should any interruption of the negotiations take place, General Bliss will, of course, apprise you immediately.

Respectfully yours,   Newton D. Baker

TLS (WP, DLC).

From James Hay, with Enclosure

My dear Mr. President: Washington, D. C. May 5th, 1916

I am herewith enclosing a proposed substitute for the Senate provision, providing for a nitrate plant.[1]

This provision has been drawn and submitted to me by Mess[rs]. Ferris, Foster and others. This matter will be taken up in the House on Monday, and if it does not meet with your approval will you kindly let me know.

Very Sincerely Yours   James Hay

ALS (WP, DLC).
[1] The Army reorganization bill was at this time in the conference committee, and the provision for the construction of a nitrate plant was one bone of contention, among others.

ENCLOSURE

AMEND SENATE AMENDMENT TO H.R. 12764, BEGINNING ON PAGE 206, STRIKE OUT ALL OF SECTION 222, AND INSERT IN LIEU THEREOF THE FOLLOWING:

That the President of the United States is hereby authorized and empowered to designate for the exclusive use of the United States such site or sites upon any navigable river, or rivers, or upon the public lands as, in his opinion, will be necessary for carrying out the purposes of this act, and is further authorized to construct, maintain, and operate at or on any site so designated or withdrawn, dams, locks, improvements to navigation, power houses, and other plants and equipment necessary or convenient for the generation of electrical or other power and for the production of nitrates or other products needed for munitions of war and useful in the manufacture of fertilizers and other useful products.

That the President is authorized to lease, purchase, or acquire by condemnation, gift, or devise, such lands and rights of way as may be necessary for the construction and operation of such plants and to take from any lands of the United States, or to purchase or acquire by condemnation materials, minerals, and processes patented or otherwise necessary for the construction or operation of such plants and for the manufacture of such products.

That the products of such plants shall be used by the President for military or naval purposes and any surplus not so required may be sold and disposed of under such regulations as he may prescribe.

That the president is hereby authorized and empowered to

employ such officers, agents, or agencies, as may, in his discretion, be necessary to enable him to carry out the purposes of this section, and to authorize and require such officers, agents or agencies to perform any and all of the duties imposed upon him by the provisions herof.

That the sum of $15,000,000 is hereby appropriated, out of any moneys in the Treasury not otherwise appropriated, available until expended, to enable the President of the United States to carry out the purposes of this Act.

That the plant or plants provided for under this Act shall be constructed and operated solely by the Government and not in conjunction with any other industry or enterprise carried on by private capital.

That in order to raise the money appropriated by this Act and necessary to carry its provisions into effect, the Secretary of the Treasury, upon the request of the President of the United States, may issue and sell or use for such purchase or construction hereinabove authorized any of the bonds of the United States now available in the Treasury of the United States under the Act of August fifth, nineteen hundred and nine, the Act of February fourth, nineteen hundred and ten, and the Act of March second, nineteen hundred and eleven, relating to the issue of bonds for the construction of the Panama Canal, to a total amount not to exceeed [exceed] $15,000,000: Provided, That any Panama Canal bonds issued and sold or used under the provisions of this section may be made payable at such time after issue as the Secretary of the Treasury, in his discretion, may deem advisable and fix instead of fifty years after date of issue, as in said Act of August fifth, nineteen hundred and nine, not exceeding fifty years.

T MS (WP, DLC).

From Robert Lansing, with Enclosures

PERSONAL AND CONFIDENTIAL:

My dear Mr. President: Washington May 6, 1916.

I enclose the official text of the German reply together with a memorandum on one point in the note which seems to me of special importance and one which should receive careful consideration.

The more I study the reply the less I like it. It has all the elements of the "gold brick" swindle with a decidedly insolent tone. I think that we should take time to scrutinize the document and give no indication as to whether it is acceptable or unacceptable until we weigh every portion with care. The first impression is bad; the second, good; and the third unsatisfactory. At least that is the way my mind has been impressed thus far. But my final judgment I am not ready to give, without further study.

Faithfully yours,   Robert Lansing

TLS (WP, DLC).

E N C L O S U R E   I

Berlin, May 4, 1916.

No. 3848. Following is the text of the note handed to me both in German and English at 5.30 this afternoon by Secretary of State for Foreign Affairs:

"Foreign Office,
"Berlin, May 4, 1916.

"The undersigned, on behalf of the Imperial Government, has the honor to present to His Excellency the Ambassador of the United States, Mr. James W. Gerard, the following reply to the note of April 20 regarding the conduct of German submarine warfare:

"The German Government has handed over to the proper naval authorities for further investigation the evidence concerning the *Sussex*, as communicated by the Government of the United States. Judging by results that this investigation has hitherto yielded the German Government is alive to the possibility that the ship mentioned in the note of April 10 as torpedoed by a German submarine is actually identical with the *Sussex*. The German Government begs to reserve further communications on the matter until certain points are ascertained which are of decisive importance for establishing the facts of the case. Should it turn out that the commander was wrong in assuming the vessel to be a man-of-war the German Government will not fail to draw the consequences resulting therefrom.

"In connection with the case of the *Sussex*, the Government of the United States has made a series of statements, gist of which is the assertion that this incident is to be considered as one instance for the deliberate method of indiscriminate destruction of vessels of all sorts, nationalities, and destinations by German submarine commanders. The German Government must emphatically repudiate this assertion. The German Government, however, thinks it of little avail to enter into details in the present stage of affairs, more particularly as the Government of the

United States has omitted to substantiate this assertion by reference to concrete facts. The German Government will only state
that it has imposed far-reaching restraints upon the use of the
submarine weapon solely in consideration of the interests of
neutrals, in spite of the fact that these restrictions are necessarily
of advantage to Germany's enemies; no such consideration has
ever been shown to the neutrals by Great Britain and her allies.

"The German submarine forces have had, in fact, orders to
conduct submarine warfare in accordance with the general principles of visit and search and destruction of merchant vessels
as recognized by international law, the sole exception being the
conduct of warfare against the enemy trade carried on enemy
freight ships that are encountered in the war zone surrounding
Great Britain; with regard to these no assurances have ever been
given to the Government of the United States; no such assurance
was contained in the declaration of February 8, 1916. The German Government can not admit any doubt that these orders have
been given and are executed in good faith. Errors have actually
occurred; they can in no kind of warfare be avoided altogether,
and allowances must be made in the conduct of naval warfare
against an enemy resorting to all kinds of ruses, whether permissible or illicit. But, apart from the possibility of errors, naval warfare, just like warfare on land, implies unavoidable dangers for
neutral persons and goods entering the fighting zone. Even in
cases where naval action was confined to their ordinary forms of
cruiser warfare, neutral persons and goods have repeatedly come
to grief. The German Government has repeatedly and explicitly
pointed out the dangers from mines that have led to the loss of
numerous ships. The German Government has made several proposals to the Government of the United States in order to reduce
to a minimum for American travelers and goods the inherent
dangers of naval warfare. Unfortunately the Government of the
United States has decided not to accept these proposals; had it
accepted, the Government of the United States would have been
instrumental in preventing the greater part of the accidents that
American citizens have met with in the meantime. The German
Government still stands by its offer to come to an agreement
along these lines.

"As the German Government has repeatedly declared, it can
not dispense with the use of the submarine weapon in the conduct of warfare against enemy trade. The German Government,
however, has now decided to make a further concession in adopt-
ing [adapting] the methods of submarine warfare to the interests
of the neutrals; in reaching this decision the German Govern-

ment has been actuated by considerations which are above the level of the disputed question.

"The German Government attaches no less importance to the sacred principles of humanity than the Government of the United States. Again, it fully takes into account that both Governments have for many years cooperated in developing international law in conformity with these principles, the ultimate object of which has been always to confine warfare on sea and on land to the armed forces of the belligerents and to safeguard, as far as possible, noncombatants against the horrors of war.

"But, although those considerations are of great weight, they alone would not, under the present circumstances, have determined the attitude of the German Government.

"For, in answer to the appeal made by the United States Government on behalf of the sacred principles of humanity and international law, the German Government must repeat once more with all emphasis that it was not the German but the British Government which, ignoring all the accepted rules of international law, has extended this terrible war to the lives and property of noncombatants, having no regard whatever for the interests and rights of the neutrals and noncombatants that through this method of warfare have been severely injured.

"In self-defense against the illegal conduct of British warfare, while fighting a bitter struggle for her national existence, Germany had to resort to the hard but effective weapon of submarine warfare. As matters stand, the German Government can not but reiterate its regret that the sentiments of humanity which the Government of the United States extends with such fervor to the unhappy victims of submarine warfare are not extended with the same warmth of feeling to the many millions of women and children who, according to the avowed intentions of the British Government, shall be starved and who, by their sufferings, shall force the victorious armies of the central powers into ignominious capitulation. The German Government, in agreement with the German people, fails to understand this discrimination, all the more as it has repeatedly and explicitly declared itself ready to use the submarine weapon in strict conformity with the rules of international law as recognized before the outbreak of the war, if Great Britain were likewise ready to adapt her conduct of warfare to these rules. The several attempts made by the Government of the United States to prevail upon the British Government to act accordingly have failed because of the flat refusal on the part of the British Government. Moreover, Great Britain has ever since again and again violated international law, surpassing all bounds in outraging neutral rights. The latest measure adopted by Great Britain, declaring German bunker coal as contraband and establishing conditions under which alone English bunker coal shall be supplied to neutrals, is nothing but an unheard of attempt, by way of exaction, to force neutral tonnage into the service of the British trade war.

"The German people knows that the Government of the United States has the power to confine this war to the armed forces of the belligerent countries in the interest of humanity and the maintenance of international law. The Government of the United States would have been certain of attaining this end had it been determined to insist against Great Britain on its incontestable rights to the freedom of the seas. But, as matters stand, the German people is under the impression that the Government of the United States, while demanding that Germany, struggling for her existence, shall restrain the use of an effective weapon, and while making the compliance with these demands a condition for the maintenance of relations with Germany, confines itself to protests against the illegal methods adopted by Germany's enemies. Moreover, the German people knows to what a considerable extent its enemies are supplied with all kinds of war material from the United States.

"It will therefore be understood that the appeal made by the Government of the United States to the sentiments of humanity and to the principles of international law can not, under the circumstances, meet with the same hearty response from the German people which such an appeal is otherwise always certain to find here. If the German Government, nevertheless, has resolved to go to the utmost limit of concessions, it has not alone been guided by the friendship connecting the two great nations for over a hundred years, but it also has thought of the great doom which threatens the entire civilized world should this cruel and sanguinary war be extended and prolonged.

"The German Government, conscious of Germany's strength, has twice within the last few months announced before the world its readiness to make peace on a basis safeguarding Germany's vital interests, thus indicating that it is not Germany's fault if peace is still withheld from the nations of Europe.

"The German Government feels all the more justified to declare that the responsibility could not be borne before the forum of mankind and history if, after 21 months' duration of the war, the submarine question under discussion between the German Government and the Government of the United States were to take a turn seriously threatening the maintenance of peace between the two nations.

"As far as it lies with the German Government, it wishes to prevent things from taking such a course. The German Government, moreover, is prepared to do its utmost to confine the operations of war for the rest of its duration to the fighting forces of the belligerents, thereby also insuring the freedom of the seas, as principle upon which the German Government believes, now as before, to be in agreement with the Government of the United States.

"The German Government, guided by this idea, notifies the Government of the United States that the German naval forces have received the following orders: In accordance with the general principles of visit and search and destruction of merchant vessels recognized by international law, such vessels, both within and without the area declared as naval war zone, shall not be sunk without warning and without saving human lives, unless these ships attempt to escape or offer resistance.

"But neutrals can not expect that Germany, forced to fight for her existence, shall, for the sake of neutral interest, restrict the use of an effective weapon if her enemy is permitted to continue to apply at will methods of warfare violating the rules of international law. Such a demand would be incompatible with the character of neutrality, and the German Government is convinced that the Government of the United States does not think of making such a demand, knowing that the Government of the United States has repeatedly declared that it is determined to restore the principle of the freedom of the seas, from whatever quarter it has been violated.

"Accordingly the German Government is confident that, in consequence of the new orders issued to its naval forces, the Government of the United States will now also consider all impediments removed which may have been in the way of a mutual cooperation towards the restoration of the freedom of the seas during the war as suggested in the note of July 23, 1915, and it does not doubt that the Government of the United States will now demand and insist that the British Government shall forthwith observe the rules of international law universally recognized before the war as they are laid down in the notes presented by the Government of the United States to the British Government on December 28, 1914, and November 5, 1915. Should the steps taken by the Government of the United States not attain the object it desires to have the laws of humanity followed by all belligerent nations, the German Government would then be facing a new situation, in which it must reserve itself complete liberty of decision.

"The undersigned avails himself of this occasion to renew to the American Ambassador the assurances of his highest consideration.

"von Jagow."

Foreign Office informs me note will be given out here to the German newspapers and American correspondents late to-morrow afternoon.

Gerard.

Printed copy (WP, DLC).

E N C L O S U R E I I

MEMORANDUM ON THE NEW ORDERS TO
SUBMARINES IN THE GERMAN REPLY.

May 5, 1916.

The German Government in its note states that it has decided "to make a further concession, adapting methods of submarine war to the interests of neutrals." (See page 6)

The extent of this new concession is to be determined by comparison of the orders which "the German submarine forces have had" (See page 3) and the order which the German Government "notifies the Government of the United States that the German naval forces have received." (See page 12)

Previous Orders	*New Orders.*
To conduct the submarine warfare in accordance with the general principles of visit and search and the destruction of merchant vessels recognized by international law, the sole exception being the conduct of warfare against enemy trade carried on enemy freight ships encountered in the war zone surrounding Great Britain.	In accordance with the general principles of visit and search and the destruction of merchant vessels recognized by international law, such vessels both within and without the area declared a naval war zone shall not be sunk without warning and without saving human lives unless the ships attempt to escape or offer resistance.

First: It is noticeable that the essential difference between these orders is that the new orders eliminate the war zone and place the same restrictions upon submarine warfare in all parts of the high seas as were in force previously outside the war zone.

Second: The new orders recite a portion of the established rules by asserting that the immunity from being sunk without warning and without saving human lives is lost if the ships attempt to escape or offer resistence. The phrase "offer resistence" is significant since it indicates that *armed* vessels possessing power of resistence are included in the general term "merchant vessels" covered by the order.

Third: In the previous orders the same restrictions on submarine warfare were in force as to all merchant vessels, both within and without the war zone, except as to "enemy freight ships encountered in the war zone." By these orders enemy passenger ships and *all* neutral ships were entitled to be visited and searched.

Fourth: It would appear that the only additional limitation placed upon submarine warfare beyond those previously in force is that "enemy freight ships encountered in the war zone" will be accorded the same treatment as that accorded to passenger ships and neutral ships in all parts of the high seas and as that accorded to such freighters if outside the war zone. It would appear, therefore, that enemy freight ships are the only beneficiaries under the new orders. It is not apparent how this is "a further concession," as asserted, "to the interests of neutrals."

Fifth: The United States' complaints have been chiefly directed against the methods employed in attacking passenger vessels. If these attacks are "in accordance with the general principles of visit and search and the destruction of merchant vessels recognized by international law," as interpreted by the German Government and applied by the German naval forces, then the new orders offer no change in the methods which the United States demands should be abandoned.

Sixth: Unless the German Government states frankly that the rule as to visit and search will be applied in the customary manner and that it will not be interpreted as it has been by the German submarine forces under their previous orders, the new orders in no way lessen the danger to life or restore to neutrals their just rights on the high seas.

Seventh: In view of the similarity of the previous orders and the new orders, and the way that the previous orders have been carried out, the new orders do not constitute a declaration of abandonment of the present methods of warfare.

CC memorandum (WP, DLC).

Two Telegrams from Walter Hines Page

London　May 6, 1916.

4256. PERSONAL. The following is Confidential for the President and the Secretary only.

Newspaper comment and private opinion here regard the German note as only another effort to prolong discussion, to embroil our Government and Great Britain and to evade the issue. The expectation of our friends here, as far as I can gather it, is of an immediate break. Else they will consider that we have yielded to evasion.　　　　American Ambassador, London.

T telegram (SDR, RG 59, 763.72/2689½, DNA).

London　May 6, 1916.

4260. PERSONAL. The following is Confidential for the President and the Secretary only.

I hear through credible channels that the recent secret session of the House of Commons brought out the feeling that the total fighting manhood of Great Britain was necessary to prevent the war ending as a stalemate. Universal conscription has given renewed confidence.

The belief is widespread here that the Germans are renewing or will renew efforts for peace on a stalemate basis which universal conscription will enable the allies to reject. Economic pressure is also more and more relied on to bring a real ally victory. Kitchener told Squier[1] our Military Attaché that without American aid the war will last another year and that with aid it would end in an ally victory within six months.

American Amb. London

T telegram (SDR, RG 59, 763.72/2694½, DNA).
[1] Lieutenant Colonel George Owen Squier, U.S.A.

From Edward Mandell House

Dear Governor:　　　　　New York. May 6th, 1916.

Your code telegram came last night about half past ten o'clock and I wrote you a hasty opinion as to what I thought best to do in the circumstances.

There is one thing I feel quite certain about and that is no formal reply should be made to the German Note. I believe, too, it would be better for you to let Lansing make any statement to the public that is considered proper.

None of the papers have brought out the real concessions that the Germans have made. This, I think, should be done and then, I believe, a rather curt statement should be made to the effect that we will deal with the other belligerents who violate international law as we see fit.

I cannot see how we can break with Germany on this note. However, I would make it very clear to the German Government through both Gerard and Bernstorff that the least infraction would entail an immediate severance of diplomatic relations, and I would let the public know unofficially that this had been done. We will then have to wait and hope for the best.

At my conference with Bernstorff yesterday I suggested that he caution his government against any further transgression. He said he would, but he did not believe any would occur. The disagreeable parts of the note he told me were necessary because of German public opinion, but he confessed that he knew it would be impossible for us to make Great Britain conform to international law in regard to the blockade. He thought you could make peace easier than you could do this.

He suggested, too, that the Lusitania incident be closed by publishing his (Bernstorff's) letter in regard to that matter which taken in conjunction with the German promise to discontinue their submarine warfare would be all that had been demanded.

Bernstorff was sorry that they did not treat the matter as he advised for he believes it would have been better for his government and for ours if they had done so.

Affectionately yours,   E. M. House

TLS (WP, DLC).

Remarks Celebrating the Centennial of the American Bible Society[1]

[May 7, 1916]

Mr. President and ladies and gentlemen: I am unaffectedly abashed when I think of the great theme which offers itself for discussion this afternoon and of my inadequacy to discuss it. But I have felt that the representative of a nation, which has been peculiarly blessed by the widespread illumination of the Word of God, was under special obligation to be present on an occasion like this and take part in the celebration in which we are participating. And there is a very great thrill of pleasure that must come to every thoughtful man who takes part in the celebration of any work which, like this, is a record of persistent and unselfish endeavor. That is what gives it dignity, nobility, and as-surance of life.

It is a very interesting circumstance—perhaps I might add a disappointing circumstance—that the world should have so late wakened to its obligation and opportunity in respect of the spread of the Scripture. We are celebrating the one hundredth anniver-sary of the American Bible Society, and there are other Bible so-cieties older than it. But one hundred years is a very small part of the history of Christianity; and this great Bible is the main vehicle of Christianity. Widespread, systematic missionary en-deavor is also modern and recent as gauged by the measures of history, and it is with a sort of feeling that we stand at the youth, at the beginning, of the hope of what may be accomplished by these means when we think of this great work and of its rapid progress and spread.

Those who weave together the thought and the ideals and the conceptions of mankind also weave together its action. They con-trol the motive forces of humanity if they can control these things. One of the things—almost the only thing—that separates races and nations of men from one another is difference of thought, difference of point of view, prompted by difference of tradition, differences of experience, differences in instruction. If all the world had a common literature, if all the world had drunk at the same sources of inspiration and suggestion, many lines of division would never have been created, and many would now disappear. And those who spread the Scripture are engaged, as it were, in drawing the world together under the spell of one body of literature, which belongs to no one race, to no one civiliza-tion, to no one time in the history of the world, but whose appeal is universal, which searches and illuminates all hearts alike. In proportion as men yield themselves to the kindly light of the Gospel, they are bound together in the bonds of mutual under-standing and assured peace.

Surely, therefore, one can easily kindle one's enthusiasm at the flame that burns upon the altar of a society like this. We are try-ing in the spread of the Gospel to make all the nations of the world of one mind, of one enlightenment, of one motive, driven through every effort of their lives by one devotion and one allegiance. Could you conceive a greater enterprise than that?

The work of the Bible societies of the world is the one great nondenominational missionary enterprise. I suppose that you can discover the lines that run between denominations in the Bible, although I must say I have never been able to discover them. They have been drawn out by differences of temperament and point of view which I take leave to say are external to the Bible itself. And this process of division and diversity ought surely to be offset and reversed by the process which sends abroad, through the earth, this opportunity to drink directly at the sources of divine inspiration, without overmuch intervention and interpretation; to drink directly from the Word of God itself the suggestion which it inevitably bears to the human spirit, no matter where you touch it.

So, that to my mind, the colporteurs, the agents of the Bible Society, the men who, tramping through countrysides or traveling by every sort of conveyance in every sort of land, carry with them little cargoes of books containing the Word of God and, spreading them, seem like the shuttles in a great loom that is weaving the spirits of men together. A hundred years cannot accomplish that miracle, a hundred years cannot realize that vision. But if the weaving goes on, if the light continues to be spread, if men do not lose heart in this great ideal enterprise, it will some day be accomplished, and a light will shine upon the earth in which men cannot go astray.

T MS (WP, DLC).
[1] Wilson spoke on Sunday afternoon in the Continental Memorial Hall of the Daughters of the American Revolution. James Wood of Mt. Kisco, N. Y., president of the American Bible Society introduced Wilson. The Rev. Dr. William Fraser McDowell, Methodist Episcopal bishop resident in Chicago, also spoke.

From Edward Mandell House

Dear Governor: New York. May 7, 1916.

Here is a letter which I shall send to Sir Edward with your approval.[1] I think it will fetch a favorable reply. It should be sent without delay in order to get an answer back in time for the purpose you have in mind.

Please re-write it in part or in whole as seems to you best.

I know Sir Edward's mind in regard to this subject as well as I know your own and have merely outlined what we all three feel.

He may not wish a statement made concerning calling of a peace conference believing that it will stimulate Germany to a maximum effort during the summer because of the certainty of a conference in the Autumn. Nevertheless, it is better for you to have both proposals come together because of the effect upon our people.

In order to force Sir Edward ro [to] accept the one with the other I have intimated that he might lose the second if he does not take the first and I have also tried to alarm him as to public feeling in America.   Affectionately yours,   E. M. House

TLS (WP, DLC).
   ¹ It is printed as an Enclosure with WW to EMH, May 8, 1916.

A Memorial to the President of the United States by the American Union Against Militarism¹

[c. May 8, 1916]

Sir: The American Union Against Militarism does not stand against sane and reasonable "preparedness" nor for "peace at any price." But, profoundly convinced that the big army and navy programs, with their accompanying propaganda, are a menace to democracy, we adopted your suggestion to "hire large halls" and ascertain how the country stands upon this grave issue. In New York City, and in ten cities of the middle west we stated our convictions as to the issue between militarism and a democracy; before great meetings in Buffalo, Cleveland, Detroit, Chicago, Minneapolis, Des Moines, Kansas City, St. Louis, Cincinnati and Pittsburgh. These meetings all gave enthusiastic endorsement to the view that the so-called "preparedness" movement is not merely unnecessary but against public interest, that in its inception and propaganda it is a dangerous expression of class and national aggression. The response was everywhere the same.

But, Mr. President, our appeal to the country found us embarrassed by questions which we could not answer. Men came to us and said: "If the President feels constrained because of the international situation to make some concessions to the 'preparedness' movement, if he asks us to uphold him in making a considerable addition to the army and navy at this time, at what point may we count upon him to resist the fanaticism and the extremes to which the movement would drive us? When will the president say to the militarists: 'Thus far shall we go and no farther?' "

We told them, Mr. President, that we would ask you.

1. Recent political events have demonstrated the existence of a strong and widespread distrust of the movement which, in the guise of "preparedness," is rapidly introducing Old World militarist institutions into American life. It is a distrust which is seeking political expression and is breaking down party lones [lines] in its search. It feels itself faced by a conspiracy of class and press, and seems determined to free itself and the country from

that conspiracy. These American citizens crave some assurance from you that under your leadership we need fear no break with the splendid anti-militarist traditions of our past.

2. May we not hope that you will choose to tell the American people that you see, as clearly as they, that much of the so-called "preparedness" movement is rooted in motives sinister and even sordid?

3. The country is facing a shrewd, presistent propaganda in favor of compulsory military service. The mass of the people—if our experience is any guide—are apparently not misled by the adroit attempts to disguise this compulsory military service as Swiss or Australian. They know this country is not Switzerland or Austrian [Australia], and that what the proponenets [proponents] of conscription really want is a military organization comparable with that of Germany. We found a widespread desire for some expression from you as to your views upon this matter.

4. You have been widely and incorrectly pictured as demanding the greatest navy in the world. Millions of people view this with dismay. To them it means an armament race with Great Britain, involving enormous taxation, and at the end of the race a devastating and senseless war. We hope that you may find, some time, an opportunity to make your position clear.

In short, we come to you, not only as the President of the United States but also as the man who has stood most firmly for the maintenance of our democratic institutions. We bring to you the evidence we have found of an abiding American spirit, tenacious of democracy, that fears the militarist propaganda as an ass[a]ult upon democracy. These people are far less fearful of an invading army than they are of the enemy in our midst. East and West, and North and South, we find good true American citizens, wage earners, farmers, members of the professions, and business men, who are stirred by a common desire to join with those in our own country and elsewhere who stand for democracy and against militarism.

At this crisis they, and we, look to you to clarify the discussion and make articulate the fundamental principles of the country.

T MS (Lillian D. Wald Papers, NN).

1 Wilson met in the Oval Office for over an hour on May 8 with representatives of the American Union Against Militarism. Besides those mentioned in the next document, the delegates present included Paul Underwood Kellogg, editor of *The Survey*; John Lovejoy Elliott, teacher and social worker of New York; Alice Lewisohn, social worker and philanthropist of New York; Frederick Henry Lynch, Congregational minister and peace advocate of New York; Crystal Eastman, feminist leader and social investigator of New York; and Charles T. Hallinan of Chicago, the executive director of the Union. The American Union

Against Militarism was an outgrowth of a pacifist, antimilitarist movement among social workers, ministers, and social reformers centering around Lillian D. Wald's Henry Street Settlement in New York. For the origins of the Union, see C. Roland Marchand, *The American Peace Movement and Social Reform, 1898-1918* (Princeton, N. J., 1972), pp. 223-48.

A Colloquy with a Group of Antipreparedness Leaders

May 8, 1916

[Lillian D. Wald] Mr. Wilson, the American Union against Militarism was organized some months ago as a protest against the spirit of militarism, which some of us felt very deeply was imperiling the democracy of our country. We felt that it was in the intention to promote the expansion of the army and navy that the propaganda was started that went deep into our life—the life of the nation—that touched our schools, attempting conscription and exercises. And those true Americans, who would gladly lay down their lives for the America that is the America of democracy, the America of opportunity and the land of promise, believed that it was their duty to stand out against militarism insofar as we believed that it would imperil our democratic institutions.

There has been some humor[1] that has entered into it, too. And at this time we should like to give you a little light and tell you how numerous some of the manifestations come that seem to be numerous when they indicate the extent to which the humor has affected the people. And then, some weeks ago, some gentlemen who are here—good Americans, good sorts—gave up pressing and important engagements to go out into the West to express this view, this protest, to audiences in the big cities.[2] And I think that your allowing us to come to you in your time of great preoccupation shows how clearly you wish to know the minds of all the American people.

There are others who would have been glad to come here after the announcement, if we had not such short notice. Mr. Spreckels[3] could not be with us. Mr. Bigelow, chairman of the state constitutional convention,[4] had started on a tour on the same subject, and Mr. [blank][5] who was in a debate tonight, and

[1] That is, black bile.

[2] About this tour, see "Swinging Around the Circle Against Militarism," *The Survey*, XXXVI (April 22, 1916), 95-96.

[3] That is, Rudolph Spreckels of San Francisco.

[4] The Rev. Herbert Seely Bigelow, Congregational minister, prominent in reform causes in Cincinnati, and president of the Ohio Constitutional Convention of 1912.

[5] Either Allan Louis Benson, Socialist presidential candidate in 1916, or Scott Nearing, Dean of the College of Arts and Sciences at Toledo, Ohio, University.

therefore could not come along. Mr. Maurer,[6] who has spoken eloquently for the laboring man, and Mr. Max Eastman,[7] who is here, will represent him.

We are here, frankly, to give back to you a report of that tour. We have prepared a little statement[8] which we think represents the thought of the committee, not only the committee but the affiliations in with us—a large committee of the laboring people in America of great importance. And, if it is your wish, Mr. President, I would speak, but it came to me after the rush of the morning began. I have only glanced at it.

(Reads the report here.)

Mr. President, would you prefer at this point to discuss this, or would you like to hear what the [people present have to say?]

[Wilson] I would very much like to hear the speeches.

[Berle][9] Mr. President, I am just about to present the physical features of this trip, which we think is important, that stood against our cause. This was a group of private citizens, unheralded by any widely known organization, having no particular grip upon the agencies of publicity, and relying only upon the sanity and soundness of the cause.

We began our meetings in Carnegie Hall, where we were said to have had between 3,000 and 4,000 people present at a meeting which was said to be as enthusiastic as almost any demonstration ever held in New York City or in Boston. We had [a meeting] in the Music Hall in Buffalo, and they closed the doors because all the standing room was [taken up] inside. And in the city of Cleveland, on a night when there was a driving snowstorm, we had 2,500 people in the Armory. In the city of Detroit, on Sunday afternoon, we had the opera house filled—said to contain 3,500 people. And Mr. Pinchot[10] and myself spoke, too; while Mr. Lynch spoke to 1,500 people in the audience, and I addressed another audience substantially filled, except the top row of people in the topmost gallery. In Minneapolis, we had the auditorium packed— said to contain 4,000 people—while Mr. Herbert Bigelow addressed 500 people on the outside. At the same time, we addressed large meetings at St. Paul and also at the University of Minnesota. In the city of Des Moines, we had 3,500 people in the Auditorium.

Nearing had been dismissed from the University of Pennsylvania in 1915 for supporting the I.W.W. Both Benson and Nearing had participated in the midwestern tour.

[6] James Hudson Maurer, president of the Pennsylvania State Federation of Labor and Socialist member of the Pennsylvania legislature.

[7] Max Eastman, poet, lecturer, and editor of *The Masses*, a Socialist monthly.

[8] This memorial has just been printed.

[9] The Rev. Dr. Adolf Augustus Berle, Congregational minister, author, and, at this time, director of the Berle Home Correspondence School of Boston.

[10] That is, Amos Richards Eno Pinchot.

In Kansas City, we had 5,000 in the Coliseum—a most remarkable meeting. In St. Louis, we had the Odeon filled.

I mention these places because you, yourself, are familiar with some of them and know exactly what these figures mean. We had the Odeon, said to contain 3,500, filled. In Cincinnati, there was a meeting of 2,500. I was not there because I had to go to Pittsburgh. At Pittsburgh X.[11]

Mr. President, I have been twenty-five years in public life. I believe that no unofficial, unheralded group of Americans ever made such a journey in order to ascertain the national, unbiased, sound judgment of the American people, ever met with so unstinting, so clear, so uncomplicated a judgment upon a public question as this tour revealed. It is my judgment, after twenty-five years of public experience as a clergyman and college professor, that no appeal which could be made could, in that territory, under these conditions, more clearly or more soundly verify the substantial truth of our claim that our country, not only does not want war, but that it does not want the militarism which is the provocation, as we believe, of war. And they, in my judgment, believe that the enormous proposed vast increase in armaments in the army and navy are the indication of an invading militarism—undemocratic, unsound, un-American, and threatening to the fundamental institutions of the land.

[Miss Wald] Mr. Pinchot.

[Pinchot] Mr. President, we found throughout the western cities that we visited, although particularly in New York, a surprising broadening of this military feeling that is going through the country, which to us seemed very important and quite dangerous, and that was the invasion of the schools by militarism. In Ohio, in Michigan, and in Minnesota and New York, we found that to be particularly true. Now those states—the three last states, the three middle western states, haven't come as far to date as New York has come. In New York, we feel that the feeling for militarism has become almost irrational and that they are acting there, in the legislature, particularly, as if the country was already in extremis, almost or at least facing the great national crisis of war now. There are before the Governor today two bills—the Welsh bill and the Slater bills,[12] the Senate and House bills, which have already been passed, waiting for signature. And those bills actually provide for compulsory military training at camps for

---

[11] One of the speakers at Pittsburgh was James H. Maurer.

[12] Introduced by Assemblyman Clarence F. Welsh and State Senator George Atwood Slater, both Republicans. The description of the bills given below is accurate. They were signed by Governor Charles Seymour Whitman on May 15. See the *New York Times*, May 16, 1916.

all boys from the ages of sixteen to nineteen. These camps are to be situated in fair grounds, suburban fair grounds, and to be under the charge of officers of the National Guard. The term of training is about fixed—a maximum of six weeks. The officers are to be, in turn, in charge of a commission of which the commanding general of the National Guard, General O'Ryan,[13] is the head, one member of the Board of Regents, and another commissioner, and a representative of the Governor, appointed by the Governor at any time.

Now, we feel that this is going further than anything we know. This is going further than any European country has ever gone in military training. We feel that it is child conscription, and that no crisis exists or is foreshadowed in this country which would justify such an extreme excursion into the militarism of the old world and beyond it. We feel that it is immensely important that children, at a time when their imagination is most fertile and most impressionable, should not be subject to the strong and more mature minds of men in the National Guard, who are, in their way, special tutors while they are in camp and who will tend to produce in the impressionable minds of these children a psychology to settle all things by force rather than by the use of the mind.

We feel that our children should grow up in a right educational system, in which the National Guard should not play an overprominent part. And we hope very much that this can be in some way checked throughout the other states, although it has gone so far in New York already that we can't hope to check it.

[Wilson] You expect it to be signed?

[Pinchot] The Governor has stated twice that he would sign it.

[Miss Wald] Mr. McSparran[14] is a farmer. Mr. McSparran.

[McSparran] I am deeply grateful, Mr. President, for the opportunity of bringing to you the attitude of the farmers. I am a farmer myself and have farmed actually for twenty years, and have only quit it since the duties which take so much time in our organization.

I want to say that I have felt very deeply about this from the beginning of this discussion more than a year ago, and went to the National Grange last November, where the delegates of thirty-two states gathered together at a national meeting. And we had the feeling from our—we can't get it from the papers—that there would be quite a strong sentiment in favor of militarism. And we went there determined, if possible, not to allow the National

[13] John Francis O'Ryan, lawyer of New York and major general in command of the New York National Guard.

[14] John Aldus McSparran, farmer of Furniss, Pa., master of the Pennsylvania State Grange.

Grange to cook up a message of propaganda. To my great surprise, when I came in there . . . there was absolutely no evidence at all among all those representatives of the thirty-two states of farming people that there was any feeling of that kind. And they adopted very strong resolutions there—three—the special points that involved a long resolution, comprehensive resolution, upon the subject covering the three points against an increase in the army and any material increase in the navy.[15]

[Wilson] Any increase in the army?

[McSparran] Any increase in the army. An immaterial increase in the navy and in favor of making our own munitions, taking away the profit that will come from this propaganda and giving it to state institutions in this country; and then, if possible, the establishment, until such time as the general peace of the world shall be given more particularly to arbitration and things of that kind, the establishment, if possible, of an international police force that can help to prevent situations that would have to be settled by war. . . .

And the papers have never given us any publicity upon that.

And so I feel very grateful today that I am able to come to you and give you that bit of experience, because it certainly must impress you, as it did me, that the rank and file of our people do not have the hysteria that our newspapers seem to reflect, and that they do not feel that they should have these undemocratic institutions fixed upon them.

[Miss Wald] Mr. Maurer, who has been on the tour and was a speaker.

[15] The delegates adopted three main resolutions offered by the "Committee on Peace": (1) All the large nations from which the United States has anything to fear whatever are busily slaughtering each other and will be in a pitiable and helpless condition at the end of the war. "And it is against those helpless nations that selfishness and men who have lost their heads and been carried off their feet are crying out for preparedness. This world's war will close with public sentiment against war as a means of settling disputes." (2) The United States, separated by wide oceans far from Europe and Asia, enjoy a security that European and Asian nations do not enjoy. (3) Preparedness that will make us efficient and strong in time of peace as well as war is a wise policy. However, militarism had destroyed Rome and Spain and is now destroying the nations of Europe. The $5 billions contemplated to be spent on the army and navy would build 1,000,000 miles of macadamized roads in the United States. "With such a road system an unlimited number of men could be transferred in motor cars and concentrated quickly where needed."

The committee offered additional resolutions favoring governmental manufacture of all munitions; opposing any increase in the standing army and "any material increase in the navy"; approving Wilson's efforts to maintain peace; favoring nationalization of all "transportation lines" and all munitions factories during wartime; and favoring the establishment of "an international police force to be contributed to by all adhering nations and to be under the direction and control of such international Court of Control as the adhering nations may decide." *Journal of Proceedings of the National Grange of the Patrons of Husbandry, Forty-Ninth Annual Session, Oakland, California 1915* (Concord, N. H., n.d.), pp. 167-69.

[Maurer] Mr. Eastman.

[Eastman] It is a special privilege, Mr. President, to take the place of an official representative of organized labor. Mr. Maurer also can tell you of the workingman's—the so-called common man's—opposition to any increase in the military aspects of our civilization. As you know, the working people have no distinct voice in the press. Papers are not published for them. They are not published for them. Therefore, it is only by noting certain rather insignificant incidents that their wishes can be taken allowance of in one or two of these incidents. The United Mine Workers, which is the biggest labor union in the country and perhaps the greatest in the world, unanimously adopted the report of their president that not only were they opposed, but it was their belief, that organized labor all over the country was opposed to the whole preparedness program.[16] And when you get a response from other classes to the proposal to increase our military branch, it misleads you as to the true sentiment of the country. If it could happen, by some extraordinary accident, for instance, that, instead of addressing the Daughters of the American Revolution, or the Women's Section of the Navy League, you had come to New York to address such a representative body as the 60,000 boat workers now on strike, I am sure you would get a response far different from this military excitement which seems to have possessed our upper and leisure classes since the European war, and more particularly since the profits of the European war began to accumulate.

[Miss Wald] Mr. President, I think I would add to Mr. Eastman's words so that these interviews do not mislead you. That may be. At our Des Moines meeting, Mr. President, we had this "St. Louis" experience. It was not, of course, without significance. It was very difficult for us to hold the meeting, because the representatives of the National Guard resorted—improvised a bowling match in order to prevent the speakers being heard. And two or three times in the course of the meeting we asked them to desist. That was hopeless. Though it was to the interest of law and order

16 Both President John P. White and Secretary-Treasurer William Green declared, at the opening session of the biennial convention of the United Mine Workers of America in Indianapolis on January 18, 1916, that the workingmen of the nation were opposed to the preparedness agitation. White denounced war and said that he was "fully convinced that the men of labor are unalterably opposed to the whole scheme of preparedness, which means war." He added that it was to be "earnestly hoped that the plans to make our country an armed camp which may be used to extend commercialism abroad and exploit labor at home will be defeated." *Proceedings of the Twenty-Fifth Consecutive and Second Biennial Convention of the United Mine Workers of America* . . . (2 vols., Indianapolis, 1916), I, 90-91.

not to prevent those speakers from gaining any hearing whatever, they succeeded.

We feel this, Mr. President, and feel this very deeply, that our organization is more than the American Union against Militarism, that being our known title, our technical title. But we are a union, and we represent, we believe, we have come to believe, a citizens' constituency throughout the Middle West, which we touched at ten points, and which constituency is fanatically in favor of the preservation of the ideals of American life, of democratic life. We sensed the spirit of the Middle West, and we found a deep-seated resentment against the whole business of [this preparedness propaganda]. . . .

Things like this, I think, Mr. President, represent a very definite conviction that there has been an absolutely indefensible participation by officers of the American army and navy in the work of army and navy propaganda. There is the feeling that the officers of the army and navy are not doing the bidding of the commands of the government but are attempting to impose policies upon us.

They are our arms, and we are their will.

In the next place, we are greatly disturbed about the attempt, and probably by now in operation, to introduce military training into the public schools, about the unblushing agitation on behalf of compulsory military service. To think, Mr. President—you know better than the rest of us—it could not have been mentioned aloud two years ago without exciting derision and contempt on the part of all sane people who believe, who truly believe, in democracy. Then we feel, Mr. President, as a result of all this militaristic talk, that the attention of the masses is being concentrated upon the militarists' method of settling our international questions, such as you are dealing with, rather than on the possibility of such adjustment and conciliation as, after all, we ought to be bent upon making possible.

We have noted, if we are not mistaken, the attempt to rewrite the entire civil service bill, giving, as you know—I think it's in the terms of the Chamberlain bill—certain preferences, most significant preferences, to men who have served under arms, and who are now civilians. I am sure that it has been said by individuals, as it has been said in the press, that the Middle West doesn't care about the whole problem, because the Middle West is safe from invasion, and because the Middle West would not gain the financial rewards which a large arms program would produce.

I feel, Mr. President, that you feel, as we do, resentment at the canard that the Middle West is any less patriotic than the rest of the country. We hold that it is not true—the notion that it is safe from invasion. What I think the Middle West has come to understand, Mr. President, is the opposite. Certain contributory motives, for example. Oh, we have no hesitation in saying to you the part originally played by the most numerous of the munitions manufacturers, to use the polite term in this phrase. The Middle West understands the capital that has been attempted to be made by the partisan-mongers—by a number of gentlemen who apparently would not be unwilling to reside themselves upon the altar of the White House for the next few years. There are forces —and the Middle West, we definitely fear, understands that because of the militaristic agitation, Mr. President—there are forces which are definitely and are repeatedly in some places frankly hostile to our institutions of democracy. And that is why we have come to you—to show that the Middle West does not care about an invasion. What America or the Middle West is rightly concerned with, Mr. President, is the invasion of America by a spirit un-American, by a spirit alien to the soul of America. The Middle West is no more opposed, as we have seen it and dealt with its representatives, to a larger army and navy, I mean, what we regard to be a sane, reasonable, forward-looking preparedness program.

But what it is concerned about, too, is this—and we are deeply concerned about it, Mr. President, as we know that you are—we feel that the acceptance by the American people now of a big army or a big navy program would simply neutralize and annul the moral power which our nation ought, through you, to exercise when the day of peace negotiations has come.

I think that moral power has always counted, and, without making any new, explicit references, such as would be confusing, that moral power still counts. We have had one recent revelation of the definiteness with which that moral power counts. We are opposed to the militarists. We feel that we have the right to call it a militarist rather than a preparedness program because we want to go—we want to go into the peace negotiations, so that we go morally in such a way that we shall have a part with our hands clean—with our hands clean, with our hands undefiled. We want to count in justice to ourselves and in goodwill to the world. We want America, yours and our own, to count for the things worthwhile, for the things of America.

[Wilson] I want to say this, Miss Wald: I don't think I have been deceived about the mind of the country. I have never dreamed for a moment that America, as a whole, or its rank and file, had got any military enthusiasm or any militaristic spirit. And I think it is very necessary, in order that we should work this thing out wisely, that we should carefully discriminate between reasonable preparation and militarism, because, if you use the two words interchangeably, then, of course, the reasonable things that we ought to do take on a wrong and sinister appearance, and we seem to be working for the wrong things, when we are, in reality, working only for the right things or the necessary things that are unavoidable in the circumstances.

I think it would be a disservice not to recognize that there is a point of reasonable preparation, and that you can go to that point without changing the spirit of the country or violating the traditions of the country, considering that the traditions of the country have not been those of a military helplessness, though they have been those of a distinct antimilitarism.

The currents of opinion, or rather the bodies of opinion, in this country are very hard to assess. For example, Mayor Mitchel of New York City and a group of gentlemen associated with him made a tour not unlike that which you made, and had meetings. And they came back and reported in the most enthusiastic terms a unanimous opinion, not for universal military service, but very distinctly for universal military training, which, of course, is a very different thing.

Now, I quite see the danger that Mr. Pinchot perceives in the laws that he referred to, because they seem to associate military training with public authority and to draw that training into some sort of connection with military organization. It is not inconsistent with American traditions that everybody should know how to shoot and take care of himself. On the contrary, that is distinctly implied in our bills of rights, where the power or the right to carry arms is reserved to all of us. And there is no use carrying arms if you don't know what to do with them.

I should say that it is not inconsistent with the traditions of the country that the people know how to take care of themselves. But it is inconsistent with the traditions of the counry that their knowledge of arms should be used by a governmental organization which would make and organize a great army subject to orders, to do what a particular group of men might, at the time, think it was best to have them do. That is the militarism of Europe, where a few persons can determine what an armed nation is to do. That is what I understand militarism to be. But a nation acquainted with arms is not a militaristic nation, unless there is somebody who can, by an order, determine what they shall all do with that force. So I think we ought to be very careful not to let these different things seem as if they were the same.

Now, when you come to ask how much preparation you can make, that, surely, is a matter of judgment, and I don't see how you can find any absolute standard upon which to determine that question. Take the mere matter of Mr. Eastman's suggestion that we might have some arrangement by which the border of Mexico can be patrolled.[17] There aren't men enough in the existing American army to patrol that border. That is the mere physical fact. We have got them all from the Philippines and everywhere else. There aren't enough men. And when men are at sixes and sevens in a neighboring country, as in Mexico, and everybody is apparently a law unto himself, there aren't men enough to safeguard that border. And, yet, it is obviously the right thing to do to keep the disorders of one country from flowing over to disturb the peace of another country. That is not militarism, that is necessity.

So I don't need to tell you that I am just as much opposed to militarism as any man living. I think it is a deadly thing to get it into the spirit of the nation. And I don't think there is the slightest danger of its getting into the spirit of this nation, only I have to determine a very practical problem. I have got to determine how large an army is not unreasonable for the United States. The largest army proposed—that of the Chamberlain bill—is 250,000 men, and, as compared with any European standard, that is extremely small in a nation of one hundred million. So that, unless you regard it as a tendency, unless you regard it as a prophecy, there is nothing extravagant in an army of 250,000 men, though I think that is more than we need.

(Rabbi Wise[18] remarked that this was an increase of 150 per cent.)

[Wilson] When you increase from something that is wholly inadequate, you are not increasing to something that is extravagant, if you are increasing 200 per cent or 150 per cent. But I am not now arguing for any number. I think that is too many. I am merely saying the point at which you stop is a point of practical necessity, or convenience, or any word you want to use about it, and not a matter of the principle, provided you go at the thing and, as far as you do go, with the right purpose and the right spirit.

The traditions of the American people have always been for a very powerful navy, because they seem to think that, if you can keep your fighting men at sea, they are not in danger of disturbing

17 Swem did not record this suggestion in his shorthand notes.
18 That is, Stephen Samuel Wise.

your peace of mind or the character of the national life. But, whatever may be the reasons, we have never been jealous of the navy, even in our most sensitive moments about threats.

[Wise] Haven't we increased it tremendously?

[Wilson] Not tremendously. You see, our tasks have increased tremendously. The amount of sea that we have found it necessary to police, to take care of our distant possessions, and be ready for exigencies of the most ordinary kind, quite independently of a foreign war, has increased tremendously. So that I earnestly hope we may not jeopardize reasonable protection in our effort to avoid militarism. And I don't think it is going to need any very great effort to avoid militarism, because I quite agree with you that there we have got the sentiment of a great body of people behind us, and that, after all, is all that we care about.

Now, as to the general thing we are all most profoundly interested in, and that is peace. We want the peace of the world. Now, I don't know, I can't speak about what I am going to speak about with any degree of confidence—I don't suppose any man can. But a nation which, by the standards of other nations, however mistaken those standards may be, is regarded as helpless, is apt in general counsel to be regarded as negligible. And when you go into a conference to establish foundations for the peace of the world, you have got to go in on a basis intelligible to the people you are conferring with.

[Berle] Mr. President, may I venture at this point to give you this information? I was in London in 1895, as Chaplain of the Ancient Company, when the company visited London—an artillery company—and of course that was at the time of the tremendous complications in Europe about Venezuela, and a great deal was made about that visit at that time. You remember, when Mr. Cleveland wrote the Venezuelan message. I was at a dinner, at which I may say here there were men like General Sir Edward [Arthur Gore][19] and other men of said rank and character. And it was said at that dinner, in my hearing, by those gentlemen, that if America at that time had had a great navy it would unquestionably have led to war, because it would have been regarded as an attempt at bullying. But at that moment it was said that the very fact that America did not have a great navy showed that the element of threat was automatically eliminated and placed it entirely on the moral issues involved in the matter and gave that message.

[Wilson] But this is not the year 1895. This is a year of madness. It is a year of excitement, more profound than the world has

[19] Inspector General of Remounts in the British army.

ever known before. All the world is seeing red. No standard we have ever had obtains any longer. Now, in these circumstances, it is America's duty to keep her head and yet have a very hard head—to know the facts of the world and to act on those facts with restraint, with reasonableness, without any kind of misleading excitement, and yet with energy. And all that I am maintaining is this—that we must take such steps as are necessary for our own safety as against the imposition of the standards of the rest of the world upon us. Now, we have undertaken very much more than the safety of the United States. We have undertaken to keep what we regard as demoralizing and hurtful European influences out of this hemisphere. And that means that, if the world undertakes, as we all hope it will undertake, a joint effort to keep the peace, it will expect us to play our proportional part in manifesting the force which is going to rest back of that. Now, in the last analysis, the peace of society is obtained by force. And when action comes, it comes by opinion. But back of that opinion is the ultimate application of force, when the greater body of opinion says to the lesser body of opinion, "We may be wrong, but you have to live under our direction for the time being, until you are more numerous than we are." That is what I understand it amounts to.

Now, let us suppose that we have formed a family of nations, and that family of nations says, "The world is not going to have any more wars of this sort without at least the duty at first, though, to go through certain processes to show whether there is anything in the case or not." And if you say we shall not have any war, you have got to have the force to make that "shall" bite. The rest of the world, if America takes part in this thing, will have the right to expect from her that she contributes her element of force to the general understanding. Surely that is not a militaristic ideal. That is a very practical, possible ideal.

[Miss Wald] Would that not, Mr. President, logically lead to a limitless expansion of our contribution?

[Wilson] Well, logically, Miss Wald, but I haven't the least regard for logic. What I mean to say is, I think in such affairs as we are now discussing, the circumstances are the logic. I remember a sentence of Burke which runs something to this effect: "If you ask me wherein the wisdom of a certain policy consists, I will say that it consists of the circumstances of that policy."

[Miss Wald] Agreeable philosophy.

[Wilson] I don't think it's merely agreeable. I mean just this, just as you can't suggest any absolute standard by which you should determine the number of men you should have in the army of the United States any more than I can. Logically, to defend an enormous territory such as ours, you should have an almost limitless armament, but practically, you don't have to have, because you have a moral force that takes its place. And so I say that is the reason I meant I didn't have any regard for logic in questions of this sort. It is not a matter which you reason out. It is a matter which you deduce from the circumstances. Now, quite opposite to anything you fear, I believe that, if the world ever comes to combine its force for the purpose of maintaining peace, the individual contributions of each nation will be much less, necessarily, naturally less, than they would be in other circumstances, and that all they will have to do will be to contribute moderately and not indefinitely.

[Miss Wald] The question of exact limits is a—I am speaking for myself, not my associates—the navy seems committed to a policy; the navy seems to be committed to a policy of huge increase.

[Wilson] Just let me say that there really hasn't been any change, any material change. The only difference is this: We have been going on, from year to year, making certain additions determined upon that year, all along looking forward to a series of years. Now, all that we have done is to evolve the rest of the program. It is not altered in its scale to any considerable extent.

[Miss Wald] But it doesn't suit the Navy League people.

[Wilson] I am not thinking about them.

[Miss Wald] The thought I wanted to leave, Mr. President, is this: Some of the people who are very confidently speaking for themselves may have very definite reasons for picking out some special cause for alarm, but there is obviously an attempt to stampede the country.

[Wilson] Yes, but it is not working.

[Miss Wald] Mr. President, there is just one point in your remarks that I can't let go unchallenged. One thing that surprised me in what you have said is your serene confidence that this country can never succumb to the spirit of militarism. It seems to me that the evidence we have that it can and may succumb is overwhelming. That a great section of our democracy like New York State could pass two laws like the Welsh and Slater bills for military training in the schools there, and no danger of invasion threatens this country, it seems to me to go all the way. We are who we are—democratic to the heart and can never be touched by militarism! Well, it is like putting your head in the sand.

[Wilson] Well, but you have just been bringing up a body of evidence that we will not be invaded by this spirit.

[Miss Wald] We want to make you feel that there is a body that will stand by you if you stand against that.

[Wilson] Now, isn't there an element of probability in this? Isn't it probable that the sentiment which permitted that to be done in New York was really a sentiment for universal training and not a sentiment for universal service? I have tried, in what I have said, to point to the difference between these. I don't think the spirit of this country is hostile to very widespread training, provided it doesn't lock people into a military organization and make it subject to autocratic use.

[Wise] Is it possible to avoid the sequel in the long run?

[Wilson] It may not be. That is the danger, and apparently they have gone a little too far in this case.

[Wise] Can I suggest—just offer a suggestion? The thing that appealed to me in that relation was this, that in military training you strike at one of the fundamental principles of democracy, in that a person, to be militarily trained, is accustomed to do what the other fellow tells him, without any particular action on his own part, and without any decision on his own part. But the fundamental principles of democracy recognize that the sovereign citizen acts on his own initiative, upon the decision of his own judgment. Now, if our boys and girls, through this military training, are to be taught to take some other fellow's idea, and to follow implicitly some other fellow's direction, can't you conceive of a condition of that kind that will immediately throw itself into our politics, that will create a condition that will ruin and undermine our insitutions?

[Wilson] Yes, if you, at the time you do that, provide—set somebody up whom they have got to obey. But suppose we had widespread training, with no authority over the man in training; he merely volunteers? Don't you see what I mean? He is not thereby bound to an organization in which he looks to some particular person to give him orders. That would be organization.

[Wise] I have never seen any system of training that did not take in as a part of its life the military idea of discipline, of obedience.

[Wilson] Only for the six weeks at a time. During the rest of the year nobody—you see what I mean?

[Miss Wald] We feel that even six weeks in the year, you might say its mere tendency, will have its effect upon our citizenry.

[Wilson] You remind me of the story of the Irishman who had a million dollars left him. He took a room somewhere and asked the boy to call him at seven o'clock in the morning and tell him that the boss wanted him. When he was called, he said "Tell the boss 'Go to hell,' I don't have to come." That was his idea of liberty!

[An Unknown Person] Mr. President, may I ask a question? How can the practical details in your talk about the maintenance of peace differ from the ideal which has prevailed in Europe all along in the matter of the piling up of arms?

[Wilson] What do you mean? It differs very radically. The ideal of the typical military nation has been Germany. She must, within years, be so armed and powerful that she could take care of her interests as against all the rest of the world.

[An Unknown Person] They have always said that they stood for peace.

[Wilson] I know. Now, for each nation to undertake to make—go to a clash of interests against the rest of the world—is certainly a very difficult program. And for the combined nations to say that no nation attacks another contrary to treaty or international investigation, surely that is very different matter. In a proportion of armament, that is radically different.

[An Unknown Person] Except that assumes at first that an international agreement is a thing just to be secured. It assumes—

[Wilson] That is true. If it is secure this time, it will not be secure without being armed. It will be secure by the profound—

[An Unknown Person] Mr. President, may I ask in regard to what you were saying before whether you do believe in universal compulsory training?

[Wilson] I didn't say I believed in it. In my judgment, to use the phrase of a friend, my mind is to let on the subject. I would say merely that it is not contrary to the spirit of American traditions.

[An Unknown Person] Mr. President, it seems to me that we have got to recognize the fact that we are just like everybody else, and that we are not the least bit less aggressive than any other nation. We are potentially more aggressive, because our economic organizations are more active, more powerful, in reaching out and grasping for the world's trade. The organization of the international corporation is one of the great facts of modern history. And it seems to me that, if you hitch up this tremendously aggressive spirit of grabbing for the trade of the world with a tendency to back up that trade, there is going to be produced an aggressive nationalism in trade which would—

[Wilson] It might, very easily, unless some check was placed upon it by some international arrangement which we hope for.

[An Unknown Person] If they get the educational thing with it.

[Wilson] I quite see your point.

JRT transcript (WC, NjP) of CLSsh (C. L. Swem Coll., NjP).

From Robert Lansing, with Enclosure

PERSONAL AND CONFIDENTIAL:

My dear Mr. President: Washington May 8, 1916.

After returning home last evening I took your draft of an answer to the German note and went over it with considerable care. I found on reading it that the same impression I had when we discussed it last evening remained with me—namely, that it expressed satisfaction and gratification, which do not appeal to me. While I think our note should be polite I feel we should omit any expression of relief on having avoided a break with Germany. I also thought the note was longer than was necessary and that it should be limited as far as possible.

With these ideas in mind I made another draft of an answer which I am enclosing,[1] together with your original draft. If final decision can be reached early today I will have Gerard instructed to deliver the note and at the same time have it given to the press for publication tomorrow morning. I hope this can be done, for I feel we should delay as little as possible in the matter.

Faithfully yours,   Robert Lansing

TLS (SDR, RG 59, 763.72/2654, DNA).
[1] It is printed as an Enclosure with the following letter.

E N C L O S U R E

Handed me by the Prest.
May 7/16 RL
The White House.

The Government of the United States notes with satisfaction that the Imperial German Government "is prepared to do its utmost to confine the operations of the war for the rest of its duration to the fighting forces of the belligerants" and that it is determined to impose upon all its commanders at sea the limitations of recognized international law upon which the Government of the United States has felt it to be its duty to insist; and it is very gratifying to the Government of the United States that the Imperial German Government has been prompted to take this action not only by its recognition of the binding force of the principles of international law involved but also by its desire to perpetuate the friendship which has so long subsisted between the two nations and by its reluctance to do anything that might bring on "the great doom" which would seem to "threaten the entire civilized world should this cruel and sanguinary war be extended and prolonged." Throughout the trying months which have elapsed since the German note of February, 1915, the Government of the United States has been guided and restrained by the same motives in its patient and persistent efforts to bring the critical questions which have since then arisen between the two Governments to an amicable settlement. The Government of the United States will confidently rely upon a scrupulous execution henceforth of the now altered policy of the German Government and the prevention thereby of further danger of an interruption of the friendly relations of the two Governments.

The Government of the United States feels it necessary to add that it takes it for granted that the Imperial German Government does not intend to make the maintenance of the policy which it now announces contingent upon the course or result of diplomatic negotiations between the Government of the United States and any other government now involved in the existing war, notwithstanding the fact that the language used in the note of the Imperial German Government of the fourth of May might seem in certain passages to be susceptible of that construction. The Government of the United States cannot for a moment entertain the suggestion that the rights of its citizens upon the high seas as affected by the acts of German naval commanders should in any way or in any degree be made contingent upon the attitude or action of any other government with regard to the rights of neutrals and non-combatants. Responsibility in such matters is single, not joint or conditional, absolute, not relative.

WWT MS (WP, DLC).

To Robert Lansing, with Enclosure

My dear Mr. Secretary,   The White House. 8 May, 1916.
    You are probably right about cutting out all "satisfaction," and I am quite content to have the note go as you have amended it. I am returning it so that it may be sent at once.
    In haste,   Faithfully Yours,   W.W.

WWTLI (SDR, RG 59, 763.72/2662, DNA).

E N C L O S U R E[1]

May 8, 1916.
DRAFT OF ANSWER TO GERMAN NOTE OF MAY 4, 1916.
The note of the Imperial German Government under date of May 4, 1916, has received careful consideration by the Govern-

ment of the United States. It is especially noted, as indicating the purpose of the Imperial Government as to the future, that it "is prepared to do its utmost to confine the operations of the war for the rest of its duration to the fighting forces of the belligerents," and that it is determined to impose upon all its commanders at sea the limitations of the recognized rules of international law upon which the Government of the United States has insisted. Throughout the months⟨,⟩ which have elapsed since the Imperial Government announced, on February 4th, 1915, its submarine policy, now happily abandoned, the Government of the United States has been *constantly* guided and restrained by ⟨the⟩ motives of friendship in its patient efforts to bring to an amicable settlement the critical questions arising from that policy. Accepting the *Imperial Government's* declaration of *its* abandonment of the policy⟨,⟩ which has so seriously menaced the good relations between the two countries, the Government of the United States will rely upon a scrupulous execution henceforth of the now altered policy of the Imperial Government, ⟨which⟩ *such as* will remove the principal danger to an interruption of the good relations existing between the United States and Germany.

The Government of the United States feels it necessary to state that it takes it for granted that the Imperial German Government does not intend to imply that the maintenance of its newly announced policy is in any way contingent upon the course or result of diplomatic negotiations between the Government of the United States and any other belligerent Government, notwithstanding the fact that certain passages in the Imperial Government's note of the fourth instant might appear to be susceptible of that construction. In order, however, to avoid any possible misunderstanding, the Government of the United States notifies the Imperial Government that it cannot for a moment entertain, much less discuss, a suggestion that respect by German naval authorities for the rights of citizens of the United States upon the high seas should in any way or in the slightest degree be made contingent upon the conduct of any other government affecting the rights of neutrals and non-combatants. Responsibility in such matters is single, not joint; absolute, not relative.

T MS (SDR, RG 59, 763.72/2654, DNA).
1 Words in angle brackets deleted by Wilson; words in italics added by him.

To Edward Mandell House, with Enclosure

Dearest Friend,   The White House. 8 May, 1916.

I hasten to return the enclosed with my approval. You could even heighten the emphasis with which you warn Sir Edward that the sympathy of this country is apt to be alienated from Great Britain in a very significant degree in the immediate future and its peace sentiment become more and more insistent.[1] It is much better for Great Britain that we should initiate the final movement than that the Pope should.

Will you pardon my correcting the last word in the letter?[2] In haste,   Affectionately Yours,   Woodrow Wilson

A reply goes to Germany to-night of which I believe you will approve.

TLS (E. M. House Papers, CtY).
[1] The letter, actually sent as a telegram (EMH to E. Grey, May 10, 1916), is printed as an Enclosure with EMH to WW, May 9, 1916 (first letter of that date).
[2] House had written "with war regards."

ENCLOSURE

Edward Mandell House to Sir Edward Grey

Dear Sir Edward: New York. May 7, 1916.

There is an increasingly insistent demand here for the President to take some action towards bringing the war to a close. Germany will foster this sentiment and if she ceases her submarine warfare and England continues the blockade, one can foresee a change of feeling towards Germany.

Will it not be said that the Allies are fighting more for the purpose of punishing Germany than for any good results that may come from further loss of blood and treasure? May it not also be said that Germany is now willing to concede as much as can be forced from her by another year of war?

If the President is to serve humanity in a large way should he not take some steps now rather than wait until the opportunity becomes less fortunate? If he could intimate that in the near future he contemplated calling a conference looking to peace, he could at the same time suggest to our people that the United States ought to be willing to do her share towards maintaining peace when it comes.

He could point the way by which this could be done. That is by a general covenant of the powers to guarantee peace along the lines you and I have so often discussed and which you expressed in your letter to me of September 22, 1915.[1]

The nations subscribing to this covenant should pledge themselves to side against any power breaking a treaty. The convention should formulate rules for the purpose of limiting armaments both on sea and land and for the purpose of making warfare more humane to the actual participants and safe-guarding the lives and property of neutrals and non-combatants.

The convention should bid the signatory powers to side against any nation "which refused in case of dispute to adopt some other method of settlement than that of war."

For reasons I cannot go into here it is important and necessary for the President to make this statement, if he makes it at all, before the first of June and I would appreciate your cabling me upon receipt of this your opinion as to the advisibility of such a move.

Unless it is done now, the opportunity may be forever lost. You could understand better why if I could explain verbally.

With warm regards and good wishes, I am,

Sincerely yours,

TCL (E. M. House Papers, CtY).

[1] E. Grey to EMH, Sept. 22, 1915, printed in n. 3 to the extract from the House diary, Oct. 15, 1915, Vol. 35.

To William Calhoun McDonald

My dear Governor: The White House May 8, 1916.

Information has reached me through the Department of Justice that Ensevio Reuteria, Paurino Garcia, Jose Rodriquez, Francisco Alverez, Jose Ranzel, Juan Castillo and Juan Sanchez, followers of Villa, who were present and participating in the recent raid at Columbus, New Mexico, having been captured by the forces of the United States under the command of General Pershing, sent back to Columbus, New Mexico, and by the commanding officer of that place turned over to the local civil authorities, have been brought to trial in the State Courts of New Mexico, convicted of murder in the first degree, and sentenced to death, their execution being set for May 19th instant.

Would it not seem, in view of existing conditions, that the execution of these men should be deferred pending the active field operations for the capture of the principal offender, Villa, whose case should be disposed of along similar lines? In view, too, of the highly excited conditions on the border and among the Mexican people, may not grossly misrepresented and exaggerated accounts of the execution be circulated and lead to acts of so-called reprisal being committed upon American citizens resident in Mexico?

I respectfully request that you consider the propriety of repriev-
ing these men for a reasonable period in order that their present
execution may not complicate the existing conditions in the
manner stated above.

Sincerely yours, Woodrow Wilson.

CCL (WDR, RG 94, AGO Document File, No. 2638774, DNA).

From Robert Lansing, with Enclosure

PERSONAL AND CONFIDENTIAL:

My dear Mr. President: Washington May 8, 1916.

I enclose for your consideration a suggested comment on the
German reply, which, if you think advisable, I might give to
the press.

In the event that we send a note to Gerard today, would you
think it well to give out the comment at the same time that we
give out the text of our instruction?

In regard to the Commissioners for the Board of Investigation
under our Treaty with Great Britain, I find that they are the
following:

United States Commissioners—
   Judge George Gray, of Delaware,
   Mr. Domicio da Gama, Brazilian Ambassador to
                        the United States
British Commissioners—
   Viscount James Bryce,
   Mr. Maxim Koveleski, Member of Counsel of
                        Russian Empire.[1]
Joint Commissioner—
   Mr. Fridtjof Nansen, Norway.[2]

Faithfully yours, Robert Lansing

TLS (WP, DLC).
   [1] Maksim Maksimovich Kovelevskii, Russian historian, jurist, sociologist, and
ethnologist. Professor in the Department of Law at the University of Moscow,
1878-87; in exile, 1887-1905; professor at the University of St. Petersburg, 1905-
16. He had died on April 5, 1916.
   [2] Norwegian Arctic explorer, oceanographer, and former Minister to Great
Britain (1906-1908).

E N C L O S U R E

SUGGESTED COMMENT ON THE GERMAN REPLY OF MAY 4, 1916.

Secretary Lansing gave out the following comment on the German note

The greater part of the German answer is devoted to matters which this Government cannot discuss with the German Government. The only questions of right which can be discussed with that Government are those arising out of its action or out of our own, and in no event those questions which are the subject of diplomatic exchanges between the United States and any other country.

The essense of the answer is that Germany yields to our representations with regard to the rights of merchant ships and non-combatants on the high seas and engages to observe the recognized rules of international law governing naval warfare in using her submarines against merchant ships. So long as she lives up to this altered policy we can have no reason to quarrel with her on that score, though the losses resulting from the violation of American rights by German submarine commanders operating under the former policy will have to be settled.

While our differences with Great Britain cannot form a subject of discussion with Germany it should be stated that in our dealings with the British Government we are acting, as we are unquestionably bound to act in view of the explicit treaty engagements with that Government. We have treaty obligations as to the manner in which matters in dispute between the two governments are to be handled. We offered to assume mutually similar obligations with Germany, but the offer was declined. When, however, the subject in dispute is a continuing menace to American lives it is doubtful whether such obligations apply unless the menace is removed during the pendency of the proceedings.

Dear Mr. Secretary
Excuse pencil. This seems to me all right. I hope you will issue it.   W.W.[1]

T MS (SDR, RG 59, 763.72/2654, DNA).
[1] Copies of this statement were given to the Associated Press at 8:45 P.M., May 8, 1916.

Herman Bernstein to Joseph Patrick Tumulty

My dear Mr. Tumulty: New York May 8, 1916.

I would be very grateful to you if you will be good enough to inform me whether the receipt of the letter from the Pope, which was autographed by Cardinal Gasparri, and which I had the honor of giving to the President, was acknowledged.[1]

With kind regards, I am,
                            Yours sincerely,   Herman Bernstein

N.B. It may interest you to know that in addition to my duties as Editor of THE DAY, the National Jewish daily, I assumed charge of THE AMERICAN HEBREW, the oldest and foremost Jewish weekly in the English language, in this country.

TLS (WP, DLC).
¹ About this matter, see H. Bernstein to WW, May 20, 1916.

Count Johann Heinrich von Bernstorff to Edward Mandell House

My dear Colonel House: Washington. May 8, 1916.

Peace talk has been revived immensely by our last note and the alleged message from the Pope.¹ I received *confidential* information that Mr. Melville Stone intends to write a letter to the Emperor suggesting peace. Considering the information you and I have with regard to this question, it seems to me perfectly useless that more people should put their fingers in the pie. Besides if Mr. Melville Stone wishes to promote the peace idea, it would be better for him to write to the President than to the Emperor.

I am informing you of the above because I thought, that you might perhaps be able to prevent Mr. Melville Stone from taking any steps. Now that the peace idea is becoming popular, everybody will want to get on the band waggon, a state of affairs which will only disturb *our* endeavors to attain the desired object.

I expect to be in or near New York next Sunday. If you intend to go out of town for the week end, I will be delighted to arrange to call on you before you leave for the country or when you return home. I should therefore, be very much obliged to you for a kind answer whether you wish to see me Friday, Saturday, Sunday, Monday or Tuesday next.

    With best wishes,
                    Very sincerely yours,   J. Bernstorff.

This has just come.   E.M.H.

TCL (WP, DLC).
¹ About this matter, see J. Cardinal Gibbons to WW, May 12, 1916.

ADDENDA

To Jabez Lamar Monroe Curry

Markham, Fauquier Co., Virginia,

My dear Sir, 15 August, 1897.

Your very kind letter of the twelfth has reached me here.[1] I am sincerely obliged to you for your generous way of speaking of my address at the Hot Springs.[2] The Bar Association means to have it printed in pamphlet form at an early date, and I will take great pleasure in sending you a copy.

Your wish that I might have been chosen President of the University of Virginia particularly pleases me,—not because I think such an election possible, but because I know how high an estimate of me your wish implies.

Yes, indeed, I have seen and own your little volume on the Southern States,[3] and value it most highly. I expect it to be of constant service to me in what I shall myself write.

With warm regard, and renewed thanks,

Most Sincerely Yours,   Woodrow Wilson

WWTLS (J. L. M. Curry Papers, DLC).
[1] J. L. M. Curry to WW, Aug. 12, 1897, Vol. 10.
[2] "Leaderless Government," printed at Aug. 5, 1897, *ibid.*
[3] See J. L. M. Curry to WW, Aug. 12, 1897, n. 4, *ibid.*

To William Jennings Bryan

My dear Mr. Secretary: [The White House] October 2, 1914

I have the letter, which I return, which General Wotherspoon[1] addressed to you. It discloses again the uncomfortable and problematical situation at Vera Cruz. But I am clear in the judgment that we ought not to linger in our departing. I think it would make a very bad impression not only in Mexico, but in Latin-America generally, and I sincerely hope that the department's correspondence with the temporary authorities at Mexico City has resulted in something definite which we can use as a basis for handing over the civil authority on our departure. My wish is to get out at the very earliest possible date.

With warmest regard,

Cordially and faithfully yours,   [Woodrow Wilson]

CCL (WP, DLC).
[1] William Wallace Wotherspoon, major general, U.S.A., Chief of Staff.

From the Diary of Walter Lippmann[1]

March 22 (Wednesday) [1916].

Met Senator Henry Hollis at White House at 11:15 A.M. Short talk with Tumulty who was bitter about "plutocracy."

Ushered in to President's office. Large circular room.

Physical bigness of Wilson. "You've come to look me over."

Please analyze opposition.

"Henry L Higginson & others who were 'insiders,' no longer inside. Roosevelt 'their kind.'"

Mexico, liberty, Virginia bill of rights.

American cormorants and liars. Morally certain Hearst is behind Villa raid.

Pan-Americanism, merchant marine, foreign credits.

"We know Germany had designs in Brazil."

No greater responsibility under Pan-Americanism than under Monroe Doctrine.

Armed ship question: normal route, normal cargo makes merchant ship.

"Greatest Navy in the world:[2] Oratorical afflatus, very endemic, ashamed."

"Show you inside of my mind."

Hw bound diary (W. Lippmann Papers, CtY).

[1] Political writer, publicist, and chief editorialist on foreign affairs for *The New Republic*. This diary entry records Lippmann's first meeting with Wilson.

[2] Wilson referred to his statement in his speech at St. Louis on February 3, 1916. The only authoritative biography of Lippmann is Ronald Steel, *Walter Lippmann and the American Century* (Boston and Toronto, 1980).

NOTE ON THE INDEX

THE alphabetically arranged analytical table of contents at the front of the volume eliminates duplication, in both contents and index, of references to certain documents, such as letters. Letters are listed in the contents alphabetically by name, and chronologically within each name by page. The subject matter of all letters is, of course, indexed. The Editorial Notes and Wilson's writings are listed in the contents chronologically by page. In addition, the subject matter of both categories is indexed. The index covers all references to books and articles mentioned in text or notes. Footnotes are indexed. Page references to footnotes which place a comma between the page number and "n" cite both text and footnote, thus: "624,n3." On the other hand, absence of the comma indicates reference to the footnote only, thus: "55n2"—the page number denoting where the footnote appears.

The index supplies the fullest known form of names and, for the Wilson and Axson families, relationships as far down as cousins. Persons referred to by nicknames or shortened forms of names can be identified by reference to entries for these forms of the names.

All entries consisting of page numbers only and which refer to concepts, issues, and opinions (such as democracy, the tariff, the money trust, leadership, and labor problems), are references to Wilson speeches and writings. Page references that follow the symbol Δ in such entries refer to the opinions and comments of others who are identified.

Two cumulative contents-index volumes are now in print: Volume 13, which covers Volumes 1-12, and Volume 26, which covers Volumes 14-25.

INDEX